Evelyn Waugh

The Later Years 1939–1966

By the same author

Evelyn Waugh: The Critical Heritage (ed.)
Evelyn Waugh: The Early Years 1903–1939

Evelyn Waugh

The Later Years 1939–1966

Martin Stannard

W · W · NORTON & COMPANY
New York London

First American edition, 1992

Originally published in England under the title, *Evelyn Waugh: No Abiding City, 1939-1966.*

Printed in the United States of America

Manufacturing by the Haddon Craftsmen, Inc.

Library of Congress Cataloging in Publication Data

Stannard, Martin, 1947–
Evelyn Waugh.

Includes bibliographical references and indexes.
Contents: [1] The early years, 1903–1939—
[2] The later years, 1939–1966.
1. Waugh, Evelyn, 1903–1966—Biography.
2. Authors, English—20th century—Biography. I. Title.
PR6045.A97Z79 1987 823′.912 [B] 87—5750
ISBN 0-393-03412-7

W.W. Norton & Company, Inc.
500 Fifth Avenue, New York, N.Y. 10110
W.W. Norton & Company Ltd.
10 Coptic Street, London WC1A 1PU

1 2 3 4 5 6 7 8 9 0

Contents

Plates

Between pages 108 and 109

Evelyn Waugh's identification card, issued just before his aeroplane crash in Yugoslavia (*University of Texas*)
Evelyn Waugh and Randolph Churchill in Croatia, on the British Military Mission to Tito's partisans (*private collection*)
Lord Lovat in November 1942, a man Evelyn Waugh came to hate (*The Hulton-Deutsch Collection*)
Fitzroy Maclean, Waugh's CO in Yugoslavia (*The Hulton-Deutsch Collection*)
Major-General Robert Laycock, Waugh's friend and CO, October 1943 (*The Hulton-Deutsch Collection*)
Moray McLaren in April 1955, journalist and playwright, who owed his post-war literary career to Evelyn Waugh's loyalty (*The Hulton-Deutsch Collection*)
Teresa, Laura, James, Auberon, Harriet, Evelyn and Margaret Waugh at Piers Court, c. 1949 (*private collection*)
Alec Waugh and Joan Chirnside on announcing their engagement in August 1932 (*The Hulton-Deutsch Collection*)
A.D. Peters, Evelyn Waugh's literary agent (*by courtesy of Catherine Peters*)
Cyril Connolly
Lady Diana and Duff Cooper at their Bognor house during the war (*photograph by Cecil Beaton courtesy of Sotheby's London*)
John Betjeman, August 1955 (*The Hulton-Deutsch Collection*)
Evelyn Waugh standing for his portrait by Simon Elwes in California, 1946 (*private collection*)
Anna May Wong, Evelyn Waugh, Sir Charles Mendl and Laura Waugh in California, 1946 (*private collection*)
Evelyn Waugh in Windsor, Ontario, during his North American lecture tour, February 1949 (*private collection*)
Evelyn Waugh's self-portrait on leaving America (*private collection*)
Laura and Evelyn Waugh at Plymouth aboard the *Ile de France* after returning from America, 6 November 1950 (*private collection*)
Graham Greene talking to Eric Portman during the rehearsal of *The Living Room*, 18 April 1953 (*The Hulton-Deutsch Collection*)
Catherine Walston, Graham Greene's lover (*photograph by Cecil Beaton by courtesy of Sotheby's London*)
Nancy Mitford in Paris (*The Hulton-Deutsch Collection*)
Evelyn Waugh and one of his follies at Piers Court (*The Hulton-Deutsch Collection*)

Between pages 236 and 237

Evelyn Waugh in his library at Combe Florey House (*photograph by Mark Gerson*)
Trompe l'oeil panel by Martin Battersby depicting Evelyn Waugh's work, presented to him by Chapman & Hall (*private collection*)
Combe Florey House, Combe Florey, Somerset (*Mark Gerson*)
Alec and Evelyn Waugh, 25 November 1953, (*Yevonde Portrait Archive*)

List of Plates

Acknowledgements

Many of the acknowledgments for *The Early Years* will also serve for this volume. Those repeated here relate to research specific to *No Abiding City*.

First on this list must come the Department of English at the University of Leicester, for providing me with the time and space to finish the book, the University Establishment Board for allowing me a year's unpaid leave to write the first half, and the Research Board for continuous support. I could have had no better Head of Department than Sandy Cunningham, no better partner than Sharon Ouditt, no better friends than Kelvin Everest, Rick Rylance and Nigel Wood, all of whom endured my obsessive interest in Evelyn Waugh with saintly patience and never wavered in their encouragement. Mary Arthur, Sylvia Garfield and Pam Ross provided excellent secretarial help. Dido Arthur kept me in touch with the rare book trade. Paul Large and Katharine Cockin typed, respectively, the first and second drafts.

Several people read the whole or part of the typescript and offered useful suggestions and corrections: Mark Amory, Stuart Ball, Bernard Bergonzi, Winnifred M. Bogaards, Tom Burns, Peter Cattermole, Paul Chipchase, Duncan Cloud, Robert Murray Davis, Kelvin Everest, Robert Kenny, Sir Fitzroy Maclean, Sharon and Sylvia Ouditt, Mark Rawlinson, Rick Rylance, Stephen Wall and Nigel Wood. My editors, Hilary Laurie and Linda Osband, have helped me to collate all these revisions and to make many more. Douglas Matthews compiled the Index.

For lengthy interviews I must thank Gillon Aitken, Tom Burns, Fr Philip Caraman, Major-General T. B. L. Churchill, Lord and Lady Donaldson, John St John, Sir Fitzroy Maclean, Viscount Norwich, Stuart Preston and Lord Walston.

A special mention must be made of two librarians whose assistance has been invaluable: Alan Bell of Rhodes House, Oxford, and Cathy Henderson of the Humanities Research Center, University of Texas at Austin. Mr Bell was the custodian of Evelyn Waugh's incoming correspondence until it was sold to the British Library. This volume draws heavily on that huge archive of largely unpublished material, and it was only thanks to his courteous assistance and his meticulous arrangement and indexing of these papers that I was able to find my way about in them quickly. Cathy Henderson has been equally helpful, particularly with the boxloads of correspondence from A. D. Peters's office.

Viscount Norwich, Artemis Cooper and Hodder & Stoughton kindly allowed me to quote from the letters of Lady Diana Cooper. The following have granted permission for me to quote from unpublished correspondence with Evelyn Waugh and others, and from a variety of unpublished documentary material: Lady Acton, Sir Harold Acton, Mark Amory, the Countess of Avon, Constance Babington Smith, the Marquess of Bath, Professor Quentin Bell, the Berners Trust, Paul Betjeman, Blanchards of Dorchester, Boston University Library (Special Collections), M. Bridget, the BBC Written Archives Centre, the estate of the late Sonia Brownell Orwell, Tom Burns, Fr Philip Caraman, the Hon. Mr Justice Cazalet, Hugh Cecil, the Controller of Her Majesty's Stationery Office for Crown copyright material in the Public Record Office, Curtis Brown & John Farquharson, on behalf of the estate of John Duggan, copyright John Duggan 1992, David Higham Associates, the Duchess of Devonshire, Lord Donaldson, Francis Greene, Mrs Daphne Fielding, HE Giles FitzHerbert, Mrs Anne Fremantle, Sir Ian Gilmour, Sir Alec Guinness, Lady Harrod, A. Norah Hartley, the Harry Ransom Humanities Research Center of the University of Texas at Austin, Bishop Hollis, the Hon. Mrs Pamela Jackson, Lady Pansy Lamb, Mrs Deirdre Levi, Lady Longford, Lord Lovat, Peter Lunn, Candida Lycett-Green, Mary McDougall, Mrs Alexandra Mayes Birnbaum, the Merton Legacy Trust, Lieutenant-Commander John Miller, the Hon. Fionn Morgan, the Earl of Oxford and Asquith, Peters, Fraser & Dunlop, the estate of John Pick, the estate of Olivia and Gwen Plunket Greene, Mrs Eva Reichmann, Michael Rubinstein, John Russell, John Sparrow, Sir Stephen Spender, Lady Stanley of Alderley, the Earl of Stockton, the University of South Carolina Library, the Trustees for Roman Catholic Purposes Registered, the late Lord Walston, Rt Revd Abbot Aelred Watkin, Mrs Virginia Sorenson Waugh, the Hon. Mrs Mia Woodruff, Archbishop Worlock and Sebastian Yorke.

The rest are most conveniently thanked under separate headings. Additional correspondence and discussion: Louis Auchincloss, the Marquess of Bath, Alan Bell, Mary Cunnane, Malcolm Gerratt, Mark Gerson, Peter Greenham, Graham Greene, H. A. I. Goonetileke, George Keyt, Paul Moor, William Myers, Adele Parks, John Phillips, Michael Power, Sir Stephen Spender, Josephine Stannard, Ralph Tanner, Margaret Vallance, F. B. Walker and Peter Waugh. Libraries: the staffs of the BBC Script Library, the BBC Written Archives Centre, The Bodleian, the British Library Manuscript Room, Cambridge University Library, the Harry Ransom Humanities Research Center, and Leicester University Library. Publishers and editors of earlier work by myself: Routledge and Kegan Paul for permission to quote from *Evelyn Waugh: The Critical Heritage* (1984).

The author and publishers also gratefully acknowledge the use of extracts from the following published sources:
Harold Nicolson, *Diaries and Letters 1930–1964*, ed. and condensed Stanley Olson (Collins, 1980); Bernard Fergusson, 'Gentlemen at Arms', *Sunday Times*, 6 May 1973; John St John, *To the War with Waugh* (Leo Cooper, 1973); 'I was Evelyn Waugh's Batman. Peter Buckman interviews Ralph Tanner', *Punch*, 19 November 1975; 'Commando Raid on Bardia', *Life* (International), 17 November 1941; Joe Dever, 'Echoes of Two Waughs', *Commonweal*, Vol. 53, October 1950; Tom Harrisson, 'War Books', *Horizon* IV, 24 December 1941; unsigned review, *Times Literary Supplement*, 21 March 1942; unsigned review, *New Yorker*, 30 May 1942; Alec Waugh, *The Best Wine Last* (W. H. Allen, 1978); Evelyn Waugh, 'Face to Face' interview BBC TV; Evelyn Waugh, 'Fan-fare', *Life*, 8 April 1946; Auberon Waugh, 'Laura Waugh 1916–1973', *Antigonish Review*, Winter 1984; Evelyn Waugh, 'Drama and the People', *Spectator*, 6 November 1942; Tom Driberg, 'William Hickey', *Daily Express*, 1 January 1943; unsigned review, *Times Literary Supplement*, 23 January 1943; Nigel Dennis, *Partisan Review*, 28 July 1943; Arnold Lunn, 'Evelyn Waugh Revisited', *National Review*, 27 February 1968; Sir Fitzroy Maclean, *Eastern Approaches* (Papermac, 1983; Penguin, 1991); Earl of Birkenhead, 'Fiery Particles' in *Evelyn Waugh and His World*, ed. David Pryce-Jones (Weidenfeld & Nicolson, 1973); *The Essays, Articles and Reviews of Evelyn Waugh*, ed. Donat Gallagher (Methuen, 1983); Cyril Connolly, *The Unquiet Grave* (Curwen Press, 1944); Henry Reed, *New Statesman*, 23 June 1946; Edmund Wilson, *New Yorker*, 5 January 1946; Julian Jebb interviews Evelyn Waugh for *Paris Review in Writers at Work* (Secker and Warburg, 1968); Evelyn Waugh, 'A New Humanism', *Tablet*, 6 April 1946; Evelyn Waugh, 'Palinurus in Never-Never Land Or The Horizon Blue-Print of Chaos', *Tablet*, 27 July 1946; John Betjeman, 'The Angry Novelist', *Strand*, March 1947 – by permission of Desmond Elliot; Evelyn Waugh, 'When Loyalty No Harm Meant', *Tablet*, 7 December 1946; Peter Quennell, 'Speaking of Books: Evelyn Waugh', *New York Times Book Review*, 8 May 1966; Evelyn Waugh,'Death in Hollywood', *Life*, 29 September 1947; Orville Prescott, 'Books of the Times', *New York Times*, 14 June 1946; Donat O'Donnell (Conor Cruise O'Brien), *Bell*, December 1946; Auberon Waugh, 'Father and Son', *Books and Bookmen* 19, October 1973; Edmund Wilson, *Classics and Commercials* (W. H. Allen, 1951); Desmond MacCarthy, *Sunday Times*, 21 November 1948; R. D. Smith, *New Statesman*, 11 December 1948; Susan Cooper, 'Snoek Piquante' in *The Age of Austerity: 1945–1951*, eds Michael Sissons and Philip French (OUP, 1986) – by permission of Peters, Fraser and Dunlop; Evelyn Waugh, 'Felix Culpa?', *Tablet*, 5 June 1948; Anne Fremantle, 'Waugh in America', *Vogue*, 15 November 1960; Evelyn Waugh,

'Come Inside' in *The Road To Damascus*, ed. John A. O'Brien (Doubleday, 1949); Robert Craft, 'Stravinsky and Some Writers', *Harper's Bazaar*, Vol. 237, December 1968; Sister M. Thérèse, ed., 'Waugh's Letters to Thomas Merton', *Evelyn Waugh Newsletter*, Vol. 3, No. 1, Spring 1969; Joe Dever, 'Echoes of Two Waughs', *Commonweal*, Vol. 53, October 1950; George Orwell, *New York Times Book Review*, 20 February 1949; Harvey Breit, *New York Times Book Review*, 13 March 1949; Edward R. F. Sheehan, 'A Weekend With Waugh', *Cornhill*, Vol. 171, Summer 1960; Evelyn Waugh, 'The American Epoch in the Catholic Church', *Life*, 19 September 1949; Elizabeth Jane Howard interviews Evelyn Waugh, 'Monitor' series, 16 February 1964, BBC TV; V. S. Pritchett, *New Statesman*, 30 September 1949; John Raymond, *New Statesman*, 21 October 1950; Frederick J. Stopp, 'Grace in Reins: Reflections on Mr Waugh's *Brideshead* and *Helena*', *Month*, August 1953 – with the permission of Elisabeth Stopp; Evelyn Waugh, 'A Progressive Game', BBC Third Programme, 17 May 1951 (BBC Script Library); Evelyn Waugh, 'The Heart's Own Reasons', *Commonweal*, 17 August 1951; David Malbert interviews Evelyn Waugh, *News Chronicle*, 11 June 1953; Evelyn Waugh, 'Our Guest of Dishonour', *Sunday Express*, 30 November 1952; Evelyn Waugh, 'It's Dangerous, Says Waugh', interview with James Dow, *Sunday Chronicle*, 15 November 1953; Evelyn Waugh, 'Frankly Speaking', 16 November 1953, BBC Home Service (BBC Script Library); Evelyn Waugh, 'Apotheosis of an Unhappy Hypocrite', *Spectator*, 2 October 1953; Tom Driberg, 'The Agony of Evelyn Waugh', *Sunday Dispatch*, 14 July 1957; Frances Donaldson, *Evelyn Waugh: Portrait of a Country Neighbour* (Weidenfeld and Nicolson, 1967); Robert Pitman, 'Mr Waugh Makes Good', *Sunday Express*, 15 May 1955; Evelyn Waugh, 'An Open Letter To The Honble Mrs. Peter Rodd ... On A Very Serious Subject' in Nancy Mitford, ed., *Noblesse Oblige* (Hamish Hamilton, 1956) – by permission of Peters, Fraser and Dunlop; Rebecca West, *The Meaning of Treason* (Pan Books, 1949) – by permission of Peters, Fraser and Dunlop; 'Is He Pinfold?', *Daily Telegraph*, 12 April 1957; Kenneth Allsop, 'Mr Waugh Wields the Scalpel', *Daily Mail*, 18 July 1957; unsigned review, 'Self Portrait', *Times Literary Supplement*, 19 July 1957; Philip Toynbee, 'Mr Waugh Shifts Gears', *Observer*, 21 July 1957; J. B. Priestley, 'What Was Wrong With Pinfold?', *New Statesman*, 31 August 1957; Thomas C. Ryan, 'A Talk With Evelyn Waugh', *The Sign*, August 1957; Evelyn Waugh, 'A Tribute to Ronald Knox', *Sunday Times*, 1 September 1957; *Daily Express*, 10 June 1958; *Daily Mail*, 12 February 1959; Sir Arnold Lunn, 'Evelyn Waugh Revisited', *National Review*, 27 February 1968; Evelyn Waugh, 'Aspirations of a Mugwump', *Spectator*, 2 October 1959; Graham Greene, review of *Knox*, *Observer*, 11 October 1959; Evelyn Waugh, 'I See Nothing But Boredom ... Everywhere', *Daily Mail*, 28 December 1959;

Kenneth Allsop interviews Evelyn Waugh, 'The Living Arts 1960', *Daily Mail*, 26 April 1960; Kenneth Allsop, 'Waugh and Peace', *Sunday Times*, 8 April 1973; Cyril Connolly, *Sunday Times*, 25 September 1960; Frank Kermode, *Partisan Review*, 20 August 1962; Evelyn Waugh, *Spectator*, 13 October 1961; 'Waugh Tests Guests', *Daily Express*, 27 February 1962; Evelyn Waugh, 'The Same Again, Please', *Spectator*, 23 November 1962; *Proceedings of the Royal Society of Literature*, 1963; Evelyn Waugh, 'The Dialogue Mass', *Tablet*, 16 March 1963; Evelyn Waugh, 'The Council: Phase One', *Tablet*, 7 September 1963, Cyril Connolly, 'Fresh Strands on the Loom', *Sunday Times*, 22 October 1967; 'And Father Came Too: Auberon Waugh interviewed by Stephanie Nettell', *Books and Bookmen*, January 1964; 'Words With Evelyn Waugh', *Sunday Telegraph*, 23 August 1964; Evelyn Waugh, *Commonweal*, 18 September 1965; Evelyn Waugh, *Commonweal*, 7 January 1966; John Raymond, 'Waugh's Last Post', *New Statesman*, 29 April 1966; *Daily Mirror*, 21 July 1966; Auberon Waugh, 'My Father's Diaries', *New Statesman*, 13 April 1973; Evelyn Waugh, *Downside Review*, April 1966.

Every effort has been made to trace the copyright holders of published and unpublished material.

Abbreviations and note on references

Unpublished letters are given full references; those published by Mark Amory in 1980 are alluded to by '*Letters*, p ...'. For convenience I have cited quotations from the Penguin Books editions of Waugh's fiction. Full reference to date and place of first publication appears in the Bibliography. For the travel books, biographies and *ALL*, page references are given to the first edition. Place of publication (for all works) is London unless otherwise stated. Where Waugh's journalism or reviews of his books have been reprinted, cross-references to *EAR* and *CH* are added. Unpublished letters between Waugh and his agent are cross-referred to Robert Murray Davis's *Catalogue* of the HRC Archive, Texas. The contractions used in the footnotes are explained below.

Abbreviations

ALI	Autograph letter, initialled
ALL	Evelyn Waugh, *A Little Learning. The First Volume of an Autobiography* (Chapman & Hall, 1964)
ALS, nd, np	Autograph letter, signed, no date, no place (i.e. no address)
AN	Autograph note
ANS	Autograph note, signed
APC, pm	Autograph post card, post marked
APCI	Autograph post card, initialled
AWD	Arthur Waugh's Diaries, BUL
B&B	*Books & Bookmen*
BBCSL	BBC Script Library
BBCWAC	BBC Written Archive Centre
BL	British Library Manuscript Collection
BUL	Boston University Library (Special Collections)
Catalogue	*A Catalogue of the Evelyn Waugh Collection at the Humanities Research Center, The University of Texas at Austin*, ed. Robert Murray Davis (Troy, New York, Whitston Publishing Company, 1981)
CH	*Evelyn Waugh. The Critical Heritage*, ed. Martin Stannard (Routledge & Kegan Paul, 1984)
C Her	*Catholic Herald*
CSM	*Christian Science Monitor*
CUL	Cambridge University Library

DE	*Daily Express*
Diaries	*The Diaries of Evelyn Waugh*, ed. Michael Davie (Weidenfeld & Nicolson, 1976)
DM	*Daily Mail*
DR	*Dublin Review*
DT	*Daily Telegraph*
EAR	*The Essays, Articles and Reviews of Evelyn Waugh*, ed. Donat Gallagher (Methuen, 1983)
EN	*Evening News*
ES	*Evening Standard*
EWAHW	*Evelyn Waugh and His World*, ed. David Pryce-Jones (Weidenfeld & Nicolson, 1973)
EWN	Evelyn Waugh Newsletter
HB	*Harper's Bazaar*
HRC	Harry Ransom Humanities Research Center, University of Texas at Austin
LAF	*The Letters of Ann Fleming*, ed. Mark Amory (Collins, Harvill, 1985)
Letters	*The Letters of Evelyn Waugh*, ed. Mark Amory (Weidenfeld & Nicolson, 1980)
MBE	Alec Waugh, *My Brother Evelyn and Other Profiles* (Cassell, 1967)
MP	*Morning Post*
MS	Manuscript
MWMS	*Mr Wu and Mrs Stitch: The Letters of Evelyn Waugh and Diana Cooper*, ed. Artemis Cooper (Hodder & Stoughton, 1991)
NR	*New Republic*
NS	*New Statesman*
NY	*New Yorker*
NYHTBR	*New York Herald Tribune Book Review*
NYT	*New York Times*
NYTBR	*New York Times Book Review*
PRO	Public Record Office
SE	*Sunday Express*
ST	*Sunday Times*
S. Tel.	*Sunday Telegraph*
Sykes	Christopher Sykes, *Evelyn Waugh. A Biography* (Collins, 1975)
TccL	Typed carbon copy of letter
TccLS	Typed carbon copy of letter, signed
TLS	Typed letter, signed

TLS	*Times Literary Supplement*
TPCI	Typed post card, initialled
TS	Typescript
UBCL	University of British Columbia Library (Special Collections)
Writers	Julian Jebb's interview with Waugh printed as 'Evelyn Waugh' in *Writers at Work* (Secker & Warburg, 1968), pp. 105–14
WTD	Auberon Waugh, *Will This Do? The First Fifty Years of Auberon Waugh. An Autobiography* (Century, 1991)

Preface

The first volume of this biography[1] left Waugh in November 1939 at Chatham Barracks, a trainee officer in the Royal Marines. He was in the third year of his marriage to Laura Herbert, who had borne him two children, Teresa and Auberon. Even before Waugh secured his commission, their house, Piers Court, had been let for the duration and they had all moved to Laura's childhood home, Pixton Park in Somerset. There they lived with her mother (Mary) and her two sisters (Gabriel and Bridget), but the house was crowded with ancient servants and evacuees. Waugh, uncomfortable in this environment, escaped to his favourite bolt-hole, the Easton Court Hotel on Exmoor, to begin writing a novel. In many ways it was a book about middle age and a sense of loss; indirectly it described the massive changes wrought in his life by his marriage to Laura and by the impending war.

Then had come the call to arms. Waugh put his manuscript away and never completed it. When the fragment was published as *Work Suspended* late in 1942, it was divided into two parts, later retitled 'A Death' and 'A Birth'. The book, indeed, marked a watershed in his life and work. In one sense, the 'Death' was that of the feudal *ancien régime* which Waugh saw as the bastion of cultural value, and the 'Birth' was that of the Age of the Common Man which he despised. In another, more personal, sense, the 'Death' was that of his frenetic bachelordom and its miserable temporary relationships, the 'Birth' that of his new, better regulated, life with Laura.

Waugh had been born into a comfortable middle-class home. His father, Arthur, was Managing Director of Chapman & Hall and had been educated at Sherborne School and Oxford. Evelyn's mother, Catherine, came from a family of soldiers, civil servants and lawyers, and was related to Lord Cockburn of Cockpen. Arthur and Catherine married on very little money and lived humbly as he tried to make his way as a writer. Relinquishing this ambition in order to support his family, he soon became a respected man of letters in the London publishing world. He was a paterfamilias of a new style, reacting against the strictures of his Victorian childhood. Amiable and theatrical, he doted on his first son, Alec, and found Evelyn's reserve distressing. As the boys grew up, Alec gravitated towards Arthur, Evelyn towards his mother. After the First World War, in which Alec served, he became a literary celebrity with his scandalous *roman à clef*,

1. *Evelyn Waugh. The Early Years: 1903–1939* (Dent, 1986; Norton, 1987; Paladin paperback 1988).

The Loom of Youth (1917), and settled happily into the beer and cricket atmosphere of the Georgian *littérateurs*. Success for Alec, however, had meant exclusion for Evelyn. *The Loom*, a book describing homosexual romance in a school that was clearly based on Sherborne, made it impossible for Evelyn to go there. Instead, he was sent to Lancing College, an establishment which he always considered inferior.

As a schoolboy, Evelyn was at first conventional, shy and pious. When he left Lancing, in December 1921, he was subversive and agnostic, having largely turned his back on the school's Anglican values. Only at Oxford did he discover what he was looking for – not scholarship and cricket but the fantastical world of aesthetes centring on Harold Acton and Brian Howard. Here, Waugh learned to drink and dress with style. He became a practising homosexual and popular jester, gay in both senses of the word. At the time he wanted to be a painter, and, going down without a degree in 1924, he returned to his parents' house in Golders Green and attended art school. Abandoning that, he thought of taking up carpentry and printing. His passion was for arts and crafts. He had no wish to enter the family trade of letters. In the meantime, however, he had plunged into debt as he tried to keep up with his smart friends in London and Oxford. Arthur Waugh, distinctly displeased, settled the debt on condition that Evelyn find himself regular paid employment. Schoolteaching seemed the only option.

By the time Evelyn left for his first post in North Wales, he had emerged from his actively homosexual phase and fallen in love with a Catholic girl, Olivia Plunket Greene. Separation from her made his isolation all the more painful. Like many women later in his life, she could not reciprocate his physical passion. Her influence, nevertheless, was deep and abiding. It was his desire to be reunited with the social world in which she moved that drove him to become a writer. It was she, more than anyone, who brought him into the Roman Catholic Church.

His escape from schoolteaching was effected by an essay he wrote on the Pre-Raphaelite Brotherhood. On the strength of this, Anthony Powell, a friend from Oxford who was then working for Duckworth's, suggested Evelyn as a biographer of Rossetti. A contract was signed, a small advance paid and, much to Arthur's amazement, the book was completed. While writing it, Evelyn amused himself by making dilatory stabs at a comic novel. He was in love again, this time with Evelyn Gardner, and in high spirits. In June 1928, with *Rossetti* published and his novel completed, the two Evelyns married. The novel, *Decline and Fall*, appeared later that year and established him as a Bright Young Author. All seemed set fair. The young couple appeared to their friends to be enviably contented in each other's company. Then, quite suddenly, in the summer of 1929, she left him for another man. It was a blow to his self-esteem from which he never fully recovered. Twelve months after filing a petition against his wife, in September 1930, he was received into the Catholic Church, and his 'conversion' generated considerable publicity. *Vile Bodies* had appeared the previous January and was a huge success. Evelyn Waugh was 'news', and he remained a public figure for the rest of his life.

Three more brilliant black comedies followed – *Black Mischief* (1932), *A Handful of Dust* (1934), *Scoop* (1938) – interspersed by travel books, short stories and another biography, of Edmund Campion, which won the Hawthornden Prize. His writing fed off his travels – to Abyssinia and British Guiana in particular – to produce hilarious and disturbing images of the conflict between barbarism and civilization. After *Vile Bodies*, he always wrote as a Catholic but without propagandizing the Faith, a stance which angered some foolish co-religionists and which he bravely defended as his artistic right. In England he moved almost exclusively among the British upper classes, often staying at Madresfield Court with Lady Dorothy and Lady Mary Lygon. Henry Yorke (the novelist 'Henry Green') became a particular friend, as did Lady Diana Cooper, and Katharine Asquith of Mells Manor in Somerset. He financed his pleasures by becoming probably the best-paid author of his generation (his agent, A.D. Peters, was a masterly entrepreneur), and, to outsiders, Waugh appeared to be the epitome of success. As a remorseless self-publicist, he went out of his way to encourage this notion. Only his closest friends knew of his depression, fear of failure, persecution mania. Until the mid-1930s, his attempts to make another enduring sexual relationship had been singularly unsuccessful. His religion did not recognize his divorce and required him to be celibate. This he found impossible, and the string of prostitutes and casual affairs which constituted his sexual life for six years rebuked his longing for orthodoxy. Laura resolved this difficulty. When his first marriage was eventually annulled, she married him in April 1937.

It was an odd union but a successful one. She was twenty, shy, virgin, aristocratic and astute. He was thirty-three, pugnacious, worldly, middle-class and rash. It was a particular sadness to Laura that Waugh could never like her brother, Auberon, for the Herberts, devout Catholics, were a close family. At first, it seems that they saw him as something of a counter-jumper. It did not help that Waugh had affectionately lampooned Pixton as Boot Magna Hall in *Scoop*. But they were eccentric, intelligent people who appreciated Waugh's eccentricities and tried to welcome him into their fold. For his part, Waugh grew to love Mary and to like Gabriel and Bridget, while preferring to keep his distance. They were all, he believed, part of a much larger family, the Household of the Faith, and in this their fellowship was perfect. He entered the war as a Catholic crusader, aching for adventure and honourable service. He emerged from the conflict feeling not only unwanted as an officer but also dishonoured by the British betrayal of Christendom. The Herberts, with their close interest in the persecuted Catholics of Poland, sympathized with his feelings on this subject and admired his relentless battle against Communism.

From 1945, Waugh began slowly to disengage himself from the modern world. His friendships – particularly those with John Betjeman, Cyril Connolly, Diana Cooper, Graham Greene and Nancy Mitford – were conducted increasingly through correspondence. He was a powerful man of great spiritual humility who possessed the gift of making people want to please him. But he was also a man tormented by his own irritability and the dryness of his soul. For years he found it difficult to pray. His power to hurt was the mainspring of his comic imagination. He was, as he admitted, least happy when he had nothing to complain about. Although he was generous and loyal, and could even manage long bursts of sweet temper, his Faith also obliged him to be charitable. It was this obligation with which he had most difficulty. The story of Waugh's later life is the story of his agonized spiritual quest towards compassion and contrition.

I

Mr Churchill's Murder Gangs: December 1939–August 1941

In the winter of 1942 Evelyn Waugh wrote to Lady Diana Cooper from a snowbound hut in Roxburghshire. 'Perhaps in the future,' he said, 'when Senator Cooper is representing the State of Free England in Washington and I am teaching English syntax to a convent school in Quebec, we may meet at Niagara. Meanwhile I live in the past.'[1] From that point he never looked forward and his love affair with the army was in ruins. Full infatuation had survived just six months. Nothing, indeed, had ever equalled the honeymoon – his first two days of service, before training had begun.

At Chatham Barracks Waugh had discovered an odd collection of temporary officers and gentlemen: a wine merchant, an accountant, a schoolmaster, people who in civilian social life he would have shunned. But the eccentricity of the selection was for him part of the charm of the Marines. As one of only twelve successful candidates from over two thousand applicants, Waugh was proud to be of the elect. The buildings were superb; the mess rewarded discipline with gastronomic luxury. A tradition of ceremonious life structured every waking moment and, for a few weeks, the conflicting aspects of his personality were fused. Silver candelabra stood reflected in heavy, polished mahogany, the port slid clockwise, and Waugh felt contented. At last, it seemed, he could be both aesthete and man of action.

Commando units were raised in 1940, after Dunkirk, as an élite fighting force. When Waugh later transferred to them he emphasized their distinction from the Marines. In fact, RM 1 (Marine Infantry Brigade) was being raised in 1939 to perform similar tasks. It was a crack battalion skilled in the techniques of amphibious landing and sabotage, trained to strike hard and fast behind enemy lines. At thirty-six, Waugh was the oldest recruit, and his enlistment in such a unit suggested that baffling combination of humility and arrogance which never ceased to shock his friends and family. How, they wondered, would the military mind cope with such an untrainable fellow? Surely that fierce independence could never be reduced

1. ALS, nd [February 1942], from 5 RM, Hawick, Roxburghshire; BL; *MWMS*, p. 76.

to conformity? He was plump and sybaritic. Could he endure the physical rigours?

All these fears were well-founded, but his romantic enthusiasm for the defence of Christendom temporarily checked his subversive instincts. Like his father, he found it painful to relinquish his hold on youth. He regarded the imminent conflict as an adventure. The Marines restored to him an adolescent immunity from personal responsibility while sanctifying their games with the holy waters of duty and discipline. Waugh was always a solitary in search of a club. Having missed the Test of Manhood in the Great War, he was determined to prove himself now. And it was, perhaps, this struggle to establish his 'masculine' credentials that led to his strangely divided self in later years, for he was always sympathetic to the 'pansy-aesthete'.

When, in *Put Out More Flags* (1942), Waugh described the 'Churchillian renaissance' reviving the spirits of red-blooded Englishmen, the ostensible butt of the humour, Ambrose Silk, is sympathetically drawn. There was something at once brave, charming and sensitive about the British upper-class 'bugger'[2] which Waugh loved. Ambrose's lament – '"... why can I not speak like a man? Mine is the brazen voice of Apuleius's ass, turning its own words to ridicule...."'[3] – was also Waugh's, although he would never have admitted it, perhaps not even to himself. Ambrose '"... wouldn't sit around discussing what kind of war it was going to be. [He'd] make it [his] kind of war. [He'd] set about killing and stampeding the other herd as fast as [he] could...."'[4] So would Waugh have done – had he been allowed.

*

The Chatham regime was rigorous: breakfast 7.30; parade 8.15; infantry drill until 9.30; lectures on military law followed by 'P.T. of a degrading kind'[5] until 12.45; luncheon was followed by another parade at 2.30 and more infantry drill. Work finished at 4.00, leaving Waugh with so stiff a spine that he found it painful even to pick up a pen.

During those early weeks, nevertheless, he wrote to Laura almost every day, hungry for her company, anxious about her health. As she recovered slowly from post-natal pleurisy, his jokes, prayers, and a strange new earnestness, raised her spirits. She respected his desire for honourable service, although the immediate future promised no adventure for her.

2. Waugh's term, reiterated affectionately in his letters.
3. *Put Out More Flags* (Chapman & Hall, 1942; reprinted Harmondsworth, Penguin Books, 1943 and 1969), p. 61.
4. *Ibid.*, p. 73.
5. Unpublished ALS to Laura Waugh, 'Tuesday' [12 December 1939], np [Chatham]; BL.

Mary Herbert and her daughters had reconstituted themselves as a family at Pixton Park, where Laura lived for the duration in the company of her children, evacuees and their 'helpers'. She had a toddler (Teresa) and new baby (Auberon), she was beset by the constant emotional exhaustion of Waugh's preparations for mortal combat, and she had lost her independence again. Piers Court was occupied by teaching nuns and Laura was burdened with something for which she was supremely ill-suited: the financial organization of the family. It was now her business to see that rents were paid and to deal with Waugh's literary agent, A. D. Peters, when her husband was incommunicado.

As Waugh leapt and squatted in his vest and plimsolls, or had his parade-ground stride measured by Colour Sergeant Smith's wooden callipers, two thoughts appear to have obsessed him: money and Christmas leave. Alarming letters had begun to arrive. Percy Popkin had been Waugh's accountant for some years, but he had never secured a straight answer from his client to forward to the Inland Revenue. The Revenue chose this moment to demand unpaid taxes, when Waugh was clearing (after mess expenses) seventeen shillings a week. A family allowance of seven shillings for the two children was intended for Laura, but was, in any case, inexplicably stopped some months later. The situation seemed desperate because, with the declaration of war, paper rationing had begun. One by one, Waugh's novels would drop out of print and he feared having to sell Piers Court to settle the tax bills.

The prospect of Christmas at Pixton also horrified him. The evacuees were enough of a deterrent, and the entire Herbert clan would be there, including Laura's (in his view) ghastly brother, Auberon. 'Will you be fit to travel to Chagford for Christmas?' Waugh wrote to Laura.

> I am sure that it could be arranged without offence by our pointing out that it would not be a family Christmas this year ..., that we should see nothing of one another at Pixton in existing circumstances, that I hope to do a little work then etc. Anyway I will undertake all the diplomacy if you will get well enough to move....[6]

Diplomacy was never Waugh's strong suit. Fortunately it was not required. Laura remained too ill to travel; Christmas was spent at Pixton and no work was done.

It was a difficult time for them both. Waugh dissuaded Laura from visiting Chatham: '... a crowded, slummy city in perpetual fog; if you came you would have to consort with the wives of the other officers whom you

6. Unpublished ALS to Laura Waugh, 'Monday' [11 December? 1939], from RM Barracks, Chatham; BL.

would not like at all. . . .'[7] But this protection of her social distinction was probably misplaced. Laura mixed easily with her cowmen and servants, often preferring their company to that of the aristocracy cultivated by her husband. She had grown up in, and grown a little tired of, high society. An introvert, she preferred the quiet life of a country gentlewoman. In later months she happily visited Waugh in various camps. His remarks seem rather to reflect his fiction of her as the aristocratic wife and to reveal his own uncertainty. If he lived out with her, he said, '. . . it would make it very much less probable of my becoming efficient & earning promotion to the staff where you wish to see me.'[8] Did she, or did Waugh?

On Christmas Eve he wrote to Lady Diana Cooper:

> You ask for news of *myself*. Well I am having a spot of leave at Pixton; it is a rough transition from the comfort & order of barracks but there was no alternative, as Laura is still bed-ridden . . . and is only now beginning to sit up for an hour a day. Pixton is full of slum children; eight professional spinsters . . . sit down to dinner with Mary [Herbert]. I eat on a tray in Laura's room. It is all highly disagreeable. . . . Everyone I see, but that is very few outside the Marines, is enjoying the war top hole. The highbrows have split – half have become US citizens, the other half have grown beards & talk of surviving to salvage European culture. . . .[9]

Here was the raw material for Waugh's next novel, which, like the letter, mocked the effete war efforts of his non-combatant contemporaries. But he was not as unsympathetic to them as he pretended. That December Cyril Connolly and Stephen Spender had produced the first issue of *Horizon*. Its editorial (January 1940)[10] proclaimed the historical moment to be 'anarchistic, conservative, and irresponsible, for the war is separating culture from life . . . the impetus given by Left Wing politics is for the time exhausted. . . . Civilization is on the operating table and we sit in the waiting room.'[11] Nothing could better describe Waugh's attitude.

Back at Chatham, Sergeant Greensmith was instructing his recruits in the use of small arms. 'When I look down the sights of my rifle', Waugh wrote to Laura, 'the foresight is indistinct & the target disappears totally. They will find this out when we start firing on the range.'[12] In unremitting fog and snow, small irritations flowered. Whenever possible, he shirked the

7. *Ibid.*
8. *Ibid.*
9. *Letters*, p. 131.
10. The first issue seems to have been available, at least in proof, as early as 9 December 1939. Cf. Harold Nicolson (ed.), *Diaries and Letters* condensed by Stanley Olson (Collins, 1980), p. 170.
11. 'Comment', *Horizon*, Vol. 1, 1 (January 1940), 5.
12. Unpublished ALS to Laura Waugh, 'Tuesday Evening' [2 January? 1940], np [RM Barracks, Chatham]; BL.

undignified PT and toadied to the Brigade commander, Colonel Lushington. He was, Laura learned, still treated as 'head boy', but had behaved very badly in '... telling the squad to parade at 2.15 instead of 2 so that I could finish my cigar....'[13] A ranker officer had dared to reprimand him. Waugh's laxity (he was in fact an obsessively punctual man) was designed to annoy the humourless and to establish him as a man of style.

On 15 January, Second Lieutenant Waugh's group moved to Kingsdown Camp (near Deal in Kent) and discovered a radical reduction of home comforts. Kingsdown was a cavernous Victorian villa, devoid of decent furniture and all carpets, surrounded by the asbestos huts of a former holiday camp. The landscape was blanketed in snow. Waugh suffered three nights of the place and trudged off with his wine merchant friend to secure temporary membership of the Deal and Walmer Union Club. It was a cheap escape for a guinea. Here he retired each evening to evade the ping-pong and radio and to write his sad letters home.

Sixty officers were at Kingsdown for a tactical course. At first Waugh shared a bedroom in the villa with four others. Within a fortnight he had moved into one of the huts in search of silence. Grey skies, slate sea with a flotilla of neutral shipping riding at anchor, the camp inaccessible to wheeled traffic, evenings in the mess raucous with gin and rugger club songs – he hated it all, and his feelings of alienation smouldered for more than a decade until they found expression in Guy Crouchback's experiences at Kut-al-Imara House in *Men At Arms* (1952). Kingsdown, for all its discomfort, provided excellent material for a novel. Here he encountered Brigadier Albert Clarence St Clair-Morford: '[He is] like something escaped from Sing-Sing and talks like a boy in the Fourth Form at school – teeth like a stoat, ears like a faun, eyes alight like a child playing pirates, "We then have to biff them, gentlemen." He scares half and fascinates half.'[14] The Brigadier appeared in the affectionately heroic guise of Ben Ritchie-Hook in *Men At Arms*. At the time, Waugh was uncertain what to make of him. This crackpot crusader could not be allowed the honour of intimidating Evelyn Waugh, who was more curious than fascinated. In the Forces he could rarely find anyone with whom to conduct an adult conversation.

Alone in his freezing hut, he pined for Laura, and they put up briefly in the Swan Hotel – another tactless move, for it was the home of the senior officers. Waugh already felt no compunction at losing touch with the camp when his daily duties were complete. He was appalled by the noise and slovenliness of his younger colleagues, irritated by not being worked harder to start fighting sooner, frustrated by the general impasse of the Great Bore War. Nothing was happening and Waugh always wanted to make something

13. Unpublished ALS to Laura Waugh, nd [8–12 January? 1940], np [RM Barracks, Chatham]; BL.
14. *Diaries*, 18 January 1940, p. 461.

happen. 'Brisk' was one of his favourite adjectives of commendation. 'Slate-grey' sprang more easily to mind in his wartime records.

He was being taught the arts of 'appreciating the situation' and 'getting in and out of the picture'. He was also picking up the Marine *argot* (wives were 'madams'). No new public schoolboy could have struggled more earnestly to learn the etiquette. In a short while, he hoped, he would escape from this muddle into command. Meanwhile, he could no longer disguise frustration and was beginning to reveal his incompetence. His myopic misfiring had been noted on the range at Gravesend; since the move to Kingsdown he had wandered about in a blizzard on the downs with binoculars and map case, attempting and failing to solve simple tactical problems. Writing to Laura he had joked about his small successes, but he could not delude himself. Unless he were rushed into action within a couple of months, he feared discovery and permanent military impotence. 'John Betjeman went to his medical exam for the RAF and was registered insane. We went out in the dark & snow tonight to practise listening to sounds at a distance. I am ashamed now that I treated Trim's [Lord Oxford's] complaints of army life so lightly.'[15]

After a month of general training and 'TEWTS' (Tactical Exercises Without Troops) round a sand-table, they were again moved at short notice, this time to Brigade Headquarters at Bisley. Waugh's enthusiasm revived under canvas 'in a landscape of burned gorse and immature conifers, prettily embellished with cartridge cases.'[16] But it was a brief respite. The local hotels were packed, so wives could not visit. The catering was appalling. 'News of the summer is bad too,' he wrote. 'Plans change so often . . . that there is no point in becoming either depressed or hopeful. What seems certain is long leave for Easter.'[17]

As an economy measure, he spent his second week-end in camp, hoping at least to be left alone. Brigadier St Clair-Morford, however, was a determined host. 'He picked us up at 12.30,' Waugh noted in his diary, 'and, driving all over the road, took us to a depraved villa of stockbroker's Tudor. I asked if he had built it himself. "Built it? It's four or five hundred years old." That was a bad start. He turns slate-grey instead of red when he is angry.'[18] Waugh recounted the tale in long letters to Laura and Betjeman, savouring its tinge of lunacy and adding a few fierce strokes of his own. Mrs St Clair-Morford, it seems, was the victim of booby traps set by her husband. 'He told us with great relish how the night before she had

15. Unpublished ALS to Laura Waugh, nd [January? 1940], np; BL.
16. 'RM Brigade', *The Globe and Laurel* (April 1940); *EAR*, p. 262.
17. Unpublished section of ALS to Laura Waugh, 'Sunday' [25 February? 1940], from RM Brigade, Bisley, Brookwood; BL.
18. *Diaries*, 26 February 1940, p. 464.

had to get up several times to look after a daughter who was ill and how, each time she returned, he had fixed up some new horror to injure her – a string across the door, a jug of water on top of it etc. However, she seemed to thrive on this treatment. . . .'[19] Each letter embellished the story (the diary reports only boots over the door). In reality it was for Waugh a painfully boring episode. After tea he had been forced to recite from a book of Kiplingesque verses compiled by the Brigadier and his wife. They were clearly intrigued by this peppery little writer who refused to be cowed by their eccentricities. Perhaps St Clair-Morford was accustomed to sycophantic laughter as he barked out his anecdotes. Waugh, instead, corrected him about not smoking a pipe while drinking vintage port. The Brigadier glared quizzically from his one good eye: '"I hope you aren't taking a lot of notes about us all to make fun of us in a book. . . ."'[20] Waugh was, of course, breaking military law by keeping a diary. Later, he instructed Laura to file his letters. If he survived, these documents were to be the stuff of fiction.

After the St Clair-Morford fiasco, Waugh spent every week-end leave until Easter in London with Laura. Sometimes they stayed at Fleming's Hotel, content with its modest luxury, dining out alone or with any friends still in London.[21] After the asperities of Marine discipline he treasured these escapes, and particularly the lazy Sundays in bed with his wife and the papers. On one of these visits she conceived a child.

At Bisley, Waugh was dragooned into becoming battalion correspondent for the Marines' house journal, *The Globe and Laurel*. The account he gives there of RM 1's activities bears small relation to reality, but, as he said, 'The profound secrecy which covers the activities of "Mr Churchill's Murder Gang" makes the duty of your correspondent a light one.' The first article was jocular propaganda: 'Moustaches are growing luxuriantly . . . battle dress lends a menacing aspect to the most peaceable characters; Easter draws near, spirits are high.'[22] In fact, as Easter approached, Waugh's spirits had plunged. 'It was a detestable week,' he wrote to Laura, 'full of minor worries & major ones too, rumours, changes of plan and exasperation with colleagues, subordinates and superiors. . . . It takes hours to make a programme and twice a day regularly changes are made which necessitate complete revision.'[23]

On the eve of his Easter leave, the Company lists came out. He had been hoping for a captaincy, second-in-command of a Company. Shortly before,

19. *Letters*, p. 137.
20. *Ibid.*, p. 138.
21. Chief among these were Betjeman, Connolly, Christopher Hollis, Douglas and Mia Woodruff, and Henry and 'Dig' Yorke.
22. 'RM Brigade', *The Globe and Laurel*, *op. cit.*; *EAR*, pp. 262–3.
23. Unpublished ALS to Laura Waugh, nd [March 1940?], from Marine Barracks, Bisley; BL.

however, he had been on a long 'route march and practical exercise which was disastrous from first to last, and at every stage of the disaster I occupied a conspicuous place.'[24] The lists confirmed his forebodings: he was given charge only of a platoon in B Company.

It was the first of many wounds to his self-esteem and it generated a mood of comprehensive gloom. He was £500 overdrawn and owed £200 to the Inland Revenue. Having looked to promotion to increase his earnings, he now had to continue on lieutenant's pay. And in the background, all the time, the war was going badly. Russia had invaded Finland, which, much to everyone's surprise, had obstructed the Communist advance. Waugh had listened eagerly to the news of these giant-killing battles and wanted desperately to be there. Easter brought the Finns' collapse and surrender: '[It] had an acutely depressing effect on me.... [There] ... seems to be ... no possible front for our specialized types of warfare.'[25] Easter Week, normally a period of spiritual renewal for Waugh, was in 1940 a miserable interlude. He spent it alone with Laura, who immediately contracted measles.

It was Waugh's lowest point for four months. After this he abandoned his unnatural anxiety about economy and military prestige and became altogether more amiable. Laura was the crucial figure in this. Throughout their marriage she somehow withstood his thunderous melancholia and restored him to equanimity. As one whose arrogance disguised a persistent fear of failure, he relied absolutely on her devotion to him as a 'great man'. In the early days of their marriage, she played the child-wife to his Victorian paterfamilias. Yet at the same time she constantly and refreshingly broke from that role with a witty riposte or a call to order. For her, he acted the old buffer who scraped a few pennies together in trade. For him she acted the gauche aristocrat who would stand no nonsense from a smart-alec parvenu. In later life Waugh would playfully criticize her in front of their children. '"Your dear mother", he would say, "is the kindest and most hospitable of women, but she has no sense of style."' Laura knew exactly how to reply: '"And *your* dear mother spoke with a Bristol accent."'[26]

Laura was not a snob but, as her son suggests, '... an awareness of her social superiority may have helped to sustain her through a marriage which was not without its reminders of her husband's success in other fields.'[27] This is nicely put, and we might add that Waugh's awareness of her sense of social distinction was intensely stimulating to him. He needed a wife

24. *Diaries*, 28 March 1940, p. 465.
25. *Ibid.*, p. 466.
26. Auberon Waugh, 'Laura Waugh 1916–1973', *The Antigonish Review* (Winter 1984), 27–32. Mr Waugh adds: 'This was cruel as it was untrue. Mrs Arthur Waugh spoke with the gentlest and most ladylike voice without any trace of regional or any other accent.'
27. *Ibid.*, p. 30.

who could correct him and he (usually) enjoyed her slaps. Too many people suffered his provocative behaviour without complaint. Laura had, in terms of the social order he idealized, an unassailable advantage by right of birth. His imitation of upper-class life was to her a lovable eccentricity and to both of them, one suspects, it remained a game. The only entirely serious room in their house was Evelyn's library. Elsewhere, in the furnishings, paintings and decorations, there was that unmistakable, mischievous touch of the grotesque which characterized his taste and his art. 'By choosing preposterous objects as possessions', he noted in 1945, 'I keep them at arm's length.'[28] Buried inside that misanthrope, whose control of language was so exactly measured, there was always the unruly undergraduate with his smutty jokes and easily wounded affections. He became Polonius but he was happier as Hamlet, and Laura knew the secret of releasing that *alter ego*. It was the fantastical child in him that she loved. Perhaps his greatest gift to her was his tacit admission that she could hurt him but that he trusted her not to. With every other human being it was Waugh who did the hurting, and she treasured as a sacred trust her power over this otherwise indomitable creature. But, for all that, the marriage was placed under considerable strain during the war. A week-end in London, at the end of March, was their last taste of unadulterated pleasure for many months.

*

The stagnant period of Waugh's military career appeared suddenly to be over. On 9 April Hitler invaded Denmark and Norway, and the Marines expected either to be sent to fight abroad or to repel invasion at home. The other ranks were categorized as 'HOs' ('Hostilities Only') and were proud of their offensive role. All were volunteers and most had signed up in anticipation of rapid engagement with the enemy. Waugh was not alone in feeling that four months of theory had weakened their initial enthusiasm. Now RM 1 was more obviously in a state of readiness, although less than half-trained as a battalion. Waugh was promoted to Captain of D Company and reported the fact proudly to wife and friends. The tone of his letters switched abruptly from the private to the public. Laura's visits to London were cancelled and he devoted himself with renewed vigour to becoming a successful officer.

> My new command means endless work as I have to work out training syllabuses for men in there [*sic*] separate grades of development, co-ordinate them with the other companies & battalions for range allocations besides doing full time on parade and in supervision; also I sit in my orderly room hearing all kinds of requests and grievances. . . .

28. *Diaries*, 20 January 1945, p. 610.

> I have no second in command at all. Result, I have to do all the work for everyone. On Saturday 60 new troops arrived for me from Chatham, 93% of whom have never fired a rifle or slept in a tent before....

But there were consolations: 'The great Chatham piss-up was highly enjoyable. I kept pretty sober but suddenly discovered that I was signing all the menu cards '"Peregrine Winstanley"'.[29]

This party was the monthly Chatham guest night. They had motored over in a charabanc to a banquet followed by free-for-all wrestling in the ante-room. Waugh had emerged badly bruised and jubilant, all reservations about the infantile behaviour of his colleagues temporarily quelled by promotion. If this club wanted him, he was prepared to engage in its rites of passage. They rocked home to the accompaniment of rugby songs and occasional vomiting and eventually reached Bisley at 5 a.m. Reveille was at 6.15. At 8.15 there was a ceremonial Company Inspection by the Colonel. Waugh was delighted to tell Laura that it 'went like clock-work as smart as bedamned.'[30]

She was not, it seems, unduly impressed. As the year wore away and austerity began to bite, she seems to have found Waugh's boyish extravagance rather irritating, and Waugh certainly sensed her resentment. Other letters were more cautious:

> It was cold in camp ... & they kept us working till 10 at night. On Saturday I was so dirty I came to London for a Turkish bath. Then I thought of Diana & Duff [Cooper] & went to Bognor for the night ... [and] ... ate plovers eggs. It was decent to be in real agricultural country again after the military sands at Bisley....[31]

The decision to go is presented as impulsive and as reasonable reward for uncongenial duty. The casual tone perhaps tries to forestall Laura's 'If you went to London, why didn't you ask *me*?' – a complaint which she made directly on more than one occasion. For some years there remained a certain awkwardness between her and Diana Cooper. 'I feel you have a shyness of [Laura],' he wrote in the 1950s 'which must be overcome if we are to see as much of each other as I ardently desire.'[32]

It is easy to sympathize with Laura. She was depressed by the discovery of her pregnancy and in need of support. Waugh wrote in more sober mood:

29. Unpublished ALS to Laura Waugh, 'Sunday' [14 April ? 1940], np [Marine Barracks, Bisley]; BL.
30. *Ibid.*
31. Unpublished ALS to Laura Waugh, 'Sunday' [14 or 21 April? 1940], from St James's Club, Piccadilly; BL.
32. Unpublished ALS to Lady Diana Cooper, 19 September [1953?], from Piers Court; BL.

> It is sad news for you that you are having another baby and I am sad at your sorrow. For myself, surrounded with the spectacle of a world organized to kill, I cannot help feeling some consolation in the knowledge that new life is being given. Your suffering will be to give life, ours, if we have to suffer, to take it. A child that is a danger & distress now may be your greatest happiness in the future. . . .[33]

This did little to cheer a twenty-three-year-old wife who had been ill for months and who now faced her third pregnancy in three years. The prospect of widowhood with young children in a besieged country appalled her. Waugh did what he could and found a cottage near Bisley where they could at least be together in the evenings. It must nevertheless have been clear to her that the misery he expressed at seeing the 'spectacle of a world organized to kill' was not unmixed with excitement.

While Laura was most miserable, Waugh was eager for battle. She had only been in the cottage a few days when the 'balloon went up' and the Phoney War was over. Waugh's diary begins again after a gap of a month on 10 May. It was a significant day in European history. Hitler invaded Holland, Luxembourg and Belgium, and Neville Chamberlain resigned as Prime Minister to be succeeded by Winston Churchill, under whose influence the spirit of the House of Commons revived. For six months, Chamberlain's funereal presence had been a profound depressant as events had obliged him to inform the Honourable Members week by week of their country's impotence. They were months of national humiliation which Waugh had felt more bitterly than most. Norway and Sweden had refused to allow British troops to cross their territory to assist Finland. Roosevelt fiercely maintained America's isolationist policy while simultaneously condemning Nazi aggression. The 5th of May had brought the shocking news that Italy threatened to join the war. 'It seems incredible to us', Harold Nicolson remarked of his fellow MPs, 'that Italy should really come in. If she does it means that Mussolini is convinced of our early defeat. . . .'[34]

Italy declared war on 10 June. Until Churchill's ascendancy, Britain and her Government had blundered on in debilitating indecision, caught between the old world and the new. They had been at war for six months but the war had been taking place elsewhere. Most wanted it to begin so that it might end the sooner. Yet its beginning, everyone knew, might mark the end of European civilization. There seemed no possibility of victory without the assistance of a major ally. A new dark age stretched ahead. Waugh, however, loved nothing better than a lost cause. Depressed by the thought of having to fight Rome, he was nevertheless exhilarated by the

33. [April 1940]; *Letters*, p. 139.
34. Harold Nicolson, *op. cit.*, p. 180.

prospect of slaughter, and in Churchill he briefly saw a leader capable of rousing the nation to honourable aggression. 'Invasion of the Low Countries received with satisfaction in camp,' he noted that night.[35]

Even so, this did not signal the sort of transition he always craved: from grey to primary colours, from waiting to doing. He was not yet a man marked down as unsuited to authority. Indeed, Lushington's report on Waugh's first five months' service described him as

> A natural commander and experienced man. He works hard and gets good work out of his subordinates but must curb a tendency to lean on his 2nd in Command. Possesses any amount of moral courage and has self confidence when on subjects he knows. A little impatient ... with more military experience ... he will make a first class Company Commander.[36]

But when the CO delivered a tirade, furious that his trainee officers had seen to their own comfort before that of their men, everyone except Waugh recognized his concluding 'Any questions?' as rhetorical. 'Would you not agree, sir,' Waugh enquired innocently, 'that it would be ever so much nicer if there were no Marine soldiers and if everyone could be an officer?' On another occasion he had asked whether it were true that 'in the Roumanian [*sic*] army no one beneath the rank of Major is permitted to use lipstick'.[37] On Lushington's report Waugh scores highest on 'Zeal and Energy', lowest on 'Judgment'.

Waugh's captaincy merely exacerbated this tendency. For while he felt leadership to be his due, he was often uncomfortable in the role. As schoolmaster and parent he could vacillate between strictness and *laissez-faire*, and this suited him perfectly. In these moods he could be charming. 'One nice thing happened,' he wrote to Laura just before his promotion. 'A young Marine asked for a night's leave to compete in a dancing competition. I refused & he pleaded so earnestly that he & his young lady had achieved the ambition of their lives by getting into the finals that in defiance of the Colonel's orders I relented. Yesterday he came back from Portsmouth with a silver cup as big as himself, Champion of the South of England.'[38] But in the Marines, as at Lancing, he could also become fatuously haughty with his underlings. John St John, a fellow recruit, remembers Waugh's attitude to his men as one of 'contempt relieved only by avuncular patron-

35. *Diaries*, 10 May 1940, p. 467.
36. Unpublished report from Lieutenant-Colonel Lushington, 18 May 1940, ref. S.260B, section III, Old Admiralty Building, Whitehall. Under sections IV and V respectively, Lushington marked Waugh down as not suitable to specialize or for accelerated promotion.
37. John St John, *To the War with Waugh* (Leo Cooper, 1973), pp. 25–6.
38. Unpublished ALS to Laura Waugh, nd [March 1940?], *op. cit.*; BL

age'. Good officers were expected to get to know their men individually. Waugh despised such familiarity.

> A petty offence could make him apoplectic. I once heard him address a parade on the question of swearing: 'The continued use of obscenities in conversation is tedious and undignified. The words punctuate your speech like a hiccup. Instead they should be savoured and reserved for the creative act itself or for moments of the most extreme frustration.'[39]

Elegantly expressed and perhaps laced with self-mockery, such gentlemanly reprimands were nevertheless misplaced. Blank incomprehension stared back at him, and some positive dislike.

*

It took the Germans just two weeks to cut through France. By 25 May they had occupied Boulogne and Calais and captured, among other notable ornaments, P. G. Wodehouse. Allied communications were completely severed to the east, and the British Expeditionary Force straggled back to the beaches of Dunkirk. Waugh's battalion was on constant alert for parachute invasion; the battalion encamped beside them suddenly disappeared one night to defend Iceland. RM 1 kept training, training, training.

In the hiatus, he and Laura snatched a couple of week-ends in the Swan at Alton, twenty-five miles away, and tried to forget the war. It was a surreal situation common to many couples. Each of these excursions, they knew, might be their last. Certainly, they were too precious to waste on Waugh's parents and, under the circumstances, it might seem odd that they squandered one of these leaves on a visit to Edrington, Alec and Joan Waugh's country house near Reading. Neither felt much warmth for Alec, but there were several long good-byes in the offing. Alec had already come close to death when bombed out of Arras, and had recently been evacuated from Boulogne. Evelyn's unit was about to move; and Joan was shortly to escape with the two children to her native Australia. The time seemed ripe for a family reunion.

Evelyn arrived stiff and smart: immaculate uniform, clipped moustache. His lean and soldierly appearance startled Alec, who, as usual, was intimidated by his brother and keen to please. The visit was a success, although apprehension punctuated their gaiety. It was a turning-point in all their lives. Joan's evacuation was not entirely the product of the invasion scare. For some time, Alec had been unfaithful to her. He was currently in love with an admiral's daughter. The marriage lasted until Joan's death and Alec always maintained a deep affection for his wife, but it was ultimately a complicated compromise and after the war he spent most of each year

39. John St John, *op. cit.*, p. 24.

abroad. Joan generally disliked his friends. He had always to think carefully before issuing invitations to Edrington. Her wealth embarrassed him. Alec feared the prospect of being a kept man and, as Evelyn's literary reputation had soared during the 1930s, Alec's had declined. He knew that he was approaching the time when he might no longer be able to support himself independently. His novel *No Truce with Time* (1940) had just been published and, although Arthur thought it the best thing Alec had written, its author knew otherwise.

Alec and Evelyn had last met in 1939 at Piers Court. The manuscript of *Work Suspended* had been lying on the desk and Alec had read through a section. He recognized excellence when he saw it. It was, however, a painful period for him, when his self-confidence was at its lowest ebb for a decade. Evelyn's genius rebuked his brother's mediocrity and Alec was tempted to abandon writing altogether and settle for the life of a country squire. If he did this, however, his financial independence would be lost and his failure complete. He did not begrudge Evelyn his literary superiority, but there was something irritating in the way the younger brother enjoyed his own success. He never told Alec that he thought him dim, but he had a supercilious way of looking, and of writing letters, which left little room for doubt on the matter. Years later, Alec generously cut several lapses into recrimination from his memoirs and, as we shall see, even from one of his father's letters.

That week-end, Evelyn was unusually convivial[40] in all respects but one. He and Laura had arrived with a brother officer and his wife. When Alec asked whether the Marines were moving to the Middle East the reply was simply 'No, no.' Evelyn took his commitment to secrecy seriously. He conveyed the impression that he was involved in a major operation, and Alec later believed him to have been *en route* to Dakar. In fact, he had no idea of his destination. He simply enjoyed appearing impressive.

May and June 1940 saw the rebirth of nationalist euphoria. Churchill growled defiance in vivid metaphors; Duff Cooper as Minister of Information ingeniously presented the ignominy of evacuating 300,000 troops from Dunkirk as a victory; every Sunday evening J. B. Priestley broadcast fraternal encouragement; Herbert Morrison, the Minister of Supply, incited the nation to 'Go to it'; and defeatist talk was threatened with prosecution. The Nazi beast, it seemed, was tensing its muscles for its final leap across the Channel and Waugh, certain that he would see immediate action, spent another month being buggered about.

40. Cf. unpublished ALS from Arthur Waugh to Laura Waugh, 19 June 1940, from 14a Hampstead Lane, Highgate; BL: 'Joan wrote us a most enthusiastic letter, describing the visit that you & Evelyn paid to Edrington. You gave immense pleasure, and Joan said that Evelyn was so kind and gracious about everything. It cheered her up a lot.... I wish I could have seen Evelyn before he moved into action; but I quite understand that it was impossible for him to come....'

When embarkation orders finally arrived on 10 June, RM 1 were sent to the destination they most dreaded: not the front-line Channel ports but west Wales. In Haverfordwest, Waugh's Company was billeted in the Drill Hall, where he spent ten more days doing nothing. Laura came down for sightseeing tours of the town. Then, two days after Paris fell, on 23 June, the battalion marched six miles to Milford Haven and clambered on to the bloodstained decks of a dilapidated cross-Channel ferry which had seen service at Dunkirk. It was overcrowded and infested with lice. Two more days passed before they sailed – with the disappointing objective of defending Northern Ireland. Morale was low. No sooner were they at sea than their orders were cancelled and they returned to port to entrain for the coast west of Plymouth.

Waugh was deeply shocked by this experience. The shambles of embarkation, the filth of the ship, the disintegration of standards of dress and behaviour among troops aboard trains, all burned into his memory to be called up in *Put Out More Flags*, *Brideshead* and the war trilogy. He wanted nothing to do with the People's War. He found it humiliating that the Marines should be occupied, with the Home Guard, in protecting nondescript Cornish resorts. 'Our task is the defence of Liskeard,' he noted with grim humour. 'None of us can quite make out why anyone should want to attack it.'[41]

At the end of July, Waugh decided to take matters into his own hands. On a week-end leave he went first to Pixton to see Laura:

> Next day I saw Brendan Bracken and the late Adjutant-General. A new force of independent volunteer companies [Commandos] is being formed under Sir Roger Keyes to which I hope to get transferred. Diana Cooper came to luncheon with us. Dined in slapdash way at a beastly restaurant with Phyllis [de Janzé] and Hubert [Duggan]. The Woodruffs came in to drink champagne with us after the cinema. They were full of tales of the interesting jobs all my friends were getting – Tom [Burns] in Madrid, Chris [Hollis] in Washington. I felt sad to be going back to the confusion of the Marines.[42]

At last he saw his chance. The independent companies sounded much more to his taste. Bracken, the acquaintance from the days of the Bright Young Things who had helped secure Waugh's call-up, was now Churchill's PPS and had promised to use his influence again.

While Waugh was itching for his transfer, RM 1 kept moving: a few miles west to Downderry, then to Bake House, then by lorry to St Germans, where they entrained for Birkenhead – all within three weeks. Exhausted

41. *Diaries*, 17 July 1940, p. 473.
42. *Ibid.*, 6 August 1940, p. 473.

and infuriated by these apparently pointless manoeuvres, he began to despair of the mail ever catching up with him. A month earlier they had been issued with tropical kit. It now seemed that they might at last be heading for the African or Mediterranean theatres of war.

*

A luxurious P & O liner, the *Ettrick*, had been converted into a troopship and there was another chaotic embarkation, this time in darkness. The cargo had to be unloaded and reloaded because the ammunition had been stacked beneath the beer. The ship was then discovered to be overladen and the captain refused to sail; two battalions had been crushed into a ship intended for one. Late on the second night, the Argyll and Sutherland Highlanders were forced to go ashore again. Thirty-six hours late, on 20 August, the *Ettrick* steamed from its berth. 'It seems clear', Waugh wrote, 'that if there is an expedition, which becomes increasingly doubtful, I shall be left to take up my transfer to the Commando while an ungenerous attempt is being made to suggest that I am leaving under a cloud.'[43]

Waugh was certainly in bad odour with some of his colleagues, and his attempt to desert them for an élite force did nothing to enhance his reputation. But still no letter arrived and he found himself in a moral quandary. He longed to be free of the Marines but he was also a man of honour; he did not wish to be seen to leave when they were about to engage the enemy. On the other hand, a major had been sent from another division to take command of Waugh's Company. Lushington by this stage plainly did not wish to see him heading a fighting force. While sailing for Scapa Flow for final exercises, Waugh was offered four choices: leaving the ship at Scapa and returning to await his transfer, becoming Brigade Intelligence Officer, becoming Battalion IO, or continuing with D Company but as second-in-command. None appealed; all offended dignity. Waugh knew perfectly well what 'Intelligence Officer' meant in his case – non-combatant secretary – and he could not bear a subsidiary role in the Company he had once commanded. If he were to leave the ship, he might be accused of cowardice. If he were to become Brigade IO, he would be returned to HQ. The only way to see action was to take the, to him, ignominious post of Battalion IO and to stay with the ship. It was a melancholy compromise.

The exercise at Scapa was to practise tactics and night assaults using the landing-craft which swung from the davits of the liner. Waugh tramped about disconsolately in the heather and rain as chief umpire. He blacked up for the night assault and waded through freezing, waist-high water to the shore. But he had been given no orders other than to follow Battalion

43. *Ibid.*, 20 August 1940, p. 476.

HQ and he had only the dimmest idea of their objectives. Breaking the rules was his one consolation. Equipment was precisely calculated to allow each man to carry the maximum weight of ammunition. Waugh's ancient batman clambered ashore with less than the normal complement of weaponry to make way for two bottles of excellent red wine. There was a row about this. When discovered quietly toping in the safety of a house while the 'battle' was in full swing, Waugh was accused of neglecting his duty. His unanswerable defence might have been that his duties were negligible. Instead, when the matter was eventually raised at a Court of Inquiry in 1945, he indignantly denied the charge that he had been smoking a cigar and drinking claret. Only when pressed did he concede that he had been smoking a cheroot and drinking Burgundy. Why, he wanted to know, should he be 'run in by an officer so ill-bred that he could not distinguish between these totally different things'?[44]

Next day, 31 August, the expedition proper began, although few aboard knew where they were going or why. They rendezvoused with other ships and sailed hundreds of miles out into the Atlantic before turning south, zig-zagging all the way to baffle U-boats. Waugh's job involved the examination and recension of intelligence reports, keeping files of cables and the Battalion War Diary, and censoring letters. It was dreary and futile work. He had discovered that their purpose was to support a Free French landing at Dakar, near Freetown, West Africa, and to install General de Gaulle as leader. It promised little more than a routine exercise. The garrison at Dakar was held by officers loyal to the Vichy Government, but it was thought to be weakly defended. The convoy represented a considerable force. Churchill was determined upon this small victory in the dark days of the war. In addition to the *Ettrick*, there were other ships carrying the rest of the Marine brigade, the Argylls, and 2,500 Free French in two Dutch liners. Two sloops, various destroyers and the cruiser *Fiji* acted as escort. Brigade command assumed that Dakar would immediately capitulate.

They were a fortnight at sea before reaching Freetown, weeks in which life on board seemed incongruously similar to that of the pleasure cruises for which the *Ettrick* had originally been designed. The febrile gaiety which often grips those approaching battle was lubricated by cheap alcohol (a double gin was ½d). Officers occupied the first-class saloons and consumed five-course meals. Goanese stewards patrolled the corridors ringing the meal-times on tiny copper gongs. There were concert parties, lectures, games. Waugh lectured on Abyssinia and spoke for the motion in a debate: 'Any man who marries under thirty is a fool.' It was defeated by an

44. Bernard Fergusson, 'Gentlemen At Arms', *ST*, 6 May 1973, 40.

overwhelming majority, much to his dismay. He despised the sentimentality of the men. As censor he was sickened by reams of illiterate discourse on 'love'. The whole scene had for him a phantasmagoric unreality. Over the ship's loudspeakers four Ivor Novello records were played in a remorseless sequence interrupted only by an officer reading the hideous news from home.

They had been at sea a week when the Blitz began. Night after night London was being devastated by an assault on the civilian population unparalleled in British history. Everyone aboard knew that this was a preparation for invasion. After their mission, there might be no unoccupied British port to receive them. By 17 September, the Battle of Britain was at its height and the day marked one of the RAF's greatest successes. Invasion seemed temporarily to have been averted. But the bombing continued throughout that winter and spring, and coastal defences were constantly on the alert. 'My worst fear', Waugh wrote to Laura, 'is that England gets into German hands & I shall not be able to get to you.... If the invasion comes, stay put at Pixton at first, then at your leisure make for Quebec....'[45]

That letter was posted in Freetown, which Graham Greene was later to make the setting of *The Heart of the Matter* (1948). Waugh, like Greene, found the place intriguing. An African greeted the ship, entirely naked save for a top hat and a placard round his neck reading: 'Fuk Dakar'. Sitting on the balcony of the sleazy Bedford Hotel, Waugh was back in good form, 'bubbling with caustic and delighted comments on the passing life in the delapidated ... streets....'[46] 'I enjoy being in Africa again', he noted, 'and among niggers.'[47]

By this time a veritable fleet had assembled, including two battleships, three cruisers, a flotilla of destroyers and the aircraft carrier, *Ark Royal* – an astounding range of fire-power to take a small town. Major-General N. M. S. Irwin, Admiral J. H. D. Cunningham and General de Gaulle commanded. Waugh's tasks remained peripheral. On the day they steamed out of Freetown, he recorded: 'Intelligence work consisted of: (1) carefully cataloguing all recent documents two days before they ceased to be secret and are scattered broadcast; (2) gridding maps.'[48] When the assault turned from grandiose strategy to farcical confusion, his quiet satisfaction at the inefficiency of his superiors was mixed with relief and shame.

They arrived off Dakar at dawn on 23 September to find the entire area in impenetrable fog. This carried a double penalty: they could not see the

45. 13 September [1940]; *Letters*, p. 140.
46. John St John, *op. cit.*, p. 48.
47. *Diaries*, 17 September 1940, p. 480.
48. *Ibid.*, 22 September 1940, p. 480.

town (or even their sister ships); even worse, the town could not see them and thus had small idea of how large a force was ranged against it. A poor start, but they decided to proceed.

The first assault was by radio. The Vichy garrison was warned to keep all French ships and submarines in port and to refrain from firing. This generous offer was declined. Dakar's commander knew something which, apparently, Irwin did not: three Vichy cruisers and three destroyers had inexplicably been allowed to slip past Gibraltar and were presently on hand to defend the town. In addition to them, the *Richelieu*, a damaged French battleship which the Allies hoped to capture as an additional prize, had operational fifteen-inch guns, ammunition for which had been supplied by the cruisers and destroyers. Far from being a defenceless colonial backwater, Dakar had rapidly transformed itself into a fortress.

This was unexpected but not disastrous. Allied forces far exceeded those of the French. All that would be necessary, it was thought, was to explain this decently. An aeroplane scattered the town with leaflets prettily printed in the colours of the Tricoleur, de Gaulle proclaimed himself over the airwaves to be the new Governor, and a Free French delegation landed at the airport. They were promptly arrested and imprisoned. Then a second delegation was sent in motor-boats flying white flags. They found the place deserted by the indigenous population and were met by two officers. After a brief and acrimonious debate, the delegation and boats withdrew and a burst of machine-gun fire seriously wounded two of the men. The next day the British issued an ultimatum and the commander replied: 'I defend Dakar to the end.' Bombardment of the town began, producing no discernible effect. Shore batteries and the *Richelieu* returned fire through the fog and it now appeared that submarines and a small air force were also at Dakar's disposal.

The *Ettrick*, being only a troop carrier, had to keep out of range, circling continuously in the mist to the strains of *The Dancing Years*. On the third day, if all else failed, they were to attempt a shore assault. All else failed. De Gaulle's landing had been repulsed at Rufisque, twenty miles further south, and a message had been received from Downing Street during the night instructing the expedition to 'stop at nothing' to achieve its objective. All morning they stood to. On one occasion they even manned the boats and set off, only to be called back by loud-hailer. Then suddenly the circling stopped, the ship headed out into the Atlantic and made full ahead back to Freetown. The mission had been cancelled.

According to John St John: 'The commanders on the spot had reached their own decision. We were running away.'[49] Back in Freetown, Irwin

49. John St John, *op. cit.*, p. 53.

issued a 'Special Order of the Day' explaining his disappointment but avoiding St John's interpretation. Waugh kept the memorandum in his papers as testament to a plain case of cowardice. 'Bloodshed', he wrote to Laura, 'has been avoided at the cost of honour.'[50] But he had, at least, learnt something from the experience:

> ... I have written again to London asking for a transfer from the Brigade because it seems clear to me that we are never going to be employed in a way I can be proud of. Also I want to see you.
>
> Mr. St. John writes pages to his artistic girl & when asked about what said 'love'. I am afraid I do not know how to write that kind of letter but I can tell you this – during the time when we expected to be sent into an operation which could only be disastrous, I realised how much you have changed me, because I no longer look at death with indifference. I wanted to live & I was pleased when we ran away.... I know that one goes into a war for reasons of honour & soon finds oneself called on to do very dishonourable things. I do not like the R.M. Brigades part in this war and I do not like the war, but I want to be back in Europe fighting Germans.[51]

They docked at Gourock, a few miles west of Glasgow, on 27 October, travelled south to billets in Kilmarnock and were given a week's leave. The next day was Waugh's thirty-seventh birthday. He spent it on a train journey to Taunton. Laura was nearly eight months pregnant and morbid. Together they visited Piers Court and found 'the house full to capacity; the chaplain sleeping in the wine cellar, the garden breast-high with weeds ... many young plants completely lost.'[52] This sense of dispossession was not relieved by their return to Pixton. Family life there had been improved by the Herberts' reserving part of the house for themselves but it was still overcrowded, and the news remained grim. The Italians had invaded Greece; national communications were in disarray; the Blitz continued.

On his return to Kilmarnock, Waugh discovered that Brigadier Laycock had at last secured a place for him in the Commandos. Since there was still no letter of confirmation, he dashed to London for a week to get firm orders. 'London looks much the same as it always did,' he wrote to Laura, 'the bomb craters at first sight might be the usual repairs & demolitions that are always going on.'[53] His vision, of course, was restricted to the smart centre. He saw nothing of the ravaged docks and streets of the East End. The St James's Club had been hit and fire bombs had demolished the

50. 26 September [1940]; *Letters*, p. 141.
51. 28 September [1940]; *ibid.*, p. 141.
52. *Diaries*, 5 November 1940, p. 485.
53. [11 November 1940]; *Letters*, p. 143.

chapel of Buckingham Palace. Other than that, he registered no architectural losses. When he spoke of people's lives being utterly different, by 'people' he meant 'Society', not the Londoners scuttling into Tube stations as the sirens wound up to screaming pitch. The Dorchester, a modern, steel-framed structure, had become an upper-class air-raid shelter. Diana and Duff Cooper had a suite there and maintained some sense of style. But guests were now tumbled together in shared rooms and there were bunks in the subterranean Turkish bath. The place seemed little more than a slum to Waugh. He was distressed to find his elegant friends not immune to panic. *He* had marched through an air-raid in search of Laycock before coming to the hotel for the night. And, after all, the day had been fruitless. Laycock, it turned out, was in Scotland, a few miles down the road from Kilmarnock, and was not contactable by telephone.

Waugh's habit of striding into offices and demanding attention irritated the military bureaucrats. He was shunted about and sternly informed that his method of confirming a transfer was thoroughly improper. During his second Kafkaesque day, he took time off to visit Maimie Lygon and at last found the aristocratic *sang froid* so miserably absent from the Dorchester herd. Maimie had, in 1939, married Prince Vsevolode, a whimsical fellow with a half-serious claim to the Russian throne, who was happily employed as an air-raid warden by night and, by day, as a director of Saccone and Speed, the wine merchants. Waugh thought him irredeemably stupid but was prepared to suffer him for access to vintage champagnes and for Maimie's company.

They had moved from her large house to a cottage behind Brompton Oratory. The scene, Waugh discovered, had all the reckless charm of Madresfield but it was somehow now incongruous and distressing:

> She is living a life of serene detachment among acres of ruin. Her minute house full of opulent furniture, a disorder of luxury – lap dogs, orchids, dishes of grapes, boxes of chocolates, about 50 mechanical toys with which she and Vsevolode play in the evenings. She, very stout, and oddly dressed, exactly like eccentric royalty. . . . It is not at all London life as Hitler imagines it.[54]

While he admired her disregard for anything as impertinently intrusive as a war, he could not fail to notice that she was becoming faintly crazy.

His infatuation with the aristocracy had begun as a reaction against his father's middle-class frugality. He had escaped from Golders Green to the ordered extravagance of adult nurseries: the Ritz and the great London and country houses. That route was now partially blocked. London was being smashed up and the ancestral homes filled with strangers. Far more serious

54. *Ibid.*

to Waugh than the destruction of buildings, however, was the disintegration of upper-class privilege which had survived largely unmolested since the Restoration. He knew in his bones that a revolution was in progress and he began to believe that no victory could ever restore these losses. He saw the aristocracy as arbiters of taste, as those who were educated to 'discriminate between similars'. He believed discrimination to be the essential faculty of the civilized mind and he would not have been surprised to find that the word, in egalitarian political usage, has become pejorative. His father's ideology of tolerance, Waugh felt, was reaping its whirlwind.

When he dutifully visited his parents for the week-end he found another odd spectacle. Highgate had been heavily bombed and the raids had damaged his mother's nerves. This formerly quiet and determined woman was now sadly agitated, while Arthur, whose temperament had always been less stable, was paradoxically rescued by deafness and sat placidly through the raids reading de Maupassant. It was a strange reversal and Waugh never again felt that intimacy with his mother which had been so valuable a resource during his unhappy early years. Alec came over. He was living in a flat above A. D. Peters's office in Buckingham Street with three girls, including the Admiral's daughter. It was a miserable affair. She did not love; he did. She was not married; he was. Evelyn appeared to be having a dramatic war; Alec was stuck in the Petroleum Warfare Department experimenting with various never-to-be-used offensive weapons. Evelyn provided a bottle of champagne (Laycock had confirmed his transfer), but there was little enough to celebrate. While the family went through the routines of convivial reunion, Evelyn was impatient to be gone.

*

On 12 November, Waugh was seconded on a six-month 'contract' to No. 8 Commando and, although he had been demoted to lieutenant, returned eagerly to Scotland to join them in Largs, some twenty miles west of Glasgow on the bleak Ayrshire coast. Laura was less happy. She was angry with him for spending a week in London when he could have visited her, and she was becoming increasingly depressed about her pregnancy and the immediate future. The prospect of his *Boys' Own* escapades merely bored her. The whole business seemed not only dangerous but also preposterous.

Waugh was a small, irascible, middle-class writer not in his first youth. He was joining a set of aristocratic toughs largely recruited from the bars of White's and Buck's. Apart from anything else, the expense of life in such a unit promised to be exorbitant. With great difficulty, Waugh was sending Laura £15 a month and she needed the money badly. She did not wish to see his income dissipated on drink and gambling. 'Your letter read rather sad . . .' he wrote to her. 'It is all wrong that we should be separated at this time.'[55] But he was never much of a husband when it came to parturition. Each time she gave birth he ensured his absence, and Laura understood and accepted that on these occasions she would be left to the ministrations of her mother. It was the only way to prevent Waugh's provoking rows with Mary and Auberon Herbert. As recompense he sent her a heavy box of chocolates, which was stolen in the post.

He arrived in Scotland to find an extravagant house-party atmosphere in the Marine Hotel. No. 8 Commando, drawn largely from the Guards, considered itself very grand. 'You need have no misgivings about my prestige,' Waugh wrote to Laura. 'Everyone in the army is competing feverishly to get into a commando and it is more glorious to be a subaltern here than a captain in the R.M. Brigade. It is also a great deal more enjoyable. The officers are divided ... into dandies and highly efficient professional soldiers.'[56] Laura knew the reputations of the leading 'dandies' – Randolph Churchill, Peter Milton (later Lord Fitzwilliam) and Henry Stavordale (Lord Stavordale, later Earl of Ilchester) – and had no doubt that her husband would gravitate towards them. It seemed hard for her, feeling ugly and in pain again, poor for the first time in her life, that Evelyn should leave at this moment to join his glamorous gang in deepest Scotland. 'I thought I detected a note of asperity in your letter ...,' he wrote disingenuously.[57]

To lessen the blow, he constantly played down the potential danger and expense:

> Liaison officer really means being on the waiting list for a job. I have done nothing so far except take a cuckoo clock to pieces.... As a result of so many chaps being so very rich I have been able to set myself up as a poor man. We get 13/4 a day allowance for food & lodging & make slightly on it instead of paying mess bills. What I do not yet know is whether I shall get marine 9/- or army 14/- pay. I will manage your £15 a month without privation.[58]

The muddle over who was to pay him continued for months as his pass book moved mysteriously between the Marine Office and the War Office.

Waugh strove to be sensible for Laura's sake. He found it humiliating to restrict expenditure, especially in front of people like Churchill. But he stayed away from the dandies' card table where hundreds of pounds regularly changed hands, and refused invitations to dine with them each night in Glasgow. The only literary project he had on hand was the possible

55. Unpublished ALS, nd [13–30 November 1940], np [Marine Hotel, Largs, Ayrshire]; BL.
56. [November 1940]; *Letters*, p. 145.
57. *Ibid.*, p. 146.
58. *Ibid.*

publication of *Work Suspended* in *Penguin Parade*. He had written nothing new for a year and Popkin was demanding £10 a month to pay off the income tax. Waugh contemplated writing a book for his own pleasure – 'a kind of modern Arcadia'[59] – but there was no opportunity for concentrated work and he appeared doomed to relative penury for the foreseeable future.

Despite his economies, Laura must have been irritated by the news that various smart wives had turned up in Largs while she was marooned in Somerset. Nell Stavordale, Peggy Dunne and Pamela Churchill had come to enjoy themselves and Waugh's suggestion that 'a minor [military] operation might be salutary to check the lotus eating' cannot have set his wife's mind at rest. The hotel was expensive and the landlady, enduring the brutal patronage of Churchill and his crew, determined to revenge herself through huge charges. 'I have been unable to find any other accommodation in the town,' Waugh pleaded. '... You must not please think of me as drinking up all your childrens money.'[60] 'Will you please try and bear your baby about Dec. 22nd,' he wrote. 'This will suit me very well.'[61] It was an unfortunate joke in retrospect. Laura gave birth prematurely on 1 December. The day before, Mary Herbert had telephoned to say the labour had started. On the 1st he struggled aboard a train, his mouth injured from having rushed out drunk and fallen down during a recent exercise, and arrived just in time to miss the baby's last flickerings of life.

'I saw her when she was dead', he recorded, '– a blue, slatey colour. Poor little girl, she was not wanted.'[62] His faith afforded distance from suffering. It was God's will and His mercy. But there is an unmistakable tightening of the lips here. The death hurt both parents as badly as such deaths always do. He often thought of that brief life with affection, possibly with envy, for he believed that Mary, as she was christened, would be in Heaven long before her father. In naming their sixth child 'Septimus', he implicitly registered her permanent place in the family.

He spent a few days with Laura, back in their familiar routine: chatting, doing the crossword, taking meals in her room. There was no time for self-pity. In early December, when his Commando was transferred from 'Operation Accordion' to 'Workshop', he was recalled and they embarked immediately on HMS *Glenroy* to begin a training exercise on the Isle of Arran.

59. *Ibid.*
60. Unpublished ALS to Laura Waugh, nd [13–30 November 1940], np [Marine Hotel, Largs, Ayrshire]; BL.
61. Unpublished ALS to Laura Waugh, nd [c. 24 November 1940], from Marine Hotel, Largs, Ayrshire; BL.
62. *Diaries*, December 1940, p. 489. Waugh had written to Henry Yorke: 'Laura is having another baby at Xmas poor girl – regretted by all'; *Letters*, p. 145.

In the company of the Buck's toughs, Waugh's spirits improved. 'After RM Brigade,' he noted later, 'the indolence and ignorance of the officers seemed remarkable, but I have since realized that they were slightly above normal army standards. Great freedom was allowed in costume; no one even pretended to work outside working hours.'[63] Their air of effortless superiority, of thorough competence beneath nonchalant swagger, their bravado in setting up as an élite within an élite, flatly rebuking the boorish regulations of an established institution – all this touched a chord in Waugh. It was precisely this attitude which had so irritated Arthur about his son's behaviour at Lancing and Oxford.

Unfortunately for Waugh, however, he was always just beyond the secret society of those he most envied. He was liaison officer rather than gentleman killer. He could not afford their games or their meals. He was excluded from confidential policy decisions. And to compensate for this failure to be at the centre of things, he endorsed the violent snobbery of people like Churchill and Eddie Fitz-Clarence, both of whom he later found weak-minded. The diary for 1940–1 ('Memorandum on LAYFORCE') is often a retrospective fantasy based on a documentary intelligence report: numbering paragraphs, cutting adjectives, packing the text with times, dates, contractions. Waugh's dream of upper-class life always circled round the same illusion: that he belonged, that he was a natural member of the clan. But he always knew, and Laura sometimes reminded him, that he didn't and wasn't.

Aboard the *Glenroy*, for instance, he happily accepted the ludicrous superiority which the Commandos accorded themselves. They were, it must be remembered, guests on the ship. Although the navy were the experts at sea, the dandies thought otherwise, and Waugh, with no naval training and on the briefest acquaintance, felt able to condemn the crew as ramshackle incompetents:

> The Pay Lt.-Commander ... had dug himself into a position of authority and trust beyond ... his ... abilities. ... The RNVR lieutenants and sub-lieutenants were a pathetic collection of youths straight from insurance offices, who had nothing in common with 8 Commando. Besides being dreary fellows to talk to, they were hopeless seamen. ...[64]

What Waugh is discussing is, of course, class, not competence. '... No 8 Commando was boisterous, xenophobic, extravagant, imaginative, witty, with a proportion of noblemen which the Navy found disconcerting; while

63. *Diaries*, 'Memorandum on LAYFORCE', July 1940–July 1941, para. 5, p. 491.
64. *Ibid.*, para. 6, p. 492.

the Navy was jejune, dull, poor, self-conscious, sensitive of fancied insults, with the underdog's aptitude to harbour grievances.'[65]

We see here developing the confusion of social grace with moral worth which was to bedevil *Brideshead Revisited*. The navy represents a breed of Hoopers. In an egalitarian age and a People's War, Waugh suffered from the prejudice that the majority of the population was (or should be) bred to be servants. It was scarcely surprising that the navy should take against Fitz-Clarence's referring to the captain as 'the old bugger on the roof' or to Philip Dunne's suggestion that the navy was like the guard on a train on which the army was a first-class passenger. Friendly rivalry between the Services was expected and encouraged, but the captain refused to suffer this sort of nonsense. As in Abyssinia, the atmosphere of Waugh's group was that of a public-school party: pranks and impertinence and jokes and treats. It shimmered with the kind of skilled immaturity he relished.

After assault training on Arran and Holy Island, they transferred to the *Karanja* for Christmas. The season Waugh hated 'passed without incident except that the Captain set the table cloth on fire during dinner and was, shortly afterwards, sick where he sat.'[66] He was already bored. In early January they put on a grand exercise to impress visiting top brass from the Admiralty and the War Office. Another shambles. 'Workshop' was cancelled. They sat about in port, more despondent than ever. Then, suddenly, their movement order came. A fortnight's leave was granted and, on their return, they re-embarked on the *Glenroy* and sailed for Egypt. Waugh had been waiting for this moment for fourteen months.

*

Egypt was only accessible via the Cape. 'We have been at sea a week now', Waugh wrote home, '& face the long voyage with patience. Wine, cigars, soda water, lime juice have all failed. I share a minute cabin with Harry [Stavordale] & Randolph both of whom have brought luggage enough for a film star's honeymoon. . . .'[67] At last he was relaxed. W. N. Roughead, A. D. Peters's partner who was running the business during Peters's absence at the Ministry of Food, had finally secured £50 from Penguin for *Work Suspended* and the money was to be forwarded to Laura to pay the tax debt for six months. Piers Court was safe from the bailiffs and Waugh settled comfortably into gentlemanly life again. He was encouraging his butler, Ellwood, to join him as his servant. In the meantime, he had a respectful young trainee surveyor in that position, Ralph Tanner.

65. *Ibid.*
66. Unpublished ALS to Laura Waugh, nd [early January 1940], from British India Line, 8 Cmdo, 4 SS Bn., APO 405; BL.
67. Unpublished ALS to Laura Waugh, 8 February [1941], from 8 Cmdo, APO 190; BL.

The myth of Waugh's unpopularity in the army relies on the image of him as a fatuous prig who had to be protected from his men. Christopher Sykes's biography endorses this notion, as does St John's parade-ground story. Dr Tanner's memories, however, are a salutary rebuff to easy generalization. Waugh was no uniformed buffoon. It was true that he stood out rather as an 'uncle'. But, when he was with people he liked, he 'fitted in very well. He was everything you'd expect an officer to be, if you were an ordinary soldier' and 'behaved as a model employer to a servant'. He only rebuked Tanner mildly for small mistakes. None of the soldiers gossiped about Waugh other than to note that 'he was a bit fond of the Honourables. He insisted on sharing a cabin with Randolph Churchill and Lord Stavordale, for instance.' He was never noticeably drunk or irascible. In fact, he was so unusually considerate that Tanner would 'wait up for him with some hot water, just to return the courtesy.'[68]

Waugh, it seems, was easily the most temperate and dignified of the dandies. Churchill lost £850 in two evenings of cards. Waugh sat quietly at another table playing for small stakes, winning and posting the profit home. Just as he had done *en route* to Spitzbergen, he grew a beard to signal his spirit of adventure. 'At present,' he wrote to Laura, 'it looks peculiarly repulsive – a mass of isolated, coarse hairs of variegated colouring, but it gives me an interest as they say, like a pot plant or a flower. . . .'[69] Sometimes he wrote to her as to a child puzzled by the mysterious life of her papa: 'I am shortly to be promoted to a very important position as Bob [Laycock]'s adjutant which, if he gets a Brigade, will see me as Brigade Major. In any case, I get a captaincy. . . .'[70] False hope. When they arrived and went into camp at Geneifa, Laycock indeed became a colonel and the unit's name was changed from 'Z Force' to 'Layforce'. But a brigade major was brought in from CHQ and Waugh was again demoted to Intelligence Officer. Someone was blocking his path.

Layforce's principal objective at this stage was 'Operation Cordite', the invasion of Rhodes. Waugh, eager for attack, took five days' leave in Cairo. There he met Sykes, lunched at the Embassy, drank vintage champagne with Joan Aly Khan and ate quails with Peter Stirling. Patrick Balfour was in town (with the RAF) and Robert Byron was due to arrive shortly. With the scent of battle in his nostrils, however, Waugh could not enjoy social life – or, at least, he made out to Laura that he could not: 'The whole town is like one huge, heterogeneous and very expensive officers' mess. . . . It all

68. 'I was Evelyn Waugh's Batman. Peter Buckman Interviews Ralph Tanner', *Punch*, 19 November 1975, 960–1.
69. Unpublished ALS to Laura Waugh, nd [c. 8 February 1941], from 8 Cmdo, APO 190 [on board *Glenroy, en route* to Egypt]; BL.
70. Unpublished section of ALS to Laura Waugh, 18 February [1941], np [on board *Glenroy, en route* to Egypt]; BL. Cf. *Letters*, p. 149.

sounds very gay but it was really flat & stale.' Had he, perhaps, caught himself out, masquerading as the young crusader? His tropical kit never fitted him. He looked absurd in shorts: 'I was much troubled by looking glasses in Cairo,' he wrote home. 'It was many weeks since I had seen myself at full length. I found a middle aged, portly, ill dressed figure which upset me....'[71]

No sooner had he returned for tactical exercises in the desert than Egypt began to panic at the German reoccupation of Cyrenaica. Layforce was rushed up the Red Sea to Port Said and Alexandria, its role suddenly reversed. The units drafted to Port Said were to evacuate Lemnos. Waugh's B Company was sent to Sidi Bish, near Alexandria, and here he sat despondently for another idle month while the Allies fell back on all fronts around him. It seemed inexplicable. They had gone out as the spearhead of an unorthodox, aggressive force. Now they were to be lumped together with the disorganized rabble, to be shunted about to block holes. 'Men had not volunteered to leave their regiments', he noted bitterly, 'in order to do general defence duties in the Middle East....'[72]

As the period of their initial 'contract' drew to a close, the Commandos began to agitate for guarantees of offensive action. Little resulted from three months of negotiation other than a series of minor raids whose farcical code-names – 'Rookery Nook', etc. – only reflected their impotence. Waugh, taken on none of these, was further saddened to see Layforce become part of the reserve of Middle Eastern Forces in mid-May. B Company, much to his relief, was exempted from this order through Laycock's loyalty to his rich friends. He kept them on Special Service, still dangling the hope of real fighting. But Waugh had few illusions left by that stage. During April he had, at last, been involved in a raid, on Bardia, which was another fiasco.

*

Bardia is on the Libyan coast. It lies between Salûm, just inside Egypt's western border, and Tobruk. The town was behind enemy lines and the main supply road to Fort Capuzzo ran through it. If Waugh's diary is to be trusted, Allied Intelligence believed 2,000 enemy troops to be stationed in Bardia guarding a transportation centre. The Commandos were firstly to destroy the stores and defences (it had large coastal guns) and secondly to create a diversion requiring the Germans to pull units back from the front. In the second of their objectives they were successful. The first was, in military parlance, a balls-up.

71. Unpublished ALS to Laura Waugh, 1 April 1941, from Layforce HQ, Middle East; BL.
72. *Diaries*, 'Memorandum ...', para. 9, p. 494.

It was a night assault of the kind Waugh had been practising for months. Their parent force was attacking further up the Libyan coast that night with 250 men in a destroyer. B Company had 150 operating in landing-craft from another converted P & O liner, the *Glengyle*. On 19 April they sailed from Alexandria and arrived at their station, four miles off the coast, at 11 p.m.

The day had been spent issuing maps and written instructions and examining air reconnaissance photographs. The orders were merciless and the schedule exact. No instructions were to be given between leaving the ship and returning to it; the operation was to be conducted in silence; each of four units had its target and had to complete the job and be back on its beach within three hours. If men were late, they would be abandoned. One unit was to cover the beach, one to cover the road, one to blow the road bridge, and the last to destroy stores and shoot up the town. Waugh's task was that of non-combatant time-keeper, although to read his own accounts of the affair, one might think that he was the commanding officer.

The conflict between these accounts – one in his diary, the other in an article published in *Life* in November 1941 – offers an amusing example of how self-aggrandisement and propaganda can twist dull fact into heroic fantasy. The article, 'Commando Raid on Bardia', caused a furore in the War Office and the Ministry of Information but not because Waugh criticized military incompetence. Had they seen the damning account in the diary they might have been pleasantly surprised by his efforts to glamorize the story in print. He wrote it up in his best *Boys' Own* style to make a fast profit. It was a scoop, the first public description of a Commando raid. It was also laced with distortion, partly to placate the censor but also to inflate the author's self-image as an independent man of action. During the voyage out, he says, each of those detailed to remain on board came to him and pleaded to be allowed to go ashore. 'I managed to fit most of them in . . .,'[73] he remarks in seigneurial style. In his article, no one appears as senior to him.

The facts were rather different. As Intelligence Officer, Waugh could have done little more than pass on such requests to his superiors. He did not lead anyone other than in his abstract capacity as an officer. Crammed into the landing-craft, astride three benches which ran the length of the boat, most of the men fell asleep. Sitting behind Waugh was an eccentric octogenarian, Admiral Cowan, small and frail, but determined to be of service. The fellow next to Waugh managed only a slight movement of the head in his direction before vomiting. Standing on the beach in a sick-stained uniform, note-book and stop-watch in hand, Waugh saw the boats

73. 'Commando Raid on Bardia', *Life* (International), 17 November 1941, 63–6, 71, 72, 74; *EAR*, pp. 263–8.

and the men out of sight, and followed battalion HQ into the darkness. They were guarding the beach. Waugh's account of the action derived from others. He saw little of it except as a distant spectacle.

Bardia is on a small promontory whose cliffs are cut by four wadis. These dry watercourses end in half-circles of sandy beach out of sight of each other. The four groups were to land on these beaches simultaneously and make their way quickly to their targets. Up to this point, everything went according to plan. Waugh landed with four detachments on 'A Beach' and they began to climb the wadi. It was steeper than expected and composed of loose stones, which avalanched noisily. Shots were fired. In a panic, the covering party killed one of its own officers before discovering that the place was deserted.[74]

As at Dakar, there had been a hopeless failure of Intelligence. Allied forces had already been through the place and spiked the coastal guns. The Italian barracks was empty. The only enemy soldiers they saw were two motor-cyclists, who, doubtless disconcerted to find themselves in the middle of a landing, drove hell-for-leather through a hail of automatic fire and escaped. Waugh was infuriated by this. Two units had failed to stop them.

The Commandos, discovering no opposition, ran about freely. There was no transportation centre, but there was at least a dump of new tyres. They set light to this, blew up a trestle bridge and dashed back to the beach. It might have been better had they destroyed nothing. The blaze lit the sky and advertised their presence. Enemy flares soon began dropping preparatory to a counter-attack. They were fortunate not to have been massacred. One party descended the wrong wadi and found no boat waiting for them. They were captured. On Waugh's beach a landing-craft ran aground and was scuppered with a grenade in the petrol tank, thus brilliantly illuminating the beach and the other men's attempts to get aboard under cover of darkness. Waugh's boat could not raise its ramp. For half an hour it 'drifted about the bay in the light of the burning MLC, full of disorderly troops and a seasick brigade major.'[75] Someone with a bayonet eventually hacked through the cable fouling the winch, but it was a close-run thing. They rendezvoused with the *Glengyle* just as the captain was about to give them up, and made full speed back to Alexandria.

This was Waugh's last Offensive Action, though not, of course, his last offensive action. Much of his misanthropic rudeness in later life can be traced to the dishonourable compromises he suffered in the Services. In many respects these were no different in kind from the 'rebuffs and injustices

74. *Diaries*, 'Memorandum . . .', para. 11, p. 496. The article describes them as being fired on by an enemy sentry.
75. *Diaries*, 'Memorandum . . .', para. 11, p. 496.

of . . . manhood' to which his persecution mania had always rendered him sensitive. But he had expected the army to be different: a mechanism through which courage could find disciplined expression. He found instead confusion and cowardice. It was at Bardia that he first encountered the model for Fido Hound in *Officers and Gentlemen* (1955):

> After this operation [he noted] there was a good deal of talk among the more responsible A Battalion officers that Colonel Colvin had behaved badly. I thought no one had behaved well enough for them to be able to afford a post-mortem and did not pass their criticism on to Bob. Perhaps if I had we might have been saved some shame in Crete.[76]

Waugh returned disconsolate to B Company's other camp at Mersa Matruh, near Alexandria. 'I am being comparatively parsimonious here', he wrote to Laura:

> – comparatively with the lavish standard of life of Pete Milton, Harry, Phil [Dunne] etc all of whom have bought racehorses – but I feel ashamed to be eating so much delicious food while you are rationed and of bathing in brilliant sun while you are cold. . . . I have been in one very minor action & emerged safely with considerable good fortune. . . .[77]

Temporal comforts went some way to assuage wounded pride. He was nevertheless consumed with home-sickness and bitter about being excluded from the Mediterranean battles. Everywhere he looked he saw betrayal: '. . . I went to my Easter confession & had to have the priest arrested for asking questions of military significance. . . .'[78]

The dandies lived in Alexandria. To avoid expense, Waugh only went into town occasionally and spent most of his time in camp at HQ with Bob Laycock. Morale was low. Laycock's rich underlings were restive under his leadership. There were no women and, although Waugh could endure celibacy with equanimity, he missed female company. Laura's letters were always four months out of date, but he kept up a one-sided correspondence with her, sharing his sadness, all pomposity gone, in whimsical, tender mood:

> The Brigade Major had his wife here for a fortnight goodness how ugly & how we envied him. Now she has been expelled & he is so sad he is playing the bagpipes. I may not be as demonstrative but I feel very strongly too. . . . If you see me again you will find a man of

76. *Ibid.*
77. 25 April 1941; *Letters*, p. 151.
78. *Ibid.*

middle-aged, uncertain temper & failing powers – but a very loving one.[79]

Waugh's view of his comrades had undergone radical change. He now considered most of them to be idle and decadent. Dermot Daly, his Company Commander, seemed happy for B Company to be dispersed. Robin Campbell, like Achilles, remained all day in his tent. Philip Dunne was leading the agitation against Laycock. Only Randolph Churchill and Waugh actively struggled to get back into the war, and Churchill's determination in this respect earned him Waugh's loyalty. In mid-May, Waugh flew to Cairo to try to get some 'time pencils' (fuses) from Peter Fleming, and brought him back to Mersa Matruh to lecture on explosive booby traps. No one was particularly interested. The Commandos had, in Waugh's words, 'exhausted every means of getting into action'.[80] But he did not have long to wait.

*

When Italy had attacked Greece in October 1940, the British had occupied Crete. In April the Germans overran both Greece and Yugoslavia. Only Crete lay between them and Egypt and they attacked the island on 20 May using a new type of warfare – paratroops. Waugh's first news of this came from Randolph Churchill. The invasion, he said, had been repulsed. Certainly the first wave was badly mauled. But as the Germans poured in thousands more soldiers, the Allied forces fell back in disarray. B Company was immediately called upon to assist.

Waugh was an impatient man who could not bear to be hurried. He also soon came to despise the nature of the operation. The Commandos had left with the intention of turning the Germans back. Now they were assisting soldiers to leave a battlefield and Waugh's diary is ruthless on this subject.[81] The British and Commonwealth troops are not described as 'evacuees' but as 'runaways' or 'cowards'. In fact, they were acting under orders and many had distinguished themselves with remarkable feats of heroism and endurance when hugely outnumbered. Waugh ignores this. The evacuation was to him a national disgrace. In some ways his military attitudes were more Japanese than British. Utterly fearless under fire, he expected all others to be the same.

Waugh's martial ardour was sharpened by working closely with Laycock.

79. 7 May [1941]; *ibid.*, p. 152.
80. *Diaries*, 'Memorandum . . .', para. 10, p. 495.
81. Cf. Anthony Beevor, *Crete. The Battle and the Resistance* (John Murray, 1991), pp. 213–32. Beevor draws on Waugh's Layforce war diary in the PRO (PRO WO, 218/166). Waugh's version of this for his own records ('Memorandum on LAYFORCE') is very similar but contains more subjective critical commentary.

From their first meeting, Waugh had been infatuated by this man who '[combined] life in the most fashionable cavalry regiment with a brilliant career at the Staff College, and such feats of toughness as sailing round the world as an ordinary seaman in a Finnish windjammer.'[82] He seemed the perfect cocktail of dandy and professional soldier, but Waugh had seen little of his idol until recently. While Laycock had risen to colonel, Waugh had remained a captain and their paths had diverged.

Waugh was as delighted by their reunion as a schoolboy to whom his favourite master is restored. As Laycock's liaison officer, he was at the nerve-centre of Combined Operations and under orders to follow his CO wherever he went. Waugh's role was again that of non-combatant secretary. This he extended to include acting as watchdog of Laycock's honour. In his shadow, Waugh himself adopted the air of high command, a spectacle which could be amusing or irritating to his chief according to the severity of their situation. Laycock was in a difficult position in relation to the other commanders of Combined Operations. The Commandos were still largely untried and had arrived in Egypt too late to fulfil their proper function. He was keen to prove their efficiency. On HMS *Warspite*, planning the Bardia raid, a solemn conference had been held at the highest level when a bearded Waugh had burst in wearing solar topee and hideous shorts. Saluting smartly, he had stood to attention. Harassed Laycock: 'What brings you here?'; Waugh: 'Merely loyalty, sir.'

On 22 May the Commandos boarded four destroyers, Waugh with Laycock and HQ aboard the *Isis*. It had been another scrambled embarkation. The order had been to take all stores, so Waugh and his staff had bundled up the Brigade files, which were later lost in the *débâcle*. The object was to land on the western section of the south coast and to march inland to join Creforce at Suda. But when they arrived they could not disembark at Castelli because the sea was too rough and no recognition signals had been received from the shore. Lying off for an hour, they returned to Alexandria, where they received new orders to base themselves at Suda for a seaborne counter-attack. This was more to Waugh's taste.

Next day they transferred to the *Abdiel* and sailed at night into Suda Bay. The notion of a counter-attack, however, was painfully inept. The harbour was crowded with the dying and wounded. Each soldier they met was stupid with fatigue, many were terrified. The harbour was also the head of a long snake of desperate men. There was nothing to do but hand over the ships for evacuation. Valuable signalling stores were pitched overboard to clear space. Liaison officers from inland units met them and

82. 'Commando Raid on Bardia', *op. cit.*; *EAR*, p. 263.

gave instructions as to where relief was required. One of these officers came from Lieutenant-Colonel Felix Colvin.

The new plan was that the Marines and the Commandos should form a rearguard covering the evacuation to Sphakia on the south coast. The route lay across thirty miles of mountain. 'We then went to Colvin's headquarters,' Waugh noted afterwards, 'gave him his orders for the line he was to hold next day; his liaison officer spoke in a quavering undertone which I learned to recognize as the voice of the force. Colvin himself did not seem particularly nervous that night. . . .'[83]

It was a chaotic scene. Laycock, Waugh, Tanner and a driver commandeered a truck and drove slowly back through the bedraggled column. German 'planes had been relentlessly dive-bombing and strafing. The men had quite reasonably lain low during these attacks and had marched – some without boots, many of them wounded – all night through the mountains. Waugh spared no sympathy for their haggard faces. That night Laycock's HQ bivouacked on a hillside, exhausted and thirsty, and dined on a packet of biscuits and some bully beef. At 8 a.m. the waves of Stukas returned and the sky was black with them all day.

Laycock sent Waugh and Tanner ahead with the driver to find Colvin. They drove to some vineyards and olive groves, where Waugh left the truck and bravely continued alone. As he wandered about no-man's-land ignoring the dive-bombers, he stumbled across various soldiers dug in against air attack. Overcoming his disgust at finding 'two officers who made excuses for not leaving their holes',[84] he eventually discovered one who would, and who took him to Colvin. The scene that greeted Waugh there remained with him for life.

'Cowardice' in the men he thought despicable but not altogether unexpected from those he always termed, with no shade of irony, the 'lower orders'; cowardice in an officer was unforgivable:

> I went into a tin-roofed shed and found two NCOs sitting at a table.
> I said, 'I was told Colonel Colvin was here.'
> 'He is,' they said.
> I looked round, saw no one. Then they pointed under the table where I saw their commanding officer sitting hunched up like a disconsolate ape. I saluted and gave him his orders. . . .[85]

Colvin was clearly suffering from shell-shock. He was perfectly rational until he heard an aeroplane overhead, when he would be paralysed with fear. His nerve had snapped. No shame attaches to this condition although

83. *Diaries*, 'Memorandum . . .', para. 13, p. 499.
84. *Ibid.*, p. 501.
85. *Ibid.*, pp. 501–2.

it is, of course, embarrassing to spectators. Waugh preferred simpler categorization: the man was an abject coward.

Only a few months earlier, however, when Bernard Fergusson was 'awaiting the invasion which never came', he had dined with Laycock and his commando in their billet in Southend. 'There was an appalling crash close by as a parachute mine arrived.... I plunged under the table with my glass of claret in my hand; and there I met Evelyn, who had had the forethought to bring not only his glass but the bottle as well.'[86] Waugh fails to mention this incident in his diary. Had he done so, he would, presumably, have excused his action on the grounds of the panache with which it was performed. To excuse Colvin's behaviour would have represented something different in kind, mere liberal nonsense. Everyone, Waugh would argue, was intimidated by bombs and machine-guns, but a gentleman should control his fear.

Waugh refused to see those whose minds were no longer governed by reason as anything other than lunatics or poltroons. If they were lunatics, they should be locked up; if cowards, then they had still made a choice: to abandon logic and the more difficult standards of courage and restraint. It was ultimately a theological question. If he allowed the psychologists to say that the sane were not always responsible for their behaviour, he believed this to be tantamount to countenancing sin. The ability to choose between Good and Evil was man's distinguishing moral characteristic. There was no room for manoeuvre in Waugh's mind here, no possibility of compromise about how one defined the categories: the Church defined them, although 'Cowardice', of course, is nowhere condemned as such in Christian teaching. The confusion results from a transfusion of military ethics (which Christ abhorred) into those of Christian teaching. Waugh still saw himself as a crusader and had a hard spiritual road ahead before he could come to appreciate a 'haunting love of failure and a sense of the inextricable interrelation of human lives'.[87]

*

Waugh was on Crete for just five days. 'We did not once ... receive an order from any higher formation without going to ask for it,' he noted resentfully.[88] Given the tumultuous military disorganization and the destruction of signalling equipment, this was not entirely surprising. In fact, he relished the independence, for it revealed a new and thrilling

86. Bernard Fergusson, *op. cit.*
87. ALS to Lady Diana Cooper, 9 February 1959, from SS *Rhodesia Castle en route* to Africa; BL; *MWMS*, p. 265. Waugh was referring here to the spiritual qualities of Maurice Baring's novels while complaining about the poor quality of his prose.
88. *Diaries*, 'Memorandum ...', para. 13, p. 502.

experience: that phantasmagoric sense of displacement in battle conveyed so brilliantly in his novels.

Waugh took Colvin back to HQ and the next day Laycock returned the sick man to his unit, some seven miles inland, to hold the rearguard. Laycock drove off in the truck. An hour later, Colvin reappeared. His unit, he said, had been ambushed. They must retreat. Waugh believed none of this but had no option but to accept a lieutenant-colonel's order. All night they marched with the column. Next morning Colvin went to ground with the coming of daylight and Waugh began to ask others for a more objective picture of the battle. Another officer's reply – 'I don't know and I don't care' – shocked him into action: 'So I went off to look for myself, leaving my servant and the intelligence section behind. It was always exhilarating as soon as one was alone; despondent troops were a dead weight on one's spirits and usefulness. I set off along the road we had come.'[89]

This was certainly courageous, but Waugh always felt happier moving against the tide. Alone, he struggled back through the column, finding more officers careless of their men's condition. He stumbled into a village: 'In the square a peasant girl came and pulled at my sleeve; she was in tears. I followed her to the church, where in the yard was a British soldier on a stretcher. Flies were all over his mouth and he was dead ... with signs, I told them to bury him....'[90] Suddenly Waugh's diary begins to read like *The Red Badge of Courage*. The experience of war was becoming stranger by the hour: its sharp alternations of noise and silence, panic and order, gluttony and starvation, stagnation and action left Waugh half-suspended in a dream. The life of the village had been brutalized by foreigners. Yet here it still pursued its tranquil course through the care of its people for the dead soldier. It was a scene enacted slowly and without words, a brief ritualistic moment of communion. Waugh did not speak their language. They had no English. But there was dignity here, and courage: a strange world in which, for a few seconds, he had stepped through a doorway out of the battle. Which was the illusion and which the reality? This was the teasing question which all his later fiction investigates. The roaring of the daily world held no attraction for him as a yardstick of the 'real', and the scene lodged in his memory to reappear in *Officers and Gentlemen*.

Beyond the village was another dream-vignette: the vision of romantic militarism which the fly-blown soldier had seemed so effortlessly to deny. 'In an arbour of sweet jasmine I found Bob and Freddy [Graham] and two brigadiers; they had had an adventure, being attacked at close quarters by tommy-gunners.'[91] Waugh, crusader again, leapt into the lorry with Laycock

89. *Ibid.*, p. 503.
90. *Ibid.*, p. 504.
91. *Ibid.*

and returned to Colvin in his road drain. Laycock relieved him of his duties and Brigade HQ was established at Babali Hani. It was another crazily enchanting place amid so much destruction: a grove of fir trees encircling a spring. As the sun burnt the surrounding scrub, they rested in the shade, drinking wine chilled in the water, smoking cigars and doing crossword puzzles to the accompaniment of the distant bombardment.

'As night fell', Waugh recorded, 'stragglers emerged from the ditches, like ghosts from their graves, and began silently crawling along towards the coast.'[92] There, beyond Imvros, he discovered hordes of men sheltering in caves:

> ragged, starving, neurotic Australians who had run away earlier. Whenever an aeroplane was heard, often when it was not, they shouted, 'Aircraft, take cover!' and shot at anyone who moved about. One could hear the wail being passed from cave to cave down the gorge. Some of them had Cretan women living with them...; at night these men sallied forth to raid ration dumps. Some were starving yet some had large stores of food they stole in this way.[93]

The scene recalls the atavism of his 1933 short story 'Out of Depth': snapped from the supporting stem of civilization, humankind is seen to collapse rapidly into savagery. It was not the brutality of institutionalized killing to which Waugh objected, it was the nightmare of life without order.

Waugh and Laycock spent their last two days like Cedric Lyne in *Put Out More Flags*, struggling fruitlessly back and forth through a ravine to GHQ to see General Freyberg and, later, General Weston. No clear orders could be obtained other than that the Commandos should be the last to leave as they had been the last to arrive. Waugh's diary records a continuous sneer at the failure of nerve among all units but his.

It was certainly a terrifying situation. The 31st of May was designated the final night for evacuation. It was thought, incorrectly as it turned out, that the German advance was too close for the naval operation to be continued without further endangering valuable ships. They had already suffered hideous casualties, and boat-loads of refugees formed an easy target for air attack. In all such operations there comes a strategic moment when chances of survival are higher as a prisoner of war and attempts at rescue become futile. That point had come. Eight thousand would be left behind and panic began to infect the ranks. They were being abandoned: no Dunkirk for them. They felt betrayed and fearful of what the Nazis might do to them. Military discipline disintegrated; the beaches thronged with ragged soldiery. To exclude stragglers, those ordered to embark held the

92. *Ibid.*, p. 505.
93. *Ibid.*, pp. 506–7.

shoulders of the man in front. It was an undignified spectacle. Waugh did not panic but, ultimately, he was not immune to the general feeling of *sauve qui peut*.

He excuses himself casuistically in the diary. Freyberg had already left, but had dictated the order of embarkation. This clearly stated that Layforce should be last. He had, however, also said that fighting troops had precedence over others. 'We interpreted this to mean troops who had maintained their arms and organization, but I believe he may have meant soldiers as opposed to civilian refugees.'[94] Waugh is trying to be honest here but does not quite succeed. Had Freyberg meant 'any soldier as opposed to any civilian' then this would only have included Layforce as the last to leave. If Freyberg had meant, as seems more likely, 'those soldiers who have been actively involved in the fighting as opposed to those whose role has been one of support for evacuation', then Layforce was again excluded. Waugh was not a 'fighting' soldier in this action. It is unlikely that he fired a shot. Laycock arguably abandoned military discipline in disregarding or 're-reading' Freyberg's instructions. At any rate, Waugh's conscience was salved by his acting under Laycock's orders to shove their way through the rabble, pull rank, knock others out of the way and embark.

Grabbing a small motor-boat, they reached the *Nizam*, a destroyer, about midnight. Here, Waugh's hypocrisy rocketed to new heights. 'There were no "fighting troops" among the officers in her', he noted later, 'and few among the men.'[95] Perhaps he was glad to find it thus. But it seems that he had already forgotten how he and Laycock had cheated. *Sauve qui peut* was a game at which Waugh was peculiarly adept: 'I think I was the only man in the ship to bring his pack away with him. . . .'[96] How could he possibly have known this? How could he ever have thought that he could have known this? Even if it were true, it would have been an entirely irrelevant indication of bravery or discipline since all men had been instructed to jettison their kit. Waugh was occasionally gripped by moments of insane self-righteousness to protect himself from complicity in failure. He never failed: he was always betrayed.

*

'The names among our officers of Jellicoe, Keyes, Beatty and Churchill', Waugh wrote a few months later, 'showed how the sons of the last war's leaders saw in the commandos the chance of reliving their fathers' achieve-

94. *Ibid.*, p. 508. Cf. Anthony Beevor, *op. cit.*, p. 220, where he discusses a similar passage in Waugh's war diary: 'This version, although closer to the truth than Laycock's, was still disingenuous. . . . The key point – the claim that all fighting troops were in position for embarkation – was definitely false.'
95. *Ibid.*, p. 509.
96. *Ibid.*

ments. There was something of the spirit which one reads in the letters and poetry of 1914.'[97] At Lancing, he had experienced a vague sense of loss with the decimation of Rupert Brooke's generation. Companionship, loyalty, a sense of purpose, a chivalric code had died. Waugh saw his own generation as sceptical and unsympathetic and, in a sense, he had always been waiting for a chance to release the romantic narcissus from that brazen cuirass which protected his adult self. He had looked to this crusade against the massed forces of Evil to effect such a release. But his statement about reliving the fathers' achievements, coming as it does after Crete, was bitterly ironical for those who knew him well and could read between these propagandist lines. The Cretan experience was for Waugh the final spadeful of earth in the grave of his military enthusiasm and, looking round himself in early June 1941, he saw not crusaders but a huddle of demoralized decadents.

No. 8 Commando had believed that its 'style' would protect it from disorder. Crete had proved otherwise. In the aftermath of defeat, they were just like anyone else. One officer, Pedder, had been shot in the back, possibly by his own men. Eddie Fitz-Clarence 'looked like a Hollywood hanger-on.... He studied psychoanalysis and had a set of opinions formed from American magazines.'[98] Waugh was forced to admit that this élite had behaved no better than its NCOs. Sergeant Lane had proved courageous and resourceful, as had Tanner, who was mentioned in dispatches. But even here there was disappointment. Lane had been abandoned. When they examined his kit, they discovered a diary expressing persistent resentment against many of his officers, especially Churchill. Tanner's experience during the evacuation had left him shell-shocked and morbid.

Waugh sat about for the whole of June, mostly in Mersa Matruh, waiting for Layforce to be wound up.

> Since I wrote last to you [he informed Laura], I have been in a serious battle and have decided I abominate military life. It was tedious & futile & fatiguing. I found I was not at all frightened; only very bored & very weary.... In danger I have only one fear, that it means further separation from you.... I read a book *Old Curiosity Shop* in which there was a pony called Whisker & it brought me near to tears.[99]

Part of his misery was that, like everyone else, he could think only of England. On the 23rd he wrote again:

> There is a very fair chance of my being able to get home.... Although I am sorry to see our force disbanded I long to shake off the sand of

97. 'Commando Raid on Bardia', *op. cit.*; *EAR*, p. 264.
98. *Diaries*, 'Memorandum ...', para. 19, p. 513.
99. 2 June 1941; *Letters*, p. 153. 'Whiskers' was Waugh's pet name for Laura.

> Egypt. Moses cannot have felt more impatient. . . . I have been . . . ill . . . with what is called a septic throat . . .: not able to eat at all or sleep much & very, very depressed & homesick & hopeless. . . . My poor Mr. Tanner has gone out of his mind and is under observation at a military hospital. . . .[100]

B Company was still involved during early July in operations at Tobruk under Philip Dunne and Dermot Daly. No one required Waugh's services. Laycock flew home on the 12th, carrying a letter from Waugh to Laura stating that he was on his way, and Waugh, a Marine again, embarked on the *Duchess of Richmond* to prepare himself for the longest sea voyage of his life.

Waugh travelled without Tanner – Mombasa, Cape Town, Trinidad, north along the American coast with an air escort, Iceland, Liverpool – a vast circuit of the Atlantic basin. Before this, Tanner had seen no signs of Waugh the writer. A servant examines his officer's kit each day: there had not even been a diary. Then, in July 1941, Waugh had bought a quarto notebook and from Cape Town he wrote to Laura:

> We are travelling slowly . . . & . . . it will be October before I get home. I have no other interest or aim than to be with you again.
>
> The ship is comfortable & pleasantly empty. I have infinite leisure and I am trying to write a novel so that if I am allowed to stay any length of time in England we can set up together as we did last year.
>
> . . . Everyone has got very excited about V for Victory here and chalks it up everywhere. It seems a light form of war work but heavier than I have done since June 1st.
>
> I found a complete set of my books, including the ones you won't read in the library here & read most of them again with great satisfaction. . . .
>
> Would you like to have the windows in the drawing room and the breakfast parlour made into glass doors? I want to start building at Stinchcombe [Piers Court] but I suppose that for years to come all building materials & labour [?] will be controlled for use in [?] making good war damage. . . .[101]

Even in these melancholy fantasies of reconstruction he knew that the world which had produced his house and books no longer existed. He was returning to a dream, an historical fiction, in which artistic and social values could be maintained only by an effort of the imagination.

100. Unpublished ALS to Laura Waugh, 23 June 1941, np [Mersa Matruh, nr Alexandria, Egypt]; BL.
101. Unpublished ALS to Laura Waugh, 3 August [1941], np [Cape Town, *en route* to England]; BL.

In *Work Suspended* he had touched on the subject and had effectively acknowledged that this new world demanded a new prose style. But 'Suspenders', as he termed it, had been abandoned and he was still uncertain whether he could complete the structure of a novel in this richer style, invading the thoughts and feelings of his characters. He was even less certain of his safe return. It was a dangerous journey and had so far been a miserable one. From Egypt to Durban they had been transporting 1,400 Italian prisoners; at Mombasa they had picked up South African troops returning for leave. The ship had been crowded, slummy and noisy, with fights and drunkenness. Beyond Durban the atmosphere had lightened and in the isolation of the South Atlantic, with the Roaring Forties and U-boats beyond his porthole, Waugh settled to his notebook and allowed imagination sway.

Put Out More Flags opens with a Jamesian description of a Great House, Malfrey, which had been 'built more than two hundred years ago in days of victory and ostentation and lay, spread out, sumptuously at ease, splendid, defenceless and provocative. . . .'[102] It was an image of a paradise lost.

102. *Put Out More Flags*, p. 9.

II

Slow Astern: September 1941–May 1942

On 4 October 1941, Arthur, Catherine, Alec and Evelyn met as a family for the last time. That night Alec was to be posted to Spears Mission (Syria) as an intelligence officer working with MI5. Arthur, at seventy-five, was obese and in failing health. It was an emotional moment for them but no fuss was made, perhaps because Evelyn, an awkward guest at such a farewell, came over for lunch.

Arthur, genial until middle age, had grown melancholy and resentful of his younger son's patronage. During 1940 Arthur had resumed the Chairmanship of Chapman & Hall, but, as he noted in his diary, that was 'more of a burden than a joy'.[1] He disliked Gatfield, the Managing Director (as did Evelyn), and felt little of his old loyalty to the firm. As the years passed, Arthur grew closer to Alec and withdrew into deafness from the modern world. It seemed hard to him that Evelyn's work should be the chief support of the firm's fiction list. He admired the technical brilliance of the novels but cared little for their subject matter or social attitudes. To the end he believed Alec to be an equally important writer, and he felt more comfortable with Alec's wife than with Laura.

Joan's departure for Australia 'was a great wrench, most of all to K. [Catherine], who as always has borne her sorrows in silence. . . .'[2] Laura, by contrast, seemed coolly superior. When she had lost her baby, all Arthur could find to remark was that 'it is impossible to say how much, or how little, she minded that.'[3] She was an enigma to him. Her stoical Catholicism seemed perversely unemotional[4] and her combination of shyness and arrogance unnerving. This was not the twilight period he had anticipated and which his sentimental diary tried to evoke: the aged P., descending the hill in the company of a devoted family 'until travelling days are done'.[5] The world and his family were disintegrating. For all Evelyn's success, he was

1. AWD, Endnote to 1940; BUL.
2. *Ibid.*
3. *Ibid.*
4. Cf. unpublished ALS from Arthur Waugh to Kenneth McMaster (an Anglican priest), 25 August 1940, from 14a Hampstead Lane, Highgate; HRC: 'She had a son [Auberon] on November 27. She is expecting another in December. The Roman Catholic priests insist upon it.'
5. AWD, Endnote to 1941; BUL.

a disappointment to Arthur. The truth was, he wrote to a friend, '[Evelyn] is thoroughly ashamed of his parents and does his best to banish them from his conscience.'[6]

Alec loyally deleted this when the letter came into his possession – and with good reason, for Arthur's statement was not true. Impatience rather than shame generated Evelyn's intemperance and Alec often found himself in the awkward position of defending his brother to his parents when he (Alec) was equally subject to rebuff. 'Do you quite realise mother dear,' he wrote in 1951,

> I wonder if any of us do quite, how considerable a contribution he has made to the culture of his day, and how much honour he has brought to the name of Waugh? The world is full of agreeably mannered people, but lamentably short of men of genius. We ought, I think, to be grateful and proud that he is what he is. We tend I think, to remember too often that he was rather tiresome between 1924–30 and forget that he is really a very important person.[7]

It was Evelyn's insistence upon being treated as a VIP that irritated. But there was no help for it. He was a burden they had to bear, and, as his parents aged, this burden fell increasingly on Alec. Normally, he would accept it gladly to maintain family unity: answering offensive letters politely, ignoring snubs, taking second place. In 1941, however, he was depressed and eager to escape.

The last year had been a painful one for Alec. The affair with the Admiral's daughter had effectively concluded with his removal from the flat over Peters's office to a top-floor apartment in White House, a new block near Great Portland Street Station. It was a sterile *pied-à-terre* rather than a home. He had not seen his wife and children for eighteen months. The post from Australia was erratic and he worried about them. On the other hand, he was unsure how he would react to their return for he remained in love with his 'giantess'[8] and, to confuse matters further, his parents had no notion of the affair or of his difficulties with Joan. They looked to Alec rather than to Evelyn to provide an extended family life in which they were welcome, and the gap between their innocent assumptions and the reality was a perpetual embarrassment in Alec's uncertain middle age.

6. ALS to Kenneth McMaster, 'Eve of St Valentine' 1941, from 14a Hampstead Lane etc.; HRC.
7. Unpublished ALS from Alec Waugh to Catherine Waugh, 11 July 1951, from MacDowell Colony, Petersboro, NH, USA; HRC.
8. Evelyn Waugh's description of the Admiral's daughter in an unpublished section of ALS to Laura Waugh [c. 6 October 1941]; *Letters*, p. 156: 'Alec Waugh is deeply & genuinely in love with that giantess who came to lunch at the Perroquet.'

The focus of this uncertainty was his continuing decline as a writer. Paper shortages and the wartime clamour for reading material meant that the small editions of new novels sold out automatically. In late October, after he had left for Syria, *Redbook* magazine bought the rights of *No Truce with Time* for $5,000. But for most of the year his literary future had seemed bleak. The novel had attracted little attention. Alec felt outmoded in both his art and his life. He was fourteen years older than his giantess and, although he would talk blithely about young women as his 'pipelines' (to youth), such affairs were small consolation when his lovers did not take him seriously. He needed a complete change.

The dismal routine of the Petroleum Warfare Department had only increased his sense of futility. There was little to do. Before midday he would often leave and meet his mother for a snack in the Lyons' Corner House in Coventry Street. They would catch a bus and go to a film in Golders Green, then return to Hampstead in time for tea with Arthur. Alec enjoyed the cosiness of those evenings, the reconstitution of the family circle (always better without Evelyn). But the arrangement was also claustrophobic, somehow undignified for a man of forty-three, and his misery was only deepened by Evelyn's seemingly dauntless success. The early Commandos were not recruited from Alec's clubs, the Savile and the Athenaeum. Evelyn never caught buses or lunched at Lyons. He did not exert himself in the emotional support of his parents. Alec felt the resentment of the good son towards the prodigal and, after that last day with Catherine and Arthur, he took his sleeper to Glasgow with a clear conscience. Let Evelyn look after them for a while.

That evening Evelyn went to the White House. He arrived punctually, looking smart and fit. Normally he avoided Alec's invitations, but this might have been their last encounter and formalities had to be observed. Alec asked him about the voyage home. It was, Evelyn said, boring. At Trinidad he had volunteered to stay on board as he had seen the island before. He had, however, finished a novel, which was with the typist. Penguin was due to publish *Work Suspended* and part of it would appear in *Horizon*. Alec was having a champagne party later. Would Evelyn care to stay for it? He refused, saying that he had an article to write on the Commandos. Brendan Bracken had given him special permission. It was an impressive catalogue and intended as such, for Evelyn never revealed his fear of failure to his brother.

*

'Alec Waugh went off last night . . .,' Evelyn wrote to Laura. 'It is sad for my parents & for me as it means I now have them on my conscience. . . . I wish I could recapture some of that adventurous spirit with which I joined at Chatham.'[9] He never did. On landing at Liverpool he had been posted to 12 RM Land Defence Force at Hayling Island and again employed as a secretary. He loathed the commanding officer, Colonel Walton, who had had the temerity to make Waugh stand to attention. Walton, doubtless warned of Waugh's erratic regard for rank, probably wished to impress upon him that there would be no such nonsense with 12 RM. After a brief leave, Waugh had been naïvely astonished to find the Colonel's attitude changed:

> [He] now treats me as the apple of his eye & continually complains of me leaving him in the lurch. He is garrulous, facetious, volatile, liable to the most frivolous & violent outbursts of rage. A most unbalanced fellow & nothing will induce me to spend the rest of the war with him.... In the mess I am treated as a likeable Chinaman....[10]

Walton had made Waugh Director of Instruction, which at least got him out of the office with a Company of juvenile Marines. But 12 RM was again a defensive force. He wrote to Brigadiers St Clair-Morford and Lushington 'begging to be taken back to the old party'[11] and eventually, on 28 October, was granted a transfer. It was his thirty-eighth birthday and the posting to 5 RM in Hawick seemed the best possible present.

Peters had also secured extraordinary terms for the article (*Life* agreed to £50 down; £50 if it passed the censor; another £100 if published). *Put Out More Flags* was being typed and Chapman & Hall hoped for Christmas publication. Waugh was solvent again and heading for a unit training for active service. All seemed set fair. In their absence abroad, he and Randolph Churchill had been elected to White's. With the promise of income, Waugh headed there in high spirits after purchasing 175 cigars, ate a grouse, got drunk and clambered unsteadily aboard the train to Scotland, hopeful that his military career was at last taking shape. In fact, six more months of agonizing frustration and a chain of disapproving commanding officers lay ahead.

*

'Things are not at all satisfactory,' he wrote to Laura on his first evening:

> I arrived here at dawn to be met by ... Col. Reading who is not an attractive man. It was he who drove poor [Peter] Belloc to die of drink.... I am Second in command of a company, not even a

9. 'Sunday evening' [6 October 1941]; *Letters*, pp. 156–7.
10. Unpublished ALS to Laura Waugh, nd [September–October 1941], from St James's Club, Piccadilly; BL.
11. [nd ('Saturday'), dated by Amory 'October? 1941' but possibly late September]; *Letters*, p. 156.

captain.... There will be no work to do. I think this is only a stop-gap job. They had to fit me in where there was a vacancy....[12]

Again, he discovered that he had been passed on – and to another CO disinclined to be charitable towards eccentrics.

Hawick was a picturesque little town which Waugh eventually came to like. Unfortunately 5 RM did not live there but in a bleak collection of huts five miles out. As the war progressed and Waugh became further alienated, he hungered increasingly for Laura's company. Whenever possible she would travel to live near him or they would snatch week-ends in London. In hotels and rented houses they could isolate themselves for forty-eight hours, lie in late and rarely go out, so that Waugh could relish the pleasure of civilian clothes. But the brevity of his stay with Walton had made such arrangements impractical and wives were not permitted to live in Hawick. Two small villas near the camp were reserved for visitors. Both were full. 'I might just as well be in Alexandria,' he wrote to her. 'I almost wish I had stayed with the mad Walton.'[13] On his second day he applied unofficially for a transfer. Colonel Reading was not pleased.

Waugh's only official activity was to train to do those things he had already trained to do. When he returned from the hills, soaked, frozen and bored, there was nowhere to relax. He shared a room with three others where the dark and cold impeded reading or writing. In the mess, the wireless blared ceaselessly. If he went into Hawick, the town was full of soldiers. 'Yesterday was a day of continuous rain & gale,' he wrote to Laura, 'and I spent it sitting in a defensive position. Today I am coughing & sneezing.'[14] No one shared his sense of humour 'but they never stop laughing.... Reading is intolerably smug, cocksure, charmless....'[15] For a man who valued silence and civilized surroundings, it was purgatory: 'My life here is one of squalor, idleness & loneliness.'[16] He was desperate. The harder he struggled to become a fighting soldier, the more that prospect receded. 5 RM promised only sea exercises.

'We must not get low-spirited,' he wrote home. 'There are so many changes that happen so unexpectedly in service life that it is absurd to look on any condition as permanent.... Please send me warm woollen pants and fur rug.'[17] 'My life is lived staring at an iron roof,' he told Lady Diana

12. Unpublished ALS to Laura Waugh, nd [1–2 November 1941], np [5 RM, Hawick]; BL. Laura knew Hilaire Belloc who had once been her father's private tutor. The Belloc referred to is presumably Peter, his son, who served in the Marines and died of pneumonia in April 1941.
13. *Ibid.*
14. Unpublished ALS to Laura Waugh, nd [November 1941], np [Hawick]; BL.
15. 16 November 1941; *Letters*, p. 157.
16. Unpublished ALS to Laura Waugh, 2 November 1941, from Hawick; BL.
17. Unpublished ALS to Laura Waugh, nd [1–2 November 1941], *op. cit.*

Cooper, 'lying under a rug away from Hi Gang and Happydrome [radio programmes]':

> Do you understand now why I would have no wireless or talk of central Europe at Stinchcombe?
>
> I have to lie & keep a jaunty front to a hundred men. Duff has to to a hundred million. Are there corners where old friends can still talk as though they were free? If there are, they must say in those corners that there is nothing left – not a bottle of wine nor a gallant death nor anything well made that is a pleasure to handle – and never will be again.
>
> The English are a very base people. I did not know this, living as I did. Now I know them through and through & they disgust me.[18]

His only distraction was a return to literary life. He wrote to the *Tablet* and *Spectator* for review books, sent a letter to *Horizon* abusing Arthur Calder-Marshall[19] and found some entertainment in the furore over his Commando article.

This first appeared, under confused circumstances,[20] in the *Evening Standard.*

18. ALS to Lady Diana Cooper, nd [February 1942], from 5 RM, Hawick, Roxburghshire; BL; *MWMS*, p. 77.
19. 'Letter: Why Not War Writers?', *Horizon*, Vol. IV, 24 (December 1941), 437–8. Waugh was replying to 'Why Not War Writers? A Manifesto' in the October issue (236–9) signed by Arthur Calder-Marshall, Connolly, Bonamy Dobrée, Tom Harrisson, Arthur Koestler, Alun Lewis, George Orwell and Stephen Spender. This proposed the establishment of an official group of war writers (like the 'war artists') who would receive 'the same facilities as journalists' and be used 'to interpret the war world so that cultural unity is re-established and war effort emotionally co-ordinated'. The language of popular sociology ('emotionally co-ordinated') was meat and drink to Waugh's savage attack. But, as usual, he deliberately grasped the wrong end of the stick. Here, he suggests, we have a group of idle, left-wing non-combatants looking for perks and jaunts rather than for fighting. He ignores entirely point 4 of their manifesto: 'A proper proportion of these writers to be of groups most actively engaged in the war.' As a serving soldier Waugh pretended that he could not sign his public letter as it dealt 'with military matters' (it did not) and he was thus able to add the extra sting of his pseudonym: 'Combatant'. Cf. *Diaries*, 28 May 1940, pp. 470–1, where Waugh records attending the Ministry of Information to meet Graham Greene and Tom Burns. Greene, 'propounded a scheme for official writers to the Forces.... I said the official writer racket might be convenient if we found ourselves permanently in a defensive role in the Far East, or if I were incapacitated and set to training.'
20. Walter Graebner of the London office of *Life* (International) had first contacted Waugh and then commissioned the article through A. D. Peters. Waugh wrote it on 6–7 October 1941 and it passed the censor, apparently with Bracken's blessing, on the 12th. Peters immediately sold the subsidiary rights to the *ES*. In the confusion that followed, the *ES* published the first part, before *Life*, on 14 November after having successfully submitted the article themselves to the censor on the 10th. They had consulted both Colonel Walter Elliott (Director of Public Relations at the War Office) and the Ministry of Information. Despite this, at noon on the 14th, the War Office seized the copyright and issued a free hand-out, a résumé of the complete story, through Bracken's Ministry of Information. A garbled version thus appeared in several papers before the *ES* could print the second half on the 15th. Result: fury on the part of *ES*, *Life* and Waugh. Waugh disliked being reprimanded when Bracken refused to support him and disliked even more the idea of losing £100 from *Life*, which was now uncertain whether it could use the story. All ended happily: *Life* printed most of the complete text on the 17th and Waugh made £250. The only discontented person was

> It had not been published an hour before the Marine Office came on the telephone to ask why I was writing for the papers. I replied 'by special permission of Rt. Hon. Brendan Bracken' and there the matter rests, but yesterday all the dailies had my story, issued by the War Office so I imagine the root of the matter is the press complaining that a news story was issued to one paper only instead of to all. I expect further unpleasantness but in a life as unpleasant as mine it will not be noticeable.[21]

Waugh's interpretation of the War Office's action may have been accurate. It is also possible that they were furious at his presumption and determined to queer his pitch. 'So far the row about the Bardia article has fallen mostly on Peters,' he told Laura later, 'I think it will be some time before official anger percolates down to my low level. . . . Anyhow I don't care a fuck. . . .'[22]

He was exhausted. After a five-mile run-and-walk he had gone into Hawick and got blind drunk on champagne. He was, he admitted, 'getting too old for this kind of thing',[23] and it was at this time that he at last made a will. He was about to embark for a fortnight's sea-exercise and there was a slim chance that this might be cover for overseas service.

*

Laura was equally miserable and was further cast down by the arrival of the will. She had seen little of Waugh for two years. She was pregnant with her fourth child in the fourth year of their marriage. At Pixton she had lost the privacy she coveted. By day she escaped the house and could be found aboard a small tractor, farming the estate, while Mary Herbert looked after Teresa and Bron. Laura's evenings were spent with her mother and sisters. She was a resilient and determined woman who was growing up fast under wartime austerity. She did not complain. But it was a dismal life and one overshadowed by her growing uncertainty about her husband's sense of responsibility.

They were utterly different characters. Part of Laura's charm was her blank unconcern with material detail. Her eyes would glaze when complex arrangements were explained. Friends often described her as 'ethereal': a fragile slimness, liquid blue eyes, gentle voice and a slow, sweet smile. As a young woman she possessed that child-like quality that Waugh had found attractive in all his lovers. Like Alastair Graham and Evelyn Gardner, she

Harold Matson, the New York agent who worked with A.D. Peters on the American market. Peters had short-circuited him and his ten per cent by commissioning the piece in London.

21. Unpublished section of ALS to Laura Waugh, Sunday, 16 November 1941; BL; cf. *Letters*, p. 157.
22. Unpublished ALS to Laura Waugh, nd [late November 1941], np [5 RM, Hawick]; BL.
23. *Ibid.*

demanded protection. But beneath this abstraction and apparent shyness her upbringing and her Faith lent her the strength which made the marriage a practical proposition in the years beyond romantic infatuation. Although much younger than her husband, she had quickly realized that she was in some respects more adult than he would ever be.

Laura loved Waugh for his eccentricities, his talent, his jokes. He released in her a suppressed hedonism and vitality, a laconic wit. She enjoyed living in his shadow, although she regarded the literary circus with contempt. When people met them and he was in good humour, their affection for each other was evident. He would be sparkish and gallant; she would relish the performance, the manipulation, the awe in which others held him. She was clearly devoted – when he was in good humour. But she had to pay for these exquisite interludes by observing an unwritten rule of the marriage: that it should not interfere with his life as an independent gentleman. Usually, this was a satisfactory contract. She often preferred to be left alone.

Waugh wanted to live two lives simultaneously. Laura provided the stable home life without which he would probably have suffered mental breakdown earlier than he did. His circle of smart acquaintances offered sensuous escape from the routine of domesticity to which, she knew, he could never be confined and in which she was herself often uncomfortable. But Waugh frequently took this arrangement to extremes and, aiming for a joke, struck the wrong note entirely. 'I shall not visit my children during [Christmas] leave,' he wrote to her. 'They should be able to retain the impression formed of me for a further three months. I can't afford to waste on them any time which could be spent on my own pleasures. I have sent them some kippers as compensation.'[24] He was by nature a displaced person, reckless and extravagant, always in search of a home, never able to settle in one. Beneath the satire of the Connollys' plebeian manners in *Put Out More Flags* there is a hint of admiration from this parvenu author for their street-wisdom. The sheer joy of exploitation never left him and Laura found this vulgar.

So intimidating were Waugh's conversational tactics that he would not so much conduct an exchange of views as turn people into characters in a private fiction. Even Basil Bennett, an eccentric and bibulous Commando friend, found it impossible to live at close quarters with him. '"I have become a marionette,"' Bennett complained. '"You make me do the most extraordinary things."'[25] An American described much the same feeling:

24. Unpublished ALS to Laura Waugh, St Nicholas Day [6 December] 1941, np [Hawick]; BL.
25. *Diaries*, 20 March 1943, p. 531.

> ... there was, on occasion, the illusion – at once pleasant and disturbing – that you were an extra, if not a principal, in the shooting of a scene from one of his books. He, seemingly as omniscient in actual living as in the novel, setting the mood and the tempo, holding all the strings and manipulating them when ready.[26]

This was precisely how Waugh in *Decline and Fall* had described the fate of Paul Pennyfeather at the hands of Margot. It represented, perhaps, his deepest fear – the loss of his ability to act independently – and with heartless precision he inflicted this torture on others. His hatred of formal interviews and of the telephone was in part related to this, for his own disconcerting technique – a barrage of unconnected questions – could thus be turned upon himself.

To the onlooker, Waugh's performances in this vein were either cripplingly funny or simply painful. Many strangers made approaches to him; none got near him. He gave nothing away. An expression of benign puzzlement would greet any enquiry, followed by a response so brief as to disrupt discussion with silence. No one knew better than Laura how ill-suited this art of embarrassment was to military life. In melancholy mood and without her to keep him in check, she knew he would inevitably blunder for he was incapable of sycophancy and, when depressed, lacked grace and tact. She could judge his temper by his letters. If they bubbled with jokes and obscenities, he was genial, no matter how dismal his circumstances. A chain of dreary notes streamed from Hawick and she feared the worst. 'I lectured on Crete', he wrote, '& the Brigadier came & got grey-faced with sorrow at my tale of shame. You will say it did me no good with him & perhaps you could be right. . . .'[27] This was not the road to promotion.

Laura liked their being an odd couple. She was a considerable eccentric herself, a distracted character, warm and generous within her own circle, but a hopeless manager and of the Mrs Jellyby school of motherhood. Waugh was an exact man. As has been said, part of the game they played was that of the buffer with the schoolgirl and it is easy to misread the patronage of his letters to her. His orders were precise and peremptory. She understood her role in this charade, even enjoyed his instruction, at least in the early years of the marriage, as evidence of his concern – and then quietly did as she pleased. She dealt with him much as Catherine had always coped with Arthur's eccentricities. Late 1941, however, was one of the occasions of Waugh's going too far.

From Hawick he sent a handsomely bound set of *The Children's Encyclopedia* to Bron:

26. Joe Dever, 'Echoes of Two Waughs', *Commonweal*, Vol. 53 (October 1950), 68–70.
27. Unpublished ALS to Laura Waugh, nd [November? 1941], np [Hawick]; BL.

> This is not to be given to the Grant children[28] or dismembered in the nursery but kept until the boy is of a suitable age to enjoy it.... In the meantime you may study it. I am sure you will find it instructive.... It was the delight of my childhood particularly the sections – 'Things to make and things to do.'[29]

One of Waugh's more amiable characteristics was that, like his father, he was a passionately educative man. He had a talent for conveying his enthusiams by the energy of his desire to impart ideas. But this letter was surely too much and the will was another case in point.

Laura was not only pregnant, suffering from fibrositis and enervated by her work, but she also had a husband who left her to manage everything and who might at any moment disappear to his death. This would have been nothing unusual had he not let their house and maintained his civilian career. It was she who in her spare time had to act as bailiff, secretary, librarian, valet and camp-follower. At this stage she was correcting the proofs of *Put Out More Flags*. His parental responsibilities apparently ended with encyclopedias and kippers. After returning from the sea exercise he had again been made Acting Temporary Captain and resumed payments to her of £15 a month, but these had always been erratic. Her own settlement of £150 a year from her mother was to run out in February 1942. The very least she wanted was the certainty of inheriting Piers Court and the income from Waugh's books. She had written to him in Egypt about the matter because he had not even thought to give her power of attorney. The will, scribbled on a piece of writing paper, alarmed her. It left the house to two-year-old Bron and, she thought, seemed to make it possible for Christopher Hollis, Waugh's old friend from Oxford, to claim half the estate.[30]

Laura's interpretation was inaccurate, but the settlement remained punitively 'aristocratic' in that Bron could legally evict his mother from Piers Court upon attaining his majority. 'The will you object to', Waugh replied tartly, 'was made under legal advice and is perfect.'[31] Nothing irritated him

28. The children of Eddie Grant and Bridget, Laura's sister.
29. Unpublished ALS to Laura Waugh, 2 November 1941, *op. cit.*
30. Cf. unpublished ALS to Laura Waugh, nd [1–4 December 1941], np [Hawick]; BL: 'This is the last will & testament of me Evelyn Arthur St. John Waugh.... I shall appoint my wife Laura Letitia Evelyn Waugh and Maurice Christopher Hollis of Mells to be the Executors & Trustees.... I devise [?] all my freehold estate unto my trustees upon trust for my son Auberon Alexander Waugh as and when he shall attain the age of 21. I give all the rest, residue and remainder of my property whatsoever unto my trustees upon trust for my wife absolutely after payment of all my just debts. Dated this twenty sixth day of November, 1941.'
31. Unpublished ALS to Laura Waugh, St Nicholas Day 1941, *op. cit.* Waugh's explanation ran: 'Hollis has no chance of benefiting by anyone's death. The property left to you absolutely goes to your heirs; if you die intestate to your next of kin, your children. You are automatically guardian of your children on my death. Piers Court is not entailed and on Auberon's dying intestate after

more than a woman attempting to correct him over matters of fact. Laura had to tread carefully.

That Christmas, as he had promised, he spent his leave without her, first in London where he wrote up his 'Memorandum on LAYFORCE'. It was a sad catalogue of betrayal and disillusionment: 'Train grossly crowded. London crowded and dead. Claridge's slowly decaying. Wine outrageous in price and quality.... Everyone justifiably depressed by the news from the East.'[32] The war was at a turning-point. Germany had invaded Russia with enormous initial success. On 7 December the Japanese had bombed Pearl Harbor and Churchill and Beaverbrook had left a week later on a secret mission to the USA. From the British perspective these developments offered two major allies and the only hope of victory. Waugh saw it differently: post-revolutionary Russia was his nation's natural enemy; America was a joke. Alliance with them was prostitution of the cause for which he had enlisted. From this point the war was no longer the defence of Christendom but a dishonourable scuffle for land.

'I age ten years as soon as I reach Stobs [Hawick],' he wrote home.

> For the first few days I was stunned dizzy by the noise & bustle. Christmas passed fairly pleasantly. The sergeants came & got drunk in our mess in the forenoon ... and Col. Reading conscientiously wore a paper cap. Does it seem odd to you that having read my novel ... [he] should make absolutely no mention of it to me?[33]

It was perfectly clear to Laura, however, that a novel like *Put Out More Flags*, appearing in the darkest days of the war, was unlikely to inspire the respect of senior officers. When Reading was promoted in February and 'left us, dressed as a brigadier and smirking obscenely',[34] Waugh got so drunk that he apologized to someone. He had just returned from a Company Commanders' course in Edinburgh (where he had met and become friends with Eric Linklater), and hoped that the change of CO might signal a change of fortune.

It was a premature celebration. Reading was replaced by another stern professional, 'a pompous booby ... with no interest in the war or in warfare.'[35] 'Col Cutler cannot make me out', he wrote to Laura, '& doesn't much like me. We had a bitter little meeting during company exercises in Hawick. I gave as good as I got....'[36] If Waugh was an educative man with

me, goes to his next of kin, yourself. If Auberon dies before me and I do not make a new will, the bequest to him is void & Piers Court goes to you.'

32. *Diaries*, December 1941, p. 517.
33. Unpublished ALS to Laura Waugh, nd [5–6 January 1942?], np [Hawick]; BL.
34. Unpublished ALS to Laura Waugh, 19 February 1941, np [Hawick]; BL.
35. *Diaries*, Company Commanders' School, Scottish Command, Colinton [Edinburgh], 5 January–7 February 1942, p. 519.
36. Unpublished ALS to Laura Waugh, nd [c. 1 March 1942], np [Hawick]; BL.

those he loved, the reverse was also the case: those he could not instruct, he could not love. And this, perhaps, lay at the root of his trouble with the military mind. In any group he sought intellectual dominance. Cutler had accused Waugh of losing company gear. If it were not found, he was told, he would have to pay for it. Waugh did not deign to institute a search but tried instead to embarrass Cutler by sending him a cheque. Another bad start – and Cutler made him pay again for his impertinence.

The Edinburgh course had, for the most part, been a pleasant relief. Laura had stayed with Waugh and been so 'piercingly sweet'[37] that he now missed her intolerably. He could not bear failure. Lonely and dispirited, he was again forced back from the world of action to the life of the mind. It was at this time that his interest in the early nineteenth century became an obsession. With each year he retreated further into history. As he later said, he longed to borrow a Time Machine, but not to pry into the horrors of the future. He would set it to 'Slow Astern ... and hover gently back through the centuries....'[38] In Edinburgh he had noted with pride the Cockburn arms[39] in a stained-glass window and discovered from this that the house in which the course was being held was Lord Cockburn's Bonaly Tower, modelled on Abbotsford. From Hawick he wrote to Lady Scott and secured an invitation for a week-end at Abbotsford itself. 'Not your style,' he told Laura, '1820 baronial on the lines of Bonaly outside but highly decorative within. Lord Cockburn stayed here in 1828.'[40]

The link between that period and his one ennobled ancestor was an integral aspect of Waugh's fantasy about nineteenth-century life. In London, cast-iron railings were being felled for scrap with oxyacetylene torches. Buckingham Palace had even relinquished a section. A 'salvage order' had been placed on the magnificent gates of Stanley Baldwin's country house and the Duke of Bedford was thought traitorous for refusing to allow the railings of his London squares to go for tank metal. It was time, Waugh felt, for a call to the orders: 'There is always dead ground immediately in front of the lines of popular taste,' he wrote to *The Times*, 'extending for the lives of two generations,' and he pleaded for the preservation of cast-iron rustic garden furniture, Gothic gateposts and Jubilee drinking fountains. This was not merely an abstract aesthetic issue. The solid craftsmanship of these ornaments testified to his dream of social order, 'the free and fecund life of Victorian England.... The railings which adorned the homes of all classes were symbols of independence and privacy

37. ALS to Lady Diana Cooper, nd [mid-February 1942], from 5 RM, Hawick, Roxburghshire; BL; *MWMS*, p. 76.
38. *ALL*, p. 1.
39. Cf. Vol. 1, pp. 15–16 and 18–20.
40. Unpublished ALS, nd [c. 8 March 1941], from Abbotsford, Melrose, Scotland; BL.

valued in an age which rated liberty above equality.'[41] 'I have bought a beautiful album of 1830 water colour drawings,' he wrote to Laura. '... You will not believe how pleased I am to get a proof of my Times letter. I have been feeling more & more strongly about cast iron since our parting.'[42] Without further ado, he booked her into a Hawick hotel.

Just before Laura arrived, Waugh heard that he was to lose his Company again. It was intensely embarrassing. Not only would he appear foolish in front of his wife, but the news had come from his NCOs. No one in authority had bothered to inform him. With his usual bravado he strode into Cutler's office. Was the rumour true? Yes, it was. Waugh then demanded to see the Brigadier. Cutler was present. The demotion, Waugh protested, was grossly unfair. He was competent to command a Company. He had done it several times already and had just completed a course on the subject. If he were to be baulked at Hawick, he requested a transfer to somewhere where he *could* command. The Brigadier was diplomatic but adamant. The trouble was, he said, that Waugh was suitable only to command a fighting unit. One further difficulty, Waugh added, was that he was even less suited to being second-in-command. Nothing to be done. Cutler had his revenge. Waugh was removed even further from the action and dumped in another office. From this point, he stayed in the hotel with Laura, travelling into camp for working hours only.[43] This was the end of his chivalric dream. 'You should remember', he wrote to Lady Diana Cooper after the war, 'that I was very patriotic though my patriotism took a different form from yours & Duffs, right up [to] 1942. Then I realized that there were two historically necessary wars going on – Russia v. Germany, U.S.A. v. Japan & that England had no part in either of them. . . .'[44] More to the point, perhaps, was the fact that Evelyn Waugh was allowed no part in either of them.

*

In these curious circumstances *Put Out More Flags* was published and, although its author did not rate the book highly, the good reviews were a welcome riposte to Cutler. 'It is a minor work dashed off to occupy a tedious voyage,' Waugh told his father in December, 'but it has good bits such as the half incestuous relationship of Basil and Barbara. . . .'[45] Arthur thought it an enjoyable read after a slow start. He and Catherine had raced through the proofs in two nights and posted off a list of misprints. A steady sale

41. 'Victorian Taste', *The Times*, 3 March 1942, 5; *EAR*, pp. 268–9. Baldwin's gates were eventually saved only by Winston Churchill's intervention.
42. Unpublished ALS to Laura Waugh, nd [c. 1 March 1942], *op. cit.*
43. Cf. *Diaries*, 13 March 1942, p. 519.
44. ALS to Lady Diana Cooper, 10 January 1947, from Hospital of SS John & Elizabeth, NW8; BL; *MWMS*, p. 92.
45. [5 December 1941]; *Letters*, p. 158.

was expected. No one foresaw a triumphant success. The 'evacuation novel' was already old fashioned.[46] Publishers were, in any case, restricted to $37\frac{1}{2}$ per cent of their 1939 paper quota, reprints were rare and authors of Waugh's political persuasion generally unpopular. Some of his wartime royalty accounts make amusing reading in retrospect. In the summer of 1941 Longman's informed him that they had sold two copies of *Waugh in Abyssinia* and that most of their stock had been destroyed by enemy action: author's profit: 7d; over-advance: nearly £200. Waugh cared nothing for this (the 'debt' was never worked off), but in 1942 he was certainly anxious about his literary career. He saw *Put Out More Flags* as an elegant pot-boiler and knew that he had backed away from the technical challenge he had set himself in *Work Suspended*. Artistically and financially it was a transitional work.

Reviews were mixed but generally favourable. Kate O'Brien voiced the uneasiness of many: that in 1942 people felt too close to the blunders of the Phoney War to laugh at 'group-presentations of the inept'.[47] Here was Waugh fooling along in his usual fashion with his cast of smart sillies but their almost heroic irresponsibility in, and irrelevance to, a world at war had become sinister. This, of course, was Waugh's point, missed entirely by the fatuous *TLS* reviewer who hinted at dark implications which were to re-emerge in Rebecca West's revised edition of *The Meaning of Treason* (1956). The characters, the *TLS* suggested, were 'such as in the years after the last war were drawn by authors dubbed young intellectuals, to the weakening . . . of the nation's faith in itself and with general disruptive effects from which its enemies are now profiting. . . .'[48] The implication was plain: that this was an obliquely treasonable work. Waugh was acutely sensitive to any imputation of disloyalty. Fortunately for the reviewer, he/she stayed clear of libel. Miss West, to her cost, did not.

Most reviewers, however, found *Put Out More Flags* a brilliant affair, Waugh's best novel to date, and detected a new seriousness in his tone. Alan Pryce-Jones (a friend from Oxford) likened the 'logic' of Waugh's world view to that of Kafka. Pryce-Jones may also lay claim to being one of the earlier commentators to detect the 'romantic' in Waugh, a term much

46. Cf. Tom Harrisson, 'War Books', *Horizon* Vol. IV, 24 (December 1941), 418: 'The war in the country, and evacuation novels. This first spate of war books began early in 1940 and consisted mainly of soft novels about the way townspeople had impacted upon and upset the countryside. Most of them showed the evacuee in a poor light; and sometimes the adult evacuee was an enemy agent, while the young evacuee often brought bad luck, upset the pattern of the village, etc. The early war books were very distinctly middle class and often distinctly unsympathetic to the "masses". Nowadays country books are kinder: usually have R.A.F. hero, villain spy. . . .'
47. *Spectator*, 3 April 1942, 336; *CH*, pp. 213–14.
48. Unsigned review, *TLS*, 21 March 1942, 137; CH, pp. 212–13.

used later to describe the nostalgia for a lost civilization in *Brideshead* and the war trilogy.

The Americans at this stage had scarcely discovered his work, but the novel sold well and Little, Brown, his American publishers since 1935, decided to invest. Alfred McIntyre, a Boston gentleman, was President of the firm and ran it with dignity and with a respect for his authors that Waugh came to appreciate. McIntyre also had a sharp eye for business. He was convinced that Waugh would soon produce a blockbuster best-seller on the American market. *Put Out More Flags* was not it, but it was moving in the right direction and, scenting dollars, McIntyre proved his good faith the following October by buying the rights of the early novels (*Decline and Fall*, *Vile Bodies*, *Black Mischief* and *A Handful of Dust*) with the intention of producing a uniform edition.

Waugh was delighted. It was a difficult market to conquer for so peculiarly English and mordantly satirical a writer. Up to this point his work had appealed only to a small East Coast audience. Farrar and Rinehart had sold little more than their first editions of 2,000 copies. And there was a similar problem with American magazines. While he was the occasional darling of *Harper's* and *Vogue*, Waugh had never stormed the citadel he most coveted: the *New Yorker*. Then, as now, it specialized in smart, anarchic humour and paid generously. But it had never liked Waugh and *Put Out More Flags* did not change its view. Its entire review occupied just ten short lines:

> Mr Waugh knows – or one would prefer to think he had invented – a class of idle, hollow, old-school-tie Englishmen and Englishwomen, who chatter and cheat their brittle way through the first year of the current war. Mr. Waugh remarks that they are a class that is dying out. A good thing too.[49]

This was the central problem of interpretation: *did* the novel applaud their demise? *Time* clearly believed that it did in suggesting that '[Waugh] has become one of the most deadly serious moralists of his generation.'[50] Even the left-wing *New Republic* found itself complimenting him on successfully, if only 'for a moment', engaging the reader's interest with this 'embarrassing' collection of 'frozen pretty boys and exhausted glamour girls'.[51] The hurdle Waugh believed he had always to overcome with American critics was their puritanical distrust of pleasure-seeking and their democratic prejudice against the privileged world of his novels' *mise en scène*. But the Yanks, as he always called them, were at last beginning to realize that this was SATIRE and that the macabre splendour of Waugh's

49. Unsigned review, *NY*, 30 May 1942, 66.
50. Unsigned review, *Time*, 25 May 1942, 90–1.
51. Dunstan Thompson, *NR*, 13 July 1942, 60–1.

comic writing derived from the cruelty of his vision. No one was immune from attack and especially not those, like Ambrose Silk, for whom he felt affection.

The introduction of Silk and the development of Basil Seal's character had added a new dimension to Waugh's bestiary. So far, readers had seen the naïfs, the smart barbarians, the rogues and the real barbarians. Basil, for instance, is the rogue who had first appeared in *Black Mischief* (1932). The Americans might have been shocked to learn that he was no invention. 'You know how I loathe Peter Rodd', Henry Yorke had written, '& everything to do with him, yet when you make him start before one's eyes in print I find myself almost getting fond of him.'[52] Waugh and 'Prod' (Nancy Mitford's husband) had never been close but, during the 1930s, he had provided the novelist with a splendid vehicle for an assault on the criminally tolerant. Seal is fleshed out here in a fashion which leaves little doubt as to the original (although Waugh always claimed his creation to be a blend of Rodd and Basil Murray). The drinking, the infidelity, the desperate attempts of parents to secure him respectable employment, the inability to hold down a job, the moody, glazed stare, mocking conventional behaviour – all were recognizably Peter.

> Basil was in the habit ... of conducting his own campaigns, issuing his own ultimatums, disseminating his own propaganda ...; he was an obstreperous minority of one in a world of otiose civilians. He was used, in his own life, to a system of push, appeasement, agitation, and blackmail, which, except that it had no more distant aim than his own immediate amusement, ran parallel to Nazi diplomacy.[53]

This description closely resembles an aspect of Waugh's early social strategy and perhaps explains Rodd's attraction. The final clause, however, places the charm of the reckless in another perspective. Basil's naughtiness has become pernicious.

At Oxford, Rodd's precocity had seemed impressive. He spoke several languages. There was no subject on which he would not pontificate. His cosmopolitan background lent him charm and poise. His blond good looks left débutantes gasping with lust across ballrooms and night-clubs. A decade later, he had done nothing but drive Nancy Mitford to despair and back. For, beneath her veneer of aristocratic disregard for bourgeois caution, she was essentially conventional, and so at heart was Waugh. Both relished the charming (and by this they did not mean the well-behaved), but both came to see charm as destructive without modesty and industry to channel it. In

52. Unpublished ALS from Henry Yorke to Evelyn Waugh, 7 April 1941 [error for '1942'], from 58 Rutland Gate, SW7; BL.
53. *Put Out More Flags*, p. 49.

the 1920s, Peter's disquisitions had drowned all opposition with an apparently inexhaustible store of first-hand knowledge. Now, repeating these adolescent performances, he had become a bore. By 1942 he and Nancy lived apart. She always defended him in her letters to Waugh during the 1940s as a kind of genius or saint, perhaps to disguise from herself the hideous mistake she had made. But everyone knew the truth about Peter. Like Brian Howard, he was a spectacular failure. The introduction of Silk thus acted as an important counterbalance.

Ambrose anticipates Anthony Blanche of *Brideshead* and personifies that other Oxford of Waugh's mythologizing memory: not the belligerent Hamlet kicking against pricks like Cruttwell, but the contemplative Hamlet, the aesthete, the delicate, easily damaged sensibility, the orphan-child crouched behind a hail of self-defensive aggression. Part of Waugh's 'romantic' retrospect centred on something he had not yet dared to write about: the tenderness of homosexual love.

So fiercely had he fought for his 'masculinity' after his broken marriage that he had tried to thrust away all that was homosexual in him. It would not die. Like Nancy, he was always intrigued by 'prancers'. Unlike her, he despised what he saw as an ineradicable strain of weakness in men like Howard and Mark Ogilvie-Grant. These delicious Firbankian figures were ineffectual against enemies like Ribbentrop. 'Pansies', along with kippers and mothers-in-law, had to remain the subject for jokes even though Waugh frequently felt closer to the male homosexual community in spirit than to abrasively masculine figures like 'Randy' Churchill. There was often a deep divide between Waugh's private and public life, between an almost religious tenderness and aggression. In his public role his mockery of W. H. Auden and Christopher Isherwood (lightly disguised as Parsnip and Pimpernell) is unrelenting. But with typical audacity, Waugh puts his own views into the mouth of a female Communist: '"What I don't see is how these two can claim to be *Contemporary* if they run away from the biggest event in contemporary history. . . ." . . . At any moment, it was felt. . ., this indecent girl would use the word "escapism". . . .'[54]

As we have seen[55], Waugh thought 'escapism' a positive quality in art. The misuse of the term by the young intellectuals in Poppet Green's studio condemns them as humourless materialists. Their parlour-Marxism has led them away from fantasy to meaningless abstraction, away from craftsmanship and design to haphazard pattern-making, away from God to a vain preoccupation with their own pathological disorders. This was, to Waugh, the primrose path to chaos. He describes a decadent world which has inevitably collapsed into war. Ambrose's complacency, his desire always to

54. *Ibid.*, p. 39.
55. Cf. Vol. 1, pp. 462–3.

be 'in the movement', has led him down that path from Cocteau and Stein to the preposterous yellow face of Poppet's painting: Aphrodite amid boiled sweets. He stands before it baffled, not by the complexities of the work (which he despises) but by finding himself in this circle of noise, an 'old queen' whose affectations now merely render him ridiculous. How did he get here? Art-for-art's-sake, has deposited him among these zanies.

It is an affectionately humorous portrait. Art-for-art's-sake was Waugh's ideal, but he would not separate it from the artist's responsibility to communicate and to preserve and enrich tradition. *Put Out More Flags* sends a highly polished boot up the pants of the experimentalists. Aphrodite was the Greek goddess of beauty, love, reproduction, born of the sea foam, mother of Aeneas, the father of Roman civilization in Britain. She is a potent, intangible creature of myth, the subject of the Venus de Milo and of countless glorious paintings. She ought not, in Waugh's view, to become that plastic, butter-coloured lump against a background of humbugs. It is a world which needs a few Basils to paint ginger moustaches on false Aphrodites.

This suggests the confusing ambivalence critics discovered in the book, and it is a problem posed by all Waugh's novels up to *Helena* (1950). There is no 'hero', no single focus of moral value. It is the art of camouflage and displacement, the Commando raid, attacking and disappearing under cover of darkness. Waugh splits his *alter ego* between Seal and Silk and gives his wartime experiences to Cedric Lyne. The need to do this perhaps reflects that persistent division in his personality between the man of the world and the aesthete. There was no better kicker of public behinds, no gentler spirit when in contemplative mood. Like Seal, he wanted to be active, offensive, unshockable; like Silk, he was persistently shocked by a world in which the skills of civilized discourse counted for nothing, and he retreated, dazed like Cedric, into the life of the mind, with the prospect only of dying in no-man's-land. But writing like this was an essentially negative business: it attacked everything, defended nothing. Waugh felt the need as an artist, as he had as a soldier, to stand up and be counted.

The presentation of the positive aspect of intellectual retrenchment was Waugh's technical experiment. It carried a little further the effects of the first-person narrative of *Work Suspended*, the complete text of which had not yet been published. Few had seen its first chapter in the previous November's *Horizon*. *Put Out More Flags* was Waugh's first complete novel since *Scoop* (1938). Yet no contemporary reviewer noted the shift in prose style. True, it maintained the flickering images and rapid cinematic 'cutting' of the earlier work, but it had also retreated towards the use of an omniscient, intrusive narrator offering extended scenic description and character analysis. Waugh was partially abandoning his technique of conveying the narrative principally through dialogue, and was experimenting with an earlier form of modernism: impressionism, Henry James's 'point of view'. The novel opens with three women's images of Basil. The focus on the perceptions of Silk is achieved by allowing the conversations around him to loom in and out of his consciousness and to blend with his whimsical retrospect. It was a technique brilliantly used two years later in *Brideshead.* The tone of *Put Out More Flags*, however, was awkwardly divided between the brutal mockery of the early work and the attempt to describe suffering sympathetically.

While he was on his Edinburgh course, Waugh had been forced to submit to a psychological examination. The doctor appears to have been told that Waugh was a drunkard and tried to impute to him (with some good reason) unhappiness and frustration during adolescence. Waugh suffered ninety minutes of this and managed at last to turn the tables. '"You have been asking me a great many questions. Do you mind if I now ask you one?" The psychiatrist offered no objection. "Why then," Waugh asked, "have you not questioned me about the most important thing in a man's life – his religion?"'[56] No space had been allowed in *Put Out More Flags* for this dimension of experience. He had regressed into well-tried negative suggestion and also into the smart private jokes. The Connolly children were a gibe at the editor of *Horizon* and his Socialist chums, as was the *Ivory Tower*, the magazine Silk edits. What was it, then, that made the reviewers sense a distinctly more serious tone?

The novel opens with a 'Dedicatory Letter' to Randolph Churchill:

> I am afraid that these pages may not be altogether acceptable to your ardent and sanguine nature. They deal, mostly, with a race of ghosts, the survivors of the world we both knew ten years ago ... where my imagination still fondly lingers. I find more food for thought in the follies of Basil Seal and Ambrose Silk, than in the sagacity of the higher command. These characters are no longer contemporary in sympathy.... Here they are in that odd, dead period before the Churchillian renaissance, which people called at the time the Great Bore War.[57]

On the last page, however, there is a disconcerting reference to this renaissance. Sir Joseph Mainwaring, a notorious duffer, pronounces that there is a new spirit abroad: 'And, poor booby,' the narrator remarks, 'he was bang right.'[58] The Dedicatory Letter, then, is a joke. The 'renaissance' is already over and the new spirit is not Churchillian but plebeian, or rather, the

56. Alec Waugh, *The Best Wine Last* (W.H. Allen, 1978), p. 213.
57. *Put Out More Flags*, p. 7.
58. *Ibid.*, p. 222.

terms have become interchangeable. The Prime Minister is indirectly mocked[59] and was soon to be identified by Waugh as his country's principal traitor. The Age of the Common Man had begun with the war and *Put Out More Flags* signalled the historical moment.

The rottenness of this society is only obliquely described but it seems to centre on the 'danger of numbers'. There is nothing new in this. It had been Waugh's main line of attack for a decade. There is, however, something new in the characterization. The Lynes are perhaps Waugh's first genuinely sympathetic figures. Mrs Lyne stumbles hopelessly through her secular waking nightmare and ends a husk. But Cedric is a precursor of Charles Ryder and Guy Crouchback: a sensitive, intelligent spirit who has withdrawn from the world into art. His grottoes are poignant but sentimental landmarks of each year's separation from Angela, just as Ryder's paintings mark stages in his love for the Marchmains. Until his foreign service, Cedric remains as ineffectual as Tony Last. On the battlefield, however, Cedric discovers something which Waugh had also experienced. He finds himself 'weary of the weight of dependent soldiery':

> As he walked alone he was exhilarated with the sense of being one man, one pair of legs, one pair of eyes, one brain, sent on a single intelligible task; one man alone could go anywhere freely on the earth's surface; multiply him, put him in a drove and by each addition of his fellows you subtract something that is of value, make him so much less a man . . . there's danger in numbers; divided we stand, united we fall, thought Cedric, striding happily towards the enemy, shaking from his boots all the frustration of corporate life.[60]

Nothing better describes Waugh's secular philosophy: 'divided we stand; united we fall'.

The hilarious agony of Waugh's earlier work had sprung from failures of communication, each character locked in solitary mental confinement. There is much of this in *Put Out More Flags*. Tragic and comic effects, however, can now also derive from the reverse: enforced comradeship. It was a subject touched upon in *Work Suspended* but not developed. Civilized man has not merely lost, but been deprived of, the key to his own front door; he can no longer control his destiny by excluding the Common Man. Waugh's mythologized reading of history assumed that this freedom had once been every Englishman's birthright. (Even Tony Last had always the option of taking control of his life.) In the dawn of a dominantly proletarian

59. Cf. ALS to Lady Diana Cooper, nd [February? 1952], np [Piers Court]; BL; *MWMS*, p. 129. Waugh here describes Churchill's BBC speech on the King's death as 'Platitudes enlivened by gaffes.'
60. *Put Out More Flags*, pp. 208–9

culture Waugh saw small opportunity for the secular exercise of free will. The army, which had first attracted him as an extension of his code of heroic individualism, had become the chief agent of a society bent on obliterating distinction. Cedric's death is futile, but he does at least discover something valuable: the inestimable gift of solitariness, the hatred of corporate life. Ultimately, this again represented Waugh's idiosyncratic application of the doctrine of Free Will. Politically it was a jumble of Catholic Action, nineteenth-century *laissez-faire* and the values of the Whig gentry. None of these conflicting ideologies belonged in the same bed, but they were forced into it by Waugh's terror of the mob.

When John Freeman asked Waugh if he wrote with a purpose in mind, he replied: 'It wouldn't occur to me to sit down and say I will now write a book to reveal the horrors of the gangs in this district or something like that.'[61] This was reflected in his method of composition:

> As for the major characters [he wrote], I really have very little control over them. I start them off with certain preconceived notions ... but I constantly find them moving another way. For example, there was the heroine of *Put Out More Flags*, a Mrs Lyne. I had no idea until half way through the book that she drank secretly. I could not understand why she behaved so oddly. Then when she sat down suddenly on the steps of the cinema I understood all and I had to go back and introduce a series of empty bottles into her flat.[62]

He always worked like this, maintaining the basic structure, inserting the perfectly cut marquetry, smoothing the joints. 'Polishing' was his favourite term for revision. It was true that his fiction sprang from an arrangement of images rather than from a desire to dramatize an argument. He had dealt with this aesthetic quandary as early as *Rossetti* (1928). But that was not what Freeman had meant at all. He was trying to suggest that an element of didacticism had crept into Waugh's novels after *Scoop* because the earlier characterization had been too insubstantial to bear the weight of what Waugh termed 'private causes of the spirit'.

Although Waugh refused a direct answer (on principle, his inquisitor had to be wrong on every point), Freeman's was a reasonable observation. The changing focus of Waugh's work was concerned precisely with a shift from the mere negation of public causes towards positive celebration of those 'private causes of the spirit'. Ambrose Silk touches directly on this when he says: '"European culture has become conventual; we must make it cenobitic."'[63] Monastic life came increasingly to fascinate Waugh. Its

61. 'Face to Face' interview, BBC TV, 26 June 1960, p. 9; BBCSL.
62. 'Fan-Fare', *Life*, 8 April 1946, 53–4, 58, 60; *EAR*, p. 303.
63. *Put Out More Flags*, p. 176. The Penguin text reads 'conventional' for 'conventual' (1st edn, p. 205).

solitude and silence, its concern for craftsmanship and discipline, above all, its regime of continuous spiritual reflection, offered a model for a way of life immured from the cacophonous modern world in timeless, masculine routine. From this point, he slowly withdrew from social life. Silk's '"I alone bear the weight of my singularity"'[64] perfectly describes Waugh's neurosis. *Put Out More Flags* was his first 'historical' novel; five of the seven novels to follow adopted this form. Waugh was no longer 'contemporary' nor did he want to be. He had set his Time Machine to Slow Astern.

*

If *Put Out More Flags* reveals the schizophrenic division of loyalties Waugh felt on returning from Crete, that psychological cleft only deepened in the following six months. In March 1942 he had not abandoned hope of seeing action, but he was falling into a fever of claustrophobia with 5 RM, and particularly with Colonel Cutler. In London, the publication of his novel had revived Waugh's celebrity and the BBC asked him to appear on 'Any Questions?'. He was rich again and in demand. In Hawick, he was a nonentity and Cutler meant to keep him that way. Waugh decamped for Easter leave, hell bent on enjoying himself, and, perhaps to demonstrate his national importance to Cutler rather than with any hope of pleasure, accepted the BBC's invitation.

In 1942 'Any Questions?' was a hugely popular radio programme and it took its responsibilities seriously. There was a resident panel of popular sages (the 'Brains Trust') – Commander Campbell, Professor Joad and Dr Julian Huxley – and each week three new guests. The routine was for the producer (Howard Thomas) and question master (Donald McCullough) to invite everyone to an informal luncheon at the Café Royal to allow residents and guests to become acquainted. Then, with the contributors mellow and slightly frisky, the recording would be made in the afternoon. This was not Waugh's style. He chose his own friends. The BBC offered twenty guineas. He instructed Peters to demand thirty – or twenty if he were excused luncheon. They accepted the latter option and Waugh lunched, more bibulously than the BBC would have thought suitable, with Frank Pakenham.

This was intended to irritate the others and succeeded in doing so. Waugh arrived punctually, eager for game. By an odd coincidence, one of the first people he met in the foyer was his preparatory schoolmaster, Aubrey Ensor, who greeted him warmly and doubtless embarrassed him with reminiscences of their days at Heath Mount. Waugh passed quickly on to the studio. Joad was his particular target. Waugh saw him as a

64. *Ibid.*, p. 61.

grotesque combination of brutish rationalism and mumbo-jumbo: 'goatlike, libidinous, garrulous . . . [he] bounced in his chair with eagerness to speak'.[65] Campbell he despised as vulgar, insincere and conceited. Huxley was perhaps lucky to be absent.

Before long, Waugh was approaching apoplexy. The questions were so general as to render brief replies meaningless. He sat cramped round the table glowering into the microphone. Having missed his chance to crush Joad on a point of logic, he waited until the recording had finished and coolly returned to a subject already discussed: equal pay for soldiers and civilians. William Beveridge[66] (another guest) and Campbell had supported it. If they were sincere, Waugh said, they should all donate their fees to a war fund. It was an awkward moment. 'They were aghast but ashamed to dissent,' Waugh wrote jubilantly to Peters, 'so I left them with that decision but the certainty in my mind that they would rat as soon as my back was turned.'[67] They did rat and Waugh claimed his twenty guineas plus first-class return fare.

That evening he escaped London for the cool silence of Mells Manor, Katharine Asquith's house, where she and Laura were waiting to offer sanctuary. This was the only world in which he now felt comfortable: Mass of the Presanctified at Downside on Good Friday; the week-end with Laura, Ronald Knox, Katharine and her two daughters, Helen and Perdita. Good conversation, good food, and a life structured by church-going were now positively preferred to the decayed dreams of chivalry. By Monday, he even felt strong enough to visit his children at Pixton. 'I found Teresa,' he noted, 'contrary to accounts, a civil, intelligent and self-possessed little girl, inarticulate and pasty-faced. I am sending her to my mother for a long visit which may, I hope, undo some of the mischief of Pixton neglect. My son was sanguine and self-confident.'[68] He felt no love for Bron. Waugh's children were strangers to him and he preferred to remain a dim, august presence during their infancy. Both parents, indeed, were remote figures. Laura 'accepted her children', Bron wrote, 'with a peculiar detachment as the people who made up her life.'[69] Small children not only bored Waugh but threatened his dignity. He stared at them curiously like a visitor to a monkey-house.

His trips to Pixton had always been marked by a certain awkwardness. It had been a tumultuous household even before the evacuees. He became restive when embroiled in its disorganization. Mary Herbert was abrasive

65. *Diaries*, 2 April 1942, p. 520.
66. Later Baron Beveridge (1879–1963), social reformer, economist and architect of the Welfare State.
67. [4? April 1942]; *Letters*, p. 159.
68. *Diaries*, 1–11 April 1942, p. 521. Waugh's visit was on 6 April.
69. Auberon Waugh, 'Laura Waugh 1916–1973', *The Antigonish Review* (Winter 1984), 32.

and sharp-witted, but she shared little of Waugh's mental or sartorial precision, and her daughters, Gabriel and Laura at least, had acquired her disregard of personal appearance. Mary's fingers were stained with nicotine. Some neighbours found the family eccentrically uncouth. As we have seen, however, this did not represent a neglect of social distinctions. 'Waugh's background', his son has remarked, 'was distinctly middle-class. Although the Waughs were an eminently respectable family ... the gulf between them and the carefree traditions of the aristocracy was as great as if he had been a fishmonger's assistant.'[70] Having overcome the Herberts' initial opposition, Waugh had gradually been accepted and, although his social pretensions always struck them as amusingly vulgar, they eventually came, with Laura, to recognize his genius. This took some time. In 1942 he was in the 'middle period' of his relationship with the family, no longer the bumptious parvenu, not yet the man of distinction. It was only after the balance of power had shifted and they valued *his* patronage that he could relax with them. Those he could not instruct he could not love.

One Herbert he could never love. During this visit, Laura's brother came over: 'Auberon has managed to plough both his [army] groups and his future was widely and wildly discussed.'[71] Auberon rarely emerged as more than a caricature in Waugh's vindictive imagination. He loathed the ugliness and awkwardness of that fleshy youth who, as a sixteen-year-old about to give Laura away, had burst into tears in the car on the way to the ceremony and pleaded with his sister not to go through with the wedding. Waugh could not forgive such things.

Auberon was a shy, faintly pompous young man of ungainly appearance, who was acutely susceptible to these waves of polite hostility. Waugh expected to be entertained and, like Ambrose Silk, craved vibrant, allusive conversation. Auberon was at first easily intimidated into silence. As he grew up, however, he came to feel justifiably resentful of this treatment. Isaiah Berlin, Malcolm Muggeridge, David Cecil and Mark Amory found him brilliantly amusing. He spoke ten languages and, failing to be accepted for the British army, joined the Polish forces, in which he served courageously. He became an authority on Polish and Ukrainian affairs. But intellectual gifts could never compensate Waugh for someone's failure to amuse *him*, and Laura found this estrangement painful. She was close to Auberon, and Waugh would not invite him to their house. After the war, brother and sister could meet only clandestinely.

Waugh spent just three days at Pixton. After 'family fun', he needed a couple of nights' hedonism before facing Cutler again. Laura, Teresa and he returned to London, where Laura took Teresa to Highgate to stay with

70. *Ibid.*, p. 29.
71. *Diaries*, 1–11 April 1942, p. 521.

her grandparents. Laura spent the night there; Waugh headed into town for caviare and black velvet with Frank Pakenham and Maimie Lygon. Pakenham had, during the early years of the war, become a Catholic and this had instantly intensified their friendship. It was a glorious evening. 'On returning to St James's', Waugh noted, 'I was so tipsy that I supported Auberon's candidature for the club. Next day I met Laura and ate oysters with her, saw part of a film, went to tea with the Yorkes; then separated.... The happiest leave of the war.'[72] At the root of this contentment lay the promise of release from 5 RM. Before leaving Hawick, a letter had arrived from Bob Laycock saying that there was a place for Waugh at Special Service Brigade HQ.

5 RM had moved to a desolate camp on the outskirts of Glasgow. Waugh escaped whenever he could to the lugubrious Western Club, where he drank vintage port in Victorian surroundings and waited for deliverance. 'Pollock Camp is frightful,' he wrote to Laura. 'All the discomforts of Stobs [Hawick] combined with industrial fumes and dirt and a horizon of proletarian suburb.'[73] He was depressed but, with the prospect of a transfer, able to turn his misery to humour: 'The bombardment of Bath depresses me more than the fall of Singapore. I dread a competition in architectural destruction but my only hope is that with their ghastly taste the Germans will concentrate on Stratford-on-Avon.'[74]

The immediate obstacle to Waugh's release was that the Marines were raising their own Commando. The Adjutant General told him that any Marine wishing to do this kind of work should either go to them or resign before applying elsewhere. Waugh hated the Marines but he was reluctant to resign because 'I thought it unlikely that any respectable regiment would take on an officer who did not intend to serve with them. However "the Blues" have accepted me so I can now grow my hair long and wear a watch chain across my chest....'[75] It was a complicated manoeuvre and one that Arthur, with his inexperience of military life, found utterly baffling. Waugh needed some regiment to accept him in order to remove himself from Cutler, who persistently blocked the secondment. Few regiments, however, were interested in accepting a new officer who would immediately disappear. Perhaps this became Laycock's trump card in arguing for Waugh's acceptance by the Royal Horse Guards (his own regiment): that they need fear no trouble from this recalcitrant novelist because Laycock would instantly take him off their hands. So Waugh became a member of the Blues.

72. *Ibid.*
73. Unpublished ALS to Laura Waugh, 'Sunday' [26 April? 1942], from Western Club, Glasgow, CI; BL.
74. Unpublished ALS to Laura Waugh, nd [c. 26 April 1942], from Western Club, Glasgow, CI; BL.
75. Unpublished ALS to Laura Waugh, 'Sunday' [26 April? 1942], *op. cit.*

Cutler did not give up easily. Waugh was not allowed to wait comfortably for his transfer but was sent on a lengthy exercise: 'For four days we have been living in a field,' he wrote to Laura, 'acting as enemy to the army who are practising invasion. I think their performance . . . must have postponed the opening of the popular front in Europe for some years.'[76] But not even this could dampen his spirits:

> I removed my moustaches half an hour ago & feel a free & happy man. The last weeks with Cutler have been very disagreeable. He did all he could to persecute me, even to putting me down for a young officers hardening [?] course to start in the highlands tomorrow. My reprieve arrived a matter of hours from the time I was to leave. The course was to have been my death. . . . To have got my transfer is like having lost a rotten and aching tooth that was poisoning me. The relief is immediate and I feel benign again to all marines.
>
> What have you done about my civilian clothes? If nothing, start at once [?], unpack, dry [?], brush, air them. They will rot otherwise and are irreplacable [*sic*]. . . .
>
> When your new son is born you shall come to Ardrossan to recuperate and we will be happy again.[77]

Waugh's mood could often be gauged by the revival of his sartorial obsession. His wardrobe was as much an eccentric work of art as his writing or his house. The dandy in him was only suppressed during periods of melancholia. In May 1942 his anticipation of happiness did not focus on the birth of his fourth child but on long hair, a watch-chain, new regimentals, and a length of ghastly Royal Horse Guards tweed to make up a suit for Laura. On the 11th he boarded a truck and drove to Ardrossan with a light heart. He was, he felt, going home to the club of upper-class toughs who were the only soldiers who could ever understand him.

76. Unpublished ALS to Laura Waugh, 'Sunday' [10 May? 1942], from Western Club, Glasgow, CI; BL.
77. *Ibid.*

III

Resignation: May 1942–January 1944

On his thirty-ninth birthday, Waugh was based in Sherborne, Dorset, near his brother's old school. 'A good year,' he recorded:

> I have begotten a fine daughter, published a successful book, drunk 300 bottles of wine and smoked 300 or more Havana cigars. I have got back to soldiering among friends. This time last year I was on my way to Hawick to join 5 RM. I get steadily worse as a soldier . . . but more patient and humble – as far as soldiering is concerned. I have about £900 in hand and no grave debts except to the Government; health excellent except when impaired by wine; a wife I love, agreeable work in surroundings of great beauty. Well that is as much as one can hope for.[1]

Unusual benignity. In fact, his recent military experience had evoked little patience or humility. The week-end before his birthday had been typical: he had umpired a field day at Sherborne School and slipped off early to dine with Basil Bennett, forgetting the commanding officer's invitation to sandwiches and beer. After two bottles of vintage port, they had arrived puffing cigars to discover a lonely CO, quietly apoplectic behind hillocks of cut bread. It was another blunder for the record. In fact, the last six months had been largely futile.

Ardrossan was on the west coast of Scotland, a few miles south of Largs where Waugh had been stationed with No. 8 Commando. The old party – Bennett, Brian Franks, Bill Stirling, Philip Dunne and Bob Laycock – had welcomed him and he was at first elated. It was there that he heard of the birth of Margaret on 10 June, although he had taken so little interest in the event that he mistook the date in his diary and left Laura to choose a name. He had travelled to Pixton, pleased to find both her and the asparagus healthy, then quickly disappeared to Matlock for 'Intelligence training': a course of photographic interpretation.

Back in Ardrossan, Waugh had found himself returned to his futile role as Laycock's Intelligence Officer, an acting temporary captain on lieutenant's pay, loyally kept on as a kind of regimental mascot. There can

1. *Diaries*, 28 October 1942, p. 530.

be no doubt of Laycock's affection for him and Waugh was an efficient administrator when he could be bothered. Like his father, he could rapidly impose order on a morass of papers. Unlike him, however, Waugh found no pleasure in performing routine tasks well. As he sat glumly behind his 'IN' and 'OUT' trays, his only entertainment had been to post letters to himself and to watch them endlessly circulating.

Laycock witnessed this frustration sadly, but there was little he could do to help. Offered encouragement, Waugh abused it. When Laycock made a national tour of Commando bases, he took Waugh along for the ride. Waugh persistently embarrassed everyone by acting as an aide-de-camp. Later he had worked briefly at Combined Operations Headquarters in London. But not even Laycock's patronage could save Waugh from himself:

> A regrettable event took place on Friday. I went to a morning cocktail party by Maimie & got a little drunk. Then Phil [Dunne] & I lunched together and we sat all the afternoon drinking old brandy & goodness we were pissed by cocktail time when we went to two cocktail parties. I have no memories after about seven o'clock but I learn that I dined with Bob & Angie & Sally Churchill & Randolph & panto [Pam]....[2]

To arrive paralysed with alcohol at his CO's table was a gross misjudgment. 'From that evening', Waugh noted, 'I began to trace a decline in my position in Bob's esteem.'[3]

Waugh had always to be engaged on a quest of some sort. A dynamic man, he could also be petulant when not the centre of attention. And during this hiatus, as ever, he had fought boredom with hedonism. For ten days after this 'regrettable event' he had drifted between the Ritz, the St James's Club and Claridge's, usually drunk, his condition grimly noted by senior officers. No, in many respects, it had not been a good year, despite his literary success. A diary entry for 28 August more accurately registers his feelings: 'I have spent the day in complete idleness, having no share in or knowledge of the current operations.'[4]

At this time, while idling around London as Laycock's representative at COHQ, Waugh had strolled into the St James's Club for breakfast to be greeted by the porter with the words: '"We thought you would be in Dieppe, sir."'[5] He was referring to the Commando raid, mounted the day before. It was the first Waugh had heard of it and the humiliation cut deeply. Clearly he was not trusted with classified information. Worse still, he learned that the thirty-two-year-old Lord Lovat had led the assault.

2. Unpublished ALS to Laura Waugh, nd [23 August 1942], from St James's Club, Piccadilly; BL.
3. *Diaries*, 27 August 1942, p. 525.
4. *Ibid.*, 28 August 1942, p. 526.
5. *Ibid.*, 27 August 1942, p. 525.

'Shimi' Lovat always failed to understand Laycock's affection for Waugh. Lovat's mother and Waugh had first met on that Hellenic Society cruise in 1933 which had proved a turning-point in the novelist's life.[6] Waugh had been pugnacious, irreverent, determined to impress; Lady Lovat and her son had maintained an icy reserve. They thought him bumptious. He found them pompous. When Alfred Duggan farted at Lady Lovat, Waugh thought that this had struck precisely the right note of response and turned his attention to the blue-blooded contingent who *did* enjoy his jokes. But he never forgot. The Lovats were 'old Catholic' gentry of the sort Waugh later eulogized in fiction; not so in his life. Mother and son became implacable enemies to Waugh, although they felt no particular animus towards him. 'I have had a very great victory in a very minor battle with Shimi', Waugh wrote to Laura in October, 'and hate him instead of Wakefield.'[7] In this case, however, Waugh's enjoyment of impolitic antagonism developed into a more serious matter than his brushes with Walton and Cutler.

Laycock had moved the Special Service Brigade HQ to Sherborne in early October and had made Lovat second-in-command. Probably to be rid of Waugh for a while, Laycock sent him on ahead to make preparations. But there was still nothing for him to do and, failing all else, he had again reactivated his literary life. He thought of writing a novel; reviewed Graham Greene's *British Dramatists*; and conducted a running battle with Marie Stopes in the correspondence columns of the *New Statesman*. For some months he had been arguing with Gatfield of Chapman & Hall to get *Work Suspended* published. Throughout that 'good year' he had found himself becoming steadily alienated from the military world.

The Greene review reflects an obsession which partly explains Waugh's failure as an officer. Much as he admired his friend's literary gifts, Waugh loathed his apparent subscription 'to the popular belief in "the People"':

> An American statesman has announced that this is 'the century of the common man', and it is not to be wondered at that during the last ten years English writers have sought conspicuously to flatter the rising, and revile the falling, powers in the land . . . in place of the old, simple belief of Christianity that differences of wealth and learning cannot affect the reality and ultimate importance of the individual, there has risen the new, complicated and stark crazy theory that only the poor are real and important and that the only live art is the art of the People.[8]

6. See Vol. 1, pp. 350–3.
7. Unpublished ALS to Laura Waugh, nd [17–18 October? 1942], np [Sherborne]; BL.
8. 'Drama and the People', *Spectator*, 6 November 1942, 438; *EAR*, pp. 272–3.

Waugh despised the spirit of classless comradeship in which the war was (theoretically) being fought and his determination to see *Work Suspended* published suggests a growing desire to provide a fictional counterblast to populist culture.

Wavell had mopped up the Italians in Cyrenaica in 1940, but since Rommel's entrance into the North African campaign, the news had been mostly bad. When his country needed him most, Waugh had been kept in his tent, and, when in November 1942 the bells of London rang out to celebrate El Alamein, he did not share the jubilation. It was the turning-point of the war. From that time, as Churchill said, British troops were consistently victorious. After the Germans had stuck in the snow ten miles from Moscow during the previous winter, Hitler had assumed command and directed his reinforced armies south. At the time Waugh was writing his bland birthday entry, the siege of Stalingrad was raging and turning the Russians' way. By February 1943 the flower of the German Wehrmacht was destroyed and the Germans were in disarray on the eastern front. Waugh cared nothing for this. German fighting Russian was in his view beast against beast and the atrocity stories which emerged that winter – of the mass execution of thousands of Russian prisoners of war, of the transportation of the Jews – came as no surprise to him. No mention is made of these events in his diary. Instead we find a continuous social round, obliterating the nightmare with wine, cigars and literary work in an effort to enjoy the last vestiges of civilized life before the brutishness stalking Europe finally overran England.

Waugh's life at this stage was a palette of violent colours in need of a canvas. He felt himself boiling up to write a *magnum opus* but had no time for serious work. His efforts to secure honourable service – with the Political Warfare Executive – collapsed ignominiously, and the fierce pursuit of pleasure only emphasized ugliness and age. Mirrors again brought him up sharp: 'I got drunk . . .', he wrote to Laura, '& seeing myself in a looking glass had a serious fright. I looked like a Chinese dragon in red lacquer – so think I was on the point of apoplexy. . . .'[9]

At Sherborne in early October, Waugh moved into Westbridge House, a dull villa with rationed food, owned by a Mrs Maxwell. Laura visited him briefly; Basil Bennett was shortly to take her place. It was a comfortable routine, with Bennett supplying cases of liquor from the Hyde Park Hotel. In peacetime Bennett managed this Victorian pile. During forays to London, Waugh began staying there at great expense and, with macabre pleasure, took the suite in which, five years earlier, four public-school boys (the 'Mayfair Men') had violently robbed the director of Cartier's of £13,000

9. Unpublished ALS to Laura Waugh, nd [17–18 October? 1942], *op. cit.*

worth of diamond rings. To these rooms he brought books and, as autumn turned to winter, his bibliophilic passion intensified: nineteenth-century illustrated books, books on architecture, everything old and well-crafted, nothing new. Cheap paper and 'War Economy Standard' book production sickened him. In a dark and congested London, the Hyde Park Hotel and White's took on the aura of magical palaces in which gentlemen could maintain isolated, orderly lives. Most of his time, however, was spent at Westbridge House, where money could not purchase extra rations or service. The single consolation was that he had overcome Gatfield's opposition and, on 21 December, *Work Suspended* was published.[10]

*

Waugh attached extraordinary importance to this book. In that letter to his father explaining that *Put Out More Flags* was a minor work, he had added: 'My major work, unfinished in 1939, appears shortly as a fragment in Penguin. A fragment of this fragment is in this issue of *Horizon*. It is about a father with whom you will be unable to trace any similarities.'[11] The Penguin deal had dragged on for months, owing partly to Waugh's insistence that both sections of the story should appear together, and had eventually collapsed. Nevertheless, the success of the *Horizon* fragment had confirmed his belief in the work and, in December 1941, he had asked Peters to reclaim the rights and offer them to Chapman & Hall.

An amusing confrontation with Gatfield ensued. Waugh had suggested a limited edition. Gatfield proposed 500 copies at a guinea. Peters immediately saw the problem: the book would sell, but a guinea for a fragment in wartime would surely invite criticism. He wrote to discourage publication: better to wait and finish it, or at least to wait until the war was over.[12] Waugh was not to be deflected:

> I think a guinea too high a price, particularly as no one in C & H has enough taste to produce a book in a really desirable form. Don't pass that on. I don't care about what I get out of it myself. See if they can't cover their costs by doing 1,000 copies at 5/- on machine made paper and paper covers.[13]

Waugh could afford to neglect profit in this case; Gatfield could not. During the year a series of rows had blown up as a result of the unexpected success of *Put Out More Flags*. The hardback edition had sold 18,000 copies;

10. Cf. Vol. 1, pp. 490–500.
11. [5 December 1941]; *Letters*, p. 158.
12. Cf. unpublished TccL from A. D. Peters to Evelyn Waugh at 'A' Camp, Pollock, Glasgow, 19 June 1942; HRC.
13. Unpublished ALS to A. D. Peters, nd [received 4 July 1942], np [Ardrossan]; *Catalogue* E403, p. 134.

the Book Society had selected it for March; Foyle's Book Club had then offered £1,000 for a massive reprinting; various parties were seeking film rights. Throughout, Waugh and Peters had been truculent with Gatfield. Paper famine prevented Chapman & Hall from reprinting. They had already used an exceptional quantity on the book. When Gatfield had attempted to claim half the Foyle's money, according to their contract, Waugh insisted that publishers who allowed titles to fall out of print should lose all rights. Gatfield, who had arranged the deal, was enraged to find that, in providing Waugh with thousands of new readers and 500 unexpected pounds, his only reward was vilification as a crook. Peters often amused himself by passing on Waugh's libellous remarks as lengthy quotations embedded in his own coolly commercial language. All publishers were fair game to Peters, who enjoyed squeezing them until they squeaked. Gatfield was conscientiously refused all but minimal courtesy.

He bore it without retaliation for the sake of trade: 1942 had produced Chapman & Hall's best figures for many years. '... Waugh's suggestion that we should use up some of our small supply of paper to produce a book that "he hopes would just pay for itself" is quaint,' he replied wearily. 'However ... if I can plan anything which would appear to give us a reasonable chance of making a profit on his unfinished novel, I'll let you know about it.'[14] Ultimately, honours were even. Peters refused 50 per cent of Foyle's bulk purchase price and settled for 1d. a copy – an astute move which made Waugh much more than £500; Gatfield eventually agreed to produce 500 copies of *Work Suspended* (8s. 6d., cloth-bound, on reasonable paper) and Waugh took the unprecedented step of writing him a cordial letter agreeing to the terms before consulting Peters.

The book appeared so late in December that there were no reviews until January. Hardly anyone noticed it. Tom Driberg, then in his first year of a new career as an Independent MP for Maldon, had kept on his William Hickey gossip column in the *Daily Express*. Waugh sent him a copy inscribed '*Nous ne sommes pas heureux à notre age*', but Driberg no longer shared the author's nostalgia for 'the lost, careless, picturesque, unjust world of our youth'.[15] England was aflame with grandiose plans for post-war reconstruction and the book's melancholy retrospect seemed a decadent gesture. 'Mr. Waugh is often amusing, sometimes acute, at times pleasantly decorative and at other times a trifle shrill with prejudice,' said the *TLS*, 'but what else this fragment is intended to convey there is no means of knowing.'[16]

14. Unpublished TLS from A. W. Gatfield to A. D. Peters, 8 July 1942, from Chapman & Hall; HRC.
15. 'William Hickey', *DE*, 1 January 1943, 2; *CH*, p. 226.
16. Unsigned review, *TLS*, 23 January 1943, 41.

The one acute analysis was published six months later by the English novelist Nigel Dennis, who had only seen the abbreviated first chapter in *Horizon*.

> 'My Father's House' ... could stand as an invisible title to everything Waugh has written.... Always the house has made the man; man has not existed apart from his roof.... And always the house has been a way of life for Waugh.... He has dwelt upon its driveways and park, the iron railings and stone walls that have stood between the house and the slaves.... And in this love of house, of continuous domicile and individual roof, Waugh appears for the defence in one of the most important struggles in English poetry and letters of the last 20 years.[17]

The left-wing poets of the 1930s, Dennis suggests, had vacated their fathers' houses as a gesture of political defiance; Waugh's was a solitary riposte, a lament for the destruction of the squirearchy, turning us back towards Pre-Raphaelite medievalism and dreams of knighthood, rebuking the supposed benefits of industrialized society.

Waugh's friends also noticed the story's extraordinary literary power. Henry Yorke, 'depressed, lonely & overworked', agreed with the dedication:[18]

> You are quite right, it is the best work you have done.... For I like Lucy Simmonds, &, knowing my tastes, you can imagine the abject state I was reduced to by Julia.... Plant is a tremendous character, he made me think of Tony Powell.... But the best thing of all is Plant falling in love. No one has ever done such a thing as well. I've read it again & am aghast at its excellence technically. You make me feel like an amateur....[19]

Edith Sitwell agreed:

> ... you are doing something in this book which is entirely new. It seems the first time that a character, speaking through his own mouth, exhibits his nature so freely without consciousness of what he is

17. Nigel Dennis, *Partisan Review*, 28 July 1943, 352–6; *CH*, pp. 228–9.
18. To Alexander Woollcott, the eccentric wit, broadcaster, critic and playwright: '... *This is the book at which I was at work in September 1939. It is now clear to me that even if I were again to have the leisure and will to finish it, the work would be vain, for the world in which, and for which it was designed has ceased to exist.*

    So far as it went, this was my best writing. Will you who in the past, have been so prodigal of encouragement, accept this fragment of what, complete, might have come within measurable distance of justifying your interest?' The dedication is dated 'Summer 1942'.
19. Unpublished ALS from Henry Yorke, 24 December 1942, from 16 Trevor Place, SW7; BL.

> doing.... It frightens me, too. By that I mean that I am frightened by the condition that one has no idea of what one is really like....[20]

Had she put her finger on something here, not only about the book, but also about Waugh? That strange, florid little figure he had caught staring back from mirrors had an accusing look in its eyes. Waugh's image of 'what he was really like' was becoming increasingly diffuse, comprehensible only in the abstract terms of the discussion of 'taste', or in the theological concept of the soul. But his physical existence – his body, his clothes, the points at which he touched others' lives – had become correspondingly vague. Nothing attached him to the world. The space which might have been filled by a sense of 'self' had become occupied by self-parody. He was, Sykes thought, 'such a *violent* man. He was a little bit mad.... And he knew it.' His terror of boredom, said Sykes, 'arose from an incapacity to take enough things seriously. People taking themselves seriously aroused the demon in him.'[21] Occasionally, and with increasing frequency now, he stumbled in his headlong course of frivolity, and, catching his fabricated image off-guard, was disturbed by his lack of control over it. The ventriloquist's doll was working the master.

*

After the birthday entry there is a five-month gap in Waugh's diary. When he resumed it he was still at Westbridge House and his mood had swung full circle:

> In my heart winter, born of idleness, loneliness, and a heavy cold in the head. It has been a drab week with Bob, Brian, Phil and Angie [Laycock] away and the office work going on in corners. Myself without any task except to open the letters and in a kind of condition of Coventry....[22]

His one consolation was voluptuous week-end visits to Daphne Vivian (later Viscountess Weymouth) and Harry and Nell Stavordale. The two young women shared a house and regularly entertained the smart officers. Waugh's Christmas had been spent in joyful isolation from his children, drinking at Sherborne and Emshot. At the latter he had found Rex Whistler, Duff and Diana Cooper, and Conrad Russell. Duff was then Chancellor of the Duchy of Lancaster. Since her return from Singapore,[23] Lady Diana and Waugh had resumed their friendship, but, as Waugh always fell out

20. Unpublished ALS from Edith Sitwell, 28 December 1942, from Renishaw Hall, Renishaw, nr Sheffield; BL.
21. Interview with Christopher Sykes, 27 December 1976.
22. *Diaries*, 20 March 1943, p. 531.
23. Duff Cooper (later Viscount Norwich) was Resident Cabinet Minister at Singapore until it fell to the Japanese.

with Duff, and Diana insisted on talking politics, intimacy was strained. Perhaps she felt a little jealous: Waugh quickly became infatuated with Daphne Weymouth. But with both women it was much the same story as it had been with Diana Guinness. Waugh's puckish gallantry secured him a permanent place in their affections. He was their loyal squire, their eunuch, their pet, paramour and licensed fool. It was flirting without tears, for he was no sexual threat. 'Lately you called me very aptly leaden,' he once wrote to Lady Diana. 'A solid, soft almost incorruptible metal, useful to keep the rain from your head, to make a round shot to defend you, a lining for a coffin. Also *please* don't forget Portia's casket.'[24] He had an unfortunate habit of loving the wives of men he found tedious, and from whom he failed to conceal his boredom. Now his eccentricities were beginning to drive even his closest friends away. Nightmares began to attack him: black rooks circling the bedroom or, the recurrent one, far worse: 'Dreams of unendurable boredom – of reading page after page of dullness, of being told endless, pointless jokes, of sitting through cinema films devoid of interest.'[25]

During a visit to Emshot, he met two other old friends. Olivia Plunket Greene and her mother lived in a cottage in the grounds of Longleat. 'I . . . found [Olivia]', he wrote to Laura, 'with no trousers on completely drunk and Gwen blacking the grate.'[26] For once, this was probably no exaggeration, although Olivia was often less full of whisky than she appeared to be. She and her mother, having grafted Communism on to Catholicism, lived a highly charged, insular life with Gwen trying to heal her daughter's neuroses but in effect only fuelling them. Olivia's renewed friendship with Waugh came to assume enormous importance to her during the 1940s. Although they saw little of each other, a lengthy correspondence began which shows Waugh in the role known only to a few: the simple man of simple faith doing good by stealth. It was as though he were ashamed of his charitable instincts. Politically, Olivia represented everything he abhorred; theologically, he believed, she existed in a terrifying maze of heresy, arrogating to herself the right to interpret Scripture without guidance. The relationship was an embarrassment to him (partly because she was yet another 'cousin' of Laura's),[27] but he remained steadfast, always answering her crazy letters, imploring her to seek instruction.

The visit depressed him: another glamorous butterfly from his youth broken by the Age of the Common Man. Everywhere he saw dissolution.

24. ALS to Lady Diana Cooper, 7 August [1953?], from White's; BL; *MWMS*, p. 179.
25. *Diaries*, 21 March 1943, p. 532.
26. 28 December 1942; *Letters*, p. 165.
27. Gwen Plunket Greene's mother, Lady Elizabeth Maude Herbert, was descended, like Laura, from the 8th Earl of Pembroke; they were distant cousins.

Randolph Churchill and his first wife, Pamela, were in the terminal agonies of their marriage. Philip Dunn, a hugely wealthy and charmless man whom Waugh liked least among the dandies, was being cuckolded by his wife, Mary, and a close member of their group, Robin Campbell. Even Bob Laycock, if Waugh's letters to Laura are to be believed, led a life of depravity. Waugh was rarely prudish about adultery. But he was, nevertheless, saddened. Despite his teasing Laura with his keenness for Angela Laycock, he clung to his wife's company as a refuge from this maelstrom of infidelity.

Another apparently lost cause of this time was Hubert Duggan. A decade earlier Waugh had tried to save Hubert's brother, Alfred, from drink. In the spring of 1943, Hubert was lying immobilized in the house of his lover, Phyllis de Janzé. Waugh had known Alfred better at Oxford but, during the 1930s, Hubert had become the closer friend. Waugh had invited him to the breakfast party before his second marriage. Both brothers had that cosmopolitan, aristocratic *chic* Waugh loved, in this case part American, part Irish-Argentinian. They were the step-sons of the former Viceroy of India, Lord Curzon, and had seemed men when Waugh was a boy. Alfred with his suicidal drinking, night-clubs and hunters had appealed to Waugh the undergraduate, in love with his kingdom of Cockayne. Hubert, Waugh observed, was a delicate Regency dandy, who had 'languished at the House [Christ Church] without feminine company and went into the Household Cavalry after two terms complaining of damp sheets and an immature society.'[28] Later he became a politician. He was always a social figure. Now he was seriously ill and Waugh was concerned, for the Duggans had been brought up as Catholics but no longer practised the Faith. Waugh was shortly to be posted to London again, where he could visit Hubert regularly. In the meantime, all he could do was pray.

*

At Sherborne, frustration and growing persecution mania oppressed him. '"I have that degree of detachment from the world,"' he told Arnold Lunn five years later, '"which would be very edifying if it led to love of Christ but is not at all edifying because it merely leads to boredom."'[29] Such small pleasure as Waugh gained from success came through his exercise of power in the literary market. In wartime, however, this counted for little in comparison with martial triumph, and 'Shimi' Lovat was taking every trick in that game. As usual, Waugh was a bad loser. To make matters worse, Lovat was a near-perfect manifestation of Waugh's gentlemanly ideal: a Lord, a Catholic and a fearless warrior.

28. *ALL*, p. 169.
29. Arnold Lunn, 'Evelyn Waugh Revisited', *National Review*, 27 February 1968, 190.

Fighting free of depression always drove Waugh, usually through drink, into a state of febrile excitement. This resulted either in mental acuity or nervous torpor: he never knew which state would overtake him. In either case, he felt partially out of control, as though someone else were performing his actions, and this determination to see life as a fiction from which he was separate, the only sane man in a world of lunatics, could make him a tactless judge of his own jokes. As an undergraduate he had once gone into Peter Quennell's room, finished his friend's champagne and flung the bottle from the window at a passer-by. Waugh enjoyed the idea of magnums exploding beneath the feet of the pedestrian. He rarely concerned himself with the pain of those he injured. The man in the street was not real to him. It was a circular mental process: the more people he offended, the more he withdrew in self-justification from the crowd of prigs and bores who complained, and the more bottles he threw – always from someone else's window. When his enemies retaliated, they were usually confronted not by Waugh but by one of his masks, or by one of his protectors. In later life Laura and Peters always stood guard. In the Forces, despite Laycock's efforts, Waugh was vulnerable to repercussion.

Nine months of Waugh's company was strong poison. Bennett was being driven crazy. Even Mrs Maxwell, a benign and diligent landlady, had to register a modest protest at his excesses and set careful limits on her services before he smashed and ate his way through everything. In response, Waugh sat down with Bennett to compose thirteen clauses of the 'Westbridge House Treaty', among them:

(1) Capts. B. and W. to dine nightly and lunch when they feel like it. (Bread and cheese.)
(2) Capts. B. and W. to eat all Mrs M.'s eggs, and all her meat ration. . . .
(6) Mrs M., when requiring a bath, will submit written application, in duplicate, to Capts. B. and W. 12 hours before the time when it is required. In no circumstances will she wash more than three times a week. . . .
(8) Cut glass tumblers to be restored to use.
(9) Mrs M. will, at all times, have her private correspondence accounts, and underclothes open to inspection by Capts. B. and W., and will furnish, in duplicate, a full written account of her life. . . .[30]

Waugh thought this fairly and amusingly expressed. Mrs Maxwell could take a joke. She was clearly fond of her officers. Bennett, however, knew that the comic patronage of this contract would offend her and refused to

30. TS, nd; HRC.

deliver it. Waugh had thrown his last bottle from Bennett's window and, shortly afterwards, he moved out and left the recalcitrant novelist to shift for himself.

Late March brought another horrific revelation:

> Headache. Basil and I drinking gin and tonic by 10.30. Two sharp blows to professional pride in finding [Tom] Churchill sent to Shetlands to brief Fynn for the operations and John Selwyn appointed assistant brigade major with hints that he will take over in near future when Brian [Franks] is to go away. Later in the morning Bob explained to me that I am so unpopular as to be unemployable. My future very uncertain.[31]

No one wanted him. Laycock constantly embarrassed by Lovat's and Tom Churchill's dislike of Waugh, tactfully shifted him back to COHQ at Richmond Terrace. This both satisfied Waugh's dignity and kept him out of the way. It also allowed him to lead a metropolitan life, which, for a short while, improved his temper.

Waugh's tastes were best accommodated by Heywood Hill's Mayfair bookshop, and it was at this time that he began a long association with the place. Nancy Mitford had recently taken a job there and Waugh, curious as ever, went to investigate. 'I was told', he recorded, 'that it is now a daily occurrence for enormous majors in the Foot Guards to come in and ask for the works of sixteenth-century Spanish mystics.'[32] Heywood Hill's was exactly right: eccentric, exclusive, well-stocked – another haven of civilized values, another club. Superior to all these attractions, however, was Nancy: *chic*, brittle, witty, efficient, who '*Darlinged*' her chosen customers and ignored the rest. Through her influence the bookshop prospered as a centre for Waugh's literary circle. Betjeman, Connolly, Raymond Mortimer, the Sitwells and Lord Berners often dropped in for a chat. Hill had been called up in December 1942 and his wife ran the shop with Nancy. It dealt not only in books but also in embroidered pictures, prints, Victorian toys and automata – exactly the kind of nineteenth-century frippery that amused Betjeman and Waugh.

He had seen little of Nancy since her marriage to Rodd in 1933. Even before that, a certain awkwardness had existed between Waugh and her after her involvement with the collapse of his marriage in 1929.[33] She had always been a determined socialite. They had met, chatted, drunk, parted, but their deep compatibility had yet to flower. Much as he enjoyed writing about Rodd, Waugh loathed his company. There had been the difficulty of

31. *Diaries*, 23 March 1943, p. 532.
32. *Ibid.*, 25 March 1943, p. 533.
33. Cf. Vol. 1, pp. 183–4.

Nancy's and Peter's affiliation with the Black Shirts. Then Nancy's politics, following her husband's again, had swung to the Left. By 1943, although she had lost none of her vivacity, she was altogether more adult, and her volatile nursery language masked a considerable history of suffering. Her marriage was wrecked on Peter's continual infidelities. Four months earlier she had entered hospital with abdominal pains, expecting an appendectomy. The surgeon, discovering an ectopic pregnancy, had performed a total hysterectomy, a mortal blow to her already fading dream of home and children. During the 1930s she had been a diligent but dilettante author, producing four light novels and two editions of letters.[34] Now that Peter was on active service, they rarely saw each other, and she found herself breathing more freely. The gap he left she filled by satisfying a long-suppressed hunger for independence and artistic recognition. The war and the bookshop revitalized her. Greeting the air-raids as a tonic, she settled resolutely for single life and a more considered approach to her writing. She wanted to produce a *good* comic novel, and in this Waugh was later able to help her.

His working day in London was monotonous. From nine until seven he was out, and at night he returned to an uncomfortable single room in Maimie's house in Montpelier Walk. Even this retreat was spoiled. Vsevolode's presence interrupted delicious, late-night gossips with Maimie. The couple's friends and dogs, above all the Prince's ineffable silliness, shattered Waugh's composure and before long he had to move out. Lenten fasting, always acutely uncomfortable for Waugh, was particularly so under these circumstances. But it had the vague benefit of reducing his pudgy figure and, he hoped, making him appear more fit for active service. 'I am working uncommonly hard', he wrote to Laura, 'and am quite worn out. I am being very efficient & conscientious sober chaste pious & I feel all washed up.'[35] She received the assurance that he enjoyed 'a position of great authority and responsibility at COHQ'.[36] Both knew this to be untrue.

Officially he was Laycock's representative. In fact, he was relegated to mundane tasks and diverted from sensitive information. His spartan regime produced only insomnia, giddiness and a stream of tactless remarks. 'I saw the new chief intelligence officer', he noted proudly, 'and told him I thought intelligence officers in the Special Service Brigade quite redundant.'[37] He had said the same thing to Tom Churchill at Sherborne. 'Really!' Churchill had replied. 'Then I'm surprised to learn that you are holding down the

34. Cf. Selina Hastings, *Nancy Mitford* (Hamish Hamilton, 1985).
35. Unpublished ALS to Laura Waugh, nd [March–April 1943], from Combined Operations Headquarters, 1A Richmond Terrace, Whitehall, SW1; BL.
36. Unpublished ALS to Laura Waugh, nd [12 April? 1943], from White's; BL.
37. *Diaries*, 26 March 1943, p. 533.

job of Brigade Intelligence Officer. That'll be all. Fall out.'[38] Waugh had already fallen out with Churchill, a professional with no time for idlers. He had called Waugh in to force him to take part in battalion exercises and to prove his capacity as an IO. A constant stream of complaints had been directed to Churchill: 'Who's that bloody man in your office who never does a bloody thing?'[39] Waugh seemed only to use his telephone for social arrangements. According to Churchill, Waugh was not so much a soldier as a 'complete joke'.[40]

When he applied in London to be a Force commander, he was ridiculed as too old for parachuting – a disability which did not prevent them from sending him on a parachuting course some months later when he had made himself even more unpopular. With General Haydon, Waugh's new CO, it had been hate at first sight. In early April 1943, Laycock had proposed the establishment of a new HQ in Scotland, preparatory to leaving for 'Operation Husky' in Sicily. Lord Lovat was to remain as CO at Sherborne. This had been the decisive factor in Waugh's moving permanently to London. But at Richmond Terrace the familiar story was repeating itself. No one wanted him. His only hope was that Laycock would fulfil his promise and ask for Waugh to join him soon in Africa.

*

April 1943 was Waugh's cruellest month. London, blitzed and half-ruined, was deluged with rain. At COHQ he suffocated beneath the multiple prevarications of bureaucracy. He liked to cut straight to the heart of a problem and to act immediately. But 'Everyone here', he noted, 'sees everything through frosted glass and hears through stuffing, so that they never quite get the point of what is said or done and write minutes to each other always just off the point.'[41] This more precisely describes others' view of him. His deafness increased in direct proportion to his boredom, and he began to make serious mistakes.

Outside office hours, Waugh sealed himself inside clubs, hotels and elegant private houses. The streets of the unreal city appalled him. He went short of nothing except by design and, as soon as Lent was over, plunged into a round of smart parties, trying to ingratiate himself with those in power. Lord Mountbatten (Chief of Combined Operations) and the Sea Lords found Waugh's earnest, irascible face unconvincingly simulating humility across the dinner table. But it was a futile bid to outflank the system and, as his mood darkened, so did his mental image of the capital.

38. Interview with Major-General T. B. L. Churchill, 26 March 1987.
39. *Ibid.*
40. *Ibid.*
41. *Diaries*, 22 April 1943, p. 536.

When the rains ceased, May sunshine greeted the news of Rommel's defeat in the desert and of the U boats in the Atlantic. Waugh saw only a dead land:

> London shabbier and shoddier in the sunlight than in shadow. The crowds uglier and more aimless, horrible groups of soldiers in shabby battledress with their necks open, their caps off or at extravagant angles, hands in pockets, cigarettes in the sides of their mouths, lounging about with girls in trousers and high heels and filmstar coiffures. . . .[42]

The scene was recreated in *Men At Arms* where, with mischievous artistic licence, the soldiers all became Americans. It was the vision of 'Lunnon' from 'Out of Depth'[43] risen hideously to life. The moment he set foot in the streets he shivered at the proximity of common humanity.

With Laycock's departure for Scotland on 28th April, Waugh had been left with no friends at COHQ but some hope. Ten days later a copy of a letter sent from Laycock to Lord Lovat arrived:

> It is my intention that Capt Waugh shall join 'HUSKY' Force in North Africa as soon as it can be arranged. I am therefore appointing Capt Bray to take his place. . . . [Bray] should . . . spend a short time with Capt Waugh at COHQ in order to learn procedure there. Capt Waugh will remain as Liaison Officer at COHQ until his embarkation orders arrive.[44]

That seemed straightforward but Waugh was by this time adept at reading between military lines. Was it an astute political move to promise action at some unspecified date while leaving him in the charge of Lord Lovat? Waugh was uncertain but still believed to the last moment that he might be included in the first draft. When Brigade HQ left London without him, he felt insulted, and determined to make Laycock's promise stick. There was, however, a cruel coincidence which necessitated his remaining in the city, at least for a fortnight. On the very day of HQ's departure, 26 June, Arthur Waugh died.[45]

*

During his two years stationed at home, Evelyn had scarcely seen his parents. His last recorded visit had been on his mother's birthday in April, another formal call. Arthur had been infirm and deaf, his face collapsed on one side, and since it was impossible to conduct a normal conversation,

42. *Ibid.*, 15 May 1943, p. 536.
43. See Vol. 1, pp. 345–7.
44. *Diaries*, p. 539.
45. *Ibid.* Waugh [or Davie?] dates it wrongly as 'July 24'; cf. *MBE*, p. 214.

Evelyn had scribbled his replies on a piece of paper. The old man's amusement at his own indignity had baffled his son. The *Diaries* depict Arthur as a helpless cripple. In fact, he had only suffered a minor stroke which affected his face and his writing hand. Otherwise he remained much the same stout figure, pottering round Hampstead Village in well-brushed overcoat and grey Homburg. He took to his bed just two days before his death. During the previous week he had spent an entire day watching cricket at Highgate School, where he had acted (in more ways than one, no doubt) as a temporary English master. To the last he was energetically reading manuscripts and advising authors for Chapman & Hall. Death had come suddenly and peacefully on a Saturday morning. Five days later Alec had received the macabre present of his father's last letter: lucid, amiable, odd words illegible as his bad hand had jerked the pen. For the two years of Alec's absence they had corresponded every four or five days. Their letters scarcely mention Evelyn other than as a public figure.

In late May, driven from Maimie's in search of solitude, he had taken Derek Verschoyle's flat in Curzon Street, Mayfair, for two months. It was a tiny, elegant apartment but cramped for two. When Laura came to town they stayed there or at the Hyde Park Hotel and spent lavishly. When she left, he always felt alienated and lonely, but not as irritable and humiliated as he felt now. Arthur's death had come with inconvenient haste. There was no option but to abandon his battle with the authorities and to go to his mother's assistance.

Waugh and Laura went to stay at Highgate. Catherine was dazed and vacant. She had been widowed just three-and-a-half months before her golden wedding anniversary and preparations for that were now gruesomely transformed into preparations for the funeral. Bron was brought up from Pixton to distract her and, while Laura ran the house (there was a cook), Waugh disappeared moodily into his father's bedroom-office to sort out the family affairs.

It was painful for him to go through Arthur's papers ('a large correspondence with very dull people')[46] and he unsentimentally destroyed many letters. This appalled Alec when he heard of it. What to Evelyn was embarrassingly second-rate was to Alec a precious archive. In Syria he received a peremptory letter informing him of the arrangements,[47] but it is

46. *Ibid.*, p. 539.
47. Unpublished ALS to Alec Waugh, nd [early July 1943], from Combined Operations Headquarters, 1A Richmond Terrace, Whitehall, SW1; HRC. Waugh explained that Arthur's estate was left entirely to Catherine, with the exception of his books, which were to go to his sons. The estate was probably worth only £5,000; inadequate, if invested, to secure an income for Catherine, and Evelyn suggests that Joan (Alec's wife) should make a covenanted allowance. No offer of financial assistance came from Evelyn at this stage. He clearly wished to impress upon Alec that it was his duty to relieve his brother of these domestic responsibilities: 'The best thing would be for you to live with her. . . .'

unlikely that Evelyn's editing was a form of self-protection. There is no evidence, for instance, of his reading his father's diaries. Had he done so, he would not have been shocked by the figure he cuts there: the social climber reckless of his father's affection. It is more probable that he would have roared with laughter. Arthur's journal uncomfortably approximates the tone of *The Diary of a Nobody*.[48] Evelyn always proclaimed that he was Lupin and, by the same token, Arthur was Pooter.

Evelyn preferred the role of father to that of son. Few parents relish the patronage of their children, and Arthur was no exception. January 1930 had marked by unfortunate coincidence both Arthur's retirement and his son's rise to celebrity with *Vile Bodies*. In those days, Evelyn's exclusive relationship with his mother had often left Arthur in melancholy isolation, but even Catherine's worship of her prodigy did not grant her immunity from hurt. As a stern teetotaller, she feared his sinking into dipsomania. As an Anglican, she was wounded by his defection to Rome. By 1939, his Catholicism had formed a permanent barrier between himself and his family. Arthur maintained a decent reserve when talking to Evelyn about religion or politics. The old man's diaries and letters, however, reveal positive hostility.[49]

Evelyn expressed no grief at his father's death. But something had changed. His father, he knew, had indirectly created the extravagant character that the son's soul inhabited. A year later Waugh wrote in *Brideshead*:

> The human soul ... enjoys ... rare, classic periods [of vision and completeness], but, apart from these, we are seldom single or unique; we keep company ... with a horde of abstractions and reflexions and counterfeits of ourselves.... We get borne along, out of sight in the press, unresisting, till we get the chance to drop behind unnoticed, or to dodge down a side-street, pause, breathe freely and take our bearings, or to push ahead, outdistance our shadows, lead them a dance, so that when at length they catch up with us, they look at one another askance, knowing we have a secret we shall never share.[50]

It had been in reaction to Arthur's timidity, 'masculinity' and respectability that Evelyn had gravitated towards arrogance, homosexuality and bohemianism. Now Arthur had gone and had left his son with this 'horde of

48. Cf. AWD, Saturday, 1 November 1930, recording Arthur's lament upon the death of his poodle, Gaspard: 'Dear darling Gappy. No more walks together on the Heath. No more welcoming barks as I open the gate. Goodbye, dear little companion of so many happy hours.'

49. Cf. unpublished ALS to Kenneth MacMaster, 24 August 1936, from 14a Hampstead Lane, Highgate; HRC: '... Evelyn is back from Abyssinia fortified with the blessings of Mussolini and the Pope. He is welcome to any comfort he can derive from such benedictions. I prithee have me excused.'

50. *Brideshead Revisited: The Sacred and Profane Memories of Captain Charles Ryder* (Chapman & Hall, 1945), p. 198. The passage was cut from the revised 1960 edition.

abstractions and reflexions and counterfeits' which constituted the masks of his public self. The romantic side of his nature, so long repressed, could be released – if not in his life, then at least in his writing. Perhaps he had foreseen this in *Work Suspended*. Arthur's death was in two respects a birth: it marked the final division between the old world and the hopeless future; it signalled the crossing of a Rubicon in Evelyn's life and art.

Addressing Lovat as 'Shimi', Waugh wrote on 5 July explaining how his superior should run the unit, with special reference to Waugh. Lovat, having encountered the novelist constantly drunk in White's bar for a week or so, and believing this to be inadequate preparation for overseas service, had instructed Waugh, through a subordinate, to attend the Depot for training. Waugh was furious:

> ... it is clear that my position ... at COHQ is not fully understood. Could you please explain to this officer [the subordinate]:-
> (1) That I am appointed Liaison Officer here by the Brigade Commander [Laycock] and have his explicit orders to remain at this post until my embarkation
> (2) That these orders were confirmed in writing to you....
> (3) That the question of my going to the Depot was raised by yourself solely with a view to my own welfare ... to get physically fit for the Theatre of Operations....
> (4) That I have good personal reasons for wishing to remain in London as long as possible....[51]

Waugh had a case. He held copies of Laycock's letters to Lovat specifically ordering Waugh's posting to Africa with the first reinforcement. What he did not understand – or refused to believe – was the real nature of that order: that Laycock had no serious intention of its being carried out. He knew, as Waugh now did, that it would be at least six weeks before a passage would be available. If Waugh were forced to attend training at the Depot, this delay would extend to three months, by which time Laycock's Sicilian campaign would be finished. This was precisely what he, Lord Lovat and General Haydon wanted.

Lovat's reply was brutally frank. Captain Mills was to replace Waugh:

> ... I recently (10 June) requested permission from the Brigade Commander in the presence of the GOCO [Haydon] for Captain Mills to act as Liaison Officer with Rear Headquarters. This was accepted.... A harmonious liaison has never been established between your department and Rear Headquarters; I saw fit to apply for Captain Mills for this reason.... You will report to the Depot on 1st August.... You

51. TLS to 'Shimi' [Lord Lovat], 12 July 1943, np [COHQ]; reprinted (with the rest of this correspondence), *Diaries*, p. 541.

will not proceed overseas unless passed physically fit by Achnacarry. I hope I have made myself clear.[52]

The Depot at Achnacarry was chiefly concerned with training the newly formed RM Commando. Its young men were worked to their limit. Waugh could never have competed, and he felt that to be returned to basic training after more than three years' experience was a snub which left no honourable response but resignation. His hand was forced. But he then made an irredeemable error, just as he had with Colonel Cutler. He attempted to go over Lovat's head by requesting an interview with General Haydon.

Haydon was not a man sympathetically inclined towards impertinent soldiers, and had never met a soldier in the least like Waugh. Already 'in a highly excited condition' when the novelist entered the office, the General listened impatiently to accusations of malpractice (which necessarily implicated him) and was soon quite unable to contain himself. '"Your Brigadier", he said, "has made a great mistake in asking for you at all and I shall see that you don't go until I am satisfied that you are fit."' Rather than accept this, Waugh enquired what he meant by 'fit'. Haydon's simmering boiled into rage and abuse. Having relieved himself of a character assassination he concluded by saying 'that I had done nothing but discredit to the Brigade since I had joined it and that for the Brigade's good he advised me to leave as soon as possible.'[53]

It was the sack. Waugh was mortified. He had entered, brimming with righteous indignation, specific orders for posting in his pocket; he left with the full horror of his senior officers' ridicule heaped upon him. And, undiplomatic to the last, he did not let the matter rest. After submitting his resignation (to 'Lord Lovat' rather than 'Shimi') on 17 July, he went straight to Harley Street, paid five guineas to get himself passed fit for active service by an independent authority, and wrote a long letter to Laycock. It was a question of honour, Waugh said. He did not wish the Brigadier to believe that Captain Waugh had betrayed him.

Doubtless this was intended to embarrass. In explaining that he did not believe Lovat's story about Laycock's authorizing Waugh's removal from COHQ, he left Laycock with only two options: either to admit that Lovat was a liar, or that he (Sir Robert) was a traitor. The letter selects items from Haydon's accusations which Waugh knew he could disprove. (He does not mention, for instance, his habit of scribbling facetious asides in the margins of important memos, his persistent use of the telephone for social arrangements or his near-total incompetence.) He tries, like the barrack-room lawyer he was, to induce guilt at this mistreatment of a

52. TLS from 'Shimi' [Lord Lovat], 13 July 1943, np [Midhurst?]; *Diaries*, p. 542.
53. TccLS from Evelyn Waugh to Brigadier Laycock, 19 July 1943, np [COHQ]; *Diaries*, p. 544.

humble and recently bereaved fellow officer. 'Since my father's death,' he says, 'my mother, aged 74, is entirely alone in London. A request has been made for my brother's return ... on compassionate grounds and until that is arranged I have responsibilities and I know that my duty is to spend as much time as I can with her....'[54] The tears in his eyes did not fool Laycock. Mrs Waugh was not alone. She had many friends in Highgate and a resident housekeeper. Laura and Bron had been there. Evelyn had stayed only a few days before leaving his wife to minister to the widow while he drank at White's. His 'duty' was rarely less than irksome and he wished to shrug it off with all possible haste.

It seemed a caustic irony to Waugh that he should have been sacked when the tide of war was for the first time running full against the Axis, but he accepted his fate resolutely and, as usual, turned love to hatred in self-defence. 'I have got so bored with everything military', he noted in August, 'that I can no longer remember the simplest details':

> I dislike the Army. I want to get to work again. I do not want any more experiences in life. I have quite enough bottled and carefully laid in the cellar.... I wrote to Frank [Pakenham] very early in the war to say that its chief use would be to cure artists of the illusion that they were men of action. It has worked its cure with me. I have succeeded, too, in dissociating myself very largely with [*sic*] the rest of the world. I am not impatient of its manifest follies and don't want to influence opinions or events, or expose humbug.... I don't want to be of service to anyone or anything. I simply want to do my work as an artist.[55]

Here, at last, we see the mature Waugh, the cenobitic aesthete, the ungentle priest-craftsman, cured of chivalry and waiting for the moment to write his great, reflective work.

*

The Royal Horse Guards, having admitted Waugh as an honorary member on Laycock's recommendation, suddenly found this irritable subversive back on their books. Uncertain what to do with him, they sent him to the Household Cavalry Training Unit at Windsor. Waugh ambled up there one day with an ailing Hubert Duggan, 'found the barracks full of fine paintings and middle-aged, embittered subalterns',[56] and resigned himself to futility. It was there that he wrote the long diary entry quoted above and within

54. *Ibid.*, p. 543.
55. *Diaries*, 29 August 1943, p. 548.
56. *Ibid.*, 10 August 1943, pp. 545–6.

three weeks he had realized (again) that he was of no use. When he applied for indefinite leave pending posting it was granted unopposed.

Waugh's one hope of posting now lay with Bill Stirling, a cousin of Lord Lovat, who was trying to raise a new unit, the 2nd Special Air Service Regiment. Whenever Stirling popped up in London, Waugh buttonholed him, pleaded, and secured ambiguous promises of release. The Laycock story was merely repeating itself. Waugh embarrassed his seniors with his earnest desire for action, but could not disguise hisun willingness 'to be of service to anyone or anything'. He simply craved adventure, anything to shatter the monotony and, while his courage was unquestioned, he was temperamentally incapable of accommodating himself to the military machine. There was no place for this Hamlet-turned-Don Quixote in the mechanized professionalism of the modern army.

Waugh's misery was deep and complex and, for once, incurable by success. He was as rich as he had ever been. During the financial year 1942–3, Peters had paid him nearly £1,200 and was holding a further £1,300. In July, Alexander Korda had agreed to give Waugh £10 a week as a retainer against the purchase price of the film rights of his next novel. Foyle's had sold 175,000 copies of *Put Out More Flags*. *Work Suspended* had been vastly over-subscribed and warmly praised by those he respected, particularly Desmond MacCarthy. Waugh's reputation had progressed securely from that of *enfant terrible* to Great Man of Letters and his social life was as glamorous as he could wish: Lord Mountbatten, Lady Diana Cooper, the Duchess of Westminster, the Earls of Antrim and Birkenhead all sought his company. Wherever he went, however, he caused trouble. Visiting the Coopers at their Bognor farm, he had sat grumpily in the blackout, feeling no elation as the RAF droned over, laden with bombs for Milan. He always argued with Duff. Next morning Waugh pursued a wrangle with his hostess: 'Logic in the early morning was more than Diana could bear ... irritation made an outburst of ill-temper and I left sad and cross with no inclination to be reconciled.'[57]

In London he lived expensively. Most days he would go to the St James's Club to pick up his letters, walk round to Nancy's shop for gossip, lunch at White's, spend the afternoon searching for lithographic books and get drunk over dinner in one of his clubs. It was at Heywood Hill's that Waugh met Sergeant Stuart Preston, a young history graduate in the US army (later caricatured in the war trilogy as 'the Loot'). It was in the bookshop that Waugh most frequently encountered Connolly and cemented a difficult, life-long friendship. With no plan of attack, however, no work, no personal role in the war effort, Waugh sank into apathy. On 8 September Italy's

57. *Ibid.*, 29 August 1943, p. 546.

unconditional surrender left him joyless: another jungle closing in. The Germans were putting up fierce resistance and Churchill's determination to thrust up through the 'soft underbelly of Europe' only signalled to Waugh the destruction of priceless works of art.[58] At home, Laura was pregnant again and, as usual, unhappy about it. In her absence, only Nancy and Connolly could raise his spirits.

Waugh saw much of himself in Connolly. Lady Betjeman has described Connolly as the best conversationalist she had ever met, and her close friends included Waugh and Maurice Bowra.[59] Connolly was better read than Waugh in everything but theology. He understood and was sympathetic to the *avant-garde*. He was, in the best sense of the word, an 'intellectual', a brilliant and cultivated man, sensitive to nuance and passionately committed to the life of the mind. *Horizon* was an act of faith and, as we have seen, the kind of venture Waugh had himself been keen to initiate in 1939. In wartime its few copies were seized by those gasping for the breath of ideas – and Waugh was no exception. He greatly admired the magazine, if not all its contributors.

Connolly had begun with enormous promise and, in some respects, had fulfilled it. For all his success, however, he was a disappointed man. A national figure, he was in close touch with the major British artists of his day, and was a fine parodist and essayist with one novel (*The Rock Pool*) to his credit. Waugh trusted his literary taste, allowing him to choose new books for him and (the highest accolade) to cut 'My Father's House' without supervision. But Waugh would not allow him to forget one crucial difference between them: that Connolly had never established himself as an artist. It was a nerve which Waugh prodded with fierce glee. He saw in this squat, pug-faced little firecracker another mirror image.

> Cyril is the most typical man of my generation. There but for the Grace of God, literally.... He has the authentic lack of scholarship of my generation. He read French while getting a third in Greats, the authentic love of leisure and liberty and good living, the authentic romantic snobbery, the authentic waste-land despair, the authentic high gift of expression....[60]

Connolly and Waugh, unfortunately for Connolly, loved each other. Waugh dined regularly at his table with the guarantee of excellent food and

58. Many others sympathized with this view. Cf. Harold Nicolson, *op. cit.*, 16 February 1944, p. 258: 'Go to supper with Rothermere. A discussion starts as to whether we should sacrifice lives in order to spare works of art. I say that we do not realise at all that works of art are irreplaceable whereas no lives are irreplaceable....' Much as he detested Nicolson, Waugh agreed with him here. See Waugh's diary entry quoted p. 97 below.
59. Interview with Lady Betjeman, 29 March 1984.
60. Waugh's marginalia on the fly-leaf of Connolly's *The Unquiet Grave* (limited edition, no. 99, Curwen Press, 1944); HRC.

wine, and conversation vivid with fantastic allusion. They laughed a great deal together but ultimately the laughs were on Connolly. Seeing an unguarded throat, Waugh tended to go for the jugular. Friends were never exempt from the power struggle which energized him. Connolly the Celt trying to be English; Connolly, the lap-dog of high society, professing Socialism; Connolly the aesthete trying to cut up rough; Connolly the modernist protecting 'culture'; Connolly the sybarite playing at asceticism – nearly all were contradictions in Waugh's own character, but it was Waugh who could nail them in someone else and thus deflect criticism.

Their major point of divergence, of course, was Christianity. Connolly, a bemused humanist, was an atheist without the courage to abandon agnosticism. Generally they avoided the topic. It was not until Waugh read *The Unquiet Grave* in 1945 that he was certain what was wrong with his friend: he was ignorant of the doctrine of the Fall of Man.[61]

*

Waugh was leading four lives which rarely overlapped: the writer on the fringes of the Heywood Hill–*Horizon* circle; the officer; the husband and father; the Catholic apologist. Wandering homeless about London he felt baffled and tetchy. Laura, often ill, must have found his brutal criticisms hard to bear: 'It has been a great sorrow to me to hear nothing of you,' he wrote in late September:

> No particular interest in your doings: to hear that Teresa has sneezed or Bron fallen down or Gabriel bought a farm does not excite me. Still I should like to feel that once or twice a week you felt enough interest in me to write & say so. I am fighting the Giant Boredom as best I can. . . . Most of my day is spent waiting for and on Bill Stirling. . . . I spent yesterday evening with my mother. She is more composed in her mind but very dull. . . .[62]

Awash with self-pity, Waugh would always encourage others to feel guilty of neglect. Mass at Farm Street and the companionship of Hollis, Douglas Woodruff and Pakenham offered some spiritual refreshment, but he was discovering subversion even within the Household of the Faith. Cardinal Hinsley, then the Archbishop of Westminster, 'a bluff, patriotic Yorkshireman,'[63] was not at all Waugh's ideal leader. Together with his Anglican counterpart, Archbishop Temple, he had launched 'The Sword of the Spirit' campaign to oppose the 'spirit of wickedness in high places'.

61. Cf. *ibid.*, Waugh's marginalia, p. 19. Beneath 'Human life is understandable only as a state of transition, as part of an evolutionary process . . .' Waugh wrote: 'Ignorance of the doctrine of the Fall of Man. Almost all Cyril's problems are fully & simply explained in the catechism.'
62. ALS to Laura Waugh, 'Tuesday Night' [28 September 1943], from White's; *Letters*, pp. 171–2.
63. Christopher Hollis, *The Seven Ages* (Heinemann, 1974), p. 156.

Its ends were noble but its means ecumenical. And when Waugh visited Pakenham working in Bruton Street for Lord Beveridge, planning post-war social security, Waugh only noted in his diary that the office was 'decorated like a hat shop with silk draperies and rickety Empire furniture'.[64] There is little doubt about the flavour of these remarks. It was to the Herberts' mansion in Bruton street that Waugh had come when courting Laura. With the outbreak of war, financial retrenchment had forced Mary to sell the place. An ancient pattern of civilized life had been broken: the country house; the London mansion; the Italian villa. Now the villa was in enemy territory, Pixton invaded, the mansion sold. Pakenham, an aristocrat and Catholic convert, spent his days extending the common man's rights in a street which had formerly been the exclusive province of the upper class. Over dinner with Betjeman, Waugh had discussed the essence of his difficulty: '... the obligation of charity to love mankind in general – an obligation we both find it impossible to meet.'[65]

Waugh's loyalties were awkwardly divided. Of those he knew socially, only the Christians accepted his premises for argument about the nature of 'reality' but he found most of his Catholic friends dull. Knox and Greene had the *flair* he loved, but Knox was a generation older, Greene an ambiguous Catholic with Socialist leanings. Waugh hardly saw them. Neither possessed Betjeman's glorious bisexual eccentricities or the exuberance of Connolly or Nancy. Few shared Waugh's interest in the aristocracy. Few aristocrats were Catholics. Those who were tended to dislike him and to misinterpret the complexity of his art. For aesthetic discussion, which always obsessed him, he had usually to turn to agnostics or Anglicans. Katharine Asquith, much as he admired her, had not the slightest notion about the mechanics of his writing.

The result was that he felt uncharitable to almost all his friends at some stage when, inevitably, their views collided with his, and he suffered agonies of remorse that he should injure them so badly. 'How right you are about not losing friends,' he wrote to Diana Cooper. 'You have stuck by yours heroically – me especially despite every sort of provocation. I lose mine fast. Not I think from not loving them but from expecting them to be different. You find something agreeable in almost everyone. I am put off by anything not wholly agreeable. Wiser & happier baby.'[66] In fact, within his circle, he was widely and devotedly loved. Waugh's generosity, like everything else in his life, was excessive. Those he helped, and there were many, were astonished at the brutal self-image he publicized.

64. *Diaries*, 29 September 1943, p. 551.
65. *Ibid.*, 23 September 1943, p. 550.
66. ALS to Lady Diana Cooper, 6 March 1954, from Piers Court; BL; *MWMS*, p. 189.

By normal human standards Waugh sometimes verged on sanctity with his relish for giving pleasure. But, a self-mortifying perfectionist, he was burdened by the sense of his sinfulness, believing himself to be an incurable egotist, arrogant rather than vain, malicious, with the schoolboy's rather than the Fascist's desire to torment. Embarrassment was funny; discomfiture his stock in trade. Occasionally, when his faith demanded sacrifices, he would overcome his distaste for 'the obligation ... to love mankind in general' and do something he disliked. Otherwise he wanted to be left alone. The parable of the camel and the eye of the needle seemed irrelevant: no virtue, he proclaimed, lay in poverty; the proposed Welfare State was fraudulent in promising what it could not deliver; no honest man could live comfortably, let alone save, thanks to punitive taxation; a man's duty was to his family, not to a plebeian rabble trying to steal the profits of dignified labour. Samuel Smiles would have applauded. But when Waugh was in this mood, friends like Connolly and Nancy, both pink Socialists, could only change the subject. For his part, Waugh (with some reason) saw their gestures towards the Left as hypocrisy, for he knew both to be unrepentant élitists. Impasse.

*

Hubert Duggan presented Waugh with that rare thing – a cause to which he could commit himself absolutely. By the autumn of 1943 it was clear that Duggan was dying, effectively alone in the world. His lover, Phyllis de Janzé, was dead. Waugh visited the Chapel Street house regularly and was distressed by what he found. Duggan was nursed by his mother (Lady Curzon), his sister (Marcella Rice) and the maid (Ellen). Marcella was hostile to the Roman Church; Lady Curzon, a whimsical Edwardian beauty, had few strong feelings about anything beyond her family, ball-gowns and the divine rights of Conservative politicians. Waugh thought her 'really a very gruesome woman'.[67] She worshipped her children and the memory of her husbands. In 1931, she had helped Hubert oust a Socialist from Acton and he was still their MP. She looked on, distraught, as he lay near death. He was only thirty-nine. Marcella was opposed to last rites. Lady Curzon did not know what to think. She was an Anglican, but if it would be a comfort to the poor boy.... Waugh saw his chance.

'The news of Hubert is very bad indeed,' he wrote to Laura.

> He is allowed to see no one. I had a long talk with Ellen about it. He never sleeps and drugs put him into a delirium but not to sleep. He is in the blackest melancholy and haunted by delusions. There is

67. ALS to Lady Diana Cooper, nd [mid-February? 1953], from Piers Court; BL; *MWMS*, p. 157.

> nothing which can be done for him medically. Supernatural aid is needed.[68]

Laura came up to London, but they were prevented from seeing the patient. After a week-end at Pixton Waugh tried again:

> Hubert very much worse. This morning, for the first time, he began to talk of religion and of returning to the Church, but he has no strength for reasoned argument and needs the presence of someone holy. I suggested a nun but nothing seems to come of it much, though Lady Curzon seems sympathetic. It seems in Hubert's mind that it would be a betrayal of Phyllis to profess repentance of his life with her.[69]

Next day Waugh went to see Fr Dempsey, Catholic Forces chaplain for West London. Waugh was not impressed, describing him (unfairly) in his diary as 'a big fat peasant'. He gave Waugh a religious medal to hide in the sick-room and promised to come when called. At Chapel Street, however, Waugh was told that Hubert could not survive the day, and at this critical moment Dempsey could not be located. Waugh rushed round to Farm Street and returned with Fr Devas, the priest who later instructed Lady Betjeman.

Waugh's interference in this delicate business was resented by Marcella and baffled Lady Curzon. Family crises usually bored him and he steered clear. Irritated by Laura's domestic hesitations, he would sometimes stride into confusion and take command. But this was rare and his odd behaviour on this occasion requires explanation. It was a special case. Waugh was no proselyte but he was passionately committed to helping those who had been, or thought of becoming, Roman Catholic. He believed in Hell and, to save his friends from it, he would gatecrash anyone's privacy. Such tactics rarely met with success. In this case, however, he achieved his aim – indeed, secured rather more than he had bargained for. Marcella's opposition overcome, Fr Devas gave Hubert absolution and his 'Thank you father' was taken as assent.[70]

Waugh retired satisfied to White's and sat drinking with Randolph Churchill till late afternoon. Devas was still there when Waugh returned, Hubert still alive, Marcella distinctly obstructive. Devas wanted to anoint Hubert. Waugh, trying to browbeat Marcella and, intent on arguing the case from first principles, only added a further charge to an already electric atmosphere:

68. [September 1943]; *Letters*, p. 171.
69. *Diaries*, 12 October 1943, p. 552.
70. *Ibid.*, 13 October 1943, p. 552.

> Father Devas very quiet and simple and humble, trying to make sense of all the confusion, knowing just what he wanted ... and patiently explaining, 'Look, all I shall do is just to put oil on his forehead and say a prayer. Look the oil is in this little box. It is nothing to be frightened of.' And so by knowing what he wanted and sticking to that ... he got what he wanted and Hubert crossed himself and later called me up and said, 'When I became a Catholic it was not from fear', so he knows what happened and accepted it. So we spent the day watching for a spark of gratitude for the love of God and saw the spark.[71]

Waugh felt that he had witnessed the operation of Divine Grace. It was irrelevant to him that Hubert was delirious, his statements ambiguous. No, it was cast-iron proof of supernatural intervention, the final experience he needed to complete the gestation of his *magnum opus*. A similar scene forms the climax of *Brideshead* with the deathbed conversion of Lord Marchmain. Antagonistic reviewers often selected this incident as evidence of Waugh's romantic disregard for realism. As far as he was concerned, it was one of the few scenes of reportage.

He did not return to Chapel Street. He had done all in his power there. Twelve days later he went to Pixton with the intention of starting his novel. Stirling, it seems, tried to play Laycock's hand and decamp, leaving Waugh with indefinite orders. Waugh, unwilling to be caught out twice, had insisted on going with him to the Adjutant-General's office to fix the posting. With Stirling gone, Waugh, theoretically on leave, expected to go abroad for up to six months.

Revenge rather than idealism inspired his military ambition now. 'I dread the prospect of organization and training and a hundred new acquaintances. But after my treatment by Haydon I must "make good" as a soldier. Nothing can upset him more than to find me promoted as a result of his intemperance.'[72] Four months were wasted on this scheme, months during which the novel was baulked and Waugh's ill-temper rose to new heights. 'I ... am ashamed that I was often petulant and ungrateful,' he wrote to Laura on his return to London. 'Thank you for being so funny & patient.'[73] On 8 November she came to town to see him off. On the 9th the operation was postponed for an indefinite period.

Waugh looked on his books as independent systems of order in a nightmare existence. And, just as he temporarily entered their sanctuary, so there had always been those silent rooms into which he could retreat from the disorderly street: galleries, Venetian palaces, Oxford colleges, country

71. *Ibid.*, p. 553.
72. *Ibid.*, 29 September 1943, p. 551.
73. ALS to Laura Waugh, 'Friday' [5 November 1943], from White's; *Letters*, p. 173.

houses, gentlemen's clubs, the officers' mess and, above all, the Church. Most had been invaded by his 'enemies'. Now even military life had to be struck from the list of protected environments. The world was too much with it. The attempted escape from mundanity and compromise into the ideal and absolute had revealed only muddle. The army, he thought, had opened its doors to the Grammar School boys and expelled the gentlemen, who, like flamboyant, overcivilized creatures, were dying in the wilderness.

This, of course, bore small relation to the truth. Waugh was the only member of his gang not to have seen offensive action. During that autumn he had met Dunne and Laycock, back from triumphs in Italy. At a No. 8 Commando reunion at the Savoy, Robin Campbell (minus a leg) had been fêted with oysters and champagne. Waugh's celebration of their heroism was publicly enthusiastic and privately resentful. As in those four shiftless years after Oxford, he felt unfairly discriminated against, an object of mockery, and now, as then, instead of accepting responsibility for his failure, he constructed a fiction with himself as hero: Waugh as Crouchback, sensitive, Catholic, bundled out of a Protestant war because he would not compromise his honour; Waugh as Ryder, the artist, besieged by Hooperism; Waugh as Scott-King, the scholarly recluse, adrift in the chicancry of international politics. Everyone else *had* to be wrong – and it was the determination to prove them so that provided the impetus of his post-war fiction. Philip Toynbee later described him as a 'mourner for a world that never was', and this perhaps touches on the melancholy of those novels whose author rejected quotidian reality as fantastic and turned increasingly to fantasy and the supernatural as more accurate registers of the real.

Waugh's last training exercise is unmistakably described in these terms: as a brief experience of spiritual release between cacophony and the flat earth. When the posting had been cancelled, the prospective members of the new SAS group (including Dunne and Sykes) had been told to report back to their regiments. Instead, most had hung around in London and, with Dunne's assistance, Waugh had contrived to have them sent on a parachuting course at a secret house in Ringway. He had arrived with 'flu and missed the two days preliminary training. But this did not deter him from making two jumps:

> The first was the keenest pleasure I remember. The aeroplane noisy, dark, dirty, crowded; the harness and parachute irksome. From this one stepped into perfect silence and solitude and apparent immobility in bright sunshine above the treetops.... All too soon the ground seemed to be getting suddenly nearer and then, before one had time to do all one had been told, one landed with a great blow.[74]

74. *Diaries*, 30 December 1943, p. 556.

'Parachuting is without exception the most exhilarating thing I have ever done,' he wrote tactlessly to Laura. 'All the tedium of the last months has been worthwhile for the few seconds of first leaving the aeroplane. I felt absolutely no reluctance to jump.... But hitting the earth was very shocking.'[75] It was like the leap of faith into that state of spiritual quietude achieved by the holy, always irritatingly beyond Waugh's reach. It was a taste of the silence of Heaven followed by an abrupt recall to mortality. On the first jump, he kicked himself; on the second, he sat on his leg and cracked the fibula. The letter was written from an RAF sick-bay. 'As soon as I get hurt,' he wrote plaintively to Laura, 'I need you enormously....'[76]

As usual, he expected her to be instantly available to repair his wounded dignity. 'Your telegram', he wrote, '... was a bitter and unexpected blow.... I do not know where to go. I am in pain & helpless and can't manage the journey to Pixton; even if I could I should need more attention than I can ask in the circumstances. Nor can I stay alone at a London hotel.'[77] As he grew older, he came to sound increasingly like his father. In this petulant mood, an injury to Waugh was an injury to the world. He had scarcely set his heart on Christmas at Pixton, nor had he injured himself badly. He did not need constant medical attention. He simply demanded attention. The broken leg was as nothing: it was the neglect that hurt, the embarrassment and isolation, the reduction to passivity. Laura's refusal he saw as betrayal, and he arrived in London hobbling ignominiously on crutches, full of recrimination. Only there did he discover to his shame that she had been ill.

She came to town as soon as she could and cured his persecution mania. Waugh was restored by two weeks of continuous entertainment at the Hyde Park Hotel. The centre of attraction again, propped up in bed, an effervescent, self-mocking host, he drew a stream of guests into an environment where he could control their responses. But with Christmas approaching, Laura had to return to Pixton and he sank again. Maimie took him in and mothered him; Vsevolode's stupidity drove Waugh, hopping painfully, from the room and eventually from the house. Back in the hotel, '... leading a more and more limited life in the vicious spiral of boredom and lassitude ...',[78] he greeted the new year despondently and was further depressed by the arrival of his son.

A sandy-haired, secretive child, Bron had lived a quite separate life from his father and was more than a little frightened of him. Waugh intended to

75. ALS to Laura Waugh, 'Monday' [December 1943], from YMCA, With His Majesty's Forces [Manchester]; *Letters*, p. 174.
76. *Ibid.*
77. ALS to Laura Waugh, 'Tuesday' [7 December 1943], np [Manchester]; *Letters*, p. 175.
78. *Diaries*, 31 January 1944, p. 557.

maintain this distance. When in November the news of the German V1's had leaked out and the further devastation of London had seemed imminent, he arranged for his books to be moved from the Hyde Park Hotel to Piers Court.

> At the same time I have advocated my son coming to London. It would seem from this that I prefer my books to my son ... the truth is that a child is easily replaced while a book destroyed is utterly lost; also a child is eternal; but most [*sic*] that I have a sense of absolute possession over my library and not over my nursery.[79]

This was Waugh's perpetual problem with human relations: they were beyond his control. He increasingly felt the need to wall off his estate so that, within its boundaries, everything might be the perfect expression of his taste. Children were to him savages, for ever threatening this order. For his own, though, he reserved a special awkwardness and puzzlement which they found hypnotic.

They grew up with an image of him that Laura encouraged: the Great Man not to be disturbed. But he was also a fantasist, larger than life; there was something of the clown and the magician about him which suggested that, beneath the crusty exterior, he was ultimately on their side, subverting the adult world and everything that took itself seriously. He taught them never to be humble, always to attack, always to scorn with wit and to be 'amusing'. He had an extraordinary power to make people wish to please him. Part of his extended joke with Laura was to describe their children from a distance like stray farm animals, each with a peculiar malfunction. Such an attitude, however, could come dangerously close to sadism. Laura spent much time deflecting his anger away from her brood and on to her own head. Bron's occasional forays into the tall story were ruthlessly condemned as mendacity. Waugh made a serious distinction between lying and fantasizing which was not always easy for his children to understand. 'The wonderful thing about children', he once told Sykes, 'is that you can tell them anything you want and watch them grow up believing it.'[80]

Waugh's peculiar paternal intimacy was yet to develop. At this stage, father and son were strangers and both displaced persons. Bron's only home had been Pixton. His formative influences during the war were his mother, his grandmother and the disorderly aristocratic ambience of the Herbert family. This gave him an air of confidence, even as a four year old, but it was a disrupted life. 'I am sorry my poor son is so morbid and secretive,' Waugh wrote to Laura. 'He has a bad heredity in that matter.'[81] Tem-

79. *Ibid.*, 13 November 1943, p. 555.
80. Interview with Christopher Sykes, 27 December 1976.
81. Unpublished ALS to Laura Waugh, 18 October [1943], from St James's Club, Piccadilly; BL.

peramental similarity failed to encourage any warmer feelings in January 1944. Laura was ill again, this time with mumps. Bron needed an oculist urgently to correct an 'alternating squint'. It did not please his father to be forced into nursery duty, hobbling around Harley Street with his swivel-eyed offspring, at a moment of crisis in his relations with the army.

Waugh was juggling several possible futures: secondment as a film writer, secondment to MI5, or taking leave to write his novel. By the 20th, all these possibilities seemed to have collapsed:

> I am about again but low spirited & without vitality. I have no news of my future. Korda has decided he dare not apply for me. In despair I have written to Brendan [Bracken] direct. M.I.5 turned me down without an interview.... Would it make you any better to have a set of Caldecott first editions 13 vols or another 16 vols bound in 4?[82]

Book purchases continued unabated, building the library into which he would retire after the war. But he detested 'meantimes' and this one had lasted for three years.

Four days later he wrote a difficult letter, unused as he was to self-effacement:

> I ... request ... leave of absence from duty without pay for three months:
>
> 1. I have reached the age of 40.... I have ... not acquired the technical training to render me of use to my regiment....
> 2. I have no longer the physical agility necessary for an operational officer....
> 3. I have not the administrative experience necessary for the type of appointment normally given to a regular officer of my age.
> 4. I have not the knowledge of foreign languages necessary for an appointment in the Intelligence....
> 5. In civil life I am a novelist and I have now formed the plan of a new novel which will take approximately three months to write.
> 6. This novel will have no direct dealing with the war ... [but] ... it is understood that entertainment is now regarded as a legitimate contribution to the war effort.
> 7. It is a peculiarity of the literary profession that, once an idea becomes fully formed in the author's mind, it cannot be left unexploited without deterioration. If, in fact, the book is not written now it will never be written.
> 8. On ... completion ... I shall be able to return to duty with my mind unencumbered either by other preoccupations or by the

82. Unpublished ALS to Laura Waugh, 20 January 1944, from White's; BL.

> financial uncertainty caused by ... supporting a large family on the pay of a lieutenant.[83]

This sad list of his demerits was his capitulation: resignation from the world of action. Copies were sent to Bracken and to the Secretary of State for War. It hurt to relinquish the opportunity for revenge, but he was determined to exact retribution in other ways.

By the end of January he was back in his old haunt, the Easton Court Hotel in Chagford, Devon, 'with the intention of starting on an ambitious novel tomorrow morning. I ... am in low spirits but I feel full of literary power which only this evening gives place to qualms of impotence.'[84] The qualms did not last. He had waited many months for this moment, the vintage of his experience ripening slowly. Now he held the bulk of a long and complex fiction in his head. The working title was *The Household of the Faith*. It became *Brideshead Revisited*.

83. TccLS, to Officer Commanding, HCTU Windsor, 24 January 1944, np [London]; reprinted *Diaries*, p. 557.
84. *Diaries*, 31 January 1944, p. 558.

IV

Conditional Surrender: February 1944–August 1945

A week before travelling to Chagford, Waugh had written to Laura:

> . . . I did not explain why your plan to live with me in a cottage at Pixton would not do and may have seemed abrupt in turning it down. The reason is that I long for your company at all times except one. When I am working I must be alone. I should never be able to maintain the fervent preoccupation which is absolutely necessary to composition, if you were at close quarters with me.[1]

This was true, but no other book had obsessed him to this degree. *Brideshead* was to be his *A La Recherche du Temps Perdu*: an intimate first-person narrative, displacing but not disguising its autobiographical base. Like Charles Ryder, Waugh's enlistment had in retrospect marked a valediction: to youth and gaiety, to a civilization which had nurtured power with grace. His hero's name had been chosen carefully. At the corner of Ryder Street and Duke Street, St James's, stood one of Waugh's favourite art dealers: Neumann's.[2] It was a symbolic point of convergence between the aristocrat and the artist.

Brideshead was to be a lament in the waste land but it was also to be a statement of faith. The end of Ryder's story is its beginning: the Epilogue confirms that he has become a Catholic and the whole focus of his sceptical, controlling voice is shifted from the secular to the theological, eating its tail, demanding a re-reading in the light of this revelation. By this simple fictional device, Waugh created a double focus in the narrative. When Charles remarks to Lady Marchmain that Catholics seem '"just like other people"', she replies: '". . . that's exactly what they're not – particularly in this country, where they are so few . . . they've got an entirely different outlook on life; everything they think important, is different from other people."'[3] This statement was of crucial importance to Waugh. It was not a question of social snobbery (although he often muddles the issues); it concerned the double focus of Catholic life in which the supernatural was the real and the material world an illusion.

1. 25 January 1944, from White's; *Letters*, p. 176.
2. Cf. unpublished APC to Lady Diana Cooper, nd [pm 18 May 1955], from Piers Court; BL.
3. *Brideshead Revisited*, *op. cit.*, p. 80.

Time was the problem: the sense of being both in time and out of it; the disbelief in the rationalists' linear time, one damn thing after another in meaningless space; the belief in all time existing simultaneously, part of a Divine Plan. Waugh wished both to convey this mystical sense of being and to confront the agony of time passing. On one level it is a book about growing old, about homelessness and the resentment, boredom and nostalgia that corrupt the languor of youth. On another, it concerns historical process, suggesting that Charles's (and Waugh's) temporal indignities correspond with the death-throes of European civilization. The thematic structure was large – too large for Waugh to control as finely as he wished – but, considering the pace at which it was written and the persistent interruptions, it is astonishingly successful.

'Up at 8.30,' he recorded after his first day's work, 'two and a half hours earlier than in London, and at work before 10. I found my mind stiff and my diction stilted but by dinner-time I had finished 1,300 words all of which were written twice and many three times before I got the time sequence and the transitions satisfactory. . . .'[4] Substantial revision at manuscript stage was strange to him and he maintained the practice throughout: 'I have fallen into a slough of rewriting. Every day I seem to go over what I did the day before and make it shorter. I am getting spinsterish about style. . . .'[5] *Brideshead* was employing a new form, the style first attempted in *Work Suspended* and then abandoned. It was also, despite his 'Author's Note',[6] intensely autobiographical. For the first time he was giving himself away. The scene of the 'Prologue' is Pollock Camp, near Glasgow: 'It is v. high quality', he wrote to Laura, 'about Col. Cutler and how much I hate the army.'[7]

Waugh had written nothing at Chagford since 1939. Carolyn Cobb welcomed him and offered the middle sitting room with a blazing, smoky fire. Everything was perfect, even the bitter winter. He preferred a chill in the air, and the hotel was full of ancient gentlewomen who lent the place that parochial anonymity in which he liked to work. Norman Webb drove to Piers Court to pick up cases of wine and Waugh settled quickly into a precise routine: mass at a nearby village; 1,500–2,000 words a day; a long walk in the afternoon; dinner at a separate table in the company of the old ladies; correction; crossword or reading in the evening.

Laura was six months' pregnant and miserable, but Waugh was not to be deflected. 'While I am working it is brief, fairly frequent visits I want

4. *Diaries*, 1 February 1944, p. 558.
5. *Ibid.*, 13 February 1944, p. 558.
6. 'I am not I: thou art not he or she: they are not they.'
7. [2 February 1944]; *Letters*, p. 176. Amory dates this as 1 February.

not solid domesticity. . . .'[8] He was as strict with himself as he was with her. The danger of military recall rendered each day precious. Like Graham Greene, he counted every word and knew exactly when he should finish the novel. At the end of his first week, over 10,000 words were complete and he was promising Peters the whole manuscript by mid-May. Had the army not intervened, this estimate would have been accurate. By 26 February, 23,000 words had gone to the typist[9] when Waugh was called to London. The book was eventually completed in five stages between interruptions.

*

The authorities were not unreasonable about Waugh's leave – but every man was needed. Southern England in February 1944 was a tumultuous international military camp preparing for the second front. Towns and trains were packed with soldiers; roads hummed with convoys of lorries, jeeps and armoured cars. The country stood in readiness, although few knew that Roosevelt and Stalin had overruled Churchill at the Tehran conference the previous November and committed the Allies to invading Europe in May. This military background, of course, directly influenced *Brideshead*. While many of Waugh's countrymen were in a state of heightened anticipation, charged with patriotic fervour, Waugh saw only a further collapse of that 'Churchillian renaissance'. He could no longer cry God for Harry, England and St George. Embittered, he stood to one side and watched the confusion with bilious eye. The Allied invasion of Italy had met with serious obstruction and the composition of Waugh's *magnum opus* coincided almost exactly with Anzio, the last major set-piece battle with the Germans on Italian soil.

The plan had been for the armies to the south to breach the Gustav Line, thus drawing forces away from Anzio and for the American General, John P. Lucas, to break out, turn south and join them. As the Germans had no major force in Anzio, the whole scheme back-fired. The Gustav Line held, thousands of Allied soldiers died in its assault, and the troops at Anzio were left as sitting ducks while Kesselring poured troops and armour into the area. On the day Waugh began *Brideshead*, the US 3rd Division, attempting to attack Cisterna, ground to a halt and sustained heavy casualties. It was a typical defeat, and the slaughter was again immense. Victory did not come until 26 May, after four months of bitter fighting which produced considerable dissension between the American and British command. General Alexander's plan had been to destroy the German forces in Italy. When the Allies were at last in a position to do

8. Unpublished ALS to Laura Waugh, nd [c. 18–23 February 1944], np [Chagford]; BL.
9. Probably the first three chapters.

this, with Anzio secure and the Gustav Line breached, the Americans irritated the British by a vainglorious dash for Rome. General Clark's ambition to be the liberator of the Eternal City can only have confirmed Waugh's view of the war as a loutish display of self-interest.

At home, with the news from Italy so bad and the preparations for D-Day, the army was naturally keen to deploy its full strength. Small sympathy was spared for gentlemen requesting leave to write novels. Waugh was made ADC to Major-General Ivor Thomas and sent to Tenterden in Kent for a week's trial period. Thomas was an affable professional who laughed off Waugh's protestations about his unsuitability for the job. Waugh thought him common; Thomas seemed determined to like him. Whatever his reasons for this, he soon changed his mind. Waugh, like his fictional Connollys, knew how to make himself unwelcome. The posting lasted just twenty-four hours. 'The primary lack of sympathy', he recorded, 'seemed to come from my being slightly drunk in his mess on the first evening. I told him I could not change the habits of a lifetime for a whim of his.'[10] The remark itself would have been sufficient provocation but it was designed to cover another gaffe: at dinner he had knocked a glass of claret into Thomas's lap.

In London, Major-General Miles Graham, 'who appears to appreciate ... the importance of a gentleman leading his own life,'[11] offered a PR job and six weeks' leave. Waugh accepted, spent a delightful week-end with Laura at Chagford, but found on her departure that he could not settle to work: 'I have spent three days of nervous depression doing practically no writing, walking a little and fidgeting. I have been buggered about in the hotel.' Lord Grantley had arrived with 'a very personable film actress'. Waugh had been turned out of his sitting room to make way for adultery and given a bed-sitting room overhead. 'I am sick at heart and lonely. ... Lord Grantley did not remember me. I spoke to him & he thought me the hotel manager. ...'[12]

Back in his room the next day, he could not recapture the sense of well-being with which he had begun writing. Weary and sleepless, he took bromide and chloral each night which left him dull-witted in the mornings. Nevertheless, in twelve days he had completed and revised another 27,800 words: 'It is always my temptation in writing to make everything happen in one day, in one hour on one page and so lose its drama and suspense. So all today I have been rewriting and stretching until I am cramped.'[13]

10. *Diaries*, 2 March 1944, p. 559.
11. ALS to Laura Waugh, 9 March 1944, from White's; *Letters*, p. 179.
12. Unpublished ALS to Laura Waugh, 'Wednesday evening' [15 March 1944], np [Chagford]; BL.
13. *Diaries*, 22 March 1944, p. 561.

He was pushing himself to the limit. 'I don't know what to do about your visit here . . .' he wrote to Laura.

> (a) I am liable to immediate recall . . . I need one day holiday in 5 from my book; I could take another day correcting typescript in your presence, so 2 days are allowable. . . . I always long for your presence . . . you read brilliantly. . . . I have scarcely been out of the house but have sat at my desk all day. . . .[14]

Rumours were circulating in Chagford that transport would be disrupted after 1 April as the second front got under way. Waugh thought it unwise for his pregnant wife to be tottering round the country. But it was her eighth month and she was determined to see him before the birth. Waugh's mind was entirely concentrated on his novel:

> Is there a Father Brown book with 'The Fisherman' handy at Pixton. If so look out the quotation at the end where Fr. Brown compares the Faith with a fishing line, copy & send. . . . The sun brings out the old women like lizards & they sit by my window & annoy me. . . . I reviewed Archbishop Spellman's book for the Tablet so offensively I think Douglas [Woodruff] won't print it.[15]

At the beginning of this session he had taken a long walk and planned the next five weeks' work. The theological structure of the book was paramount and he had written to Ronald Knox requiring detailed information about the deconsecration of private chapels.[16] Waugh had no intimate acquaintance with ancient Catholic families and he followed the priest's advice exactly when he came to Cordelia's description of Lady Marchmain's Requiem,[17] a crucial image marrying the sense of homelessness with the themes of spiritual and historical discontinuity. But that was still 30,000 words hence. By the end of March he had only completed five chapters when, after Laura's visit, he was again recalled to London.

'I saw the Colonel I was told to see,' he wrote to Laura. 'It seems I must be a "conducting officer" for journalists.'[18] He then met Peter Rodd, 'who claims to command a detachment devoted to works of corporal charity',[19] and hoped for more honourable employment. Nothing came of either

14. Unpublished ALS to Laura Waugh, 'Passion Sunday' [26 March 1944], np [Chagford]; BL.
15. *Ibid.* Woodruff did not print it.
16. Cf. unpublished TLS from Ronald Knox to Evelyn Waugh, 14 March 1944, from Aldenham; BL. Knox advised that private chapels in great houses were not consecrated nor as a rule dedicated, just blessed; that it would be unusual and probably 'against the rules' to have a stone altar, the altar stone generally lying loose on the surface of 'any old table'; that the holy oils should be removed or burnt.
17. *Brideshead, op. cit.* (reprinted Harmondsworth, Penguin Books, 1951, 1960, 1973), pp. 211–12.
18. Unpublished APC to Laura Waugh, nd [1 April? 1944], from White's; BL. The job was to conduct journalists round the second front.
19. Unpublished ALS to Laura Waugh, 'Holy Saturday' [1 April 1944], from White's; BL.

posting. Lent was drawing to a close and Waugh added spice to Easter by rewriting an article on Harold Laski 'to make it more personally offensive to him'.[20] So long as the journalists' job remained a fiction he was free to sit in the Hyde Park Hotel and correct his typescript. 'My Magnum Opus', he told Peters, 'is turning into a jeroboam. I have written 62,000 words.... The original scheme of the book was three sections of which two are complete.... Should I be well advised to expand what I have written ... & publish it as Vol 1, leaving the second for next year?'[21] Peters thought not, despite the paper famine, and Waugh spent a fortnight getting drunk.

He did not want PR work, but when none was found for him, gratitude for neglect quickly soured into persecution mania. In desperation he wrote to Laycock, who was on leave from Italy, and on 1 May went to see him. Nothing could be done. Waugh, it seemed, was doomed to writing as his only sphere of influence and the next day he found himself in the Dorchester, an unwilling guest at a dinner given by Douglas Jerrold for Cardinal Griffin, the new Archbishop of Westminster, to meet the 'flower of Catholic literature'.

Robert Speaight and Graham Greene were the only other guests he knew. Hollis and Woodruff had defected to Claridge's and Waugh felt betrayed and vulnerable, 'very ill at ease in these rotarian surroundings'. Compton Mackenzie's sycophancy towards Griffin seemed profoundly misplaced:

> His Grace had clearly never read anything except a text-book in his life, but was not nonplussed. With complete self-assurance he praised the conduct of the House of Commons on the Education Bill ... said what an august lot we were – and by God we weren't – and sat down. He is a man of mean appearance, sly, pleased with his job, absolutely philistine, absolutely charmless.[22]

The fraternity of Catholic authors with its proletarian sympathies made Waugh restive. Griffin, it must be admitted, was to many others an unsympathetic figure. For much of his career as Archbishop he appeared to be senile and his business was conducted by Mgr Worlock.[23] Griffin and Worlock, ecclesiastical outflankers, were an unpopular team with Waugh's cronies. But the Butler Education Act (1944), restructuring the state secondary school system and opening more Grammar School places to poor families, was welcomed by most. Waugh felt alienated from both

20. *Ibid.* Cf. 'Marxism, the Opiate of the People', *Tablet*, 22 April 1944; review of Harold Laski, *Faith, Reason and Civilization* (Gollancz, 1944); *EAR*, pp. 277–80. Laski's argument sees Christianity merely as an historical phenomenon similar to, and no better than, Marxism.
21. [Received 3 April 1944]; *Letters*, p. 182.
22. *Diaries*, 2 May 1944, p. 563.
23. Now Archbishop of Liverpool.

populist political reorganization and the camaraderie of his Church. He left London gratefully to sink back into his fiction.

The next chapter, he knew, would be the most testing, for it would deal openly for the first time with erotic love. *Work Suspended* had avoided the issue by making Lucy pregnant.[24] Sebastian's homosexual love had been presented as platonic.[25] The difficulty in describing Julia's adultery with Charles was twofold: there was the 'question of modesty' facing a Catholic author, and a certain awkwardness which Waugh felt in his own heterosexual relations. It is possible that he was, like Betjeman, bisexual, refusing to acknowledge ineradicable homosexual tendencies. Whatever the reason for Waugh's mixture of sexual shyness and arrogance, the scenes with Julia on the liner are embarrassingly coy.

It took him six days to write those painful 12,000 words:

> ... the most difficult part of the book so far, and in spite of some passages of beauty I am not sure of my success. I feel very much the futility of describing sexual emotions without describing the sexual act; I should like to give as much detail as I have of the meals, to the two coitions – with his wife and Julia. It would be no more or less obscene than to leave them to the reader's imagination, which in this case cannot be as acute as mine.[26]

The ancient conflict with Oldmeadow about obscenity[27] was always at the back of Waugh's mind and he accepted the moral responsibility that Catholic writing should not titillate or deprave. When Fr D'Arcy saw the typescript of this scene and of the earlier one in the night-club, he was clearly shocked and advised revision.[28] As we shall see, Waugh reluctantly accepted his view and obliterated the first coition, only restoring it in the 1960 revised version.

Waugh's remark about the fervour of his sexual imaginings might seem to lay the ghost of his latent homosexuality, but it rather points to an adolescent obsession with women as stereotypes. Ryder's descriptions of Celia reek with disgust – not only for her hygienic sexual habits and debased language but also for her 'female rites', which he sees as subverting 'the

24. See Vol. 1, n. 48, p. 500.
25. Cf. *Brideshead* (Penguin), p. 208, where Brideshead asks if '"there is anything vicious in my brother's connexion with this German [Kurt]?"' and Charles replies: '"No. I'm sure not. It's simply a case of two waifs coming together."'
26. *Diaries*, 9 May 1944, pp. 564–5.
27. Cf. Vol. 1, pp. 336–42.
28. Cf. unpublished ALS from Fr M. C. D'Arcy, 23 June 1944, from Campion Hall; BL: '... I am sure a number will object to p. 118 – because of its open talk of sleeping with a woman as an adventure for young men. The steamer scene & [?] passage p. 233 will be too vivid & coarse a picture for many & the paragraph on p. 264 [?] will be objected to for this same reason – especially "white breast & [?] narrow loins"....'

august, masculine atmosphere of a better age'.[29] This, centred on Oxford's predominantly homosexual ethos and on those parts of Brideshead Castle not infected by women, is opposed to the 'intimate feminine modern world',[30] and it is this intimacy which Ryder cannot bear and which he discounts as not merely frivolous but dangerous. Julia is acceptable because, to all intents, she is a man or, at least, the very image of Narcissus which had always obsessed Waugh. She is effectively a clone of Sebastian, who was the 'forerunner' in Ryder's sexual imagination. A Freudian interpretation might suggest that in making love to Julia, Ryder is merely displacing his desire to make love to Sebastian and that it is this dishonesty which results in the embarrassing immaturity and strained, passionless vocabulary of his description of the coition.

The first public edition read: 'I took formal possession of her as a lover. . . . Now on the rough water, as I was made free of her narrow loins . . . while the waves still broke and thundered on the prow, the act of possession was a symbol, a rite of ancient origin and solemn meaning.'[31] The sexual act, then, is an act of possession for the homeless Ryder and no parody could improve on the lamentable phallic imagery of the ship. The revised version, currently in Penguin, might have been written by a solicitor: 'Now on the rough water there was a formality to be observed, no more. It was as though a deed of conveyance of her narrow loins had been drawn and sealed. I was making my first entry as the freeholder of a property I would enjoy and develop at leisure.'[32]

It is generally foolish to assume a character's voice to be his author's. In this case, however, there is considerable evidence to suggest that Ryder's heterosexual awkwardness, masquerading here as comfortable dominance, was Waugh's own or, at least, a metaphor for Waugh's own. He impressed many of his female friends as low-sexed and boyish, and was all the more attractive for being unthreatening in this respect. The writing of the scene was 'painful' for Waugh, surely, not because he feared Catholic repercussions, but because it described the one area of sensual activity in which he had never felt at ease. If he was happier as father than son, he was also better content as master than lover. Unfortunately, beyond his family, few accepted his leadership, and it was the army's refusal to let him take command which ruined his love affair with military life.

*

29. *Brideshead* (Penguin), p. 133.
30. *Ibid.*
31. *Ibid.*, 1st edn, *op. cit.*, p. 229.
32. *Ibid.* (Penguin), p. 248.

After finishing his chapter, Waugh was again called to London – this time to be offered two even more ignominious jobs. He accepted the least obnoxious[33] and scuttled straight round to Laycock at COHQ, pleading for release. Laycock, embarrassed by their earlier difficulties, was pleased to help. He telephoned Bill Stirling and secured Waugh a posting to No. 2 SAS, the unit he had been with when he fractured his fibula. Six weeks' leave was granted, more than enough to finish the novel, and he returned to Chagford on 12 May in high spirits. The next day, as he worked on the 'private view' chapter, Laura gave birth to Harriet. He did not disturb his routine for this. Writing vigorously again and with the promise of active service, he kept his head down and by the end of the week had finished 15,000 words: 'I think perhaps it is the first of my novels rather than the last. . . .'[34]

Waugh first saw Harriet nine days after the birth. He had instructed Laura not to allow the Herberts to bother him until she was well again, and had a habit of talking about 'my baby' when it suited him and 'your baby' when it did not. Irritated by his wife's failure to inform him of 'my baby's' name, he was further annoyed by her choosing her mother's secretary, Miss Haig, as a godparent. Miss Haig, who Waugh felt lacked social distinction, had originally come to Pixton to oversee the evacuees. The other godparents were more suitable: Countess Coudenhove, Basil Bennett, Nancy Mitford and, as a thank offering for the SAS job, Bill Stirling. The childless Nancy took her responsibilities to Harriet seriously, and all were present for the christening on the 28th. But Waugh felt odd returning to this predominantly female atmosphere where his authority was marginalized. Laura now led a quite separate life and refused to be awed by the magnificence of his literary project. An alien presence in the family, he was also faintly suspicious of Stirling's assurance that leave could be extended for as long as it took to complete the novel.

Stirling's promise naturally relied on his retaining authority. Three days later, Waugh discovered that Stirling had argued with his superiors and been replaced by Brian Franks. Franks, another friend from No. 8 Commando, was even less certain about Waugh's military competence. No one could avoid the fact that he was looking less and less like a soldier. In London, after the christening, he got so drunk that he was sick in his hotel bedroom, fell in the fireplace and bruised his head. The next day, still half-drunk, he had met Franks, who eagerly offered more leave. Waugh left for Chagford, took a treble sleeping draught and woke on 3 June to begin the last section[35] feeling decidedly shaky.

33. Intelligence Officer, Chemical Warfare Department, War Office.
34. *Diaries*, 21 May 1944, p. 566.
35. This began with 'Book III, Chapter Three', although in the first public edition this was 'Book Two, Chapter Three'. In the 1960 version Waugh returned to the original scheme of the manuscript.

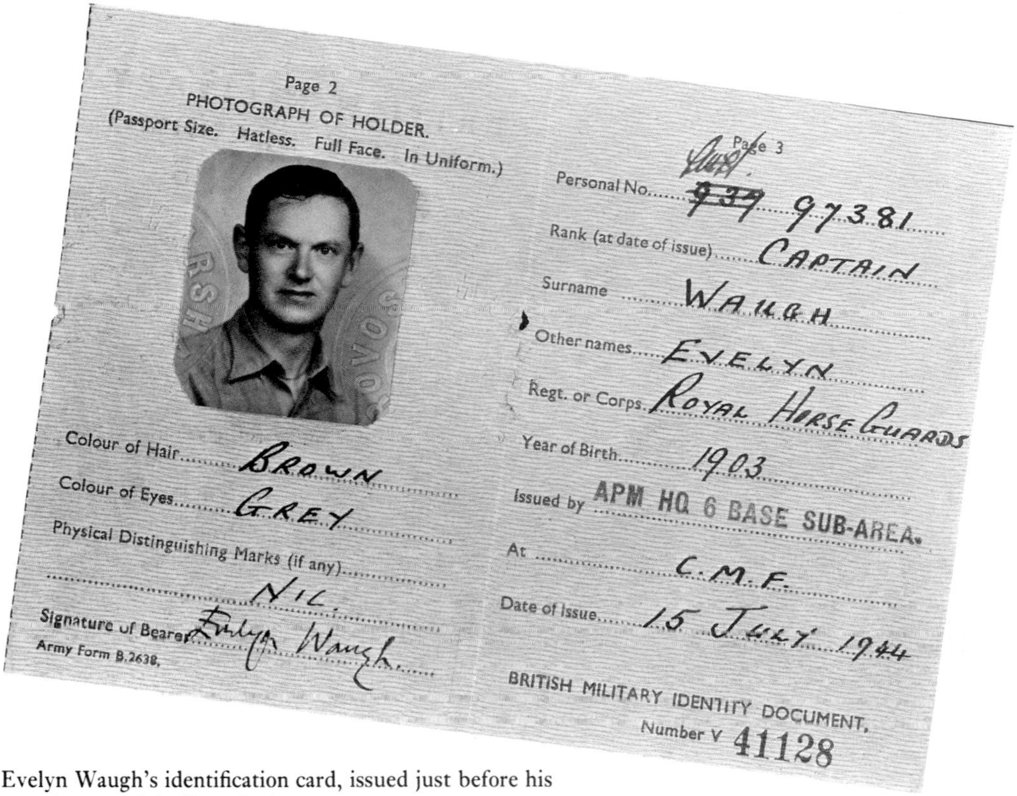

Page 2
PHOTOGRAPH OF HOLDER.
(Passport Size. Hatless. Full Face. In Uniform.)

Colour of Hair .... BROWN
Colour of Eyes .... GREY
Physical Distinguishing Marks (if any) ....
NIL.
Signature of Bearer Evelyn Waugh
Army Form B.2638.

Page 3
Personal No. .... ~~939~~ 97381
Rank (at date of issue) .... CAPTAIN
Surname .... WAUGH
Other names .... EVELYN
Regt. or Corps. ROYAL HORSE GUARDS
Year of Birth 1903
Issued by APM HQ 6 BASE SUB-AREA.
At .... C.M.F.
Date of Issue .... 15 JULY 1944

BRITISH MILITARY IDENTITY DOCUMENT.
Number V 41128

Evelyn Waugh's identification card, issued just before his aeroplane crash in Yugoslavia

Evelyn Waugh and Randolph Churchill in Croatia, on the British Military Mission to Tito's partisans

(*Above*) Lord Lovat in November 1942, a man Evelyn Waugh came to hate

(*Above right*) Fitzroy Maclean, Waugh's CO in Yugoslavia, described in the *Diaries* as having a 'shaved head and devil's ears'

(*Below*) Major-General Robert Laycock, Waugh's friend and CO, on taking over from Lord Mountbatten as Chief of Combined Operations, October 1943

(*Right*) Moray McLaren in April 1955, journalist and playwright, who owed his post-war literary career to Evelyn Waugh's loyalty

(*Above*) Left to right: Teresa, Laura, James, Auberon, Harriet, Evelyn and Margaret Waugh at Piers Court, c. 1949

bove) A. D. Peters, Evelyn Waugh's
erary agent

ec Waugh and Joan Chirnside on
nouncing their engagement in August
32

(*Left*) Cyril Connolly

(*Opposite page*) Evelyn Waugh standing for his portrait by Simon Elwes in California, 1946

Lady Diana and Duff Cooper at their Bognor house during the war

(*Left*) John Betjeman, August 1955

(*Opposite page*) Left to right: Anna May Wong, Evelyn Waugh, Sir Charles Mendl and Laura Waugh in California, 1946

Evelyn Waugh in Windsor, Ontario, during his North American lecture tour, February 1949
(*Right*) Evelyn Waugh's self-portrait on leaving America
(*Below*) Laura and Evelyn Waugh at Plymouth aboard the *Ile de France* after returning from America, 6 November 1950

Graham Greene talking to Eric Portman during a rehearsal of *The Living Room*, 18 April 1953

(*Left*) Catherine Walston, Graham Greene's lover

(*Below*) Nancy Mitford in Paris

Evelyn Waugh and one of his follies at Piers Court

He did not get far. As he sat down to describe Julia's and Charles's retrospect of their two years' unmarried bliss, composition was interrupted by a persistent thumping on the ceiling: 'A Belgian airman is having a passionate honeymoon over my head,' he wrote to Laura. 'I have had to have him moved so it stopped work yesterday. They left bed for only $\frac{3}{4}$ hour at lunchtime.'[36] Waugh apparently saw no irony in this carnal intrusion into the idealized world of his fiction. In fact, he saw nothing, could think of nothing, but the theological structure of this section of his book which renders all human passion '"merely hints and symbols; ... doors that open as in a dream to reveal a further stretch of carpet and another door...."'[37] The 'low door' *Alice in Wonderland* imagery, used earlier to describe the magic of Oxford, is here combined with a Keatsian vision of the mind as a many-roomed mansion. Unlike Keats, however, Waugh was not interested in the limitless vistas of consciousness. Down those corridors madness lay, the frigid paradoxes and hopeless optimism of humanism. He insisted instead upon seeing in pain and confusion the mysterious workings of Divine Purpose. The passage goes on to forge a link with Charles's earlier remarks on the individual soul:[38] '"... perhaps you and I are types and this sadness which sometimes falls between us springs from disappointment in our search, each straining through and beyond the other, snatching a glimpse now and then of the shadow which turns the corner always a pace or two ahead of us."'[39] Everything, even sex, was translated into an aspect of the quest for the City of God.

Waugh knew the agony of which he was writing: the sense of sinfulness, the stain which betrayal and, more particularly, adultery could spread through a life. In addition to the aborted relationships with Audrey Lucas, Teresa Jungman and Hazel Lavery, and to the string of prostitutes during the 1930s, at least two other women had fallen in love with him and been discarded. He usually took his lovers to Chagford. One had woken there to find Waugh gone. He had left a note. 'Evelyn dear,' she replied:

> That was the unkindest cut of all. Was it absolutely necessary to leave me when I needed you so badly? I suppose it must have been because I can't believe you would willingly kick me so hard once I was down. My hand is so shaky this morning I can hardly hold the pencil steady

36. Unpublished ALS to Laura Waugh, 'Monday' [5 June 1944], np [Chagford]; BL.
37. *Brideshead*, 1st edn, *op. cit.* p. 265.
38. See ch. 3, p. 84 above.
39. *Brideshead*, 1st edn, *op. cit.*, p. 265; Penguin edn, p. 288. This section in the Penguin text corresponds with the first edition. The earlier part of the paragraph, however, was revised as: '"... perhaps all our loves are merely hints and symbols; vagabond-language scrawled on gate-posts and paving stones along the weary road that others have tramped before us...."'

> but the doctor's given me some soothing medicine which may help. And God do I need it after your note this morning....[40]

Like Sebastian, Waugh often used to run away from women, and it seems that their sexual power, what he saw as their sticky sensual and emotional demands, threatened his 'manhood' and his self. Before Laura, he had been trying, with considerable difficulty, to find his way with the opposite sex, and he clearly did not object to adultery in his pursuit of experience.

Early in 1936, for instance, at the height of his chaste courtship of Laura, he had been sleeping with a married woman. Two years later, tied to a husband she could not love, her passion for Waugh still raged. Laura was pregnant with Teresa when he received a letter from his abandoned lover. She was still obsessed, distraught. His marriage had hurt her badly; Laura's pregnancy only emphasized the irrevocable nature of that union. Through two-and-a-half closely-packed quarto sheets the poor woman spilled out her agony. She followed his advice, she said, and thought of him whenever she was making love. But his voice, body, everything about him was still so vivid that he seemed to start to life beside her.

It might be a secular version of Julia Flyte's monologue. Waugh's correspondent saw her life as finished. She still longed to have a child by him but, of course, it was all too late: he had started again with a younger woman and cast off his messy alienation from 'decency'. In the 1930s, it seems that he attracted effusive, flamboyant women and, although most felt sexually indifferent to him, he was charmed by their gaiety and spontaneity. Women, he thought, should be 'quick', sharp, smart. Laura was droll but rarely quick or smart. She could not write letters like Nancy Mitford or Penelope Betjeman and he sometimes found his wife's relative dullness irritating. Ultimately, however, he was grateful to her for her stoicism. The kind of erotic torment expressed in the letter he found distasteful and unnerving.

The experience of adultery in *Brideshead* is recorded in Julia's monologue, using this language of obsession but translating it from a sexual to a religious context. We hear of her physical passion by report only, although, as we have seen, he would have liked to have written more comprehensively about Ryder's lust. Waugh, it seems, was not interested in this side of women's nature. Sex was for him, as for Ryder, an act of possession; to Waugh the Catholic it was also a function of propagation. The male, Waugh believed, should command the female. Women who expressed lustful feelings sought to usurp the male 'right' of possession and were thus dangerous: criminally naïve, bestial or evil. And in Laura he found someone who very nearly suited his impossible demands: quiet, astute, usually obedient in the early

40. Unpublished ALS, nd, from Easton Court Hotel, Chagford, Devon; BL.

years and, when his lust had subsided, tough and sardonic. He had married someone, in fact, who bore a marked temperamental resemblance to his mother.

Brideshead is an 'all passion spent' novel. It anticipates nothing pleasurable but the dim prospect of the Second Coming. Waugh completed it in the week during which his nation rode on a tide of euphoria: the Americans had liberated Rome and the second front had opened. He was in ebullient mood. He had, he thought, completed a masterpiece. 'I have never been happier. . . .' he wrote to Laura. 'I see nothing but innocent pleasure ahead.'[41] The remark, however, did not refer to the rest of his life or to the future of Europe. He was in White's, with three days to polish his manuscript before travelling to Scotland,[42] and he was experiencing a deep, malicious thrill to be publishing a work proclaiming a hopeless future while the ignorant majority saw only a Brave New World. They needed, Waugh thought, simply to look out of the window. London was being terrorized with a new secret weapon, flying bombs, which disturbed even Waugh's equanimity.

*

From Bill Stirling's hunting lodge in Perthshire he advised Laura not to go to London during the bombardment:

> . . . The danger is negligible but the annoyance grave and almost incessant. The bombs make a noise like a motor-car then stop & fall with a pop. One gets into the habit of listening to motor-cars & wondering if they are bombs, which distracts one from rational pleasure during the day & keeps one awake at night.
>
> I did not at all enjoy my few days in London. . . . After the industry, repose and domestic bliss of Chagford it was very unnerving. Now I have come to a place of complete repose. . . .[43]

With his return to military life, his rumbustious self-assurance revived, but he had, at last, accepted that he was no longer the social animal he had been. Archdullary Lodge seemed ideal: a small, cosy house in an empty landscape of lochs, pine woods and grouse moors. He was alone there with Franks and with nothing to do; the regimental orderly room was twenty-five miles away. Two years earlier he would have been furious with frustration. Now he was as content to be as idle as low spirits would allow. 'I

41. Unpublished ALS to Laura Waugh, 17 June [1944], from White's; BL.
42. Waugh submitted the completed manuscript to Chapman & Hall on 20 June 1944 and left for Scotland with Brian Franks the next day.
43. Unpublished ALS to Laura Waugh, 23 June 1944, from Archdullary Lodge, Strathyre, Perthshire; BL.

am not very well,' he wrote home. 'I cannot make out whether it is my teeth or my eyes that are aching.'[44]

This, he tried to convince himself, was an excellent appointment. He was free to do as he liked. When Bennett and Sykes arrived, Waugh immediately began to plan another novel.[45] In the event, his tranquillity survived less than a week and he wrote nothing but letters. Even in this close group, he was an irritant. 'Basil and Christopher are solid friends,' he told Laura. 'Bryan [*sic*] very loyal but plainly much embarassed [*sic*] to have me under his command and shows all eagerness to get me out of his way which I should resent if I did not know its cause.'[46] He did not know its cause. Franks wished to be rid of Waugh because he was a hopeless soldier.

Waugh was struggling to reform: 'I have given up drunkenness for life.... It is a cutting of one of the few remaining strands that held me to human society....'[47] He wrestled with (relative) abstinence for some months, but, as he suspected, this only deepened his isolation. Clear-headed in the company of boozers, he found their jokes flat and their conversation fuddled. When drunk, Waugh could be amusingly offensive; sober, he was caustic and melancholy. He wanted to visit Pixton for a week but, before Laura could reply, frantic cables began arriving from Randolph Churchill. He was in London at the Dorchester. Did Waugh wish to join him on a military mission to Croatia? Waugh left Scotland immediately.

'I visited your mother yesterday', he wrote to Alec, 'to say goodbye – I am just off on a jaunt to the Balkans – and borrowed your His Second War. You asked for my opinion. I must congratulate you on keeping so much in the fashion in spite of your exile. 'Documentaries' are all the rage now and I rejoice that the bourgeoisie should step in and take a little proletarian cake....'[48] Poor Alec, languishing in Syria, fearful for his diminishing literary reputation, had knocked out the book in his spare moments and was himself depressed by its low quality. Cassell had at first refused it, pleading paper shortage. Alec had not experienced such a rejection since his first attempts to publish *The Loom of Youth*. If he accepted the decision, he thought, he would be finished as a writer and so, foolishly, he insisted

44. *Ibid.*
45. Cf. unpublished ALS to Laura Waugh, Monday, 25 [error for '26'] June [1944]; np [Archdullary Lodge, Strathyre, Perthshire]; 'I think very soon I shall start a magnum or minor opus.'
46. *Ibid.*
47. *Ibid.*
48. Unpublished ALS to Alec Waugh, 4 July 1944, from White's; HRC. The letter continues: 'I don't see, given the limitation you accept, that the book could be improved except in two particulars (a) I don't like the playing about with the time sequence ... (b) I don't like the third person "one" or "you" which you certainly employ where "I" is the only suitable word.... All your slang is unfamiliar and uncongenial to me – such verbs as "to tuck" or the transitive use of "to breakfast" ... seem to show the strain of the U.S.A....'

that, as an established author, he deserved better treatment. Cassell's backed down. The reviews were dreadful. Evelyn's letter can only have driven his brother to the whisky bottle. Beneath the thin rhetoric of praise, the mockery is plain. The correct use of the English language had become an obsession, at once 'old-maidish', as he admitted, and *avant-garde*. Linguistic 'slippage' signalled philosophical muddle and Alec's Americanisms were as shocking as his unstructured religious belief.

*

Less than a week after receiving Churchill's telegrams, Waugh was with him aboard a York aircraft, taxiing down the runway of Hendon aerodrome. Their route lay through Algiers, Sicily, Naples and, finally, Bari, on the Adriatic coast of Italy. Bari was the Rear HQ of Fitzroy Maclean's military mission, whose business it was to assist Tito's army of resistance, the Partisans, to eject the Germans from Yugoslavia.

By this time (July 1944), the whole of the southern Mediterranean coast and much of Italy were controlled by the Allies and in northern Europe they were pushing on towards Paris. But the German armies, although caught in this pincer movement, were far from defeated and their hold on Greece and the Balkans was crucial to the Mediterranean theatre of war. Within a few hours Waugh moved from peace and luxury to lands still ravaged by conflict. At the Embassy in Algiers Diana and Duff Cooper held a kind of French court for General de Gaulle. Peacocks strutted round the Arabesque villa and the Coopers entertained lavishly before moving on to take over the Paris Embassy in September.[49] Waugh spent three days with them. Bloggs Baldwin, Waugh's friend from Madresfield days, was there, as was Mary Hemingway (whose immodest bathing dress embarrassed Waugh). There were dinner parties and bedroom parties in dressing-gowns and pyjamas. Waugh disliked Algiers (full of Americans), but he relished his return to a centre of politics and fashion. General Maitland ('Jumbo') Wilson (Commander-in-Chief Middle Eastern Forces) was in town and Randolph made contact with him. After years on the sidelines, Waugh at last had access again to top-secret information and his sense of military dignity escalated proportionately.

Naples, overrun by often unscrupulous soldiers, seemed barbaric by contrast. In the ruins of the city, starvation and disease reduced many Neapolitans to the condition of scavenging animals. Drinking water was scarce; mothers offered their daughters for the price of a meal. Bari, though less savage, Waugh saw as a ramshackle dump of cowards. This was nonsense. The town was certainly used as a rest-camp for the battle-weary

49. Paris was liberated on 23 August 1944; the Coopers flew to the Embassy on 13 September.

but it was far from being a safe posting for idlers. A huge airfield sent regular, dangerous missions to the Balkans and Greece. It was from here that Waugh flew to Vis, an island off the Dalmatian coast, and met Tito for the first time.

'A great banquet for Tito at HQ,' Waugh recorded in his diary that night:

> (a modern villa with all conveniences except water), a bagpipe band, much gin and wine and kümmel.... [Tito] in brand new cap and uniform of Russian marshal with Jug badge. Hammers, sickles and Communist slogans everywhere... Randolph very drunk.... Maclean dour, unprincipled, ambitious, probably very wicked; shaved head and devil's ears.... Too early to give any opinions but I have as yet seen nothing that justifies Randolph's assertion to the Pope that 'the whole trend' was against Communism.... Tito like Lesbian. Randolph preposterous and lovable....[50]

Waugh's mind was, as usual, cluttered with fictions. Tito's uniform was Yugoslav, not Russian, and his gender was far from indeterminate. Waugh usually preferred a lively story to the truth. In the early days of Maclean's mission, over a year before, no one had been certain whether Tito even existed, let alone whether this mythical figure were male or female. This tiny seed of gossip fuelled years of Waugh's malice and, far from retracting the slander, he took every opportunity to embellish it. In Tito, however, Waugh had met his match. Clearly he had been up to mischief already on that first day, spreading rumours about the Partisan leader's genitalia. Everyone had been bathing. Tito emerged from the sea wearing a costume so brief as to leave no further doubt on the subject, strolled up to Waugh and Maclean and said: 'Will you please ask Captain Waugh why he thinks I am a Lesbian?' Captain Waugh was dumbfounded. He had not expected humorous self-assurance in a Communist and he never forgave Tito for ridiculing him.

Tito remains a difficult man to judge. In retrospect, he has appeared to many as a cynical tyrant, no more averse to genocide than Stalin. 'Broz' was, nevertheless, a remarkable man – courageous, adaptable, dignified, relentless in pursuit of his political ambitions but gifted with wit and inspired by a humanist idealism quite alien to Waugh. Whatever one thought of his politics, he was undeniably impressive. Waugh was a fake 'hard man'; in Tito and in Maclean he met the genuine article and they shocked him with their toughness. The respect between Maclean and Tito was beyond Waugh's understanding as, it seems, was the complexity of Yugoslavian politics.

50. *Diaries*, 10 July 1944, pp. 571–2.

Maclean's record reads like a John Buchan novel. Risen from the ranks to brigadier, he had seen action with the Long Range Desert Group and his exploits were legendary. During the 1930s, as a diplomat in Russia during Stalin's purges, he had travelled widely and recklessly without a permit. In 1941, in order to escape diplomacy for fighting, he had first contrived to become elected as a Conservative MP (parliamentary service being the only claim which the Foreign Office recognized as superior to its own) and had then enlisted as a private. This tall, languid Etonian possessed the kind of style and had achieved the sort of worldly success Waugh craved. But he made no allowance for the courage, industry and intelligence which had won the man distinction. The fact of his being Lord Lovat's brother-in-law perhaps had something to do with this. Maclean, a natural linguist, spoke French, German and Russian before beginning this mission. In a year he had acquired fluent Serbo-Croat and had risked his life daily. Tito's respect had been won by shared danger. Waugh and Churchill strode into this delicate situation with all the diplomacy of two Sir Toby Belches.

Maclean's first action on being appointed had been thoroughly to acquaint himself with the history of the country. Waugh seems not to have bothered with such homework. Maclean had parachuted into Yugoslavia in 1943 to attempt to elucidate for Winston Churchill what the hell was going on – and found that hell *was* going on. Mihailović was then Britain's ally, leading the Četniks as a resistance force. He represented the army of King Peter, the titular head of state to whom the British had given sanctuary and with whom they had diplomatic relations. Mihailović professed allegiance to the Allied cause and hatred of the Germans. Tito was an unknown quantity and, for all Maclean knew, an unreliable renegade.

Maclean soon discovered, however, that Mihailović was ineffective where Tito was not. The Četniks's policy of appeasement was not to Churchill's taste. The object, as Waugh once remarked, was to kill as many Germans as possible, and Tito was the more determined to do this. Maclean knew a ruthless professional when he saw one. He also recognized a charismatic leader who inspired passionate loyalty in his Partisans. There was no question in Maclean's mind but that Britain should switch military aid to them.

It was a potentially embarrassing change of horses. Neither Maclean nor Churchill was eager to see the establishment of a Communist state principally allied to Russia. First, however, the war had to be won and Russia was already an ally. It would have been hypocritical to refuse to side with Tito on political grounds. So Maclean returned to the Prime Minister and explained the situation, emphasizing the likelihood of a Marxist regime in the event of victory. Churchill listened patiently and agreed to back the Partisans. His response to the problem of Yugoslav Communism was precise and ruthless: '"Do you intend", he asked, "to make Yugoslavia your home after the war?" "No, Sir." ... "Neither do I...."'[51]

*

Despite his encounter with Tito, Waugh anticipated keen pleasure from his expedition. There were minor irritations. Both his arms ached from inoculations. He had brought no cigars with him, expecting to purchase them freely in Italy, and had found none for sale. The resulting hunger drove him constantly to the snack bar for sausage rolls. His resolution not to get drunk did not entail not drinking, and the local liqueurs had made him ill. But, in general, he was content to be ambling round Bari's churches, eating in a black market restaurant and waiting eagerly for the galley proofs of *Brideshead*. He had a large double room, bathroom and balcony to himself. Churchill was touring the country and rarely bothered him. Nothing suited Waugh better.

Laura had dispatched him with a religious medal, but the silver chain stained his neck green. On the day before his departure he wrote to her saying that he would soon abandon it. If he did, he doubtless attributed what happened next to a foolish neglect of supernatural powers. 'I am just setting out', he wrote to her on 16 July, 'and will give this [letter] to the airman when we arrive so that when you receive it you will know that we are safely on the ground.'[52]

During the early days of the military mission, Maclean and his staff had dropped at night into enemy territory, guided by signal fires. The 'planes flew perilously close to the ground, allowing barely enough time for a parachute to open. By June 1944, these dangers were largely over and extensive areas had been liberated by the Partisans. Airfields had been built in Croatia; Waugh and Churchill were entering relatively safe territory. Their Dakota transport flew in unopposed after sunset and prepared for a routine landing. At the last moment, however, the pilot thought he saw an obstruction and attempted to pull out. No one knows exactly what happened but they crashed from about four hundred feet and the 'plane burst into flames. The first Waugh knew of the accident, he was wandering in a corn field lit by blazing wreckage with someone at his elbow telling him to rest. Somehow the survivors had freed themselves or been thrown clear. Of the nineteen people aboard, two were killed. Waugh made little of the incident in his diary. His chief emotion was suppressed rage at this interruption of

51. Sir Fitzroy Maclean, *Eastern Approaches* (Cape, 1949; reprinted Penguin, 1991), pp. 402–3. For an entertaining account of the Yugoslav situation, see pp. 275–532. Other brief assessments can be found in *Diaries*, pp. 569–70; *Letters*, p. 185, n. 2; and Sykes, pp. 262–6.
52. Unpublished ALS to Laura Waugh, 16 July [1944], np [Bari]; BL.

his plans. His burns necessitated a return to hospital in Bari, but, much worse, his kit had been destroyed.

Realizing that the crash would be reported in the London papers, Randolph had thoughtfully sent a message to Laura through his father. Randolph had jarred both legs so badly that he could scarcely walk and suffered considerably from fluid on the knee. Waugh was blistered about the head, legs and arms, but, anaesthetized by shock, felt no great pain. Mummified in bandages, however, he could neither write nor move about easily and he watched his companion's boisterous antics in the hospital – drinking, chasing the night nurse, plastering American propaganda photographs on the walls – with glacial distaste. When, after six days, Randolph hobbled off to recuperate with the Coopers in Algiers, Waugh breathed a sigh of relief. Dorothy Lygon, then in the WAAF, came to visit and cheered him a little. But nothing put him in a worse temper than enforced passivity. Wait, wait, wait.

A fortnight later he was heading for Rome with 'Coote' Lygon, who spent her leave with him there. Diana Cooper turned up with Bloggs Baldwin and it was in Rome that she heard of the liberation of Paris. A pang of remorse and guilt had struck her at the news. It marked the end of the frivolous luxury of Algiers, the advent of responsibilities in a grey, post-war Europe. Like Waugh, she never entirely recovered from this sense of belonging to a dead world. Through the 1940s and 1950s, as her depression deepened, she tried to cling to Waugh as a vital force. At this stage he rarely responded with equal enthusiasm, divorced as he now felt from the glitter of her metropolitan world, longing for his wife and the isolation of his Wemmick's castle. Her visit was not a success. Another infirmity had struck in the form of an agonizing carbuncle on the back of his neck. At one stage he required penicillin injections every three hours, and he preferred to be alone, wandering in the shade of Roman churches. Only architecture could refresh him, although even these excursions were spoiled. His shoes had been burnt with his luggage and the indignity of his 'creepers', both made for the same foot, became an obsession.

While in Rome he wrote a report on the food conditions in the city and, probably for the first time, visited a slum for a purpose other than the search for prostitutes. Poverty had never held any political or philosophical attraction for him. The noble savage and the worker-hero were alike to Waugh, glorifications of the uncouth, and he stared at the anonymous man in the street from the windows of his ordered rooms with cool indifference. In Rome, however, he could no longer remain entirely unaffected before '... scenes of pitiful distress which gave me the less relish for my own meals.'[53] That was the limit of his sympathies at this stage. But it was a

53. *Diaries*, 26 August 1944, p. 576.

seed that grew. The Displaced Person develops in his later fiction from the image of the molested aesthetes of *Brideshead* to include all suffering humanity, all refugees.

At the end of August, Randolph popped up again and drove Waugh to Naples in a jeep. The Prime Minister's son was everywhere fêted as a celebrity and ambassador and he did not hesitate to take full advantage of his privileged status. They flew to Sicily for a luxury tour at the Americans' expense, were put up in a hotel suite, each with his own sitting room, were showered with gifts of whisky, cigars and underclothes, and taken on a hair-raising tour round corniche roads with a motor-cycle escort. All this Waugh might have enjoyed three years earlier. Now he was both bored by such garish exhibitions and unhappy to play second fiddle to Randolph. Any gratitude Waugh felt towards the Americans was overwhelmed by his rage at their linguistic infantilism. The great virtue of his present appointment, he felt, was that the military missions were likely to be the first units to be disbanded and sent home. 'My longing for you', he wrote to Laura, 'is the ghost at every feast. I never drink a glass of wine or bathe in the sea or look at a fine building without missing you at my side. It is a quite small part of me that is jaunting about. All the rest is with you.'[54]

Ten days later he was back in Bari to find a pile of letters from her and from his friends. He sorted hers into chronological order and savoured each scrap of family gossip. In the oppressive heat, he lovingly created a mental picture of her at Pixton on the wooded autumnal slopes of Somerset. The news was not all good. Bridget's husband, Eddie Grant, had been seriously ill. The 'plane crash had thrown everyone into a fluster, not least McIntyre of Little, Brown, who had read of the accident on the same day he had received the typescript of *Brideshead*. But Peters sent glad tidings from the USA. *Town and Country* had bought the serial rights, and Waugh was unexpectedly £1,000 better off. He was so unusually contented that he at last gave Laura full power to cash cheques on his account and even wrote to his mother telling her to draw on Laura for any money she needed. She had left Highgate for the safety of Midsomer Norton. A large part of Waugh's family was now congregated in the West Country.[55]

During his month's delay, the military situation in Yugoslavia had swung even further in the Allies' favour. The Russians and Tito were cutting off the Germans' retreat and it was now only a matter of time before they were defeated. In the south and east the Russians were converging on Belgrade and it seemed possible that the war might end during the autumn. Waugh was a liaison officer, second-in-command to Randolph, and both acted as

54. Unpublished ALS to Laura Waugh, 1 September [1944], np [Sicily]; BL.
55. Cf. unpublished ALS to Laura Waugh, 9 September [1944], np [Topusko]; and unpublished ALS to Catherine Waugh, 10 September [1944], from Force 399 CMF [Topusko]; BL.

military ambassadors between the British army and the Partisans. Large quantities of stores and weapons were regularly dropped by British and American 'planes. An extensive network of military missions had been established. It was Waugh's task to distribute the stores, to observe and report the progress of the war, and generally to act as go-between: fielding enquiries, succouring the refugees, trying to keep the peace between the Catholics and the Communists in the internecine struggles of an emergent state. Bill Deakin, a history don from Wadham College, Oxford, had been one of the old hands at these negotiations, preceding even Maclean in the Allies' contact with the Partisans. Deakin had won the Communists' respect by his combination of courage, a brilliant intellect and, as Maclean put it, 'a gift for getting on with everyone'.[56] This was not a gift shared by Waugh or Churchill.

They were based in the village of Topusko, a blitzed spa in Croatia, the predominantly Catholic province. The baths still operated; there were ornamental walks and pretty houses. The indigenous population had fled or been killed. Tito used the place as a rest camp for his soldiers and as his Croatian headquarters. The Allies used it as the final link in their POWs' escape route from the Balkans. It was a quiet place and in its lazy atmosphere Waugh's gaze fell cruelly on the gangs of young Partisan men and women, chanting songs and slogans. A fierce asceticism characterized their ideology. Drunkenness was almost unknown, sexual promiscuity punishable by death. Here, Waugh thought, was a dangerous combination of naïvety and duplicity which bore a grotesque resemblance to Puritanism.

In Waugh's view, the Yugoslav high command had

> . . . no interest in fighting the Germans but are engrossed in their civil war. All their vengeful motives are concentrated on the Ustashe [*sic*] who are reputedly bloodthirsty. They make slightly ingenuous attempts to deceive us into thinking their motive in various tiny campaigns is to break German retreat routes.[57]

Certainly the Partisans sought the death of Germans and the Catholic Ustaše with equal fervour. From both, Tito's forces and tens of thousands of civilians had suffered savage reprisals. Germans, Italians, Ustaše – all were, to the Partisan mind, Fascist oppressors. Even the Četniks in Bosnia and Montenegro had collaborated, fighting 'side by side with the Germans and Italians against the Partisans, while captured documents provided evidence of the contact which existed between the commands.'[58] There were old scores to settle. Waugh's superficial grasp of the situation did not,

56. Sir Fitzroy Maclean, *op. cit.*, p. 321.
57. *Diaries*, 16 September 1944, p. 579.
58. Sir Fitzroy Maclean, *op. cit.*, p. 322.

however, hamper his instinct to make snap judgments and attempt hasty resolutions. Everything was always painfully simple to him and, as a result, simply painful to those trying to persuade him otherwise. It was, he felt, perfectly straightforward, the same story as in Spain and Mexico: a barbarian assault upon the True Church. In that struggle, he knew where he stood.

After three days in a log cabin in a chestnut forest, Waugh and Churchill moved their headquarters to a farm on the outskirts of Topusko and, although Waugh missed the isolation and silence of the cabin, he much preferred their new home. Randolph was already beginning to irritate, and in Topusko Waugh had a room to himself. They had four rooms, a small verandah and very little to do. Rain often kept them indoors. Waugh attended mass with forty peasant women; Churchill blustered and drank and tried to compensate for his ignorance of Serbo-Croat with displays of grandiloquent patronage towards the Partisans. From his earliest days there, Waugh was keen to observe any signs of religious persecution and finding none merely added to his ill-temper as the war began to drag on for another winter.

The news from western Europe was of stalemate and failure. In mid-September, the attempt to capture Arnhem and break the German line had resulted in a bloodbath. Allied soldiers the world over huddled anxiously round wireless sets. Waugh listened to the bulletins with scarcely a flicker of interest. It was the huge advances on the eastern front which obsessed him. Waiting for the end, he was like a Chekhov character: bored, sceptical and trapped in uncongenial company. Time passed slowly. He longed for letters, particularly those from Laura and Nancy Mitford. No post came for weeks. Lying in bed every morning staring at the sunlight flickering through the vine leaves round his window, he became engrossed by a Proustian reflection. For a fortnight the pattern had inexplicably filled him with joy and reminded him of his childhood holiday home in Midsomer Norton. '. . . I have compared it to the border round a text, to my grandmother's illumination, to the tones of chromolithograph. I have just realized that it is quite simply the light through the vine that used to hang round the smoking-room verandah. . . .'[59] Slow astern, Waugh's mind was cruising back again to that comfortable mid-Victorian atmosphere. 'My theme is memory,' says Charles Ryder. '. . . These memories, which are my life – for we possess nothing except the past – were always with me. . . .'[60]

59. *Diaries*, 24 September 1944, p. 581.

60. *Brideshead* (Penguin), p. 215. In the revised edition, a paragraph on this subject is cut: 'These memories are the memorials and pledges of the vital hours of a lifetime. These hours of afflatus in the human spirit, the springs of art, are in their mystery akin to the epochs of history when a race which for centuries has lived content, unknown, behind its own frontiers, digging, eating, sleeping, begetting, doing what was requisite for survival and nothing else, will, for a generation or two,

Nostalgia for a lost England was becoming a habit of mind, and with Waugh in this delicate mood, it is small wonder that he and Churchill infuriated each other. Only Freddy Birkenhead's arrival with Stephen Clissold prevented violence.

Birkenhead reported back:

> I discovered Major Randolph Churchill and Captain Evelyn Waugh ensconced in a snug little farm building pleasantly heated by the usual tall china stoves fed by logs of wood. Their wants are attended to by an imposing retinue of menials, both English and Yugoslav.... The [spa] waters have remarkably soothing effects upon the nervous system and helped to preserve the harmonious atmosphere of the mission.[61]

The last statement was, of course, a diplomatic lie. Birkenhead, a friend from the 1930s,[62] came bearing gifts: a letter from Laura, shoes, hairbrushes, cigars. Temporal comforts, and the chance to leave Birkenhead to suffer Randolph's company, improved Waugh's spirits slightly. He spent his time with Clissold, whom he described with quiet patronage as '... a gentle ex-schoolmaster from Zagreb, political advisor to Maclean....'[63]

In fact, Clissold was probably the most important member of the party, chosen for his talent rather than for his social distinction. A mild-mannered fellow, he had been a lecturer at Zagreb University, was fluent in Serbo-Croat and an expert on the Partisans. After the war he produced standard works on Yugoslav history. He must at first have been puzzled and amused by this extravagant White's Club atmosphere transplanted to a bombed-out bathing establishment in Croatia. Later he lost patience. Most nights Birkenhead and Churchill drank themselves into fractious mood and regaled the company with recitations from Betjeman, Belloc, Macaulay 'and other

stupefy the world, commit all manner of crimes, perhaps, follow the wildest chimeras, go down in the end in agony, but leave behind a record of new heights scaled and new records won for all mankind; the vision fades, the soul sickens, and the routine of survival starts again' (1st edn, pp. 197–8).

61. 'Balkan States. Secret. December 20, 1944, Section 1. [R 21384/11/92] Lord Birkenhead to Sir R. Bruce Lockhart – (Received in Foreign Office 20th December, p. 1)'; PRO 371/48910. Birkenhead's report, dated 23 November 1944, continues: 'The discipline in the partisan army is stricter, and its behaviour more impeccable, than any army I have ever seen.... Of humour in the partisan movement there is none. The cause is too holy.... The attitude of the partisans to our propaganda is polite but restrained. They are ... deeply suspicious of British intentions and have to be handled gingerly. Many of them are obsessed with the idea that we intend to interfere with the internal affairs of the country, notably in trying to foist the King [Peter] back on them.... They are suspicious of the oblique approach of the English, and nauseated by sycophancy and the simulation of Left-wing sympathies, so perhaps it was healthy for the comrades to cope with a Conservative M.P., a Conservative peer and a reactionary Roman Catholic....' (pp. 1–4).
62. Cf. ALS from Waugh to Lady Diana Cooper, 'Whitsunday' [24 May] 1953, from Piers Court; BL; *MWMS*, p. 171. Waugh describes Birkenhead as: 'Never an intimate of mine but a crony in the early thirties at boxing matches & supper parties.'
63. *Diaries*, 13 October 1944, p. 583.

classics', as Waugh recorded with gloomy irony.[64] Neither had any thorough understanding of the military situation and Clissold received the dubious benefit of being taken under the wing of an Evelyn Waugh suffering from manic depression. A fifth, even less sortable, character completed their entourage: Leo Mates, a young English-speaking Communist, attached to the mission as a liaison officer from the Partisans. He later became Yugoslav Ambassador to the United States and Vice-Minister for Foreign Affairs. Waugh only registered Mates's futile wrangles with Churchill, '... a fiery and insane patriotism side by side with his Communism',[65] and despaired of both men.

In civilian life Waugh often found Churchill stimulating, an eccentric eager for life, volatile, courageous, sentimental. In wartime this preposterous schoolboy seemed sadly diminished and, like Birkenhead, unable to crawl from beneath the weight of his father's fame:

> Of conversation as I love it – a fantasy growing in the telling, apt repartee, argument based on accepted postulates, spontaneous reminiscences and quotation – they know nothing. All their noise and laughter is in the retelling of memorable sayings of their respected fathers or other public figures.... [Randolph's] American slang, his coughing and farting make him a poor companion in wet weather.[66]

It amused Waugh to learn in 1957 that the BBC had offered Churchill the chairmanship of a TV programme entitled 'Conversation'.[67] And so greatly had Waugh come to despise him in 1944 that his jaundiced imagination turned an ordinary wartime incident into a demonstration of his friend's failure of nerve.

The anecdote is legendary but too significant to omit. During a brief air-raid everyone but Waugh sensibly scampered into a slit-trench. Waugh, in white duffel coat, stood motionless as six or seven 'planes bombed and strafed the mission and the village, Churchill all the time screaming at him to take cover. Having already suffered Waugh's sarcasm and realizing that he was certain to resent such instructions, Churchill apologized afterwards for the tone of his orders. '"It wasn't your manners I was complaining of,"' Waugh remarked, '"it was your cowardice."'[68] The tale was spread gleefully by Birkenhead. Waugh's companions always ran the risk of becoming enshrined in some fantastic tale as the buffoon to his straight-man. But it was Waugh who was in error here, unwisely brave, threatening to draw the enemy fire. Churchill had many faults. Cowardice was not one of them.

64. *Ibid.*, 23 October 1944, p. 585.
65. *Ibid.*, p. 584.
66. *Ibid.*, p. 585.
67. Cf. *LAF*, pp. 210–11.
68. The Earl of Birkenhead, 'Fiery Particles', *EWAHW*, p. 161.

In search of solitude, Waugh would rise at eight, two hours before Churchill began typing and telephoning. After the raid, Churchill became convinced that, as the PM's son, he was a significant target for the German war effort. They had, he believed, pinpointed his unit for an assassination campaign. Tito's HQ had been attacked in this fashion five months earlier when he was driven out to Vis. Apprehension woke Churchill early and he began to interfere with Waugh's one tranquil period. Tempers flared, rain crashed down, and Waugh took Clissold out for walks, thinking only of repatriation.

Waugh's one escape was into the mind and, as he brooded about Laura, Pixton and Piers Court, the Victorian dream of 'English Gothic' increasingly dominated his thoughts. 'Have conceived idea of keeping my aunt's home at Midsomer Norton as a working studio,' he had noted a few days earlier.[69] Writing to Laura, he eagerly expanded the idea: she wanted to farm; he needed isolation to write. Why should they not sell Piers Court and buy a farm near her sister, Bridget? The Midsomer Norton house would be willed to Alec, himself and their Tasmanian cousin. The others could be bought out for £1,000:

> I could then make the house into a museum of Victorian art, put Ellwood there as permanent housekeeper . . . keep my library there & write my novels there. It would be a secret house to which no guests would come. I have the photographs of the rooms as they were in 1870 & I could gradually restore them to that splendid state. It, and the tranquillity of a provincial town, would be precisely suited to the mood in which I work. . . .[70]

'You would', he added as an afterthought, 'of course be always eagerly welcomed there. It is not an attempt to set up a separate household. . . .'[71] Laura was plainly annoyed by this and, when Waugh pressed her to respond, she seems to have squashed the proposition. It consorted ill with her idea of family life and, although she would go to unusual lengths to accommodate her husband's whims, she was not prepared to go this far. The problem, however, did not disappear. Waugh's obsessive desire to vacate Piers Court led him six months later to annoy Laura again.

In *Brideshead*, Charles Ryder remarks that: 'There is no candour in a story of early manhood which leaves out of account the home-sickness for nursery morality. . . .'[72] Waugh never overcame that nostalgia, and the enchantments of Oxford, Madresfield and the Ritz had prolonged, with a

69. *Diaries*, 18 October 1944, p. 583.
70. ALS to Laura Waugh, 17 October [1944], np [Topusko]; *Letters*, p. 190.
71. *Ibid.*
72. *Brideshead* (Penguin), p. 61.

kind of masochistic infantilism, the glamour of an imagined pre-lapsarian existence. Since his remarriage in 1937, the 'rabble of womankind'[73] had invaded this predominantly masculine world with its domestic demands and Grimes's nightmare: 'the hideous lights of home and voices of children'.[74] Waugh had accepted the intrusion with the loss of youth as an inevitable sacrifice to the conventional decencies of the heterosexual world. And, looking about himself in 1944, he was certain he had made the right decision. His mind, nevertheless, was divided and was to remain so for the rest of his life. Part of the charm of the army, and particularly of the Commandos, had been the opportunities for regression to childhood games and discipline. Part of its surreal irrelevance to the threat posed by the Age of the Common Man he also saw in these terms. 'We grow backwards in war time,' he wrote to Laura on 5 November. 'First it was public school life in the Marines, then prep. school at COHQ, now nursery – with picnics postponed for rain, everyone with his nose pressed to the window, time dragging, occasional treats. . . .'[75]

With his mind sharper than ever, the hiatus of Topusko infuriated him. There was so much he wanted to write: '. . . a child's history of Christendom and a short story, drawn from my present experience, of a man who gave up drink and became so clear sighted that he could not abide any of his friends & had to take to drink again.'[76] Above all, he thirsted to revise work: *Scoop* and the early-middle chapters of *Brideshead*. *Brideshead* was being bound at his own expense in a limited, paper-covered edition of fifty copies as Christmas presents for family and close Catholic friends. Waugh had instructed Peters to inform Gatfield that further large-scale alterations would be made for the first public printing. And when, on 20 November, a parachute drop brought the proofs, Waugh grabbed the parcel greedily and disappeared into his bedroom.

It took him just a week to complete the corrections, with Churchill constantly bursting into the room. To quieten him, Birkenhead and Waugh had each bet Churchill £10 that he could not read the entire Bible (of which he was largely ignorant) in a fortnight. This merely resulted in perpetual commentary ('God, isn't God a shit!')[77] and ultimate surrender during this crucial week. Not to be outdone, Churchill set about composing poetry: 'He sat with a glass of *rakija* stinking beside him, grunting, counting the syllables on his fingers and in the end produced the line: "Nostalgia for the limbo of the oblivion of your love." Later he became abusive, and

73. *Ibid.*, p. 23.
74. *Decline and Fall* (Penguin), p. 102.
75. 5 November [1944]; *Letters*, p. 192.
76. ALS to Laura Waugh, 24 October 1944, np [Topusko]; *Letters*, p. 191. Neither was written.
77. *Diaries*, 11 November 1944, p. 591.

later comatose.'[78] Birkenhead and Clissold had disappeared to Bari leaving Waugh, desolate and *désoeuvré*, alone with Churchill. Snow fell. American airmen began to come through on the escape route, making it increasingly difficult to evacuate the Jewish refugees encamped in the region. Waugh's one spark of hope lay in release. He had asked Clissold 'to suggest in Bari that I move elsewhere'[79] and on Waugh's birthday, 28 November, authorization for his departure at last arrived.

That birthday, his forty-first, was his gloomiest since 1933 (when Teresa Jungman had rejected his proposal), and he wasted no time in leaving. As soon as the road to Split was open, four days later, he took it, regardless of the dangers. Free of Churchill, he felt immediately relieved and his diary account of the journey celebrates the colours and texture of landscape in unusual, luxuriant detail. By early December he was back in Bari, anticipating a little cosmopolitan pleasure. He dined with Constant Lambert and summoned Dorothy Lygon, but luxury and old friends could no longer generate the pleasure he sought. A banquet had been arranged for her which Waugh was too exhausted to enjoy. Fatigue killed appetite and he was glad to see her leave.

Waugh's weariness was as much a state of mind as of body. His new mission was to be in Dubrovnik. He had signalled to Maclean for authority to write a report on the religious situation there and received a positive response. Much of his time was consumed by interviewing officers with experience of the area and by collecting stores. All this was tedious, but much more debilitating was his impotence in the face of Communist successes. The Russians had taken Belgrade and were advancing on Zagreb. Their victories rendered the Allied assistance paltry in comparison and left no doubt as to the post-war balance of power in Yugoslavia. In Greece the Communists were conducting a civil war as the Germans retreated and were happily shooting Allied soldiers. 'Freddy Birkenhead, Bill Deakin, John Clarke and I in a mood of black despair', Waugh noted on 14 December, '– the war going the wrong way, the situation in Greece insoluble, the casualties in Italy approaching last war level, the Americans becoming unfriendly ... no personal future for any of us.'[80] 'My days in Italy are nearly up', he wrote to Laura, 'and I go back quite readily. After the trafficless snow bound [*sic*] world of Croatia I find the warm rain & ceaseless flow of military vehicles very exhausting. Also I meet so many old friends & that over excites me and keeps me awake at nights. . . .'[81] He read

78. *Ibid.*, 25 November 1944, p. 593. 'Rakija' or 'raki' was the local spirit, potent & strong-smelling. No other alcohol was available.
79. Unpublished section of ALS to Laura Waugh, 2 November [1944], np [Topusko]; BL; *Letters*, p. 192.
80. *Diaries*, p. 597.
81. Unpublished ALS to Laura Waugh, 13 December [1944], np [Bari]; BL.

The Woman in White and dreamed of solitude and silence. Three days later, the Battle of the Bulge began.

*

Waugh seems not to have been unduly perturbed by this battle. Whoever won, he felt, Europe was already lost. He was not wanted in the front line and no longer wished to be there. Ahead lay real work, behind the lines, in the defence of Christendom. While the battle was raging in the Ardennes, he was bucketing across the Adriatic in a landing-craft towards Dubrovnik (Ragusa). Here the rear headquarters of Floydforce, a new Combined Operations unit of brigade strength, was organized to help cut off the German retreat. Waugh had last visited the city on his Hellenic Society cruise and he anticipated a treat: Venetian architecture in a Catholic stronghold.

Waugh's vaguely defined task was to run another military mission, a tiny operation, but, as usual, he took his responsibilities seriously. The officers with whom he worked were invariably of higher rank and attached to Floydforce, directly involved in the fighting. Waugh's primary function was to act as intermediary between them and the Partisans, whose gratitude to the British was limited. Tito's forces needed help, but they neither trusted Winston Churchill nor appreciated imperial condescension. For their part, the British were irritated by the Partisans' casual attitude to western aid. The Russians, who donated much less, received a warmer response. Cases of British stores were often re-marked with Soviet insignia (Sir Alec Guinness wrote to Waugh in 1961, explaining that he had regularly witnessed this).[82] It was a delicate situation and Waugh soon realized that there was no hope of his exerting influence. As he watched the pale, scared faces of the citizens, he developed an intense loathing for the Partisans.

To Waugh, the refugees, to whom 'victory' offered only dispossession, became kindred spirits. Discovering for the first time the pleasure of charity, he threw himself into the business of distributing small comforts. 'I am entirely alone,' he wrote to Laura on Christmas Day:

> which next to being with you is what I like best. . . . I came here last week and am happy enough. . . . I have a jeep, an Italian servant, a female Dalmatian servant, a first class Dalmatian cook: the quarters are in a slum and are exceedingly cold but I have managed to get an oil stove; I have also a great quantity of red & white wine and an Alsatian dog. . . . The town is quite undamaged by war, though not improved by having all its public buildings scrawled over with

82. Cf. unpublished ALS from Sir Alec Guinness, 21 October 1961; BL. Sir Alec had commanded a landing-craft in the Adriatic, ferrying stores to Yugoslavia from Italy.

> partisans slogans in red paint, nor is the face of the place lightened by the juveniles of both sexes, armed with sten guns, who saunter about oafishly. But it is a joy to be surrounded by first class architecture again. The Churches are going full blast and absolutely packed at all hours – not partisans....[83]

On the same day he wrote to Nancy Mitford: 'I dined alone sitting opposite a looking glass & reflecting sadly that the years instead of transforming me into a personable man of middle age, have made me into a very ugly youth.'[84]

*

The obsessive concern of this ugly youth was his *magnum opus* and its reception. He sent back the proofs *via* Downing Street and fretted until 7 January, when F. B. Walker cabled their safe arrival at Chapman & Hall.[85] From this moment Waugh's letters to Peters become less hesitant. Another American offer came in: £250 from *Harpers* for further serialization. They would, he insisted, have to use the corrected proof version: 'If they wish to present the extracts as the whole work, they may not do so at any price.... The corrections are extensive & very important. It is essential that the Americans use this version for their book publication....'[86] Poor McIntyre was appalled by this news. Little, Brown had already set up the type, but they obeyed Waugh's instructions, believing that *Brideshead* was likely to be his first huge success on both sides of the Atlantic. Anticipating international celebrity, he commissioned a portrait bust of himself.

As Mr Paravicini scooped handfuls of grey clay from a rucksack and plastered a wire frame, his subject looked on with bemused vanity. The portrait grew slowly, revealing a face not always to Waugh's taste – sometimes petulant, more often suggesting the priggish benignity of an Anglican headmaster bishop. Another description reached Laura after a sheaf of complimentary letters about *Brideshead* had arrived:

> It [the bust] is very masterly & rather bad tempered in expression but most forceful like Beethoven rather. It will be a lovely possession for you & indeed a series of possessions for all as I propose to have it cast in bronze and terra cotta & lead & iron and to travel with it as Gerald

83. Unpublished ALS to Laura Waugh, 25 December 1944, from 37 Military Mission, CMF [Dubrovnik]; BL.
84. *Letters*, p. 194.
85. Cf. unpublished ALS to Laura Waugh, 5 January 1945, np [37 Military Mission, CMF Dubrovnik]; BL.
86. Unpublished ALS to A. D. Peters, 7 January 1943 [error for '1945'], from 37 Military Mission, CMF [Dubrovnik]; *Catalogue* E433, p. 140.

> Wellesley used to travel with the bust of his great ancestor. You can imagine what an interest & excitement it has been to me.[87]

He could never resist lampooning his own self-esteem. The bust later stood, mockingly topped by his forage cap at a rakish angle, on a sideboard at Piers Court: another preposterous possession.

It was at this stage that he began to fix the mould into which the rest of his life would flow: solitude, interrupted only by family, church, occasional visitors and infrequent jaunts. After the war, contact with his friends was principally through correspondence. He filed their letters more carefully, would rarely answer the telephone and, then, angrily. After the Post Office tried to telephone cables to Piers Court, he insisted upon receiving written messages, even if this meant their late arrival. 'When I use [that devil telephone],' he wrote to Lady Diana Cooper, 'I feel absolutely isolated and loveless – no sense of contact and communication.'[88] The written word obsessed him and in this he lived entirely. Words on paper were to him almost tactile, malleable, subject to control. He felt safer with them but they also held their terrors. He thought in words,[89] in perfect sentences; the loose construction of the world in colloquial speech and rationalist debate infuriated him. During his brief but intense periods of literary composition, words continually echoed in his head. These dancing symbols, shuffling themselves into order, would wake him at night and force him to pad down to the library to make corrections. Nothing sensible, he believed, could be conveyed through inaccurate grammar, and theology, the Queen of Sciences, was the grammar of the universe. Small wonder, then, that he saw the quality of his writing as indivisible from its spiritual content. Hooper's linguistic dereliction is symbolic of the state of his soul.

Brideshead was Waugh's first sustained attempt at a dense and allusive use of language and his first overtly apologetic novel. Its reception was thus crucial to his sense of self in the bleak future. He expected hostile criticism of the public edition and thought himself immune to 'humanist' insult. But he was deeply concerned that his friends and co-religionists should register the extent of his commitment to a new style and vision in the private edition.

All but one sensed his nervousness and responded with generous praise if, privately, they expressed reservations: 'A dull letter from Laura, and a bright one from Nancy . . .,' he noted on 7 January and wrote immediately to correct his wife:

87. Unpublished ALS to Laura Waugh, 4 February 1945, np [37 Military Mission, CMF, Dubrovnik]; BL.
88. ALS, 19 October [1955], from Piers Court; BL; *MWMS*, p. 209.
89. Cf. *Writers*, p. 111.

> Darling Laura, sweet whiskers, do try to write me better letters.... I simply am not interested in Bridget's children. Do grasp that. A letter should be a form of conversation; write as though you were talking to me.
>
> ... What do you think of the book? Your copy is still binding but you must have seen ... [Eddie Grant's]. You know I have not seen one. Tell me what it is like. It is dedicated to you. Are you pleased to see it in this form? Are you curious to know what changes I have made in the final proofs? ... Can you not see how it disappoints me that this book which I regard as my first important one, and have dedicated to you, should have no comment except that Eddie is pleased with it? ... Don't send any more of these catalogues of family facts....[90]

While Osbert Sitwell, Greene, Sykes and Nancy were explaining why they believed *Brideshead* to be a masterpiece, Laura had preferred not to stumble into the minefield of literary criticism. She had read the book as it was written and admired it. Waugh knew that. What more was there to say? Unfortunately, owing to postal delays, another of her chatty epistles was sent before his arrived.[91] 'A bitterly disappointing letter from Laura,' he recorded on receiving it.[92]

Laura's family were impressed by the book and, although Auberon, Eddie and Gabriel wrote to say so, they were not people whose judgment Waugh admired. Mary Herbert's description of the Pixton household's devouring *Brideshead*,[93] however, must have delighted him. From this point the awkwardness between Waugh and Mary evaporated and a warm friendship developed. It had taken nearly eight years for him to shed the role of parvenu. He respected her for putting him to the test; she now admired his perseverance and his genius. That little power struggle over, Waugh adopted the dominant role and the victory gave him immense satisfaction.

The literary signals returning from England were generally favourable. As we have seen, D'Arcy was ruffled by the 'coarser' passages. Knox was also 'at first antagonistic'.[94] But they soon accepted the novel as a major work of apologetics. D'Arcy reported that the community at Campion Hall thought *Brideshead* Waugh's best work; Dom Hubert van Zeller was perpetually placing it in people's hands with hearty recommendations, and

90. 7 January 1944; *Letters*, p. 195.
91. Cf. unpublished ALS from Laura Waugh, 26 December [1944], from Pixton Park; BL.
92. *Diaries*, 8 January 1945, p. 607.
93. Unpublished ALS from Mary Herbert, 17 January 1944, from Pixton Park; BL.
94. Cf. unpublished ALS from Fr M. C. D'Arcy, 21 April 1945, from Campion Hall, Oxford; BL: 'Daphne Acton was "ecstatic" about *Brideshead*. She told me too that Ronnie was at first antagonistic, but was in tears over the deathbed scene, & by the last chapter an ardent convert....'

Knox intended to quote Julia's monologue about sin to the Westminster clergy on their Day of Recollection.[95] Knox wrote:

> The book is of course so good that I just don't feel competent to assess, let alone judge it.... Reading it you move neither in real life nor in Faery, but in Metroland, which is a beastly place anyhow.... I read all the book out loud to Daphne [Acton], only skipping two turns of phrase to save my own blushes rather than hers. I don't know if I shall have the courage to admit this if Oldmeadow starts getting his gun out....[96]

That ancient ghost did not rise. Waugh's friends now ran the Catholic periodicals and they saw to it that the book was well-reviewed.

Publication, however, was delayed for some months[97] and there was, for all this early adulation, a sense of suppressed embarrassment among some of Waugh's friends. Knox had deferred writing, and the blushes of the stricter Catholics hurt Waugh. Laura agreed with D'Arcy's reservations[98] and Katharine Asquith had found the book painful: 'I can hardly bear your writing about modern people.... I suppose I'm too old for novels....'[99] Both letters cut deeply.

> Katharine [Waugh wrote to Knox] who detested the book to the end & beyond, and expressed her disgust with feminine ruthlessness, had the same thing to say – that the characters did not exist either in real life or faery. The sad thing is that 'Metroland' is my world that I have grown up in & I don't know any other except at second-hand or at a great distance.[100]

This description bears small relation to Mrs Asquith's remarks, but a morbid sensitivity to criticism from that quarter drove him to neurotic overstatement.

His Catholic contemporaries had no misgivings. The novel was welcomed as a weapon for the Church Militant. Sykes, included among the early

95. Cf. unpublished ALS from Lady Acton, 23 April 1945, from Aldenham Park, Bridgnorth; BL. After reporting Knox's praise she adds that: 'the Woodruffs liked *Brideshead* and [Robert] Speaight [later, biographer of Belloc] says "What can I do to make Evelyn talk to me? I hate not being on speaking terms with so great a man.... It seems to me like writing to tell Shakespeare I think well of Macbeth....'
96. Unpublished TLS to Waugh, 'VE ii', from Aldenham Park, Bridgnorth; BL.
97. Partly owing to paper shortage; mainly owing to Waugh's insistence that the revised proofs be used.
98. Unpublished ALS from Laura Waugh, 26 December [1944], *op. cit.*: 'I do agree with Father D'Arcy's criticisms in his letter – not the one about the scene with the tarts but the others. I think it is a pity when you have written such a great work that it should be able to upset or debar everyone [*sic*] from reading it....'
99. Unpublished ALS from Katharine Asquith, 1 January 1945, from The Manor House, Mells, Frome; BL.
100. 14 May 1945; *Letters*, p. 206.

readers, replied with explosive praise, relishing the prospect of a scrap between Waugh and Bloomsbury. 'Feeling in London is running high,' he wrote. '"Roman tract" is being hissed in intellectual circles, and Basil Bennett is now under instruction. Connolly is very upset. . . . A Byronic exile is all I can safely prophesy for you. . . . Come back and attack someone. . . .'[101] More news of Connolly came from Lady Diana Cooper, with whom he had been staying for three weeks at the snow-bound Paris Embassy 'being fêted as tho' he were Voltaire returned. He blossomed beneath the warmth, & regretted his *Unquiet Grave* a book of so heavy a mealancholly [*sic*] that reading one half of its groan sent me to bed for a fortnight.'[102] Nancy Mitford had written to Waugh before Christmas asking what he thought 'of Grave I ache to know'.[103] At the time he had not the faintest idea what 'Grave' might be. She soon sent him a copy. It was an unfortunate coincidence for Connolly to be published simultaneously with the private circulation of *Brideshead*. Waugh was bored in Yugoslavia, his mind razor-sharp, eager for prey.

*

Two days of storm offered ample opportunity to scrutinize *The Unquiet Grave* – 'half common-place book of French maxims, half a lament for his life. . . .'[104] – and the copious marginalia in Waugh's copy present an intriguing glimpse of feelings he usually suppressed. Connolly's adoption of a *nom de plume*, Palinurus,[105] fooled no one. The pretence that the manuscript had been 'submitted anonymously to HORIZON' and 'seemed unusual enough to warrant separate publication'[106] merely rendered the appearance of these *pensées* slightly more embarrassing for his friends than they might otherwise have been. Everyone knew that this was the voice of sad Cyril, the desperate throw of a disappointed man who had not quite lost faith in his genius.

Effectively a form of diary, written by one who has abandoned religion but retained a sense of sin, *Grave* is certainly melancholy. There is no redemption in Connolly's waste land, only ceaseless fishing in the dull canal, waiting, thinking, turning over the dead leaves of a lifetime's mistakes. The form is that of a fragmentary word cycle, a prose poem masquerading as documentary writing with its quotations and footnotes. Politically it

101. Unpublished ALS from Christopher Sykes, 27 December 1944, from White's; BL.
102. ALS from Lady Diana Cooper, 18 January [1945], from British Embassy, Paris; BL; *MWMS*, p. 81.
103. Unpublished ALS from Nancy Mitford, 12 December 1944, from 12 Blomfield Road, W9; BL.
104. *Diaries*, 9–10 January 1945, p. 608.
105. Aeneas's pilot, lost overboard during a storm and later murdered, hence (or so Connolly presumably meant to suggest) a voice from the underworld, a distant and objective observer on human affairs like Eliot's Tiresias.
106. [Cyril Connolly], *The Unquiet Grave* (Curwen Press, 1944), from 'blurb' on front cover flap.

marks a shift from his earlier flirtations with Socialism towards a horror of the attack on individualism by the corporate state, but he finds himself constantly trapped by guilt at his own selfishness and sloth, ashamed yet unable to apologize for his detachment.

Connolly's depression had brought him to the political position Waugh had adopted fifteen years earlier. Indeed, Waugh applauded such sentiments as: 'I do not "find fulfilment through participation in the communal life of an organised group" – that is tyranny. . . .'[107] 'Well said, Palinurus' is scribbled alongside, and there are many similar signs of approval. As we have seen, Waugh believed Connolly's character and the nature of his melancholy to be uncomfortably close to his own: 'always tired, always bored, always hurt, always hating',[108] claustrophobic,[109] loathing the enforced fraternity of a rationalist culture, believing that the only object of art should be to produce a masterpiece, that the artist must work alone, that friendship had been destroyed by the sickness of the age which 'developed sympathy at the expense of loyalty'. But, for all this, there was something fundamentally unsympathetic to Waugh in Palinurus's grumbling.

To Waugh there was no accurate language of contemplation but that of Christianity and he faced here the apotheosis of those voices – rationalist, Bloomsbury, sentimental – which had always screamed in his ears, insisting that Catholicism, representational art and an hierarchical society were the fictions of a collapsed and vicious culture. Connolly's articulacy, which often transported Waugh by the beauty of its rhetoric, represented a direct challenge to Waugh's orthodoxy. *Grave* attacks not only the concept of Original Sin, but also Christianity and Christ in particular, preferring Taoism as a system of thought. Waugh read the book carefully, at least twice, marking his copy in pencil and in blue and red ink like a schoolmaster correcting the essay of a talented but ill-informed Downside sixth-former. 'There can be no genuine self-knowledge', he wrote at the top of the first page, 'without some knowledge of God. But Cyril's elaborate [?] "self-dismantling" is not the fruit of knowledge.'[110]

Waugh's riposte was threefold: stylistic, sociological and theological, although ultimately the third category of argument subsumed the other two. Connolly's grammatical inaccuracies and plunges into jargon were

107. *Ibid.*, p. 77.
108. *Ibid.*, p. 18.
109. Cf. *Ibid.*, p. 8. Beside three paragraphs containing the following, Waugh wrote 'Good', 'Better', 'Best': . . . 'In youth the life of reason is not in itself sufficient; afterwards the life of emotion, except for short periods, becomes unbearable. . . .

'Yet sometimes at night I get a feeling of claustrophobia; of being smothered by my own personality, of choking through being in the world.

'It is like being pinned underneath the hull of a capsized boat. . . . In those moments it seems that there must be a way out, and that through sloughing off the personality alone can it be taken.'
110. *Ibid.*, p. 1.

picked out mercilessly and his subjective generalizations (particularly about women) condemned as populist nonsense or personal hysteria.[111] The whole style of the work irritated Waugh and his notes reveal his struggling for words to define this distaste. In one respect it was simply a question of the book's tone, the élitist air of the Bloomsbury intellectual:

> All these quotations – or most of them – are snobbish in their choice. I mean Palinurus is. For they might have been said in English by almost anyone at almost any time. But their *origin* gives them a dandyism. It is more than the repetition of platitudes that have fallen from august lips – Palinurus wears their wisdom & swaggers about in it '– you like this tie? It came from Charvet last time I was in Paris.'[112]

But the violence of Waugh's reaction is not satisfactorily explained by this alone. Even *Grave*'s assault on Christianity would not have demanded the level of engagement he gave it. The arguments were predictable and he had dispensed with them before. No, it was surely that in Connolly, as he said, he saw himself. There but for the Grace of God, literally ... and he needed to dispatch that embarrassing phantom trying to link him with weakness and fallibility.

When Palinurus talks of those things nearest to his heart – loneliness and lost love – Waugh sneers coolly in the margins: 'Enter the woman novelist, a recurrent character....'[113] Ruminations about the nature of romantic love held no interest for Waugh. Where Connolly fed off the pain of his broken marriage, Waugh had buried the memory of Evelyn Gardner. 'We love only once ...', Palinurus says, 'And on how that first great love-affair shapes itself depends the pattern of our lives.' No one's life better illustrated the second premise than Waugh's. 'Nonsense,' he wrote beside it, never doubting his perfect grasp of the truth. 'Perhaps one should be more tolerant of second-hand, half-understood knowledge ...,' he notes. 'It is not obnoxious when it refers to zoology or anthropology.... But it must not introduce its own bastard vocabulary & that is what psycho-analysis does.'[114].

Again, language, like theology, is seen to be exact: anyone tampering with these absolutes, Waugh believed, did so at his peril. Yet one senses in this bullying omniscience a range of suppressed fears, unanswered questions, that would not be silenced. If he could throw all free-thinking from the casement with a clear conscience, shouting after it 'Gollancz', 'Left Book Club', 'woman novelist', he was not silly enough to believe that

111. E.g. by 'Women are different from men, and to break with the past and mangle their mate in the process fulfils a dark need in them' (*ibid.*, p. 14), Waugh wrote: 'Ethel M. Dell + Peter Q[uennell]'.
112. *Ibid.*, p. 58.
113. *Ibid.*, p. 9.
114. *Ibid.*, pp. 22–3.

he could express hatred of Palinurus's open mind while simultaneously honouring the traditions of free and civilized discourse which the book supports. Waugh's only solution is the unsatisfactory one of avoiding the paradox by pretending that a series of alien voices – Joad, Victor Gollancz, Clive Bell, etc. – has interrupted Connolly's cultured common sense, and by creating another series of fictions about Connolly himself. 'Very much better towards the end,' Waugh wrote beneath the last paragraph:

> First Joad & the woman novelist are shaken off. Then the middle-writer of the weekly reviews, and finally the delicate plaintive poet of the decadence is left having at last found a silence [?] where [?] he can be heard. The last paragraphs are exquisite, after a penultimate lapse, the intrusion of all the wrong people together ... jostling in, jostled out after an embarrassing five minutes, through the closing door, like a party of actors in a charade who have mistaken their cue and spoiled the scene.[115]

'Why should I be interested in this book?' he asked himself. 'Because I have known Cyril more than twenty years and enjoy drinking with him? Because, alone in Dubrovnik, I have not much to occupy me? Rather because Cyril is the most typical man of my generation ... ':[116]

> Here he is in war-time, strait-jacketed by sloth, in Bloomsbury, thinking of Jean [his first wife] & the South of France, peaches and Vichy water, instead of Lys [his lover] & syrens [*sic*] and official forms. Quite clear in his heart that the ills he suffers from are theological, with the vocabulary of the nonsense-philosophy he learned, holding him back. The Irish boy, the immigrant, homesick, down-at-heel and ashamed, full of fun in the public house, a ready quotation on his lips, afraid of the bog-priest; proud of his capers; the Irishman's deep-rooted belief that there are only two final realities – Hell and the U.S.A.[117]

In this private dialogue Waugh seems more to be trying to convince himself that he has conquered Connolly's dandyism and nostalgia, silenced the questioning voices and withdrawn from the community into 'a silence where he can be heard'. The actors, false prophets and nonsense philosophers are firmly ejected from Waugh's library, leaving him alone with God and his art. The available space within which rational pleasure was possible was continuously contracting and he knew as he sat in Dubrovnik reading *Grave* that his fascination with alien cultures was finally exhausted. An alien culture cavorted in the streets of London and beyond the windows

115. *Ibid.*, p. 94.
116. For the rest of this quotation see p. 89 above.
117. *Ibid.*, written on flysheet beneath 'THE UNQUIET GRAVE' and across his own dating 'Evelyn Waugh. Ragusa 8 Jan. 45'.

of his country house. The savage at home was no longer a joke or a literary device, no longer a warning, because it was too late.

On the dust-jacket of *Brideshead* he noted the change:

> When I wrote my first novel . . . my publishers advised me . . . to prefix the warning that it was 'meant to be funny'. . . . Now, in a more sombre decade, I must . . . state that *Brideshead Revisited* is *not* meant to be funny. There are passages of buffoonery, but the general theme is at once romantic and eschatological.
>
> It is ambitious, perhaps intolerably presumptuous; nothing less than an attempt to trace the workings of the divine purpose in a pagan world. . . . The story will be uncongenial alike to those who look back on that pagan world with unalloyed affection, and to those who see it as transitory, insignificant and, already, hopefully passed. Whom then can I hope to please? Perhaps those who have the leisure to read a book word by word for the interest of the writer's use of language; perhaps those who look to the future with black forebodings and need more solid comfort than rosy memories. For the latter I have given my hero, and them . . . a hope, not, indeed, that anything but disaster lies ahead, but that the human spirit, redeemed, can survive all disasters.[118]

This might serve as a rebuff to Connolly on almost every point. Waugh saw him as schizoid: a pagan addressing theological problems; a dandy hedonist turned eccentric don; a fat man with a thin man inside, struggling to get out; a skilful writer whose style unaccountably rotted with cheap sentiment. Did Waugh know that all these paradoxes applied to himself? *Brideshead* and *Grave* are in many respects complementary works, the same vision from different angles: both nostalgic, both 'romantic', both sentimental and deeply prejudiced, yellow with hatred and self-pity. *Brideshead*, most would argue, is infinitely superior as a work of art. As a register of its author's frame of mind, however, it does little to assure us that he did not share Connolly's schizophrenia. The 'voices' would not be silenced, although it took nine years for them to erupt from Waugh's unconscious.

*

During January, he had settled into an undemanding routine, sitting impatiently for Paravicini, pottering off to take supplies to a Dominican convent, answering cables from Italy. 'I spend many hours a day listening

118. *Brideshead*, 'Warning' on inside flap of dust-jacket; *CH*, p. 236, n. 1.

to the sad stories of refugees,' he wrote to Laura.[119] But there was little he could do.

> It seems to comfort them to come & tell me how miserable they are; it saddens me. But is it not odd? Would you have thought of me as having a kind nature? I am renowned for my great kindness here. At my headquarters in Bari ... I am looked upon as very troublesome and offensive.[120]

A week earlier Waugh had attended the Catholic festival of St Blaise's Day with mixed feelings, delighted by the energy of the people's simple piety, downcast by their hunger and fear. The Partisans had looked on disapprovingly but had not interfered. Unknown to Waugh, however, 3 February had also marked two less happy events. It had been the first day of the three-power conference, when Churchill had met Stalin and Roosevelt in Yalta and effectively betrayed the Poles. The dribble of refugees Waugh was dealing with in Dubrovnik was shortly to become the flood of Displaced Persons washing across eastern Europe. By the 15th, one-and-a-quarter million Poles had been deported, many sent by cattle truck to labour camps or imprisoned in Russia. On the local level, too, the date signalled a significant change. Dubrovnik's dull commander was replaced by a younger man hostile to the British, and to Waugh in particular. Waugh's preferential treatment of Catholics; his assistance to the refugees rather than to the Partisans; above all, his ill-disguised sense of superiority were deeply irritating to the new man. Waugh described him in his diary as 'a pubescent cretin named Antoravić'.[121] We can only guess what Antoravić called Waugh. Open rows erupted. Antoravić requested Bari in the strongest terms to remove this pompous subversive and they eagerly complied.

A week after Antoravić's appointment a cable arrived instructing Waugh to return. He ignored it, replying that the order had not come from his command. Headquarters were furious. They had already suffered a barrage of William Bootish signals marked with four Qs (i.e. only to be decoded by a senior officer) concerning such important matters as the supply of soap. Antoravić's reports left no doubt as to Captain Waugh's complete unsuitability to his job; now he was refusing orders. Waugh, however, knew what he was doing. He was playing for time, and it was at this point that he revived the plan to write a report on the Church by signalling Maclean for permission to get on with it before final expulsion. Maclean agreed because he hoped that it would distract Waugh from interfering with more volatile political issues. Everyone at Headquarters knew that a few priests had been

119. Unpublished section of ALS to Laura Waugh, 23 January 1944; BL; cf. *Letters*, p. 198.
120. ALS to Laura Waugh, 10 February 1945, np [Dubrovnik]; *Letters*, p. 201.
121. *Diaries*, 12 February 1945, p. 615.

'executed', but then so had thousands of others of all religious and political persuasions and, in a country so ravaged by war, this religious 'persecution' seemed a tiny, almost irrelevant issue. The chief concern was to secure political stability and here the British were in the business of compromise. Compromise was anathema to Waugh. To him, these deaths and the atheism of the Partisans were the essence of Yugoslavia's story, and the British support for Communism a further betrayal of Christian civilization.

It was plain to all, and Waugh appears to have made no secret of it, that he preferred the interests of the Church to those of the British Government. The local bishop gave him a secret letter to forward to the Vatican and Waugh relished his role as a Campion figure, working under cover for the secret and glorious aims of the Faith. He conducted a few interviews, made some notes and, by the time Bari had cabled back the unambiguous sack, he was ready and more than willing to leave. '... I was expelled from Dubrovnik by the Partisans', he wrote to Laura, 'for interference in civil affairs, spent three days in the mountains in the snow, then got permission to leave, returned to Dubrovnik, waited four days for a ship and arrived back at Bari yesterday after a very rough crossing in a flat-bottomed invasion ship....'[122] His 'got permission to leave' is amusing. No hint of his real incompetence was passed on to Laura, nor the depth of his seniors' animosity towards him. No, it was all the fault of the Partisans. 'I was not quite sure of myself when I went to my headquarters,' he added, 'as I thought it might be felt that I had made a balls of things but they were all most cordial.'[123]

> The day after tomorrow [he told Laura], I fly to Rome for a week to intrigue with the Pope on behalf of the distressed clergy of Croatia.... My present ambition is to be made consul in Dubrovnik. This is for reasons of honour. I was expelled for arrogating consular authority to myself so I think it will be a good sucks for the bloody partisans if I return as consul by right. Also there are numbers of wretched people who had looked to me for help whom I don't want to desert.[124]

His charitable instincts were unhappily mixed with vengefulness and, although he did not desert one family of refugees who continued to write to him for many years as though to Father Christmas, he was ultimately delighted when his application was refused. It had, of course, never been seriously considered, especially after the Foreign Office had received his report.

*

122. Unpublished ALS to Laura Waugh, 22 February 1945, np [Bari]; BL.
123. *Ibid.*
124. *Ibid.*

Waugh returned from his Roman holiday to Bari, primed with religious enthusiasm, to begin writing. Half of the report was written there, half in London. Hearing that Maclean was due to be posted home from Belgrade, Waugh decided to return to England, where he could more easily contact his commanding officer. By a fortunate coincidence, it turned out that Maclean no longer *was* his CO.

Waugh arrived in London on 15 March to find himself a rich man. Peters had just sent £760 to his bank and the £1,000 for the *Town and Country* serial had come in. Waugh immediately set up in the Hyde Park Hotel in Basil Bennett's personal suite and began spending furiously. Laura arrived the next day and between them they got through £15–20 a day for three weeks. A new collecting mania absorbed him: the purchase of gold watches for £50 and more. He bought three in the space of a month, not daring to tell Laura of his final purchase – a repeater for £125. Punctuality had always been an obsession but watches kept failing on him. Time, like grammar and theology, had to be precisely calculated. There was little enough of it left, he felt, for civilized life.

As he completed his report – a lengthy affair of some 7,500 words – the last rocket bombs of the war could be heard falling. One, dropping near Marble Arch, blew out the windows of his sitting room. It was the end of an era. Lloyd George died the following day; Lord Alfred Douglas, Oscar Wilde's lover, had died during the previous week. Those aunt sallies of his youth – liberalism and bogus aestheticism – were now history. There were new enemies to attack, and his 'Church and State in Liberated Croatia' was a suitable preliminary barrage before the major offensive of *Brideshead*.

These new enemies were everywhere: in the godless Communist world, in the cultural vacuum of America, in his own Government, often (perhaps especially) in the Conservative Party. Everyone who was not a Catholic was an actual or potential foe and, as Easter approached, he made his case for the British to act honourably towards the Yugoslav Catholics, knowing full well that there was little hope of the Foreign Office sharing his opinions. Christopher Sykes gives a lurid account of the FO's attempts to discredit Waugh's report. Sykes writes of a 'proposition to have Evelyn court-martialled'[125] and of the idea that 'British opinion ... hesitated to accept the unwelcome fact that Tito's regime was not with Communist influence in it, but *was* a Communist regime.'[126] 'That protest against persecution and massacre', he continues, 'should be dismissed with irritation and

125. Sykes, p. 277. He implies that the FO believed Waugh to be a spy who had 'no scruples about conveying "information gathered in the course of duty to outside persons"' and that it was on this basis that they wished to have him court-martialled. In fact, the question of court-martialling Waugh as a traitor is never openly raised in the extant FO memos.

126. *Ibid.*, p. 278.

condemned as bias within the walls of a British ministry would have surprised and pained an earlier generation.'[127] Was there a scandal here, truth and justice suppressed by bigotry? Did Waugh's military career nearly end in public disgrace?

Waugh certainly irritated the FO. His avowed intention to inform Catholic editors and MPs of the contents of the report was unapologetically insubordinate. The point at issue, however, was straightforward and covered by the Official Secrets Acts. 'I should have thought', wrote a bemused official, 'that the material in the report was "information ... which he has obtained owing to his position as a person who ... has held office under His Majesty", and that for him to communicate it to an unauthorised person would constitute an offence under Section II(i) of the Act of 1911.'[128] This, and an irate memo from Sir Orme Sargent, the Permanent Undersecretary, is presumably what Sykes construes as an attempt to have Waugh court-martialled. In fact, they seem merely to have been mulling over various legitimate threats which might be used to prevent Waugh from breaking the law and rocking the Government's diplomatic boat.

Waugh had first been to see Douglas Howard, 'a timid but civil bureaucrat'[129], who refused a straight answer to the proposal to 'publish'. Howard recorded:

> I pointed out that this report was bound to be considered an official one as it was written during his period of service ... and submitted through Brigadier Maclean. I should have, therefore to ... give him an answer in due course. Capt. Waugh was very petulant about this, & said that even if he could not [show the report] ..., presumably we could not prevent his talking to his Catholic friends.[130]

It was at this point that Sargent asked for Maclean's views and became slightly apoplectic:

> I see no reason why we should agree that the author should use ... the report as propaganda against the Govt's policy. Not only must it not be published but he should be told that if he shows it to persons outside the F.O. and W.O. he does so without our consent and at his own risk.[131]

A Foreign Office official giving any other advice would, surely, have been failing in his duty. What really annoyed them, however, was that by a legal

127. *Ibid.*, p. 280.
128. FO R 5927/1059/92, memo dated 30 March 1945, p. 118; PRO 371/48910.
129. *Diaries*, p. 623. Howard was head of the Southern Department in the FO, covering Yugoslavia, Albania, Bulgaria, Romania, Turkey and Greece, a crucial diplomatic position in 1944.
130. FO R 5927/1059/92, memo dated 29 March [1945], p. 115; PRO 371/48910.
131. *Ibid.*, p. 117

accident Waugh's case appeared to fall outside their jurisdiction. Not only had Maclean ceased to be his CO but, by leaving Italy, Waugh had also ceased to be part of the mission when the report was completed. It was thought unlikely that the Official Secrets Acts would cover these circumstances.

Maclean sagely advised caution. It would, he told the FO, 'be unwise to attempt to coerce Captain Waugh by threats. Captain Waugh is . . . a clever man and . . . would be likely to respond to such treatment by making as much trouble as he could.'[132] This was indubitably correct, and Maclean had to be careful. He had not appointed Waugh personally, but had been directly responsible for Waugh's actions. If it were discovered that 37 Military Mission had been harbouring a subversive, the reputation of the mission as a whole might have been tarnished. Maclean's view was, therefore, that 'the report gives a reasonably fair picture'.[133] Relations between the two men were strained but polite. Waugh later invited Maclean to lunch at the Hyde Park Hotel to present him with a copy of *Brideshead*. Was there an element of revenge in this apparently benign gesture? It soon became clear that Waugh held Maclean responsible for betraying the Yugoslav Catholics. For his part, when the *Diaries* were published, Maclean allowed the libels to stand but answered in copious footnotes which leave the reader in no doubt as to his view of Waugh's grasp of the Yugoslav situation. The report was plainly, and rather naïvely, prejudiced and no one knew this better than Maclean. He was glad to be able to pass it on to the FO with the excuse that he was no longer head of the mission.

The FO, having reached this impasse, sent the report to Ralph Skrine Stevenson, newly appointed as the Ambassador in Belgrade, for assessment by a specialist. The FO could only manage such remarks as:

> I should not be in the least surprised if the Partisans have in fact bumped off large numbers of Catholic priests in Croatia; but I should be inclined to think that such executions were of local significance only at this stage and were not part of a deliberate and centrally directed policy. The exclusion of Catholic influence from the schools is more probably deliberate policy. We should, however, have no ground at all for intervening to preserve the Church's hold over education – that would be gross interference in the internal affairs of the Yugoslav state.[134]

This turned out to be an accurate appraisal, but they needed a more substantial case if they were to dissuade Waugh from making his 'disclosures'.

132. *Ibid.*, memo from J. M. Addis, 5 April 1945, p. 118; PRO 371/48910.
133. *Ibid.*
134. *Ibid.*, memo from J. M. Addis, 28 March [1945], p. 113; PRO 371/48910.

These were not, of course, in any sense shocking revelations to anyone who understood Yugoslav politics. Maclean had always known of Tito's intentions to found a Communist regime, as had Churchill and the FO. The last suspected that, despite Tito's allegiance to Stalin, the new Yugoslavia would not be modelled on Russia – and they were right, as his row with Stalin later demonstrated. There was no shamefaced skulduggery in Whitehall as Sykes suggests. Indeed, with an open-faced liberalism Waugh would probably have despised, the London officials often expressed concern at the points raised. True, Waugh was ignoring the simple diplomatic fact that British intervention in the internal affairs of Yugoslavia was neither legal nor possible. But the question remained: was his atrocity story accurate?

Stevenson's reply (to Anthony Eden) offers a detailed and intelligent analysis of the evidence. He accepted that the Partisans had 'behaved with unnecessary brutality towards the Catholic Church'. He could not, however, accept Waugh's interpretation of these events.[135] Sykes dismisses this as mere prevarication: 'Couched in that anodyne style of which the diplomatic service is master ... it suavely diminished the pretensions to gravity of Evelyn's report.'[136] But this is unfair. Stevenson deplored the persecution. The difficulty was not to establish whether atrocities had been perpetrated, but whether (a) they signalled a post-war policy of organized oppression and (b) the report deliberately omitted information which might have damaged its case.

On the first point, Stevenson was unequivocal:

> The new regime is determined to restrict the activities of the Catholic Church in Yugoslavia to a minimum. At the same time they will try to eliminate all those elements of the Church which have actively collaborated with the enemy. The officials of the new regime will, within the limits of their mentality, carry out their instructions from above to allow freedom of religious worship. The regime should therefore be judged by the extent to which they distinguish between collaborators and guiltless members of the Catholic Church and how far they interpret fairly the phrase 'freedom of worship'. To expect a concordat mutually satisfactory to two such irreconcilable bodies as the National Liberation Movement and the Catholic Church is beyond the bounds of reason.[137]

135. FO R 8555/1059/92 (no. 66), 'Mr. Stevenson to Mr. Eden (Received 17 May [1945])', Belgrade, 2 May 1945, p. 10 (p. 129); PRO 371/48910.
136. Sykes, p. 277.
137. 'Mr. Stevenson to Mr. Eden ...', *op. cit.*, p. 10 (p. 129); PRO 371/48910.

Nothing could be plainer, but Stevenson could not avoid pointing out (and it seems that he was right) that

> Catholic priests played a leading part in the Ustaše movement. This activity is minimised quite arbitrarily in Captain Waugh's report. Priests not only led the Ustaše rising in certain districts in 1941, but they acted unceasingly as agents, couriers and purveyors of funds for the Ustaše for many years before the war, not only throughout Europe but in North and South America.[138]

The Partisans' resentment towards them, then, was understandable and Sykes, while describing the Ustaše as a terrorist organization, omits to mention that they were also a band of fanatical Catholics. In the Dalmatian region, according to Stevenson, where Waugh was based while collecting his information, the Catholic clergy had shocked the population of Dubrovnik by doing all they could to assist the Italians and Ustaše during the occupation. The Dominicans and the Franciscans were the worst offenders, and it was to these people Waugh had turned and to whom he channelled supplies. A local priest, Mgr Ritoig, who was openly sympathetic to the Partisans and welcomed by them, is effectively dismissed by Waugh as ancient and untrustworthy. Of the Ustaše he says little other than that 'the only available evidence about them comes from violently antagonistic sources. It is thus impossible to give any documented or impartial account of them.'[139] This did not, however, prevent him from using equally prejudiced sources to provide the 'evidence' for a plot to initiate a campaign of genocide.

Stevenson thus had good reason to suspect the impartiality of 'Church and State':

> The Catholic clergy of Dubrovnik [he noted] provide the source of a large part of the information contained in Captain Waugh's report. The evidence produced by them was translated for Captain Waugh by Mr. Carey, the assistant press secretary at this embassy, who points out that significant passages of their evidence have been omitted. The priests were unable entirely to gloss over the fact of their collaboration, for this was universally known. . . .[140]

Even without this knowledge, no intelligent reader of the report could fail to detect bias. Waugh does not lie about those facts which contradict his thesis, he merely ignores them. Even a casual glance at his typescript reveals

138. *Ibid.*, p. 130
139. Printed version of Waugh's 'Church and State in Liberated Croatia', '4. The Ustase', p. 3 (p. 122); PRO 371/48910.
140. 'Mr. Stevenson to Mr. Eden . . .', *op. cit.*, p. 11 (p. 130); PRO 371/48910.

his hand on the balance, at every opportunity ignoring the Catholics' culpability and placing the full weight of guilt on the Partisans.[141]

Eden accepted Stevenson's advice to ignore 'Church and State...', but the FO could not suppress the information it contained. Maclean felt that if they 'behaved to Waugh with a show of generosity, he would be likely to respond to a request that he should only show his report to a few selected individuals in strict confidence. . . .' The FO could circumvent their difficulty by insisting 'that if public reference is made to any information contained in the report, the fact that it was collected by a member of a British Military Mission would be concealed.'[142] Waugh grudgingly complied with these restrictions, although furious that his research could not appear in the *Tablet* or the *Catholic Herald*. The drift of Maclean's idea was that, by appealing to Waugh's better nature, circulation of the atrocity stories could be restricted to a few individuals. Such appeals rarely moved Waugh. He went straight to an MP, John McEwen, who stood up in the House of Commons on 30 May and asked Eden what he intended to do to protect Croatian Catholics from Tito. The phrasing of a supplementary question came almost verbatim from the report. No satisfactory reply was received. Nothing was done. But Waugh had made his point and continued his campaign against Tito for several years.

*

'I find I enjoy things more every year,' Waugh had written to Laura from Yugoslavia. 'Things like pictures not things like cocktails. I eat less and less & am wrinkled & old, crotchety, peppery and obsessed with the splendour of my literary work. A great change.'[143] In London he gluttonized, drank himself into a stupor during Laura's absences and became increasingly irritable. No totalitarian likes being thwarted by totalitarianism of another persuasion. And so it was with Waugh and the Partisans, the FO and the War Office. He mooched discontentedly around London over Easter, feeling no elation as the war drew to a close, haunted by the news of the Communist dismantling of eastern Europe. Most days he would spend silently in the Hyde Park Hotel, a seclusion broken only by an hour in White's or in Heywood Hill's. Victorian fiction was the staple diet of his

141. Cf. TS of Waugh's 'Church and State . . .', *op. cit.*, with A emendations and addition, p. 1 (p. 163); PRO 371/48910. Describing the Partisans' characteristics as 'extreme youth, hardiness, pride in the immediate past' etc., Waugh inserts 'ignorance' between 'youth' and 'hardiness'. On p. 2 (p. 164), describing the Partisan army, he alters 'commands' to 'formations', thus reducing their status. On p. 4 (p. 166), he originally stated that 'there is abundant evidence that many wholly unworthy men are attracted to the order [of Croat Franciscans]', but altered 'many' to 'several' and 'are' to 'were'.

142. Memo from J. M. Addis, 5 April 1945, *op. cit.*, p. 118; PRO 371/48910.

143. Unpublished ALS to Laura Waugh, 22 February 1945, *op. cit.*; BL.

reading. He found himself utterly estranged from most contemporary writing.

Henry Yorke had published *Loving* in December 1944 and had sent it to Waugh with a letter of commentary on *Brideshead*, but the package had gone astray: 'It was so very enjoyable to see you both the other evening,' Yorke wrote in late March. '... How curious it is that we should both now be writing on lines [?] odious to each other. Me with servants & children, you with the dilemmas of the Church.'[144] He sent another copy 'for old time's sake because, alas, you won't like it'[145] and repeated his remarks about *Brideshead*.[146] Waugh liked neither book nor letter. He would not brook criticism from an agnostic about the theology of the *magnum opus*; Loving he found 'obscene'.[147] After their second meeting, Waugh recorded: 'Henry and Dig [his wife] came to dinner. He talked about the lower classes and Russia, which he thinks will collapse from internal corruption in ten years.'[148] Waugh's belief in Yorke's genius had waned. In 1945 Yorke was at the height of his literary reputation and in the middle of a very productive phase which only ended with *Concluding* (1948). But he had always been depressive, uncertain of himself and in need of support from other writers. He did not get it from Waugh. Yorke's abandonment of the manners of his class were to Waugh tantamount to betrayal. The 'obscenity' of *Loving* lay partly in the fact of Yorke's having made heroes of domestic servants.

Waugh was himself tense as he sat out the next few weeks waiting for *Brideshead* to appear. VE day, by unfortunate coincidence, also loomed near: not a celebration for Waugh but a ghastly carnival of the Common Man. He hoped to escape it. Another *magnum opus* was waiting to be born and frustration and depression were curiously mixed with the buoyant expectation of critical success. Everyone seemed to want to know him. Even Clive Bell, whose name Waugh had taken in vain in the margins of *Grave*, sought him out. Connolly arranged a dinner party for Waugh to meet Edmund Wilson and Elizabeth Bowen. Three years earlier, Waugh had

144. Unpublished ALS from Henry Yorke, 20 March 1945, from 9–13 George Street, Manchester Square, London, W1; BL.
145. *Ibid.*
146. Cf. unpublished ALS from Henry Yorke, Xmas Day 1944, from 16 Trevor Place, SW7; BL. Yorke's first letter, which eventually turned up, was full of praise, qualified only by distaste for the ending: 'You can imagine how shocked & hurt I was when the old man crossed himself on his deathbed. But when he sent the priest out the first time I had an idea it was too good to last. In fact through the whole of the end (when I thought Ryder was winning) I kept on saying to myself Evelyn is reconverted to the fold & there will be wailing & gnashing of teeth in Farm Street over this. But it was no go.... I wish I had been in love with Oxford when I was up. I see now what I have missed.' In his second (20 March 1945, *op. cit.*, quoted in part by Sykes, p. 251) Yorke adds: 'One thing irritates me. There is a great house in my book & I fear you have done yours better.... I did not like your nanny who I thought was over written, though the relationship with the grown-up children was perfect....'
147. *Diaries*, 31 March 1945, p. 624.
148. *Ibid.*, 2 April 1945, p. 624.

tried to ingratiate himself with the former in the hope of conquering the American market and Wilson had responded in March 1944 with a generous retrospective review of the early novels being reprinted by Little, Brown. McIntyre had been considerably excited by this. It was the first time that the *New Yorker* had taken Waugh up and this promised large sales for *Brideshead*. Waugh had good reason to be grateful to Wilson. The dinner party was a disaster. Wilson's novel, *Memoirs of Hecate County*, had been refused by his British publishers on the grounds of obscenity. Waugh, informed that no one should mention the subject, and well soused with champagne, hounded Wilson into admitting the truth and concluded by advising publication in Cairo.[149] The next day, Waugh chucked his promise to show this 'insignificant Yank'[150] around London. It was the end of his brief association with Wilson, who, henceforth, was in the vanguard of hostile critics.

Towards the end of April, Waugh finally heard that his application to return to Yugoslavia as a consul had been refused. '... I am well content', he recorded:

> Honour is satisfied. I am glad to have done all I could to go back and glad not to be going. The end of the war is hourly expected. Mussolini obscenely murdered, continual rumours that Hitler's mind has finally gone. Communism gains in France. Russia insults USA. I will now get to work on St. Helena.[151]

This was to be his next *magnum opus*, a novel about the mother of Constantine the Great. It was a subject pleasantly remote from the new dark age. On a visit to Campion Hall ten days before, he had recommended that Catholics should take to the catacombs. Meeting Belloc at Pixton, Waugh could only see him as a redundant propagandist for ancient prejudices: 'Perhaps in forty years' time I shall make myself tedious denouncing Communism in this way.... He is conscious of being decrepit and forgetful, but not of being a bore.'[152]

'I try to sequestrate myself from public affairs,'[153] he wrote to Laura after his first day's work on the new novel and, in the deep silence of the Devonshire countryside, he could face his future, if not the rest of the world's, with equanimity and a large dose of self-deception:

> It is pleasant to end the war in plain clothes, writing.... I regard the greatest danger I went through that of becoming one of Churchill's

149. The anecdote is told fully, and hilariously, in Sykes, pp. 284–5.
150. *Diaries*, 12 April 1945, p. 625.
151. *Ibid.*, 1 May 1945, p. 627.
152. *Ibid.*, pp. 626–7.
153. Unpublished ALS to Laura Waugh, 'Nones of May' [7th] 1945, from Easton Court Hotel, Chagford, Devon; BL.

young men, of getting a medal and standing for Parliament; if things had gone, as then seemed right, in the first two years, that is what I should be now. I thank God to find myself still a writer and at work on something as 'uncontemporary' as I am.[154]

154. *Diaries*, 6 May 1945, p. 627.

V

Transition: May 1945–January 1947

Over the next three years Waugh became an old man. 'Would you say I was . . . very ill-tempered & self-infatuated . . .?' he wrote to Nancy Mitford in 1947 after receiving an unsympathetic review. 'It hurts.'[1] The end of the war and the publication of *Brideshead* could have provided release and contentment. He came home, if not as the conquering hero, at least rich and successful, to Laura and a beautiful house. But, as he told Lady Diana Cooper, 'I found returning to [Piers Court] with many sentimental tremors that my love for it was quite dead, as so many soldiers found about their wives but not me thank God. Perhaps all my ex-service resentment got concentrated on the house unjustly.'[2] London had long since ceased to be habitable. Now England herself, bespattered with dishonour and bent upon pleasing her proletariat, was equally insufferable. Against Laura's wishes, he determined to emigrate. He *was* often ill-tempered and self-infatuated, and for two years she had to deal with a husband scarcely recognizable as the man she had married.

The appearance of *Brideshead* on 28 May marked a turning-point in Waugh's career. Apart from J. D. Beresford's extraordinary complaint that Waugh's themes were 'adultery, perversion, and drunkenness',[3] the early British reviews expressed cautious pleasure. Some were confused by Waugh's new approach. The *TLS* thought it doubtful that he had traced 'the workings of the divine purpose' with 'any marked clarity' and that 'the decorations of the tale' (Sebastian's dipsomania, Charles's father) were more successful than the working out of the grand theme.[4] But Henry Reed in the *New Statesman* found the novel 'deeply moving in its theme and its design' and, although 'flagrantly defective at times in artistic sensibility', 'a fine and brilliant book':

> The subjects of *Brideshead* . . . are the inescapable watchfulness of God, and the contrast between the Christian (for Mr. Waugh, the

1. 26 December 1947; *Letters*, p. 264.
2. ALS to Lady Diana Cooper, 12 January 1947, from Hospital of SS John & Elizabeth, NW8; *MWMS*, pp. 93–4.
3. *Manchester Guardian*, 1 June 1945, 3; *CH*, p. 233.
4. Unsigned review, *TLS*, 2 June 1945, 257; *CH*, pp. 233–6.

> Roman Catholic) sinner, and the other kind of sinner described in the cant term of our day as 'pagan'. Boldly, Mr. Waugh writes throughout from the point of view of the pagan, which he . . . has not forgotten. . .[5]

Such literary courage won Waugh respect. The *Spectator*, applauding his wit, even felt that while 'the book has a powerful religious purpose it has no shadow of Catholic exclusiveness',[6] an idea which many later critics would have found obtuse.

Waugh received these accolades with resignation. Few reviews in the 'rationalist press', as he termed it, took his religious theme seriously. None registered that *Brideshead* was the retrospective narrative of a Catholic convert. The notices were good for trade but the result of this was that the first edition sold out overnight and immediately went out of print. Thanks to the paper shortage, his other novels were also unavailable. At a time when Chapman & Hall could have sold thousands of copies of each, and when paper was squandered on pulp fiction and propaganda, the public was prevented by government order from immediately making Waugh a rich man. He did not, however, have long to wait for his wealth. In June, Peters heard from a delighted McIntyre, whose attempts to sway the judges of the Book-of-the-Month Club had been successful. American publication was delayed until September, Randolph Churchill wrote a piece on Waugh for the *Book-of-the-Month Club News*, and all was set fair for celebrity in the United States.

The selection had a dramatic effect on Waugh's life. 'It is impossible now to be rich', he wrote to Graham Greene when *The Heart of the Matter* was chosen in 1948, 'but it is possible to be idle, and this American coup relieves you of work for about fifteen years.'[7] In Waugh's case the £20,000[8] meant that he could fix his income for five years at £5,000 a year, double his previous earnings. Without the stimulus of needing to earn an annual salary, however, he found it difficult to write.

His first week's work on *Helena* had concluded with such deep depression that he abandoned the novel for seven months. It took nearly five years to complete. There were many reasons for the delay, not the least of which were his obsessive desire to do the subject justice and the research involved. Even so, no one realized more acutely than Waugh that the luxury of the space afforded by the American money was in some respects bad for him both as man and writer. He worked well under pressure, enjoyed huckstering in the literary market. The energy derived from spending more

5. *NS*, 23 June 1945, 408–9; *CH*, pp. 239–41.
6. V. C. Clinton-Baddeley, *Spectator*, 8 June 1945, 532; *CH*, pp. 237–8.
7. 3 May [1948]; *Letters*, p. 278. Fifteen years was an exaggeration.
8. £10,000 payment and the expectation of a further £10,000 from ordinary sales and cinema rights. Waugh could also expect at least £1,000 a year from his other writings.

than he earned had always prodded him into action. For the foreseeable future, he would have enough loose cash to encourage prodigality, yet not enough to be entirely careless of expense.

Any compromise rendered him irritable and in his frustration he constructed an image of England as an occupied country. His siege mentality, inward- and backward-looking, caused the ordinary events of daily life to dissolve into chaos. Order lay only in art and theology; sanity in isolation. Politics were rationalist nonsense. Anglicans went to Hell. England was a slave-state. European civilization had been wrecked by the pagan onslaught. It was what he had believed since 1930 but had rarely articulated in anything other than savage jokes. Conservatism, in the sense in which he understood the word, meant saying 'No'.[9]

The Labour Party had been doing precisely that at their Blackpool conference a week before *Brideshead* appeared. Churchill had suggested to them that the National Government should remain in power until the end of the incongruously named Pacific War. In rejecting the proposal, Labour forced a general election on 5 July. Waugh watched the preparations with near-catatonic indifference, but as the delayed count drew nearer, excitement began to infect even him. Many of his friends were standing. It was clear that the new Parliament would shape the future of post-war Britain for decades. In London, the smart set were to make a social event of election day and Waugh, keen to be at the centre of things, invited Laura to London: 'It will be much more exciting than anywhere else. We are asked to Lady Rothermere's . . . champagne & tape machine & buffet lunch. No speech would be expected of you. All you would do would be what you like doing – sit in a corner with me and watch and listen.'[10] Laura refused.

They could not repossess Piers Court until September and Waugh would not live temporarily at Pixton. This was mildly insulting but Laura was a patient woman. She had to stay there because of the children; the children and her brother deterred Waugh. Under these circumstances, she felt, it was better not to have him glowering at the two Auberons. But while Waugh was spending £100 a week in the Hyde Park Hotel and hundreds more on *objets d'art*, Laura was feeling shabby and neglected. She had had no new clothes for five years and, although she could suffer this silently, she found it increasingly difficult to endure his egotism. The money and kudos brought by *Brideshead* had turned Waugh into a dictatorial husband.

9. In *The Unquiet Grave* (*op. cit.*, p. 46), Connolly quoted: 'Presque tous les hommes sont esclaves, par la raison que les Spartiates donnaient de la servitude des Perses, faute de savoir prononcer la syllabe *non*. Savoir prononcer ce mot et savoir vivre seul sont les deux seuls moyens de conserver sa liberté et son caractère.' Beside this Waugh wrote: 'Waugh knows well how to do both these things.'

10. Unpublished ALS to Laura Waugh, 21 July 1945, from White's; BL. Polling day was 5 July, but the count was delayed until 26 July to allow for the collection of the Service vote.

Without consulting her, he had arranged to purchase a castle in Ireland and, as they had already been looking at alternative houses, he had expected her joyful compliance. Laura had not complied. The idea of living with a sea-crossing between herself and her children's schools was intolerable. She was a West Country woman and wanted to remain near her sisters and mother. Waugh, considering none of this, had replied with a schoolmasterly rebuke which had depressed her further. Another rebuke followed, thinly disguised as sympathy:

> The aim of my letter was not to make you unhappy, still less to make you despair, but simply to rouse you from the trivial torpor into which you have sunk & make you think. Please go on thinking, however painful it is.... I telephoned you today but heard only the unctuous tones of Auberon [Herbert]. Cheer up & wake up.[11]

This approach somehow failed to restore her vitality. Nevertheless, she had allowed herself to be persuaded to come to London. Waugh was always keen to smarten her up, show her off and make her fit in, an aspect of his patronage which she found either pleasantly naïve or vulgar according to her mood. Waugh's entrée into upper-Metroland was his badge of success and he wanted her to share the thrill it gave him. She never could. The world of press barons, politicians and writers she found merely tiresome. After a few days she returned to Pixton with a compromise arranged. She would visit the Irish castle; he agreed not to take it if she disapproved. It was an awkward moment in their marriage and Laura's refusal of the Rothermere invitation made it clear to Waugh that his wife was not to be ignored. If the past five years had altered him, they had also changed her. She had entered the war frail and dependent, overwhelmed by her husband. She had emerged from it an independent woman.

'You should have come ...,' he wrote later. '... the spectacle of consternation as the details of the massacre spread, was a strong intoxicant.... Ann's party was full of chums dressed up to the nines and down in the dumps....'[12] The Conservatives were routed. For Winston Churchill the reward of military victory was parliamentary defeat. It seemed to the rich a demonstration of astonishing national ingratitude. But Churchill's popularity could not overcome the long British memory of suffering. The Conservatives had effectively governed for most of the inter-war period. They were seen to be responsible for the unemployment and appeasement which had led, respectively, to the Depression and to the ultimate conflict. The Labour Party promised work, education and a national insurance system in an egalitarian society and, after nearly six years of death and

11. Unpublished ALS to Laura Waugh, 14 July 1945, from White's; BL.
12. *Ibid.*

deprivation, this seemed a glorious prospect. Labour was returned with a massive majority.[13] Churchill resigned immediately and the dim figure of Clement Attlee became Prime Minister.

Most of Waugh's friends failed to get elected. Randolph Churchill turned up in Waugh's room at 7.30 the next morning, bloodied but unbowed, hopeful of being adopted by another constituency. It was altogether a bad time for him. He and his wife, Pamela, had separated and he was setting up house with the remnants of the furniture at Ickleford Rectory in Hertfordshire. Waugh had warmed to his boyish refusal to repine, the Yugoslavian breach had been healed with the thinnest of scar tissue and Randolph had invited Waugh to share the Rectory while waiting to return to Piers Court. Neither lived in confident expectation of domestic harmony, particularly given the political context of their arrangement. Randolph, still an ardent advocate of his father's virtues, was boiling with fury at the Socialists. Waugh, who had not voted, was equally distressed but refused to show it. Nothing pleased the anarchist in him better than a *débâcle*, particularly when it proved him right. With the savage detachment of his schoolboy sense of honour, he felt that the Conservatives had received their just deserts, not only for failing to fight harder against an enemy he had persistently warned them about, but for Winston's betrayal of eastern Europe and the Balkans. There was only one ray of hope: two Catholic friends had been elected: Hugh Fraser and Christopher Hollis.

During Waugh's stay with Randolph the bombing of Hiroshima was announced and the six o'clock news on 6 August threw the popular newspapers into a mood of feverish optimism. Nuclear fission was presented as a benevolent scientific revolution. No details were revealed other than to describe the force of the bomb in terms of conventional armaments. No mention was made of the hideous long-term effects. It was seen as a weapon to end wars. The technology promised a massive new source of energy. Boundless prosperity was forecast. 'Randolph', Waugh wrote to Laura, 'is greatly over-excited about the atomic bomb. We heard the news at the Melchetts who claim to have made it in their garden.'[14] Waugh, to his credit, realized that this was no joking matter. Following the style of one newspaper, he began to date his letters by the days of the atomic age and was wholly sceptical of its supposed benefits. 'Papers, catching up with public opinion,' he noted three days after the first holocaust, 'now express consternation.... Everyone seems impelled to make a public statement about his own opinion of the atom bomb. Even I, left alone, began to write a note for *The Tablet* ..., but recovered my good sense and destroyed it.'[15]

13. Labour: 393 seats; Conservatives: 213; Liberals: 12.
14. Unpublished ALS to Laura Waugh, nd [August 1945], np [Ickleford Rectory, Hitchin, Herts.]; BL.
15. *Diaries*, 9 August 1945, p. 631.

Three years later he hinted at what he might have said. Ronald Knox's *God and the Atom* (1945), he revealed, 'inspired me; it came at a time of deflation and blew into me a clear breath of reason and wisdom.'[16] The bomb, he thought, vindicated his and Knox's warnings about the dangers of rationalist optimism, but it also 'seemed to cast doubt on the hypothesis of causality and the five classical Thomist proofs of the existence of God.'[17] The attack on Hiroshima represented a 'wound in the civilized mind' apparently subverting Faith, Hope and Charity. For once, Waugh was in line with popular opinion which felt an 'unquiet ... based on the deepest philosophical grounds'.[18] The assault on Faith and Hope did not bother him. His Faith was unassailable and he was inured to living without Hope for the survival of civilization. The possibility of the destruction of Charity, however, did disturb him for it struck at the root of his ideology. He lamented the fact that the individual no longer had a place in the crusade for a just cause. On the battlefield, chivalry had died; in peacetime the function of private charity had been usurped by the Welfare State. All this articulated a typical Conservative nostalgia for enlightened patronage and the traditions of service. But Waugh soon drove his argument to such extremes in order to fix its terms that even his right-wing Catholic friends thought him a little mad. A few months later, Douglas Woodruff had to return the typescript of a review, requiring corrections because Waugh had stated that Tito's prohibition of private charity had caused a famine.[19]

When the review was published[20] the statement about the famine had been removed but numerous equally offensive remarks remained. Many British liaison officers, he said, had been 'hoodwinked as to the true nature of the force they were supporting. There were sinister influences in London and Bari ... in 1944.' It was effectively an attack on Fitzroy Maclean.[21] The book, Waugh remarked, told a story of 'candour, modesty and chivalry', implying that it described a lost age when such virtues were still possible. Mihailović is seen as 'a loyal soldier of his king, aiming at the restoration

16. 'Mgr. Ronald Knox', *Horizon*, 17 (May 1948), 326–38; *EAR*, pp. 347–56.
17. *Ibid.*, p. 350.
18. *Ibid.*, p. 349.
19. Cf. unpublished TLS from Douglas Woodruff, 1 May 1946, from Tablet House, 128 Sloane Street, SW1; BL.
20. 'Failure of a Mission', *Tablet*, 11 May 1946, 241; review of Jasper Rootham, *Irregular Adventure*; *EAR*, pp. 307–9. Major Rootham wrote of his time at a British mission attached to Mihailović's army, before the British switched their support to Tito.
21. Waugh had written to *The Times* on 23 May claiming that 'The peoples now overrun by the forces of Marshal Tito are predominantly Roman Catholic' and that when the truth was revealed, his regime would be seen to have 'all the characteristics of Nazism'. So as not to breach the Official Secrets Act, Waugh signed it 'A British Soldier Lately in Yugoslavia'. Another British officer from Yugoslavia replied on 26 May, demolishing these views as 'half-knowledge disguised as expert knowledge' and Waugh, jubilantly assuming his assailant to be Maclean, fired off another volley on 5 June. Waugh's aim was wide: Sir Fitzroy did not write the letter. Cf. *EAR*, pp. 282–5.

of the monarchy', and Waugh thus neatly linked Christian morality, monarchism and Conservatism. This unity, he suggests, was brutally sundered by betrayal. 'I think any honourable man who was involved in this small corner of the war feels a sense of guilt . . . and Major Rootham has written what may be read as an apology for them all.'[22] Waugh was later to write his own apology in the stories about Major Gordon and Guy Crouchback. In the meantime he tried in vain to wash his hands of the modern world.

*

At the beginning of September, Laura began to receive further abrupt instructions: 'Wake up. Before leaving Pixton finally see that the tombstone is placed on your daughter's grave. I am gravely displeased with you for not writing.'[23] 'Will you please take great pains to ensure that *all* my possessions at Pixton, clothes, books, bookplates etc. are included in your luggage. It will be very disagreeable if anything is left behind.'[24] Two nights spent in a nearby inn while the nuns finally removed themselves from Piers Court irritated him further. He stalked about with a hangover in the ruined gardens, inspected the cellar for theft, ticked off each scratch and stain. Dispossession had been a form of rape and Laura's delight at their homecoming was spoiled by his ill-temper: '[she] saying how perfect everything looked, I detecting losses and damage everywhere.'[25]

When the nuns were packed off (later to receive a bill for over £100), Waugh began to restore order. The library was his priority and by the end of the week he could sit at his desk surrounded by the shining calf bindings of his manuscripts and architectural books, face to face with a bronze of Queen Victoria and the oil painting of George III. The house, like its master, had a Georgian exterior and Victorian interior. Both presented a blank and formal face to the world, concealing a tumult of intricate sentimentality. Having outgrown worldly ambition, Waugh struggled during the next decade to transfer allegiance from his public to his private identity. He valued his Metroland reputation but was all the time tormented by the knowledge that everything there was vanity. He loved his wife and needed the ordered silence of his home like a drug, but he could not shut out the roar of the street for long before boredom broke him. Most weeks he would travel to London, ostensibly to get his hair cut but really to find someone to talk to.

Waugh was a creature of routine. As we have seen, part of his London round had been a morning stroll to Nancy Mitford's bookshop. His

22. *Ibid.*, p. 308.
23. Unpublished ALS to Laura Waugh, 1 September 1945, from White's; BL.
24. Unpublished ALS to Laura Waugh, 4 September 1945, from White's; BL.
25. *Diaries*, 1 September 1945, p. 634.

departure for Gloucestershire was followed shortly by hers for Paris[26] and, deprived of the cocktail-party atmosphere she engendered, he became morose. She would, he knew, make her home abroad and, although a long correspondence ensued, he lost both the company of a close friend and her London gossip. 'I do think its a waste for you ... to live among worthies and worzles,' she wrote, 'instead of glittering away in Paris with birds in your hair.'[27] But he would not be persuaded, and when she came to stay, shortly before leaving the country for good, it was clear that their lives had irrevocably divided.

Nancy was an incurable optimist and agnostic. She loved flattery, saw herself as a Socialist, was a friend of Connolly, Quennell and Spender. For holidays she sought the sunshine of the Lido. In Paris, she enjoyed rubbing shoulders with 'intellectuals'. Above all, she was infatuated with French culture – its *chic*, its food and wine, its social calendar. She could not understand why this should not be exactly to Waugh's taste. Waugh, however, could only survive such a life in small doses. He quickly became over-excited, then dazed, then sleepless, and when this point of nervous exhaustion was reached, he began to insult everyone. He thought her Socialist friends traitors and the rest second-rate. He now disliked being lionized, loathed 'intellectuals' (loathed even the word), and hated the French. The damp silence of Gloucestershire better protected his privacy, and Nancy's girlish glamour was entirely out of place at Piers Court. During her visit she slept so late that Laura had to bring her breakfast in bed; when she rose, she spent her two days shivering before the fire. Waugh and Nancy's relationship could only continue on the common ground of fantastical letters. Each relished seeing the other as a character from fiction. The reality was less easy to endure.

Piers Court at first had had no water and no cook; Waugh had no cigars. The kitchen, he told Laura, was entirely her concern and she battled vaguely with the culinary art, emerging shame-faced with a variety of burnt or otherwise indigestible dishes. But life gradually returned to normal. Laura's cooking improved; the demobbed butler returned to clean and press and polish, and his master's spirits rose with the sheen on the mahogany. Food rations were supplemented by the few eggs Laura's chickens produced[28] and, failing all else, dinner was always available at the

26. She went to Paris in September 1945 and stayed until November writing her novel *The Pursuit of Love* (December 1945). On her return to London she decided on permanent emigration and set about disposing of her flat, 12 Blomfield Road, W9. She stayed there, it seems, until her return to Paris in March 1946.

27. Unpublished ALS from Nancy Mitford, Easter Day [21 April 1946], from Hôtel de Bourgogne, Rue de Bourgogne, Paris 7; BL.

28. Cf. *Diaries*, 2 October 1945, p. 637: 'We have practically no meat – two meals a week – and live on eggs and macaroni cheese (made by Laura), bread and wine; very occasionally we get a rather nasty fish.'

local inn. Cigars arrived from Randolph, who had taken a lucrative job in America as a gossip columnist.

Waugh's chief pleasures were his cellar and his wife's company. Margaret and Harriet at first remained at Pixton; Teresa and Bron were soon dispatched to boarding-school. At Ickleford Rectory, Waugh had invited his son to stay and, apart from falling into a bonfire, his behaviour had been exemplary. Encouraged by this success, he had decided to develop the experiment by dragging his five year old around London sights and offering him a packet of triangular stamps. When, at Highgate that evening, his grandmother had enquired whether he had had a delightful day, Bron had replied: '"A bit dull."' It was not a remark in which his father detected gratitude. 'I have regretfully come to the conclusion', he informed Laura, 'that the boy Auberon is not yet a suitable companion for me . . . that is the last time for some years I inconvenience myself for my children. You might rub that in to him.'[29]

Waugh kept his promise. One obstacle to his relinquishing Metroland was that he could never be a conventional paterfamilias. 'Don't be depressed about your children,' Nancy had written. 'Childhood is a hateful age – no clouds of glory – & children are generally either prigs or gangsters & always dull & generally ugly. . . .'[30] But he *was* constantly depressed by them. He watched them suspiciously during their brief spells in his presence: 'The elder girl has a precocious taste for theology which promises well for a career as Abbess; the boy is mindless & obsessed with social success.'[31] As we have seen, Bron's slightest dishonesty was rigorously investigated, and his father's sense of moral rectitude was often indistinguishable from his sense of social charm. Bron's squint had been enough to deter Waugh during the boy's infancy and when Teresa came home with middle-class manners and speech ('serviette' for 'napkin') he lost all patience: 'My children weary me. I can only see them as defective adults; feckless, destructive, frivolous, sensual, humourless.'[32]

When not uncovering the lost paths in his garden, he shut himself up in his library. Most of his time at Piers Court he spent alone, taking stock, and throughout that autumn Yugoslavia haunted him. He re-read his Lancing diaries with shame and put *Helena* to one side, attempting instead a school story set in 1919. Even in this, Serbia tugged at his imagination. The fragment of 'Charles Ryder's Schooldays'[33] is an elegant reworking of his diaries but too close to the original documents to rescue it from dullness

29. 25 August 1945; *Letters*, p. 211.
30. Unpublished ALS from Nancy Mitford, 7 January 1945, from 12 Blomfield Road, London; BL.
31. ALS to Lady Diana Cooper, 3 January 1946, from Piers Court; BL; *MWMS*, p. 82.
32. *Diaries*, 26 December 1945, p. 640.
33. TccL in HRC; first published, with an Introduction by Michael Sissons, *TLS*, 5 March 1982; reprinted in *Work Suspended and Other Stories* (Harmondsworth, Penguin Books, 1982 and 1985).

and confusion. It contains only one substantial fictional invention: the hero's mother dies in the Serbian uplands of Bosnia during the First World War. She had gone there for patriotic reasons which Charles's father finds incomprehensible. How Waugh intended to use this *leitmotif* we shall never know. But it seems clear that he wished to relate Charles's sense of alienation to the death of chivalry in general and to Yugoslav political history in particular.

Abandoning this, Waugh turned to the editing of his travel books, pruning out blasphemy and digression, for a single volume, *When the Going Was Good* (1946). Its preface laments the recent, lost glories of Europe, before travel and currency restrictions and the Cold War.[34] While working on this he dutifully toured the country to speak at the Catholic societies of the Universities of London, Oxford and Cambridge, criticizing the British betrayal of Mihailović. By Christmas, the first three chapters of *Helena* were complete and were published in heavily edited form by the *Tablet*.[35] This, too, was a form of exorcism. He had chosen, against historical probability, to make St Helena British, daughter of Old King Coel, and to leave her living in Dalmatia. 'Constantius Chlorus of course', he wrote to Lady Diana Cooper, 'is Fitzroy Maclean....'[36]

'Yes, I am serenely happy,' Waugh remarked bitterly, 'swathing myself in layers of middle age; the crisis over, the doctor's bag packed, I placidly doing cross-word puzzles at the bedside of the patient for whom all hope has been finally abandoned. After ten years' fretfulness I am quite reconciled to the decline of the West.'[37] He had emerged from Yugoslavia bruised by neglect and tormented with guilt. Somehow, in that deeply divided mind searching for straight answers, the retreat to nursery morality had to articulate the wound inflicted by the war upon the civilized mind, and the only way he could do this was to construct myths from history. Helena's period is seen to be exactly analogous with his own. The Christians in their catacombs face the barbaric decadence of a declining empire and the clarity of the Faith is threatened by the logic-chopping dualism of the Gnostics. Waugh felt that it was his task, as it had been Helena's with her no-nonsense insistence upon historical proof, to find the True Cross and to knock everyone's silly head against it. '"There's two sorts of Emperor you see,"' the young Crispus informs his mother, '"bad and good."'[38] This approximated Waugh's view: the world, he felt, had forgotten the simplest distinctions.

34. Cf. Vol. 1, p. 348.
35. 'St. Helena Meets Constantius: A Legend Retold', *Tablet*, 22 December 1945, 299–302.
36. ALS, 3 January 1946, *op. cit.*
37. *Ibid.*
38. *Helena* (Chapman & Hall, 1950; reprinted Harmondsworth, Penguin Books, 1963 and 1984), p. 74.

Waugh's literary energy sprang from anger. And since he could only write amusingly when he had something to complain about, he needed constantly to extend the range of his enemies. In late 1945, however, at a time when European Christianity was in crisis, he had never had fewer assailants. Everyone (except Quennell) seemed to admire *Brideshead*. Even Clive Bell had offered undiluted praise.[39] Waugh not only needed to be irritable, he needed to irritate, and the sense of his acceptance as '*cher maître*', while it flattered his self-esteem, left him feeling uncomfortable, beyond the walls of his castle, a common property he had never intended to become.

Beneath all this, deeply buried, there lay that seed of guilt: guilt at his failure to do more in Yugoslavia; guilt at his lack of affection for his children; guilt at his instinctive cruelty; above all, guilt at not *feeling* guilty. There was a religious dryness in his soul which hurt him, a lack of contrition, and he found it difficult to pray. His faith remained one of intellectual conviction rather than of emotional release. Belief often only brought him pain; in offering the prospect of salvation it emphasized an image of life on earth as a bestial interruption of unity with God. But if he could not share the contrition and compassion of more receptive souls, he could at least observe and value them in his art. This was to be Waugh's literary penance: the celebration of simplicity, even of dimness, in a chain of oddly assorted figures from Helena to Crouchback to whom the glamour of Metroland meant nothing.

He felt overwhelmed by the presumption of the enterprise. 'Of course you must go on with St Helena,' Woodruff insisted after the excerpt in the *Tablet* had appeared; 'Ronnie Knox says it is the only book . . . he has ever read which gave him the feeling of what upper class 3rd century life was like: you have a wonderful spiritual theme. . . .'[40] Thus encouraged, Waugh returned to his fable, doubtless amused by Woodruff's last sentence: 'I ought to add that I have had a good deal of protest about some of the passages. . . .'[41] Waugh had mischievously invented horse-riding sexual fantasies for his heroine and was soon conducting an intriguing correspondence with Penelope Betjeman on the subject.

Waugh's obsession with literary discipline extended, it seems, to the literature of discipline. During the 1930s he and the Betjemans had giggled

39. Cf. unpublished ALS from Clive Bell, 12 June 1945, from Charleston, Firle, Sussex; BL: 'It is a masterpiece, the best novel written in English, or in French either I strongly suspect, since . . . since I don't know when. If I was to say The Lighthouse you would accuse me of family prejudice. . . . What old Peter Quennell may be up to I'm sure I don't know. . . .' Quennell had reviewed *Brideshead* in *DM* (2 June 1945, 2) and expressed reservations about the novel's Catholic exclusiveness. Waugh knew Bell as a casual acquaintance at the Beefsteak Club.
40. Unpublished ALS from Douglas Woodruff, 1 January 1946, from 199 Park West, W2; BL.
41. *Ibid.*

over copies of *London Life*, a magazine devoted to the pains of the flesh. Waugh kept in his library (under plain wrapper) a copy of a pornographic doggerel poem celebrating the well-whipped buttocks of small boys. Part of the game of his relationship with Lady Betjeman had always been that they used to share an interest in bondage:

> Many months ago I wrote to ask your help with the hipporastic passages of my life of Helena. The *Tablet* had the fruits of my unaided invention. I should welcome detailed criticism.... I describe her as hunting in the morning after her wedding night feeling the saddle as comforting her wounded maidenhead. Is that O.K.? After that she has no interest in sex.[42]

Lady Betjeman entered eagerly into the spirit of the enquiry:

> I never received any communication from you ... about horse sex.... Personally I found it very difficult to separate sex & religion after I married & frequently used to drive a severely-bitted carriage horse in flights of fancy with an Anglo or Roman priest seated at my side.... I know two persons v. interested in the subject, one the brother of a distinguished war leader. He once sent me a picture of a girl in boots & spurs riding a stallion bareback & I told him I was no longer interested in such things. Pray consign this to your kitchen boiler when studied....[43]

Waugh loved trying to shock his female friends and loved them better for refusing to blush. He delighted in asking the most intimate questions under the guise of casual enquiry[44] and it was no secret that Lady Betjeman was the model for his heroine. 'St Helena Betjeman in characteristic form,' Nancy wrote after a visit to Wantage. 'Everybody sorry for the poor old fathers who run the Tablet & don't know smut when they see it – awful of you, it is thought, to trade on their saintly innocence like this....'[45] But there was scholarly research on hand too. He sought out a Jewish historian in Golders Green and wrote to Robert Henriques: 'I am at work on a description of the Empress Helena's visit to Jerusalem in about 330 AD. My authorities are all either Christian or atheist. Can you ... put me onto any Jewish books ... that would help? What I need is a description of the

42. 15 January [1946]; *Letters*, pp. 217–18.
43. unpublished ALS, 23 January [1946], from Farnborough, Old Rectory, Wantage, Berks.; BL.
44. Cf. unpublished ALS from Nancy Mitford, 2 May 1948, from 7 Rue Monsieur, Paris VII; BL: 'Darling Evelyn, *Masturbation*. I used to masturbate whenever I thought of Lady Jane Grey, so of course I thought about her continually.... This sublimation of sex might be recommended to Harriet, except that I don't think it changed anything & I still get quite excited when I think of Lady Jane. (Less & less as the years roll on)....'
45. Unpublished ALS from Nancy Mitford, 29 January 1946, from 12 Blomfield Road, London; BL.

Jews in Palestine after the destruction of the temple....'[46] By this time Waugh had completed the first 'book' of *Helena* (chapters 1–3) and was reading hard for the second and third. The precision of his literary marquetry generated deep pleasure.[47] After a dismal Christmas with his family, he had settled happily to work again.

The change of mood sprang from several sources: no children, the restoration of his friendship with Lady Diana Cooper after seven awkward years, and the American publication of *Brideshead*. Little, Brown's edition had appeared in December and it was Book-of-the-Month Club selection for January, guaranteeing financial success. No one, however, had expected an avalanche of praise from the American 'quality' papers. 'Mr. Waugh's finest achievement,' said the *New York Times Book Review*,[48] and similar plaudits echoed from every side. The only dissenting voice was Edmund Wilson's. Like the other critics, he admired the Oxford sections, the flavour of which, 'seen now from the bleak, shrivelled 'forties ... has taken on a remoteness and pathos'. But the book as a whole was 'a bitter blow' to him after his delight in the early novels. It degenerates, he suggests, into 'mere romantic fantasy' when Waugh 'abandons his comic convention' and the writing of the early chapters, 'felicitous, unobtrusive, exact', runs to '... dispiriting clichés' and 'stock characters'. At the root of the objections lay his disgust with Waugh's 'beglamoured snobbery', his 'cult of the high nobility' in a 'Catholic tract'. Wilson lamented the absence of Waugh's old, brutal truths: 'something essential has been left out ... and the religion that is evoked to correct it seems more like an exorcistic rite than a force of regeneration.'[49]

Waugh was as delighted to discover a new enemy as he was to reclaim Lady Diana's friendship. He had sent Wilson a copy of the novel with a genial note, hoping that he would forget the insults at Connolly's party and be flattered into log-rolling. But if the American chose to be antagonistic, nothing suited Waugh better. Wilson-baiting became a life-long pleasure[50]

46. 24 January 1946; *Letters*, p. 219. Henriques was a friend from the Commandos, a writer and one of the few practising Jews of Waugh's acquaintance.
47. Cf. *Diaries*, 12 January 1946, pp. 640–1: 'Yesterday I had to mention the fall of Palmyra. Longinus was executed there. I brought this in as decoration and made Helena have heard of him. Today I rewrote a paragraph of the first chapter making the tutor mention him. Then, because Mr. Hodges, my nurse's father, was a fabulous figure to me, I gave Helena two fables: first of the nursery, the exemplary soldier; secondly of the schoolroom, the stupendous pundit. Then I introduced to the Longinus paragraph the fact that Helena felt his death as a bereavement, the final end of her education. Then I introduced into the passage about Tetricus's betrayal the sense that Helena thought the grave of her nurse's father dishonoured. So the book prospers.'
48. John K. Hutchens, *NYTBR*, 30 December 1945, 1, 16; *CH*, pp. 241–5.
49. *NY*, 5 January 1946, 71, 74; *CH*, pp. 245–8.
50. Cf. *Writers*, p. 113: 'Have you found any professional criticism of your work illuminating ...? Edmund Wilson, for example?' 'Is he an American?' 'Yes.' 'I don't think what they have to say is of much interest, do you?'

while critical success promised foreign gold. And since Waugh cared only for the Americans' cash, he discovered a delicious opportunity to abuse them for rewarding him. 'I [am] deeply content to be home,' he wrote to Raimund von Hofmannsthal, 'and am busy on a story which begins rather like Sir George Sitwell's, on a rainy May morning in the year 273. It will put the lid on this disgusting popularity in the U.S.A.'[51] Much the same attitude was adopted in his correspondence with Peters: 'I'm glad we have shaken off Edmund Wilson at last.... "The Quest of the Empress Dowager" is one third written & very good.... The yanks will think it awful. If Littlejohn [McIntyre] gets cocky we will send it to him as a novel.'[52] *Helena*, like 'Charles Ryder's Schooldays' and the attacks on Picasso,[53] were rebuffs to those eager to welcome him into the brotherhood of 'contemporary' artists.

Waugh's reputation in America had previously ensured a small but steady sale to a few thousand devotees. Suddenly, he found himself heading the best-seller lists with a massively increased public and sheaves of 'fan-mail'. The intimacy of the latter shocked him, although not as much as he pretended. As the water-supply began to fail at Piers Court again and he had to take to filling his bath with hand-pump and hose, the composition of insulting letters to harmless American housewives and schoolgirls offered some compensation for domestic discomfort.[54] He was enjoying himself hugely. The Americans became characterized in his imagination as savages, mad children to be treated with stern sympathy. A vast new nation had opened up as a source of comic capital and Waugh felt it his duty to make it hate him.

When Elizabeth Reeve of *Life* magazine wrote suggesting 'a photographic feature dramatising character and scenes from your novels' to tie in with the Book-of-the-Month Club selection, she had assumed that Waugh would be grateful for the publicity. He was not:

> I have read your letter ... with curiosity, and re-read it with compassion. I am afraid you are unfamiliar with the laws of my country. The situation is not that my co-operation is desirable, but that my

51. Unpublished ALS, 11 January [1946], from Piers Court; private collection.
52. 16 January 1946; *Letters*, p. 219. The last sentence, might seem to suggest that Waugh did not think of *Helena* as a novel. The suggestion is rather (a) that it was a fable (i.e. a fiction based on history) and (b) that Waugh was prepared, so long as McIntyre was suitably deferential, not to count *Helena* against the contractual promise to publish his next two novels with Little, Brown. Waugh expected McIntyre to be disappointed with *Helena* after the best-selling *Brideshead*. He was not.
53. Cf. Vol. 1, p. 231.
54. Cf. *Diaries*, 6 March 1946, p. 643: 'An offensive letter from a female American Catholic. I returned it to her husband with the note: "I shall be grateful if you will use whatever disciplinary means are customary in your country to restrain your wife from writing impertinent letters to men she does not know."'

> permission is necessary.... You say, 'Without consulting you the project will be like blind flying.' I assure you it will be far more hazardous. I shall send a big blue incorruptible policeman to look you up....[55]

Not so easily deterred, *Life* set the redoubtable Mr Osborne from their London office on the trail. 'I don't know how I have given you and Mrs Reeve ... the impression that I seek popularity for my books among those who cannot read,' Waugh wrote to him. 'I have tried to give the literate all the information they need about my characters. If I have failed, I don't believe you can help me.'[56] But the tone was amiable. Waugh understood, he said, about bosses. Poor Mr Osborne was not to fret about his instructions from America. If, however, the project had to be pursued, perhaps Mr Osborne would care to visit? The invitation might have come from William Boot to Salter: 'I cannot ask you to stay as I have no cook or housemaids; there is a neighbouring inn. Have you a bicycle? I live seven miles from Stroud station. I am always here and can give you a glass of port on your arrival and plenty of dry bread. Please do not telephone.'[57] The approach to his house was presented as a quest to baffle casual enquirers.

Waugh had waited a long time to be in this position. *Brideshead*'s success had completely altered his relationship with the press. After years of being an eager, if pugnacious, client, he could now afford to be careless of such custom. Should journalists seek to trade with him, they would do it on his territory, in his time, at his prices, and he would dictate the subject. After his dry bread letter he expected to hear no more. Osborne's deferential but determined response, however, rather won Waugh's respect. Mr Osborne had a motor-car? Well, that was quite different. In fact, the journey was pleasant: 'Steer for Tetbury.... My house is approached through shabby white gates at the cross-roads. I can very well put you up for the night.'[58] 'I told the balmy fellow to apply to you for terms,' he wrote to Peters afterwards. 'Make them stiff.'[59] He did ($1,000), and Waugh reluctantly agreed to a modified proposal which became 'Fan-Fare',[60] a rare and important statement of his artistic aims. The deal was also significant for other reasons: it began Waugh's fruitful relationship with the Luce publishing empire, which took him to America and the Holy Land; it almost wrecked his friendship with Peters.

55. 31 January 1946; *Letters*, p. 221.
56. 7 February 1946; *Letters*, p. 225.
57. *Ibid.*
58. Unpublished ALS to Mr Osborne, 15 February 1946, from Piers Court; Time-Life-Fortune Collection, University of South Carolina (Special Collection).
59. 25 February 1946; *Letters*, p. 225.
60. Cf. Vol. 1, pp. 245, 320, 378, 379–80, 471, 490.

Waugh was a recalcitrant customer in 1946. Peters was required to find him evening studs and to arrange for McIntyre to send cigars. Illegal shipments of the latter, packaged as books, soon came through. While waiting, however, Waugh, suffering withdrawal symptoms, began to bark and bite, and the arrival of the cigars coincided awkwardly with a one-sided row between author and agent. Peters had never wished to pursue *Life*'s suggestion. Waugh had proceeded against advice. Now he was complaining that *Life* was breaking its contract by wishing only to pay $500 for the manuscript and $500 if it printed it. The correspondence with Osborne, Waugh insisted, made it clear that the full $1,000 was immediately due.

> Armed with these documents [he instructed Peters], and fortified if need be by counsel's opinion, you must take out a warrant for debt against him. . . . If you can in any way implicate a woman named Mrs Reeve in the legal proceedings I should be pleased. . . . It is plain that McIntyre does not understand the nature of tobacco. No first class cigar is ever wrapped in cellophane. They are shipped in bundles in a cabinet. . . .[61]

Peters was not used to being addressed in this tone; nor did he require instruction about tobacco or the proper conduct of business. But he had a long fuse where good customers were concerned and he was a masterly diplomat. Rather than retaliate, he sent Waugh some of his own *Romeo y Julietas*. 'Thank you very much for the cigars,' Waugh replied, disconcerted but refusing to retract. '. . . I cannot understand your treatment of Osborne . . . you seem to have been bamboozled by Yankee impudence.'[62] As in his dealings with Korda in 1937, Waugh had become obsessed by the notion that he was being cheated and in this mood was blind with fury. Peters poured oil. Waugh wrote to Osborne: 'Mr. Peters' gullibility and pusillanimity in the matter nearly led to the severance of a long connection. I go abroad at the end of this week. I hope very much that you will visit us again in the summer. . . .'[63] It was as near as he ever came to an apology.[64]

*

61. Unpublished ALS to A. D. Peters, 19 March [1946], from Piers Court; *Catalogue* E473, p. 147.
62. Unpublished ALS to A. D. Peters, 22 March 1946, from White's; *Catalogue* E474, p. 147.
63. Unpublished ALS to Mr Osborne, 27 March 1946, from Piers Court; Time-Life-Fortune Collection.
64. Waugh did not forget an imagined hurt. Thanking *Life* for sending an off-print of 'Fan-Fare' with the ensuing correspondence, he continued his assault: '. . . It is a sad thing that these simple, illiterate immigrants should have been taught to read. They clearly do not understand a word of the language. Surely I recognize the familiar poison pen of [Elizabeth] Reeves in the phrase "antediluvian relic of the fascist mentality"? . . .' (unpublished ALS, nd [May? 1946], from Piers Court; Time-Life-Fortune Collection).

Waugh's foreign destinations – Nuremberg and Paris – in many ways epitomized the division in his mental life. A casual meeting with Mervyn Griffith-Jones in White's had produced an invitation to the war crimes trials and Waugh grasped it as a rare opportunity to escape the 'accursed soil'[65] of England. It seems that he was interested in writing something which would include the Nuremberg experience, perhaps a new kind of travel book – a post-war, melancholic tour of dead Europe? – to contrast with the exuberance of *When the Going Was Good*. Nothing came of it. Waugh flew out by troop carrier and spent two days as a VIP sitting in the front row of the gallery. The sense of righteous purpose which inspired the British lawyers seemed to him absurd. Nuremberg was to Waugh neither glorious retribution nor the 'injudicious travesty'[66] some people thought it at home. It was simply an irrelevant 'surrealist spectacle'[67] and the images that sprang to mind in that luxurious courthouse amid 'a waste of corpse-scented rubble'[68] were again those of the schoolroom:

> Ribbentrop was like a seedy schoolmaster being ragged, who knows he doesn't know the lesson, knows that the boys know, knows he has done the sum wrong on the blackboard, knows he has nothing to hope for at the school, but still hopes . . . he can hold out to the end of term to get a 'character' for another post. He lied instinctively and without apparent motive.[69]

Waugh left, disappointed, and took an American military 'plane to Paris.

His invitation was to the Embassy, 'a house of dazzling beauty, Borghese decorations in a Louis XV structure, brilliantly rearranged by Diana.'[70] The Coopers, outdoing the French for *chic*, had become the focus of fashionable life in the city. Waugh detected ominous signs: Auberon Herbert was another guest; Quennell arrived that night. But Lady Diana, at her most charming, maintained the peace and, after filling Waugh with champagne, even persuaded him to be pleasant to his brother-in-law: 'I pursued Auberon downstairs . . . and told him I liked him. He believed it.'[71] Maurice Bowra was there, and Nancy. All this should have ensured pleasure. Waugh, however, disliked being one of many. He preferred to be the focus of

65. ALS to Lady Diana Cooper, 13 December [1946?], from Piers Court; BL; *MWMS*, p. 90.
66. *Diaries*, 31 March 1946, p. 645.
67. [April 1946]; *Letters*, p. 226.
68. *Diaries*, 31 March 1946, p. 645.
69. *Ibid.*, 1–2 April 1946, p. 646. 'I shall not after all be writing about Nuremberg,' he told Peters. 'Would [?] you please inform Duckworth & Little, Brown' (unpublished APCI, nd [pm 11 April 1946], from Piers Court; *Catalogue* E477, p. 147). Waugh generously passed over his impressions to Randolph Churchill for his American gossip column, drawing on the diary and adding considerably to it, asking Churchill not to quote. Cf. *Letters*, p. 226.
70. *Ibid.*, [3 April 1946], p. 646.
71. *Ibid.*, p. 647.

attention and to have his women friends to himself. When Nancy took him to Mme Bouquet's salon, he felt 'a fish out of water'.[72]

The French translation of *Brideshead*, soon to be published, had carried its reputation before it. Waugh, flattered as an English Mauriac, was an unhappy object of worship, stranded between languages. And when Julian Huxley (the absent Brains Trustee in 1944) turned up, any fragile pleasure in the visit evaporated. 'It was very agreeable to see Huxley, who is head of all education and science for Uno, a crypto-Communist who regards himself as a world-force, treated on all sides as a zoo-keeper, by myself from malice, by everyone else in genuine goodwill.'[73] Laden with cheese, wine, scent, toys and an extraordinary hat sporting stuffed doves,[74] Waugh left France early and gratefully. 'You were hell to go like that,' Nancy wrote to him:

> everybody was furious it was such fun with you here. Marie Louise does a wonderful turn on your appearance at her house. 'He came in & just sat down & told us about Nuremberg & there we were at Nuremberg – s'était génial.' ... You can't imagine what a lion you are....[75]

'Paris was heaven ...,' he replied disingenuously.[76]

He was turning his back on Europe. Seven months earlier, Woodruff, requiring more corrections, had accurately characterized Waugh's mood:

> It would be a pity to have the N[ew] S[tatesman] and co. saying 'intelligent converts to Rome like E. W. have frankly and publicly despaired of their [?] religion having any future in Europe' when we are in fact encouraging central European Christians [?] not to despair but to keep up their resistance as far as they can....[77]

The *Tablet* had changed after the war from being a predominantly literary and theological magazine to one packed with dry political discourse. This was Woodruff's way of encouraging the eastern European Christians. Waugh found it indigestible and, discovering his friend in the Beefsteak one day 'like a dying orang-outang',[78] tackled him on the subject and invited him to stay at Piers Court. There the attack was renewed. A magazine,

72. *Ibid.*
73. *Ibid.*, p. 648.
74. The hat was for Nancy's sister 'Debo', now Duchess of Devonshire. Waugh selected it, tried it on and paid for it with a loan from Nancy, foreign currency being difficult to obtain.
75. Unpublished ALS from Nancy Mitford, 13 April 1946, from Hôtel de Bourgogne, Paris VII; BL.
76. [18 April] 1946; *Letters*, p. 227.
77. Unpublished ALS from Douglas Woodruff, 10 November 1945, from 199 Park West, W2; BL. Woodruff was thinking of printing the text of Waugh's speech to the university societies (see p. 156 above), but ultimately decided against it.
78. *Diaries*, 26 April 1946, p. 649.

Waugh insisted, was only of use in so far as it was readable. Woodruff stuck to his guns and, although Waugh's loyalty to the *Tablet* was deep, the disagreement explains his eagerness to help Fr Caraman launch the remodelled *Month* two years later.

Back at his desk, Waugh had several projects on hand. Saccone and Speed, the wine merchants for whom Prince Vsevolode worked, had offered payment in kind for a history of their firm. The work was dreary but the terms generous (one dozen bottles of champagne per thousand words), and this was the kind of job Waugh now sought in order to evade income tax. As he plodded through *Wine in Peace and War*, however, *Helena* remained his preoccupation. His original estimate for completion had been May. Now (April) he hoped to finish by the autumn and he was writing to private presses:

> ... Only about three facts are known ... about this lady. The work is therefore primarily one of imagination.... I have in mind a small folio with three illustrations and decorated openings ... and a number of decorated initials in the text, not more than one thousand copies at four or five guineas each. The profits accruing to myself are of secondary interest; my first interest is to see the book beautifully produced, for it is one over which I am taking great pains.[79]

At the same time, in Swiftian mood, he wrote 'What To Do with the Upper Classes: A Modest Proposal' and sent it to the *New Statesman* in the hope of annoying its editor, Kingsley Martin.

In all his writings at this stage, Waugh was obsessed by craftsmanship and by the relationship between language and class. Reviewing Orwell's essays, 'a work of absorbing interest', he discovered an approach diametrically opposed to his own. They represented, he said, 'at its best the new humanism of the common man' whose critical practice attacked hierarchical classification.[80] While respecting Orwell's talents,[81] however,

79. Unpublished ALS to Christopher Sandford at the Golden Cockerel Press, 18 April 1946, from Piers Court; Bodleian Library. The three illustrations were to mark the three sections. When Waugh sent the first section on 7 May his concept of the book had changed. It was to be in four sections: three more books of the same length named 'Ilium', 'Rome' and 'Jerusalem'.

80. 'A New Humanism', *Tablet*, 6 April 1946, 176; review of George Orwell, *Critical Essays* (Secker & Warburg, 1946); *EAR*, pp. 304–7: 'It is a habit of mind rather than a school. Mr. Edmund Wilson ... is an exponent.... The essential difference between this and previous critical habits is the abandonment of the hierarchic principle. It has hitherto been assumed that works of art exist in an order of precedence with the great masters Virgil, Dante and their fellows, at the top and the popular novel of the season at the bottom. The critic's task has been primarily to preserve and adjust this classification.... This, I believe, is still the critic's essential task....'

81. Cf. *Diaries*, 31 August 1945, p. 633: 'I read and greatly enjoyed Orwell's *Animal Farm*.' Waugh wrote to him the day before, thanking him for sending a copy 'of your ingenious & delightful allegory' (*Letters*, p. 211). Orwell also sent *Nineteen Eighty-Four* and received another appreciative letter (17 July 1949) in which Waugh expressed admiration for the 'ingenuity' of the writing but: '... I think your metaphysics are wrong. You deny the soul's existence (at least Winston does) and

Waugh envisaged only the disintegration of literary language if the principles of these essays were generally applied.

Waugh's position was straightforward: the English language was a refined and delicate instrument whose purity was preserved by 'a high civilized society, where it [is] spoken and given its authority and sanctity' and by 'a thin line of devotees', artists 'who [make] its refinement and adornment their life's work.'[82] It followed that this symbiosis required a social hierarchy for language to prosper; the refinement of language was thus in danger of extinction from the decay of a stratified society.[83] T. S. Eliot would have agreed. When discussing books, Waugh put the conservative case astutely.

'A Modest Proposal' mockingly posits a future for the aristocracy in the social engineering of 'what was once Europe': the creation of 'native reservations' for them where they 'could support life by agriculture and the arts, subsidized by the fees from tourist-visas paid by those who visit them.'[84] But beneath the mockery he was taking his argument about language and class a stage further. Waugh had always been fascinated by any complex, internally coherent social system with its own language and etiquette. (A good novel, in his view, reflected this and he admired Hemingway's slang as much as the parochial niceties of Jane Austen or Trollope.) Some systems, he believed, were intrinsically more 'valuable' than others and, with his back to the wall, Waugh would defend the 'best' against threat from others. The suggestion is, however, that in a well-regulated (hierarchical) society, the fascination of all linguistic and cultural systems is released and shared. Class structure is seen to be exactly analogous to linguistic complexity; it is 'elaborate and flexible', 'the growth of centuries',[85] a beautiful thing, eternally fascinating. Waugh's essay is a lament for his being forced to relinquish his pleasure in other tribal dialects and customs. Oddly it is an intensely class-conscious attack on class-consciousness, a phenomenon he believes to have been introduced by egalitarian politics. Before this pernicious development had corrupted the intricate social balance of European life, the poor man, Waugh seems to suggest, sat happily at the rich man's gate and gazed reverentially at the

can only contrast matter with reason & will. It is now apparent that matter can control reason and will in certain conditions. So you are left with nothing but matter. But the predicament is not entirely new. We have always accepted the existence of insanity, where reason & will fail to operate, but no one denied that lunatics had souls' (*Letters*, p. 302).

82. 'Fan-Fare', *Life*, 8 April 1946; *op. cit.*
83. 'The Writing of English', *Tablet*, 3 June 1943, 8–9; review of Robert Graves and Alan Hodge, *The Reader Over Your Shoulder: A Handbook for Writers of English Prose* (Cape, 1943); *EAR*, pp. 275–7.
84. 'What To Do with the Upper Classes: A Modest Proposal', *Town and Country*, 1 September 1946, 41, 260–1; *EAR*, pp. 312–16. Waugh was apparently successful in annoying Kingsley Martin and, indeed, all the British editors that Peters first tried. Matson eventually sold it in America. The joke about 'tourist-visas' became reality with the assistance of the National Trust and the lions of Longleat.
85. *Ibid.*, p. 312.

intricacies of its wrought iron. Consciousness of class was an entirely different thing from class-consciousness. The latter derived from envy. Knowing one's place was the prerequisite of a stable society.

In his memoirs, Anthony Powell has said that Waugh really believed in stereotypes: the poor scholar etc. Certainly he always wanted to believe in them and his art extended this imaginary world into a dream of British upper-class life. There is a hint in 'A Modest Proposal', though, that the playfulness which had originally inspired his fantasies has run out of control. To preserve the internal consistency of his dream, he not only needs to manufacture historical and political myths but also to pretend that they are fact. And at this point, the detachment of his critical writing disappears, to be replaced by a scarcely disguised persecution mania. One senses that, like Ribbentrop, he 'knows he doesn't know the lesson' but dare not admit it. The fiction Waugh had created of the world now had its own momentum. To break free from it into common sense would have involved an intolerable loss of face. To remain inside his fantasy, knowing it to be such, building its walls slowly and painfully, was his only option. And that way, he knew, lay madness.

'God I wish I had some neighbours I could bear to speak to,' he wrote to Nancy.[86] Walled up in Piers Court, he was dying of inanition. Beyond his estate the European civilization which had meant so much to his Romanitas was largely inaccessible and, he believed, collapsing into chaos. During March he had received the first of his letters from Hilde Bertram, a Catholic refugee he had tried to help in Yugoslavia. She had been shunted through a chain of prisons to a Displaced Persons' camp in Austria. Her husband had 'disappeared'; she had an eight-year-old daughter and another female relative to support from menial work. Her letters arrived irregularly from 1946 to 1950, thanking Captain Waugh for his concern and relating a fearful catalogue of persecution and frustration. In 1947 she reminded him of 'what you told me on departing, in this world decent people can only look for a few other friends with the same mentality and then hide. . . .'[87] But isolation Waugh found tedious. 'Though I make-believe to be detached from the world', he had noted at Christmas, 'I find a day without post or newspapers strangely flat, and look forward to tomorrow's awakening, with Ellwood laying the papers by my pillow.'[88]

Waugh read *The Times* each day with growing apprehension. 'A Modest Proposal' had been an attack on the Labour Government. As the months

86. Unpublished ALS to Nancy Mitford, 11 May 1946, from Piers Court; private collection.
87. Unpublished ALS from Hilde Bertram, 9 July 1947, from Konstanz am Bodensee, Baden 46, Markgrafeusts 39, Zone Français; BL.
88. *Diaries*, 26 December 1945, p. 640.

passed, he came to see it as an army of occupation. The 8th of June was Victory Day:

> [Attlee] is driving round in a carriage with Churchill, behind the Royal Family, at the head of a procession of Brazilians, Mexicans, Egyptians, Naafi waitresses and assorted negroes claiming that they won the war. . . . I hope it rained hard and soaked Attlee. None of the 'Communist' countries sent representatives.[89]

When Woodruff offered Waugh a free trip to Spain, he jumped at it. Anything to smash the monotony.

*

The year 1946 marked the fourth centenary of the birth of Francisco de Vittoria, founder of International Law. Spain, having kept out of the war and emerged from it with both a record of support for Fascism and a Fascist leader, wished to placate the liberal democracies. One way of doing this was with a 'conference', particularly one celebrating so liberal and democratic an institution as International Law. The *Tablet* was approached in its capacity as a leading Catholic journal (de Vittoria had been a Dominican friar), and two tickets were offered for the paper's correspondents.

Neither Woodruff nor Waugh had the slightest interest in de Vittoria, and Woodruff made it clear that this was to be a jaunt for the sunshine and the wine. True, neither knew quite what to expect but, as they were required to do little but attend banquets, it promised well. They were met in Madrid, as planned, by Catholic students and taken to their hotel. There they discovered that the Congress had been delayed for five days and, to amuse the delegates in the meantime, a tour of Spanish cities had been arranged. To Woodruff, this was a bonus; Waugh thought otherwise.[90]

From the minute they arrived at Croydon airport, Waugh had been on his guard. For him, air travel had long since crashed into his cesspit of modern inventions designed to embarrass and intrude. The checking of documentation (a great deal of it in those days), currency and baggage made him impatient; the VIP lounge made him laugh; being strapped into a confined space with people he did not know made him pompous. Professor Brierley of All Souls, Oxford, had travelled out with them. He had been met by 'suave lawyers' and taken by car to the Palace Hotel. Waugh and Woodruff had been conducted by their students to the 'low-class' Hotel Nacional. Then had come the news of the five-day hiatus and 'it . . . became

89. *Ibid.*, 8 June 1946, p. 650.

90. Additional information about this trip derives from an interview with Douglas Woodruff, 16 June 1976. 'I was annoyed with [Christopher Sykes]', he said, 'because [when he described] that outing to Spain I took Evelyn on, he never checked with me. He just took Evelyn's very over-written account [in the *Diaries*].'

plain that the Francisco de Vittoria Association was a luxury tour for international jurists in which Douglas and I were not included.'[91]

Woodruff, of course, had never pretended that they *were* members of the Association, merely that they were to attend a congress organized by the Association. As hangers-on, it was not surprising that they should have been omitted from the list for the coach tour. Despite this, Waugh became convinced that there were two conferences and that they were attached to the wrong one. It was plain to Waugh that his friend had been duped and that the celebrations were a sham. If they were honoured guests, he wanted to know, why were they not the centre of attention? How was it that these dreary academics should be accorded better treatment than an eminent novelist? Woodruff struggled to maintain his equanimity and smiled broadly at his hosts. After a few polite enquiries, no objection was raised to these curious Englishmen joining the tour.

'Instead of the pious & peaceful retreat at Salamanca which I expected', Waugh wrote to Laura, 'I find myself whirled round Castile to a series of mayoral receptions conducted tours & endless drives in a decrepit charabanc. The Pax Romana Congress is postponed ... so Douglas & I have gatecrashed a quite different party of international jurists.'[92] At every stage he was determined to find fault: the coach was undignified and over-heated; meals were supplied irregularly; the company consisted predominantly of ancient bores; the mayoral hosts were 'young shits, not worthy burgesses'.[93] But it amused him to be addressed as 'Professor' and to disappoint expectations. 'Conversation with bearded Spanish Jesuit,' he wrote home. ' "Vous êtes professeur de Oxford M. Waugh?" "Au contraire, mon père, j'étais chassé de l'Université sans degré et à cause de ça, suis devenu romancier." "Mon professeur je trouve que vous tenez [?] les plaisanteries [?]." (Collapse of middle-aged party).'[94]

Woodruff was annoyed. He had provided this outing as a treat, only to be rewarded by complaints about mismanagement:

> Waugh was always very conscious that he was there on false pretences, that he wasn't a Professor of International Law and therefore he was always looking out for subtle social discrimination against people like himself. And the only thing was that, very naturally, the Spanish lawyers paid more attention to a genuine Professor like Professor Brierley ... than to a literary man of whom they had presumably never heard. But otherwise, officially, we were very well treated.[95]

91. *Diaries*, 15 June 1946, p. 653.
92. 18 June 1946, from Hotel Parador, Condestable, Burgos; *Letters*, p. 231.
93. *Diaries*, 16 June 1946, pp. 653–4.
94. Unpublished APCI to Laura Waugh, nd [pm 25 June? 1946], from Salamanca; BL.
95. Interview with Douglas Woodruff, *op. cit.*

This was perfectly reasonable – but not to Waugh. The discriminating man should discriminate. Surely something awful must have happened to excite Waugh's disgust?

> Nothing very bad [said Woodruff] except, at the very end ... all the people who had been engaged to look after the guests disappeared and, rather like in 'Cinderella', the coach and everything had gone and you were left to make your way out of the country. . . . I knew the Foreign Minister quite well and we had no trouble in getting our visas and places on the 'plane. But for a moment it crossed Evelyn's mind how easily we might have been stranded. So that's what he makes happen in *Scott-King*. . . .[96]

The delay in departure was all Waugh needed to fire his imagination. There was, he felt, a story in this about everything that had troubled him since leaving the army, and *Scott-King's Modern Europe*[97] was to be his revenge on his hosts.

*

Waugh returned in mischievous mood to discover that, two days before, Laura had produced a second son, their fifth child, James. Although it had been an agonizing birth and she was still ill, her husband stayed away. He refused at first even to telephone on the grounds that he could not speak to her. Instead, he telegraphed and wrote affectionately, promising presents – rubber corsets, surgical stockings, a hot-water bottle, two bottles of sherry, a pair of Toledo scissors – and four days later, after ordering a couple of new suits, took a leisurely taxi to Somerset: 'I hope you will appreciate this great act of self-sacrifice – heat-wave, week end travel.'[98]

It was another miserable time for Laura. Shortly afterwards Waugh returned to London and a storm destroyed her corn and hay. The omens, it seems, were not good at James's birth. He fitted uneasily into this extraordinary family. Years later, Woodruff visited his godson at prep-school and witnessed a conversation between the boy and the headmaster's wife: 'What is it like being the son of a famous author?' 'Mrs Dix,' James replied solemnly, 'you have no conception. It is utter hell.'[99]

Waugh was more concerned with his own pleasure than baby or wife. Summer signalled the London 'season' and, as he now felt too old for balls

96. *Ibid.*
97. *Scott-King's Modern Europe* (Chapman & Hall, 1947); first printed in abridged form in *Cornhill*, 162 (Summer 1947), 321–64, and as 'A Sojourn in Neutralia', *Hearst's International/Cosmopolitan*, 123 (November 1947), 67–70, 73–4, 76, 78, 80, 83–4, 86, 88.
98. Unpublished ALS to Laura Waugh, 4 July 1946, from White's; BL. Laura had ordered the surgical appliances herself, and Prince Vsevolode sent the sherry to the wrong address. The only vaguely interesting item was the scissors. Waugh gave them to his mother.
99. Interview with Douglas Woodruff, *op. cit.*

and parties, he decided to set up his own court. A suite of rooms was booked at the Hyde Park Hotel and there, for three weeks, he gave a series of elaborate dinners and drank his way through several dozen of the bottles of champagne received for his wine book. This private season became his practice for some years. The guest list for luncheon would alternate: one day his friends; the next, those to whom he felt he owed hospitality. It was an efficient means of clearing social obligations, keeping himself in the public eye and having a damn good time. Laura rarely joined him.

Waugh professed not to care that, on average, he found one new friend a year and lost two. But this obsessively private, offensive man loved nothing more than to please and he feared that the lovable clown in his nature was dying beneath the weight of his melancholy. In his suite, in control, host not guest, he could relax and indulge in his old demonic practice of encouraging others to excess.

No new friends emerged in 1946. Grateful as he was for the loyal appearance of old chums, there was a morbid predictability about these occasions. Sykes was a regular attender. He had all the appropriate qualifications: high birth, an irreverent wit, literary talent, a good war record and ultra-conservative Catholicism. He was well able to withstand bullying and was in his own right a member of that eccentric literary élite for whom Waugh had become The Master.[100] Sykes was a friend of Graham Greene and of T. S. Eliot. His acquaintance bridged the same disparate worlds Waugh had known: Oxford, White's, the Commandos and the Catholic intelligentsia. As an editor and later as a BBC executive, he was in touch with many writers Waugh snubbed – Quennell and Spender, for example – and, like Nancy, was a fund of malicious gossip about them. Only Waugh and Bowra could out-do Sykes in the Beggar Your Neighbour game they all played and Waugh enjoyed his aggressive snobbery. But there was something 'jaggering' about Sykes which Waugh seems to have found wearisome. Like Connolly, Sykes collected the friendship of more talented men and acted up to them. 'My last day in London & goodness I am pleased,' Waugh told Nancy. '. . . It is six weeks now I have been sitting about in hotels & clubs bored bored bored.'[101]

To jerk himself from lassitude he had fired a second barrel at Connolly[102] and for once hit the bulls-eye in political discussion. 'Palinurus in Never-Never Land Or, The Horizon Blue-Print of Chaos'[103] was a withering response to the Editor's 'Comment' in the June issue. *Horizon*, Waugh

100. Nancy Mitford, Greene, Connolly, Bowra, Betjeman, Lord Berners, the Sitwells and Henry Yorke.
101. 7 August [1946], from Hyde Park Hotel; *Letters*, p. 232.
102. Waugh had already reviewed *The Unquiet Grave* mockingly: 'A Pilot All At Sea', *Tablet*, 10 November 1945, 255–6; *EAR*, pp. 281–2.
103. *Tablet*, 27 July 1946, 46; *EAR*, pp. 309–12.

says, had been a glorious thing during the war. It 'came to represent to countless soldiers the world of culture which they had left. . . . Somewhere, we believed, in the minds of the editors of *Horizon* there existed a free and wise society of which we were all members.'[104] *Post-bellum*, Waugh implied, Connolly had lost his reason. First he had exhorted his readers to vote Socialist. Now he was offering a ten-point plan suggesting the basic objectives of a civilized state. 'It is a somewhat baffling document,' Waugh says, with the kindly euphemism of an executioner.

Connolly's points of liberal doctrine were not related by a political thesis; Waugh related them. The result was hilarious and stung Connolly badly. For some time he refused to read it, although baited by mutual acquaintances with its existence. But Waugh would not let the matter rest. If they were to remain friends, Connolly had to respond, yet to respond was to acknowledge humiliation. Waugh, an expert judge of these fine gradations of pain, hounded his quarry, perhaps irritated by the competition from Connolly's high reputation in America.[105] Ultimately, the critic, preferring friendship to dignity, was rewarded by retaining Waugh as a contributor to *Horizon*.[106]

It was not spite, however, that drove Waugh to such attacks. He was conducting a crusade in which he was prepared to cast himself into isolation by sacrificing social for religious loyalties. 'I suppose you are right in setting morality above friendship and art,' Lord Berners had written after Waugh had savaged *The Unquiet Grave*.[107] And this, for someone as profoundly loyal as Waugh, was not an easy course. But it had its consolations. Grateful letters were beginning to arrive thanking him for the salutary religious influence of his books. During April, Elizabeth Pakenham had been received into the Church. *Campion*, she told him, 'gave one a really warm feeling for the Church & her heroes, comparable ... in strength to my loyal conviction that she was right. Frank & I are both so pleased that you are Catherine's Godfather. . . .'[108] If Waugh's circle of pagan acquaintance was contracting, his group of friends within the Household grew steadily. A

104. *Ibid.*, p. 309.
105. Cf. unpublished ALS to A. D. Peters, 29 July [1946], from Hyde Park Hotel; *Catalogue* E495, p. 150: 'Edmund Wilson proclaimed Connolly the greatest English writer and "The Unquiet Grave" the greatest book published for 20 years. Since then some Yanks have taken him seriously. Do you think one of their high-brow papers would care to publish this debunking ["A Pilot All At Sea"]? ... Anyway I would like the review to appear in USA (even cheaply). . . .'
106. Cf. unpublished ALS from Cyril Connolly, nd [1946], from *Horizon*, 2 Lansdowne Terrace, Guildford Street, WC1; BL: 'I have found & read the Tablet article which I think is very good & most reasonable – I would certainly have printed it in Horizon as a reply. . . . The reason I minded your reviews so much is that I thought you fought unfairly i.e. pretending not to know who Palinurus was so as to insult me. . . .'
107. Unpublished ALS from Lord Berners, 27 December 1945, from Faringdon House, Berks.; BL.
108. Unpublished ALS, 24 April 1946, from 8 Chadlington Road, Oxford; BL. Waugh had sent her daughter, Catherine, a golden spoon, fork and knife as a christening present.

recurrent theological motif appears in his letters and journalism: his belief in 'an all-wise God who had a particular task for each individual soul, which the individual is free to accept or decline at will, and whose ultimate destiny is determined by his response to God's vocation. . . .'[109]

Helena was to be Waugh's grand study of vocation. His new sense of the seriousness of his work centred on the idea that he had been 'called' to do it, and he prized those letters which demonstrated its direct influence. Something approaching missionary zeal possessed him and, while he never proselytized, he would explain. He watched his non-Catholic friends cautiously. If he saw a fissure in their beliefs through which the Grace of God might enter, he would pounce. A malicious rumour ran round literary London that the Church had set its prominent members 'conversion targets'. Waugh's was supposed to be Connolly, and Boots (as Connolly was nicknamed) was shaking in his shoes. But he need not have worried. Waugh thought him beyond redemption.

*

That autumn, loyalty was a problem on all fronts. Having resumed his seat on the board of Chapman & Hall in 1945, Waugh had turned up once a month to sit there bored and largely useless. Chapman & Hall, under J. L. Bale's influence, had become predominantly concerned (as it still is) with technical and scientific books. The firm had been bought up by Methuen and, while continuing to publish under its own imprint, was increasingly becoming the technical division of the parent firm. Even the premises had moved from the rambling Henrietta Street terrace to Methuen's block in Essex Street. The whole development of the firm had made Waugh uncomfortable.

During the war, an affable and efficient fellow, F. B. Walker, had taken over many jobs including that of Production Manager of the General side. After Gatfield's sudden death in 1944, Walker had effectively run this department although he was not on the board. It was he who had seen *Put Out More Flags*, *Work Suspended* and *Brideshead* through the press and he and Waugh had a comfortable professional relationship. Waugh gave him inscribed copies of his books, often of the special editions, and Walker was the only person left at Chapman & Hall for whom he felt the slightest sympathy. He would drop in to Walker's office after meetings, usually in glum mood. Asked how it had gone on one occasion, he sighed: 'Oh figures, figures, figures.'[110] Business details were beyond him and, therefore, beneath him.

109. 'Palinurus in Never-Never Land. . .', *op. cit.*
110. Interview with F. B. Walker, 9 February 1984.

Waugh was on the board as literary adviser for the General publishing. Very few manuscripts were sent to him, but he could, at least, use his influence to get his friends' work into print. To the end of his life, Moray McLaren remained grateful for Waugh's efforts on his behalf. McLaren had emerged from a 'Judas-like job' in Poland in 1945. 'I had to run between [the Poles] and my own bosses at the F. O. until the final betrayal,' he had written to Waugh. 'At the end I drank a good deal....'[111] His marriage broke up, his health broke down and he lost his Catholic faith. Wanting to begin a new life as a writer, he had sent his manuscript to Waugh, who had generously offered detailed technical advice and was fascinated by the book's autobiographical description of 'demoniac possession' and exorcism.[112] In these small ways he could be loyal. For the firm itself, though, he felt no warmth and he was looking for an excuse to desert it.

The opportunity for this had arisen at the August board meeting. Waugh had been shocked to see in the chair an 'entirely new figure ... fat with shiny plebeian face and crescent-shaped glasses....'[113] This was Nutcombe Hume of Charterhouse (who had bought Methuen). The 'Appointment to the board of Mr McDougall' was on the agenda and it was clear that his acceptance as Director of the General side was a foregone conclusion. Waugh had not been consulted. Methuen had arranged this, bringing in McDougall from Chatto. Waugh had wanted Walker. Was Walker's loyal record to be ignored? Yes, it was, and Waugh left the meeting enraged, having registered his disapproval. A month later he resigned and sought out a trade paper interested in publishing the inside story.[114] He also wanted to remove his custom to a 'respectable' firm like Macmillan's. Hume was clearly angered by Waugh's attitude.[115] Chapman & Hall only kept Waugh through McDougall's assiduous diplomacy. Under his patronage, the novelist was treated with regal courtesy and, gradually, Waugh softened. McDougall had a powerful intellect. He was a classical scholar and an indifferent businessman, sympathetically inclined towards the literary book, often backing failures. Waugh found this a refreshing change from Gatfield's stony pragmatism. Ultimately, 'Jack' became one of his closer friends.

It did not, however, escape Waugh's attention that Chapman & Hall was glad to be relieved of his managerial influence, and this saddened him. With his departure, he relinquished his last attempt to be a man of affairs, and

111. Unpublished ALS from Moray McLaren, 15 July 1945, from Murray House, Perth, Scotland; BL.
112. Cf. ALS to Lady Diana Cooper, 3 January 1946, *op. cit.*; *MWMS*, p. 83.
113. *Diaries*, 24 August 1946, p. 658.
114. Cf. 'Mr. Evelyn Waugh Resigns Chapman and Hall Directorship', *The Bookseller* (London), 12 September 1945, 582.
115. Cf. unpublished TLS, 6 September 1946, from the Chairman [Nutcombe Hume], Chapman & Hall, 37 Essex Street, WC2; BL.

turned instead to what he did best. 'I am writing a bright little short story and a would-be bright long one,' he told Peters.[116] As he wrote, his mind was 'aflame with Ireland'[117] and with the spectre of a desecrated Europe.

> Why do I contemplate so grave a step as abjuring the realm and changing the whole prospects of my children? What is there to worry me here in Stinchcombe? I have a beautiful house furnished exactly to my taste; servants enough, wine in the cellar. . . . Apart from taxation and rationing, government interference is negligible. . . . Why am I not at ease? Why is it I smell all the time wherever I turn the reek of the Displaced Persons' Camp?[118]

Helena was again put to one side. The experience of Spain; the stories of Hilde Bertram and Moray McLaren, the continuing battle against Connolly and Socialism, the disgust at Chapman & Hall's technical publishing and its betrayal of Walker all needed to find expression before the hatred died. The short story, 'Tactical Exercise',[119] was his last in the pre-war vein. It is a study of hatred, perhaps as a corrective to the author's besetting sin. The longer piece was *Scott-King's Modern Europe*.

In 'Tactical Exercise' the hero, John Verney, is a villain who has conceived and nurtured a loathing for his wife. He plots her death only to be murdered by her. Verney had ignored the fact that his own hatred would breed counter-violence. In contrast, Waugh was acutely aware of the dangers of his own ill-temper and, although the story is a fantasy, the description of Verney's frame of mind is clearly based on its author's: '. . . the intermittent, invisible sheet-lightning of hate which flashed and flickered deep inside him at every obstruction or reverse.'[120] *Scott-King* offers a more benign vision of a violent world; its ascetic, cenobitic central figure came closer to the resignation Waugh was struggling to achieve.

Scott-King is a solitary, middle-aged bachelor teaching Classics in a respectable but inelegant public school. Like Chapman & Hall, the school has increasingly made concessions to the modern world and promoted technical and scientific subjects. The traditional education of the English gentleman has been subverted and Scott-King marginalized in the school until he has become something of a joke to the boys. 'But [he] did not repine. On the contrary he found a peculiar relish in contemplating the victories of barbarism. . . .'[121]

116. Unpublished ALS, 1 October 1946, from Piers Court; *Catalogue* E508, p. 152.
117. *Diaries*, 10 November 1946, p. 662.
118. *Ibid.*
119. 'Tactical Exercise', *Strand* (March 1947), 45–54; in USA as 'The Wish', *Good Housekeeping* (March 1947), 22–3, 319–26, 328; Harmondsworth, Penguin Books, 1962, pp. 193–247.
120. 'Tactical Exercise', *Strand, op. cit.*, 45.
121. *Scott-King, op. cit.*; reprinted in *Work Suspended and Other Stories, op. cit.*, pp. 193–247.

Sykes believes that this hero has nothing in common with Waugh and, at first glance, one is inclined to agree. Scott-King 'was of a type, unknown in the New World, but quite common in Europe, which is fascinated by obscurity and failure. "Dim" is the epithet for Scott-King and it was a fellow-feeling, a blood-brotherhood in dimness, which first drew him to study the works of . . . Bellorius.'[122] No one could describe Waugh as 'dim' or as cultivating obscurity. A radical change in his life was nevertheless taking place. Scott-King is sympathetically characterized and Waugh could now only enjoy glittering in Metroland for brief periods. Perhaps as a result of this, his hero represents a kind of intellectual decency: scholarship, loyalty, and the strength to stand alone in the fight for civilization.

In fact, a kind of dimness had always fascinated Waugh. From Paul Pennyfeather to the lugubrious and alienated Ryder, Waugh had continuously written of those molested by power-brokers. Ryder's fierce snobbery had articulated that of the novelist. Scott-King's gentle determination derived from that other side of Waugh's personality: the deeply religious, contemplative man; the craftsman fascinated by linguistic discipline and by eccentricity, tricks of speech, odd habits; the loyal friend; the amateur scholar. The 'voice' behind *Brideshead* which pretends to cool reflection is really that of the testy colonel; here, it is that of the eccentric don. The tone is quizzical, amused, parodying the dear-readering of nineteenth-century fiction. A donnish narrator leads us through the maze: 'Something must be known of this history if we are to follow Scott-King with understanding. Let us eschew detail and observe. . . .'

The history we learn is that of Neutralia – a country undisguisedly modelled on Spain, although Waugh tried to throw readers off the scent (and towards Yugoslavia) by making it a former kingdom of the Habsburg Empire run by an autocratic marshal. Scott-King is invited there as an expert on Bellorius, a minor seventeenth-century poet who left to posterity 1,500 lines of Latin hexameters. 'The subject', says the narrator, 'was irredeemably tedious – a visit to an imaginary island of the New World where in primitive simplicity, untainted by tyranny or dogma, there subsisted a virtuous, chaste and reasonable community.'[123] Bellorius had lived, in happier days, under the rule of the Habsburgs; by 1946 his native town has been incorporated into Neutralia, whose government has decided to celebrate the quartercentenary of the poet's death.

For Scott-King, attendance at the celebrations is a pilgrimage; for the other delegates it is a jaunt; for the Neutralian government it is a confidence trick to gain international prestige. Scott-King is photographed as a British representative laying a wreath on the vaguely described 'National Monu-

122. *Ibid.*, pp. 195–6.
123. *Ibid.*, 196.

ment'. When it is discovered that this commemorates the execution ten years earlier of fifty leaders of the now dominant party, the other delegates leave. Scott-King, faithful to Bellorius, remains as the sole representative at the unveiling of the poet's statue. He gives a lengthy peroration in Latin, praising Bellorius's vision of a united world. The unveiling, however, reveals a travesty figure, a decaying nineteenth-century sculpture, rescued from the mason's yard. The government changes. Scott-King cannot leave the country. Eventually he escapes, disguised as an Ursuline nun, through the agency of a rapacious 'underground' organization. But he is not sent to England. One of his former pupils, Lockwood, eventually discovers him in a Jewish illicit immigrants' camp in Palestine.

At home again, Scott-King is approached by the headmaster. The decline of classical students has continued. Would Scott-King be willing to teach economic history?

> 'Parents are not interested in producing the "complete man" any more. They want to qualify their boys for jobs in the modern world. You can hardly blame them, can you?'
>
> 'Oh, yes,' said Scott-King. 'I can and do.... If you approve ... I will stay as I am here as long as any boy wants to read the classics. I think it would be very wicked indeed to do anything to fit a boy for the modern world.'

The headmaster thinks this a short-sighted view. Scott-King begs to differ: '"I think", he says, "it the most long-sighted view it is possible to take"'[124]

The moral is plain. *Scott-King* is a fable, dextrously told, rippling with the literary muscle of ingenious allusion. Classical culture; the citizenship of Europe; the pleasures of wine, food, travel, courtesy and fine feeling – all have been prostituted.[125] It is a comic expression of Waugh's bitterness about the sack of Europe, and particularly about the war, 'a sweaty tug-of-

124. *Ibid.*, pp. 246–7.

125. Bellorius's 'vision' for example, parodies the post-war idealism typified by NATO and the United Nations; the use of the conference setting, with disconnected gangs of foreigners arriving and disappearing, parallels the European nightmares of 'Displaced Persons swept up in the machinery of "social engineering"' (p. 232). This theme is given specific political point by making Dr Antonic a refugee and emphasizing the benign influence of imperialism. Asked if his country is 'Jugo-Slavia', Antonic corrects the definitions: '"I am a Croat, born under the Habsburg Empire. That was a true League of Nations. As a young man I studied in Zagreb, Budapest, Prague, Vienna – one was free, one moved where one would; one was a citizen of Europe. Then we were liberated and put under the Serbs. Now we are liberated again and put under the Russians"' (p. 218). There are also tiny, delicate touches. Lockwood was formerly a prize pupil in Scott-King's Greek set, a sitter for the Balliol scholarship. With the declaration of war he had abandoned this and gone into the army. By 1946 he has become a doctor – another triumph for science over classical culture – in the latest site of massive 'social engineering'. Britain was a leading proponent of the creation of Israel and the denationalization of Palestine. Waugh showed considerable foresight in using this as a focus for the chaos which could be caused by 'social engineering'.

war', as the narrator terms it, 'between teams of indistinguishable louts'.[126] Waugh, however, was dissatisfied with the tale and ultimately one must disagree with Sykes[127] and accept Waugh's misgivings: it is a slight thing by his standards. The jokes are often schoolboyish and leaden,[128] sometimes reworked versions of old material.[129] None of Scott-King's disasters had been Waugh's. His fantasy here is not a metaphor for direct experience but generated by a sense of persecution so acute that he overplays his hand and writes amusing propaganda. As Sykes points out, the form of the tale, the long short-story, was Jamesian. Nancy Mitford had sent Waugh a complete set of James and for the last year he had been steadily reading the Master. 'What an enormous, uncovenated blessing', he recorded while at work on *Scott-King*, 'to have kept Henry James for middle age. . . .'[130] But Waugh was not yet ready to use a similarly cool, ruminative style. His story was too brief for the range of the subject and he needed distance from his raw material to maintain objectivity. That distance was becoming increasingly difficult to achieve.

*

A complete change was needed. Earlier in the year Peters had written to say that Hollywood was interested in *Scoop*. Waugh, feeling little affection for the book but less for the moguls, tried to choke them off with preposterous conditions (absolute veto over script and casting). Since they persisted, it amused him to play with them. He did not need the money. MGM (UK) had paid him £10 a week during the war. This retainer had guaranteed the option on his next novel (*Brideshead*) and his services as a screen writer after the cessation of hostilities. On leaving the army he had written, grudgingly declaring himself available for work, but Korda's resignation early in 1946 had resulted in a major reorganization. The writers he had signed up were paid off. Peters had secured Waugh £3,000 free of tax which, with the money already received, came to £4,250 for doing and selling precisely nothing. *Brideshead* had since become a best-seller and was thus Waugh's most valuable property. Having regained the option fortuitously, he guarded it fiercely. Nevertheless, it tickled his entrepreneurial instinct to think that he might sell the novel back to MGM for another fortune. Better still, he could now dictate terms: '. . . I should like

126. *Scott-King*, *op. cit.*, p. 197.
127. Cf. Sykes, pp. 297–9, where he suggests that the story is underrated, 'a masterly minor work'.
128. The mistake, for example, in the typing of the place-card as 'Dr. Scotch-Kink' (p. 217) and the parody of Betjeman in Whitemaid's eulogy of Miss Sveningen (p. 216).
129. The political satire centring on Arturo Fe (a feeble allusion to *auto da fé*?) is scarcely distinguishable from that centring on Benito in *Scoop*. The same comic device – sending the visitors to a false destination – is used; a similar counsel of war between the exploited parties takes place in a hotel bedroom.
130. *Diaries*, 17 November 1946, p. 663. Waugh was reading *Portrait of a Lady* at the time.

to take Laura for a jaunt to Hollywood in February,' he had told Peters, '... a tax-free trip, lecture-free, with a minimum of work of any kind at the other end. Luxury not lionization is the thing.... The sum paid is not of great interest....'[131]

In October, Peters went to New York carrying with him Waugh's expression of willingness to talk. It was a difficult embassy. The moguls were bemused and negotiations protracted. The offer for *Scoop* had clearly been bait. It was *Brideshead* that they wanted. Did Mr Waugh wish to sell or did he not? Peters struggled to convince them that they were not paying for a free holiday and eventually emerged triumphant having secured at least $2,000 a week for approximately four weeks' discussion with no obligation. If they bought the rights, the price would be $145,000, less the expenses already incurred. A problem, however, remained:

> I must tell you that you have the reputation here – both at MGM and everywhere else – of being a difficult, tetchy, irritating and rude customer. I hope you will surprise and confound them all by behaving like an 18th Century ambassador from the Court of St. James's. They are children; and they should receive the tolerance and understanding that you show to children ...[132]

– an unfortunate analogy in Waugh's case.

His desire to give Laura a jaunt was not entirely unselfish. She was jaded, ill-dressed and at loggerheads with him over his still firm intention to move to Ireland. He wanted to placate her and he badly needed a holiday himself. 'I am anxious to emigrate, Laura to remain & face the century of the common man,' he wrote to Nancy. 'She is younger, braver & less imaginative than I.'[133] She was also more pragmatic and had no desire to be cast into Celtic twilight with Waugh in his current frame of mind. He seemed to be turning into a parody of himself, tormented by self-contradictions. He looked on, horrified, as the 'grey lice'[134] of Socialism infected his imagined Old England, yet, as he admitted, he was largely untouched by government interference. Arranging to emigrate to Ireland, he was simultaneously warning Nancy against the artistic sterility of exile in Paris.[135] He liked to think of himself as worldly, immune to despair and shock, but constantly discovered a deep strain of priggishness that could be triggered by minuscule breaches of decorum: the

131. 3 October 1946; *Letters*, p. 235.
132. Unpublished ALS from A. D. Peters, 15 November 1946, from The St Regis, 5th Avenue and 59th Street, NY; HRC.
133. 16 October 1946; *Letters*, p. 236.
134. Cf. *Diaries*, 23 November 1946, p. 663: 'The French called the occupying German army "the grey lice". That is precisely how I regard the occupying army of English socialist government.'
135. 24 October [1946]; *Letters*, p. 237: 'Your literary future is insoluble I think. You see even the most bookish & meditative minds, like A. Huxley's, decay in exile.'

use of bad grammar or an oath.[136] It was not simply another country house that he wanted but a castle. Laura watched her husband's behaviour with growing concern. He remained rational but, like Pinfold, his reason was operating on false premises.

Waugh perfectly understood the impression he was creating. 'I do not feel entirely at ease in the role of nouveau riche invader of an historic property,' he wrote to the owner of Gormanston Castle.[137] He knew that he would be accused of aping the aristocracy and he accepted that, after a fashion, he was. But he buried misgivings beneath the glory of the dream. If Laura's trustees could be convinced that Gormanston was a sound investment, he was determined to take it. 'In any case, I mean to sell up in England and emigrate to some Christian country. . . . Liberty, Diversity, Privacy are what I seek. Shall I find them?'[138] The whimsical Patrick Balfour, who had inspected the house for Waugh, was unable to say. Having arrived after dark and been conducted round the vaulted interior by candlelight, all he had carried away was an impression of vastness. Waugh was intrigued. Laura accompanied him glumly to Dublin. Only the last-minute discovery of Billy Butlin's plans for a nearby holiday camp prevented Waugh's exchanging contracts.

This near-disaster, however, did nothing to discourage him. Even Betjeman, not noted for his caution, had written pleading circumspection. Waugh, he suggested, should rent a house first to see if he could bear living abroad. Caution had never troubled Waugh. Piers Court was advertised for sale and a second excursion to Ireland was postponed only because Christmas and Hollywood were upon him. He felt threatened. Public images of him were appearing which he did not, could not bear to, recognize as himself. Harold Acton had sent him the section of his memoirs[139] which embarrassingly raked over the first marriage to She-Evelyn. Waugh was curiously vulnerable to the slightest criticism from friends. 'My dear Evelyn,' Nancy reminded him, 'think what many have endured uncomplainingly from you, & not least poor Harold himself. I don't think you have much come-back there. *Think* of your inhumanity to poor boots [Connolly] who is *very* fond of *you*.'[140] It did no good. Waugh simply failed to understand why people could not distinguish between cruelty and honesty. At Christmas and birthdays he sometimes lamented,

136. Cf. ALS to Henry Yorke, November 1946; *Letters*, p. 239. Commenting on Yorke's novel *Back*, Waugh exempted from general praise 'the Grand Siècle' interpolation, objecting to its grammar and syntax: 'People did not write like that in civilized ages. It is like the time you told me poor Andrew Scott was a "cunt". . . . You will think me a prig of course. . . . Well I suppose I am.'
137. Unpublished ALS to Peter Lunn, 18 November [1946], from Piers Court; private collection.
138. *Ibid.*
139. *Memoirs of an Aesthete* (Methuen, 1948).
140. Unpublished ALS from Nancy Mitford, 18 August 1946, from Hôtel de Bourgogne, Paris VII; BL.

like a melancholy orphan, the miserable quantity and quality of his presents. He was fastidious and exorbitant in *his* gifts. Why, he complained, were these expressions of love not reciprocated?

Osbert Lancaster's cartoon is an interesting case in point. Waugh struggled to overcome his resentment of it by saying that it was good in conception but poor in execution, and by securing the original and hanging it in his library. In fact, he was offended by this stumpy elf, glaring from the steps of White's. It revealed an ugliness that hurt. So too did Rose Macaulay's essay in December's *Horizon*, attacking *Brideshead* and calling *Waugh in Abyssinia* a 'fascist tract'.

That December, Betjeman gave a radio talk on Waugh, later rewritten round the Lancaster cartoon when both appeared in the *Strand* the following March as a preface to 'Tactical Exercise'. It was a polite and accurate portrait:

> . . . you are not looking at an old High Tory. There is nothing emotional about Evelyn Waugh. He has no sentimentality. He has all the logic of the Celt. As a man interested in people and the visible products of their brains he demanded a logical framework for existence. . . . So . . . he was received into the Roman Catholic Church which supplied the logical framework he needed. . . . I write this as an Anglican, aware of the compromises of the poor old C. of E., but as one who can see that for . . . Waugh's logical mind the Roman Catholic Church is the full solution.[141]

This struck Waugh as desperately frigid. Was it true? 'I was listening last night in my Palladian villa,' he responded. 'I borrowed a loud-speaking machine from my children's nurse and for the first and last time it sounded in the drawing room.'[142] Clearly he disliked what the voices were saying and, in response, he was soon to turn that ruthless logic on Betjeman.

It was, perhaps, a sense of his own ugliness and imperfection, curiously spliced with vanity, that drove Waugh to sign up at a private hospital for a quite unnecessary operation. For some years he had suffered from fibrositis and a variety of pains in his legs and feet. Now he had developed piles and had decided that this condition was not to be borne amid the trials of family life:

> I do not see [my children] until luncheon, as I have my breakfast alone in the library, and they are . . . well trained to avoid my part of the house; but I am aware of them from the moment I wake. Luncheon is very painful. Teresa has a mincing habit of speech . . .; Bron is clumsy and dishevelled, sly, without intellectual, aesthetic or spiritual

141. [Sir] John Betjeman, 'The Angry Novelist', *Strand*, March 1947, 42–3.
142. Unpublished ALS to [Sir] John Betjeman, 15 December [1946], from Piers Court; UBCL.

interest; Margaret is pretty and below the age of reason.... The prospect of Christmas appalls me and I look forward to the operating theatre as a happy release.[143]

Every aspect of his life was tainted by this theatrical sense of decay. A month earlier he had sent Roughead the draft of a brief article, 'Words To Live By'. As his text he had taken three lines by Richard Crashaw:

Life, that does send
A challenge to his end,
And when it comes, say, 'Welcome, friend.'

The moral, Waugh added, 'which needs more emphasis in this century than in any of which we have record, is that a complete life can only be lived when the fact of Death is kept steadily in mind....'[144] Death was the 'friend' Waugh wished to welcome and it was in this mood, awaiting the horror of another family Christmas, that he began his famous correspondence with Betjeman, trying to bully him into the arms of Holy Mother Church.

A pamphlet had come Waugh's way, 'Five Sermons by Laymen', to which Betjeman had contributed, 'expounding Protestant devotional practices'.[145] Betjeman was a member of the Anglo-Catholic community in Wantage and believed it to be as much part of the Catholic Church as the Roman variety. But he had doubts, particularly about the Incarnation, sometimes about the Resurrection. Waugh, believing his friend's soul to be in danger, attacked his theology:

It is no good saying: 'I don't happen to be logical.' Logic is simply the architecture of human reason. If you try to base your life & hopes on logical absurdities YOU WILL GO MAD ... people are going mad & talking balls to psychiatrists not because of accidents to the chamber-pot in the nursery, but because there is no logical structure to their beliefs. Vide Smarty-Boots-Connolly passim.[146]

The argument followed Waugh's usual line: the Church was 'unique & indivisible & nothing is remotely like it'; Protestants could be right, atheists might be right, but it was impossible for Betjeman's 'handful of homosexual

143. *Diaries*, 23 December 1946, pp. 667–8.
144. Unpublished MS, A. D. Peters's file, 29 November 1946; HRC. The piece continues: 'Our ancestors were superior to us in never losing this consciousness that life is terminable; that our tenure of the world is not by freehold but a precarious tenancy revocable by the Landlord from one hour to the next; that we are by nature lodgers on probation; that our ultimate destiny is elsewhere. Only when this is held as the first postulate of all our propositions can they be seen in true perspective. In the greatest & smallest human affairs remember that Death is at the elbow.'
145. 22 December 1946; *Letters*, p. 242.
146. *Ibid.*

curates' to be right and Waugh wrong; the resemblance between Anglo-Catholics and Roman Catholics was entirely superficial. 'It would be a pity to go to HELL', he concluded, 'because you prefer Henry Moore to Michelangelo. THIS GOES FOR PENELOPE TOO.'[147] Betjeman, shocked by the force of this assault and astounded that damnation should be pronounced on all outside the Roman Church, consulted Christopher Hollis. Was Waugh's assumption an article of faith among intelligent Catholics? No, Hollis said, it was not.

Marooned in hospital, Waugh corrected and refined his terms: 'No one is damned except by his own deliberate act . . . but it is doubtful how many formal heretics really commit the sin of heresy – of seeing the truth and denying it.'[148] This shaft went home. All other accusations Betjeman could counter but his humility left him perpetually open to this charge. 'As to your letters,' he replied, 'I deeply appreciate your zeal on my soul's behalf. Indeed I have never been more exercised by a correspondence . . . I am really grateful to you for forcing me to look into all this though it makes me v. miserable.'[149] He was desperate, and Waugh, sensing this, pressed his advantage: 'All this "waiting for God's good time" is intolerably wet. Time is a human conception & limitation. We make God's time for him. . . . But there is ten years painful transition ahead for you if you decide to follow your mind instead of your emotions. You may shirk them.'[150] Eventually, Betjeman, like Connolly before, was forced to respond to specific points, although he sidestepped the essential accusation:

> I have delayed answering your letters because I have been thinking about this a great deal. All I can do now is to read, pray and study the life of Our Lord. That I am doing. I feel that it is not so much a matter of which church, as of loving God & I still think of us as *both* right, which is why I emphasize the importance of the validity of our orders in the C. of E.[151]

There the matter rested until Waugh's return from America. It was as though he were trying to convince both Betjeman and himself that divorce from Anglican roots was logically essential. Lancing is condemned along with Protestant muddle in general. The aesthetic appeal of Anglicanism is seen to be delusory. Writing to Sykes about his *Four Studies in Loyalty* (1947), Waugh made it plain that his hatred of Robert Byron had centred

147. *Ibid.*, pp. 242–3.
148. 9 January 1947; *Letters*, p. 244.
149. Unpublished ALS from [Sir] John Betjeman, 12 January 1947, from Farnborough Old Rectory, Wantage, Berks.; BL.
150. 14 January 1947; *Letters*, pp. 246–7.
151. ALS from [Sir] John Betjeman, 23 January 1947, from Farnborough Old Rectory etc.; BL; partially reprinted *Letters*, p. 247, n. 5.

not only on his anti-Catholicism but also on his buggery.[152] Waugh was not unreasonable in disavowing the conduct of his youth; it was more dangerous to pretend, as he was beginning to, that these things had not happened to him but to some other person with his name. His position was now so absolute, so precisely controlled within a self-regulating, eccentric intellectual system, that to admit any compromise would have been to bring the castle crashing round his ears. He did not like what the voices were saying but he could still manage to ignore them. It was, of course, not Betjeman who was going mad, but Waugh. He both feared and courted the advent of lunacy, just as he stared with fascinated disgust into those mirrors reflecting his physical decay. Decline of intellectual power threatened him with poverty and ridicule from the horde of enemies he had cultivated – but cultivating them was his principal entertainment.

After three weeks of humiliation and agony in hospital he embarked on the *America* 'full of cocaine, opium and brandy, feeble and low-spirited' and examined his recent behaviour: 'I took no advice ... just went to the surgeon and ordered the operation as I would have ordered new shirts. In fact I had behaved wholly irrationally and was paying for it.'[153] Vanity, it seems, had prompted surgery. Laura and he normally slept in separate rooms. On this trip they would be continuously at closer quarters and he had wanted to be free from the embarrassing application of ointments. He wasn't. As they set off, the gap between the glamour of the expedition and the ignominy of his condition was painfully evident. He felt ridiculous.

152. Cf. unpublished ALS from Christopher Sykes, 28 December 1946, from 90 Eaton Terrace, SW1; BL: 'I am surprised you attach so much importance to his buggery. Oddly enough I never thought anything about it until right at the end of his life. . . .' In Waugh's review of the book ('When Loyalty No Harm Meant', *Tablet*, 7 December 1946, 308–9; *EAR*, pp. 319–20) he avoids expressing his loathing for Byron but suggests that '"Loyalty" is not a happy word. It serves too conveniently to cover mere extensions of egotism ... or brutish tolerance of bores. "Fidelity" is perhaps a better word for what Mr. Sykes seeks to illustrate. . . .' (p. 319).
153. *Diaries*, 25 January 1947, pp. 668–9.

VI

Abjuring the Realm: January 1947–October 1948

Waugh arrived in New York still feeling ill, ignored a call to attend a press conference and slipped ashore, thus confusing the poor young man MGM had sent to meet them. They were treated royally: booked into a suite at the Waldorf Astoria, taken to the theatre, and invited to dinner with Carl and Carol Brandt.[1] Little of this pleased Waugh. He thought the suite cramped, the food tasteless; he left the play after the second act and patrolled the streets searching (successfully) for a drug store which would breach state regulations and provide the sleeping draught Dial without a prescription. Even the Brandts' hospitality failed to save them from criticism: 'Mrs Brandt is a woman of no intellectual interests. Brandt three-quarters civilized with a taste for Trollope. . . . [She] is a secretary raised to its highest power. She did not disguise that her services to us were personally distasteful but she performed every service brilliantly.'[2] Carol Brandt was an abrasive, 'fast-track' New Yorker. She drove herself hard to please the Waughs and a letter from Laura confirmed Mrs Brandt's belief that she had been the perfect hostess. When, thirty years later, she read Waugh's *Diaries*, his remarks galled her.

America, however, soon began to release in Waugh a curiosity about human behaviour he had thought long dead. Interviews with magazine editors left him not angry but amused. Herbert Mayes of *Good Housekeeping* was to publish 'Tactical Exercise' but had changed the title to 'The Wish'. Why? '"People would think it dealt with the war."'[3] Were the Americans, Waugh wondered, so obtuse a race as not to bother to read the first sentence of a story? He was intrigued and saw scope for teasing. Mayes had paid $2,500 for the illustration. '"But you could have got a real picture for that,"' said Waugh.[4] Mayes, missing the joke, got down to business. Would Mr Waugh like $4,000? Certainly, but what for? An advance – on another

1. Both were literary agents. Earlier they had worked together as Brandt & Brandt, and acted as A.D. Peters's American representatives. Peters had since transferred his business to Harold Matson but remained on cordial terms with the Brandts, who now worked separately, she running her own agency.
2. *Diaries*, 1 February 1947, p. 670.
3. *Ibid.*, 3 February 1947, p. 671.
4. *Ibid.*

story. '"But"', said Waugh, bemused, '"I may not write another story suitable for you." "Well it won't break us if you don't. We're easy people to do business with. Maybe in two–five years you'll write us something."'[5] Waugh's eyes sparkled. This maniac, apparently with money to burn, could perhaps be cajoled into colluding in a tax-evasion scheme. Waugh suggested that half the amount should be paid in the form of a new station-wagon to be delivered to Ireland. Mayes agreed. America was looking up. Only later did Waugh discover this editor's intransigence when, not unreasonably, he insisted that acceptance of largess represented contractual obligation. The station-wagon story rolled on for years.

In genial mood, Waugh and Laura entrained on the *20th Century* and headed for Chicago. Matson, Waugh's American agent, had stockpiled $3,500 pocket-money, $2,000 of which Laura had already spent on clothes. Waugh had purchased champagne, brandy and sherry to take west, assuming that nothing of reputable quality would be available in the desert. He was in a state of mild bafflement about his American experience. Normally he would have assessed a foreign country, particularly one against which he harboured so violent a prejudice, within ten minutes of having his passport stamped. But some New Yorkers, he had to admit, possessed a certain *chic*; the train was undeniably luxurious, its cuisine excellent. True, it was 'all thin aluminium and one hears coarse native laughter through the walls.'[6] Even so, there was something appealing about the child-like seriousness of Americans and something healthy in their sense of temporary habitation. '*Non enim habemus hic manentem civitatem*';[7] death at the elbow; life as brief exile from felicity[8] – these religious preconceptions had always channelled Waugh's scepticism. In the dining-car, pulling out of Chicago, he explained to the *maître d'hôtel* that he was a foreigner. '"We are all foreigners in this country,"'[9] the man replied.

Before leaving Chicago, Waugh had caught the attention of a stranger. Marguerite Cullman and her husband Howard, also travelling from New York to Hollywood, had met several old acquaintances on the train and had lunched with them during the stop-over. Brooke Marshall and her husband were among them. The Marshalls proposed a drinks party in the lounge car. Returning to the train, Howard Cullman noticed an odd figure in a

5. *Ibid.*
6. *Ibid.*, p. 672.
7. 'Here we have no abiding city', which Waugh attempted to quote in ALS to Randolph Churchill, 22 December [1946]; *Letters*, p. 243. The quotation comes from the official Roman Catholic Latin Text (the Vulgate) of what Waugh would have styled the Epistle of St Paul to the Hebrews, ch. 13, v. 14. The sentence concludes: '... sed futuram inquirimus', and the Douai version of the whole reads: 'For we have not here a lasting city, but we seek one that is to come.' The tag was also used as an epigraph for the manuscript of *Brideshead* (HRC).
8. Cf. unpublished section of ALS to Robert Henriques, 2 February 1946; *Letters*, p. 222.
9. *Diaries*, 4 February 1947, p. 672.

plaid coat striding vigorously up and down the platform. A railroad detective? Indeed not: at the party their host introduced Evelyn Waugh. Mrs Cullman was impressed. She had no greater literary idol. Waugh responded gallantly and, according to her account,[10] steered her away from her husband to an easy chair and perched happily on its arm. The conversation ran a predictable course: a flattering discussion of his novels. '"Actually this wasn't too convenient a time . . .," Waugh explained, "we have a new baby . . . haven't really had a good look at it."'[11] Mrs Cullman was aghast. '"Oh, that probably was my own fault . . . the pram was pushed past my window often enough, I just never got to look in."'[12]

The next morning they met again in the club car. He was eager for information about the Hollywood moguls. She warned him that a lavish dinner would be designed to leave him in their debt, thus making the deal easier to negotiate. Waugh had already been invited: '"How does one cope with it? What shall I do in self defence?"'[13] Mrs Cullman offered the unnecessary advice that he should pretend to expect far more than they could provide. Like many before her, she sensed that she had become a marionette in his private theatrical. But there was charm in his mock innocence, teasing irreverence rather than rudeness. She told him not to miss the huge pets' cemetery – landscaped grounds, headstones, mausoleums, marble statues. When she read *The Loved One* in 1948, she realized that he had been listening more carefully than she had thought.

She watched him leave the train at Pasadena with a mixture of affection and amusement, and a distant chain of connections brought the story via Alec to his mother: '. . . Evelyn's appearance at Los Angeles [*sic*] station was fantastic. The sun was shining, tropical flowers were in bloom, all the young people were dressed in shorts and slacks and open shirts and there was Evelyn in a stiff white collar and a bowler hat, carrying a rolled umbrella. . . .'[14] To his family, Evelyn was no less a creature of fantasy than to the Americans. California was like nothing he had ever seen. As he stared impatiently from the window of MGM's limousine, the only comparison that sprang to mind was Egypt: Cairo with a dash of Addis Ababa. He was equally surprised by the comfort of the Bel Air Hotel. Even the local

10. Marguerite Cullman, 'A Waugh-Time Memory', *HB* (US), Vol. 90 (February 1963), 109–10, 162. This is an extract from her *Occupation: Angel* (Norton, New York, 1963). Mrs Cullman was a 'Broadway angel', an actress and writer. According to Waugh's account (*Diaries*, 4 February 1947, p. 672), he met 'A swarthy flashy man with a bright wife' and Howard Cullman introduced himself. The implication is that they forced themselves on his attention.
11. *Ibid.*, 109.
12. *Ibid.*
13. *Ibid.*, 110.
14. Unpublished ALS from Alec Waugh to Catherine Waugh, 22 February 1948, from Hotel Algonquin, NY; BUL. Alec had heard the story from McDougall's mother-in-law at a party given by Mrs Marshall.

wine (Paul Masson's Pinot Noir) was potable. But fortunately there was something to complain about. The suite reserved for him was not available and Laura and he were given temporary accommodation in a pretty attic room with bath.

The occupants of the suite, a charming old couple, had arranged to vacate it the day before Waugh's arrival. Then the husband had collapsed with a paralytic stroke. They were a much-loved pair and regular customers. The management, understanding that the patient could not be moved and sympathetic to the wife's distress, insisted that she stay until the crisis had resolved itself. Waugh was apparently told another story: rheumatic fever had felled the ancient; all would be well within a few days. Registering his extreme discontent, the novelist stalked off. Each morning he would appear in his bowler to demand access. Each morning the flabby young manager returned the same answer: the old man was still sick. '"Your guests' health"', Waugh replied, '"is no concern of mine!"'[15] and he stepped up the war of nerves. Even the hard-boiled executive who had arranged the visit was shocked by this. Mr Waugh, he told Peter Quennell, 'had gravely disappointed him'.[16]

This, of course, was precisely Waugh's intention. Taking Mrs Cullman at her word, he had appeared for his reception at Louis B. Mayer's house, surveyed its Petronian luxury and declaimed: '"How wise you Americans are to eschew all ostentation and lead such simple, wholesome lives! This really is delightful. Who'd even want to live in the main house when he could have this charming gatehouse instead!"'[17] Waugh delivered his speech with a smiling face of cherubic innocence. No one knew what to say. '"I can tell you," said Mrs Cullman's informant, "it was all rather unnerving. Now we don't quite know how to deal with him, even on a business level. . . ."'[18]

Business with Mr Waugh was clearly going to be difficult. On his first day he had been taken to Culver City, the site of MGM's studios, by Leon Gordon, one of the producers unhappily organizing the *Brideshead* project. Waugh saw the canteen, with its high table for executives and stars, as a grotesque version of Oxford, and the 'story conferences' as nothing previously known to civilized discourse. A screenwriter appeared who turned out to be Keith Winter, whom Waugh had mocked in Villefranche in 1931.[19] 'He wore local costume', Waugh recorded, '– a kind of loose woollen blazer, matelot's vest, buckled shoes. He has been in Hollywood for years and sees

15. Peter Quennell, 'Speaking of Books: Evelyn Waugh', *NYTBR*, 8 May 1966, 2, 23. Quennell repeated this story in what was effectively an obituary.
16. *Ibid.*
17. Marguerite Cullman, *op. cit.*, 162.
18. *Ibid.*
19. See Vol. 1, p. 274.

Brideshead purely as a love story. None of them see [*sic*] the theological implication....'[20] From this moment Waugh knew that the film would never be made. The trick was to keep the Americans on the wrong foot while he imbibed Hollywood's extraordinary atmosphere. Winter had already become a rough sketch for Dennis Barlow in *The Loved One*.

For a week, Waugh lived quietly, paying respectful, non-committal calls at the studio, visiting the Jesuits at Loyola University and taking tea with Anna May Wong (his 'favourite film star' in 1930).[21] The tendency of hotel servants to engage him in amicable banter was beaten off and, apart from the acrimony over the suite, the holiday was having the desired effect. Laura was invited out separately, spent liberally and was entirely revived from her torpor. He relished seeing her smart and light-hearted and, when the Elweses arrived, a new perspective on Hollywood society opened for him.

Simon Elwes, an artist related to Sykes by marriage, had long been a distant friend. He painted Waugh's portrait and introduced him to the English colony. The portrait – its subject straddled in the sunlight with bowler and cane – seems to allude to Charlie Chaplin, and there is certainly a sense in which Waugh saw himself as the baffled clown refusing to repine in the face of Hollywood's dismal rapacity. Waugh considered Chaplin and Disney to be the only artists Hollywood had produced and he loyally paid homage to both.[22] But that was a small part of his business. The English colony, with its cricket club and snooty expatriates, for ever engaged in the struggle for social distinction, was a mine of delicious eccentricity: a displaced culture with a private language. Its absurd sense of the fine shifts of good form, its Chaplinesque pathos, intrigued him and he made detailed enquiries into its etiquette which were not, it seems, appreciated.[23] Having alienated three sets of, as he saw them, parasitical hosts – the hoteliers, the moguls and the colony – he felt content. His defence of Chaplin pushed Waugh further into the chilly distance he preferred to inhabit and, as negotiations proceeded, it amused him to beat worldly Hollywood with the stick of its hypocritical puritanism.[24]

20. *Diaries*, 7 February 1947, p. 673.
21. Cf. Evelyn Waugh, 'My Favourite Film Star', *DM*, 24 May 1930, 10; *EAR*, pp. 68–70: 'She has in the highest degree that subtlety of movement and restraint of expression which the film particularly nurtures.'
22. Cf. *Diaries*, 7 April 1947, p. 675. Waugh was taken to supper at Chaplin's house by Lady Diana Cooper's friend, Iris Tree: she was, he told Lady Diana, '... sickly & cranky, living in a peasant [?] hut in the hills with a goat & a giant & a grandchild & two new motor cars, teaching yokels to act Macbeth ...' (ALS, 10 May [1947], from Piers Court; BL; *MWMS*, p. 95). Waugh saw a private performance of *Monsieur Verdoux* (which he thought brilliant). Later he visited Disney's studio.
23. Cf. *ibid.*: 'We antagonized most of the English colony who were guiltily sensitive of criticism.'
24. Cf. 'The Man Hollywood Hates', *ES*, 4 November 1947, 4; review of *Monsieur Verdoux*; *EAR*, pp. 337–9: 'Charlie Chaplin is not merely unpopular in Hollywood. For many years he has been

The dicta of the Johnston-Hays Office had long been an object of European mockery. Its function was to eliminate impurity from moving pictures. No graded censorship existed in America for fear of reducing audiences and, when the *Brideshead* script was condemned as likely to undermine the conception of Christian marriage, Waugh grasped the excuse he needed and refused changes. An impasse of the Americans' own making thus got him off the contractual hook and left him free to enjoy himself.[25]

After a month's unsuccessful campaign to enter the Bel Air suite, Waugh, assisted by Sir Charles Mendl, moved to a luxurious set of rooms in the Beverly Hills Hotel. From here, he instructed his MGM driver to take him not to the studio but to the pets' cemetery and, as a natural progression, visited its elaborate counterpart for the defunct plutocracy. 'I am entirely obsessed by Forest Lawns [*sic*]', he wrote to Peters, '& plan a long short story about it':

> I go there two or three times a week, am on easy terms with the chief embalmer & next week am to lunch with Dr. HUBERT EATON himself. It is an entirely unique place – the *only* thing in California that is not a copy of something else.... Aldous [Huxley] flirted with it in *After Many a Summer* [1939] but only with the superficialities. I am at the heart of it....[26]

Hubert Eaton, the 'visionary' manager, had foolishly allowed Waugh free run of the place. Mr Howells (the Chief Embalmer) introduced him to the chilled Loved Ones, propped up, painted and grinning back with Howells's 'personality smile'. Waugh was transported with delight. The place symbolized for him the paganism at the heart of the American Dream: if Forest Lawn were California, and California were America, America was the cemetery of the humanist fallacy.

The 'Bible' of Forest Lawn was Eaton's *Embalming Techniques*. Waugh was presented with a signed copy and read it with close attention, marking,

the victim of organized persecution. A community whose morals are those of caged monkeys professes to be shocked by his domestic irregularities.'

25. Cf. 'Why Hollywood Is a Term of Disparagement' and 'What Hollywood Touches It Banalizes', *DT*, 30 April 1947, 4, and 1 May 1947, 4; republished together under former title in *EAR*, pp. 325–31: 'The story was of an unhappy married man and woman who wished to divorce their respective partners and remarry one another. They institute proceedings, but in the end refrain from remarriage precisely because they come to realize that this would not constitute Christian marriage' (p. 330). Dr Gallagher notes: 'This story strongly suggests *Brideshead*.... On 15 March, 1947 [Waugh] telegraphed A. D. Peters, "Censor forbids film of *Brideshead*...."' In Waugh's diary (7 April 1947, p. 675), he places the responsibility for this impasse on Gordon: '... when the censor made some difficulties he accepted them as an easy excuse for abandoning the whole project.' Gordon, doubtless pleased to be rid of Waugh, was nevertheless only responding to the novelist's intransigence.
26. 6 March [1947]; *Letters*, p. 247.

annotating.[27] Every sweetly euphemistic line typified the vacuous ideology inspiring the author's 'dream'. Undertaking, in Eaton's hands, had become the art of evasion. Forest Lawn was not so much a graveyard as a way of life. There, death was no welcome 'friend', life no exile from felicity. The place tried to invert Waugh's theological preconceptions: the sting of death, Eaton suggested, could be disarmed by concentrating on the perfectibility of terrestrial life. Indeed, his principal concern was to obscure the fact of death altogether. Waugh saw gloriously developing in his mind the metaphor he needed to crystallize his thoughts about Hollywood and, by extension, artistic exile and the American Dream. Here was the end-product of Bellorius's vision in *Scott-King*.

*

Waugh returned from America primed with artistic enthusiasm but otherwise depressed, and went for his Easter retreat to Downside, concerned about the welfare of his soul. During his absence, Britain had suffered the worst winter of the century and a political crisis. This merits scarcely a mention in his diary; the Socialists' failure, he felt, was drearily predictable. His gaze now rarely travelled beyond the boundaries of his estate and, even in that enclosed world, 'the expectation is that something has decayed further.'[28] He wanted to be gone: from Piers Court, from England, from life. Detachment had become such a habit of mind that he felt alienated from all fellow feeling. If he could only gain pleasure from hurting, no one would love him. This he could accept. But if he could feel no contrition for his lack of compassion, even God could not love him, and this Waugh found painful. 'How to reconcile this indifference to human beings with the obligations of Charity. That is my problem. But I am sure that Dickensian geniality is as far from Charity as my indifference.'[29]

Waugh was a generous man who needed to castigate himself with the belief that he was not guilty of liberal humanism. The supertax regulations gave him the excuse he required. Journalism was onerous and now financially unnecessary, but he continued this labour mainly for charity. Two

27. Waugh was particularly attracted to descriptions of gruesome practical detail, and those making incongruous allusions to artistic vocation and the profit-motive. The following passages, for instance, were marked: 'The nose is sometimes turned to one side. This may have been caused by wrapping the sheet too tightly about the face ...' (p. 13). 'The world's greatest artists have never been able to paint their masterpieces so that they will look well under any but subdued light.... An indirect light is usually found best for viewing bodies upon which Restorative Work has been done' (p. 22). 'The writer prefers to embalm all [children's] bodies even though the family cannot afford to pay the embalming fee.... Numerous cases are recalled where this treatment has earned the gratitude of the bereaved families ... [especially] ... where the mother survived but a few days as it made it possible to place the baby's body in the mother's arms in the casket' (p. 62).

28. *Diaries*, Easter Monday, 7 April 1947, p. 674.

29. ALS to Lady Diana Cooper, 2 June [1946], from Piers Court; BL; *MWMS*, p. 88.

articles on Hollywood for the *Daily Telegraph*[30] and a piece on death for *Life* obstructed *The Loved One*, which he was itching to begin. Peters had secured generous terms from *Life*; Seymour Berry had offered £100 each for the *Telegraph* essays. Waugh gave it all away to the Jesuits. Fr D'Arcy (by this time elevated to Reverend Father Provincial) was constantly amazed at the stream of cheques. Waugh had insisted on the American printing of *Campion* in 1946 so that Campion Hall might capitalize on *Brideshead*'s success;[31] he wrote *gratis* for the *Tablet*, and donated the serial rights of *Scott-King* and many translation rights. It would be tedious to itemize his hundreds of gifts, but this became the pattern of his professional life to the end. Tens of thousands of pounds, a small fortune even after supertax, went for apostolic work.[32] And he was generous also in small causes. Before leaving for America he had written to Hilde Bertram wishing her a happy Christmas and asking if there was anything he could send her from the States. There was – and the food parcels duly arrived.

None of this raised Waugh in his own estimation:

> The gentle effects of Easter have worn thin and my temper has been short, my prayers tepid. . . . I have no human contacts here. Laura is busy and happy with agriculture and has lost all her Californian chic. My children afford me no pleasure. . . . Mystics spend half their lives in doubt and despondency, half in exultation. How can one claim that one half is valid evidence and not the other? But to aim at anything less than sanctity is not to aim at all. Oh for persecution.[33]

No one persecuted Evelyn Waugh more relentlessly than himself, and in search of additional enemies he continued the attack on his American hosts. What he had found at Forest Lawn still seems extraordinary. The astonishing thing about *The Loved One* article is its documentary cor-

30. *Op. cit.*; see p. 190 above, n. 25.
31. See Vol. 1, pp. 388–9. All the money from *Campion* went to Campion Hall. The biography had appeared in the USA in 1935 but only in a small Sheed & Ward edition of imported sheets and it had gone almost unnoticed. The 1946 printing caused a considerable stir in the wake of *Brideshead*. Edmund Wilson renewed his attack. 'Mr. Waugh's view of history . . .', he said, 'is, in its main lines, more or less in the vein of *1066 and All That*. Catholicism was a Good Thing and Protestantism was a Bad Thing' (*NY*, 13 July 1946, 81; *CH*, pp. 179–80). But other Americans were more generous. Richard Sullivan wondered 'if this excellent little study . . . did not . . . foreshadow the profound eschatological concerns which much later the author was to exhibit in his fiction' (*NYTBR*, 7 July 1946, 6; *CH*, pp. 176–8), and *Time* thought it done 'skilfully with full respect' (1 July 1946, 39).
32. Waugh arranged all these contracts so that the money never passed through his hands. He was thus able to donate the full amount. Supertax would have left him with 4s. 6d. in the pound, which would still have amounted to a considerable sum.
33. *Diaries*, 19 April 1947, p. 676. At Downside, Waugh had consulted a monk, 'Tusky' Russell, about his spiritual predicament and had been persuaded to read the autobiography of Thérèse de Lisieux. Against expectation, he did not find the style repulsive – but neither did the book offer the revelation he sought.

respondence to his *Life* article. The novel reads like grotesque fantasy; 'Half in Love with Easeful Death' explains that Forest Lawn was little different. To the casual tourist, however, those spacious grasslands behind the largest wrought-iron gates in the world might have signalled no particular horror. It took Waugh's relentless scratching to enter its inner sanctums and unearth its contradictions.

The grounds, he points out, are 'judiciously planted with evergreen (for no plant which sheds its leaf has a place there). . . .':

> Even the names given to . . . [the] various sections – Eventide, Babyland, Graceland . . . are none of them specifically suggestive of the graveyard. The visitor is soothed by countless radios concealed about the vegetation, which ceaselessly discourse the 'Hindu Lovesong' . . . and the amplified twittering of caged birds. It is only when he leaves the seven and a half miles of paved roadway that he becomes aware of the thousands of little bronze plates which lie in the grass. Commenting on this peculiarity in the *Art Guide of Forest Lawn with Interpretations* Mr Bruce Barton, author of *What can a man believe?*, says: 'The cemeteries of the world cry out man's utter hopelessness in the face of death. Their symbols are pagan and pessimistic. . . . Here sorrow sees no ghastly monuments, but only life and hope.'[34]

'The Christian visitor', Waugh adds wryly, 'might here remark that by far the commonest features of other graveyards is still the Cross, a symbol in which previous generations have found more Life and Hope than in the most elaborately watered evergreen shrub.'[35]

Waugh sent Betjeman a copy of Eaton's astonishing catalogue. It was all there – America's largest collection of marble statuary (mostly of animals, children and toys), the Italianate Mausoleum, the Tudor-style Administration Building ('Class A steel and concrete', to counter all conceivable hazards of fire and earthquake) – just as it was to appear in the novel. 'My hat!' the poet had replied, 'what a subject. . . . No, I can't sleep either & am v. gloomy. Your letters started it. . . .'[36] They had also started something else. Lady Betjeman dated her interest in Catholicism from reading Waugh's

34. 'Death in Hollywood', *Life*, 29 September 1947, 73–4; reprinted as 'Half in Love with Easeful Death. An Examination of Californian Burial Customs', *Tablet*, 18 October 1947, 246–8; *EAR*, pp. 331–2. Gallagher reprints the *Tablet* version. *Life* required changes, though the major insertion resulting from these was also included in the *Tablet* piece ('Secondly, the Park . . . most conspicuous monument'; *EAR*, p. 335). It seems that *Life* wished the author to emphasize that the peculiarities of Californian life were not typical of the USA. Waugh sent the addendum to Peters on 19 June, but Mr Coughlan of *Life* still quibbled. 'What a bore these yanks are,' Waugh wrote. 'If the money were not for the Church I would tell them to go & boil their heads' (unpublished APCI to A. D. Peters, pm 11 June 1947, from Piers Court; *Catalogue* E542, p. 157).
35. *EAR*, p. 332.
36. Unpublished ALS from [Sir] John Betjeman, Maundy Thursday, 3 April 1947, from Farnborough Old Rectory, Wantage, Berks.; BL.

letters to her husband. Betjeman came to see this as a grievous betrayal. Waugh had invited him to go castle-hunting in Ireland at the end of April and, presuming their rift to be healed, he had accepted. In the event, Waugh went alone. A 'secret' correspondence with Penelope had begun which was doubtless no secret to Betjeman. 'I have seen Fr. Matthew several times and he has been to stay here,' she wrote in June.[37] Having decided on reception, her problem was both to prevent her husband from over-reacting and Waugh from further persecution.

Her now regular letters to Waugh were an hilarious mixture of Church and spade, with the brusque irreverence for earthly powers captured so well in Helena's character. 'I desperately want to come and take ploughing lessons from Laura but John will think it all a Roman Catholic plot. . . . I thought all children hated you as you hate them but [Candida] has conceived a passion for you. . . .'[38] Against this background, Betjeman's jealousy and depression festered and no one was more acutely aware of the delicacy of his mental balance than his wife. Her intention to be received, she explained to Waugh, must be masked from Betjeman until he had survived this mood. But Waugh, jubilant at having her hooked, could not resist another jerk on Betjeman's line: 'One deep root of error is that you regard religion as a source of pleasurable . . . sensations. . . . I wouldn't give a thrushs egg for your chances of salvation at the moment.'[39] 'Believe me,' came the sad reply, 'I find it no pleasure. . .',[40] but when Betjeman's sense of persecution deepened to crisis-point, 'Propeller' (as he called her) stepped in with the hairbrush: '. . . you know John well enough to perceive that reason has no effect upon him. . . . Has Laura made any silage? . . . LEAVE JOHN ALONE. IT IS THE WISEST POLICY.'[41] That concluded the assault but not Betjeman's agony. His wife's reception nearly broke their marriage – and he felt that he had Waugh to thank for this. It says much for the poet's loyalty that he never complained to his torturer and ceaselessly promoted him as the finest living writer of English prose.

'I am by nature a bully and a scold', Waugh replied, 'and Johns pertinacity in error brings out all that is worst in me. I am very sorry. I will lay off

37. Unpublished ALS from Penelope [Lady] Betjeman, 1 June 1947, from Farnborough Old Rectory etc.; BL.

38. Unpublished TLS from Penelope [Lady] Betjeman, 9 April 1947, from Farnborough Old Rectory etc.; BL. Some five months earlier Waugh had visited the Betjemans' 'stuffy, cold, poky rectory among beech woods overlooking Wantage', where he had discovered 'Harness everywhere. A fine collection of nineteenth-century illustrated books . . .' and 'A daughter [Candida] of grossly proletarian appearance and manner' (*Diaries*, 31 October 1946, p. 660).

39. ALS to [Sir] John Betjeman, nd [May 1947]; *Letters*, p. 250.

40. Unpublished ALS from [Sir] John Betjeman, Whit Monday [25 May 1947], from Farnborough Old Rectory etc.; BL. In a long letter he repeated that the focus of his religious struggle was the desire to keep faith with village C. of E. life and its tiny number of regular church-goers.

41. Unpublished ALS from Penelope [Lady] Betjeman, Trinity Sunday [1 June 1947], from Farnborough Old Rectory etc.; BL.

him in future.'[42] It saddened Waugh to have to threaten friendship with orthodoxy. Although loyalty to the Church superseded all other loyalties, kindred spirits were rare. It was as though he had seen a friend drowning. The desire was to save with whatever force was necessary. And it was the same motive, in secular form, which prompted Waugh at this time to defend an odd collection of heroes and martyrs: Chaplin, Beerbohm and Wodehouse.

Beerbohm lived close to Piers Court, near Stroud, and was one of Sykes's friends. Waugh had met Sir Max seventeen years earlier under embarrassing circumstances[43] but never since. Now he persuaded Sykes to engineer another encounter. Beerbohm's works had fallen from favour, and Waugh was determined to offer support.

On the great day, Carol Brandt lunched with the Waughs. Tea with Beerbohm came as an immense relief, rather as tea with Francis Crease had used to after the harsh competitiveness of Lancing. 'A delicious little old dandy,' Waugh recorded. '... A touch of Ronnie Knox and of Conrad [Russell] and of Harold Acton.'[44] Afterwards he wrote expressing his gratitude. 'You are wrong about "high privilege",' Beerbohm replied. 'It was mine.... And you are wrong about "homage" too; for you are a more gifted man than ever I was ... you are a master of language when you write for print: it is only when you write a letter or inscribe a book that you go astray!'[45] Wherever Waugh sought a humble place, he received a similar response. As he struggled to protect his modesty, praise was a constant occasion of sin. Pride and Sloth persistently tempted him.

Wodehouse was another at whose feet he tried unsuccessfully to sit. He believed 'Plum' to be a supreme artist persecuted by the Age of the Common Man and exiled to America. During the war, Wodehouse's broadcasts for the Germans had been condemned by the Ministry of Information under Duff Cooper, and 'Cassandra' had conducted a hate campaign in the *Daily Mirror*. While Waugh was at Nuremberg, he had discovered British lawyers still eager to bring the creator of Bertie Wooster to trial. In May 1947, just before Waugh began *The Loved One*, he wrote to Wodehouse expressing solidarity.

This came as a pleasant surprise to 'Plum', who was in America partly to evade tax and partly because he loved the country. He re-read Waugh's books every six months. The Master, it seemed, was again writing to the pupil with misplaced humility. 'I can't tell you how much I appreciated

42. ALS to Penelope [Lady] Betjeman, 4 June [1947]; *Letters*, p. 252.
43. See Vol. 1, pp. 192–3. In n. 29 I suggested that the meeting took place in late 1929. Evidence which has since come to light establishes the date as July 1930. Cf. unpublished ALS from Sir Max Beerbohm to Evelyn Waugh, 17 July 1930; BL.
44. *Diaries*, 18 May 1947, p. 679.
45. ALS from Sir Max Beerbohm, 22 May 1947; reprinted Sykes, pp. 258–9; BL.

your letter . . .,' Wodehouse replied. 'I gather from what you say that [in London] the brickbats have been flying about once more, though I had hoped the brickbat season was over. But I don't care what the papers say, so long as people like you are on my side.' In fact, he said, everything was fine. The New York press was 'uniformly friendly', the magazine market picking up, he had 'three shows lined up for the autumn' and, best of all, the joke was on the persecutors. 'I find that the War Department here were using my broadcasts as samples of anti-Nazi propaganda throughout the war at the U.S. Army Intelligence School at Camp Ritchie. . . .'[46] No cause for alarm, old boy, but thanks awfully. Waugh, for the time being, would have to look elsewhere for his martyr.

He was rather lonely in his eminence. While he needed the comradeship of other writers, he increasingly found among his friends only deference and self-distrust. Nancy and Connolly were both racked by a sense of artistic inferiority; Yorke had, as far as Waugh was concerned, gone off the rails; Powell seemed formal and distant. Only Greene offered the kind of support Waugh needed, and he was rarely in the country. Isolation Waugh could survive; he had chosen his Irish house, Lisnavagh, an early Victorian baronial pile in Co. Carlow,[47] and was preparing to abjure the realm. But there was something more worrying: the increasing anxiety that he might be losing his reason. When Rose Macaulay wrote to him about reprinting her *Horizon* essay, his complaints verged on mania.

This correspondence suggests that Waugh's political attitudes had by mid-1947 become a closely co-ordinated network of prejudice and fantasy which few intelligent people could take seriously. History was the problem. The deductive, logical part of his mind saw history as the sheet anchor of empirical data which ultimately secured his Faith. Yet his inductive, imaginative faculties always shaped and selected this information as they would have transformed the raw material for a novel. History in his hands became something approaching a fairy-tale pageant of the struggle between Good and Evil and he was in the impossible position of arguing both for empiricism and for the fairy-tale. Rose Macaulay clearly found the naïvety of his position staggering.

He believed, for instance, that she represented a Liberal, anti-Catholic school of thought, and that 'Liberals always support the communist side'. Behind this strain in English culture he saw a radical division between the oldest universities. She replied:

> Oxford & Cambridge. I don't believe in your dichotomy. I think it an Oxford fantasy; no Cambridge person would accept it. 'The austere,

46. Unpublished TLS from P. G. Wodehouse, 31 May 1947, from 53 East 66 Street, NY; BL.
47. Owned by Lord Rathdonnell; price: £20,000. The house had twenty-two bedrooms, five bathrooms, twelve acres and a 'luggage entrance'.

> atheist, marxist, scientific, functional Cambridge' conveys no picture of the Cambridge of the poets, the aesthetes, the humanists, the classics, the literary giants & the eccentrics.... Myself. I see you don't know me at all if you say I don't like gluttony & tawdry gilt ornaments. I love both.... Agnostics. They don't deny the possibility of communion with God; they keep an open mind about it....[48]

But Waugh's mind was closed. He would never back down. His sanity depended on his being right.

The long antagonism with Professor Hugh Trevor-Roper (now Lord Dacre) also began that summer. Waugh read *The Last Days of Hitler*, hated it and prepared an assault. To be certain of safe social ground, he wrote to Bowra about his Oxford colleague.

> Trevor-Roper is a fearful man [Bowra wrote], short-sighted, with dripping eyes, shows off all the time, sucks up to me, boasts, is far from poor owing to his awful book, on every page of which there is a howler.... Please persecute him as much as you can. Something in The Tablet would wound him a lot. He is very thin-skinned....[49]

Waugh did not wait for this reply. Trevor-Roper had already received a brief, offensive letter followed by 'something in the Tablet'.[50]

*

The Loved One was written against this background. He began it cautiously, painstakingly, on 21 May, broke off to fly to Dublin to see Lisnavagh, and finished the first draft by 6 July. 'The Forest Lawn novelette goes on slowly & well,' he wrote to Peters. 'When it is finished I shall need your advice as to whether to publish it at all in the U.S.A. It will cause great offence & it might be injurious to make myself abominable there.'[51]

Peters was growing weary of Waugh's barracking the Americans. During the last year, *Campion, When the Going Was Good* and the last novel of the Uniform Edition, *Black Mischief*, had appeared in the States. Little, Brown

48. Unpublished TLS from [Dame] Rose Macaulay, 3 June 1947, from 20 Hinde House, Hinde Street, Manchester Square, London; BL. In an earlier letter (31 May) she wrote: '... As to anti-Catholic bias it is sad [that] you think [?] that [?]. Because I *like* Catholicism ... as to taking up any position myself to shoot at Catholics [?] – surely *no*!...' Graham Greene had advised her to cut examples of 'lush passages' in her article in that this represented unfair selection. She agreed to do this for the reprinting.
49. Unpublished TLS from [Sir] Maurice Bowra, 1 July [1947], from Wadham College, Oxford; BL.
50. 'The Last Days of Hitler', *Tablet*, 28 June 1947, 335; letter adding a note to Fr J. Brodrick's review and attacking Trevor-Roper's interpretation of a quotation from Newman: 'There is not the smallest reason why Mr. Trevor-Roper should introduce Catholic theologians into his nasty story. They are dragged in ignorantly, maliciously and irrelevantly. Mr. Trevor-Roper had a sensational subject. Apparently he thought it too good an opportunity to be missed for giving wide currency to his prejudices....'
51. Unpublished ALS to A. D. Peters, 1 July 1947, np [Piers Court]; *Catalogue* E 545, p. 146.

was planning a collection of short stories. The ball was rolling but there were ominous signs. Edmund Wilson was not the only influential critic to have condemned Waugh. Orville Prescott of the *New York Times* felt that Waugh's reputation 'had been overinflated',[52] and there was a serious danger that the bubble might burst if Waugh continued to provoke.

He worked carefully through two more drafts, expanding the text slightly. In September he submitted the second to Peters, who advised against American publication. 'I am sorry you don't like The Loved One,' Waugh replied:

> I have been sweating away at it and it is now more elegant but not less gruesome. I enclose a yank opinion ... from a woman of high Boston origins lately become a best seller. But I am not headstrong in this matter & don't want to antagonize future customers. The tale should not be read as a satire on morticians but as a study of the Anglo-American cultural impasse with the mortuary as a jolly setting....[53]

The 'woman of high Boston origins' was Helen Hans-Allen (Helen Howe), one of the few people Waugh had liked in Hollywood. Meticulous as ever, he had written asking for corrections to American slang and for her opinion as to the book's long-range effect on his literary reputation. Flattered to be asked, she took her task seriously and replied quickly:

> ... I have read 'The Loved One' with delight.... Don't worry about US public response. The readers who really will chatter like monkeys in a rage are the English colony in Hollywood. Are you aware that there is only one Dame living in the U.S. ... Dame May Whitty. Her friends will inevitably associate 'the caustic dame' with her, and are

52. 'Books of The Times', *NYT*, 14 June 1946; review of *Campion* and *Black Mischief.* In a later piece (6 January 1947), reviewing *When the Going Was Good*, Prescott remarked: 'His [early] books were entertaining, but they were permeated with an intellectual and social snobbery which was distasteful to many.... In spite of the drastic editing ... [of *When the Going*] ... it contains many random jottings of little interest....' A similar backwash of critical disdain for *Brideshead* was breaking on British shores. Rose Macaulay in *Horizon* (December 1946), while not denying the importance of 'divine purpose', had objected to the idea that Waugh seemed to 'equate the divine purpose, the tremendous fact of God at work in the universe, with obedient membership of a church' (372–6; *CH*, pp. 253–5). It was Donat O'Donnell in the *Bell* (December 1946, 38–49; *CH*, pp. 255–63), who had taken the argument a stage further by noting that 'one of the secrets of Mr. Waugh's comic genius was his keen interest in humiliation'. If we laugh, he suggests, we are a party to prejudice. 'Mr. Edmund Wilson ... condemned the snobbery of *Brideshead* ... but he had swallowed with delight the snobbery implicit in the early novels.... Snobbery was quite acceptable as an attitude: the critic objected only when it was formulated as a doctrine.' O'Donnell elucidates the confusion caused by this sentimentality in Waugh's theology and politics, and his phrase 'Neo-Jacobitism' was taken up by later critics, particularly Kingsley Amis, to suggest this brand of wistful romanticism. But it was O'Donnell's remark – 'In Mr. Waugh's theology, the love of money is not only the root of all evil, it is a preliminary form of the love of God' – which provoked the considerable debate in the *Bell* to which Waugh contributed, admitting snobbery in so far as he preferred 'the company of the European upper-classes' (July 1947, 77; *CH*, pp. 270–1).
53. ALS to A. D. Peters, 14 September [1947]; *Letters*, p. 259.

> not going to like ... seeing the old lady suffer by so much as a pin-prick. You undoubtedly know this....[54]

As other letters came in, it became clear that on several counts the novel might be subject to libel proceedings.

In the meantime, Waugh had offered the first printing to Connolly, asking for only two concessions in return: that it should appear as a complete issue of *Horizon*, and that Waugh's 'subscription' (i.e. free copies) should be maintained. Connolly, of course, accepted. It was a *coup* for the magazine but to its editor it meant a great deal more.

For many months Connolly and Waugh had not been on speaking terms and, although they missed each other, neither was humble enough to admit as much. Connolly lived in confused domestic circumstances and constantly heard echoes of Waugh's mockery. Waugh had prepared the ground for reconciliation by sending a message through Sykes: abuse of the Connolly women, he said, was directed against Janetta 'Barefoot' Woolley[55] not Lys Lubbock (Connolly's lover).[56] This alone would scarcely have repaired the breach. But Waugh had followed it with an invitation to Piers Court – for Connolly and Lys. At first they had refused. Waugh pressed them.

The visit had been a success. At the time, Waugh was nearing the end of the first draft of *The Loved One* and had mentioned it briefly. Connolly's ears had pricked up. On literary matters they understood each other and it also appeared that Boots was shifting his ground, recanting Socialism and developing a guilty predilection for expensive porcelain. 'May I record', he wrote afterwards, 'how delightful, suitable & commendable I found your *train de vie* – fine books, fine wine, fine view – I am sorry you will have to move them all to an Irish equivalent....'[57] Connolly had suggested that Waugh contribute an essay to the *Horizon* series in which Rose Macaulay's had appeared: 'The Best and the Worst'. Waugh, rather mischievously, chose Ronald Knox and, though subject and treatment were out of keeping with the series,[58] Connolly accepted and tentatively asked if he might also

54. Unpublished ALS from Helen Hans-Allen, 1 September 1947, from 1666 Summit Ridge Drive, Beverly Hills; BL.

55. Janetta Woolley, alternatively known as Blue Feet because she had once opened the door to Waugh wearing no shoes, later married Robert Kee, writer and broadcaster. She lived in Connolly's house during 1947 and, after her marriage to Kee, Connolly shared a house with them in Sussex Place.

56. Cf. unpublished ALS from Christopher Sykes, 2 June 1947, from High Elms, Farnborough, Kent; BL. Connolly's amatory muddles had amused his contemporaries for years. Cf. unpublished ALS from Nancy Mitford, 13 April 1946, from Hôtel de Bourgogne, 7 Rue de Bourgogne, Paris VII; BL: 'Stephen Spender – I suppose you hate him. He told me an awfully funny story about when Cyril was living with Jean [his first wife] & ******** & caught them both out having affairs ... & said to Steve, almost in tears, "It is hard, here have I been absolutely faithful to 2 women for a year & they've *both* been unfaithful to me...."'

57. Unpublished ALS from Lys Lubbock and Cyril Connolly, 3 July 1947, from *Horizon*, 6 Selwyn House, 2 Lansdowne Terrace, WC1; BL.

58. The object was to select a contemporary author whose faults as well as virtues were an obsessive

have a story. The response had been more generous than he had dared hope.

The dealings over the essay and *The Loved One* finally healed the wound. Connolly threw himself energetically into the correspondence; Waugh was happy to reclaim so sympathetic an acolyte. During July, *Scott-King* had appeared (abridged) in Quennell's *Cornhill*:[59] 'Curiously enough much as I enjoyed & agreed with your Cornhill story – it is the Strand one ['Tactical Exercise'] which haunts me – very subtle & perfect – the girl has great sex-appeal ... – but it must be delicious to be murdered, when you find life as intolerable as your hero....'[60] Both Waugh and Connolly recognized themselves in the misanthropic John Verney. 'Est, est, est! ...' Connolly replied after reading the second draft of *The Loved One*. 'One of your very best I think. I shall be honoured to publish it.... Is the obscenity of Aimée wagging her tail (piece of tail, slang for cunt) deliberate? You must beware of making ... [Dennis] ... sound too heartless. He knew her death was his fault....'[61] Waugh allowed Connolly to correct the slang and grammar, even to edit it for publication and to write a prefatory note – all unsupervised, a huge compliment – but there was to be no change to the callousness of the central figure. 'You will see that I have followed most of your suggestions. There is an ineradicable caddishness about all my heroes – Dennis too, I'm afraid.'[62]

In this and in his other correspondence of the period Waugh displayed an unaccustomed humility. During the autumn of 1947 a change had come over him. Persecution mania had subsided. The Easter retreat, it seems, had borne late fruit and another aspect of his character began to emerge, described by his son as 'the occasional almost religious gentleness which made his gloom such a cause for despondency in everyone else.'[63] Distance had been achieved from the torturing sense of military betrayal and, with distance, humour had returned. The first stage of the transition period was over.

*

On completing the first draft of *The Loved One*, Waugh had accepted an invitation to tour Scandinavian capitals at the *Telegraph*'s expense.[64] It was

concern and about whom the essayist could not make up his or her mind. Waugh's piece ('Ronald Knox', *Horizon*, 17 (May 1948), 152), promoting a literary priest as one of the great writers of the day, was straightforward eulogy.

59. *Cornhill*, 162 (Summer 1947), 321–64; reprinted as 'A Sojourn in Neutralia', *Hearst's International Combined with Cosmopolitan*, 123 (November 1947), 67–70, 73–4, 76, 78, 80, 83–4, 86, 88.
60. Unpublished ALS from Cyril Connolly, 7 July 1947, from *Horizon*, 6 Selwyn House etc.; BL.
61. ALS from Cyril Connolly, nd [September 1947–January 1948], from *Horizon* etc.; BL; partially quoted *Letters*, p. 260, n. 2.
62. Unpublished ALS to Cyril Connolly, nd [c. 10 January 1948], from Piers Court; private collection.
63. Auberon Waugh, 'Father and Son', *B & B*, 19 (October 1973), 10–12.
64. 17 August–2 September 1947.

merely a jaunt and an excuse to be away from Piers Court during his mother's annual visit. One way of spending untaxed translation moneys was to stockpile them in 'nest eggs', as he called them, in their country of origin. He had anticipated little pleasure from the visit and had gained little. But the tour marked a watershed in his life. He felt a calmness bordering on compassion for these strangers who would never understand him, and, in this mood of relative benignity, perhaps recognizing in Scandinavia more powerfully than ever before the disadvantages of being a foreigner, he abruptly abandoned his plan to move to Ireland.

He explained the reasons for this in purely rational terms which circle the issues cautiously without settling on a satisfactory answer.[65] The decision to recant had been impulsive, and his wife's anxiety surely prompted it. Although he could not admit that he had been wrong, a certain guilt nagged him: guilt at his rashness and carelessness for others, particularly for Laura.

While he was away, Laura had received a letter: 'I asked Hatty [three years old] to break the news to you that I have decided to live in England for a bit longer. I hope she broke it gently.'[66] Laura was immensely relieved to find him back on form. With typical disregard for her comfort he had invited forty orphans to tea in his absence and merely left a note of the arrangement on his engagement pad. Laura had seen it at the last moment when two coachloads were due with eight nuns and a priest. A few weeks earlier, she would have been depressed by the prospect. With her husband's Irish madness cured, she relished the ludicrous solemnity of the event and 'phoned a neighbour for emergency assistance. After the mob departed, Laura and her friend attacked the strong drink in a fit of giggles. It was at this moment that Waugh had returned bearing a stuffed animal and a large German mechanical organ.[67] His fixed intention now was to embellish Piers Court with amusing and educational artefacts. These oddities were the first instalment.

It was a happy reunion against a background of continuous strain in the marriage. Their contentment, however, was short-lived. Towards the end of September, Eddie Grant died and Laura went to stay with her widowed

65. *Diaries*, 25 August 1947, p. 689: 'Reasons: (1) Noble. The Church in England needs me. (2) Ignoble. It would be bad for my reputation as a writer. (3) Indifferent. There is no reason to suppose life in Ireland will be more tolerable than here. My children must be English. I should become an anachronism. The Socialists are piling up repressive measures now. It would seem I was flying from them. If I am to be a national figure I must stay at home. The Americans would lose interest in an emigrant and the Irish would not be interested.'

66. 20 August [1947]; *Letters*, p. 258.

67. Cf. unpublished TLS from Teresa M. Forrest to Alec Waugh, 17 March 1970, from Manor Place, Chilgrove, nr Chichester, Sussex; BUL. Mrs Forrest was the neighbour. She also recounts her first dinner at Piers Court, after the war, when Waugh opened by asking her what she thought of the picture over the fireplace. There was no picture – only the outline of the space where one had hung. 'I shall always remember the Waugh family in my prayers,' she wrote, 'so gifted, so natural, so lovable.'

sister at Nutcombe. There, doubts again assailed Laura. She felt that, for the first time, she had been of use to someone and that Waugh did not treat her with the special privilege due to a wife. More than this, she wrote to tell him. 'Let me assure you . . .', he replied, 'that I can recall numerous occasions . . . when you have been of use to your own children & several when you have been of use to me. So shake off these morbid scruples and return to duty. . . . There is no question of my not "doing more for you than for others". . . . Don't be so bloody wet.'[68] Small comfort in that 'several'. He blustered his way out of her accusations, but it seems that he recognized their validity.

Alone and low-spirited, he had revised *The Loved One* and dug the garden, only to be poleaxed by fibrositis. On Laura's return she had propped him up in the library before a blazing fire and, in this helpless condition, he had received a letter from Penelope Betjeman. She had just begun instruction but, while he rejoiced in this, her other news troubled him.

> John is in a dreadful state . . . as I don't think he has fundamentally enough faith in his own church to overcome the inevitable difficulties of this period, especially with regard to the children. If it were not for the fact that I can now hear Mass regularly I should long ago have expired . . . during the past three weeks the situation has become acute. . . .[69]

Did Waugh feel another stab of remorse? Certainly he did not covet responsibility for wrecking a Christian marriage, and Betjeman was in danger of celebrating the day of his wife's reception by packing his bags.

Waugh looked about his own home. He had, he knew, taken too little care of this. Nancy often wrote asking after her godchild, sending presents. He examined Harriet for his report and the indifference with which he had previously regarded his offspring was now replaced by affectionate humour: 'I cannot tell you her precise age but I can describe her condition. She walks & speaks volubly but unintelligibly. A manic-depressive with marked theatrical tendencies. Highly popular with other children, hated by servants. Extremely droll. I think the most interesting of my children.'[70] Although never a dandler, Waugh was far from careless of his flock. He had a precise idea of their individual natures and, from this time, involved them in the exotic fantasy life of Piers Court. Strangers found themselves pierced by several sets of elfin eyes awaiting Papa's signal to flatter or torment. At mealtimes, visitors would be intimidated by the younger Waughs relent-

68. ALS to Laura Waugh, nd [October 1947]; *Letters*, p. 261.
69. Unpublished ALS from Penelope [Lady] Betjeman, Sunday, 12 October 1947, from Farnborough Old Rectory etc.; BL.
70. Unpublished ALS to Nancy Mitford, 23 October [1947], from Piers Court; BL.

lessly grinding the Victorian organ. It became a close family, a conspiracy against the outside world.

*

Waugh settled, if not happily, at least with resignation to the final revision of *The Loved One*, determined to make Piers Court his home, and his family the centre of his life. He had found an artist, Stuart Boyle, to illustrate the text, invited him down and told him exactly what to draw. Even when the manuscript was temporarily lost by Connolly's office, Waugh suffered the crisis without rage. He felt suddenly much older; he was beginning to listen to the 'voices'.

When *Scott-King* was published in hardback that December,[71] the reviews were generally tepid.[72] An advance copy had been sent to Desmond MacCarthy, who had read it eagerly. 'I know how loyal you are to the European tradition,' he replied, 'but I was delighted to discover your respect for "dim" people.'[73] On this basis, Waugh had hoped for high praise from him in the *Sunday Times*. Instead, the book was judged by John Russell, a writer whose dimness was to Waugh so complete that he had never heard of him. Worse still, Russell used his piece as an opportunity to attack *Brideshead*: 'More recent novels by this master of detached comedy have disclosed a deutero-Waugh; and our original interlocutor, who combined within himself the qualities of Horace, Martial and Propertius, has often been shouted down by the voice of an irritable and self-infatuated child....'[74] 'I am annoyed', Waugh recorded, 'to find myself continually described by people whom I have never set eyes on as bad-tempered.'[75] As we have seen, 'self-infatuated' hurt, especially after his struggle for rectitude, so he broke with custom and replied.

The response cannot have cheered him. He soon discovered that Russell was neither fool nor sycophant:

> You make religion appear like a department of good form. In the same way your upper classes are like the English nobility in a Portuguese farce.... Ryder is not really so very far distant from Mottram, that's why he detests him so much; he has the same arriviste's outlook, but

71. 10 December 1947.
72. Peter Quennell praised *Scott-King* in the *DM* (13 December 1947) and the anonymous *TLS* and *Tablet* reviewers (possibly Sykes and Woodruff, respectively) liked the book. But the general view was reflected by Illtyd Evans in *Blackfriars* (February 1948, 107): '... a novelist's fair copy: skilful, slight, an extended note in the margin.'
73. Unpublished ALS from Desmond MacCarthy, 8 December 1947, from Garrick Villa, Hampton-on-Thames, Middlesex; BL.
74. *ST*, 21 December 1947, 3; *CH*, pp. 293–4.
75. *Diaries*, Boxing Day 1947, p. 692.

> he uses a less primitive ladder. The vulgarity of Ryder and the vulgarity of Mottram are the same.[76]

This cut uncomfortably close to the bone for a parvenu and a convert, as did Russell's later remarks about the book's lack of charity and failures of verisimilitude,[77] but Waugh unhappily battled on with his enquiry. This was all very well, he replied, but Russell had not answered his point. Why did he think Waugh 'self-infatuated'?

The reply was brutally frank:

> An author is self-infatuated, as I see it, when he is so suffused with the beauty of his own position that he cannot any longer judge whether or not he is being his own best advocate. . . . I should not . . . have presumed to speak so bluntly if you had not . . . given me leave to do so.[78]

This was also not far from the truth and Waugh knew it. Engaging in such correspondence was an aspect of self-mortification. He did not complain when the lash fell justly, and he did not abuse Mr Russell afterwards.

Scott-King sold well despite the growing ground-swell of disapproval for Waugh's 'political' attitudes. There was a subscription of 9,300; telephone repeats poured in. By Christmas, sales had reached 14,000. McDougall of Chapman & Hall (already on first-name terms) had set aside the maximum paper allowance for the reprinting of the early novels in a Uniform Edition, for which there was a subscription of over 3,000 apiece. Although Waugh felt his spiritual condition to be parlous, his finances had never been more robust. In December, a curious letter had arrived from Derek Jackson: 'I would like to buy the animal outright,' he said, 'and enclose a cheque for £700. I will ask the appropriate people . . . about ownership of the horse. . . . Possibly the simplest would be for him to continue to run in your colours.'[79] Was Evelyn Waugh extending his interests to the turf? Not a bit of it: 'horse' was tax-evaders' code for 'car'. Having abandoned Ireland, Waugh was selling Mayes's station-wagon for a clear profit.[80]

76. Unpublished ALS, from John Russell, 19 January 1948, from 3 St Alban's Grove, W8; BL.
77. *Ibid.*: 'If you take religion and good breeding from a manual of etiquette, and you disallow the possibility of grace from anybody who drinks beer before dinner instead of cocktails, you take away the dignity of your favoured characters and you take away the dignity of yourself. The whole of life becomes a charade in which you attempt to emulate an imaginary mode of life – but one in which the Christian virtues of charity and freedom from pride never begin to appear.'
78. Unpublished ALS from John Russell, 20 January 1948, from 3 St Alban's Grove, W8; BL.
79. Unpublished ALS from [Sir] Derek Jackson, 20 December 1947, from Russeltown Park, Carlow, Co. Carlow, Eire; BL. Professor Jackson, husband of Pamela [*née* Mitford], was an eminent physicist and amateur steeplechaser, known in the racing world as the 'Galloping Professor'.
80. The car could not be imported without the payment of duty but neither could Jackson's cheque be cashed without the payment of tax. It was illegal to sell a new car within a year of purchase. Waugh, it seems, said nothing of this money to his accountant.

The Loved One was to appear in the February 1948 issue of *Horizon*. Connolly's nerves were prickling. At the beginning of the new year he had suggested that he write a 'Comment' 'introducing the story and making it clear that it is to be regarded as Swiftian satire on California burial customs. The mention of Swift sets a precedent for a certain savagery. The use of the word Californian makes it clear that you are not attacking America as a whole. . . .'[81] Waugh, of course, *was* attacking America as a whole, but he let Connolly have his way. More potential libel issues had emerged[82] and, against Peters's advice, Waugh had decided to proceed with US publication. *Horizon* was printing 9,500. 'I wish it were 19,000,' Connolly wrote.

> They all seem to be over-subscribed. . . . Zero hour any moment now! I am as interested as a parent whose son has just gone up for a scholarship and seems . . . to have actually won it. One thing I think you will enjoy will be the praise of those 'highbrow' critics who irritated you somewhat about *Brideshead*.[83]

'I was in London for two days this week', Waugh replied, '& hoped to see you. Perhaps I did see you. I cannot tell, for I got very drunk at once & remained drunk causing, rather than collecting, gossip.'[84] One minor friction with Connolly had been his recent refusal to write Waugh a 'London letter' on the grounds that he (Connolly) took no pleasure in gossiping about the calamities of friends. Waugh thought this priggish, particularly as it was also untrue; Connolly had apologized but had reminded him that '. . . you have a basic sense of security to laugh at other people's misfortunes. I always feel "There but for the grace of God" – or even "Your turn next. . . ." '[85] That, he said, was the reason why he could not write like Nancy. Waugh took the point; it was a fault in him, not Connolly, and the brief awkwardness was over.

'With regard to *The Loved One*:' Waugh continued, 'I anticipated ructions & one reason, apart from the predominant one of my affection for yourself, for my seeking publication in *Horizon* was the confidence that its readers were tough stuff.'[86] The *New Yorker*, *Good Housekeeping*, *Atlantic*

81. Unpublished ALS from Cyril Connolly, 1 January 1948, from *Horizon* etc.; BL.
82. Cf. unpublished ALS from Cyril Connolly, 2 February 1948, from *Horizon* etc.; BL: '. . . I don't think it would matter if Forest Lawns [*sic*] took offence but our printer's lawyer thinks that Aubrey Smith might have a case which would be awkward as he can probably bring it in the English courts. I imagine the answer . . . would be that being President of the Cricket Club was but one attribute of many taken from all kinds of English actors.' Waugh did not alter Sir Ambrose Abercrombie's (rather similar) christian name. Nothing came of the matter.
83. *Ibid.*
84. 2 January 1948; *Letters*, p. 265.
85. Unpublished ALS from Cyril Connolly, nd [16 December? 1947], from White's; BL.
86. 2 January 1948; *Letters*, p. 265. Connolly quoted liberally from this letter in his 'Comment', including this statement and the following, cautiously omitting the bracketed sections: 'The ideas I had in mind in writing were: 1st & quite predominantly over-excitement with the scene [of Forest Lawn]. 2nd the Anglo-American impasse – "never the twain shall meet". 3rd there is no such

Monthly and *Town and Country* had all refused it[87] and McIntyre, although finding it brilliant, required small changes for the American edition. Waugh nevertheless knew that he had produced a masterpiece. 'The more I re-read [it],' he had written to Peters, 'the better content I am with it.'[88] He had to wait until November for the British 'highbrow' accolades, but the book was an instant success. *Horizon* sold out overnight and it was a source of pride to Waugh that, of the well-thumbed issues passed eagerly from hand to hand, one apparently belonged to Princess Margaret.

He sent copies to all his friends. The book was dedicated to Nancy, whose joy at the honour and attempt to read it over lunch nearly choked her: '... I've been utterly shrieking ever since it arrived ... combined it happily with a banana & am now in despair at having finished it....'[89] Even Katharine Asquith approved, a great relief to Waugh who had expected her to think the novel in bad taste. Betjeman, generous as ever, proclaimed it Waugh's finest work: '... what I like so much about it is its complete exposure of American materialism ... [it is] not a country at all but a pool of ancient refugees lapsed into their antique paganism.... I am proud to know you.... I heard Cyril has had a heart attack....'[90] He had – or a minor seizure of some sort – brought on by over-eating. When his doctors prescribed a drastic diet at a clinic in Tring, Waugh took this as a salutary warning, curiously apposite to the subject of his book.

After all the nervousness about its American reception, *The Loved One* was the only one of Waugh's novels to appear first in hardback on the other side of the Atlantic, an accident dictated purely by commercial considerations. In fact, McIntyre had delayed publication until the libel issues had been cleared with the lawyers. The reason this edition beat the British one to the post (by three months) was simply that it was ready too soon after *Scott-King*, which was still selling briskly. The latter had not appeared in America. For the 'Yanks', *The Loved One* was the long-awaited

thing as an American. They are all exiles, uprooted, transplanted & doomed to sterility. The ancestral gods they have abjured get them in the end. I tried to indicate this in Aimée's last hours. 4th the European raiders who come for the spoils & if they are lucky make for home with them. 5th Memento mori [old style, not specifically Californian]' (pp. 265–6). 'Now if we talk of the "Anglo-Californian impasse"', Connolly added judiciously, 'and say there is no such thing as a Southern Californian, there is nothing in Mr. Waugh's phrasing with which many Americans would not agree' (*Horizon*, 17 (February 1948), 76–7; *CH*, p. 299).

87. Cf. unpublished TccL from Harold Matson to A. D. Peters, 10 December 1947, from 30 Rockefeller Plaza, NY; BL; forwarding *Town and Country*'s comments: '... The latter part is quite unpublishable, I think, by anyone.... And, too, Mr. Hearst doesn't like to have death mentioned....'
88. [December 1947]; *Letters*, p. 264.
89. Unpublished ALS from Nancy Mitford, 9 February 1948, from 7 Rue Monsieur, Paris VII; BL.
90. Unpublished ALS from [Sir] John Betjeman, 28 February 1948; from Farnborough Old Rectory etc.; BL.

successor to *Brideshead*: it would be widely reviewed and was sure to provoke comparison and controversy.

The American reaction surprised Waugh: no 'ructions'. The only unfavourable notices came later from the British. *Time* found faults (in the dialogue and 'in the intricate inanities of Whispering Glades') but was generally enthusiastic, devoting six columns to a review and a survey of Waugh's career, a compliment which, if McIntyre's memory served him well, had never before been accorded to a living author.[91] The more radical *New Republic* considered it 'strong medicine' but, technically, 'nearly faultless' and 'as satire ... an act of devastation, an angry, important moral effort that does not fail.'[92] The novel suggests that Americans are handicapped by a puritanical mirthlessness which allows them to take seriously a world of substitute values. They are eminently shockable, complacent, ignorant of their vulnerability and corruption, the standardized products of the mass media. But, in anticipating a scandal, Waugh had underestimated their ability to laugh at themselves. Edmund Wilson attacked the book later – but he had a score to settle.[93]

It came to British reviewers with a long history of rumour. Most were delighted. Even the Americanophile Alistair Cooke could remark that 'The writing is matchless, the mood finished and serene.'[94] The *TLS* gave it extensive coverage and for the first time placed Waugh in the front rank of writers opposed to liberal humanism. His apparent return to a more allusive, 'two-dimensional' style suggested (wrongly) to their critic that Waugh had 'finally accepted his métier'.[95] Only MacCarthy, however, compensating for his failure to puff *Scott-King*, pointed to the implicit metaphysics behind the work: 'a ruthless exposure of a silly optimistic trend in modern civilization which takes for granted that the consolations of religion can be enjoyed without belief in them ... and seeks to persuade us that there is nothing really tragic in the predicament of man....'[96] This was Waugh's perspective. Ultimately his satire aimed to establish theological rather than

91. *Time*, 12 July 1948, 40–2, 44; *CH*, pp. 301–2.
92. *NR*, 26 July 1948, 24; *CH*, pp. 303–4.
93. Wilson's *Classics and Commercials. A Literary Chronicle of the Forties* (W. H. Allen, 1951) was a collection of his reviews including two sections on Waugh: 'Never Apologise; Never Explain: The Art of Evelyn Waugh' and 'Splendours and Miseries of Evelyn Waugh'. The latter included his attacks on *Brideshead* and *Campion* and Wilson added a few paragraphs on *Scott-King* and *The Loved One* (pp. 304–5) to bring his survey up to date. He found both 'sketchy and incomplete': 'To the non-religious reader, however, the patrons and proprietors of Whispering Glades seem more sensible and less absurd than the priest-guided Evelyn Waugh. What the former are trying to do is ... merely to gloss over physical death; but, for the Catholic, the fact of death is not to be faced at all....' Cf. *CH*, pp. 316–17, where *Scrutiny*'s John Farrelly defends Waugh's book against this attack.
94. *Manchester Guardian*, 19 November 1948, 3.
95. *TLS*, 20 November 1948, 652; *CH*, pp. 304–7.
96. *ST*, 21 November 1948, 3; *CH*, pp. 308–9.

'sociological' truths. The theme of 'tragedy' indicated by the subtitle ('An Anglo-American Tragedy') was largely ignored.

No one noticed that a European, Catholic tradition was opposed to an American, Protestant one; a vital culture (shadows of which emerge in Aimée and intrigue Dennis) is drowned by materialism. In the terms of Waugh's earlier writing, it is the conflict between the Mediterranean South and the cold North, between classical civilization and the frigid rationalism of post-Reformation Europe. Aimée is 'Greek'. The story rewrites Scott-King's plight in an American context by taking a Jamesian theme, as Waugh reminds us with a delicious self-referential joke. '"Through no wish of my own,"' Dennis informs the brutal Mr Shultz, '"I have become the protagonist of a Jamesian problem.... All his stories are about the same thing – American innocence and European experience.... [They] are all tragedies one way or another."'[97] Mr Shultz has no time for tragedies. Mr Waugh insists that, whether Shultz likes it or not, he is implicated in one.

The book is so funny and so brief that there is scarcely room for such serious themes to take root. But they are there for all that, skilfully woven throughout the fabric. The recurrent jokes need no explanation and in many respects their ironies have been the staple of American fiction from Hawthorne to Vonnegut: America as Substitute Land – its puritanism hypocritical, its freedom a mockery, its art counterfeit, its language debased. It was an ancient literary routine.[98] Indeed, one of the extraordinary aspects of this novel is its resemblance to the work of Nathanael West. There is no evidence of Waugh's having read *Miss Lonelyhearts* (1933) or *The Day of the Locust* (1939), yet the Guru Brahmin and the Hollywood scenes are informed by the same lurid surrealism. It was not the subject matter that made *The Loved One* unique but its Catholic perspective. By shifting James's 'Anglo-American impasse' into an implicitly theological context, Waugh broadened the sense of the tragedy to include that shared by all mankind: the aboriginal calamity through which Adam and Eve bought knowledge at the expense of innocence.

As in his early fiction, this post-lapsarian perspective affords Waugh distance, and his mockery is savage. From Mr Heinkel's formal evening wear to the parrot in an open casket, the book laughs 'Damned!' from every page. The Californians, British or American, are barbarous refugees in their

97. *The Loved One: An Anglo-American Tragedy*, first printed *Horizon*, 17 (February 1948), 78–159; (Chapman & Hall, 1948; reprinted Harmondsworth, Penguin Books, 1951 and 1969), p. 96.

98. Cf. *NS*, 11 December 1948, 528–9; *CH*, pp. 309–12. This, the only unfavourable review in a major British paper, came from R. D. Smith: 'The plot is ingeniously and vividly worked out, but the work as a whole is uneven, in planning, execution and feeling. Hollywood, funeral hypocrisy, and the ad-man's domain of nutburgers, Jungle Venom perfume, and peaches without stones are themes that have been well worked over before, more effectively indeed, by Mr. Aldous Huxley, Mr. Sinclair Lewis and by various hands in the *New Yorker*, notably Mr. S. J. Perelman.'

desert, disconnected from qualitative standards. In the studios, as in the mortuaries, these actors play God, making and unmaking, 're-creating personality'.[99] They cannot see that The Happier Hunting Ground and Whispering Glades are, in all spiritual respects, identical and that both are the same as the Guru Brahmin. Whispering Glades becomes a parodic vision of Eden, even of the Kingdom of Heaven with the Dreamer as its God and Joyboy as St Peter. It is the *reductio ad absurdum* of the humanist belief in life's perfectibility, the dead fruit of the American Dream. From the pioneers to the cinema men to the crones seeking sunshine retirement, all had migrated westward, away from Europe, in search of this vision.

The appalling irony of this dream, Waugh suggests, is that it represents both an inarticulate terror of death and a secular form of Redemption. Forest Lawn exists to pretend to the slothful that death does not exist,[100] and Waugh, in another of his Hamlet roles, leaps gaily into the grave to thrust a skull into their faces. At every turn the significance of this traditional *memento mori* is stressed. Just as Dennis smashes the goat's skull and then Aimée's, so Waugh lays about him with an intellectual poker and points relentlessly to the furnace.

It is a remarkable *tour de force* to render such a theme amusing and Waugh manages this by flattering the reader's cultural snobbery. The very act of reading such a work and understanding the jokes sets us apart. European readers are seduced into guffaws at the Americans' expense (just as Bostonians and New Yorkers were seduced at the Californians' expense). Waugh, however, has an unpleasant habit of turning the gun on our complacency, and even on his own. The book opens with another self-reference, lampooning the magazine in which the story first appeared: no safe European ground there. And it is Aimée who remarks innocently: '"Once you start changing a name . . . you see, there's no reason ever to stop. One always hears one that sounds better."'[101] Nothing more accurately reflects Waugh's conservative approach to language and human relations. Throughout the novel, suffering and suicide reward the secular quest for totems. For here, by implication, we have no abiding city. Again, we witness the human tragedy of missed connections,[102] but something has been added

99. *The Loved One*, *op. cit.*, p. 47.

100. Cf. 'Half in Love with Easeful Death', *op. cit.*; *EAR*, p. 335: 'Here on the ultimate sunset-shore [Californians] warm their old bodies and believe themselves alive, opening their scaly eyes two or three times a day to browse on salads and fruits. They have long forgotten the lands that gave them birth and the arts and trades they once practised . . . and round them congregate the priests of countless preposterous cults to soothe them into the cocoon-state in which they will slough off their old bodies. The ideal is to shade off, so finely that it becomes imperceptible, the moment of transition, and it is to this process that Forest Lawn is the most conspicuous monument.'

101. *The Loved One*, *op. cit.*, p. 73.

102. Waugh emphasizes this neatly by two similar scenes – one near the beginning, one near the end; one funny, one macabre – which counterpoint each other. Dennis, receiving Mrs Heinkel's lunatic telephone call about the death of her Sealyham, lays the receiver on his blotting pad until her

to Waugh's 'bodiless harlequinade'. In Aimée's eyes, grey-green and distant, a memory lingers in the 'rich glint of lunacy'. She, the 'sole Eve in a bustling hygienic Eden',[103] is a decadent, still connected, however tenuously, to the traditions her ancestors abjured. Her tragedy is that she has no theological or cultural language with which to articulate these sensations. Dennis treats her cruelly, and at first we are encouraged to approve. What begins as a European joke, however, ends with our feeling no more for him than we do for her. The price of his artistic vision is another loss of innocence.

Waugh well understood the spiritual expense of his craft. His novel was too slight to bear the weight of his melancholy, but the 'ineradicable caddishness' of Dennis was something Waugh recognized, and repented, in himself. Hamlet holds up the skull of the jester and, in similar fashion, Dennis was perhaps Waugh's way of rebuking himself. He never wrote another 'cruel' book. From this point his work represented a form of *pietas*. There was something that, despite himself, he had found intriguing in American innocence.

*

The year 1948 was a strange one for Waugh. Every misery he had predicted under Socialism had come about. Austerity had continued unabated after the crippling winter and subsequent floods: severe rationing (petrol, meat, bread) still enforced and becoming harsher; desperate attempts to feed the country on whalemeat and indigestible 'snoek';[104] a ban on foreign travel. A huge balance of payments deficit was supported by equally huge dollar loans. The previous year had seen the granting of independence to India and Pakistan. The Empire was contracting to its centre. Britain was becoming what it now is: a massively indebted satellite of the United States while simultaneously suffering, in this pinched condition, advertisements proclaiming American prosperity. The 'spiv' in drape suit and kipper tie, dealing on street corners from a roll of fivers, glamorized petty crime as an ingenious struggle against 'Authority'. Waugh was not unusual in his political misanthropy. It was a bad time for Labour politics and for the country as a whole.

In April, Sir Stafford Cripps, newly appointed as Chancellor of the Exchequer to resolve the crisis, had switched the emphasis from direct to

grief has expended itself (p. 18); Mr Slump, receiving Aimée's call, places the instrument on the bar for the amusement of his drunken colleagues. In the latter instance, 'Tiny utterances rose from the stained wood' (p. 114), and when Slump eventually resumes the dialogue, he tells her to kill herself.

103. *Ibid.*, p. 46.

104. Cf. Susan Cooper, 'Snoek Piquante' in Michael Sissons and Philip French (eds), *The Age of Austerity 1945–1951* (Hodder & Stoughton, 1963; reprinted OUP pb, 1986), pp. 39–42. A snoek was a long, slender South African fish with fearsome teeth. Millions of tins of it were imported under government contract and an unsuccessful propaganda campaign begun to promote sales.

indirect taxation, escalating the price of luxuries and attacking inherited wealth. Wives like Laura, with more than £2,000 in trust funds, found their share income rendered negligible. Waugh pretended to care but, somehow, he did not. He was financially secure. Indeed, his problem was how not to earn too much and, like the spiv, it amused him to cheat restrictions. He watched what he took to be his country's death-throes with something approaching good humour and turned his face towards America. Something was happening there which he had failed to account for in *The Loved One*.

Looking back from his forty-fifth birthday he saw only an 'unproductive and unhealthy year'.[105] He had written little and suffered much. Piles had been followed by an agonizing attack of nettle rash. His teeth were giving him trouble. 'Success', he had remarked gloomily in August, 'has brought idleness as its dead fruit.'[106] But this was more self-mortification than truth. He had been far from idle. He had simply deflected his attention from his own writing to that of others and from an obsession with decay to the passionate refurbishment of his home.

When Betjeman ordered a funereal wallpaper and found it overbearing, Waugh snapped it up. '[It is] very remarkable,' he wrote to the Marchioness of Bath (later Daphne Fielding), 'very dark 1860 Gothic. . . . Please come & stay when the room is finished. It will be a nightmare.'[107] He had the woodwork painted pink and scoured London for Victorian subject paintings.[108] On the sideboard stood the Paravicini bust with its forage cap. Every image told a story and was, in its new context, a joke about the collapse of civilization. The house became in part a comic chamber of horrors, a museum of *memento mori* designed to unsettle, and in this playfully gruesome atmosphere Waugh felt contented. Piers Court was the opposite of Forest Lawn.

The year had opened with his buying a set of Beerbohm's works and spending all day in bedroom slippers, cigar in hand before the library fire, re-reading the Master. Bliss. It continued with his attempting Proust (in English). Bafflement. Nancy tried to convince him of Proust's merits and was shocked to learn that Waugh could not read French accurately. But it

105. *Diaries*, 28 October 1948, p. 703.
106. *Ibid.*, 16 August 1948, p. 698.
107. 27 January 1948; *Letters*, p. 267.
108. A matched pair, 'The Pleasures of Travel', by Robert Musgrave Joy, and the Viennese Swoboda's 'The Connoisseurs'. The 'Joys' represented a stagecoach being robbed in 1751, and a train carriage in 1851 with its upright and unmolested citizens. Waugh later commissioned a complementary third: 'The Pleasures of Travel in 1951', depicting panic in the packed cabin of a crashing airliner. The Swoboda depicted 'a group of savants, perhaps identifiable, disputing the authenticity of an old master before the agonised widow whose future penury or prosperity depends on their decision' (unpublished ALS to Cyril Connolly, nd [mid-January? 1948], from Piers Court; private collection).

was no use. Every year, it seemed, he aged by a decade. *Brideshead* had lingered sentimentally over the 1920s; *The Loved One* over the sort of English poetry Arthur Waugh used to recite to his sons in the period of Georgian *belles lettres*. The essay on Knox suggests loyalty to the generation of golden intellects extinguished by the Great War. Everything he had hated in his youth, Waugh now cherished. Soon he would be Victorian. By the end of his life he was back where he felt he belonged: in the Counter-Reformation and, finally, the catacombs.

'I go out shopping after luncheon a bit tight', he wrote to Nancy, '& buy such peculiar things – 3 tie pins, a $\frac{1}{2}$ ton marble 2nd Empire Clock, a solid silver 1830 candelabrum as tall as myself, a pearl grey bowler, six pounds of church candles – they keep appearing in my [hotel] bed room in the most disconcerting way. Perhaps it is not drink but insanity.'[109] In fact, he had never been saner or more approachable. The Marchioness of Bath, the Plunket Greenes, Pansy Lamb, Graham Greene and Lady Diana Cooper re-emerged at the centre of his life (or, rather, at the centre of his correspondence, which was much the same thing). That year saw the beginning of his affection for Ann Fleming and Elizabeth Pakenham (now Lady Longford). When Penelope Betjeman was about to be received in March, the warmth of his welcome to the Household could scarcely have been surpassed.[110] Visiting the Marchioness at Longleat and finding a house roaring with children and jazz, the Marquis reading lubricious passages from the *Sexual Life of Savages* to his daughter, Waugh loved it all: 'The dinner party was just what I like to think my youth was like (and it was not for it was full of melancholy & self-distrust) all light and sweetness.'[111]

While there, Waugh agreed to write something for the Marquis's birthday book, and later sent a rendering of 'a little nightmare that troubled me recently'. 'I never slept a wink last night,' Bath replied, 'having read your nightmare. To be quite frank I had an emission – the first time for years – I couldn't be more grateful....'[112] Waugh's account was indeed extraordinary:

> Extract from unpublished autobiography by Evelyn Waugh.... At this time my father made a further attempt to settle me in a profession by purchasing some secondhand dentist's instruments and a small

109. 7 April 1948; *Letters*, p. 276.
110. [7 March 1948]; *Letters*, p. 271: 'May you live happily ever after. I am sure you will ... but what you cannot know until Tuesday is the delight of membership of the Household, of having your chair at the table, a place laid, the bed turned down, of the love & trust, whatever the family bickerings, of all Christendom.... It is a particular joy for me to be able to welcome you home ... please pray for me.'
111. April 1948; *ibid.*, p. 275.
112. Unpublished ALS, 18 April 1948, from Sturford Mead, Warminster, Wilts.; BL.

> practice in a Northern city. I was not a success, for my coarse manners and manual clumsiness soon alienated my few patients but it was during this period that I encountered a problem which seems to be unique in dental history. A man came to me & complained that his teeth had lately become so prominent as to excite general ridicule. I measured them & found they were $\frac{1}{8}$ of an inch longer than was normal. During the period when I had him under observation they grew steadily. It was not that the gums receded but that the teeth actually lengthened at an astonishing rate. I began by filing them but one day I decided on extraction. I had the man under gas & taking my pincers pulled strongly at an eye-tooth. To my alarm it moved easily but, instead of roots, more tooth appeared. I had drawn it to a length of six or seven inches when he 'came to' & complaining bitterly left my operating room. Later his back teeth grew proportionately so that I was obliged to remove the lower jaw entirely. The upper teeth then grew steadily & swiftly making a kind of paling which eventually penetrated his chest near the collar bone causing a lingering and painful death.

Freudians may make of this what they will. There is no evidence to suggest that it is any less fictional than Bath's emission. But, given that 1948 was for Waugh a year of friendship and benevolence, and one which ended with his revising his attitude to America, the tone of the piece, and the fact that it was sent to an aristocrat, are interesting factors.

At Longleat, Waugh had been further reminded of his unhappy youth by a visit to the Plunket Greenes: 'Olivia $\frac{1}{3}$ drunk, $\frac{1}{3}$ insane, $\frac{1}{3}$ genius.'[113] Shortly after his return, the Marchioness wrote to him – Gwen had rung; Olivia felt that she must now face the world: 'I sent a car for her. She arrived, clutching a whisky bottle. The moment she got within the portals, she fell flat on her face – from fear, and not, I think, from drink ... talked a lot about you, Communism & free love ... she is expecting you on the bus, pour le five o'clock at any moment....'[114] Waugh boarded no bus, but neither did he shirk his responsibilities. Olivia's soul, like Betjeman's, was in danger, and Waugh was prepared to fight for it.

In the lengthy correspondence which ensued, Waugh was cast strangely back into that feminine atmosphere in which he had first tasted Catholic life and fallen in love with a family. 'I always remember you ...,' Gwen wrote, 'beginning a book – just 5 sentences it was – in that look out house on Lundy Island – how many years ago, do you remember ... just a few

113. *Diaries*, 4 May 1948, p. 698.
114. Unpublished ALS from Daphne, Marchioness of Bath, 16 April 1948, from Lismore Castle, Co. Waterford, Eire; BL.

lines about Silenus. . . .'[115] He remembered: Easter 1925, a hopeless future, schoolmastering, the book Kegan Paul refused, and agonies of frustration over Olivia; he, the young man from the suburbs, at play and slightly uncomfortable with the upper crust; they, easy, laughing; jazz, drink and passionate discussions long into the night. It seemed a century ago. These two strange women had drifted into esotericism: isolated, poor, half-crazed as it seemed to Waugh. He was master now. Olivia raved through lengthy, near-illegible letters ('O Evelyn I do so adore being an invalid maiden lady living in a hut in a remote forest . . .'), plunging between arrogance and compassion: 'I loathe *obedient* people – horrible sheep all *toeing the line* . . . it is only the Mary in me that allows me to be Martha at all. . . .'[116] She was a Communist living on unearned income, a Catholic who refused the discipline of the Church. But she remained warm, brave, amusing, sharp.

Waugh tried. He explained the contradictions in her theological position. He insisted that it was impossible to be both Communist and Catholic. Inevitably the argument became overheated. 'Darling Evelyn, Balls to *you*. Of course capitalism is a crime.'[117] He responded in kind; she was left, he said, with only the Saints Lucifer, Rimbaud and Paul Robeson; she was a traitor to the Faith. At first the energy of the discussion abstracted her from her misery. Then it broke her. Waugh aligned her with Judas. 'I think it possible', she replied, 'that a day will come when you are going to come to me on your *knees* to apologise. . . . Until that day I think it best we close our correspondence. . . . I want to send *lots* of love to you & let us leave it at that. . . .'[118]

They left it at that. Gwen wrote later to say that poor Olivia had consulted a priest to ask whether she was a traitor to the Church for contributing money to *Labour Monthly*. No, the priest had said, she was not. Waugh's tactics in theological debate were ruthless. Madness, he thought, stalked everywhere. Nancy wrote from the Rue Monsieur like a china doll in a firestorm, one moment describing 'the Hell of the Harveys'[119] and all 'Society' with its bags packed and sandwiches cut in imminent expectation of a Russian invasion; the next, humbly submitting that Communism was a high human ideal. But Waugh's rebukes rarely deflected his friends' desire to please him.

Ultimately, politics was a side issue in these relationships. Right or Left, Waugh's cronies loved him and craved his love. Lady Diana Cooper, having

115. Unpublished ALS from Gwen Plunket Greene, nd [April 1948], from Aucombe, Warminster, Wilts.; BL.
116. Unpublished ALS from Olivia Plunket Greene, 22 April 1948, np [Aucombe etc.]; BL.
117. Unpublished ALS from Olivia Plunket Greene, 24 April 1948, from Aucombe etc.; BL.
118. Unpublished ALS from Olivia Plunket Greene, 1 May 1948, from Aucombe etc.; BL.
119. The new Ambassador to Paris and his wife. He had been appointed by Ernest Bevin to replace Duff Cooper. The Coopers rented a house at Chantilly, where they continued to entertain lavishly,

lost her role as the ornament of Duff's public life, had also lost her looks and, she thought, her sense in deciding to live permanently in France. Deeply depressed, she chased Waugh's affection as relentlessly as did Olivia. When Hollis broadcast a right-wing Catholic polemic, Gwen had written to Waugh anticipating a slanging match: '... he has made me into an enthusiastic communist. How could anyone so ignorant dare to speak on the subject ...?'[120] Waugh's reply surprised her, especially as she had not realized that Hollis was a friend: a 'delightful, amusing & utterly kind & patient letter.'[121]

Waugh recognized these qualities in others, never in himself. Indeed, he fictionalized others' sanctity to reinforce his own sense of sin. In January he had met Graham Greene at mass in Farm Street. Tall, shambling, unshaven, Greene had just 'emptied his pockets into the box for African missions'[122] and Waugh had taken him to the Ritz for a cocktail. To read this account, it might be Mr Brownlow encountering Oliver Twist. But Greene, of course, was far from penniless and almost as far from altruism. During 1948 he moved into the supertax bracket with the American success of *The Heart of the Matter*. At the outbreak of war, he had left his wife and children to continue an affair with a rich and glamorous American. He was well-established and distinctly worldly, much more so, in fact, than Waugh. In 1947 Greene had been looking for a Queen Anne house, having rented one on Clapham Common during the war until it had been bombed. He had an elegant flat in the Albany, Piccadilly. It seemed possible that he might follow the same road to rural seclusion as Betjeman and Waugh.

Greene and Waugh had become friends in 1937 when they were both working for *Night and Day*.[123] Since then their relationship had remained warmly formal. Each respected the other's work. Indeed, Greene regarded Waugh as the commanding officer of their literary generation. Self-distrust, perhaps, had kept Greene at a respectful distance. Waugh encouraged him. Each recognized in the other a manic-depressive tendency and a love of the macabre; both were Catholic converts, Oxford contemporaries, writers whose chief concern was the spiritual struggle between Good and Evil. Greene, however, was troubled by the fact that they approached this struggle from opposed political viewpoints.

Greene was broadly 'Left' and cared little for country-house priests like Knox. There was no allegiance to a 'European tradition' in Greene's writings, nothing supporting the Church Militant. His Church was not a

Nancy Mitford being one of their regular circle. Nancy always worshipped 'Lady Di', but became alarmed by her heroine's deepening melancholy.

120. Unpublished ALS from Gwen Plunket Greene, 4 July [1948], from Aucombe etc.; BL.
121. Unpublished ALS from Gwen Plunket Greene, 7 July [1948], from Aucombe etc.; BL.
122. *Diaries*, 11 January 1948, p. 694.
123. See Vol. 1, p. 439 *et passim*.

precise organization with absolute rectitude on its side but a tangle of paradox and heretical temptation. In the clashes between authority and the individual in his novels, authority usually corrupts. Greene was on the side of, or at least obsessed by, the small man in a muddle, the dim and provincial, everything in fact that he, like Waugh, had struggled to escape. As a writer he felt the need, even within his Faith, to live on the borderline, owing no loyalty which would demand the faithful lie. The novelist, he felt, needed anonymity, like the spy, to observe clearly and to move freely. And he was not only dangerously 'unorthodox' in his work. He was in love with his American, a married woman who still lived with her husband. Whatever, Greene wondered, would Waugh make of all this?

The answers began to come in June. Waugh had asked Woodruff to reserve the *Tablet* review of *The Heart of the Matter* for him, and Tom Burns wrote suggesting a piece combining Greene's novel with Sykes's.[124] Burns's remarks on Greene's work condemned it as Jansenist and fell not far short of an attempt to dissuade Waugh from accepting the commission. Greene had clearly angered conservative Catholics, especially those who knew the details of his private life. Neither Burns nor Sykes considered Greene a 'religious novelist' and Burns expected Waugh to agree with this view.[125] He did not; and in the light of Burns's letter, Waugh's review stands out as a courageous defence:

> There are loyal Catholics who think it the function of a Catholic writer to produce only advertising brochures ... [for] Church membership. To them this profoundly reverent book will seem a scandal. For it not only portrays Catholics as unlikeable human beings but shows them as tortured by their faith. It will be the object of controversy and perhaps even of condemnation.[126]

All this was presumably directed at Burns and the call to order was sharpened by the implicit reference to *Brideshead*. Waugh was sympathetic to those 'tortured by their faith'.

124. *Answer to Question 33* (Collins, 1948). It was dedicated to Evelyn and Laura, and Waugh thought it 'most enjoyable' (*Letters*, p. 275).

125. Cf. unpublished ALS from Tom Burns, 18 June 1948, from 4 Victoria Square, SW1; BL: 'I find Christopher's very nearly good where G.G.'s is very nearly bad. C. contrives a spiritual vacuum, G.G. uses all the apparatus of the Catechism & bad sermons twanging away on an exhausted id & irritated nerves to produce a sham spiritual dilemma: a caricature conventional Catholic couple is very cruelly trotted out to cut capers in the world of apprehensions much more the novelist's than their own. He almost turns things upside down & hates the sinners whilst he loves the sin. G.G. is becoming a sort of smart-Alec of Jansenism. Christopher would be shocked at the idea that he was a religious novelist.... But I'm not your Editor & if you don't want to take his book in tow leave it alone.' Burns was co-owner of the *Tablet* with Woodruff, who was absent in Germany.

126. 'Felix Culpa?' *Tablet*, 5 June 1948, 352–4; *Commonweal*, 16 July 1948, 322–5; *EAR*, pp. 360–5.

The review was unusually long (3,000 words), carefully considered and enthusiastic. Heinemann's could have produced no better advertisement had they written it themselves: 'Of Mr. Graham Greene alone among contemporary writers one can say without affectation that his breaking silence with a new serious novel is a literary "event".... [He] is a story-teller of genius.'[127] The CO here was not simply welcoming a new officer to the Staff but generously stepping down. And this was not false modesty. Waugh had informed Peters that, after *The Loved One*, he could expect nothing for some years. *Helena* progressed only slowly. Beyond that, Waugh believed, just two shots remained in his locker: a war novel and his autobiography,[128] but they might never be written and Greene was at the flood-tide of his powers. At forty-four, Waugh had quite unnecessarily resigned himself to decline and he found in Greene's work a salutary grimness. In 'earlier and healthier ages', he remarks, '... the path to salvation [was] exceedingly narrow and beset with booby-traps....' Greene challenged the 'soft modern mood' by never allowing his reader to forget Hell: 'the reek of brimstone [is] everywhere.'[129]

With the new weapons of self-abnegation, Waugh continued the battle for his modesty. For years he had sought a contemporary Master and was delighted to have discovered one at last. There is a penitential thoroughness about his review, seeking out and confronting the points of literary and religious orthodoxy on which he had to be satisfied. Was Greene a Jansenist, a dualist, a subversive constructor of paradoxes? No, he was medieval in his theological rigour. Was his style not rather 'modern', brashly journalistic in places? No; it was not Waugh's approach, but it was equally valid:

> Literary stylists regard language as intrinsically precious and its proper use as a worthy and pleasant task.... [To Greene] words are simply mathematical signs for his thought ... no relation is established between writer and reader.... Nor is there ... an observer through whom the events are recorded.... It is as though out of an infinite length of film, sequences have been cut which, assembled, comprise an experience which is the reader's alone, without any correspondence to the experience of the protagonists. The writer has become director and producer. Indeed, the affinity to the film is everywhere apparent.... Perhaps it is the only contribution the cinema is destined to make to the arts.[130]

127. *Ibid.*, pp. 360 and 362. The final remark was worth a small fortune. It has appeared for many years on the Penguin reprints.
128. Cf. *Letters*, p. 238.
129. 'Felix Culpa', *op. cit.*, p. 360.
130. *Ibid.*, pp. 361–2.

The same could be said of Waugh's early work. By a different route, it is suggested, Greene and he had arrived at the same effect.

The remarks display an almost perverse loyalty. Greene's novels certainly challenge the inflexibility of Catholic doctrine. He did not believe in Hell. There *is* an intrusive narrator. And what of the political impetus towards sympathy with the Common Man? Waugh describes this as Greene's 'preoccupation with the charmless' and simply absorbs it into a shared acceptance of the doctrine of Original Sin: 'The children of Adam are not a race of noble savages who need only a divine spark to perfect them. They are aboriginally corrupt. Their tiny relative advantages of intelligence and taste and good looks and good manners are quite insignificant.'[131] Christian humility and compassion were rooted in the Fall, but it was a root which had so far found but stony soil in Waugh's heart. Much of his adult life had been spent trying to demonstrate how 'taste' was intrinsic to Christian civilization. The dandy in him never died.

With these difficulties patched up, or sidestepped, Waugh moved on to the one serious obstacle. Did Mr Greene intend us to regard Scobie as a saint? Waugh believed that this was the case. If so, the book could be seen as either blasphemous or naïve. Greene had prefaced it with a quotation from Péguy's *Nouveau Théologien*: '*Le pécheur est au coeur même de chretienté.... Nul n'est aussi compétent que le pécheur en matière de chrétienté. Nul, si ce n'est le saint.*' ('The sinner is at the very heart of Christianity.... No one understands Christianity better than the sinner. No one, unless it be the saint.') Waugh had no taste for modernist theology. How, then, did he deal with this? His response was ingenious: an attack on Péguy rather than Greene, and an astonishingly *avant-garde* dismissal of authorial intention which might have come (in secular form) from Roland Barthes. Mr Greene's artistic intentions, Waugh insisted, were irrelevant; the author was dead: '[His] opinion on [the] matter [of Scobie's sanctity] is of no more value than the reader's.'[132] The potential heresies, he suggests, were not Greene's responsibility. 'Mr. Greene has removed the argument from Péguy's mumbled version and restated it in brilliantly plain human terms; and it is there, at the heart of the matter, that the literary critic must resign his judgement to the theologian.'[133]

Small wonder Greene was pleased. Aboard an airliner to New York where he was to draw up a lucrative contract for the novel, he scribbled Waugh a note:

> You've made me very conceited – thank you very much. There's no other living writer whom I would rather receive praise (or criticism)

131. *Ibid.*, p. 361.
132. *Ibid.*, p. 363.
133. *Ibid.*, p. 365.

> from. A small point – I did not regard Scobie as a saint, & his offering his damnation up was intended to show how muddled a mind full of good will could become when once 'off the rails'.[134]

That settled the matter. Waugh instructed the *Tablet* to remove the imputation in reprints and wrote a public letter effectively apologizing for his suggestion.[135] Greene proposed himself for a visit on his return and their friendship took a large stride forward.

In the event, Greene was so busy and distraught that he could not get down to Piers Court. As his professional life rolled on from success to success (1948 also saw the première of *The Fallen Idol*), his domestic affairs became increasingly messy. Apprehension about Waugh's reaction to adultery held Greene back, but not for long. In September he asked if they could meet in London. Waugh proposed White's; Greene disposed of this idea. Marble halls bored him, but that was not the main issue on this occasion. Would Waugh come to the Albany flat? A friend, Catherine Walston, wanted to meet him. Waugh cocked an eyebrow and agreed.

It was a delicate situation. Earlier in the year Waugh had met Mrs Greene (Vivien, *née* Dayrell-Browning) at Campion Hall. His review had drawn attention to Scobie's sacrilegious communions. Greene was in a state of Mortal Sin and either in Scobie's position or, as he remained to the end of his life, non-communicant. Neither condition was likely to inspire Waugh's admiration. How much, Greene wondered, did Waugh know of the affair? During the year, Waugh had become friendly with Jack and Frances Donaldson, country neighbours who knew Greene well (they had a flat in the same Albany building as Greene's). Had they dropped any hints? Had Sykes or Burns said anything? It was not yet a subject Greene felt able to broach, but he craved honesty with Waugh. Until he knew the details, their relationship would be infected by deception or, at least, embarrassment.

Waugh arrived at the Albany to find that the Walstons rented a flat next door to Greene's. John Hayward, the crippled companion of T. S. Eliot, was there, clearly an old friend. There was a rhythm of established intimacy in the air with Catherine as the presiding spirit, trying to draw Waugh into the circle:

> She sat on the floor and buttered my bread for me and made simple offers of friendship.... Finally, I was asked to go with her to the country. I couldn't that afternoon as I had to dine with the editor of the *Daily Express*. Very well they would pick me up after dinner. I

134. ALS from Graham Greene, nd [July 1948?], 'In Flight A. A. American Airlines'; published in part in *Letters*, p. 280, n. 1.
135. *Tablet*, 17 July 1948, 41. Waugh had been eager for Peters to find an American publisher for the review, regardless of fee. *Commonweal*, a 'progressive' Catholic journal, had accepted, but Greene's letter presumably arrived too late for the correction to be made to this.

> couldn't do that as I was lunching with Father Caraman next day. Very well she would send a car for me at 2.30.[136]

Waugh was intrigued and flattered by her determination. She was rich, pretty, smart, gentle, intelligent, eccentric. Greene and she were obviously close. But the invitation was to her marital home. It was all very rum, and Waugh had to wait an agonizing twenty-four hours before the next instalment.

During that luncheon he probably talked about his other London appointments, for they epitomized his chief concerns now that *The Loved One* was published: tax evasion and *pietas*. The *Express* was sponsoring a Film Tribunal for the 'Judgement of Films of All Nations'. Waugh had been on the selection committee since May and, although he would earlier have found such publicity ventures tedious and intrusive, in milder mood he was happy for the excuse to see four free films a week and to draw on Beaverbrook's expense account. It killed time. It gave him a press pass to see *The Fallen Idol*, 'which was clever and funny and original'.[137] (Had he better understood Greene's divided loyalties, Waugh might have found the film rather darker in tone. The meeting with Fr Caraman, however, represented more serious business.

Fr D'Arcy had decided to sharpen up the *Month*, the Jesuit periodical, and to instal Fr Caraman as Editor. D'Arcy had arranged Caraman's first appointment with Waugh a week earlier, when they had discussed the form the magazine should take. Waugh's generosity to the Jesuits was legendary, as were tales about his rebarbative personality. Caraman was tentative in his approach and delighted by the response. It was the beginning of a lifetime's friendship. Caraman was to celebrate Waugh's last mass.

Negotiations continued through September and October. Waugh suggested that the *Month* proclaim itself Jesuit but was worried about direct competition with the *Tablet*. Despite his growing impatience with its political articles, he wished to remain loyal to Woodruff and Burns. Caraman scotched all fears on this subject. 'I want to produce a Catholic review of literature and the arts,' he wrote, 'with a supporting interest in theology and philosophy: an HORIZON, with Catholic thinking in place of the fluff. . . .'[138] This was exactly Waugh's objective – a counterblast to 'Smarty's Own Mag', as Nancy called it – and he startled Caraman further by immediately offering extracts from *Helena*. The new editor found himself off to a spectacular start. In his first number, Greene was also to review *The Loved One*.

136. *Diaries*, 28 September 1948, p. 701.
137. *Ibid.*, p. 702.
138. Unpublished ALS from Fr Philip Caraman, 12 October 1948, from 114 Mount Street, Grosvenor Square, W1; BL.

It was with this scheme echoing in his mind, then, that Waugh was transported to Thriplow Farm for chapter two of the Catherine Walston saga. He was not disappointed. 'I went to such an extraordinary house . . .,' he wrote to Nancy, 'very rich, Cambridge, Jewish, socialist, high brow, scientific, farming. There were Picassos on sliding panels & when you pushed them back plate glass & a stable with a stallion looking at one.'[139] Waugh was fascinated. The house was a modern range of wooden bungalows; Carolean silver in a setting of contemporary books, gramophone, wireless; an intercom connected the rooms by telephone. Mrs Walston, he discovered, had five children, three of whom were at home. Her husband, Henry, was a senior civil servant (later a life peer) and gentleman farmer. There was no sign of him. Instead, the three of them dined with Twinkle, the nanny, who conversed freely over champagne and lobster about masturbation and lesbianism. 'Mrs Walston barefooted and mostly squatting on the floor. Fine big eyes and mouth, unaffected to the verge of insanity, unvain, no ostentation – simple friendliness and generosity and childish curiosity.'[140] Waugh thought it odd but charming. 'Not drunk but tongue pleasantly loose,' he recorded. 'We talked all the time of religion. She and Graham had been reading a treatise on prayer together that afternoon. Then she left the room at about 1 and presently telephoned she was in bed. We joined her. Her bedside littered with books of devotion.'[141]

Waugh stayed the night, wandered their fields in the morning and returned to London for Knox's sixtieth birthday party. Nothing had been said about the crucial issue, but Catherine's elaborate invitation seemed to have been engineered to please Greene, and shortly afterwards he met Waugh again. At last, Greene appears to have approached the subject directly. Waugh listened patiently. The news, of course, came as no surprise. Greene's anguished modesty, struggling against his passion, was endearing. Waugh did not approve, but he did not judge: Betjeman and Olivia had taught him the penalties of intervention. 'You relieved my mind enormously,' Greene wrote. 'Thank you so much.'[142] And with that, their deep affection for one another was sealed.

'I did not mean to be taken seriously re Quennell and the Beefsteak,' Ann Fleming had written in July, 'I thought it might be an opportunity for you to show compassion, which according to *Time* magazine is the only quality you lack. . . .'[143] Perhaps, she suggested, he could call round and be

139. 4 October 1948; *Letters*, pp. 283–4.
140. *Diaries*, 29 September 1948, p. 702.
141. *Ibid.*
142. Unpublished ALS from Graham Greene, 9 October 1948, from 5 St James's Street, London; BL.
143. 18 July [1948]; *LAF*, p. 69. She had suggested that Waugh put Quennell up for the Beefsteak Club.

'brilliantly nasty'[144] about her friends. But Waugh was trying to abjure this reputation. During the year, he had performed countless acts of quiet compassion. He had given all future translation rights to charity and helped refugees and friends with his cash, influence, sympathy or literary advice.[145] In every sphere of his life he was attempting to cultivate benevolence and good humour, feelings strangely mixed with his revived interest in the dim and the absurd. He even became Chairman of the Parish Council, assisted the Dursley Amateur Dramatic Association,[146] and promised to judge the annual essay competition for the British Matchbox, Label and Booklet Society.

*

Behind this struggle for compassion lay another obscure figure: a young American monk, Thomas Merton. The rights to his autobiography, *The Seven Storey Mountain*, had been bought by Burns,[147] who had passed it on to Waugh for an opinion. Waugh, however, had already read the American edition and had written to Harcourt Brace enclosing a review and corrections. It was, he believed, an important work whose linguistic imprecision might confuse a European audience. 'I've asked HB to let me have the list of your suggested cuts,' Burns wrote. 'I doubt whether the author will allow it but I must try. . . .'[148] In fact, Merton had already contacted Waugh ('. . . I need criticism the way a man dying of thirst needs water. . .')[149] and from these formal beginnings, a friendship developed.

Burns and Merton allowed Waugh freedom to cut the text and he relished the task, not simply as an exercise of professional skill but as an act of homage: the more he cleaned up the prose, the brighter shone its significance. It took him just a week. He removed about a third, polished what remained[150] and later produced a Foreword. By the time the British edition,

144. *Ibid.*
145. Waugh, for instance, offered Hilde Bertram a place in his household and assisted Zarita Mattay (a distant Catholic relative) to escape European transit camps for Australia. The correspondence with Mrs Mattay continued for years although they never met. Her mother, Mrs Percy Waugh (?), appears to have been too old either for the journey or to be an acceptable candidate for emigration, although, with Waugh's help, she later joined her family. In the meantime, he saw to it that she was safely placed in a Surrey convent and contributed to the expenses. He used his influence with Frank Pakenham to expedite the Australian passage for Mrs Mattay's family of six. 'I do not think', she wrote, 'I shall ever be able to express to you in words what I feel about your attitude to us & our problems' (unpublished ALS, 2 October 1948, from Emigration Centre Bl. 54–20, (20a) Fallingbistal [?]; BL).
146. Waugh had been the 'sleeping' President of DADA since 1937 when he first moved to Piers Court.
147. For Burns, Oates & Washbourne.
148. Unpublished ALS from Tom Burns, 4 August 1948, from 4 Victoria Square, SW1; BL.
149. Unpublished TLS from Frater M. Louis Merton, OCR [Thomas Merton], 2 August 1948, from Our Lady of Gethsemani, Trappist, Ky.; BL.
150. Cf. R. M. Davis, 'How Waugh Cut Merton', *Month*, 6 (April 1973), 150–3.

Elected Silence, appeared in 1949, it had already become a best-seller in America. Waugh, with typical modesty, remarked only that this 'very remarkable autobiography' had been 'very slightly abridged', refusing even to say by whom.

What was it that so intrigued him? Merton's was the story of a spiritual quest. From a cosmopolitan childhood he had moved on to Columbia University and lived a rakish life. Finding himself repelled by the modern world, he had withdrawn from it to a Cistercian monastery in Kentucky. There, he lived under the strictest discipline, allowed to sit at his typewriter for only a few hours a day, required to participate fully in the rigorous routine of prayer and manual labour. His worldly trade was that of writer and it gave him no more kudos in the monastery than bootmaking or carpentry. All this appealed strongly to Waugh's sense of the writer's craft being a practical and relatively unimportant matter in the larger context of a coherent spiritual life. He shared Merton's disgust with contemporary society and his desire for isolation. But there was something else – Merton's nationality – which struck Waugh as important. 'Americans no longer become expatriates in their quest for full cultural development,' he wrote:

> They are learning to draw away from what is distracting in their own civilization while remaining in their own borders. . . . To one observer at least it seems probable that the USA will shortly be the scene of a great monastic revival. There is an ascetic tradition deep in the American heart which has sometimes taken odd and unlovable forms. Here in the historic Rules of the Church lies its proper fulfilment. . . . As in the Dark Ages the cloister offers the sanest and most civilized way of life.[151]

This effectively signalled a further act of contrition borne of his admiration for Merton.

It was an odd friendship. They met only twice. Waugh sent him *The Reader Over Your Shoulder*[152] and discussed points of style like a benevolent schoolmaster. Merton, bewildered with gratitude, was in literary matters a penitent to Waugh's confessor. But their discussions quickly broadened to include spiritual experience and here the roles were reversed. Merton never knew the 'masks of burlesque' with which Waugh defended his privacy, only a humble, self-lacerating soul, tortured by his sense of sinfulness. 'Like all people with intellectual gifts,' Merton wrote to him, 'you would like to argue yourself into a quandary that doesn't exist. Don't you see that

151. Foreword to *Elected Silence* (Burns, Oates & Washbourne, 1949); *EAR*, pp. 368–9.
152. Robert Graves and Alan Hodge, *The Reader Over Your Shoulder*, *op. cit.*; see ch. V, p. 166 above.

in your anxiety to explain how your contrition is imperfect you are expressing an intense sorrow that it is not so – and that is true contrition.'[153]

Merton's book had an immediate impact. Even before Waugh began editing it, he had contacted Clare Booth-Luce through Randolph Churchill, expressing an interest in writing an article for *Life* on the Catholic Church in America. Later he explained his ideas: 'It seems to me likely that American monasticism may help to save the world.' He wished to inform 'European Catholics about the character of their future leaders. . . .'[154]

The Luces' response was enthusiastic. *The Loved One* had rocketed into the best-seller list and maintained Waugh's stock in the celebrity market, but *Life* must have thought his custom lost to them. Their last contact (over 'Fan-Fare') had concluded acrimoniously. Now they found Waugh approaching them as an entirely different character: amiable and industrious, keen to do business on reasonable terms. Their Berlin correspondent flew to England to discuss a contract. Waugh entertained him courteously at Piers Court and they found themselves in complete agreement about the nature of the project. Only one problem remained: Waugh was convinced 'that an article of this kind cannot be lightly undertaken. My knowledge of the USA is very superficial. . . .'[155]

He had already planned to go to Baltimore at the end of January. The Jesuits of Loyola College there had awarded him an honorary D. Litt. the year before and he had been prevented from attending the ceremony by British currency restrictions. This time he knew better. Tickets were bought in the States and posted to him. He was to travel as the Jesuits' guest, give a lecture and meet prominent Catholics. He proposed to *Life* that they fund a preliminary visit. He wanted to travel 'first in a purely private capacity so that I can get the feel of the problem and know what subjects to raise with the Bishops and Professors when I meet them.'[156] He would then come back to England having submitted a questionnaire to *Life*'s research department. On his return to the States he would pick up their answers, complete the Jesuit tour, work out a synopsis and submit the finished piece by the end of April. For this he required expenses, travel and accommodation arrangements and 'a modest fee'. The magazine now understood Mr Waugh's ideas about 'payment in kind'. They made him an honorary correspondent with full access to research facilities, provided free travel and $5,000 pocket-money ($4,000 discountable as expenses, most of the remainder as agent's fee).

153. Unpublished ALS from Fr Louis Merton [Thomas Merton], 22 September 1948, from Our Lady of Gethsemani etc.; BL.
154. ALS to John Shaw Billings of *Time & Life*, 3 September 1948; *Letters*, p. 283.
155. Unpublished ALS to John Shaw Billings, 5 October 1948, from Piers Court; Time-Life-Fortune Collection, University of South Carolina (Special Collections).
156. *Ibid.*

Pietas and tax avoidance thus magnificently combined, Waugh boarded the *Queen Elizabeth* at the end of October for the oddest quest of his life. Less than a year after completing *The Loved One*, he was returning to the country his book had savaged in search of spiritual enlightenment.

VII
American Dream: November 1948–November 1950

'Seagulls are flying round the ship,' Waugh wrote home, 'and the American passengers are as excited as Noah when the dove brought back a leaf.'[1] News of Truman's re-election was coming through, much to the distress of the Republicans in the first class. But Waugh, heading for another country bent on left-wing social reform, was benignly undisturbed by the prospect. There were larger, spiritual, issues at stake. Amid the furore of this extraordinary election, his days aboard the *Queen Elizabeth* followed a strict routine: '. . . Mass, breakfast, swim, drink, luncheon, sleep, Turkish-bath, drink, dine, cinema, bed. . . . I sit alone', he informed Laura, 'and think of you.'[2]

Margaret Case of *Vogue*, acting for the Luces as Waugh's nursemaid and social secretary, filled his cabin with carnations and fluttered round him in a dream of hero-worship. On his first night ashore, he was whisked off to dine with the Luces. 'It was not a great success,' Waugh reported wearily:

> caviar, dover soles flown that day from England etc but neither aware of what they ate or drank. He handsome, well mannered, well dressed, densely stupid. She exquisitely elegant, clever as a monkey, self centred. She came back with me & sat in my suite talking about religion for a long time but complained later that I had no heart.[3]

Waugh was already fractious. A peaceful crossing had calmed his nerves and cured his nettle rash. No sooner had he landed, however, than a large carbuncle began to erupt in the small of his back and his week in the city was spoiled by pain and penicillin injections.

Ignoring his tetchiness, the Luces stuck firmly to their task of introducing Waugh to the cream of Eastern, and particularly Catholic, society. He could have had no better promoters. Henry Luce was the founder and Editor-in-Chief of *Time*, *Life* and *Fortune*. His wife, Clare Booth Luce, was famous in her own right as a playwright (*The Women*, 1936), journalist, and hostess. (Later she became a Congresswoman and Ambassador to Italy 1953–6.) Mrs Luce was a Catholic. Both were arbiters of New York's fashionable

1. Unpublished ALS to Laura Waugh, 4 November [1948], from RMS *Queen Elizabeth*; BL.
2. *Ibid.*
3. ALS to Laura Waugh, 9 November [1948]; *Letters*, p. 288.

world. They arranged a rota of suitable guests to call at the Plaza while Miss Case fielded unwelcome enquiries.

First to knock on his door was Anne Fremantle. He had known her in his youth as Anne Huth-Jackson, an Englishwoman on the fringe of the Bright Young Things who had been the unhappy recipient of a proposal of marriage from C. R. M. F. Cruttwell.[4] Her refusal of this might alone have secured Waugh's affections, but she possessed the additional attractions of being clever, pretty and a Catholic convert with several books to her name. They soon found themselves chatting amicably over Bristol Cream and caviare.

'"Your first wife",' she told him, '"was my *bête noir* when I was a girl." ... "Evelyn Gardner? Why?" "Her mother ... was a great friend of my mother who was always coming back from lunching with her to sing Evelyn's praises and tell me how much she wished I would ... behave like that charming Gardner girl."' '"You didn't, I hope,"' Waugh answered guardedly. '"Far from it. And when you got divorced I was pleased."'[5] This dangerous ground he circumvented by abruptly introducing Laura's name into the conversation, and the meeting inaugurated a long, if distant, friendship. Anne Fremantle was a leading Catholic 'intellectual', able both to keep Waugh in touch with the climate of religious opinion in her new country and to promote his works. Quite apart from this, he relished the idea of an army of smart women whose dedication to his art came teasingly close to sexual attraction. Like many men whose ferocious social self-confidence disguises sexual timidity, he was an unrepentant flirt. '... I like the middle aged rich women,' he told Lady Diana Cooper, 'particularly if they are childless....'[6]

His next caller was less welcome. 'Alec Waugh came to see me at six. He is greatly taken up with some woman, dressed with inappropriate gaiety, talking in an unusual & unbecoming drawl.'[7] New York was now Alec's professional base. Although his wife and two children continued to live at Edrington, Joan and he were effectively separated. Evelyn did not approve. Alec's emotional difficulties, not the least of which was his struggle to reactivate his literary career, were as nothing to his brother, whose formal politeness barely disguised contempt. Alec always appeared to him to be hopelessly second-rate: a bad husband and a bad writer, salving a bad conscience with bad philosophy. That evening, after his brother's departure,

4. Waugh's history tutor at Oxford, whom he came to despise and mocked in his pre-war novels with a series of ludicrous characters bearing the don's name; cf. Vol. 1, pp. 78–9.
5. Anne Fremantle, 'Waugh in America', *Vogue*, 15 November 1960, 54, 65, 66. Mrs Fremantle conflates Waugh's trips to the USA in late 1948 and early 1949, assuming that Laura was with him on this excursion.
6. ALS, 24 November [1950], from Piers Court; BL; *MWMS*, p. 110.
7. *Op. cit.*; *Letters*, p. 288.

Evelyn went dinnerless to bed feeling ill and sad, having foolishly accepted an invitation to meet again. Three days later Alec received a letter: 'I was so sorry to miss your party last night. I dressed to come & went to a dinner party where a native woman spilt red wine over my shirt. I thought in that condition I should let you down so reluctantly stayed away.'[8] Good manners were preserved, but it was an excuse and both brothers knew it.

Waugh's experience of New York was oddly mixed. The evenings were spent in an exhausting relay of parties, plays and dinners, high on champagne and the oxygen of celebrity; the days were devoted to business. There were terms to be settled with *Life* and contracts to be signed with Matson. Waugh had also come prepared with a list of Catholic addresses drawn up by Fr D'Arcy. Prominent among these was that of Dorothy Day. A member of the Catholic Labour Movement and co-founder and Editor of the *Catholic Worker*, she ran a soup kitchen with a fleet of pious young men in the city's slums. Waugh wanted to meet her to see what the radicals had to say for themselves.

Perhaps to tease, perhaps with misplaced benevolence, he invited her to the best restaurant in town. 'Please forgive my class consciousness,' she replied. 'Chambord's is as formidable to me as 115 Mott Street probably is to you. Can we meet half way at Angelo's, Mulberry Street? Quiet and good food.'[9] Waugh complied and, after ordering two new suits, set off for the Bowery in the Luces' Cadillac. 'I gave a great party of them luncheon in an Italian restaurant . . .,' he wrote to Laura, '& Mrs Day didn't at all approve of their having cocktails or wine but they had them & we talked till four o'clock. . . .'[10] Waugh encountered in Mrs Day a personality as tough and autocratic as his own, yet infinitely less selfish – a disarming combination. Confronted by this genuine ascetic whose entire working life was devoted to practical charity, he discovered a more sympathetic version of Olivia's argument: that the aims of Christianity and capitalism were fundamentally opposed. It was not an idea he cared to ponder for long, but he retreated to the Plaza somewhat chastened.

Waugh was in something of a quandary. For years he had refused his seat on the literary gravy train – the PEN (international writers') Club, the publishers' parties, the interviews, aspects of the profession into which Alec threw himself energetically. Three years later Waugh mocked Spender's desire to 'be a poet' (as opposed to writing poems). What Spender meant by this, Waugh suggested, was 'going to literary luncheons, addressing youth rallies . . . saluting the great and "discovering" the young, . . . flitting

8. Unpublished ALS to Alec Waugh, 11 November 1948, from Knickerbocker Club, 807 Fifth Avenue; BL.
9. Unpublished cable from Dorothy Day, 10 November 1948, from New York; BL.
10. 14 November 1948; *Letters*, p. 290.

about the world to cultural congresses ... the penalties of eminence which real writers shirk....'[11] It was crucial to Waugh's sense of himself as an independent artist (a 'real writer') that he should abjure the cliquish comradeship of the Left and its shared authorship. Yet from 1928 he had been an ardent self-publicist and, as he looked about him in 1948, he saw most of his friends engaged in Spenderish promotional tactics. Betjeman had become a 'radio personality'; the Sitwells were rampaging round New York, hiring the Philharmonic Orchestra for readings and netting a fortune. When Waugh complained to Nancy Mitford about this degrading behaviour, she accused him of jealousy. 'Gel-gel be bugbuggered,' he replied. 'No sane man could envy Sir Osbert his ostentatious progress through U.S.A. Nor do the Americans respect him for it.'[12] But she had a point. Apart from MGM's disastrous attempt to ingratiate themselves, this visit represented Waugh's first experience of being fêted by a vast publicity machine, and he rather enjoyed it. If he could not be a real Lord, he could at least be treated like one in America. The party at which his shirt had been stained had been given by Anne Fremantle: a huge bohemian gathering in an attic where Waugh had met Auden for the first time and found him surprisingly amiable: not at all like Parsnip or Pimpernell. Waugh's quandary had several distinct aspects: artistic, political, religious and, perhaps above all, financial.

There were no immediate financial worries but, in a period of crippling taxation at home, Waugh looked to the future with blank dismay. The day after that party, he travelled to Boston to meet Alfred McIntyre, the President of Little, Brown, for the first and, as it turned out, the last time (he suffered a fatal seizure shortly after Waugh's departure). One of the last acts of his professional life was to entertain the novelist and explain the firm's accounts and plans. Waugh had good reason to be grateful to him, not only for courteous hospitality but for consistent support. It had been McIntyre's decision to buy up the early titles and to produce a Uniform Edition. It was he who had nagged the Book-of-the-Month Club into choosing *Brideshead*. He had backed *The Loved One* against Peters's advice and, also against Peters's advice, was about to produce *Scott-King* as a single volume. Business was good. *The Loved One* was a best-seller. *Brideshead* had made a fortune which, through constant additions from other sales, had remained effectively untouched. Almost $100,000 stood to Waugh's credit in Little, Brown's account and one of the issues under discussion (they were arranging a new, three-novel contract) was how much should in future

11. 'Two Unquiet Lives', *Tablet*, 5 May 1951, 356–7; review of Spender's autobiography, *World within World* (Hamish Hamilton, 1951); *EAR*, p. 395.
12. 10 January [1949]; *Letters*, p. 294.

be paid each year into Waugh's English bank. He was tempted by their suggestion of $20,000, but, nervous of taxation, settled for $15,000.

The prospect was dim, Waugh believed, because *Scott-King* was unlikely to sell well and his work in progress (*Helena*) unlikely to sell at all. That $100,000, he insisted, was all that stood between him and destitution. McIntyre had more faith, but there were ominous clouds on the horizon. The market for *Brideshead* and *The Loved One* was almost exhausted. For the last six months of 1948, Waugh's American sales had totalled only $257.18. At that rate, he could anticipate less than eight years of financial security. To compound this anxiety, he felt both that his artistic powers were waning and that he could never write another best-seller. Something would have to be done about this on his return but, as yet, his economic ingenuity failed him. It was Peters, as usual, who came to his rescue with a brilliant tax-avoidance scheme.

In the meantime, these American tours could do Waugh nothing but good and he began this preliminary excursion with the vigour of a man twenty years his junior. From Boston, he travelled to Baltimore, visited Merton at his Kentucky monastery and went on to New Orleans. At each stop, however, finding no letter from Laura, he had sunk further into depression. At first, he had tried to encourage her to fly out and share the passage home. He liked to think of her at Piers Court following his glorious progress, but when, in desperation, he cabled for news, all he received was an enigmatic reply from the butler: 'Madam in Scotland. All well here.' Her single, brief epistle had concerned the death of her cow. Away from the epicentres of cosmopolitan life, Waugh missed her badly; '. . . the long silence', he replied reproachfully, 'makes you seem very far away.'[13] Like his father, Waugh became neurotically anxious when separated from his wife at the slightest interruption of their plans for communication. Laura did not resent his continual absences. Indeed, there was a tacit recognition between them that these breaks were essential to the vitality of the marriage. Laura needed relief from the intensity of his company as much as he craved constant change. She steered her own course. Neither blamed the other for this need to escape and the drug usually worked. Only once, some four years later, did the strategy go badly wrong.

Back in New York a week later, he was buoyant again. A sheaf of chatty letters from Laura and the ferocious sycophancy of the smart set restored his spirits. He visited the Vincent Astors and

> . . . went to try & see Father Divine the nigger who has proclaimed himself God but he was away and I only saw an angel called Endeavour. I lunched with Harold Acton & Sargeant Preston. Yesterday I saw a

13. Unpublished ALS to Laura Waugh, 1 December 1948, from The Roosevelt, New Orleans; BL.

> play called 'Streetcar Named Desire' which is thought v. modern & was v. long. And when I came home I was sick though I had drunk and eaten nothing at all. I think it was the nervous exhaustion with all my social life.[14]

Waugh did nothing by halves. On his first day back in town, Anne Fremantle had driven him out to Princeton to meet Jacques Maritain. Bowling through the frozen countryside, she had been inspired by a sense of mission: the Great French Catholic Philosopher was to meet the Great English Catholic Novelist.[15] But when she pointed out rust-red barns rising from the snowfields, her allusions to Grandma Moses were ignored. Waugh averted his eyes: '"I am so horrified at the dreadful thing you've done I can't possibly pay attention to scenery...."' Whatever could it be? '"Every human being", he continued, "is born in sin. Original Sin. But every American is born in extra sin – the sin of treason to the British crown ... you, with full consent, have deliberately committed this horrid act."'[16] Tea with Maritain was an equally prickly affair. As it was the Eve of the Feast of the Immaculate Conception, Waugh refused food and it quickly emerged that philosopher and novelist had nothing in common beyond their faith. Mrs Fremantle gingerly manoeuvred the conversation off the rocks of the Spanish Civil War and the Social Encyclicals and escaped with her guest into the darkness.

'I am afraid I have committed a great Herbertry in telegraphing to you to know your plans,' he wrote shortly afterwards to Laura. 'In order to satisfy the tax gatherers I have had your name put jointly with mine on the lecture contract. This does not mean that you must come but that you *may* & I hope you will.'[17] Autocratic manners might suffice for the Americans but he now had to exercise caution with Laura. If he wanted her to do something, he had at least to make a show of considering her feelings. In effect, such consideration rarely went beyond show. When a dock strike prevented his returning by sea in time for Christmas, elaborate excuses were fabricated to defend his refusal to switch to an air passage. If he did this, he said, 'I should be unable to bring home the purchases you require – so it is a choice between Christmas presents late or no presents & me. I think you would all prefer presents.'[18] He was probably right but, as it turned out, he brought her no gift. Her American trip, he informed her,

14. Unpublished ALS, nd [December 1948], np [New York]; BL.
15. Maritain's *Introduction to Philosophy* had intrigued Waugh in the early 1930s; see Vol. 1, p. 310.
16. Anne Fremantle, *op. cit.*, 65–6. Mrs Fremantle had become an American citizen.
17. Unpublished ALS to Laura Waugh, 10 December [1948], from Plaza Hotel, NY; BL. The 'Herbertry', or idiotic mistake, was presumably to place on record (in the telegram) the fact that Laura was not committed to the project and thus was obviously not his secretary or fellow lecturer. He had earlier described her in the contract as a lecturer on Sophocles.
18. Unpublished ALS to Laura Waugh, 1 December 1948, *op. cit.*

was to be her present. He did not, however, forget the children, nor even the children of his friends. Among the New York stores' dazzling displays, his eye settled on dolls which wet themselves and the Beau Alarm, a device to deter sexual harassment. 'Catherine sends her fervent thanks', wrote Elizabeth Pakenham, 'for the horrifying police siren you so kindly sent her. . . . Frank and I send you and Laura our best wishes for another Joyous Year under Socialist rule. . . .'[19]

Mr Waugh was back on top, gorgeously delinquent, and Laura was delighted to find him restored by the voyage. Stepping on to the boat, he had even granted an interview in a moment of good humour he came bitterly to regret.

> Evelyn Waugh . . . [said] 'it is almost impossible for a man to lead a good life in the United States' but admitted that he was going back next month for a series of lectures at $550 apiece. . . . 'They heat their rooms to seventy-five degrees, then nail the windows down so that you suffocate. They have coloured bubble gum. Their radios are on all day. And they talk too much.' . . . Mr. Waugh said that he was relieved to be back in England because he was afraid that should he die in the United States, the Morticians Union of America would refuse to bury him because of . . . *The Loved One*. . . .[20]

This was precisely the impression he did not wish to create and, so furious was he at the misrepresentation, that he published, if not an apology, at least an explanation: 'It so happens that I like visiting America, love and respect countless Americans, and, knowing their peculiar sensitiveness, take pains not to make the kind of criticisms of them that I should freely make of any other nation, most of all my own.' A young woman, he said, had cornered him. He had lectured her for an hour on monasticism. The most impressive place he had visited, he told her, was the Trappist monastery in Kentucky: 'It is a subject I have at heart because I believe that we are returning to a stage when on the supernatural plane only heroic prayer can save us. . . .' Finding her baffled by this advocacy of austerity, he had pointed out the 'painful features' of her own way of life – 'overheated rooms, radio and so forth'.[21] She had cabled her report to London. After the sub-editor had finished with it, all that had remained were the facetious remarks. He should, he knew, have known better than to have opened his mouth, but the incident confirmed an unpleasant suspicion: a large section of the popular press, he believed, was now determined to defame him.

*

19. Unpublished ALS, 31 December 1948, from 10 Linnell Drive, Hampstead; BL. Waugh also sent a siren to Edith Sitwell.
20. *NYHT*, 31 December 1948, 11.
21. 'Kicking Against the Goad', *Commonweal*, 11 March 1949, 534, 536; *EAR*, pp. 371–2.

Persecution mania seethed beneath a façade of implacable good humour. Even his oldest friends were backing off before his ruthless orthodoxy, losing their taste for his rebukes. Savage jokes had somehow ceased to be funny in the 1940s. 'Don't be so cross & don't tease me about not having children,' Nancy had written.

> ... I suppose you think me a whore & my immortal soul is in danger. About once a week, for a few minutes it worries me that you should think so. That I can understand, though what seems so unlike you is that Harold Nicolson attitude of disapproval because I live among the flesh pots. . . .'[22]

Even Betjeman had timorously answered back – 'Though I hardly dare tell you, I really do not think Edith Sitwell is so good a poet as Mr. Auden. I think she is vastly overrated. . . .'[23] – and was no more prepared to abandon his Anglicanism under Waugh's onslaught than Nancy was to apologize for her agnosticism or for her affair with Gaston Palewski.

Apostolic efforts among the Bright Middle-Aged Things invariably provoked resentment. And at the other end of the spectrum there was Olivia, mad and holy, but equally beyond the reach of Waugh's icy doctrine. In his absence, a raving sixteen-page letter had arrived from her describing a recent visit to Heaven[24] and, while he did not mock mystical experience, he remained sceptical of this. Somewhere between the beatific vision and the flesh-pots he was caught with his arid soul hungering for contrition and compassion to ease the burden of his faith. Romantic England was dead and gone, could not even live on in the fictions of his ancient loves. All that remained was a form of cenobitic existence: the library and the garden; Laura and the farm; the embellishment of his house; the education of his children; the construction of a 'huge, grim and solitary jest'[25] from what was left of his life.

Waugh's version of the 'monastic' life, of course, appeared profoundly hypocritical in the Age of Austerity. The popular press could accept him

22. Unpublished ALS from Nancy Mitford, 11 January 1949, from 7 Rue Monsieur, Paris; BL.
23. Unpublished ALS from [Sir] John Betjeman, 17 January 1949, from Farnborough Old Rectory, Wantage, Berks.; BL.
24. Unpublished ALS from Olivia Plunket Greene, nd [November 1948?], from Aucombe, Warminster, Wilts.; BL: 'I was suspended in air after having stepped off the last step of the ladder of life [&] was in a horrid & morbid turmoil for a long time – Satan writhing & gnashing his teeth in the Abyss – (I didn't know this at the time because God mercifully blinded me so I only looked upwards because Jesus own eyes had looked into mine a little while before & after that I saw only God – but my eyeballs has [*sic*] to be circumcized first. Ah that's a long story – the story I want to tell you one day). Well you see in this struggle for my soul & body somebody suddenly put a strong arm round my body and drew me up in the air & my feet went up in the air & ... I was taken through a golden door & put down ... and I knew I was in Heaven. I know it was St. Peter who had put his kind arm around me. . . .'
25. Cf. *Work Suspended*, p. 117; cf. Vol. 1, p. 495.

as a spendthrift genius but it resented his hectoring the declining West for lacking those Christian virtues with which he seemed singularly ill-endowed. It was difficult to promote asceticism with a cigar in one hand and a glass of champagne in the other. If his version of the monastic life meant living in Piers Court, travelling the world at other people's expense and being paid $550 for an hour's talk, then the Common Man, with some reason, felt well-prepared for its rigours. In the late 1940s, displays of wealth were regarded with suspicion and Waugh, ever eager to baffle intruders, hammed up the squirearchical role with music-hall ostentation. The great art of public presentation, he felt, was that people should never know what to make of you. A contract existed between author and public: 'The writer sweats to write well; the reader sweats to make dollars; writer and reader exchange books for dollars.'[26] That was the end of the matter. The public had no claim on an author's affections nor was he obliged to feel grateful to his readers. If they did not like his books, they could stop buying them. In a period when the need to appear 'ordinary' had dragged writers from their desks and into the radio studio, Waugh seemed either charmingly anachronistic or disgustingly snobbish. This did not trouble him in the least. The public, he felt, was always intrigued by an enigma and the masks of burlesque kept the mob beyond his walls. What did matter, however, was the kind of misrepresentation which imputed bad faith, religious hypocrisy.

Waugh's incoming correspondence during this period is enough to demolish such charges. His obsessive concern was the maintenance and propagation of the Catholic faith. As we have seen, he donated vast sums for these aims and further depleted his resources by working for nothing. Before going to the States, for instance, he had sent the *Month* a free short story. On his return, Waugh reviewed J. F. Powers's *Prince of Darkness* and agreed to write another piece for Caraman on Knox's new translation of the Bible. During 1949 he edited Knox's sermons, a second book by Merton, and humbly confessed his spiritual odyssey in an anthology about conversion. 'I look back aghast', he wrote, 'at the presumption with which I thought myself suitable for reception and with wonder at the trust of the priest who saw the possibility of growth in such a dry soul.'[27] If his thirst for luxury were the occasion of sin, that, he felt, was a matter between himself and God, and while his asceticism may have seemed absurd from the public bars of Fleet Street, it was real enough to him. After scarcely a month in England he was preparing to return to his American mission.

26. 'Kicking Against the Goad', *op. cit.*, p. 372.
27. 'Come Inside', *The Road to Damascus*, ed. John A. O'Brien (New York, Doubleday, 1949), pp. 17–21; *EAR*, pp. 366–8.

'Don't want to be published at all by communist countries,' he informed A. D. Peters's office. 'They might use *Loved One* as anti-American propaganda.'[28] 'I go back,' he wrote to Alec, 'dutifully and sadly – but I think it will be a beneficial holiday for Laura.... Please urge your literary friends to take in *The Month*, a new counterblast to *Horizon* in which I am interested.... Mrs Percy Waugh is in a convent at Petersfield. I expect she would welcome a visit....'[29] There is little evidence of the egocentric here. Waugh paid this distant relative's fees at the nursing home until she could rejoin her family who were soon to emigrate to Australia, helped on their way by his £250 cheque. The short story he had sent to Caraman directly concerned similar refugees and the author's Yugoslavian experience. It dealt with a British officer's frustration and guilt as he tried to release a party of Jews from a Displaced Persons camp run by the Partisans. The text was eventually incorporated, almost intact, into *Unconditional Surrender* some twelve years later, and its title – 'Compassion' – was significant, suggesting both a major theme of *Sword of Honour* and the object of its author's spiritual struggle.

*

Waugh and Laura docked in New York at the end of January to be greeted by a firestorm of publicity. *Scott-King* and *Work Suspended and Other Stories* were about to be published. America was still humming with controversial debate about *The Heart of the Matter*, a work Waugh was to address directly in his talks. His subject was 'Three Vital Writers', Chesterton, Knox and Greene. 'The U.S.A.', Waugh said in his advertising material, 'is assuming the leadership of the "West", which historically was formed by Christianity, predominantly Catholic Christianity':

> The 'West' is incomprehensible unless one understands the CHURCH – which is identical everywhere: a single supernatural body. Great diversity, however, exists in this essential uniformity.... English Catholicism is the natural bridge of understanding between American and European Catholicism. The particular character of the CHURCH in England can best be illustrated by examining the lives and work of three eminent Catholic writers ... Chesterton who came from non-conformity and 'Merrie Englandism' ... Knox, the fine flower of autocratic [*sic*] classical culture, who came by way of High Anglicanism ... Greene, the modern par excellence, who came by way of despair and doubt....

28. [Received 18 January 1949]; *Letters*, p. 295.
29. Unpublished ALS to Alec Waugh, 18 January 1949, from Piers Court; BUL.

The object was to explain how each, 'so enormously different, are all in complete accord in the essentials of philosophy.'[30] Coming from almost anyone else, this might have seemed a lowering diet. Coming from the celebrated author of *Brideshead* and *The Loved One*, a close friend of Greene, it was a show-stopper. Packed houses greeted him everywhere – and he did not disappoint them.

Waugh's first two engagements were not humble affairs: at the Waldorf Astoria and the New York Town Hall. Robert Craft was at the latter. The squeaky voice which had made Waugh nervous of radio broadcasts in his early career had in his maturity completely disappeared. In fine, fruity tones, and with an air of easy authority, he spoke lucidly from half a page of notes. It was, Craft recorded, 'the coolest performance of the sort I have ever seen, even though he disparages it.'[31] Several days later, Craft tried to discuss the matter over dinner. He, like Anne Fremantle, was eager to engineer a meeting between Waugh and another eminent Christian. This time, the Great English Novelist was to meet the Great Russian Composer. Stravinsky was in town.

Craft, a conductor and writer,[32] invited the Waughs to his hotel. They arrived, spectacular in evening dress, saying that they were going on to a late party at the Astors: 'Mrs W. . . . fair and lovely, Mr W. pudgy, ruddy, smooth-skinned, rather ramrod and poker-faced.'[33] The trip was already benefiting Laura; Waugh was awkward and defensive, eyeing up the composer of the *Rite of Spring* with undisguised suspicion. Craft made the introductions and manoeuvred uneasily between the two couples. When he tried to draw Waugh on the lecture, conversation was quickly deflected. After his outrage at the newspaper report of his earlier visit, Waugh proceeded to reinforce the statements he had denied: his rooms were too hot; the fervent hope of the morticians' union, he insisted, was that he should die on American soil. Mr and Mrs Stravinsky sank into hushed conversation in Russian. No one was fooled by her elaborate display of rummaging in her bag, pretending to talk about cigarettes. Clearly, they were discussing the Waughs.

It was a freezing night and the restaurant was a block-and-a-half away. Waugh stumped along, glum and coatless. His spirits seemed marginally to rise with the discovery of a funeral parlour but quickly dropped again on entering 'Maria's' – dark and crowded, with no one else in evening

30. From an original advertising 'flier' for Waugh's lecture at the Walkerville Collegiate, Windsor, Ontario, 16 February 1949.
31. 'Stravinsky and Some Writers', *HB*, Vol. 237 (December 1968), 101–2, 105–6, 108.
32. Robert Craft founded the Chamber Art Society in New York in 1948 and had met Stravinsky in Washington that year. He later collaborated with the composer to produce books recording their conversations.
33. 'Stravinsky and Some Writers', *op. cit.*, 105.

Evelyn Waugh in his library at Combe Florey House

(*Above*) Combe Florey House, Combe Florey, Somerset

Trompe l'oeil panel by Martin Battersby depicting Evelyn Waugh's work, presented to him by Chapman & Hall

(*Above*) Alec and Evelyn Waugh, 25 November 1953

(*Above*) Evelyn Waugh, Ian and Ann Fleming, guests of the Coopers at Chantilly

(*Opposite page*) Left to right: Margaret, Harriet, Evelyn, Auberon, Laura, Teresa, James and Septimus Waugh at Combe Florey House, 195

(*Left*) The Duchess of Devonshire and Evelyn Waugh at the Foyle's launch of *The Ordeal of Gilbert Pinfold*, 1957

Ronald Knox as a young man

(*Right*) Laura Waugh at London Airport, 11 June 1958, prior to her departure for Cyprus to tend her wounded son, Auberon

Evelyn Waugh in 1963 and his portrait bust, executed in Yugoslavia in 1945

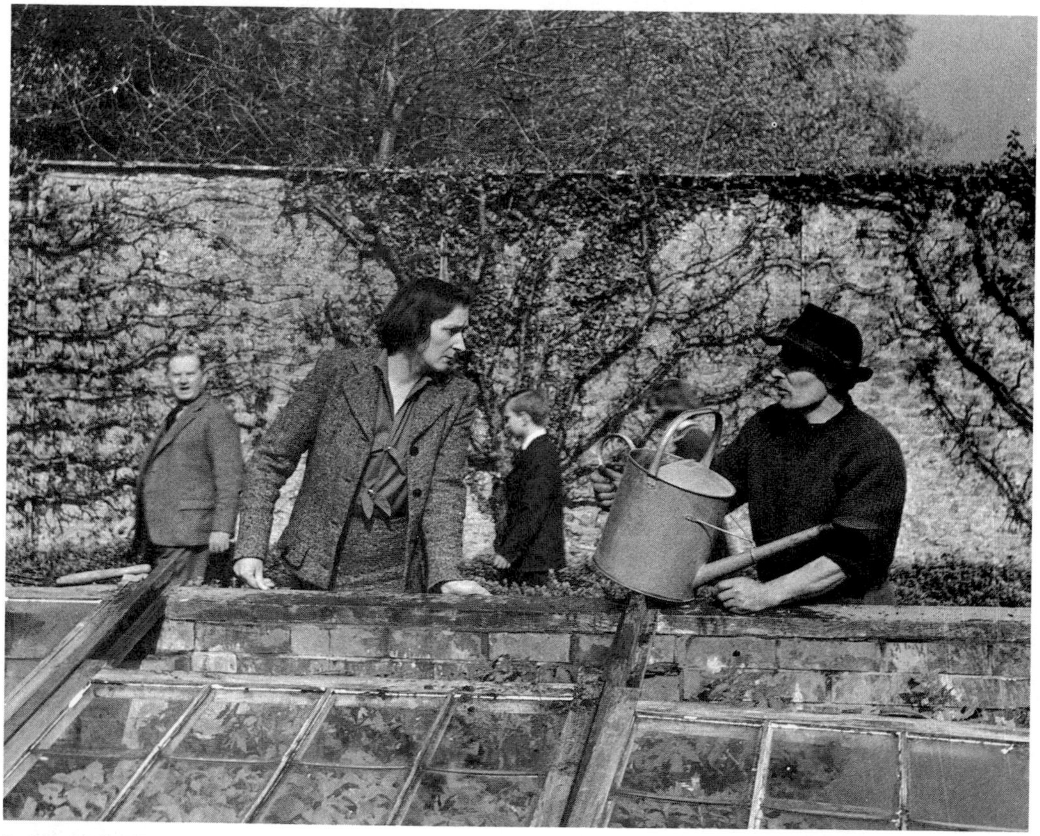

Left to right: Evelyn, Laura and James Waugh with the gardener at Combe Florey House

Evelyn Waugh's interview with John Freeman in the 'Face to Face' series, June 1960

Evelyn and Laura Waugh attending the wedding of their son, Auberon, July 1961

Evelyn and Margaret Waugh on her wedding day, October 1962

(*Left*) Evelyn Waugh and Edmund Blunden after receiving the C.Litt. at the Skinners' Hall, 25 June 1963

(*Right*) Evelyn Waugh and Justin D'Arms, the son of Teresa and John D'Arms, Combe Florey House, summer 1965

Evelyn Waugh in Victorian moo
Combe Florey House, 1963

dress. Craft feared the worst, but soon discovered how quickly wine and good Italian food could warm Waugh's heart. He began to act gallantly with Mrs Stravinsky and, turning the conversation to the Church, was delighted by the composer's response. 'Here', Craft noted, 'I.S. shines, showing himself to be at least as well-read in Chesterton and Péguy, and at least as prone to believe in the miraculous emulsification of Saint Januarius's blood.'[34] Thus encouraged, the Stravinskys admitted to having read and admired Waugh's complete works. Another palpable hit, and another Waugh began to emerge: 'as magnanimous and amusing as the old one was unbending and precise.'[35] Ultimately the evening was triumphantly convivial. There was only one further hiatus. Mrs Stravinsky invited the Waughs to the forthcoming première of her husband's *Mass*. No, no, Waugh said abruptly, it couldn't be done; tickets for their return passage were already booked. And lest the Stravinskys press the point, he added: 'All music is positively painful to me.'[36]

It was the same everywhere he went. A chain of conflicting anecdotes followed him from Baltimore to New Orleans: he was frank and amiable; he was dismissive and discourteous; he was the prophet of doom and the celebrant of Faith. Certainly the Americans did not know what to make of him and, when he crossed the border to speak in Ontario, the Canadians were equally baffled.

At Windsor he stayed at the most expensive hotel, but only briefly, and, deserting Laura, boarded for the remainder of his visit with the Basilian Fathers at Assumption College:

> ... he did not mix with the students. He didn't even bother to talk to any of them. He was this distant figure who sat with the priests at their own table in the refectory.... Waugh liked to go for a ride every afternoon. This proved tricky. The Basilians had only one community car which was booked with great regularity. To make matters worse, Father Murphy[37] didn't know how to drive. This meant that he had to pull a student out of class or, worse, a confrere.... They would go out into the countryside ... and drive through all the sleepy towns and hamlets. When they motored down the main street of Lasalle,

34. *Ibid.*
35. *Ibid.*
36. *Ibid.*
37. In 1934 Fr J. Stanley Murphy, CSB, had founded the 'Christian Culture' series of lectures, to which Waugh contributed. Its object was to broaden the horizons of fellow Catholics and to reach out to those traditionally hostile to the Church. Over the years, 'Father Stan' attracted a host of celebrities to the tiny college. In 1949, Assumption College was a small liberal arts college affiliated to the University of Western Ontario, 120 miles away in London, through which Assumption students received degrees.

> Waugh commented 'And that's Lasalle.' He said the same thing for every place they saw.[38]

Moving on to Chicago and Milwaukee Waugh found it impossible to disguise his boredom with the Mid-West and, in an effort to discover something amusing, had written ahead to John Pick of Marquette University. Could he arrange for Waugh to meet some Indians, preferably on a reservation? Unfortunately the reservations were hundreds of miles away. The best Pick could offer was waxwork figures in the public museum. This was wholly unsatisfactory: Waugh wanted them alive.

> After I met him and Mrs Waugh at the train I tried to take them to see the sights of Milwaukee – but instead he paid attention to the conversation of two of my students in the front seat of the car; one ... was telling the other that his family were vacationing in Florida and had sent him a small ... alligator. Waugh asked: 'Do you feed it shells to harden its skin? ... Where do you keep it?' The student said, 'Well, in my room, of course.' 'Why, at Oxford,' Waugh replied, 'we would have had to keep it in a kennel.'[39]

Forewarned, Pick made scrupulous arrangements for the dinner party: the silver was polished, the wine chilled, the candles lit.

> All went well till toward the close of the meal he whispered – audibly – to ... Laura across the table making queer gestures with wiggling his fingers. She tried to ignore him and conversed more and more audibly with her dinner partner. Waugh repeated. Repeated again. Finally, Laura saw what his predicament was and said, 'Evelyn, to the kitchen tap, my dear, to the kitchen tap.' ... I had thought of every detail except the finger bowls. ...[40]

The only source of fascination for Waugh was Catholic gadgetry – the commercialization of piety such as devices for counting rosary beads. 'Another anecdote from the Springfield town-diocese shop,' he wrote later to Merton. 'A traveller came in with a new type of plastic crucifix and said: "Its great advantage is that it is so strong you can throw it on the ground and stamp on it."'[41] That found its way into the *Life* article and might have seemed perfectly in keeping with a generally flippant approach. But what the public could not see, what he would never allow them to see, was the

38. Unpublished TLS from Michael Power, Assumption College, 16 September 1987.
39. Unpublished TLS from Professor John Pick to Frederick J. Stopp, 13 December 1954, from Department of English, Marquette University, Milwaukee, Wisconsin; CUL.
40. *Ibid.*
41. 27 May [1949], from Piers Court; Sister M. Thérèse (ed.), 'Waugh's Letters to Thomas Merton', *EWN*, Vol. 3, No. 1 (Spring 1969), 1.

missionary purpose of this tour. Waugh's mind was entirely concentrated on forming an impression of Catholic America. He was not trekking round glamorous institutions but small, independent Catholic universities. And he did not spare himself. From Milwaukee, he travelled a thousand miles south to New Orleans, then more than six hundred miles north again to St Louis. He went out of his way to visit Merton again and J. F. Powers in St Paul. On his return to New York, Waugh gave another lecture. Everywhere, he made himself available to the press. The whole business was purgatorial to him and particularly so because, the more he saw, the more presumptuous his project appeared. No coherent history of American Catholicism existed and he had impetuously undertaken to cover this massive subject in a magazine article. He felt that he could not possibly do justice to the rich variety of religious life he had witnessed and could thus not repay the generosity of his hosts. The burden of this guilt did not leave him for some months.

'He came and went,' wrote Joe Dever after the finger bowls incident, 'infuriating the self-conscious and the jingoistic, amusing and nettling the discerning. He came in archness, bristles, and with [a] ... sweetness that could disarm the cautious, winning them to his standards. ... And always, when he had gone, the provincials were left in their provinces – a little thrilled, a little awkward. ...'[42] Waugh happily left them confused. He was not, however, happy with the notices of *Scott-King*, which began to come in during February and March.

In his first, and only, review by George Orwell, Waugh had found himself mocked for political obtuseness: '... one must always regard with suspicion the claim that ignorance is, or can be, an advantage. In the Europe of the last fifty years the die-hard, know-nothing attitude symbolized by Scott-King, has helped to bring about the very conditions that Mr Waugh is satirizing.'[43] 'One feels that Waugh wrote this as he went along, without much care,' another critic suggested, 'to get it done and over with.'[44] Although Waugh could afford to ignore complaints (the book was selling well), the spectre of failing powers took more solid shape. Orwell had reinforced the idea that *The Loved One* was an ill-natured attack on America. Waugh had left a trail of angry reaction in his wake. To lose his American audience would be to lose both his prosperity and his authority as a spokesman for the Church. Few things made him nervous, but the prospect of poverty was one of them. Orwell's piece had appeared in the *New York Times Book Review*. An interview with the same paper, Waugh hoped, might set the record straight.

42. 'Echoes of Two Waughs', *Commonweal*, Vol. 53 (October 1950), 68–70.
43. *NYTBR*, 20 February 1949, 1, 25; *CH*, pp. 294–6.
44. John Woodburn, *NR*, 21 March 1949, 23–4; *CH*, pp. 297–8.

It was another masterly performance. He gave nothing away:

> No matter how you look at him [Harvey Breit wrote afterwards], Mr ... Waugh is a deceptive man: what meets the eye is at variance with what meets the ear. A remark ... suggests cynicism, ... but [his] face – bland, pink and cherubic – suggests only innocence. In fact, expression on Mr Waugh's face is at a minimum – a flicker of amusement, of naughtiness, an infinitesimal hint of wonder.[45]

Breit, perhaps embarrassed by Orwell, struggled to flatter *Scott-King*: 'It's first-rate satire.' 'Really, you liked it? I'm sure there's a good thing hidden away in it somewhere. ...' Benignity and arrogance were alarmingly indistinguishable in Waugh's remarks and Breit, like all the rest, was confounded. The great man spoke only when spoken to and talked of his book as though it 'had been written by a not-too-promising colleague'.[46]

Preliminary sparring over, Breit came timorously to the point: 'George Orwell ... said you had been rude to America ... but ... equally rude to Europe in *Scott-King*.' 'Not equally. People said I was harsh toward America. Not at all. I was harsher toward Europe. I've more despair for Europe than for America. There's much more wrong there than here.' At last Waugh had reached his subject and was off and running. American writers? He admired Thomas Merton and J. F. Powers. 'Christopher Isherwood', he added mischievously, 'is a good young American writer. ... The best, of course, ... is Erle Stanley Gardner. ... Do I really wish to say that? By all means.'[47] And he could not resist a final flourish: 'I'm a very lazy man. My whole life's a vacation, occasionally interrupted by work. Though I suppose I do want to write a novel about the war. It would be a study of the idea of chivalry.' In an unguarded moment, he had let slip a considerable scoop: the first public expression of his grand scheme for *Sword of Honour*, slowly germinating since the completion of 'Compassion'. Waugh covered his tracks. What he really wanted to do, he added, was to write a detective story like Gardner or Agatha Christie: 'I admire very much books of pure action.' 'Perhaps,' Breit suggested hopelessly, 'that is because your books aren't like that, but rather are quite the opposite?' Waugh responded slowly and slyly. 'Yes,' he said, 'there is some thought in them, I imagine.'[48]

45. *NYTBR*, 13 March 1949, 23.
46. *Ibid.*
47. *Ibid.* Waugh's admiration for Gardner was sincere. Eleven years later, Waugh wrote to him as 'one of the keenest admirers of your work', attempting to correct his use of 'davenport' (*Letters*, 21 July 1960, p. 546). Gardner, a longstanding fan of Waugh's work, could not at first believe in the authenticity of the signature. Waugh confirmed his praise and Gardner was blissfully flattered. He refused, however, to withdraw his use of 'davenport'. It was, he insisted, correct American usage for 'sofa' and did not only signify 'a small writing desk'. Waugh did not pursue the point.
48. *Ibid.*

He was tired and irritable. New York was beginning to weary him and there was still that last lecture on the night before he sailed. To keep his spirits up he ate caviare at every meal (including breakfast) and made sport of his guests. Anne Fremantle, invited to lunch at the Plaza, asked if a friend might join them afterwards. Waugh had seemed keen on publicity. The friend was Virgilia Peterson, hostess of a TV chat show. He grudgingly permitted her an audience over coffee and, punctually, she arrived. 'Go away,' said Waugh, 'I'm still eating. Come back at three.' Punctually, she returned. 'Why did you come back?' he asked, intrigued. 'I suppose because I'm a masochist ... but also because I wish to ask you if you would do us the honour of speaking on "The Author Meets The Critics".' 'How much do I get? Would you give me $500 to give to Dorothy Day?' 'I'm afraid you get nothing, ... our authors are *guests*.' 'Do *you* get paid?' 'Yes I do.... It's the way I make my living.' 'Could you not do something else? Domestic service, for example? There's a great shortage of domestic servants here, I believe.' 'I do that at home ... but no one pays me.' 'Isn't Howdy Doody also on your programme?' 'Why yes, he is, or rather the man who waggles him.' 'Do you mean to say that you pay a beastly puppet and would not pay me? I will certainly not speak for you.'[49]

The next day the Luces had arranged a dinner party before the lecture to wish the Waughs good-bye. Waugh invited Mrs Fremantle, who arrived much scalded about the face from an exploding pressure cooker. No one took much notice. Clare Luce provided her with a spangled veil and, comfortable to be exotically conspicuous, she watched her hero's antics. After the lecture, careless of her condition, Waugh packed her off in search of sleeping pills. He sailed early in the morning. Without drugs, he insisted, he would get no rest. As usual, they were difficult to procure without prescription but she eventually returned triumphant. As he read the directions, his face clouded. 'This is no earthly use. It's full of valerian. The only function of that is to attract cats. And there's a warning on it that an overdose will produce eruptions. No use at all.'[50]

His American friends were accustomed to him by this time. One did not react to Evelyn Waugh as one would to any normal human being. Rudeness was part of his social test and they loved him for this as much as for his sweet-tempered moments. He kept the pills, as she knew he would, and later a pen-and-ink self-portrait arrived: E.W. leaving the country with as much dignity as he could muster, in bowler hat, with a plague of boils and a posse of cats.[51]

*

49. Anne Fremantle, *op. cit.*, 66.
50. *Ibid.*
51. *Ibid.*

Waugh returned to England profoundly depressed by the prospect of *Life*. '... I am in deep misanthropy,' he wrote. 'I can't bear anyone else being alive at all & when a man goes past the window with a barrow or a child shuts a door upstairs I fall into an extremity of rage.'[52] Barrow and man belonged to Midland Gardens. Waugh was, as he put it, having his grounds 'made much uglier at terrible expense'.[53] In his absence, he had left the firm at work, constructing a sort of Victorian Disneyland. On his return, and without enquiring into the cost, he expanded his plans: a Gothic fernery, a serpentine walk and two centrepiece follies, the 'ruin' and the 'grotto'. The ruin was a miniature Greek temple, diagonally facing the front of the house, with broken Ionic columns, erect or artfully disposed about the grass. The grotto (or the Edifice, as it became known) was a more elaborate affair: 'a complex of pillared, classical walls about five feet high, an ornate obstacle course without roof, pediment or apparent purpose. Surmounting the walls were several small statues.'[54] A visiting American later asked what they represented. 'They are the ... virtues,' Bron replied. 'Oh? Temperance? Chastity –?' 'No ... they are the ... minor virtues.'[55] The visitor suspected teasing.

Everything about these embellishments was a tease, a puzzle, something to intrigue and entertain, divert the eye, structure the landscape. They were the logical extension of those rich ambiguities inside the house, all of a piece as glimpses of lost civilizations, yet each self-mocking and mocking its owner, each a *memento mori*. Another American noticed half-a-dozen spikes along the top of the colonnade. 'Do you know what I plan to put up there?' Waugh asked him. 'No.' 'Skulls. I've already inserted advertisements in *Country Life* and the *Tablet*.'[56]

Waugh's attitude to Americans was becoming confused. To Nancy Mitford he confessed a pantomime loathing, '... americans are louts and ... Catholic Americans are just a little better than panglossist americans.'[57] A month later he wrote to Merton in more sober mood: 'I am struggling with the *Life* article ... feeling daily that it is an intolerably presumptuous undertaking.'[58] Two chastening experiences had intervened between these letters: another Easter retreat at Downside and a visit to Paris. The first had reminded him painfully of his spiritual inadequacies, the second of his hatred of Metroland. He belonged, it seemed, to neither world.

52. ALS to Nancy Mitford, 12 April [1949]; *Letters*, p. 296.
53. ALS to Lady Mary Lygon, 7 June [1949]; *Letters*, p. 300.
54. Edward R. F. Sheehan, 'A Weekend with Waugh', *Cornhill*, Vol. 171 (Summer 1960), 209–25.
55. *Ibid.*, p. 216.
56. Unpublished TLS from Paul Moor to Martin Stannard, 27 September 1987, from 78 Parnassus Avenue, San Francisco. Waugh also advertised in *The Times*.
57. *Op. cit.*, *Letters*, p. 296.
58. ALS, 27 May [1949], *op. cit.*

Waugh lived for jokes, but he had alienated so many of his friends that there was now scarcely anyone with whom to share laughter. 'Women don't understand pomposity,' he complained to Lady Diana Cooper. 'It is nearly always an absolutely private joke – one against the world. The last line of defence.'[59] His incoming correspondence is a monument to the loyalty and hero-worship he inspired but, at this stage, it makes dull reading. Of his female friends, only Nancy Mitford and Penelope Betjeman could manage the sustained levity he needed and both were now cautious.

Among these letters, however, one series stands out. 'Darling Whiskers,' one runs:

> It's an age since you paid no attention this way ain't it? Found a new fuck or what is it? The Lord Chancellor's back so it's standing up time for this pretty girl, and there's my cousin too, shocked the domestic servants, he did, staying with som Erl in Ireland. O well, never say die, that's my motto. . . . Written any of your books lately? . . . I like straight laughs like in your Campion. Well toodleoo Whiskers. Stick to me if you like sticking.
>
> Yours ever devotionly,
>
> Edwina Quennell.[60]

Who was it dared to address the great man thus? No dark lady but Christopher Sykes in the persona of Peter Quennell's blowzy 'cousin'. It was the kind of fiction Waugh loved and, although unhappy to be addressed as 'Darling Big-cock,'[61] he nevertheless entered into the spirit of the correspondence. The period 1948–51 was the only one during which Waugh and his future biographer were close friends. After a reprimand about foul language, Sykes changed his persona to that of Waugh's manservant and it was in this role that he wrote to his master arranging the trip to Paris.

Sykes gives an excellent account of the excursion[62] – of Waugh's unhappy encounters with the poet Paul Claudel and the modernist theologian, Père Couturier; of Waugh's teasing Duff Cooper until he finally yelled: 'It's rotten little rats like you who have brought about the downfall of the country.' Waugh apparently sat unmoved through Cooper's tirade. '. . . Nancy and Evelyn and I', says Sykes, 'left Chantilly and returned to Paris under a cloud. None of us was ever quite clear as to why.'[63] At each stage, the trip had been disastrous, thanks to Waugh's relentless provocation. And when Nancy had asked him why he needed to be so cruel, Waugh had merely offered his now famous response: 'You have no idea how much

59. ALS, 'Winter Solstice' [21 December 1949], from Piers Court; BL; *MWMS*, p. 105.
60. Unpublished ALS from Christopher Sykes, 13 October 1948, from 90 Eaton Terrace, SW1; BL.
61. Unpublished ALS from Christopher Sykes, 4 November 1948, from 90 Eaton Terrace, SW1; BL.
62. Sykes, pp. 331–4.
63. *Ibid.*, p. 334.

nastier I would be if I was not a Catholic. Without supernatural aid I would hardly be a human being.'[64]

Sykes does not convey, however, Waugh's own misery at his failure to be companionable and, worse, at his failure even to feel sorry for having behaved like a dog. Their disgrace did not result from the quarrel with Cooper. That was an effect rather than a cause. For some months, Lady Diana had again been trying to restore comradeship with Waugh and somehow he had managed to offend even her. It was this which irritated Cooper and the background to the story is complicated.

Cooper's biographer[65] believes that Lady Diana was uninjured by her husband's infidelities. In 1949, his affair with 'Lulu' (Louise de Vilmorin) was an open secret. When 'Prod' was in Paris, wasting Nancy's money and obstructing her work, he and Cooper would frequently stay out all night casino-crawling and conclude proceedings in a brothel.[66] But while Nancy was keen to see the back of Peter, Lady Diana remained besotted with Duff, and so much so that she refused to blame him for adultery. She was no longer the most beautiful woman of her circle. Part of Duff's attraction was his virility and recklessness. She had, in any case, always regarded sex as an overrated pastime. His lovers thus relieved her of responsibility in this respect. These facts, she felt, had to be faced. So long as he always returned and always loved her, she was prepared to ignore his private life. Duff's part of this unarticulated bargain appears to have been that he should never confront her with the more unpleasant facts and that she should remain principal among his affections. She was thus able to maintain the veneer of cosmopolitan *chic* and to maintain ultimate control. One of the penalties of having an affair with Duff, Nancy once remarked (not of herself), was that, after it was over, one had then to suffer Lady Diana's coming round to sympathize. She made close friends of her husband's lovers.

This 'sympathy', perhaps, was a way of emphasizing that in this power struggle she was Queen. Her public image of flibbertigibbet *femme du monde*, crackling with energy, charmingly neurotic, could thus remain untarnished. Beneath this implacable surface, however, Mrs Stitch's small store of self-confidence was crumbling. For all her positive qualities – and she was, everyone agrees, a 'life-enhancer', a rare eccentric spirit, witty and pugnacious – she was fragile. Her letters to Waugh are cries for help: child-

64. *Ibid.*
65. John Charmley, *Duff Cooper* (Weidenfeld & Nicolson, 1986).
66. Cf. unpublished ALS from Nancy Mitford to Waugh, 14 December 1949, from 7 Rue Monsieur, Paris VII; BL: 'Brothels. Well if there aren't any where do Prod & Duff go when Prod gets back at 7 a.m. saying Duff was on all fours barking like a dog? Oh, yes, brothels all right.... I can't work when ... [Prod] is here.... He has no respect for work & wanders in and out chatting. I do think he's awfully unwell and awfully blind & halt ... but of course we are all old now.'

like pencil scribbles from 'Baby' to 'Bo', desperately jolly or honestly hopeless. She could not face old age with equanimity. With no court of male admirers, no role as Ambassador's wife, no love for France or even pleasure in regarding her own image, she often felt empty and alienated. She yearned to reclaim Waugh as an old suitor. On his previous visit, he had seemed tractable enough, positively gallant on the occasions when she could keep him and Duff apart. She had prepared for Bo's arrival with keen anticipation, only to find herself rebuked.

What he said, we shall probably never know. Perhaps he made some acid remark about her complaisance. He was unsympathetic to her marital predicament and since the 1930s had been trying to persuade her to become a Catholic. She was, he thought, in a false dichotomy: the fate of her soul lay in her own hands. She should love God, not Duff, who was in Waugh's eyes little more than a bumptious undergraduate; her allegiance should be to the Church rather than to an adulterous husband. Certainly, this was the line he took with her later and nothing could strike more fiercely at the root of her delicate self-esteem. Her marriage was her Church. Whatever Duff did, nothing could corrupt her belief in him as her temporal God. There might also have been Waugh's perennial complaint: 'If only you could treat friends as something to be enjoyed in themselves not as companions in adventure we should be so much happier together. . . . I do wish sometimes you could just sit quietly ... instead of always thinking of something amusing to do.'[67] The details of the scene are ultimately irrelevant but their effect was not. It precipitated another rift lasting over a year and, on his return, he discovered that Cooper was disinclined to leave the insult to his wife unrebuked.

'Have you heard of Cooper's Master Stroke in revenge,' Sykes wrote, 'for OUR alleged misbehaviour at Chantilly? He has got Lord Stanley of Alderley to propose Peter Quennell for White's, & himself seconds. This ... is to get us to resign – so high and bitter is the feeling (to me utterly incomprehensible). . . .'[68] Cooper was not without a sense of humour. 'I doubt if it is on account of your alleged inhumanity to Honks [Diana],' Nancy told Waugh, 'as he has been giggling away about it for many a long moon. . . .'[69] But the tease struck home. Like Randolph Churchill, Waugh could dish it out but did not like taking it. To Cooper, this business was nothing more than an exercise in sophisticated 'needling', deliciously Waugh-like in its subtlety. To Waugh, it was an affront to his dignity and he tried to rally a blackball gang. Connolly, Bowra and Lord David Cecil were invited down to Piers Court – all to no avail. Connolly rushed

67. ALS to Lady Diana Cooper, 10 April 1948, from Piers Court; BL; *MWMS*, p. 101.
68. Unpublished ALS from Christopher Sykes, 31 May 1949, from White's; BL.
69. Unpublished ALS from Nancy Mitford, 5 June 1949, from 7 Rue Monsieur etc.; BL.

straight back to London and voted for Quennell, who was elected without opposition.

It was a trivial incident but it disturbed Waugh and revived his persecution complex. He detected another plot. Particularly unwelcome was the realization that Quennell was now demonstrably more successful as a social figure. His acceptance by the innermost sanctum of the gentlemen's mafia set the seal on his triumph. Waugh found himself in the awkward position of being jealous of someone he despised. Swearing that he would never return to Paris, he concentrated his attention again on American Catholicism.

*

The topic still proved unmanageably large. Waugh's deadline had come and gone before the visit to Paris. Anxious letters had arrived from *Life* and he had been forced to request their leniency. As a craftsman he prided himself on his ability to turn out any form of writing punctually. But this was the most serious journalistic assignment of his life and he was determined to get it right. The 6,000 words of 'The American Epoch in the Catholic Church' took him almost three months to complete – astonishingly slow by his normal standards – and, in the end, he thought it drearily pedagogic: just the sort of thing the Americans would love.

They did. When the article appeared in September, it met with huge success and revealed a depth of humble piety in Waugh which few Americans had suspected. He had been widely reported as hating their country. Here he was springing to its defence. The general argument has already been discussed – the collapse of European culture beneath an onslaught of rationalism; the rise of the USA as world leader opposed to the Communist threat – but not its enormous personal significance to Waugh. To the sceptical reader, the piece might appear insincere. It was not. Indeed, it represents a massive shift in his views on the relationship between civilization and faith.

During the 1930s, Waugh's defence of tradition had emphasized a reciprocal relationship between European culture and Roman Catholicism.[70] Like Eliot, he had developed unrepentantly élitist aesthetic predilections. And as aesthetic preference had hardened into social preference, and social and religious preference had merged in his concept of discrimination, a divide had appeared in his spiritual life. Christianity teaches humility and compassion, but little children who came unto him had invariably been made to suffer. He had rarely turned the other cheek or loved his neighbour. He had felt unable to honour his father and, lately, even his mother. Charity

70. Cf. Vol. 1, p. 231.

was the problem and, labouring under this combative personality, Waugh agonized over his failures of contrition.

Shortly after finishing his article, he read Merton's *The Seeds of Contemplation* and wrote to him about it:

> I am greatly impressed by your assurance. You write as if you had been a director of souls for a lifetime. Except perhaps that an experienced director would not ... press the need for contemplation on all so eagerly. Is it not rather a question of rate of growth? Of course the contemplative's ideal is what we must all come to before we reach heaven, and of course if one can it is convenient to stop wasting time and get through as much as possible of purgation here. But don't you think that most souls are of slow growth? Is it not the most precocious child whom the parent loves most? Is there not a slight hint of bustle and salesmanship about the way you want to scoop us all into a higher grade than we are fit for?[71]

There can be little doubt that Waugh was referring to himself here, a soul of painfully slow growth, a Prodigal Son. His anarchism was deeply ingrained, incurable, the necessary attack on boredom. There is an unmistakable relish in his fiction for the pathologically deranged. A glamour attaches to their child-like recklessness, displacing perhaps their author's sense of his own 'ineradicable caddishness'. Unlike their creator, however, they lived unmolested by self-reflection. Evelyn Waugh was a tormented man. He hurt people and somehow could not stop himself from doing it. It was the power to hurt that made him a writer and exerted a demonic fascination. Power shimmered from him like heat and, with the schoolboy's delight in the electric-shock handshake, he loved the effect. Formerly he had been able to regulate the current to fine gradations, prickling the skin with the encouraging tease or instantly deterring with a thump of high voltage. In this way he had chosen his friends, testing their resilience. A form of love for him became the craving to be one of those he would not injure. Of late, however, his judgment of the gap between the tease and the injury had become erratic and this distressed him. He believed in the power of Evil. Like St Augustine, he wished to be made good – but not yet.

If he could not be good, and was temperamentally incapable of being careful, he could at least use his literary power in the service of the Church. Where his profession was concerned, the battle against Pride was won. 'I am a bigot and a philistine,' he wrote to Lord David Cecil.

> (I fail heavily in your test of sensibility – love of Scott, Hardy and Wordsworth) and I feel you can't *hint* at God. You must either affirm

71. ALS to Thomas Merton, 28 August [1949], from Piers Court; *EWN*, Vol. 3, No. 1 (Spring 1969), 2.

> or deny. If affirm, the soul is born with a longing for God and Beauty, Harmony and Order are only desirable as attributes of His. I can't think of a single Saint who attached much importance to Art. . . .[72]

The letter goes on to attack the 'mysticism of Art' and the heroic status accorded to artists in a secular age. It also helps to explain the violence of his reaction to sycophants. Fan-mail was not merely a temptation to Pride but an invitation to heresy.

'The American Epoch' is penitential in its austerity, affirming his faith that

> The Incarnation restored order. In place of his bloody guilt-offerings man was given a single, complete expiation; in place of his magic, the sacramental system, a regular service of communication with the supernatural; in place of his mystery-cults, an open, divinely-constituted human society in which to live and multiply.[73]

There was little room for jokes here, no desire to use this platform for self-display. Waugh conscientiously parades the whole range of his prejudices against America only to demolish them as ignorance. Some Catholic readers, he suggests (with, perhaps, a side-glance at Graham Greene), may feel antagonistic to the country. Its Constitution enshrines the division of Church and State; its historical tradition is anti-Catholic; its society can be seen to manifest 'a psychopathic antagonism to paternity'.[74] All this, however, is seen to be irrelevant. The Church was universally in a minority, constantly under attack from 'enemies inside or outside her body'.[75] What mattered was that 'Catholics are the largest religious body in the United States, the richest and in certain ways the most lively branch of the Catholic Church in the world . . . firmly grounded in a neutral, secular state.'[76] One of the more moving sights of his tour, he says, had been in New Orleans on Ash Wednesday. The Roosevelt Hotel was packed with tourists oblivious of the significance of Lent:

> But across the way the Jesuit Church was teeming with life all day long; a continuous, dense crowd of all colours and conditions moving up to the altar rails and returning with their foreheads signed with ash. And the old grim message was being repeated over each penitent:

72. 27 July 1949; *Letters*, p. 303. Cecil had sent Waugh a copy of his inaugural lecture as Goldsmith's Professor of English Literature, Oxford, which argued that: 'a true work of art appeals to us because, deliberately or not, it is an image of Divine Perfection and so, in some sort, a revelation of God. This reflects no special credit on the artist: he is a mere vehicle.'
73. 'The American Epoch in the Catholic Church', *Life*, 19 September 1949, 135–8, 140, 143, 144, 146, 149–50, 152, 155; reprinted *Month* (November 1949), 293–308; *EAR*, pp. 377–88.
74. *Ibid.*, p. 379.
75. *Ibid.*
76. *Ibid.*

'Dust thou art and unto dust shalt thou return.' One grows parched for that straight style of speech in the desert of modern euphemisms. . . .[77]

The phrase 'all colours and conditions' is significant. In order to make his American argument coherent, Waugh had to qualify the hierarchical principle on which so much of his thinking had been based.[78] Where aesthetics, literary criticism and the authority structures of Church and State were concerned, the principle could be maintained. But Waugh was confronting here the root of his prejudice against the Common Man. He does not overcome it but he does at least confront it. In America, most Catholics were the descendants of slaves or of impoverished immigrants from the Old World. Many were still poor. Their faith was associated in the popular mind with a redundant heritage, 'with the smell of garlic and olive oil and grandfather muttering over the foreign-language newspaper. . . .'[79] Europeans, Waugh warns, should be cautious of sneering. He praises 'the heroic fidelity of the Negro Catholics'[80] and defends humble piety. In the context of the Church, and there was for Waugh no other context, he had learnt a form of humility. No humanist argument could ever convince him of the merits of egalitarianism, but he had to accept that all men were equal in the eyes of God: 'A youth who is inarticulate in conversation may well be eloquent in prayer. It would be an intolerable impertinence to attempt to judge. . . . The Church does not exist in order to produce elegant preachers or . . . artists or philosophers. It exists to produce saints. God alone knows his own.'[81]

Waugh's role as the celebrated author in the glossy magazine is thus consistently debunked in favour of those contemplatives whose life of prayer attaches them to a higher reality. In the present phase of humanist, competitive materialism, he suggests, these solitaries are the power-house of Faith. 'The Church and the world need monks and nuns more than they need writers. These merely decorate. The Church can get along very well without them.'[82] Nothing could be further from the implicit connection between high culture and Faith which permeates *Brideshead*, and in this chastened mood he returned eagerly to work on what he termed his 'masterpiece', a novel which had already been five years in the making: 'The Quest of the Empress Dowager', or *Helena* as it became.

*

77. *Ibid.*, p. 382.
78. See Ch. V, pp. 165–7.
79. 'The American Epoch . . .', *op. cit.*, p. 383.
80. *Ibid.*
81. *Ibid.*, p. 386.
82. *Ibid.*, p. 387.

'I wish I could tell you that Helena progresses,' Waugh wrote to Peters in July. 'All I can truthfully say is that I am working on nothing else. Great sloth in the middle climacteric may be healthy, you know. There are so many sad cases of deterioration and collapse through overwork at this delicate period.'[83] Peters had still only received sixty-three pages of typescript but he knew better than to harry his best client. By the end of December, the second section of the novel, a further sixty-four pages, was submitted. The last word was not written until March 1950. It was meticulous, precisely modulated work. 'I write a sentence a week . . .,' he informed Anne Fremantle in September. 'It will be interesting only to the very few people who know exactly as much history as I do. The millions who know more will be disgusted; the few who know less, puzzled. Americans will inevitably fall into these two classes only.'[84]

His novel obsessed him – but there were unavoidable distractions to concentration. Returning from America, he had piously resolved to accept all Catholic invitations for a year. For some months he had escaped persecution. By the autumn, however, the news had leaked out and requests poured in, not only from universities and convents, but from friends seeking help with their books. The letter to Mrs Fremantle concerned her *Desert Calling*, a biography of Charles de Foucauld, which Waugh had just read in proof. Most of the next year was like that: a tidal wave of unpaid work for others – Caraman, Alfred Duggan and Thomas Merton in particular. And as he squandered energy thus, he grew increasingly anxious about money. During 1949 he felt for the first time seriously threatened by financial collapse.

Waugh and Laura were equally reckless with cheques. She ran a separate bank account. Neither knew what the other was spending. Whenever Peters sent Waugh copies of contracts 'for his records', he invariably returned the papers saying that he kept no records. Nor did he, other than to stuff odd letters and annual statements into envelopes with the more precious correspondence from friends and loonies. Bank statements were far too dull for serious consideration. His sole financial concern was whether Peters and Little, Brown still held money for him 'in the kitty'. When overdrawn, Waugh would request another wad to be paid into his account, rarely enquiring what the money was for or how much was left. As a result, his financial affairs were chaotic. For three years, he had been unwittingly overspending by approximately £2,000 per annum. Enter Percy Popkin, the accountant who was invited to Piers Court and tortured with the mechanical organ.

83. Unpublished ALS to A. D. Peters, 20 July 1949, from Piers Court; *Catalogue* E626, p. 170.
84. 14 September [1949], from Piers Court; *Letters*, p. 310.

Popkin was a patient man. The Inland Revenue inspector at Stroud, with whom he dealt on Waugh's behalf, was not. No proper returns had been made for those three years and Popkin found himself involved in awkward negotiations between equally belligerent spirits. Waugh disdained all demands as an intolerable invasion of privacy; the inspector had smelt a rat and was determined to scratch it out. Popkin had written earlier:

> You see, I realise what we are up against in cases of this kind. I rather imagine you do not when you speak of fighting the Inspector in a Court of Law.... A fighting attitude will not help us. It would if we had kept proper A/Cs and evidence to support our items.... I very much doubt whether the *total* expense of 5 servants (keep of four) would be allowed in the apportionment.[85]

Then had followed the week-end at Piers Court from which a bemused Popkin had reeled home to resume his battle with the paperwork: '... [my visit] has made this claim for expenditure', he wrote, probably not without irony, 'so much clearer to me.'[86] But all they had definitely resolved was to double Waugh's Deed of Covenant to his mother to £13. 15s. 0d. a month – a clarification scarcely calculated to impress the inspector.

Popkin's only hope of a straight answer was to deal with Peters. Here, however, he encountered another autocrat. Peters was a busy man with a fine sense of social distinction who disliked being pestered for details. He would state what Waugh had been paid in any financial year but would not examine the records. Poor Popkin was constantly requesting replies to letters sent two months earlier. And when Peters finally scribbled a perfunctory note, he merely repeated what was already known, ignoring the finer points of the enquiry. In desperation, Popkin sent him Chapman & Hall's account: 'Will you kindly return same to me and tell me whether I can now inform the Inspector.... I am sorry to trouble you, but Mr Waugh's official has always proved to be ... very fussy....'[87] Then, eleven days later: 'Could I have a reply to my letter of 22nd April? Inspector is pressing. Kind regards.'[88]

A week later, Peters's office paid £4,400 into Waugh's account at his request, being the money that they were holding for him for the next tax year: 'You usually do not like to be bothered with statements but if you would like to know how this rather large amount is made up we shall ...

85. Unpublished TLS from Percy Popkin, 11 September 1948, from 131 Main Road, Romford, Essex; BL.
86. Unpublished TLS from Percy Popkin, 18 September 1948, from 131 Main Road etc.; BL.
87. Unpublished TLS from Percy Popkin to A. D. Peters, 22 April 1949, from 131 Main Road etc.; HRC.
88. Unpublished TPCS, Popkin to Peters, 3 May 1949, from 131 Main Road etc.; HRC.

be pleased to send you a detailed account.'[89] Waugh did not want to know and Peters did not furnish Popkin with the detailed account. Instead, Peters apologized for the delay. He had, he said, had no chance to sort out Waugh's figures, but he would reply no later than 11 June.[90]

A reply came at last in August. Peters was stalling while Waugh spent money like a drunken sailor. He bought two Victorian paintings, paid Midland Gardens nearly £1,000, took Bron on an unhappy summer holiday to France and continued to entertain lavishly. In the meantime, his agent was trying to sell film rights to balance the books. 'I have no tenderness towards *Scoop*,' Waugh wrote,

> and would sell ... for whatever is now a large sum. But the difficulty will be to avoid taxation.... If the purchaser is American we could make it part of the price that Laura and I had a luxurious holiday in New York ostensibly collaborating. If English there is so [?] little they can offer. Perhaps they could put in a lot of architectural garden work here pretending they were going to photograph it....[91]

'Film companies', Peters replied, 'are scared to death of any kind of legal hanky-panky. The days are gone when motor cars and houses were given to authors in lieu of cash.'[92]

The trip to France had been financed by the Parisian 'nest-egg' and by Peters's transferring money from another author's account. But Waugh, of course, had overspent, and returned still trying to encourage his agent to arrange payments in kind: 'A chum of mine has secured (tax free) a sailing yacht and a villa in Capri from a well-known English film company in the last year.'[93] Eleven days later, with classic understatement, he was requesting more cash because he 'seem[ed] to be short'.[94] Peters sent another £2,000 of the £4,000 still due, making a grand total since April of £8,457. When informed of this figure, Waugh displayed signs of panic: 'Too much. I can't afford to earn like this. Please pay no more money to me until further notice. This is getting desperate. We must get rid of the whole of the cinema rights of *Scoop* on the Jesuits if the deal goes through.'[95]

Peters was also becoming nervous. Waugh now gave so much away and worked so often for nothing that his resources were rapidly diminishing.

89. Unpublished TccL from Margaret Stephens, 11 May 1949, from A. D. Peters & Co.; HRC.
90. Unpublished TccL, Peters to Popkin, 21 May 1949; HRC.
91. Unpublished ALS to A. D. Peters, 20 July 1949, *op. cit.*
92. Unpublished TLS from A. D. Peters, 22 July 1949; HRC.
93. Unpublished APCI to A. D. Peters, received 14 September 1949, from Piers Court; *Catalogue* E634, p. 172. Graham Greene had a villa in Anacapri.
94. Unpublished APCI to A. D. Peters, received 26 September 1949, from Piers Court; *Catalogue* E635, p. 172.
95. Unpublished APCI to A. D. Peters, nd [c. 4 October 1949], from Piers Court; *Catalogue* E638, p. 172.

Searching the records at last, Peters discovered that John Sutro's film company had contracted to pay a further £1,500 for *Put Out More Flags* which had somehow been forgotten. Peters demanded it; Waugh nobly cancelled the debt. And so it went on: furious expenditure; modest income. During November, Waugh borrowed Tom Burns's house to throw a party for Clare Luce. 'I have been an invalid for a week recuperating from a brief visit to London,' he wrote to Nancy.

> I get so painfully drunk whenever I go there (Champagne, the shortest road out of Welfaria) and nowadays it is not a matter of a headache and an aspirin but of complete collapse, with some clear indications of incipient lunacy. I think I am jolly near being mad.... My great party for Mrs Luce was very expensive....[96]

Peters was worried about him, as was Nancy. In the new year she heard more bad news:

> My new Holy Year opens with the prospect of financial ruin.... Well last week I said to Laura 'are you sure you aren't over-drawn at the bank?' 'No, I don't think so. I'm sure they'd tell me, if I were.' 'Well do ask.' So she did and, my dear, she had an overdraft of £6,420 which had been quietly mounting up for years. There is no possible way to pay it off, as her capital is in trust ... its a sad prospect isn't it. I shall have to go to prison but that is hell nowadays with wireless & lectures & psychiatry. Oh for the Marshalsea.[97]

He could afford to joke about this because he still had about £20,000 in Little, Brown's account. But with his British resources exhausted, that suddenly seemed a very small amount indeed. *The Quest of the Empress Dowager* was a beautifully written book and Peters admired it. Both author and agent, however, realized that it would not restore Waugh's fortunes. There was, of course, always money to be made out of his reputation. Nancy supplemented her income with a weekly column for the *Sunday Times*; Connolly later became a book reviewer for the same paper. These were the jobs Waugh predicted for his twilight years. But to be forced into such employment at the age of forty-six seemed cruelly precipitate. It never occurred to him that he might spend less; that if he restricted himself to his original goal of £5,000 a year, he could live comfortably for the foreseeable future on more than five times the average professional wage. *Folie de grandeur* was in danger of undoing him. He *was* going a little mad and only Peters's calm good sense averted catastrophe.

96. 5 December [1949]. *Letters*, p. 315.
97. 11 January 1950; *Letters*, p. 319.

During October and November, letters had begun to arrive from Penguin Books. Waugh had often been troubled by publishers seeking rights for cheap reprints and had usually dismissed them, believing that more money was to be made from hardback sales. 'Thanks for your letter about Penguins,' he replied. 'I am totally indifferent in the matter. Do whatever you think best and transfer the Penguin rights bodily to Fr. D'Arcy's Jesuits if you decide to sell.'[98] Penguin had published most of Waugh's early novels but they had fallen out of print during the war. *A Handful of Dust* and *Brideshead* were not on their list and no large profit had ever resulted. Waugh's attitude to paperback sales was that they were a last resort, to squeeze a few final pennies from old titles. He did not realize that the whole market was changing. Very few people did. Penguin was offering to reprint Waugh's entire fictional opus and Peters's indifference to the proposal at first almost equalled his client's. McDougall was worried that Chapman & Hall's new Uniform Edition[99] might be swamped and he and Peters agreed to hang fire.

In less than a fortnight, however, this decision was reversed. The enterprising Allen Lane had pointed out that for the last few years Penguin had been 'spotlighting' particular authors. To celebrate Shaw's ninetieth birthday they had republished ten of his works, each in 100,000 copies. The writings of H. G. Wells and Agatha Christie had received similar treatment. Block publication, Lane insisted, provided better publicity than the appearance of isolated titles and none of their selected authors had sold less than a million copies in the first year. 'McDougall wants to go ahead with the Penguin proposition,' Peters wrote.

> All his travellers and associates feel that Penguins would not hurt your ordinary sales and might increase the demand for your future books. [They] want to put out ten ... novels in 1951.... As there is quite a lot of money involved, I suggest that you assign these cheap rights to a Trust for the benefit of one or more of your children. You save tax, ensure their future to some extent, and can also draw on the income for [*sic*] the Trust for their education and maintenance if the Deed is skilfully drawn up.[100]

It was. This was the best piece of advice Peters ever gave Waugh.

A solicitor with the deliciously Dickensian name of W. Evill drew up the final terms of the Deed by August 1950 and, long before this, Waugh, sniffing profit, was referring to it as the Save the Children Fund. In fact,

98. Unpublished APCI to A. D. Peters, nd [received 25 November 1949], from Piers Court; *Catalogue* E640, p. 172.
99. Seven volumes were printed in March 1949.
100. Unpublished TLS from A. D. Peters, 8 December 1949; HRC.

it did a great deal more to save the father. Waugh committed Penguin's £1,000 advance to it, soon added all his copyrights and even briefly considered including all his property. Peters and Evill were the trustees, the Waugh children the only beneficiaries. Any money controlled by the Trust was therefore no longer the property or even the earnings of Waugh or of his wife. Peters was adamant about this in his dealings with Chapman & Hall. The first payment into the Trust account was £360[101] for the second stage of the advance on *Helena*. The money belonged, Peters insisted, '... not to Evelyn Waugh but to the Trustees.... As far as Chapman and Hall are concerned, [he] will receive no further payments from them.'[102] This had the singular benefit of evading surtax on these payments (Evill thought that Waugh would save around £700 a year). But it could only work so long as all interest of the father was eliminated in perpetuity. What, then, did Waugh propose to live on?

The answer for the Inland Revenue was simple: future writings and American money. American contracts were more susceptible to 'legal hanky-panky' in that, of any total amount paid, only a proportion was declared. The rest could be siphoned off as 'expenses'. Peters was arranging a contract like this with Sam Marx for the film rights of *A Handful of Dust* while the Deed was being drawn up.[103] A substantial part of Waugh's American income could thus be tax-free. Even with this benefit, however, the total revenue was inadequate to keep Waugh for more than a decade in his customary style. If he were not to squander his American nest-egg, he had somehow to gain access to the money tied up in the Deed, not just to its interest. Its terms stated that none of the capital could be touched until

101. £400 less Peters's ten per cent commission.

102. Unpublished ALS from A. D. Peters to John McDougall, 14 August 1950; HRC. Peters was having a rare battle with McDougall and with Duckworth's on Waugh's behalf. Duckworth's had sold *When the Going Was Good* to the Reprint Society in 1948 and had made a small fortune, Waugh's share of which (twenty per cent) came to just over £2,000. The market, they believed, was now effectively exhausted and they had been foolish enough to admit as much to Peters. When Peters requested reprinting rights for Penguin, Duckworth's had demanded fifty per cent of the profits. Peters squashed that and also tried to rewrite the longstanding 50–50 reprint agreement with Chapman & Hall. 'I think this far too high a proportion', he informed McDougall, 'in the case of this special edition. Evelyn's own view, as you know, is that publishers ought not to get any share at all on books published by others ...' (TLS, 8 June 1950; HRC). This, Peters agreed, was perhaps going too far: a 75–25 division would be fairer. McDougall, however, would not budge: 50–50 had been the basis of the negotiation and 50–50 it would remain. He seems, indeed, to have been shocked by Peters's hustling and for the first time a distinct coolness enters their gentlemanly correspondence.

103. '... we could make a deal, provided the $3,000 [advance] is paid to [Waugh] as expenses in connection with what might be called his "services"; and that in the event you exercize your option, $7000 of the balance would be charged as payments for Waugh's services for working on the script, and the remaining $10,000 as the purchase price for the rights.... Actually his "services" would be nominal, and he wouldn't be required to do any writing ...' (TLS, Peters to Marx of MGM Pictures, 24 May 1950; HRC). The deal went through (with the advance reduced to $2,000), but the film was never made.

the last child came of age. Laura was pregnant again and due to give birth in the summer of 1950. That meant that, at the very least, the money would be entailed until 1971, by which time, Waugh thought, correctly, he would be dead. It was probable, should he survive, that his children would not see him starve as they pocketed their inheritance. It was useful to have their school fees covered by the interest. But this arrangement provided no luxuries, and luxuries Waugh required as others did air.

The resolution of this difficulty was as simple as the problem was complicated, and Waugh went straight to it with a street-trader's acuity. At first, Evill was risibly correct in his dealings. What, he enquired, should he and Peters buy with the money – some stocks, perhaps? No, no; Peters thought that rather a bad idea. Better to leave the capital fluid and to consider the matter carefully. Then, during the year after the Trust was executed, bills began to arrive: from silversmiths and art dealers, interior decorators and Universal Aunts. Waugh had discovered that he could buy whatever he wanted and charge it to the Trust. So long as the goods purchased belonged to the Trust, he was (or, legally, Peters and Evill were) using the children's money to improve their investment. Later, Waugh devised a subtler refinement. Anything that remained his property he could sell to the Trust. Some of his manuscripts were thus 'bought' to release tax-free capital from what in any case would have been willed to his family. Basil Seal might have been proud of the scheme.

*

Tax inspectors, like dons, were to Waugh fair game. The killjoy in Stroud was, he thought, attempting to rob an honest man through the legislation of a degenerate democracy. Waugh felt he was only playing by the same rules to reclaim what had rightfully been his in the first place. In most instances, it must be emphasized, he was scrupulously honest, and he was, after all, breaking no laws. Throughout this difficult period, his generosity to friends and co-religionists never wavered. He had needed money badly when he cancelled Sutro's debt. He had needed isolation more to complete his novel yet had answered each call on his services. When he was about to leave on a tour of Scottish universities (nine lectures in nine days) he had received an SOS from an old flame, Baby Jungman: his old Commando friend, Peter Beatty, was going blind and suffering acute depression. Would Waugh come to Mereworth where a house-party was assembled, trying to dissuade Beatty from suicide? Waugh dropped everything and went. On the train two days later he opened *The Times* and was shocked to learn that Beatty had thrown himself from a sixth-floor window of the Ritz.

There was much tempting Waugh to despair at this time. Beatty's death must have recalled David Plunket Greene's a year or so earlier. Gwen and

Olivia had set up house with him in the cottage on the Longleat estate, hoping that restoration to family life would cure his drug addiction. Then one day he had walked into the lake. Olivia had since grown madder by the hour while Waugh wrote patiently, regularly, to remind her of the first principles of her Faith. Indeed, only first principles kept him determinedly believing in a beneficent God. In April 1949 he had spoken at the Newman Society against the motion 'That this house considers itself in duty bound to participate in the government of the country'.[104] Where earthly powers had failed him, strict adherence to the letter of the Catholic law preserved his sanity while driving him further into eccentric isolation. Tom Burns remembers him in restaurants during Lent, producing miniature scales at the table to weigh out precisely the quantities of allowable food. In all things Waugh was punctilious: Beatty was not brave, Waugh thought, he was mad.

Each day, killing time, Waugh read his newspaper from front to back and did the crossword. Often he would use up his afternoons in the darkness of Dursley cinema. The news he was reading (and seeing) can only have confirmed *Brideshead*'s political pessimism. Lord Bath opened Longleat to the public; Prince Aly Khan deserted his wife to marry Rita Hayworth. In September 1949 the Russians exploded their first atomic bomb and it was discovered that traitors had been feeding the eastern bloc with deadly secrets. In England, Klaus Fuchs was convicted; in America, Hiss and the Rosenbergs. Senator McCarthy initiated his witch-hunt; the Korean War began. At home, in February 1950, a general election failed to rout Labour, leaving them instead with a majority of six and Britain with an unstable government. Waugh turned his back on it all. Election day saw him in Peters's office, arranging the terms of the Trust and still looking to American Catholicism as the only hope for the world. It would be easy to see him at this time as the die-hard, know-nothing philistine of Orwell's review, selfish and bitter. Melancholy and boredom sometimes overwhelmed him and in these moods his temper could explode. But more frequently he was possessed by a kind of gruff geniality. 'In [*Pinfold*],' Paul Moor wrote after a visit to Piers Court, 'Waugh described himself as an "essentially kind man". On due reflection, . . . I think I'd have to agree.'[105]

Moor's story is worth telling as a stranger's account of Waugh's domestic regime. In 1949, Moor was a penurious young American writer, eagerly planning a first trip to Europe. He knew Carl Van Vechten, who offered introductions to his European friends: Alice B. Toklas and Waugh. Hoping

104. Christopher Hollis spoke for the motion. Waugh found himself increasingly estranged from Hollis since his entry into Parliament. Cf. unpublished TLS from Hollis to Waugh, nd [1948], p. 265 below.
105. Memorandum from Paul Moor to Martin Stannard, September 1987.

for nothing, Moor wrote off and was astonished to discover a charming letter from Waugh waiting at the *poste restante* in Dublin. If Moor were a man of means, Waugh suggested, he should drive down to Gloucestershire for a few days. Moor took a third-class train and found a hired limousine waiting for him at the station.

> A butler in impressive livery opened the front door and dextrously extracted the borrowed week-end bag from my ... perspiring hand. Behind him, almost at once, appeared Waugh – dressed for dinner, naturally, in an old-fashioned tuxedo, replete with dancing pumps embellished with dainty little gros-grain bows. With breath bated, I tremulously waited my idol's first words. After an elaborate reaction of exaggerated astonishment, there came, 'But I thought you'd be black!' 'I don't understand.' 'I thought all Carl Van Vechten's friends were black! What a disappointment! My wife and I had both counted on dining out for months to come on our story of this great, hulking American coon who came to spend the week-end. Ah well.' Then he brightened. 'Don't dress for dinner if you don't want to.' He paused, then added somewhat hesitantly, 'Ah – we always do.'

Waugh noticed the young man's discomfiture and enjoyed it. Moor did not own a dinner-jacket and, shamefaced, allowed Ellwood to conduct him to his room. In the adjoining bathroom, fixed to the toilet cistern, was a hand-lettered card: 'The handle should return to the horizontal when the flow of water ceases. Should it fail to do so, agitate it gently until it succeeds. E.W.' The precision of the command engraved itself permanently on Moor's memory. He unpacked, fearing the worst. In his bag, however, lay the secret of his success: not clothes, but food. Strict rationing was still enforced. In London, he had stayed with a friend on the staff of the American Embassy, whose commissary was stocked to bursting with delicacies only available to Britons on the black market. The friend had opened his refrigerator and told his guest to take whatever he wanted. When Moor shyly presented his array of exotic comestibles, Waugh was visibly moved, and fierceness dissolved into gentle teasing.

Moor quickly came to understand the game in which he was involved. At dinner that night, Laura, in full-length evening gown, was charming, Waugh mischievous. As the butler began to fill Moor's wine glass, Waugh halted him with a grand, sweeping gesture and said, 'I'm sure you'd prefer iced water', waving towards the sideboard where a large jug of the stuff waited. Moor declined the offer. 'But we've gone to such trouble!' Moor stood firm. Waugh tried again: 'At breakfast tomorrow I expect you'll want Popsy Toasties or something like that, won't you?' Moor said that he would prefer an English breakfast. Waugh, affecting disappointment that his guest had not come up to his expectations of a typical American, relinquished this line of attack.

Conversation was uphill work with only the three of them at table. When the question of religion arose, Moor said that he had been brought up a Baptist. At this, husband and wife stopped eating and stared at him with intense curiosity. 'Perhaps it's different in America,' Waugh remarked, 'but in England only the lower classes are Baptists.' Moor refused the bait and, as the evening progressed, the atmosphere warmed a little. They talked about farming. 'My wife takes care of the farm, all the masculine things,' Waugh said with a smile, 'and I look after all the feminine things – decorating and so on.'

After dinner, Waugh suggested a stroll, suddenly stopping his guest in the hallway: 'Would you like to pee?' The downstairs toilet revealed the master's decorative taste – an ornate commode, its arms upholstered in leopard skin, was superimposed over the conventional toilet basin; the walls blazed with Abyssinian paintings. Outside, Moor was taken on a tour of the follies (it was he whom Waugh tried to shock with the spikes and skulls). Then they rejoined Laura before a roaring fire in the drawing room.

> Waugh continued smoking cigars, I smoked cigarettes as did his wife. They sat on either side of the fireplace, I facing it, with all of us perhaps six feet away from it. I looked for an ashtray within reach, but found none; neither could I see one anywhere in the room, but since both my host and hostess smoked, I decided to wait and follow their example. . . . Mrs Waugh, when the ash on her cigarette grew to an alarming length, made a sort of throwing gesture with her smoking hand in the direction of the fireplace, sufficient to . . . send the ash at least on its way towards the hearth.

Waugh did the same so Moor followed suit, constantly fearful of burning the carpet. Prodigal hospitality at Piers Court always carried an edge of discomfort for strangers. No allowance was made for their ignorance of household codes.

Waugh had a regular entertainment programme for casual acquaintances. The next morning he again hired the car and took Moor to visit Gloucester Cathedral.

> He had on the most outrageously loud suit I have ever seen – a rough tweed with enormous brownish red checks – and a heavy gold watch-chain across his paunch. As I stood rapt before one of the ornate stone tombs inside, I heard his voice directly over my shoulder: 'King Edward the Second. Great aesthete, you know.' He pronounced it ees-thete, and added for my possible benefit: 'patron of the arts, you know.' He spoke in so uninhibitedly conversational a tone that several

> of the hushed, whispering tourists nearby, most of them elderly ladies, looked our way. At the same level of volume, he continued: 'Homosexual, you know – died near here at Berkeley Castle with a red-hot poker thrust up his anus.'

Everyone within earshot gaped and stared. Waugh, delighted, strode on.

His private conversation was equally unsettling. Whenever Moor tried to speak to him about writing, Waugh deflected the questions. In view of the American success of *Brideshead* and *The Loved One*, he insisted, he had no necessity or desire to write any more. During the ride to Gloucester, he had startled his guest by saying that *The Times* traditionally hired Communists as correspondents; that they had sent a Communist to cover the Spanish Civil War and his reports had done 'incalculable harm'.[106] When the talk turned to books, Moor confessed that he read slowly to savour the silent pronunciation of each word. Suddenly, he found Waugh briefly confidential. He had, he said, always done the same thing and had never seen any reason to do otherwise.

After the Cathedral, Moor was taken to a pub and a humble antique shop. Waugh, disappointed when the dealer told him frankly that he did not remember him, was searching for pictures – 'Victorian scenes of family life' – but found none, and that evening Moor began to understand better his host's obsession with genre painting. Another guest arrived, Maurice Bowra (of whom Moor had never heard), bearing a pound of bacon. Waugh showed him a recently acquired work, *La Question Embarrassante*, and invited his guests to divine its narrative. The canvas depicted three people: a Catholic priest, a man and a woman, all in the priest's study. The men appeared to be waiting for a response from the woman in an atmosphere of profound contemplation. Bowra pondered it for a while in silence and then said: 'The man and the woman have come to the priest to arrange their marriage, and the priest has just asked her whether she has been married before. She has. For all three of them, the priest has just asked *la question embarrassante*.' Waugh found this plausible but did not commit himself to an interpretation.

What fascinated him, apparently, was the play between narrative and interpretation. The painter's business, like the writer's, was to construct coherent structures of 'pure action'. These structures codified the artist's feelings but it was an invasion of the viewer's or reader's autonomy to

106. Probably a reference to G. L. Steer, a fellow correspondent with Waugh in Abyssinia (1935–6), who was unsympathetic to the Italian invasion and whose anti-Fascist views were equally evident in his later Spanish reports. Waugh reviewed Steer's books unfavourably in the *Tablet* (23 January 1937; *EAR*, pp. 188–9; and 26 September 1942; *EAR*, pp. 271–2). It is extremely unlikely that Waugh knew the secret of *The Times*'s correspondent who *was* a Communist but who paraded his sympathy for Franco as cover for future espionage: Kim Philby.

attempt to dictate such intentions. 'The feelings', Waugh explained in 1964, 'should be the reader's, the customer's. You tell him or her the facts and if it is properly told, the story, they'll quickly pick up what the feelings are.'[107] In this case, the feelings Bowra had discerned were peculiarly embarrassing to Waugh and this effect was perhaps intentional. Moor sensed Waugh's attachment to 'scenes of family life'. Bowra had jabbed fiercely at the illusion by an oblique reference to Evelyn Gardner.

That night, Moor sat silently, listening. He knew nothing of the prickly competitiveness which had always coloured Bowra's relationship with Waugh. Discussing royal honours, Waugh confessed that he would be contented with a knighthood. Bowra did not rise to this (he was to have his revenge in 1950) but quickly grasped an opportunity to reciprocate patronage. He was an accomplished linguist; his host was not. Waugh left the room to take a continental telephone call and they could hear him distantly conversing in hesitant French. 'Evelyn gets along very well', said Bowra, turning to the embarrassed American on Waugh's return, 'when he speaks French. I remember once he found himself paired off with a man who spoke nothing but French, and Evelyn got the conversation going by simply taking his arm and saying "Parlons du vin."' 'More bad news,' Waugh muttered gloomily, explaining to Laura the imminent arrival of another visitor.

Making a virtue of ignorance, however, was one of Waugh's more alarming tactics. Left to himself one day, Moor had ambled into the drawing room to discover a 'baby grand'. He had been a modest musical *wunderkind* and, the sight of the instrument offering too strong a temptation, he sat down and played. After some minutes, he discovered Waugh's face at the window, glaring in.

> When I had finished the piece . . ., I turned and looked at him for the first time. He reacted only by staring at me, popping his eyes with deliberate exaggeration, and then going away without a word. Later, at dinner, when the subject of music came up, he said emphatically, 'I don't like music' and, pausing for the proper formulation . . .: 'I despise it.'

Moor did not touch the piano again.

107. BBC TV interview with Elizabeth Jane Howard, 16 February 1964, 'Monitor' (BBCSL). Waugh continued: 'In my youth there was a tremendous blind alley a whole lot of good writers went down . . . they tried to give what was called "stream of consciousness" in that they gave what everyone was thinking and feeling apart from what they were saying and doing. The novelist deals with speech and action and time sequence. It isn't the novelist's business to feed the reader with emotions. If your novel's any good, the reader should get emotions from it, perhaps not the ones you intend, but they should be there.'

As this assault-course week-end drew to a close, the young man was, needless to say, uncertain as to the impression he had made. Had he been an intruder and a bore? When he mentioned on Sunday that he would be leaving after lunch, he was prepared for signs of unrestrained joy. The response was again startling. Waugh appeared to be genuinely dismayed: 'Must you go? . . . Stay as long as you like.' Moor wisely resisted the offer and left, sadly, carrying away an impression of a generous but immensely lonely man.

*

After completing *Helena* in March 1950, Waugh, restless and *désoeuvré*, became consumed with a passion to spend Easter of Holy Year in Rome and invited Penelope Betjeman to join him. It would, he thought, provide an excellent opportunity for her to secure the full plenary indulgence she wanted. 'About Rome:' she replied, 'isn't one much more certain of gaining [an indulgence] if one goes in great discomfort . . .? I feel I would be more likely to gain my principal intention (after the wiping out of my own sins) i.e. John's conversion if I were to be as uncomfortable as possible. How do you intend to travel?'[108] The question needed no answer and perhaps served as an affectionate rebuke. Both knew that the proposed arrangement could only irritate her husband. The invitation was in part a tease, as was the response. During April he set off alone and luxuriously, leaving Laura behind, seven months' pregnant.

In Paris he repaired relations with Nancy and dined convivially with her, Palewski and Connolly. She met Waugh off the train, pampered him mercilessly and took him to the Rome Express. In Rome he stayed at the Embassy with the Victor Mallets, visited Count Bompiani (his Italian publisher) in search of 'nest-egg' lire, and intrigued (unsuccessfully) in the Vatican for permission to construct a private chapel at Piers Court. Other Catholic business included lunch with John Somers Cocks of the British Legation to the Holy See. For some months Waugh had been encouraging Church authorities to make Knox a cardinal in recognition of his translation of the Bible. Somers Cocks was asked to bring more direct pressure to bear on the Vatican and he happily pursued the matter of 'the hat'. It was an energetic period for Waugh but it was, inevitably, another valedictory tour, kissing good-bye to the ruins of pre-war Europe.

Travelling with Mallet to the Herbert villa in Portofino, Waugh began making mental notes for the first volume of his trilogy. Mary Herbert had invited them over for the annual St George's Day *festa* and Altachiara was packed with guests – Gabriel, Osbert Lancaster and the actor Alec Clunes

108. Unpublished ALS from Penelope [Lady] Betjeman, 'Candlemas' [2 February 1950], from Farnborough Old Rectory, Wantage, Berks.; BL.

among them. Waugh found the *festa* delightful. 'Say what you like for your snooty frogs,' he wrote to Nancy, 'the wops are top nation for simple fun & prettiness. It really was lovely & gay & holy all at the same time.'[109] His last St George's Day there had been on his honeymoon: 'So I was deeply . . . moved . . .' he told Laura, '& thanked God & St George for you with a very full heart.'[110] The entertainments over, however, he soon turned his jaundiced eye on the villa as another victim of barbarism. Laura's grandfather, Henry, fourth Earl of Carnarvon, had shipped all the building materials from England. 'Johnny Churchill's awful frescoes are all that survived the German occupation. They thought they were Giottos and reverently covered them with six layers of canvas . . . while they were wrecking the charming Victorian interiors.'[111] It was cold, Gabriel irritated him, and a middle-class Englishwoman had audaciously purchased one of the local houses and had taken to prancing round the neighbourhood like the lady of the manor. What Waugh thought he remembered, the glory and the dream, had fled. Perhaps it had only ever lived in his imagination and there, refugees together, St George, St Helena and early Victorian England merged into an elaborate fiction of European history out of which *Men At Arms* was growing.

Even in Florence and Verona with Harold Acton, Waugh felt uncomfortable and, after more good-byes – to the Sitwells nearby and to Beerbohm at Rapallo – he returned to England in late May. Laura soon disappeared to Pixton for her confinement. He settled into a period of mild depression among servants and younger children, correcting the proofs of *Helena*.

As Laura's baby obstinately refused to be born, Waugh first invited Connolly down and then went off to speak at a cultural week during the Holland Festival. There he met Paul Moor again. Coming to Amsterdam, Waugh said, he had left his wife expecting to give birth at any minute. 'In fact, she may have already. Shan't know till I get back.' Moor studied him quietly, sceptically. How could this nonchalance square with the man's obvious love for Laura? It must, Moor assumed, be a pose. Waugh looked away and stared blankly across the canal.

Returning in ill-temper (all his illegally purchased sterling had been confiscated at Harwich), he found himself still the father of only five children. The baby was now seriously overdue and Mary Herbert, not a woman given to panic, was anxious. Even her concern, however, failed to persuade him to visit Pixton. With extraordinary detachment, he merely watched *The Times* each morning for an announcement and, in the meantime, moved into the Hyde Park Hotel for his London season. Charming,

109. 26 April 1950; *Letters*, p. 324.
110. *Ibid.*, p. 325.
111. *Ibid.*, p. 324.

gossipy letters were dispatched to his wife describing the great beauty of the women and when, on 9 July, Septimus eventually emerged, Waugh allowed another week to elapse before travelling down, stayed only a couple of days and returned to London for Ann Rothermere's party. 'I did love seeing you,' Laura wrote plaintively, 'do come back, I miss you sorely.'[112]

By this time, James and Hatty had arrived and were surprised not to find Septimus already walking. No one was surprised by Papa's absence, least of all Laura.

> I have been thinking deeply about whether it would be a good thing for you to come & visit me again & though I long for it I don't think it would be if Auberon is going to be here ... the mixture of all the children and him would be intolerable to you & even though I know you would be polite to him I should be in a fever & miserable, feeling that things were not right.... Please write & describe all your parties....[113]

He did, although his euphoria did not outlast the month. Dressed as an admiral at Debo Cavendish's fancy-dress ball, he had gone on to breakfast at Warwick House as Ann Rothermere's party was drawing to a close, lunched with Greene and Burns at White's and tippled with them all afternoon. But the stamina for thirty-six hours' drinking had long since deserted him: '... melancholy, insomnia, nervous nausea, lack of appetite, sore eyes, breathlessness and other painful symptoms set in & got worse. A sad lonely Saturday, a sadder lonelier Sunday, a Monday of despair.'[114] Collapse of middle-aged party.

Septimus's birth was a milestone in Waugh's life beyond which the last, fragile connections with the world of his youth finally broke. In October, Francis Crease died; Italy and Harold Acton had been unable to alleviate torpor. Those 'mentors' of Lancing and Oxford were now ghosts, like Olivia. 'I think you must be associating with a very bad lot of Catholics,' she had written angrily to him when he sent her a copy of *Elected Silence*. The book, she thought, was dull, pompous, escapist, self-aggrandizing; she was appalled that Waugh had written a supportive preface. Had he lost his senses?

> Why Evelyn did *I* ... convert you to the roman catholic church [*sic*] because my religion is just the *SAME* type & outlook as it was when you became a Catholic *through* me so you tell me.... You used to call

112. Unpublished ALS from Laura Waugh, 21 July [1950], from Pixton Park; BL.
113. Unpublished ALS from Laura Waugh, nd [July 1950], from Pixton Park; BL.
114. ALS to Laura Waugh, 26 July [1950]; *Letters*, p. 332.

> me a prophetess when I was very young & my nature is the same today. I wish you would believe in me again.[115]

He couldn't. Even his faith had changed in character, contracting to a dry kernel of dogma. 'Far from people outside the Church having no purpose in the Divine scheme except to be damned,' Hollis had written to him, 'I agree with St. Augustine that heretics are necessary to confirm our faith and the Church can only be kept up to the mark by being continually debated against, nor could heretics perform this essential service if they were all dolts or knaves or spiritually blind.'[116] Among the Catholic intelligentsia, this Conservative MP was considered a traditionalist. To Waugh, his friend's views on damnation were liberal eyewash.

Of his non-Catholic friends, only Nancy remained close and that, perforce, at a distance. They shared the same savage humour at others' expense. Both were flirtatious dandies, cautious about physical contact.[117] Both, however, were also tiring of parties (Waugh faster than Nancy) and becoming increasingly uncertain of the value of their sharp social skills. Fierce rebukes met anyone attempting to gate-crash their golden circle of professional children set up in the 1920s, yet both now recognized this closed shop as infantile nonsense. 'Prod', a wreck of a man, literally a blind drunk who attempted to lay the ruin of his life at Nancy's door, was a constant reminder to her of the delusory attractions of recklessness. It is true that, despite him, this was probably the happiest period of her life. Her translation of *La Petite Hutte* became a West End success. Her *Sunday Times* articles on Parisian life were popular. Parisian life itself was a constant joy to her with Palewski in attendance. She could afford to buy her clothes from Dior. She was about to begin another novel. But, like Waugh, she realized that if everything were to be touched with fancy, with that *style* they both coveted, it had to be bought with self-discipline. Beneath their gaiety there was a Victorian strictness driving both to an obsession with forms of etiquette (dress, manners, language). Bohemianism, especially when seen as an essential aspect of artistic life, was anathema – and on this subject they shared a satirical butt: Smarty Boots.

'Cyril is here,' Nancy had written in 1948.

> I like to see him, but unfortunately he forms part of a joyeuse bande de noctambules & I can't stick the rest of the bande – a sort of bogus

115. Unpublished ALS from Olivia Plunket Greene, 11 October 1949, from Aucombe, Warminster, Wilts.; BL.
116. Unpublished ALS from Christopher Hollis, nd [1948?], from Mells; BL.
117. Cf. unpublished ALS from Nancy Mitford, 30 September 1950, from 7 Rue Monsieur, Paris VII; BL: 'Cyril [Connolly] says the trouble with you [Nancy] is one can't imagine you sitting on one's lap – have you ever sat on anyone's lap? No I said with some vehemence, nor have I ever allowed anybody to kiss me (almost true)....'

> Gauguin with one leg called [Robin] Campbell, Mary Dunn, Joan Rayner etc. etc. all very dirty, some disfigured by a taxi accident & covered in blood – you know, just what *ONE* doesn't care for.[118]

Waugh knew.

> I saw the inside of *Horizon* office full of horrible pictures collected by [Peter] Watson & Lys [Lubbock] & Miss [Sonia] Brownell working away with a dictionary translating some rot from the French. That paper is to end soon. Everyone I met complained bitterly about the injustice of having to earn a living. . . .[119]

Connolly, stranded between his life-long involvement with bohemia and his infatuation with the English upper class, ended by feeling that he belonged in neither camp. Beyond *Horizon*, with an inheritance and revived literary ambitions, he thought at last that he had come down on the side of the mandarin artists with Nancy and Waugh:

> I spent the week-end with the Campbells. Philip Toynbee was there – I suddenly saw them through your eyes – smug complacent intellectually arrogant jollying up with gin each other's pretensions based on nothing. It depressed me terribly and I couldn't sleep. I realise that I have found it convenient to pity everyone because it makes them rather touching . . . and while one is still excusing oneself one will be suddenly dead and nothing done. I shall have drastically to revise my calling list. How much I enjoyed my visit to you. I slept so much . . . for at last I was in surroundings so congenial that I could do what I had been most wanting to for weeks. . . . It is horrid here [London], you are quite right to spurn us, & we are horrid too.[120]

But this confession did nothing to elicit pity from Waugh or Nancy. Much as they loved Boots, gossip about his sex life, irregular clothing and general embarrassments remained a staple of the correspondence between Piers Court and the Rue Monsieur. 'Cyril went to see a flat here', she wrote, 'belonging to somebody I know with a view to renting it. The concièrge said "you can't let it to him" "Why not?" "Well he had a beard & high-heeled shoes & looked like an assassin."'[121]

Such spiteful gaiety might provoke a chuckle on a grey Gloucestershire morning but it could no longer sustain Waugh as he turned increasingly to the spiritual life. And in that respect, Nancy was worse than useless to him,

118. Unpublished ALS from Nancy Mitford, 25 November 1948, from 7 Rue Monsieur, Paris VII; BL.
119. 10 October 1949; *Letters*, p. 311.
120. Unpublished ALS from Cyril Connolly to Evelyn Waugh, 19 June 1950, from 53 Bedford Square, WC1; BL.
121. Unpublished ALS from Nancy Mitford, 30 September 1950, *op. cit.*

religion a no-go area of discussion. There had, however, been some recent consolations. Eddie Sackville-West and Alan Pryce-Jones had followed Penelope Betjeman into the Church. Nothing cheered Waugh more than to welcome friends to the Household and, among such reclamations, Alfred Duggan's story seemed gratifyingly to illustrate the working of Divine Purpose in a pagan world.

Alfred was the brother of Hubert, at whose deathbed God had, Waugh believed, divinely intervened. Waugh and Alfred had been Oxford contemporaries when the young man from Golders Green had been awestruck by his friend's extravagance. But the glamour had soon faded as Duggan ran through his inheritance and succumbed to chronic alcoholism. In 1933 he had returned to Catholicism and during the 1930s, through Waugh's influence, had begun writing for the *Tablet* until one day, after another 'blind', he had failed to send in his copy. After that, he had dropped from the novelist's life, seemingly a burnt-out case, until the summer of 1949.

Duggan had emerged from the war a man purged. Having enlisted as a private and suffered badly during the retreat from Norway in 1940, he had been invalided out, his health permanently impaired, and had worked in an aircraft factory. Reckless arrogance had been replaced by humility bred of religious devotion. In the spring of 1945 he had happily begun an ex-serviceman's apprenticeship to train as a cowman at £4 a week. Then, when he felt his life at long last settled, his mother, Lady Curzon, had insisted that she was too ill to live alone and he had returned without complaint to care for her in Sussex. There, at Bodiam Manor, he had spent his spare time in the library and had developed a considerable knowledge of medieval history and theology. For want of anything better to do, he wrote an historical novel, more to amuse himself than with any hope of publication, and Faber offered him a contract. It was at this point that he wrote to Waugh, thanking him for advice about establishing a literary career. A man of extraordinary industry, Duggan simply wanted something to do. 'Actually I am extremely happy,' he wrote. 'It is the financial result of being teetotal that is astounding. Nowadays I always have money in my pocket.'[122] If he survived his mother, he said, he intended to enter the Christian Brothers or some other teaching order.

A long correspondence ensued, concluding only with Duggan's death in 1964, by which time he had written 'fifteen historical novels ..., three biographies and seven historical studies for young readers'. This proud listing is from Waugh's panegyric, delivered first on the radio and then published prominently in the *Spectator*.[123] It was an astonishing accolade.

122. Unpublished ALS from Alfred Duggan, 8 August 1949, from Bodiam Manor, Robertsbridge, Sussex; BL.
123. 'Alfred Duggan: An Appreciation by Evelyn Waugh', Home Service, 2 July 1964, 8.15–8.30 p.m.;

Reading it quickly, one might think that Waugh was speaking of a close friend whom he considered a great writer. In fact, he ingeniously avoids stating either proposition while implying both. His literary chums were baffled. Why this ceaseless promotion of a widely (and they believed, justly) neglected author? Had Waugh's fine sense of aesthetic discrimination deserted him? Was this not merely a pathetic display of his clinging to the coat-tails of the aristocracy, come what may? The answer, surely, was simpler and more creditable to Waugh. The article, indeed the whole relationship, was another act of *pietas*.

Waugh kept some fifty of Duggan's letters, replied to them all, sent him his own new books and offered generous encouragement in reviews. It was immensely satisfying for Waugh to watch this former wastrel, a man who at Oxford had professed Marxism and atheism, settling into Catholic domesticity and earning his living by the humble trade of letters. Duggan married, adopted a child, and lived for the rest of his life on a few pounds a week. Waugh attended his funeral, cared for his widow and organized a trust fund. But the social circles of the two men rarely intersected. Waugh and Laura went to tea in 1952 to meet the fiancée, but the two men never visited each other's houses. Indeed, during those fifteen years they scarcely met. Cured of drink and extravagance, Duggan perhaps seemed an admirable but dull character to one cured of neither, and Waugh politely side-stepped further invitations. Duggan no longer moved in 'society'; his patron only felt comfortable with those who did. A week-end in Hay-on-Wye, trying to make conversation with Mrs Duggan would, Waugh knew, end in disaster, and it was essential for him to preserve his object of *pietas*. He had no illusions about Duggan, who was neither a great writer nor a particularly sympathetic personality. But that was not the point. Here, Waugh felt, was a further example of divine intervention. Duggan had overcome his 'inherited weakness' 'partly by the aid of a physician, partly by his power of will, partly by his new-found love as a husband, but essentially . . . from supernatural grace.'[124]

In 1949 Duggan's story came as a welcome reinforcement of principle. Looking back over his forty-seventh year, Waugh felt that the latent enthusiasm which had fuelled a lifetime's jokes was all but exhausted. 'You still have the delicious gift of seeing people as funny', he wrote to Nancy,

'Alfred Duggan', *Spectator*, 10 July 1964, 38–9; *EAR*, pp. 625–8. The BBCSL version contains small emendations in what appears to be Christopher Sykes's hand, toning down the text's élitism. After Waugh's emphasis on Duggan's youth in four great houses, for example, the following is added: 'But, as I have remarked he did not attempt to use these advantages to make himself a career in the world of power.' It is unclear whether these corrections were made from Waugh's dictation. Some of them are ignored and some retained in the printed text.

124. *Ibid.*; *EAR*, p. 627.

'which I lost somewhere in the highlands of Scotland circa 1943.'[125] His jokes in the future would derive mainly from *accidia*. It was the end of an era, the point at which he seems to have moved from the boyish to the decrepit, omitting middle age altogether. With his last child and the Trust, a line was drawn, and it was fitting that he should have crossed it with his last visit to America and the publication of *Helena*.[126]

*

'I originally planned the trip as a stimulant for [Laura] after childbirth,' he wrote to Nancy, 'but it is now I who need it the more. It is the most wonderful health resort in the world. I look to it to revivify me. In fact at the moment I am like a patient lying comatose waiting for the doctor to come round with his needle.'[127] The drug worked.

Waugh and Laura arrived at the Plaza to the jubilant greetings of mink-coated Catholics and a fanfare from the press. Stanley Salmen, in McIntyre's place at Little, Brown, had instituted a more vigorous regime which Waugh first encountered in the form of a publicity campaign to launch *Helena*. Peters had packed his star client off with £500 pocket-money; Salmen topped this up with $1,500 against a contract which, in a careless moment, Waugh had signed, agreeing to write a book on the 'American Scene'.[128] Eighteen days of lectureless luxury restored him to sustained high spirits, possibly for the last time in his life. In boisterous mood he fulfilled Salmen's schedule of interviews, and went to *Kiss Me Kate* with Alec and his 'reasonable girl'.[129] 'That was such a gay rich evening,' Alec wrote. 'I did enjoy myself: the dinner, the play and the sight of Elsa at the microphone. And it was very very pleasant seeing you and Laura again.'[130] Wherever Evelyn went, the conversation bubbled with fantasy, expense seemed limitless. With Laura relaxed and for once well-dressed, he bathed in adulation.

The climax of the trip was a party at the Plaza to celebrate the master's birthday. Anne Fremantle was dazzled: '... It was all most gala and glorious.... You touch these shores, & presto, life is a party & we all dance as though at the Waterloo Eve Ball.'[131] An intimate gathering, the party

125. [December? 1950]; *Letters*, p. 343.
126. *Helena* (Chapman & Hall, 1950; reprinted Harmondsworth, Penguin Books, 1963 and 1984).
127. 27 September [1950]; *Letters*, p. 336.
128. Cf. unpublished TLS from Stanley Salmen to Margaret Stephens of A. D. Peters & Co., 27 October 1950; HRC.
129. Cf. unpublished ALS from Alec Waugh, 22 September 1950, from Edrington, Silchester; BL. Alec suggested *Kiss Me Kate* and promised to collect 'a reasonable girl' to make up the party. According to Sykes (p. 335), Evelyn was 'entranced by the ingenious and admirable entertainment' and visited the London production at least half-a-dozen times.
130. Unpublished ALS from Alec Waugh, 8 November 1950, from Algonquin Hotel, NY; BL.
131. Unpublished ALS from Anne Fremantle, Feast of Christ the King [29 October 1950], from 252 E. 78th St, NY; BL.

consisted mainly of Republican society, with a dash of English eccentricity added by Osbert and Edith Sitwell. Alec was not invited. Louis Auchincloss, however, was puzzled by his inclusion. A lawyer and novelist, Auchincloss had attended Waugh's 1949 lecture at the Waldorf and had met him briefly over cocktails at Brooke Marshall's. 'Why [he] should have asked me ... after so brief an acquaintance I do not know; Stuart Preston may have had something to do with it. At any rate I went like a shot.'[132] The mystery was solved after Waugh's return. Jack Pierrepoint had recommended Auchincloss's writing and, after reading his *The Injustice Collectors* (1950) during the voyage home, Waugh wrote a letter of generous praise.[133]

It is a tiny anecdote but a significant one. On the American market Waugh's stock was high, not only for his own work but also for his support of American letters. In 1949 he had engaged in an acrimonious dispute over V. S. Pritchett's review of *Elected Silence*;[134] during 1950 Waugh's defence of Hemingway's *Across the River and into the Trees* against the almost universal condemnation of British critics[135] had been partially reprinted by *Time*[136] and had prompted William Faulkner to write in support.[137] True, Waugh did not much care to have Faulkner on his side – 'It is so encouraging', he wrote to Auchincloss, 'to find an American reverting to the high

132. Unpublished ALS from Louis Auchincloss to Martin Stannard, 23 September 1987. Both Stuart Preston and Auchincloss were friends of Nancy Mitford, but Auchincloss was wary of the cynical favouritism with which the English upper-class cultivated Preston: 'London society never really treated Stuart as anything but a mascot. When Nancy ... once made a crack about him and I reproached her, saying that I had thought that she was a friend of his, she replied: "Yes, but never forget, my dear, that we are a nation of warriors, and we do not call our real friends men who spent the war having tea with Sibyl Colefax"' (Auchincloss to Stannard, 9 September 1987). See also p. 88 above.
133. 13 November [1950]; *Letters*, p. 340: 'The conception of every story is alarmingly mature and most skilfully achieved. It is hard to believe they are the work of a beginner.'
134. Cf. *NS*, 20 August 1949, 197; 3 September 1949, 245; 10 September 1949, 274. This last letter was followed by Pritchett's reply: 'It is not for Mr Waugh to lay down what a Protestant must believe, and I cannot tell what he understands by the labels he wishes to fix. I will confess to a distaste for totalitarianism in religion; and it seems to me also odd that [Merton] should enter a silent order, to engage in autobiography' (274). Waugh replied (17 September 1949, 302): 'Mr. Pritchett's letter is entirely satisfactory. He withdraws his claim to be a Protestant and re-appears as one (like myself) "of Protestant upbringing". He admits that he has so far forgotten what he was taught, that "the existence of God, the truth of the Bible, the reality of prayer" are meaningless phrases to him. He does not know whether Vocation exists. Yet he does not feel any doubt about his competence to review a book on the subject. Try him on Mathematics. I am sure a lot of American books on that subject get overpraised.'
135. *Tablet*, 30 September 1950, 290, 293; *EAR*, pp. 391–3: 'Mr. Hemingway is one of the most original and powerful of living writers.... [This is] not his best book, perhaps his worst, but still something very much better than most of the work to which the same critics give their tepid applause ... it was not only the inventions of technique that impressed us in *Fiesta*. It was the mood.... Mr Hemingway has melancholy, a sense of doom. His men and women are as sad as those huge, soulless apes that huddle in their cages at the zoo. And that mood is still with us.' (The analogy with the apes might suggest a further interpretation of Humboldt's Gibbon in *Work Suspended*; see Vol. 1, p. 500.)
136. 30 October 1950, 1.
137. 'Faulkner to Waugh to Hemingway', *Time*, 13 November 1950, 1.

standards of James, Sturgis, Wharton, Pearsall Smith & disregarding the deep South and the *New Yorker*'[138] – but it was all good publicity to promote his serious interest in American Catholic culture, and American readers, it seems, responded warmly to their eccentric knight-errant.

Waugh left New York triumphant. *Helena* was selling well and his apostolic mission was complete. Although he never visited America again, he never reneged on his belief that she would act as the focus of Catholic Christendom during the dark years that lay ahead. But the glitter of New York was not for him. He could not, like Alec or Nancy or Greene, live as an expatriate, and he returned to defend the Faith on the European front. 'I have felt so very feeble in recent weeks', he wrote to Nancy two months later, 'that at last I called in a doctor who took my blood-pressure & pronounced it the lowest ever recorded – in fact the pressure of a 6 months foetus. In an access of sudden hope I said: "Does this mean I shall die quite soon." "No. It means you will live absolutely for ever in deeper & deeper melancholy."'[139]

138. *Op. cit.*, *Letters*, p. 340.
139. 6 January [1951]; *Letters*, pp. 343–4.

VIII

Recessional: October 1950–September 1952

On the dust-jacket of *Helena* Waugh stated that 'Technically this is the most ambitious work of a writer who is devoted to the niceties of his trade', a remark which surprised contemporary critics and continues to amaze. To the end he believed *Helena* to be his best book because, quite simply, it was the best-written and dealt with the most interesting subject. This was no tease to wrong-foot impertinent reviewers. Christopher Sykes has stressed that the novel's 'indifferent reception ... was the greatest disappointment of [Waugh's] whole literary life....'[1]

Certainly many notices echoed the *Spectator*'s: 'This is a lightly devotional, decorative, frequently entertaining, but not very substantial work of fiction'.[2] The *TLS* felt that Waugh had taken on too much for the scope of a 'single, comparatively brief fable'.[3] The 'Angela Brazil accent'[4] of the heroine and her general appearance as 'one of [Waugh's] favourite vices in the way of characterisation – the clear-eyed, clean-limbed daughter of Diana, with a niche in Debrett',[5] was found amusing but limited as a fictional device. And there were more fundamental problems: 'While Graham Greene's characters make the frontal approach to Catholicism – undergoing the betrayal on the pier or the Pascalian agony in the shrubbery – Waugh's converts generally get to Heaven the back way through having the right kind of nanny.'[6] The old *Brideshead* problems, some thought, were erupting again: rampant élitism masquerading as piety.

Such accusations were deeply irritating to Waugh for during 1950 he had re-read *Brideshead* and been disgusted by its prose. David O. Selznick was trying to buy the film rights. Greene had been mentioned as a script-writer. Waugh, desperate for money, had tried to encourage him to accept the proposal. Thanks to Greene's loathing for Selznick, nothing came of the scheme and ultimately Waugh was thankful for this. (In 1959, he

1. Sykes, p. 337.
2. R. D. Charques, *Spectator*, 13 October 1950, 388.
3. *TLS*, 13 October 1950, 641.
4. *Ibid.*
5. John Raymond, *NS*, 21 October 1950, 374; *CH*, pp. 320–1.
6. *Ibid.*; *CH*, p. 321.

thoroughly revised the novel, expunging sentimentality.) *Helena*, he hoped, was an entirely different kind of book, an act of contrition rather than of revenge.

Greene rushed to the defence:

> I . . . write . . . to say how much I like *Helena*. The truncated version in The Month didn't do it justice. It is a magnificent book. I think particularly fine & moving was Helena's invocation of the three wise men. How it applies to people of our kind – 'of all who stand in danger by reason of their talents.'[7]

This was some consolation, as were the warm letters of appreciation from friends and family, but even here there were quibbles: 'The only thing that puzzles me', wrote Betjeman, '. . . is the saintliness of Helena. She doesn't seem to me like a saint. Not that it matters. . . .'[8] It mattered to Waugh. 'Saints are simply souls in heaven,' he replied:

> . . . We all have to become saints before we get to heaven. That is what purgatory is for. And each individual has his own peculiar form of sanctity which he must achieve or perish. It is no good my saying: 'I wish I were like Joan of Arc or St John of the Cross'. I can only be St Evelyn Waugh – after God knows what experiences in purgatory.
>
> I liked Helena's sanctity because it is in contrast to all that moderns think of as sanctity. She wasn't thrown to the lions, she wasn't a contemplative, she wasn't poor & hungry, she didn't look like an El Greco. She just discovered what it was God had chosen for her to do and did it . . . by going straight to the physical historical fact of the redemption.[9]

The theme of vocation, then, combined with the impediments to contrition raised by the heroine's class and talents, made her peculiarly fascinating to him.

It was the book's gentler tone – mellow, distant, resigned – which disappointed many. *Time*, for instance, thought *Campion*, *Brideshead* and now this were unfortunate aberrations from Waugh's first-class satirical talent, a largely unsuccessful attempt to 'clear the satiric brambles out of his literary field, and to plant in their stead the herb of grace.'[10] Waugh's ascetic mood seemed at best worthy, at worst insincere. 'More of the same' was the general cry, and by this was meant more of the jubilant malice that

7. Unpublished ALS from Graham Greene to Evelyn Waugh, nd [late October [?] 1950], from 5 St James's Street, London, SW1; BL.
8. Unpublished ALS from [Sir] John Betjeman, 9 October 1950, from Farnborough Old Rectory, Wantage, Berks.; BL
9. November [1950]; *Letters*, p. 339.
10. *Time*, 23 October 1950, 44; *CH*, pp. 129–30.

had spiced *The Loved One*. But he never returned to the manner of his youth in his full-length books, which, from this point, all concerned vocation. Purgatory obsessed him, the painful road towards his destiny as St Evelyn Waugh.

'The book's dust jacket may seem to some readers to be in doubtful taste,' wrote the otherwise enthusiastic Gerard Hopkins. 'The title and the author's name are shown against a background of grained wood which, presumably, is intended to suggest the timber of the True Cross.'[11] Indeed it was. Hardly a reviewer touched on the spiritual implications of Helena's quest, despite the fact that Waugh was so obviously struggling to emphasize the physical reality of the True Cross and thus to relate the Crucifixion to a specific time and place. As Sykes has noted, Waugh's fundamentalism attracted him to the post-war movement in the Church towards devotionalism. Pius XII had suggested that the Assumption, 'hitherto accepted as a pious legend or an allegory, to be believed or otherwise according to taste', should have 'the force and status of a defined doctrine'.[12] Sykes disapproved of the 1950 encyclical letter defining this doctrine. Waugh was strongly in favour and argued fiercely with his friend, accusing him of crypto-Protestantism, of atheism, of being a Communist sympathizer. As we have seen, Waugh's mind was divided between an obsession with the *facts* behind Christian belief and the notion that rational analysis was ultimately irrelevant to faith. To embellish the 'facts' he would happily rewrite history but then sidestep criticism by denying his authority as an historian. He had performed a similar disappearing act with *Campion*. *Helena*, he remarked ambiguously, 'is just something to be read; in fact a legend'.[13] Setting aside the logical and theological difficulties here, it is worthwhile pausing over the literary effects of these attitudes on Waugh's 'novel'. Was it an aberration or does it support its high claims for its technical complexity? The year 1951 saw Penguin Books' publication of ten Waugh titles. *Helena* was the only novel omitted and it was not added to the list until 1963. Few people read *Helena* today; it is rarely included in the canon of Waugh's major works. Sykes himself passes it by without comment.

F. J. Stopp was the only critic in the early 1950s to discuss that major theme which had emerged in *Brideshead* and *The Loved One*: the supernatural as the real. For others, this was an external theological question. Stopp took the proposition seriously as a basis for literary criticism:

> The alleged incongruity [in Waugh's fiction] is in fact a congruity, that between the supernatural and the natural.... For Mr. Waugh ... any book about St. Helena must show the intimate fusion of the

11. *Time & Tide*, 14 October 1950, 1025.
12. Sykes, p. 336.
13. 'Preface', *Helena*, *op. cit.*, p. 12.

> historical and the personal in a unique act in time, and the no less intimate consonance of the supernatural and the natural which made this act a miraculous and saintly one.[14]

This delighted Waugh, and an enthusiastic correspondence began which led to Stopp writing the first authorized work on the novelist. Waugh offered him unprecedented access to his files and manuscripts, and even invited him to Piers Court for an interview. Stopp and his wife, Elisabeth, were Cambridge dons, German scholars. They were clever, humble Catholics, with no connections in the grand world beyond the Senior Combination Room. A less likely choice for the invader of Waugh's privacy it is difficult to imagine. The Stopps, nevertheless, became family friends. The Waugh they knew was the Waugh known by Merton and the priesthood: tough and ingenious, but a man of simple faith, and one increasingly confused by the garish masks of his public persona. Stopp had struck a chord by emphasizing the spiritual rather than the analytical habit of mind.

It is interesting to take Stopp's argument a stage further. For if the material world, and time itself, were illusions *sub specie aeternitatis*, so were the literary tricks of realism. Waugh never credited fiction with the status of 'truth'; novels to him were not a branch of the social sciences. As Raymond Mortimer put it: 'Admit, while you are reading this book, his point of view, and you may conclude, as I do, that it is his finest achievement.'[15] Far from being an anachronism, *Helena* can be seen to be a vital technical experiment, neither modernist nor realist, but postmodernist, metafictional.

Waugh had spent longer on *Helena* than on any other novel. As Carolyn Cobb reminded him: 'You talked about her [Helena] even before D Day.'[16] His casual prefatory remarks – 'A novelist deals with the experiences which excite his imagination. In this case the experience was my desultory reading in History and Archaeology'[17] – were modestly disingenuous. Long letters in response to his researches had come from Frs Martindale and Caraman. Waugh constantly found himself directed to a mountain of additional reading. And to the end he was eager for precision, writing to Betjeman about the number of Anglican parish churches dedicated to the saint and including the information in the last page of the typescript.[18]

14. Frederick J. Stopp, 'Grace in Reins: Reflections on Mr. Waugh's *Brideshead* and *Helena*', *Month* (August 1953), 69–84; *CH*, pp. 324–34. Dr Stopp was a scholar of Renaissance German and a Fellow of Gonville and Caius College, Cambridge.
15. 'A Cryptic Saint', *ST*, 15 October 1950, 3.
16. Unpublished ALS from Carolyn Cobb, 14 October 1950, from Easton Court Hotel, Chagford, Devon; BL.
17. 'Preface', *Helena*, *op. cit.*; p. 9.
18. Unpublished ALS to [Sir] John Betjeman, nd [c. 20 March 1950]; UBCL. He replied on 23 March 1950, having asked his secretary to examine *Crockford's*, that there were 136 such churches.

Helena, then, is deceptively simple. At once contemporary and 'historical', it is a novel whose shifting tone disrupts the conventions of realism as it disrupts the chronological progression of history. The narrative opens as timeless fairy tale:

> Once, very long ago, before ever the flowers were named which struggled and fluttered below the rainswept walls, there sat at an upper window a princess and a slave reading a story which even then was old: or, rather, to be entirely prosaic, on the wet afternoon of the Nones of May in the year (as it was computed later) of Our Lord 273, in the city of Colchester, Helena, red-haired, youngest daughter of Coel, Paramount Chief of the Trinovantes, gazed into the rain while her tutor read the Iliad of Homer in a Latin paraphrase.[19]

Immediately there is a stylistic collision between what the narrator later terms 'the opposed faces of history and myth.'[20] The mundane *facts* (history) confront their fictional reconstruction. Indeed, the whole book concerns this collision: the dispelling of darkness, the mists of pagan Britain and Rome, the dangerous confusions of the cult of Mithras and the heresies of the Gnostics, by the effulgent light of the Christian revelation.

Helena's refusal to suffer the stuff of dreams is constantly articulated in blunt expletives: 'Bosh', 'Rubbish'. She wants the facts; she wants openness. '"All my life"', she tells the good Lactantius, '"I have caused offence to religious people by asking questions."'[21] And, at last, she receives from him a straight answer to a straight question. '"Tell me, ... this God of yours. If I asked you when and where he could be seen, what would you say?"' '"I should say"', Lactantius replies, '"that as a man he died two hundred and seventy-eight years ago in the town now called Aelia Capitolina in Palestine."' '"... How do you know?"' '"We have the accounts written by witnesses. Besides that there is the living memory of the Church."'[22] The seed sown, Helena is baptized. Feeding off that living memory and guided by a dream, she seeks out the 'solid chunk of wood'[23] of the True Cross with which to crush the enemies of the hypostatic union. The movement is from the world of Faery to the actualities of history. The Pre-Raphaelite princess begins in her mist-haunted castle awaiting her prince (Constantius); she ends her life as a tough, resigned Roman matron, apolitical, long since disillusioned with the glamour of power, amid the huge machinery of state, organizing the excavation of the cistern and disrupting the building of Constantine's latest church. A conservative

19. *Helena, op. cit.*, p. 13.
20. *Ibid.*, p. 131.
21. *Ibid.*, p. 85.
22. *Ibid.*
23. *Ibid.*, p. 128.

subversive, she finally sinks back into myth, mysterious, intangible, leaving to posterity her one great act of vocation.

We thus reach the first difficulty in interpretation. In what *genre* is this book written? Is it myth or history? Is it an 'historical novel'? Where is the borderline here between fact and fiction? In an interview during his American trip Waugh touched on this:

> Of course [he said], *Helena* is a very different kind of book from *Brideshead* ... less explicit.... The whole thing is done in anagrams and cyphers; it's full of hints and allusions, and little jokes tucked away in it ... [which is] one reason why *Helena* won't be as well understood in America as Europe.... It's definitely a European book.[24]

American reviewers, he thought, had not understood a word of it, and this ingenious cross-referencing leads us, in turn, to question the distinctions between fact and fiction. Mortimer pinpoints the difficulty:

> At a crucial point, [Waugh] is seized by timidity. Nothing is known, he tells us, about Helena's conversion; and for once he refuses to invent. But he makes her reject other religions because their mythology was not based upon ascertainable historical facts. From this we may perhaps gather the chief purpose of the novel, which is never explicit. Mr. Waugh ... is telling us that we should accept Christianity not because it is beneficent or beautiful, not because it may make us happy or good, but because it is factually true.[25]

Waugh, one suspects, would not have been entirely happy with this. Certainly he saw the temporal cornerstone of his faith as the historical specificity of Christ's life. But that specificity gave authority to more significant spiritual experience; it was a doorway through which the action of the supernatural on the natural could be glimpsed. Waugh surely *was* trying to suggest that Christianity was beneficent and would (or could) 'make us good'. The root of the heresy he imputes to Constantine is the denial of the doctrine of Original Sin. The madder the Emperor becomes with the vanity of power, the less real become the facts of life. The lot of man, Waugh stresses, is suffering and death. Constantine, by establishing his new churches in the East, insanely hopes for a fresh start: '"You can have your old Rome, Holy Father,"' he tells Pope Sylvester, '"with its Peter and Paul and its tunnels full of martyrs. *We* start with no unpleasant

24. 'Evelyn Waugh Comments on *Helena*', *Anno Domini* (Fall 1950), 5–7. As a favour to Anne Fremantle, Waugh agreed to the interview with Demetrius Manousos and David Marshall, her co-editors of the magazine. This was the first number and the scoop of a Waugh interview was used to launch it.
25. Raymond Mortimer, 'A Cryptic Saint', *op. cit.*, 3.

associations; in innocence, with Divine Wisdom and Peace."'[26] At one point he even dares to believe that he will not die. To Helena (and to Waugh), Constantine represents the eternal humanist fallacy. The only way to avoid it is through the remorseless fact of the lump of wood to which Christ was nailed in agony. Accept this, and the need for his redemption, and the other 'facts of life' which suffer constant interpretative variation and render human experience 'unintelligible and unendurable without God' become merely relative. Without the context of eternity and of ultimate unity with the Mystical Body, without that tunnel to the secret door, human experience *is* absurd. With the 'correct' perspective, Waugh believed, the artist was at liberty to create myths and symbols from experience, which, while not adhering strictly to the facts, nevertheless reach closer to the ultimate, supernatural truth.

What had seized him, then, was not timidity but boldness: the courage to admit that almost everything in his book beyond the sketchy framework provided by Roman history was invention. The 'novel' thus turns in on itself and subverts the reader's humanist expectations. Sykes, in his own contemporary review, perhaps describes this effect better than Mortimer:

> Historical novels usually fail because they are more like fancy dress parties than anything more likely to have occurred in the course of time. This one succeeds, despite some blemishes, because the reader can hardly help feeling that, though the story is probably not true, something like it did happen and that thanks to this strange act of imagination we are now nearer to the reality, whatever that was.[27]

To the non-believer this may seem to be special pleading. Sykes's point, however, can be developed in another direction, for the truth or otherwise of Waugh's account is irrelevant to purely literary analysis. To Waugh, all fiction was myth, most history myth[28] and fictionalizing history was therefore a legitimate device to produce a sense of the higher reality he sought. In Waugh's writing this can be seen as a technical experiment towards

26. *Helena*, *op. cit.*, p. 125.
27. Christopher Sykes, 'A Legend of St. Helena', *Tablet*, 21 (October 1950), 351. Sykes was unhappy with the treatment of time-sequence in the middle passages, feeling that too much historical detail had been crammed in: '... parts of the centre of this short book are like a violent drive over a surface not made for speeding' (352).
28. One particular object of attack is Edward Gibbon, as Nicholas Joost pointed out in *Explicator* (April 1951, Item 43). Lactantius, explaining to Helena how it is '"equally possible to give the right form to the wrong thing and the wrong form to the right thing"' says: '"Suppose that in years to come, when the Church's troubles seem to be over, there should come an apostate of my own trade, a false historian, with the mind of Cicero or Tacitus and the soul of an animal,"' and he nodded towards the gibbon who fretted his golden chain and chattered for fruit. '"A man like that might make it his business to write down the martyrs and excuse the persecutors"' (p. 80). Gibbon and Helena are ironically drawn together at the end of the novel, when he sits on the steps of the Church containing her bones, just outside Rome, and meditates on history (p. 158).

creating a new kind of theological realism, but, for the non-Catholic reader, the formal properties of the novel remain equally fascinating for their subversion of literary realism. Postmodernist writing draws attention to its fictional status. Waugh, it seems, thoroughly understood these devices in the late 1940s and believed that various forms of such self-reference had always been integral to fiction. He approved of the accurate representation of the material world. But this was not at all the same thing to him as believing that the techniques of realism or naturalism comprehended the 'reality' of the situation observed. That lay elsewhere.[29]

Helena, then, while seeming so different from Waugh's other novels, in fact reflects their characteristic feature: the terrifying formlessness of the rational, 'adult' world when seen through the eyes of a naïf. Helena is Waugh's Alice, and like Carroll, Waugh reverses the zones of safety and danger by emphasizing linguistic slippage. The fairy-tale world threatens because through it the 'real' world is revealed naked and crazy. Thus the imagined becomes more real than the 'real', becomes an image of that truth which the 'sanity' of rationalism conceals. The naïf becomes the repository of wisdom; the child knows more than the adult. This is, of course, no Wordsworthian theme. Quite the reverse. Nothing could be further from Waugh's thinking than the pantheism of the early Romantics. It is a Christian theme emphasizing the essential simplicity of faith. '"That is why your religion would never do for me,"' Helena tells Marcias. '"If I ever found a teacher it would have to be one who called little children to him."'[30]

The brilliant Marcias, formerly her slave-tutor, finds freedom and celebrity as a Gnostic preacher. Befogged by abstractions, his language becomes unintelligible to common sense and carries force only as incantation with its mystique of high learning. Helena knows more although, literally, she knows less. And similar reversal tricks are played throughout. Her 'prince' turns out to be a shifty and unscrupulous materialist; the Rome she longs to see as a child dissolves like a dream beneath the onslaught of internecine feuding to be replaced by the ideal of the Eternal City; as *civitas* decays and the mob rules, the concept of citizenship takes on the wider meaning of membership of the Household of the Faith, universally applicable, beyond the walls of empire, race and history.

The reader will, perhaps, see by now how deeply personal this novel was to Waugh. It explained not only the roots of his fundamentalism but also the way in which the Church was for him continuously contemporary. Time in *Helena* is not the linear invention of man. There is no progress, only

29. Cf. the passage cut from 'Part Two' of *Work Suspended* concerning the 'algebra of fiction'; quoted Vol. 1, p. 496.
30. *Helena*, *op. cit.*, p. 84.

change within a continuum. The way out, the 'light, release, purification'[31] sought by Constantine, will not be granted by a better future; '"... they don't realise"', says the idiotic Fausta, '"they've got to move with the times."'[32] Moving with the times was to Waugh to travel further from God and from *romanitas*. The way out was the way back. Ahead lay only power without Grace. '"I don't suppose you are much troubled by controversy at Trèves,"' the complacent Bishop of Nicomedia remarks to Helena, trying to persuade her that Rome is finished as a centre of spiritual life. '"We are conservatives there,"' she replies.[33] Waugh's peculiar conservatism, best explained by her, had equally little to do with political power or materialist ideology.

An unbroken thread of Waugh's theological polemic, from *Campion* onwards, had been the desire to present British Christianity as continuously Catholic. The four centuries since the Reformation were to him a brief interregnum. Helena was thus crucial to his argument, as was her characterization as an odd blend of twentieth-century, horse-mad, upper-class girl and Pre-Raphaelite stunner. Here, Waugh's two icons of British female beauty were fused. Helena's 'horse-sex' fantasies are described with relish. (No analysis of her character could ignore the narrator's obvious delight in her potential as a dominant female, whip in hand.) Waugh, while teasing the reader of an ostensibly 'devotional' book with his openness about sexual 'perversion', constructs a mythology of British frankness. Bluff, no-nonsense enquiry is opposed throughout to the egotistical tricks and evasions of imperial Rome. The supposedly barbarous British are seen to be rooted, through Coel's connection with Priam and Troy, in a sensibly more fruitful culture than Roman paganism. Helena is linked to Helen through the references to the *Iliad*, and to her own magical culture of 'rich poetic legends'.[34] Helena's Trojan horse, however, is the more solid timber of spiritual reality, an authentic relic rather than the dubious souvenirs of Ilium.

Helena is thus not an 'historical novel' in the strict sense of the term for it does not describe completed, past experience but a world in which all experience co-exists. The witches' song disrupts historical continuity by referring to Napoleon's exile on St Helena in an argot yet to be invented.[35] The narrative constantly plunges backwards and forwards through time,

31. *Ibid.*, p. 65.
32. *Ibid.*, p. 95.
33. *Ibid.*, p. 99.
34. *Ibid.*, p. 115.
35. Waugh appears to make a technical error here in allowing Constantine and Helena to understand what they hear. 'These verses', Waugh explained in a series of notes for his publisher, '... are written in the style of popular songs of the negros [*sic*] of the British West Indies'; HRC. He explains that 'bones' means 'dice'; 'natural': 'a winning score'; 'chop': 'food'; and 'snake's eyes': 'bottom score'.

emphasizing the fragility of the material present. The packing of the text with puns and literary allusions from all ages reinforces this. More significant for our purpose, however, is Waugh's creation of an ancient world in a theological vacuum which is directly paralleled to that of post-war Europe. *Helena* can be read as an entirely 'contemporary' work offering a complex analogy with modern times. In many respects it is Waugh's (displaced) spiritual autobiography, a dry-run for the *Sword of Honour* trilogy.

Three literary figures appear: Longinus, Marcias and Lactantius. All suggest elements of Waugh's post-war dilemma as a writer. Like the young Marcias,[36] Waugh lived through correspondence; like Longinus, he felt neglected by a society careless of literary craftsmanship. All three are exiles. But it is Lactantius, 'the greatest living prose stylist',[37] who emerges as a self-portrait:

> He delighted in writing, in the joinery and embellishment of his sentences, in the consciousness of high rare virtue when every word had been used in its purest and most precise sense, in the kitten games of syntax and rhetoric. Words could do anything except generate their own meaning. 'If only I were a little braver,' Lactantius sometimes thought, 'if I had dared stay nearer the centre of things . . ., I might have been a great writer.'[38]

Waugh was nagged by similar self-doubt. The guilt of Yugoslavia never left him. Like Lactantius, he 'had outgrown ambition but he believed that it would not be convenient to be entirely forgotten'.[39] With a wife and six children to support, Waugh could not afford the anonymity he now coveted. And there were the larger issues: the struggle for the Church's lost territory, his place in that battle, the thousand tormenting opportunities for betrayal. Lactantius lacks the courage of the martyr and suffers in that knowledge. So did Waugh.

Helena's world, then, *is* Waugh's. It is the world as it always has been and always will be. The same conflicts arise as in the main body of his 'contemporary' fiction. The atmosphere is one of confusion, darkness, arbitrary violence produced by a 'progressive' culture. Rome is cluttered with apartment houses peopled by an aspirant, materialist middle class. In the streets and slums the mob rules. In Constantine's salon the artists have lost the skills of representation and are sliding into a chaos of pure abstraction. The latest imperial architecture consists of windowless slabs

36. *Helena*, *op. cit.*, p. 13.
37. *Ibid.*, p. 78.
38. *Ibid.*, p. 79.
39. *Ibid.*, p. 78.

like that soon to rise, to Waugh's horror, on the South Bank. Palaces ignore their function as homes, ceilings vault beyond sight, dwarfing and threatening their inhabitants; shadows hide conspirators. Everything in imperial culture is 'got up to look like something else'.[40] Constantius's description of Aurelian's triumph – 'partridges made of sugar, peaches of mincemeat'[41] – recalls the scene on the liner in *Brideshead*: the swan made of ice, the atmosphere of pernicious absurdity, divorced from moral or aesthetic standards. There are 'no private lives';[42] marriage and divorce have become a solely material concern. Spies scuttle from doors; murder is commonplace, vanity all; spiritual values are neglected or endangered by schism. Waugh even nails his narrative firmly to twentieth-century military history. The witches' song begins with 'Zivio!', an echo of 'Zivio [Long live] Tito', Helena lives most of her life in Dalmatia; the journey she makes from the interior to the coast, across the plain of the Lika, is the one Waugh made as a soldier carrying his burden of guilt away from the Jewish refugees. *Helena* is about courage and moral cowardice, epitomized respectively by the heroine and her husband, and it is a book entirely relevant to the international politics of 1950.[43]

The way forward, then, was the way back, the literal or metaphorical pilgrimage to the Holy Places, and, having finished his novel, Waugh wished to retrace his heroine's final steps. The American trip had not been entirely for pleasure. In New York he had arranged another *Life* contract: $5,000 expenses, paid in dollar cheques, and a similar deal for Sykes, who was to accompany him as 'interpreter' on a trip to the Middle East.[44] Waugh was to write a 'Defence of the Holy Places'; Sykes's article (never published) was to be on Turkey.

*

40. *Ibid.*, p. 55.
41. *Ibid.*
42. *Ibid.*, p. 74.
43. One of Waugh's typical 'embellishments', suggesting an ancient British (Catholic) vitality confronting the decadence of totalitarianism, can be seen in the intricate symbolism associated with the sobriquets of Helena and her husband Constantius: 'Stabularia' and 'Chlorus'. Greenness – inexperience, envy, nausea, effeminacy (greenery-yallery) – is always associated with Constantius, culminating in the image of Constantine's absurd green wig. Horses – vitality, Troy, passion (hipporastic fantasies), openness (galloping across open countryside), Britishness, control, hunting (the Quest) – are associated with Helena, culminating with the final image: 'Hounds are checked, hunting wild. A horn calls clear through the covert. Helena casts them back on the scent' (p.159). The two sequences of symbols are brought together at two crucial points: when Helena lampoons the green wig and when Constantine ridiculously makes one of Christ's nails into a snaffle and sticks the other in his hat. Ultimately, the nails themselves draw together the horse and the Cross. Constantius Chlorus's characterization, as we have seen, was based on Sir Fitzroy Maclean.
44. Cf. unpublished ALS from Evelyn Waugh to Walter Graebner, 14 December 1950, from Piers Court; BL.

Sykes and Waugh were closer at this stage than they had ever been or were ever to be again. Disappointed by *Helena*'s reviews, Waugh had asked Sykes to dramatize it for radio production, and negotiations for this alternated with travel plans in a high-spirited correspondence. Sykes wrote to Waugh as to a distracted schoolboy likely to forget his pyjamas; Waugh wrote to Sykes as to a sex-crazed adolescent: 'I know what it is you want to stay where you can have women in your rooms you filthy beast well you wont not with me see we are going somewhere respectable with no goings on. . . .'[45] Sykes arranged everything, not, as he suggests, because he lived in London, but because he was employed mainly to act as travel agent and companion. So long as this remained a joke all was well and they set off on 20 January in a buckish mood: Golden Arrow to Paris, dinner with Nancy, train again to Rome, flight to Lydda in Israel and on to Tel Aviv.

'Last Friday [2 February]', Waugh wrote to Laura from Jerusalem, 'the Consul took us across the no-man's-land into the Kingdom of Jordan. We are in a solid, simple Arab hotel and the food is delicious compared with what we were given in Israel. I have had no return of lassitude. We are both well, busy, happy.'[46] The divided city, split by a war zone, nevertheless saddened him and excited his distaste for the Jews.

According to Sykes, crossing to Jordan irritated Waugh because they lost their status as celebrities and became anonymous pressmen. The letter to Laura suggests otherwise. An incident with the Arab Custos ('I took umbrage because I thought ... [he] did not treat me with the respect I deserved')[47] is played up by Sykes, but Waugh seems generally to have been happier on Arab territory. 'Tonight we plan to keep vigil in the Sepulchre which should be an experience to remember & boast about.'[48]

Both men were deeply moved. Waugh, at first affecting nonchalance, quizzed a humble Franciscan who explained the ceremonies at early supper. The Greek and Armenian offices would be followed by the Catholic. '"I see,"' Waugh replied, '"11.30 pm Heretics and Schismatics woken up."'[49] But there is no mistaking the reverential tone of the article he wrote afterwards. In the Sepulchre he felt himself to be at the omphalos of Christendom. Here, even his distrust of the Eastern Church dropped away temporarily amid the smells of candle wax, incense and new-baked bread for the Host.

> In the Levant [he wrote] there works an alchemy the very reverse of the Armenian melting pot. Different races and creeds jostle one

45. APC [January 1951?]; *Letters*, p. 344.
46. 7 February 1951; *Letters*, p. 345.
47. *Ibid.*
48. *Ibid.*
49. Sykes, p. 339.

another for centuries and their diversity becomes only the more accentuated.... But our hope must always be for unity, and as long as the Church of the Sepulchre remains a single building, however subdivided, it forms a memorial to that essential hope.[50]

This campaign to preserve the Holy Places in lands torn by the conflict between Jews and Arabs obsessed him. Like Helena, he was fighting for restoration and conservation. The Franciscan plan for new, separate buildings for each sect horrified him. The United Nations had promised international status to Jerusalem and failed in this objective. Now, he believed, was their chance. They should ensure the internationalization of the city and fund the restoration of the crumbling Church of the Holy Sepulchre. But he held out little hope. 'Both Jerusalems are full of huge cars flying UNO flags', he wrote to Laura, 'while both countries starve. Here there are half a million absolutely destitute & hopeless Arab refugees from Israel. Israel, starving & houseless, is importing 25,000 Jews a month from ... everywhere.... All are stark mad & beastly & devoid of truth.'[51]

Waugh's 'anti-Semitism' is notorious. Sykes draws attention to his companion's racial prejudice, and other friends became worried about this as a sign of incipient madness. To Waugh's enemies this tendency was of a piece with his earlier 'Fascist' sympathies. In fact, this aspect of his racism was a relatively recent development in 1951. 'You mustn't be against European Jews,' Nancy pleaded with him. 'I'm sure Palestine is too awful but you might as well be against the English because of America now do admit....'[52] 'Yes, I am afraid I must admit to a shade of anti-jew feeling,' he replied. 'Not anti-semite. I rather like Arabs. It dates from my visit to Israel.... It was there I realized that all Jews are not like John Sutro and Lord Rosebery.'[53] This is a delicate subject and there is no point in trying to pretend that Waugh was *not* 'anti-Jew'. As with his purported 'Fascism', however, his 'anti-Semitism' was a far cry from Hitler's: a conservative Catholic view rather than a Nazi, northern European one.

As a Christian, Waugh, like Shakespeare and Dickens, had inherited a European folk-lore prejudice connecting Judaism to usury and to cupidity. But (also like Dickens) he came to regret this inheritance. He loathed Fascist anti-Semitism just as much as he did the persecution of Christians by Communists. In the Christian tradition, the Wandering Jew was the man who refused to help Christ as he stumbled beneath the weight of the

50. 'The Plight of the Holy Places', *Life*, 24 December 1951, 58–65; reprinted and expanded as 'The Defence of the Holy Places', *Month* (March 1951), 135–48 and in *The Holy Places* (Queen Anne Press, 1952); *EAR*, pp. 410–20.
51. *Op. cit.*, [7 February 1951]; *Letters*, p. 345.
52. Unpublished ALS from Nancy Mitford, 12 February 1952, from 7 Rue Monsieur, Paris VII; BL.
53. [15] February [1952]; *Letters*, p. 369.

Cross. In one legend, Helena imprisoned him in a well until he revealed the whereabouts of the True Cross. Waugh changed all this, making him an amiable, street-wise trader, attractively vulgar, who offers the information *gratis*. He stands simply for mammon. Relics mean good business. Waugh's racial prejudice was on the level of the average English schoolboy keen to reduce anyone different to a comic stereotype. His political and religious distinctions, however, were more deeply felt and if he is to be accused of anti-Semitism, it is on these grounds that the charge must be made.

Criticism of Israel was for many years scarcely supportable in the West. The country's creation in 1948 somehow shifted an immense burden of European and American guilt. Having suffered so horribly, the Jews could do no wrong. More recently, opinion has shifted. The Palestinians, many now believe, were brutally dispossessed and, as Waugh's letter suggests, it was this dispossession which troubled him. To Waugh, the social engineering conducted by the Allies and Israel in the Middle East was no different in kind from Fascist or Communist policy. His prejudice was anti-Zionist rather than anti-Semitic. Post-war Europe had been cynically parcelled up with no respect for the delicate fabric of national cultures. The continent was awash with Displaced Persons. Waugh saw the same cancer spreading to the Holy Land. It seemed illogical to him that Palestinians should lose their land to Jews from other countries. He did not care for the way the Arabs had been stampeded from their homes. Despite the Holocaust, the whole resettlement seemed against natural justice and UNO as guilty as the Kremlin.

As a younger man, Waugh might have conducted an eccentric campaign to make his point. By 1951 he had lost all faith in the possibility of talking sense to the armies of lunatics who governed the world. And there was also the shade of a worry that he might himself be going mad. He returned refreshed and fat, but he felt increasingly harried, pressed on all sides. A few months earlier the editor of a Viennese periodical had written to ask him to contribute to a symposium: 'Where are we going to? Has our civilization come to its end? Is the actual pessimism only a passing phase and are we going to a new situation in which Technic will be mastered and the freedom of the human being will be guaranteed? With one word can we give any hope to the men?'[54] Waugh filed the letter as an absurdity. All such questions were to him inappropriate – all, that is, except one. His 'one word' was 'God' and, where the organizers of the Festival of Britain appeared not to recognize this, Waugh allowed no one to forget it.

*

54. Unpublished TLS from Friedrich Hansen-Love of *Wort und Wahrheit*, November 1950; BL.

His single contribution to the festivities mocked them. The National Book League had selected 'the hundred best books' by contemporary authors and exhibited their manuscripts alongside examples of printing and book design. As the most authentic expression of Waugh's genius the judges – Rose Macaulay, V. S. Pritchett and C. Day-Lewis – had chosen his frivolous first novel, *Decline and Fall.* Waugh had savaged Day-Lewis's *The Mind in Chains* in the 1930s, had tangled with Rose Macaulay over *Brideshead* and Pritchett over *Elected Silence*. Was this their revenge? If so, Waugh rose to the bait and, extraordinarily, agreed to make a radio broadcast.

'A Progressive Game' takes the catalogue of the exhibition and turns it into a party game: two marks for each book one possesses or has read; three for each book owned and read; maximum score: 300. The ostensible aim of this was to gauge the level of one's cultural awareness. The secret aim is suggested by the pejorative adjective of the title. He claimed his score to be 171, somewhere in the middle range. Among his friends, the highest score was Graham Greene's (216) and the lowest Henry Green's (142). Maurice Bowra managed 200. Surely any score below 200, Waugh remarked innocently, was disgraceful?

Not a bit of it. The problem lay with the judges and with the age. Three quarters of the exhibits, he said, represented

> dreariness relieved by frivolity ... there is a woeful absence of glory and also ... a complete divorce from life. For absence of glory we cannot blame our judges. There are no towering geniuses.... We happen to have struck a bad patch.... But the separation of life and art argues an unhealthy civilization or some obscurity of judgement in the committee.[55]

The judges, he believed, were all inclined to the Left and were 'progressive'. In a more civilized age the 'hundred best books would consist of an average of four or five books from twenty or twenty-five writers'.[56] The judges had chosen only one book from each and had confused the question of British nationality by including foreigners and expatriates. Waugh's various lines of attack ultimately led to the same implicit point: that the exhibition was a levelling, humanist exercise omitting Divinity entirely. Divinity, 'the Queen of Sciences, the mainspring and deep abiding channel of human thought...' is relegated to the category of 'specialized'[57] writing, irrelevant to the purposes of these New Statesmen and women.

55. 'A Progressive Game', BBC Third Programme, 17 May 1951, 7.50–8.10 p.m.; BBCSL; reprinted in revised form in *Listener*, 31 May 1951, 872–3; *EAR*, pp. 398–402.
56. *Ibid.*, p. 398.
57. *Ibid.*, p. 402.

On one level, we see Waugh here continuing his campaign for Christian representational art and using the talk as a dismissal not only of the Left but also of Sir Maurice Bowra. (Much to Waugh's chagrin, Bowra's name had appeared in the New Year's Honours List of 1951 and also on the NBL's roll of honour.) Reading between the lines, however, we can detect elements of that persecution complex which drove Waugh to madness over the next three years. The tone is urbane and mischievous, but uncertain. Leaking from it is a small cry of pain and of fear: pain at exclusion and dismissal; fear of failure.

He had, for instance, been forced to change the text of his talk. Ronald Lewin, his long-suffering producer, had pointed out that

> ... you set up an Aunt Sally in order to throw things at her ... the distinction between a hundred best writers and a hundred representative writers is surely important ... you are firing at the wrong target.... Comments on the personalities of the selectors ... raise ... certain questions of taste ... and as far as my information goes, what you say about Day-Lewis is not the case: nor is Pritchett on the staff of the New Statesman....[58]

Waugh backed off a little, growling:

> Yes, I think your complaints about misrepresenting the judges' aim are just. You will see that I have changed this.
>
> By 'expatriates' I don't mean Auden who is simply a foreigner. I mean Duff Cooper, Aldous Huxley, Maugham, Norman Douglas, etc. etc.
>
> Day-Lewis announced his membership of the Communist party in 1937 and has not since announced his resignation. I consulted him since getting your letter. He says he has 'quietly slipped out' of the party.[59] I have accordingly changed the text. Pritchett succeeded Mortimer as Literary editor of the New Statesman. If he has been sacked since let us by all means change the reference to 'closely associated with'.[60]

But a further retreat was necessary. When Waugh made his broadcast three days later, the NBL complained of distortion. The talk had implied that the NBL was a business cartel whose function was merely to sell books, any books. Before the piece could be printed in the *Listener*, changes would have to be made. Lewin rang up Piers Court. Waugh refused to

58. Evelyn Waugh's Talks File I, 1928–62, unpublished TLS from Ronald Lewin to Evelyn Waugh, 10 May 1951, from Broadcasting House; BBCWAC.
59. Day-Lewis wrote to Waugh on 10 May 1951, thanking him for good wishes for his (Day-Lewis's) marriage and stating that he left the CP in 1937 or 1938.
60. Unpublished ALS to Ronald Lewin, 14 May 1951, from Piers Court; BBCWAC.

speak to him and indignantly asked Peters to confirm that he (Waugh) was right. Peters refused to do so. Incensed and humiliated, Waugh responded sharply: 'The information about the National Book League was given me by YOU,'[61] but, reluctantly, he allowed the first paragraph to be altered. 'Very difficult,' Lewin scribbled in an internal memo. 'Waugh is almost impervious to suggestions, and liable to make inaccurate critical observations which need careful checking. His sense of his own importance makes production very difficult ... a producer should think more than twice before approaching Waugh. NB. he demands a very high fee.'[62]

Persecution mania had, of course, been with Waugh since Oxford and he had exhibited the symptoms of schizophrenia after his first wife's desertion. With the reception of *Helena* these began slowly to re-emerge. 'Most of the reviews...', Waugh wrote to Greene, 'have been peculiarly offensive. I don't believe this modern kind of chastisement is really salutary. It is just like being jostled about in a crowd.'[63] In fact, no reviews had been offensive, most were at least respectful, and many warmly appreciative. True, the literary press had been deluded by the book's mask of simplicity and had found little of interest in the theological themes, but that was only to be expected: 'It is you & six or seven others', Waugh had informed Betjeman, 'whom I seek to please in writing.'[64] No, something else was happening here. By constructing a fiction of the book's 'failure' at the hands of the barbarians, Waugh could generate a fiction of himself as martyr. 'HELENA continues to go well,' Salmen wrote to Peters in January 1951. 'You will remember the author's worry that it would not sell well in this country, but it has already reached 15,626 copies and promises to continue.'[65] Judged objectively, *Helena* was a success.

Waugh and Sykes had returned to England in March 1951. The Festival of Britain opened on 4 May, marking the centenary of the Great Exhibition. When Harold Nicolson visited the central feature, the South Bank Exhibition, he was 'entranced from the first moment....'[66] Not so Waugh, who with Sykes and Woodruff sent a letter to *The Times*:

> Whatever the sum, whether it is 13m. or more, that the Government have spent on the festival, it is to be presumed that they are anxious

61. Unpublished APCI, 25 May 1951, from Piers Court; *Catalogue* E706, p. 182.
62. 'Comments from Mr. Lewin', 17 May 1951; BBCWAC. Lewin won most of these battles. The whole section 'When I say "divorce from life" ... a minor literary exercise' was added after he had complained that there were not enough examples of books in which 'Life' and 'Art' *were* happily married. Isherwood's name was deleted from the list of expatriate 'fugitives from welfare'. Waugh's fee for the twenty-minute talk was £59. 16s. 6d.
63. 16 November [1950]; *Letters*, pp. 340–1.
64. 9 November [1950]; *Letters*, p. 339.
65. Unpublished TLS from Stanley Salmen of Little, Brown, 8 January 1951; HRC.
66. Harold Nicolson, *Diaries and Letters*, *op. cit.*, 4 May 1951, p. 349.

> to recoup as much as they can. The South Bank exhibition is posted as open to 11.30 p.m. Why then were we turned away at 10.40 p.m., ... the illuminations blazing, the grounds conspicuously empty, but not one of the very numerous uniformed attendants at the turnstiles empowered to take our money?[67]

The sub-text of this is Waugh's vision of England as occupied territory. Here was Attlee squandering the nation's wealth on a vulgar celebration of the Common Man, and the image lodged in Waugh's imagination to frame the bitter 'Epilogue' of the *Sword of Honour* trilogy: 'Monstrous constructions appeared on the south bank ..., the foundation stone was solemnly laid for a National Theatre, but there was little popular exuberance among the straitened people....'[68] Nothing better demonstrates the constriction of that Gothic arrow-slit through which Waugh now glared at the world. 'I have never seen people so cheered up or so amused' was Nicolson's view.[69] While many Britons were welcoming a new era of post-war expansion, Waugh only saw his country plummeting towards catastrophe.

*

The prospect of personal financial ruin was at the root of this. In February, Percy Popkin's name had emerged again in Peters's correspondence: 'The Inspector asks me to confirm that all fees etc. from all sources for ... [Evelyn Waugh] pass through you.'[70] Peters had replied circumspectly, confirming 'that all fees etcetera due to ... Waugh from his literary work pass through my hands.'[71] The inspector was still stalking his rat. He wanted to know whether he could rely on Peters's annual returns as a register of Waugh's total income. The agent's reply ingeniously avoided this trap by adding 'from his literary work' for, thanks to the Trust Fund, Waugh no longer owned his earlier fictional writings. The money from them was therefore not due to him, but to the Trust. Peters's formulation also avoided mentioning the non-literary work (advisory roles for film companies), translation fees (nest-eggs) and the 'expenses only' trips for *Life*. That kept the lid on things temporarily, but Waugh's public profile was far too high for the Revenue to remain satisfied with this. Penguin Books, after all, were about to print a million Waughs with his face on every cover. He had never been more famous and, apparently, more prosperous.

67. 'The South Bank at Night', *The Times*, 24 May 1951, 5.
68. 'Epilogue', *Unconditional Surrender* (Chapman & Hall, 1961; reprinted Harmondsworth, Penguin Books, 1964 and 1967), p. 237.
69. Harold Nicolson, *op. cit.*, p. 349.
70. Unpublished TLS to A. D. Peters, 14 February 1951; HRC.
71. Unpublished TLS, 16 February 1951; HRC.

At the end of 1950 the Trust Fund account had stood at £533 but Waugh, instead of regarding it as insurance for a lean future, had spent it as fast as he could: a fireplace, silver, paintings – the bills streamed in. Peters entered into the fun of successful tax evasion ('By all means install a new fireplace. It is essential to keep the children warm'),[72] but he was clearly anxious and the more cautious Evill distinctly nervous:

> When you write to Mr. Waugh will you please ... [state] that the articles which are being delivered to him are the property of the Trustees ... and are liable to be delivered up to them at any moment and that meanwhile we are prepared to let him have the use of such articles provided he undertakes to insure them.... Such a letter should be written every time we deliver to Mr. Waugh on loan articles which he is capable of enjoying in person.

No one, of course, expected Waugh to 'deliver up at any moment' a fitted fireplace, but, so long as these formalities were observed, they believed themselves safe. (The insurance, amusingly, was against fire.) Shortly afterwards a list of eighteen art objects totalling £1,500 was proposed and approved for purchase by the Trust. Waugh already owned them all.[73]

Peters's worries for his client had been temporarily alleviated by the international financial situation. Whenever Waugh was on the point of irretrievable extravagance, it seemed, fortune favoured the reckless. As we have seen, at least half of his income came from America in twice-yearly instalments. During 1949, in an attempt to bring dollars into Britain, Sir Stafford Cripps had devalued the pound, dropping it from $4.03 to $2.80. This Socialist measure instantly increased the value of Waugh's American savings by almost a third. One might have expected some expression of ironical gratitude. Instead, his fury at being 'robbed' by supertax, escalated to new heights[74] and his sense of poverty became obsessive.

In 1951 Waugh was forty-eight, ready for death and keen to set his affairs in order. One American item still nagged his conscience: the station-wagon

72. Unpublished TLS from A. D. Peters, 14 December 1950; HRC.

73. 'Objects Now At Piers Court Suitable For Purchase By The Trust Fund: 1. Silver Candelabrum by Storr-Mortimer 1830, purchased for 200 guineas in 1947 before appreciation of silver now worth £250. *The following original oil paintings*: 2. Large view of Rome by Van Vitallius £100. 3. The Connoisseurs by Swoboda (purchased from Neumann ... SW1) £150. 4. The Lost Child by Arthur Hughes (purchased from Leicester Galleries) £150. 5. The Flower Cart by Atkinson (purchased from Leicester Galleries) £150. 6. Baptism of Jewess by Furze £50. 7. Cows by Cooper £50. 8. Cistercian Monk by Zubarán £50. 9. The Young Patient – Austrian School 1830 £50. 10. King George III English School 1770 £50. *Original Watercolours*. 11. Durham Cathedral English School 1800 £25. 12. Portrait of E. Waugh by Osbert Lancaster. £25. *Original drawing* 13. Spirit of the Rainbow by D.G. Rossetti reproduced in Watts Dunton's "Life" £250. 14 and 15 Pair of Oil Paintings by Thomas Musgrave Joy "The Pleasures of Travel" £150. 16. Into the Cold World by George Smith (oil) £50. 17. Marble group by Amodori of Romeo and Juliet (slightly damaged) £100....'; HRC.

74. Cf. 'Tax on Dollar Earnings', *The Times*, 6 February 1952, 5.

affair and the debt to Herbert Mayes. 'Compassion' and *Scott-King* had been offered; both had been refused. Mayes was needling Matson for the return of his money. 'I keep squeezing the old lemon for a short story', Waugh wrote to Peters after finishing *Helena*, 'but not a drop comes.'[75] Two months later he reported with relief that he was 'just finishing a fairly funny short story. I shall take a copy to the good housekeeper in New York. . . . I think the *Sunday Times* might want it.'[76]

But Mayes's response had been curt: 'It seems to me sad that this man's talent should be wasted on such a story. How nice it would be if Evelyn Waugh went back and read . . . ['Tactical Exercise']. It might give him some idea of the kind of story a large magazine might be able to publish.'[77] Ian Fleming's reply from the *Sunday Times* was more polite but amounted to the same thing: the situation was different from when they last spoke – newsprint cut, circulation pegged. He *hoped* to make an exception for Waugh but Lord Kemsley would have to decide. Matson sent the story on to the *New Yorker*. 'The theme is almost implausibly apt for satire by Waugh', they replied, 'and yet his handling of it is, for the most part, dull-witted and tedious.'[78] The story was called 'A Pilgrim's Progress'. Waugh looked at it again and hurriedly withdrew it from the market. That light, wicked touch, so profitable in the past, had deserted him.

On his return from the Levant he had settled to his *Life* article and determined to 'try again . . . that long short story about the youth in the Euthanasia trade. . . .'[79] But he could not develop the theme satisfactorily, tinkered with it for two more years, and on its eventual appearance as *Love Among the Ruins* was the first to admit its weakness. Horrified by this degeneration, he believed he could at the same time only write 'seriously' in a fashion calculated to secure lasting oblivion for his declining years. In fact, during 1951 he earned £10,000 and his powers, far from declining, had matured in a new direction. His loathing of familiarity, and his sense of living in an alien culture bent on his extermination, were integral to the frame of mind which produced the peculiar qualities of his next major work.

'Yes will write short life of T. More for good pay', he informed Peters towards the end of May, 'but not today as I am off to Monte Carlo and then will stay in France to begin novel.'[80] That biography was never begun,

75. Unpublished ALS to A. D. Peters, 2 August [1950], from Piers Court; *Catalogue* E679, p. 178.
76. Unpublished APCI to A. D. Peters, nd [pm 3 October 1950], from Piers Court; *Catalogue* E688, p. 179.
77. Unpublished ALS to Harold Matson, 27 October 1950; HRC.
78. Unpublished TLS from Gus Lobrano of *New Yorker* to Harold Matson, 13 November 1950; HRC.
79. Unpublished APCI to A. D. Peters, nd [7 March 1951], from Piers Court; *Catalogue* E698, p. 181.
80. Unpublished APCI to A. D. Peters, nd [25 May 1951], from Piers Court; *Catalogue* E706, p. 182.

nor another he later proposed of Ignatius Loyola. The novel became *Men At Arms*.

*

If Waugh and Laura *were* worried about money, they did not respond by economizing. As in his undergraduate days, Waugh's reaction to financial embarrassment was to spend his way out of it. Laura accompanied him to Monte Carlo for a gambling holiday. He then travelled back to Calais with her before returning to Paris. John Sutro, Nancy and Diana Cooper eagerly greeted him, fêted him and dined him. There was something electrically exciting in his presence when he was about to begin a new novel, and for once he was genial. Lady Diana drove him to a quiet hotel nearby in Chantilly and he gathered his wits for a final onslaught on serious fiction. 'You are a wonderful companion in pleasure and in pain,' he wrote to Laura. 'Thank you for all your patience & for making everything so delightful.... Yesterday I spent reading all my war diaries & recapturing the atmosphere of those days. Today I began writing & it came easy.'[81]

This facility did not last. 'My book has not gone very well in the last few days,' he reported towards the end of June. 'I think it is because I am trying a new method of writing which does not work for me. I hate leaving a trail of unfinished shabby work behind me so I have decided to revert to my old habit of writing each page finally and completely.'[82] Death, he felt, was nearer his elbow than ever. The 'pain' referred to was an attack of the rheumatism which was to plague him for the rest of his life. Writing 'each page finally and completely' was the literary effect of his preparation for sudden collapse. But his later manuscripts reveal that this was far from the end of the process. From *Brideshead* onwards they become meticulous collations of holograph foolscap sheets and pasted-in typescript. As the range of his subjects widened, so too did his scope for impatience with handwritten drafts, and his literary joinery became increasingly complex. *Men At Arms* was planned as the first volume of a saga, an epic sequence of novels in three or four volumes. It was to be his *maximum opus*, his swan song, his counterblast to the enemies of *Helena*. Anthony Powell's *A Question of Upbringing*, the first volume of his *A Dance to the Music of Time* sequence, appeared in 1951 and, earlier in the year, he had visited Piers Court, house-hunting, ready to settle in the West Country to complete his life's work. Waugh, it seems, had a similar strategy for his literary future.

Men At Arms was not completed until December 1951 after seven months' steady labour. His opinion of it varied. 'I am writing an interminable novel

81. [June 1951], Hôtel du Château, Rue Connétable, Chantilly, Oise, France; *Letters*, p. 351. The first two sentences are omitted by Amory.
82. SS Peter and Paul [29 June 1951]; *Letters*, p. 351.

about army life,' he wrote to Greene in August, 'obsessed by memories of military dialogue. I was greatly encouraged . . . to read that Bendrix thinks 1000 words a good day's work. I used to write 3,000 & can still sometimes do 1200. But I suspect Bendrix writes better than I.'[83] The reference to the hero of *The End of the Affair* suggests a wry compliment to Greene. Waugh was one of the few who knew of the novel's autobiographical origins.

When Laura took the children to Italy at the end of August, Waugh invited Greene to stay. 'Catherine of course welcome', a postscript added, 'but warn her of Swiss Family Robinson Life.'[84] Greene replied:

> Your account doesn't in the least deter me. I like boiled or scrambled eggs and can do without hot water indefinitely. I can't drive . . . but Catherine can and if she manages to come we could drive and see Knox. . . . Nor do I even mind a dinner jacket. The Swiss Family Robinson life is exactly what Catherine and I used to live when the world allowed us to. So that won't put her off. We are both drinkers rather than eaters. . . . I look forward so much to this visit. Perhaps I'll be able to work again.[85]

Whatever the cause of this hiatus, it was not a religious crisis resulting from his affair. 'It didn't worry me in the least to be non-communicant', he maintained, 'because I was always a doubter. It is those who have a real and dogmatic belief who suffer from a crisis.'[86] The Catholic clergy kept a watchful eye on him, some (not Fr Caraman) fearful of the apostasy of so public a figure. Reports had come to Waugh that Greene had lost, or was losing, his faith. He had been apprehensive about Waugh's reaction to *The End of the Affair* (published that August) and overjoyed to learn that he thought it a masterpiece. 'No contribution I have ever received has given me such pleasure . . . as your review of Graham's book,' Caraman wrote to Waugh. 'I thought [the novel] beautifully written and a great technical achievement, but I read it with sadness.'[87]

Waugh perhaps shared this sadness. 'Of course I don't often agree with you,' he had written. 'I can never hope to do that this side of death.'[88] His way of supporting Greene through his difficulties was to leave him alone with his conscience in the security of the Household. Waugh's review had emphasized technical innovation and the 'brave invention' of using 'active beneficent supernatural interference. . . . His voice is listened to in many

83. 18 August 1951; *Letters*, p. 353.
84. 21 August [1951]; *Letters*, p. 353.
85. Unpublished TLS from Graham Greene, 22 August 1951, from 5 St James's Street, SW1; BL.
86. Unpublished TLS from Graham Greene to Martin Stannard, 5 November 1990, from La Résidence des Fleurs, Avenue Pasteur, 06600 Antibes.
87. Unpublished ALS from Fr Philip Caraman, 27 May 1951, from the *Month*, 114 Mount Street, W1; BL.
88. 17 March [1951], from Piers Court; *Letters*, p. 346.

dark places and this defiant assertion of the supernatural is entirely admirable.'[89] Greene later regretted this 'interference' as artistic impropriety and he might have been embarrassed by Waugh's fundamentalist reading which claimed the book as an unequivocal assertion of Faith. It is, Waugh insisted, 'addressed to the Gentiles. It shows them the Church as something in their midst, mysterious and triumphant and working for their good.'[90] Both men knew, however, that it had grown out of Greene's experience with Catherine and her husband, a confusion of loyalties which had not resolved itself in the romantic fashion of the fiction. Indeed, Catherine's sister had been so struck by the similarity between Henry Miles and Harry Walston that she had advised him to sue.[91]

Sensitive to Waugh's dilemma, Catherine wrote to clear the air before accepting his invitation:

> . . . my coming with Graham causes difficulties for some of our friends, and I would perfectly understand if you also felt this. I am thoroughly used to this problem, and as you have always been so good to and about us, I wanted to make sure that I was in no way causing you embarrasement [*sic*]. Please don't tell Graham that I have written.[92]

Waugh's reply was gentle and humble:

> Of course I won't tell Graham. . . . I met you first as a friend of Graham's but I hope I can now look on you as a friend in my own right. . . . Please believe that I am far too depressed by my own odious, if unromantic, sins to have any concern for other people's. . . . But when you say Graham is sometimes happier without you, that is another matter. You know & I don't. I did detect in his letters a hint that he looked forward to a spell of solitude. Only you can decide whether that mood is likely to persist. If you think it a bad time, come later when Laura is home. . . .[93]

In the event, she stayed for three days, Greene for a week. 'G. Greene behaved well and dressed for dinner every night,' Waugh informed Nancy, '. . . [he] spent his time patrolling the built-up areas round Dursley noting the numbers of motor-cars. He takes omens from them.'[94] Waugh engaged his guests in practical tasks – manuring the lawn, nettle weeding – and

89. 'The Heart's Own Reasons', *Commonweal*, 17 August 1951, 458–9; also as 'The Point of Departure', *Month*, 6 September 1951, 174–6; *EAR*, pp. 404–6.
90. *EAR*, p. 406.
91. Interview with Lord Walston, 13 December 1988.
92. Unpublished TLS from Catherine Walston, Friday [24 August 1951], from Newton Hall, Newton, nr Cambridge; BL.
93. 25 August 1951; *Letters*, p. 355.
94. September [1951]; *Letters*, p. 356. The last two sentences were a humorous allusion to Bendrix's obsession rather than to Greene's.

rewarded them with his special cocktail, gin-pink-lemon. He took them to films and to dinner with the Donaldsons. 'In spite of our private problems,' Catherine wrote afterwards, 'I was very happy staying with you for you cheer Graham enormously and I like being with you.'[95] At home, sorting children's underpants, her Cambridge life seemed tedious in comparison with the wonders of Piers Court. Greene returned to London refreshed and moved by Waugh's loyalty: 'I enjoyed myself with you so much & you eased what would have been a very bad period for me. I wish I'd been a better fertiliser for your garden.'[96] Greene had turned his back on the sort of 'garden' represented by Waugh's household – wife, children, a regular domestic regime within the Faith. Where Waugh travelled less frequently, Greene soon began to move restlessly about the globe from one conflict to another. Despite his family, Waugh was an immensely lonely man. Greene, rarely lonely, was homeless, and glad to be so.[97]

The visit seems also to have cheered Waugh. During August, depressed by the dullness of his novel, he had sent the first section to Chapman & Hall. '... No, not too boring', McDougall had replied, '– your best form.... It really is magnificent....'[98] 'My novel is unreadable & endless,' Waugh had informed Nancy three weeks later. 'Nothing but tippling in officers' messes and drilling on barrack squares. No demon sex. No blood or thunder.'[99] His children were at home. With their departure and Greene's arrival, Waugh's spirits had revived: 'I am scribbling away hard at my maximum opus. I think it is frightfully funny. A bad sign.'[100]

It was in this more skittish mood that he accepted an invitation to stand as Rector of Edinburgh University. 'I don't suppose I shall get in', he told Peters, 'but it might be amusing.'[101] A few days earlier he had learnt that the Inland Revenue had been awarded a minor judgment against the Waugh trustees, but, with his novel going well at last, he could jovially remark to his agent that he hoped they might all stay out of prison. Chapman & Hall put up £75 for election expenses; a hand-out was printed in the style of a Penguin cover bearing the legend 'The Rector. Evelyn Waugh' and Waugh

95. Unpublished TLS from Catherine Walston, 'Tuesday morning' [September 1951], from Newton Hall, Newton, nr Cambridge; BL.
96. Unpublished ALS from Graham Greene, nd [September 1951], from 5 St James's Street, SW1; BL.
97. Cf. unpublished TLS from Graham Greene to Martin Stannard, 5 November 1990, *op. cit.*: 'I never envied Evelyn's security.... I wandered from one conflict to another because I was enjoying dangerous situations.... The last thing I wanted was a permanent home.'
98. Unpublished ALS from Jack McDougall, 10 August 1951, from Chapman & Hall, 37 Essex Street, Strand, WC2; BL.
99. [24 August] 1951; *Letters*, p. 354.
100. ALS to Nancy Mitford, September [1951]; *Letters*, p. 356.
101. Unpublished APCI to A.D. Peters [17 October 1951], from Piers Court; *Catalogue* E719, p. 184.

plunged into the affair with an ebullient undergraduate promoting his cause.

As everyone now knows, Waugh lost, but he was probably more disappointed by the result than he cared to admit. With Bowra's knighthood in January, Waugh's thirst for some form of public recognition had intensified. This slightly absurd but none the less important title seemed just right for him. The election, traditionally a barbarous process, appealed to his combative temperament, and it had the added advantage of being conducted at the same time as a general election which Waugh despised. His electoral address emphasized his Scottish ancestry and his superiority to the rapacious egotism of contemporary politics:

> This is not a Parliamentary Election, in which the voter deliberates how he can best benefit himself by his choice. It is a conference about the disposal of an Honour. I have no policy in regard to your affairs . . . it is not my ambition to meddle uninvited in your business.
>
> I am asking you to give me an Honour. Why I want it should be plain enough. I am a Scot of the diaspora. Less than two hundred years ago my great-great-grandfather took part in that most successful action of Scottish Nationalism – the conquest of England by peaceful penetration. Since then we have always looked on ourselves as Scots. However kind strangers may be, a man looks to the place of his origin for the recognition he values most.[102]

The tone of mock pomposity was that of his undergraduate speeches and, just as then, he found himself caught between the hunger for power and an inability to take power structures seriously. As professional jester and prose stylist he was without equal. By combining the two he had gained power of a sort. This, however, he no longer found a satisfactory public image and it represented an irreconcilable division in his mind. It was the sort of thing which left him vulnerable to correction from BBC bores. He yearned to be cherished by a nation, the majority of whose subjects he despised. 'When I come to itemize my claims to your suffrage,' he told the students, 'I find them mostly negative':

> I have never gone into public life. Most of the ills we suffer are caused by people going into public life. I have never voted in a parliamentary election. I believe a man's chief civic duty consists in fighting for his King when the men in public life have put the realm in danger. That I have done. . . . It seems to me essential to your repute among the great Universities of Christendom that you should choose a man connected with the arts. I am opposed by a poet. If he writes better

102. Unpublished section of Waugh's electoral address, dated 10 November 1951; CUL.

> than I, please vote for him. But do not, I beg, choose anyone connected with commerce or with the fabrication of noisy, dangerous or quite ephemeral machinery. Do not choose a man in public life. Do not choose a pure clown. . . .[103]

With these thrusts Waugh hoped to dispose of the opposition. John Cameron, Dean of the Faculty of Advocates, was standing on the Nationalist ticket; Sydney Goodsir Smith was the poet; Sir Andrew Murray the businessman; Jimmy Logan the clown. No serious competition lay there, Waugh thought. As things stood when he wrote his address, he had an excellent chance of winning. At the last moment, however, Sir Alexander Fleming and the Aga Khan entered the hustings. Waugh came fourth behind them and Cameron.

'It was just a joke that didn't come off,' he wrote to Nancy.[104] This was, perhaps, not the entire truth, and the defeat can only have added to his already boiling sense of outrage. A few days earlier, Fr Gerald Meath had reviewed Dorothy Sayers's *The Emperor Constantine*, suggesting its superiority to *Helena* and referring to 'Evelyn Waugh' rather than 'Mr. Waugh'. Worse still, he had said that 'Miss Sayers feels no need to be smart and she shows us a woman who was made a Saint not by her aristocratic inheritance so much as by the power of the Holy Spirit. . . .'[105]

Waugh's temper exploded. 'I take him to mean', he replied, 'that I hold a contrary opinion. May I ask Meath to substantiate or deny this odious imputation?'[106] Nothing stung like an accusation of heresy from a co-religionist. But this reaction, even by his own standards of intemperance, was extraordinary. Other reviewers had made remarks similar to Meath's; authors were rarely addressed 'correctly' in reviews. Waugh disliked these trends but they were usually beneath his contempt. His instinct in this case, however, was immediately to drag the priest through the courts and to make him pay heavily. Meath, he considered, had 'ostentatiously' omitted the prefix. Thus Waugh's reply ostentatiously omitted Meath's. Woodruff was embarrassed and angered by Waugh's high-handed attitude. If Waugh wanted his second letter printed, he was told, he would have to drop an 'altogether too offensive' remark about Meath.[107] The letter also insulted Woodruff:

> As you well know, to write of a man without his 'Mr' or other prefix is to proclaim him, to the educated reader, as either a felon or a

103. *Ibid.*, from the section reprinted in *The Times*, 8 November 1951; *EAR*, p. 406.
104. November 1951; *Letters*, p. 360.
105. 'Mysteries and Moralities', *Tablet*, 27 October 1951, 295.
106. 'St. Helena', *Tablet*, 3 November 1951, 324.
107. Unpublished ALS from Douglas Woodruff, 12 November 1951, from 10 Evelyn Mansions, Carlisle Place, SW1; BL.

professional athlete – or, else, as dead. But I should not have asked your space to instruct your reviewers in the proprieties of journalism. That is your task.[108]

Controversy erupted. The heavy guns of D'Arcy and Knox thundered in Waugh's defence; various members of the public thought his approach vindictive and undignified. Eventually Meath backed off. No action was brought and Waugh, trying to emerge from the business with dignity and without directly apologizing to Woodruff, sent him a facetious disclaimer to sign.[109] Woodruff, it seems, was not amused.

Waugh's solicitor dealt patiently with him. Yes, there had been a sneer which fell within Fraser's definition of libel but there were also problems: 'As you will know, where literary and artistic criticism is concerned, the law allows extreme latitude to expressions of opinion....'[110] Meath might plead 'Fair comment on a matter of public interest' or, still more embarrassing were it upheld, that he had been making a joke. If Waugh were to sue anyone, he would have to sue the *Tablet* and defend himself against Meath's finding 'even a colourable suggestion to the effect that the high birth of St. Helena had influenced your tribute to her sanctity....'[111] On all these counts, even if he won, Waugh was likely to appear more foolish than otherwise.

He was, of course, justified in his anger at misrepresentation but the astonishing element of this case was his barefaced hypocrisy. (Waugh was not, contrary to popular opinion, usually hypocritical. He was blunt, rude, often self-deluding and distressingly honest but he was not a hypocrite.) Defamatory remarks exposing others to 'hatred, ridicule and contempt' were his stock-in-trade. He rarely stopped short of accusations of heresy. Earlier in the year he had lampooned Stephen Spender's autobiography in an hilarious fashion calculated 'to injure him in his office, profession or trade' ('... to see him fumbling with our rich and delicate language is to experience all the horror of seeing a Sèvres vase in the hands of a chimpanzee').[112] In the same piece he had attacked an old Hertford

108. 'St. Helena', *Tablet*, 17 November 1951, 364.
109. 'Copy of text sent (facetiously) to Douglas Woodruff after correspondence in *Tablet*: I deeply regret that I allowed Fr. Meath to use opprobrious language about Mr. Waugh. I aggravated the offense [*sic*] by my levity in printing the impertinent letters which certain correspondents wrote. I fully acknowledge that nothing in Mr. Waugh's *Helena* affords any justification for Fr. Meath's reference to it. I was not influenced by the facts that the publishing firm of which I am a director, failed to secure the rights they sought, to publish the book; nor by the fact that it was serialized in the *Month* instead of the *Tablet*. I ask Mr. Waugh's pardon and that of my readers. [Sign here].' MS in HRC.
110. Unpublished TLS from H. F. Rubinstein of Rubinstein, Nash & Co., 23 November 1951, from 5 & 6 Raymond Buildings, Gray's Inn, WC1; BL.
111. *Ibid.*
112. 'Two Unquiet Lives', *op. cit.*; *EAR*, p. 395.

contemporary and fellow Catholic convert, John Miller, accusing him effectively of heretical claims to mystical experience. Miller, deeply offended, both on his part and on Spender's, had written to Waugh to tell him so. But a sense of humour colours his complaint. Such mockery, Miller accepted, was part of the rough-and-tumble of literary life. It lent reviews their personal voice.[113] Waugh's was full of factual misrepresentation (John Auden, for instance, wrote to correct the myth of his brother's having fled to America 'at the first squeak of an air-raid warning').[114] No one had ever attempted to sue Waugh for these missiles fired from the near-impregnable fortresses of the review columns. Libel cases had been brought but they were rare. Waugh's was the art of embarrassment. If victims complained, he considered them wet. He was, nevertheless, becoming increasingly sensitive about receiving hostile treatment himself. Finding it difficult now to separate himself from his disguises, he became gripped by an obsession with the rectitude of his public image. The masks were sticking to the skin.

The intensity of his fury with Meath is partly explained by an unfortunate coincidence. The review appeared as Sykes was completing negotiations for the dramatization of *Helena*. Waugh was looking to this to refocus attention on his, as he thought, unfairly neglected novel as a great work of apologetics. The last thing he wanted at this juncture was an accusation of heresy.

Sykes had fought for much of 1951 to produce a good script (he wrote it, Waugh revised) and to secure the best available actors. The BBC not being favourably disposed towards Waugh, he needed a friend at court. Like Connolly, Sykes thirsted, sometimes to the point of indignity, for the Great Man's affection, and the magnetism of Waugh's character was so strong that, in his genial moods, he could produce temporary clones. Friends imitated his fantastical manner, were sucked into his snobbery, would dare the playful insult. Then he would grow bored with people aping him or telling him he was the cleverest, most sensible man in the world and would throw them away. A sudden, bitter rebuke would smash the

113. Cf. unpublished ALS from John Miller, 16 June 1951, from PO Box 340, Nairobi; BL: 'I must write a note of protest at the disgraceful review you wrote.... But ... in spite of the outrage you have committed on my own shy suggestions I was naturally consumed with giggles at what you said. There is something irresistible in your so pleasantly alliterative reference to "the mood in which Mr. Miller approached the Ministry"! ... Bless you. I am quite furious: but howling with laughter.'

114. Cf. unpublished ALS from John B. Auden, 5 September 1951, from c/o Grindlays Bank Ltd, 54 Parliament Street, W1; BL: 'That story also went around in the war but it is incorrect. He had already decided by August 1938, when I was staying with him in Bruxelles, to become an American citizen, and he left I think for the States in Feb. 1939 – surely somewhat in advance of the squeaks. It seems a failing [?] to introduce malice of that type with your wit, when your ground in most essentials about most of that gang is so sure and unassailable.'

intimacy and restore solitude. This was to be the end of Sykes's three-year period as principal courtier.

Sykes's colleagues at 'the Broadcasting', he informed Waugh, were being 'very common-minded'[115] about the whole business. The comic fiction was that of a Protestant plot to undermine the project by employing bad actors. This Sykes successfully 'overthrew' by securing the services of Flora Robson (Helena), John Gielgud (Constantine), Isobel Jeans (Fausta) and James McKechnie (narrator). 'Mr. [Wilfred] Pickles is unable to act the part of the Wandering Jew, in spite of your encouragements . . . but I have obtained an equally vulgar man called Ted Ray. The Wandering Jew was never a major problem on account of our vast national supplies of vulgar men. . . .'[116] This sort of thing went down very well as did snippets of gossip which enhanced Waugh's glory:

> Now for the Stravinsky business . . . he has a tremendous cult for what he calls 'Vok'. He has a perfectly enormous book . . . which he keeps in a chapel . . . in the basement of his house. . . . The book contains all criticisms of or written by you, all your articles in the papers, all photographs published of you, references to you by other people . . . and this is the man's great cult wherein he believes is to be found the pinnacle of human wisdom and a solitary hope of redemption. . . . 'Vok' is Slavonik for the Scottish name of Waugh. This was told by an entirely unimaginative and intimate Russian friend of Stravinsky to the Devil [Harman] Grisewood, and the Devil repeated it to me.[117]

Then had come the ignominy of Meath and Edinburgh. Waugh's mood changed. Negotiations with Sykes chilled. He tried to dissuade Waugh from attending rehearsals; Waugh insisted on meeting the actors. His desire to promote *Helena* overcame the growing discomfort of allowing third parties to meddle with his work and, to defuse accusations of levity or heresy, he offered to broadcast a prefatory talk.

'Tomorrow evening', he began, 'a very distinguished company are going to broadcast a play based on the second half of [my] novel. . . . The book was not as popular as I had hoped. Several frankly enquired why I had written it. This evening I will try to give my reasons.'[118] If listeners were anticipating a light-hearted historical romp, they were sorely disappointed. Waugh's talk turned into an attack on cheap fantasy and, indirectly, on

115. Unpublished ALS from Christopher Sykes, 16 August 1951, from Pembroke Arms Hotel, nr Salisbury, Wilts.; BL.
116. Unpublished ALS from Christopher Sykes, 14 October 1951, from 90 Eaton Terrace, SW1; BL.
117. Unpublished ALS from Christopher Sykes, 19 October 1951, from 90 Eaton Terrace, SW1; BL.
118. 'St Helena Empress', recorded BBC Bristol, 23 November 1951, for transmission 15 December 1951, 9.15–9.35 p.m., Third Programme; BBCSL. Abridged text printed in *Month* (January 1951), 7–11, and as the first essay in *The Holy Places*, *op. cit.*; *EAR*, pp. 407–10.

Dorothy Sayers and Meath.[119] *Helena*, Waugh suggested, represented his contemplation of the life of a saint. It offered no vicarious thrills. The reader or listener would not be able to 'identify' with her because, like each human being, she was unique, with a unique vocation. Helena's riches were unsought and irrelevant to her spiritual quest; indeed, they were a source of pain and uncertainty for her: 'She accepted the fact that God had his own use for her. Others faced the lions in the circus; others lived in caves in the desert. She was to be St. Helena Empress, not St. Helena Martyr or St. Helena Anchorite.'[120]

On 16 December, Waugh sat glumly by his servants' radio and was appalled by the play. Afterwards, he wrote to Flora Robson, congratulating her on her performance, but accused Sykes, only half-facetiously, of 'acting under the direction of Fr. Meath'.[121] Sykes's reply was restrained. Angry and disappointed, he was unwilling to rebuke: '... though I am conscious of many drawbacks ... I doubt if it was as horrible as you think.'[122] That was as far as he was prepared to go. Reviews had been good. For over a year he had exhausted himself in Waugh's service, only to be rewarded by blank ingratitude. But Waugh had promised the dedication of his work in progress and Sykes, anxious not to forfeit this place in literary history, hung fire.

*

By October, Waugh had put 52,000 words of his novel into shape under the working title of 'Honour'. He expected to be at work on it for several months hence.[123] After the rebuffs of public life, he had returned vigorously to work, bumping up his production to 4,000 words a day. By early December, he had rewritten the early chapters and sent the first complete typescript to McDougall. The rest of that month had been spent cutting and polishing, waiting unhappily for Sykes's production and Christmas at home. It had been a bad year for him, and the election of a Conservative Government in October had depressed him further. This transfer of power, he felt, merely installed a new set of buffoons willing to soak the rich in order to bribe votes from the 'labourers'. Churchill was Prime Minister;

119. Cf. *ibid.*, BBCSL, p. 1: 'Heavy apparatus has been at work in the last hundred years to enervate and stultify the imaginative faculties. First, realistic novels and plays, then the cinema have made the urban mentality increasingly subject to suggestion. It lapses effortlessly into a trance-like escape from its condition. Great popularity in fiction and in film is only attained by works in which reader and audience can transpose themselves and be vicariously endangered, loved and applauded. This kind of reverie is not meditation....'
120. *Ibid.*, p. 5.
121. Sykes, p. 352.
122. Unpublished ALS, 18 December 1951, from 90 Eaton Terrace, SW1; BL.
123. Cf. unpublished ALS and APCl to A.D. Peters, 19 October 1951, from Piers Court; BL; *Catalogue* E720 and E721, pp. 184–5.

R. A. Butler, Chancellor; Harold Macmillan, Minister for Housing; Anthony Eden, Foreign Secretary. They presented themselves as gentlemen of the people, concerned for the poor yet eager to expand the economy. The days of austerity, they said, were over, and when, in February, George VI died, a new Elizabethan age was proclaimed: an expansionist future, freeing the spirit of Old England after twenty-one tenebrous years. Waugh despised the whole pack of them, especially as the new year had opened with disastrous financial news.

The Inland Revenue had caught up with him at last. Peters had driven to Piers Court to explain, as patiently as he could, that to ignore tax inspectors did not make them disappear. Waugh provided a luxurious week-end and evaded the issue. 'I wish that the results of our deliberations could have been more satisfactory,' Peters wrote on his return,

> but it takes an awful long time to learn that there is practically no relationship . . . between earning power and spending power. Even so, if you can maintain a spending figure of £4000 a year, as I am sure you can, the reduction of your standard of living need not be quite so drastic as you think. You should be able to keep a reasonable staff to run the house and still come out square. The hardest thing of all is to pay back income tax out of current earnings. That is practically impossible.[124]

It was always so difficult to correct a man for exorbitance whose main 'fault' was generosity. Peters had stayed at a local pub to avoid social complications and had left his chauffeur to pay the bill. Only later did he discover that Waugh had quietly picked up the tab.

The Revenue was demanding the unpaid supertax on Waugh's film contracts since 1944. He sent them a hefty cheque, reduced his household and complained to Nancy that he was ruined. But he had no intention of cutting expenditure to £4,000 a year. During 1952, various measures were taken to raise extra money. He spent some weeks in Brighton with Carol Reed working on a film;[125] he asked Handasyde Buchanan down to Piers Court to catalogue and value the library, presumably with a view to selling it to the Save the Children Fund;[126] he offered a volume of his more savage uncollected reviews to Ian Fleming's Queen Anne Press under the title *Offensive Matter*. None of these projects came to fruition. The year 1952 marked the beginning of a steady contraction of the grand style at Piers

124. Unpublished ALS from A. D. Peters, 19 January 1952; BL.
125. Possibly *The Man Between* (1953); cf. *Letters*, n. 3, p. 378. Waugh's name did not appear on the credits. He was paid £2,000. Nicholas Wapshott in his biography of Reed (*The Man Between* [Chatto & Windus, 1990], p. 254) suggests that the film was *The Tangiers Story*.
126. Cf. unpublished ALS from Handasyde Buchanan, 3 June 1952, from G. Heywood Hill Ltd, 10 Curzon Street, W1; BL. The library was valued at £3,200.

Court, and Waugh associated this new phase of persecution with the betrayal of Conservative politicians.

'I've quarrelled with so many of my friends,' he remarked a year later.

> One makes friends up to one's thirties, quarrels with them between 45 and 55, and makes new ones in the sixties. Between 45 and 55 is an irritable time. In middle age one thinks of the young with distaste as a poor imitation of oneself. When one is older one realises that they are quite different people and they become interesting.[127]

This was a brutally accurate self-assessment. During 1952 he managed to alienate most of his friends. Connolly had finally divorced Jean, deserted Lys and married Barbara Skelton. He lived in poverty in Barbara's four-room cottage in Kent, was predictably suffering a writing block and became the butt of many cruel jibes. Nancy had made the mistakes of discussing Catholicism in the *Sunday Times* and being optimistic about the 1950s. Harold Acton had confused the travel arrangements during Waugh's visit to Sicily in February 1952 and been treated to outbursts of rage. Diana Cooper had picked Waugh up in Nice and had driven him back to Paris, paying too much attention to guide books, relentlessly pointing out sights of interest which her companion found tedious. For her, the reclamation of her old beau had drenched the trip in golden light and her febrile letters seemed alarming to Waugh in his cool withdrawal. He wrote politely thanking her. 'Darling Wu,' she replied,

> I waited with impatience for yr. letter because you being so unpredictable I had not a sure belief in what spirit it would be written. So you will see how glad it made me....
>
> I do not want to forget the book. I'll try & wipe away the tears. I'll hold tightly to my heart the cheer of yr. pink smile & pinker carnation on the Nice platform – the streams of sun-jokes at Willie's [Maugham's] & at his catamite – the flowers & sea, Villefranche & the Golden Lion – the window open to the moon – the Enos & the orange sticks.... Forget the drawing of Ingres's lady's throat, the snow on our lashes, the Mistral – the escape from one another to bedrooms on the Avignon [?] afternoon.... Remember ... the reading aloud running thro' all. Forget, O quite forget 'however-long-the-journey' let's get back in a day for poor baby's health.... We had the blizzard & our neurotic spoilt natures as luggage.... dearest Wu – Harold Acton says you're mad – I agree but I like it that way....[128]

127. Interview with David Malbert, *News Chronicle*, 11 June 1953, 8.
128. ALS from Lady Diana Cooper, 10 April [1952], from Château de St Firmin, Vineuil, Oise; BL; *MWMS*, p. 133–4.

Greene, according to Acton,[129] thought Waugh a saint. At each stage travelling north with Lady Diana, Waugh had read aloud from *Men At Arms*; at each stage, perhaps reflecting the development of the book, his mood had darkened.

Waugh still hated France. Unable to understand his preference for America, Nancy always maintained a light-hearted Francophile's battle with him. 'Yanks are madly interested in religion,' he had replied in 1950. 'Frogs are behaving (& have since 1789) very improperly . . . & it is wicked to encourage them.'[130] The running joke revolved around Nancy as class traitor, abandoning her country to Socialist rule and hypocritically supporting it from the safety of Paris. During 1952 the joke began to run out of control as Waugh apparently came to believe his reductivist history. Dictatorial and offensive, he spoke to everyone who tried to correct him as though to an infant. 'Anyway,' he told Nancy, 'your "France" is pure fantasy',[131] oblivious of the fact that the same could be said of his 'England'. She could not let this pass. 'Really what rubbish. Is England the England of Shakespeare? Is Germany the Germany of Goethe? You are not very accurate in all your statements. . . .'[132]

It was at this point that she had picked him up on his anti-Semitism. Something was clearly going wrong with Evelyn and she was worried. He was suffering acute physical pains and refusing, as usual, to see a doctor. Benevolent mockery seemed the best remedy in the short term.

> Total to me is the mystery why you don't live in Ireland. . . . Never have I seen a country so much made for somebody as *it* is for *you*. The terrible silly politeness of the lower classes so miserable that they long for any sort of menial task at £1 a week. The emptiness, the pretty houses of the date you like best, the agricultural country for Laura, the neighbours all low brow & armigerous – all 100 miles away. The cold wetness, the small income tax, really I could go on for ever. . . . I remember you went to look at a Castle, so what happened? Perhaps you saw an elemental and fled incontinent?[133]

What had happened, as everyone saw when *Men At Arms* was published in September, was that Waugh had nailed his colours to the fiction of Old England.

*

129. Cf. unpublished ALS from Sir Harold Acton, 19 April 1952, from La Pietra, Florence; BL.
130. Unpublished APCS, nd [September 1950?], from Piers Court; private collection.
131. 27 January 1952; *Letters*, p. 367.
132. Unpublished ALS from Nancy Mitford, 29 January 1952, from 7 Rue Monsieur, Paris VII; BL.
133. Unpublished ALS from Nancy Mitford, 26 April 1952, from 7 Rue Monsieur, Paris VII; BL.

Advertised as the first volume of a trilogy, *Men At Arms* had a mixed reception. John Raymond's remark that 'however much below form, any new novel from [Waugh] is bound to add immeasurably to the gaiety of his own nation'[134] was typically ambivalent. The book was somehow flawed, most felt, by schoolboyish humour, but it seemed churlish to complain when Waugh wrote so well. Only Ronald Knox made high claims, comparing the book favourably with the *Iliad* as war fiction.[135] It was the strangely placid tone which struck, and disappointed, many. 'Because [Guy] is in love,' Tangye Lean suggested, 'Mr. Waugh is gentler than usual.'[136] Raymond agreed: 'On the whole "Men At Arms" is good-tempered Waugh – and therefore Waugh at his second best.'[137] Most sensibly reserved judgment – this was, after all, only one third of a novel – and, by contemporary standards, Waugh had begun well enough.

American critics were more fiercely divided: *Time* preferred the new style:

> Reading 'Men At Arms' is like hearing a full keyboard used by a pianist who has hitherto confined himself to a single octave. Waugh is fully alive to the fact that no modern war is just a soldier's war. The drawing rooms, kitchens and clubs of the home front interest him just as much as the barracks and the tents ... & if his trilogy continues as well as it has begun, it will be the best British novel of World War II.[138]

The *New York Times*, however, and the *New Yorker* thought the book uneven: 'The raffish note of the barracks, which enlivens the middle portion ... yields to the note of Newman, and under the circumstances the reader can't help feeling disappointed.'[139] Left-wing magazines found the social attitudes distasteful. 'If one had no other information on the subject,' wrote Delmore Schwartz, 'the beginning of ... "Men At Arms" would convince one that the Second World War occurred solely to rescue Englishmen from boredom and decadence.'[140] Joseph Frank felt that: '... Waugh's latest novel illustrates the unhappy predicament of a satirist who has fallen in love with his subject ... for the most part the book may be described as a discreet orgy of adolescent sentiment.'[141]

On both sides of the Atlantic reviewers were confused by the variation of tone. Comparisons were made in an attempt to locate *Men At Arms* in

134. *NS*, 20 September 1952, 326–7; *CH*, pp. 338–40.
135. *Month* (October 1952), 236–8.
136. *Spectator*, 12 September 1952, 342.
137. *Op. cit.*; *CH*, p. 339.
138. Unsigned review, *Time*, 27 October 1952, 58–9; *CH*, pp. 341–3.
139. Unsigned review, *NY*, 1 November 1952, 117; *CH*, pp. 343–4.
140. *Partisan Review*, 3 November 1952, 703–4; *CH*, pp. 344–5.
141. *New Republic*, 10 November 1952, 19–20; *CH*, pp. 345–7.

literary history – Ford Madox Ford, Kipling, Ian Hay, Saki, Wodehouse, Yeats-Brown, Henty – and a division emerged between the tradition of the serious war novel and that of the school story. Supporting both was the theological superstructure that recalled 'the note of Newman'. This mixture of styles was, of course, deliberate and carefully controlled. Waugh even wished to tease his readers further: 'I think your idea of a school-story or P. G. Wodehouse wrapper is terrible,' his publisher wrote. 'True, a half-dozen connoisseurs wd. be amused, but it wouldn't do at all.'[142] Waugh saw sense and settled for a coat of arms on a solemn red background. But the stylistic ambiguities remained intrinsic to the desired effect. Honour, by implication, had become as outmoded as the school stories which had celebrated it.

One of the first critics to notice this was Connolly. Unlike the Americans, he disliked the barrack-room farce:

> After an admirable hundred pages. Mr. Waugh slips into a vein highly reminiscent of [Hay's] 'The First Hundred Thousand' with touches of 'Stalky & Co.', and the P. G. Wodehouse of 'Ukridge'. Atwater is not so much a comic character ... but a private joke, and for the first time I found myself bored by the central section of a Waugh novel.... One raises the silver loving cup expecting champagne and receives a wallop of ale. Once we accept that it is beer, a chronicle rather than a novel, it is of its kind perfect....[143]

Waugh, he felt, had failed to establish relationships between his military characters; the book did not resolve the discord between love and aggression as successfully as did Hemingway's *The Old Man and the Sea* (published at the same time). Waugh agreed. During its composition he had often referred to his novel as 'Mrs Dale's Diary'. But he could not resist correction:

> I thought your review of *Men At Arms* excellent. It is a pity you called 'Apthorpe' 'Atwater' throughout and credited him with two aunts (whereas it was one of my humdrum comic effects that he had only one) because it will make your readers think you did not give full attention to the book. You plainly did, and have clearly defined all that I dislike [in it]. 'Beery' is exactly right.
>
> The [religious] medal is not ... going to play much part in the story, nor will the pace quicken much, but all the subsidiary characters, like 'Trimmer' & 'Chatty Corner' & 'de Souza' will each have a book to himself. Anyway the theme will see me out – that is the humanizing

142. Unpublished ALS from John McDougall, 8 February 1952, from Chapman & Hall Ltd, from 37 Essex Street, WC2; BL.
143. *ST*, 7 September 1952, 5; *CH*, pp. 337–9.

> of Guy. . . . I am so delighted that you admired . . . *Old Man* as I did. Apart from [Hemingway's] skill, it is his piety & chivalry I recognize.[144]

Poor Connolly was covered with shame, as indeed Waugh intended him to be, and the novelist's society supergrasses, Nancy and Ann Fleming, snapped up the incident greedily. 'I saw Connolly's review well really I suppose, considering . . . your dedicace with which all Venice rang, it could have been worse. I really don't feel inspired to read the great master work about a fish.'[145] Mrs Fleming, in the doldrums of post-natal depression, was positively enlivened by the fracas: 'The day after the presentation copies I lunched . . . with Connolly, he was hopping mad with rage at your dedication and needed much soothing with slices of smoked salmon.'[146] During the war, Connolly had defended his country with *Horizon* and by firewatching. Waugh had inscribed his copy: 'To Cyril, who kept the home fires burning.' And to extend the tease, the next volume opened with a group of progressive novelists, dressed as firemen, ineffectually squirting water into the blazing morning room of Turtle's Club.

Oddly, this little skirmish served temporarily to reunite Connolly and Waugh. Of all Waugh's male friends (and they were few), he probably loved Cyril the best. The dear, sad man, so talented in youth, having failed in his final attempt to become an artist, unhappy in his second marriage, dispirited and drinking too much, had settled to the hack-work of weekly reviewing. With *Horizon* behind him and little ahead, he remained to Waugh a fascinating character whose conversation glittered with savage wit. Neurotic himself, Waugh warmed to neurosis in others. Connolly's sensitivity to insult, his narcissism, his hypochondria, all registered him as a Great British Eccentric, and such characters seemed thin on the ground in 1952. When Knox proposed a letter of complaint about the review, Waugh dissuaded him on the grounds that the criticisms were just. Desperate for money, Connolly had accepted a $1,000 commission from *Time* to write a profile of Waugh, a purgatorial task, promising further rebukes, but even this Waugh was prepared to forgive. At forty-nine, both anticipated their sixth decade as their last and discovered a grimly humorous, if distant, companionship in decline. 'I would like to see you on my 50th birthday,' Connolly wrote, 'but couldn't bear to give a party again ever. One should at 50 think only of the little one has done and the little time left and dine alone. . . .'[147]

144. ALS to Cyril Connolly, 8 September [1952]; *Letters*, pp. 382–3.
145. Unpublished ALS from Nancy Mitford, 27 September 1952, from 7 Rue Monsieur, Paris VII; BL.
146. Unpublished ALS, 20 September 1952, from White Cliffs, St Margaret's Bay, Dover; BL.
147. Unpublished ALS, nd [late 1952?], from Oak Cottage, Elmsted, Kent; BL.

Waugh was well satisfied with the reception of his novel. All whose good opinion he coveted – Mary Herbert, Nancy, Connolly, Eric Linklater, Sykes, Knox, Greene – admired the book. He had even attracted a new disciple, Angus Wilson.[148]

> You're completely crazy [Greene wrote] when you think it not up to the mark – I think it may well be the beginning of your best book.... As for style you've never, except in isolated passages, written better or, I believe, as well ... – & I'm no indiscriminate fan – there are two books of yours I don't like! It rains here most of the time & Catherine is ill with bronchitis & I am 48 today – & I don't like any of these inescapable facts. But I love Men At Arms.[149]

True, the Betjemans had maintained radio silence, but it was generally clear that Waugh's misgivings were ill-founded and his anxiety about failing powers relaxed for a few months.

In this newly buoyant mood, he began his diary again after a gap of nearly two years, recording a journey to meet Belloc which Waugh and Laura made during a brief holiday. It was something of a state visit to the Sussex farmhouse:

> Younger boy went to fetch 'Granda' [?] Sounds of shuffling. Enter old man, shaggy white beard, black clothes garnished with food and tobacco. Thinner than I last saw him, with benevolent gleam. Like an old peasant or fisherman in French film. We went to greet him at door. Smell like fox. He kissed Laura's hand, bowed to me saying, 'I am

148. Waugh had written to Wilson in August praising *Hemlock and After*; then to Caraman asking to review it for the *Month*. By the time he came to write the review in September, Waugh had read the book three times (cf. *Letters*, p. 380). Caraman replied (11 August 1952; BL) that Wilson might become a Catholic and that, if Waugh bore this in mind, the *Month* would be pleased to print a notice. The review ('A Clean Sweep', *Month*, 8 [October 1952], 238–40; *EAR*, pp. 421–3) was glorious. Waugh saw Wilson as the only important member of the new generation of writers – '*Hemlock and After* is a singularly rich, compact and intricate artifact [*sic*]' (421) – but was suspicious of what he took to be a neo-Marxist, apocalyptic tone suggesting the ultimate worthlessness of all the characters. Struggling to assist Wilson into the Church, Waugh read Mrs Sands as the 'Conscience of the book', and an expression of Divine Grace: 'All that is lacking ... is the name of the new life-giving power' (423). Sir Angus never became a Catholic but admired *Men At Arms* nevertheless: 'Your remark that it was dull and the knowledge that it was upon military life had made me apprehensive that this would not be among my favourite of your books, but far from it. I found the whole scene far more familiar than I had expected. I think that to be new in the Army must have so much of preparatory and public school that although I have had but three days under arms myself ... it was as though much of what you wrote had been with me potentially all along. Although the ideas of your principal character are ... not mine, I find him an infinitely moving man.... My brother ... (... a very 1914 type ..., of a fine but embittered kind) had a preparatory school at Seaford, indeed, he died there just about the time (1940) you describe of complications from his 1914 wounds. In a most curious way, these two aspects of my brother's life combine for me in your chapters on the school ...' (unpublished ALS, 17 September 1952, from The Reading Room, British Museum, WC1; BL).
149. Unpublished ALS, 2 October [1952], from Villa Rosaio, Anacapri; BL.

> pleased to make your acquaintance, sir.' Shuffled to chair by fire. During whole visit he was occupied with unsuccessful attempts to light an empty pipe.[150]

Waugh, immaculate in tweeds, listened with increasing irritation to the ancient's mumbled generalizations. It all, Waugh thought, belonged to a dead world, imperfectly recalled: 'Still talking of arrogance of the rich. Nothing about religion.'[151]

Afterwards they drove over to Frank and Elizabeth Pakenham, which was another mistake. The house was cluttered with children, and Pakenham, depressed by the labour of writing his autobiography,[152] had unwisely asked Waugh to read sections:

> We both got cross. I overstated the badness of the writing. I said I wasn't shocked at a politician writing like that, but at a don's. It might be work of a second-year undergraduate at BNC. I had in the preceding days taken a physical revulsion of the MS and couldn't bring myself to touch it. When challenged to find clichés, failed. Left on bad terms and with the feeling that all Frank's protestations of friendship are blarney, and his sense of Catholicism, 'uplift'.[153]

'I am just completing my 49th year . . .,' he wrote to Greene. 'It is the grand climacteric which sets the course of the rest of one's life I am told. It has been a year of lost friends for me. Not by death but by wear & tear. Our friendship started rather late. Pray God it lasts.'[154]

It did. But another had recently collapsed. 'Clarissa's apostasy', he wrote to Ann Fleming, 'has upset me more than anything that had happened since Kick [Hartington]'s death. I can't write about it, or think of anything else.'[155] Clarissa Churchill, Winston's niece, had earlier in the year married Anthony Eden.[156] This was the apostasy: she had been brought up a Catholic; Eden was divorced, and they were married outside the Church in Caxton Hall registry office. Infatuation, jealousy and, most important, a horror of apostasy perhaps drove Waugh to assume a greater intimacy with Clarissa than existed. Whenever he had come to London they had lunched *à deux* together and she was clearly very fond of him. However, his letters to her, frank and zealous, were something of an embarrassment. To one she replied:

150. *Diaries*, 28 September 1952, p. 703.
151. *Ibid.* Cf. also ALS to Nancy Mitford; *Letters*, p. 385, and to Lady Diana Cooper, *MWMS*, pp. 145–6.
152. *Born to Believe* (Cape, 1953).
153. *Diaries*, 28 September 1952, p. 704.
154. 7 October [1952]; *Letters*, p. 386.
155. 1 September [1952]; *Letters*, p. 380.
156. On 14 August 1952.

> You know what our unfortunate mutual friends are like. I would never show or read any letter of yours to any of them. My husband, who I love, admire and respect, & who needs me very much, would not consent to an annullment of his marriage. Randolph [Churchill] asked about my Catholic relatives and I told him that all of them, as well as Trim, David Jones & a few others, had sent messages of love & wishes for my happiness with the exception of yourself. This does not mean that I do not know you acted rightly in writing to me as you did.[157]

Waugh's response was startlingly honest:

> ... I don't think it presumptuous to believe that I might have influenced you, if I had not fallen in love.... As a friend I might have shown you – but I dont like amitiés amoureuses with a religious flavour. I can think of several & they stink.
>
> I am haunted by the memories of another not very distant tragedy, when I did give advice, disasterously [*sic*]. An American Catholic girl married outside the Church.... Then she was widowed, repented & was received back. She asked me what she should have done and I said: 'If you want to commit adultery or fornication & cant resist, do it, but realize what you are doing, and dont give the final insult of apostasy.' Well the girl followed my advice next time & was killed eloping. So my advice isn't wasn't much help....[158]

This was the 'Kick' (Kathleen) Hartington story which had been nagging Waugh's conscience since her death in a 'plane crash in 1948.[159] Waugh had been similarly infatuated with her and appears to have blamed himself for her death as though the hand of God had smitten her for heeding his counsel.

This retreat into an almost child-like literalism had odd effects. Graham Greene recalls a dinner with Carol Reed, his wife 'Pempy', Catherine Walston and Alexander Korda. In the middle of the meal, Waugh was suddenly and violently rude to Korda. Greene, never having witnessed this aspect of Waugh's character before, later demanded an explanation. 'He had no right to bring his mistress to Pempy's house.' 'But', replied Greene, 'I was there with my mistress.' 'That is quite different. She is married.' Greene described this as 'a curious, ... almost Edwardian attitude' and was

157. Unpublished ALS from Clarissa Eden (Countess of Avon), 2 September 1952, from 1 Carlton Gardens, SW1; BL. 'Trim' was Katharine Asquith's son, the second Earl of Oxford and Asquith; David Jones was the Catholic poet and painter.
158. ALS to Clarissa Eden (Countess of Avon), 6 September 1952; *Letters*, pp. 381–2.
159. Kathleen Kennedy, eldest sister of President Kennedy, had married the Marquess of Hartington, heir to the Duke of Devonshire, in 1944. Four months later he was killed in action.

convinced that Waugh was not 'wearing his comic mask'.[160] The statement had been made bluntly, as a matter of fact.

Waugh retreated before Clarissa's snub, although he tried to make bad blood about her marriage until Ann Fleming told him to shut his trap or forfeit gossip. (Access to ministerial circles was crucial to her role as society hostess and she would be damned if she would allow Evelyn, much as she loved him, to ruin that intimacy by repeating her stories.) The incident marks Waugh's final withdrawal from the metropolitan *salon*. 'Do you feel that communications are ceasing', he wrote to Diana Cooper, '– not between us two thank God – but generally with most people. No one listens or wants to understand anything that anyone else says. That was what upset me in U.S.A. Now it seems to be here. I return from my rare trips to London feeling as if I had spent the time in a diver's suit trying to shout at other divers at the bottom of the sea – and no treasure to salvage. Only coral bones.'[161] The end of September found him in the Royal Crescent Hotel, Brighton, giving Laura her 'annual jaunt', making his unhappy visits to Belloc and Pakenham, and writing to Nancy requesting the destruction of an unpleasant letter he had written about Clarissa.[162] Another escape was in view – a trip to India – and another campaign. President Tito had been invited by Eden to visit London as a guest of honour. Waugh determined to make his experience of Old England as uncomfortable as possible.

160. Interview with Graham Greene, 14 September 1980.
161. ALS to Lady Diana Cooper, 22 October [1952], from Piers Court; BL; *MWMS*, p. 148.
162. Cf. *Letters*, p. 385.

IX

Mr Pinfold Sees It Through: September 1952–January 1955

The third round of the 'Tito tease' began in November 1952: Mr Waugh in the blue corner, Anti-Christ in the red. Rounds one and two had gone to Tito. Waugh's attempts first to cast doubt on his opponent's sex (on Vis, 1944) and then on his political credentials (in the suppressed report, 1945) had failed. Tito's position was stronger than ever, and so much so that he had dared to break with Stalin. As an independent Communist state and (theoretically at least) an ally, Yugoslavia was Britain's crucial pawn in the Cold War chess of eastern Europe. When a state visit was offered to cement diplomatic relations, Waugh sprang from his stool with the glint of battle in his eye. 'Would any popular paper print an article from me abusing Eden for inviting Tito here?' he asked Peters. 'If they would, the price would not be important provided I could be as truthful as I liked in the words I liked. A letter to the *Times* has been ignored & I want to let off steam.'[1]

It remained a difficult period in Peters's relationship with Waugh. The financial crisis, the dispute with Mayes, and now this produced small but cumulative irritations on both sides. Peters's business had expanded to become one of London's major literary agencies. J. B. Priestley, C. S. Forester, C. Day-Lewis, V. S. Pritchett, Julian Huxley and Nancy Mitford were also on his books and doing excellent trade. Much of the list reads like a roll-call of Waugh's 'enemies', a fact which perhaps embarrassed Peters in his dealings with other clients. But it was Waugh's insistence on outraging potential customers and on being treated with a deference normally only accorded to a reigning monarch that stretched his agent's patience to the limit. A restrained sigh seems to breathe through his reply: 'I really cannot tell whether I could place an article about Tito but if you care to write it I will do my best.'[2] '. . . Of course you can't know whether anyone wants . . . [it] . . . unless you ask them,' Waugh responded angrily. 'I shall be writing as a papist to complain at insult to papists. . . . Pray investigate [newspapers'] interest.'[3] And by way of rebuke he signed his letter 'Evelyn Waugh'. Peters passed the enquiry on to one of his young

1. Unpublished ALS, 19 November 1952; *Catalogue* E770, p. 193.
2. Unpublished TccLS, 20 November 1952; HRC.
3. Unpublished ALS, nd [c. 22 November 1952], from Royal Crescent Hotel, Brighton; *Catalogue* E771, p. 193.

assistants. Increasingly he left John Montgomery or Margaret Stephens to deal with Waugh.

Montgomery did well, securing Waugh a platform in the *Sunday Express* and, swallowing his distaste for Beaverbrook, Waugh let rip. 'Our Guest of Dishonour' is in his finest vein of barrack-room invective:

> [Tito] was busy [in 1944], as now, in the work for which he has a peculiar aptitude – hoodwinking the British. The Germans were then in retreat from the Balkans. Their only use for Yugoslavia was an escape route. The partisans lurked in the hills and forests and left the main roads to the Germans. They had two civil wars on their hands – against the Serbian royalists and the Croat nationalists. Tito's job was to persuade us to arm him for these wars under pretence of fighting the Germans. He succeeded.[4]

Cooking the facts was Waugh's speciality. The Partisans *did* fight the Germans before the retreat, and obstructed their regrouping elsewhere. The implication is that a braggart confidence trickster leading a band of cowards had swindled the British, but, as we have seen, Churchill and Maclean had clearly understood Tito's post-war objectives. Waugh was justified in suggesting that his Christian nation had colluded in setting up a Communist state. As usual, however, he wanted to have the argument both ways: the British had not only acted dishonourably but were also innocent dupes.

Waugh's picture of modern Yugoslavia plays with McCarthian zeal upon the horrors of Communist rule: '. . . with all the familiar, sickening concomitants of secret police and judicial murder.'[5] He ignores the 'judicial' murders by the Ustaše; he also refuses to distinguish between Stalin's and Tito's regimes. Tito, he says, has merely 'sought to postpone the fate which devours each Communist hero in turn, by the desperate step of quarrelling with Stalin.'[6] Courage is dismissed here as a motive. No, the break with Russia was an act of cowardice, even betrayal. Waugh recalls a vivid memory of Tito on Vis. He had just received his Marshal's cap from Stalin. 'It was not becoming by any standard. But Tito waddled about the island as proud as a dog with two tails because it came . . . from his Russian heaven.'[7] The man was thus condemned not only as swindler and poltroon, he also lacked breeding, had no 'style', was an oafish Common Man of the lowest variety, a snarling underdog snapping at the heels of his betters.

4. *SE*, 30 November 1952, 6; *EAR*, pp. 426–8.
5. *Ibid.*; *EAR*, p. 426.
6. *Ibid.*
7. *Ibid.*

Not surprisingly, a bullish coterie of English gentlemen in White's saw the pure reason of this argument and praised Waugh highly for it. Randolph Churchill led the pack. Sykes sent warm congratulations, condemning Wilson Harris's 'feeble' response in the *Spectator*.[8] Among the White's gang Eden became known as 'Jerk' and they were doubtless delighted by Waugh's taunt: 'Only when Christianity is at stake do our leaders show bland indifference.'[9] The scandal surrounding the Foreign Secretary's remarriage (roundly condemned by the *Church Times* as a breach of Canon Law) had set a precedent for public figures which Princess Margaret dared not follow with the divorced Peter Townsend. Waugh cared nothing for such Anglican wrangling, only for Clarissa's apostasy from *the* Church. Randolph, her cousin, cared little for either. Both men relished the opportunity to tear at the wound of Eden's embarrassment. It had been Eden, of course, who had refused Waugh permission to publish his report.

Two difficulties, however, obstructed Waugh's presentation of a serious case against injustice: he had always supported an hierarchical social system popularly supposed in 1952 to be unjust; and he had never shaken off his clownish persona. Earlier in the year, reports of his jokes had still been worth half a column. When he was writing the film script with Carol Reed, for instance, the *Express* had regurgitated a remark made on Waugh's return from California in 1947: 'It is the work of a great array of Hollywood film writers to distinguish the individual quality of a book, separate it – and obliterate it.'[10] Jokes against him were also good copy. Reaching even further back, A. P. Herbert had recalled in an after-dinner speech a story about Waugh's visit to the Pope (in 1945?): '[He] explained in detail to his Holiness why he had changed his faith. He spoke at some length. The Pope tried gently to intervene once or twice. Then he said firmly, "But, Mr. Waugh, you must remember that I am a Catholic too."'[11] The anecdotes are an interesting register of Waugh's public image, part of which (the rebarbative, conservative wit) he had consciously created, and part of which had run out of his control. In 1952 the popular press still maintained an affectionate esteem for his eccentricities. From this point, however, and the 'Tito tease' had a great deal to do with this, Waugh detected an element of mockery. A certain shrillness creeps into his tone here, a crack in his urbanity, which spoiled an otherwise strong case against religious persecution. It was the *Daily Express*, the sister paper of his vehicle for 'Our Guest . . .', which soon emerged as his chief enemy.

Waugh's public image bore small relation to the quiet routine of his

8. Unpublished ALS, 6 December 1952; BL.
9. 'Our Guest of Dishonour', *op. cit.*, p. 427.
10. *DE*, 18 June 1952, 3.
11. *Yorkshire Post*, 29 April 1952, 4.

private life. After publishing *Men At Arms*, he had settled to the completion of two minor literary projects: *The Holy Places* and *Love Among the Ruins*. The former comprised two essays and a brief preface, and was produced as a Christmas book by the Queen Anne Press in an elegant limited edition full of misprints. The latter was a reworking of the heap of rejected typescript (formerly entitled 'A Pilgrim's Progress') into a tighter but still trivial 9,000-word story. He was not proud of either book. *The Holy Places* contained little that was new;[12] *Love Among the Ruins*, he told Peters, '... is better, not perfect, but has hung about so long I have gone stale on it.'[13] Waugh pottered about the house and garden. Three hours a day he would spend at his desk, irritated by failing memory, rather pleased by increasing deafness, tinkering with these books or turning out elegant reviews. It was a silent, ordered life, governed by Faith and spiced by gossip from London and Paris. But it was a routine also regularly interrupted by the return of his children from school. By late November, with the Tito article accepted and *Love Among the Ruins* sold to Lilliput (no one else wanted it), Waugh was gripped by his perennial desire to be absent from 'family fun'.

'For 30 days from Dec. 3rd', he wrote to Montgomery, 'there is a great Popish festival at Goa – the final exposition of the body of St. Francis Xavier. I should dearly like to go for a week but plainly no paper would foot the bill ...?'[14] It was his forty-ninth birthday. Depressed and bored, he had suddenly struck on this expedition for a Christmas treat. Would Montgomery make enquiries at the Portuguese Embassy? He did so. The Ambassador knew of only one ship and that had sailed. Perhaps Mr Waugh would like to telephone to discuss the matter personally? In the meantime, Montgomery tried the old channels and suggested that *Life* commission an article. *Life* refused. *Everybody's* refused. By the time *Picture Post* accepted, Waugh was already in India, having flown out at his own expense on 15 December.

At a time when the strict embargo on foreign travel was still in force and peers of the realm were reduced to 'caravanning' in the South of France, it is worth asking how Waugh always managed to escape in such style. His own bank had refused to give him even £20 in rupees, explaining that only £10 of currency was allowed. The £310 he needed came from Coutts, who

12. The first essay, 'St. Helena: Empress', was the text of Waugh's radio talk; the second, 'The Holy Places', was his *Life* article. Only the preface, 'Work Abandoned', was new. In that he refers to a youthful scheme for his life's work: successive volumes tracing England's connection with the Holy Land through the lives of 'St Helena, Lord Stratford de Redcliffe, General Gordon etc.' (cf. Vol. 1, p. 415). These books, he says, would now remain unwritten: Britain's recent record in the Holy Land had been shameful.
13. Unpublished ALS, 12 November 1952, from Piers Court; *Catalogue* E768, p. 192.
14. Unpublished ALS, 28 November 1952, from Piers Court; *Catalogue* E772, p. 193.

held the Trust, in the form of travellers' cheques: £210 was for Portuguese India; £100 for the Sterling Area. Waugh was not allowed to draw cash from the Trust except to buy goods for his poor children. Did Peters sidestep the rules to allow a loan against future income? If he did, he did not use his own money (Coutts was not his bank), nor was Waugh entirely successful in recouping his outlay. *Picture Post* agreed to only 150 guineas – half the sum Montgomery was seeking at first – although for 1,200 words it was a handsome enough contract.

Ensconced in the luxurious Mandori Hotel, Waugh began to realize, perhaps for the first time, that his market value was falling. *Picture Post* wanted him to cable a sketch to accompany their photographs by 3 January at the latest. It was all very unsatisfactory. 'Cable communications with Goa are very bad,' he replied, having wired his story but discovered no arrangements by the magazine for 'collect' transmission. 'I had to get a local doctor to stand surety for the large sum involved. It is therefore important that there should be no hitch in this for my personal honour & the honour of England.'[15] Peters must have smiled at this, but Waugh did not appear to be joking.

Away from what he now took to be the land of his persecution, Waugh could happily stand on his dignity. The Goanese he found 'very soft & friendly'[16] and eager to treat him deferentially. Since his time with Fr Mather in British Guiana (1933),[17] Waugh had been consistently drawn to embattled outposts of the Faith. Goa, still a Portuguese dependency, a tiny enclave on the west coast of Nehru's independent India, was holding out against the Hindus and Moslems. This warm-weather pilgrimage to a thoroughly Catholic culture suited Waugh perfectly. During the 1930s his ideas about Catholic internationalism had been influenced by Belloc. The experience of vital religious cultures in Mexico and in America had changed all that. Waugh was no longer an 'in the steps of Caesar' man,[18] but one who celebrated all Catholic strongholds of whatever racial origin. 'Convent of S. Monica vast and fascinating,' he noted in his diary, 'Belloc "Europe and the Faith" my foot.'[19] True, the cultures he admired still derived from the Mediterranean, but, as he became increasingly insular in his private life, so he became more of an internationalist in religious matters.

The diary and letters of this period give an odd impression of Waugh as a kind of first-class refugee: the citizen of the world who is simultaneously a Displaced Person. As a visiting celebrity he received priority treatment

15. Unpublished ALS, 2 January 1953, np [Mandori Hotel, Goa]; *Catalogue* E775, pp. 193–4.
16. ALS to Laura Waugh, 21 December 1952; *Letters*, p. 388.
17. Cf. Vol. 1, pp. 322–3.
18. Cf. Vol. 1, p. 440; also pp. 426 and 435.
19. *Diaries*, 22 December 1952, p. 708.

from the Archbishop coadjutor and the Patriarch. The Indian Consul-General provided a government car. Waugh had come supplied with trade-goods, copies of *Campion* and *The Holy Places*, which he dispensed liberally. Respectful servants were in plentiful supply. But temporal comforts, so crucial in England, seemed marginal in Goa. Like Assisi in 1936, Goa was full of the Grace of God. And in this mood, at home in the Household, he could even become sentimental about his family, blowing epistolary kisses to his children, feeling slightly maudlin over his solitary Christmas dinner. His isolation, as he explained rather unfeelingly to Laura, was not painful – 'I am happy alone so long as there are new things to see. . . .'[20] – but it was isolation nevertheless. Like Crouchback, he was not *simpatico*.

What he saw impressed him deeply. In the 1930s he had been fascinated by Alfonso de Albuquerque as 'a man of the Crusades', a kind of military missionary,[21] and had excused the brutality of his regime. Now Waugh was willing to admit that 'Portuguese rule was violent in its early days, neglectful later; only in the present generation has it begun to redeem its past.'[22] St Francis Xavier was Albuquerque's near contemporary and spiritual counterpart. The celebrations were to mark the four-hundredth anniversary of the death of this Jesuit priest, whose body had, until the eighteenth century, remained miraculously uncorrupted. Waugh dwelt eagerly on this physical evidence of divine intervention, rather disappointed, it seems, that the magic had worn off and that the body could now only be described as 'the relics': 'One brown stump of toe emerging from white wrapping. Body fully vested, one grey forearm and hand, and grey clay-like skull visible. I postponed my own veneration until I could make it more privately.'[23]

Returning next day to the Cathedral transept, Waugh found it equally crowded. He was led to the head of the queue, kissed the foot and retired to a five-course luncheon at the Patriarch's palace. Goa was flooded with pilgrims. The closing date of the exposition had been twice extended. 'Natives still reverence statues, kissing and leaving coins even when in museum.'[24] Such simple faith came as a draught of vintage after the spiritual desert of England. 'I see no reason to exhaust myself & spend a lot of

20. 26 December [1952]; *Letters*, pp. 388–9.
21. Cf. Vol. 1, pp. 440–1. Albuquerque was a Portuguese *conquistador* who for six years (1509–15) was in supreme command of the Portuguese Indies from the mouth of the Red Sea to the Malay Peninsula. Waugh liked Elaine Sanceau's biography of the man but had one reservation: 'She is apt to treat his devotions as a quaint conceit of the times, rather than as an essential of his character. . . . Nor is there any reason to suppose that in his last hours, with the cross in his hands, he was . . . broken hearted. . . . He was simply a dying soldier making his peace with God' (*Nash's Pall Mall Magazine*, 24 November 1936, 16).
22. 'Goa: The Home of a Saint', *Month* 10 (December 1953), 325–35; *EAR*, pp. 448–56. In America it appeared in *Esquire* 40 (December 1953), 83, 226–9.
23. *Diaries*, 19 December 1952, p. 705.
24. *Ibid.*

money when I am so content here,' he wrote to Laura.[25] But within five days impatience had erupted:

> I have changed my plans & propose to leave here early next week ... having come so far & perhaps never being able to afford to return, I think it foolish not to see some of the splendours of Southern India. So I shall go to Mysore and move about from there as opportunity arises.[26]

He did, and opportunity arose for an exhausting motor tour of Indian erections: the fifty-foot statue of Gomateshwara, for instance, a single stone which he approached, swinging, shoeless and uncomfortable, in a wicker chair on the shoulders of bearers, up 600 steps. Hassan, Belur, Halebid, Hoysaleshwara, Bangalore, Madura, Trivandrurm – the tour of medieval buildings progressed relentlessly, and, ultimately, Waugh was grudgingly impressed, although Oriental art rarely moved him and the obscene sculptures he had sought after reading Huxley's *Jesting Pilate* had proved disappointing. He flew back to Bangalore, spent a dreary half-day in Bombay buying trinkets for his children and took a 'plane to Rome.

Before leaving England, Waugh had promised, on his return, to be Alfred Duggan's best man. Still an impoverished and obscure author, Duggan clung to his relationship with Waugh not only out of love but also because it represented a purchase on the world of 'influence'. Duggan was in a difficult position, a man with a history of weakness caught between two strong-minded women. His mother, Lady Curzon, opposed the match; his fiancée, Laura Hill, was equally determined on rapid consummation. Lady Curzon could only see Alfred as a waif requiring her protection. Both women, it seems, regarded the other as predatory and claustrophobic. Into this emotional vortex Waugh had been drawn as arbitrator and protector.

Waugh's stamp of approval had apparently convinced Lady Curzon of the social credentials of the alliance. She had emphasized to Alfred, however, that, should he marry before securing salaried employment, she would not attend the ceremony. Unable to imagine his ignoring this ultimatum, she had settled to the comfortable anticipation of indefinite delay – with her son still safely under her roof. But she had reckoned without Miss Hill's next strategy, which was to rent Alfred a bed-sitting room in London and to concentrate his mind on the date of the ceremony: 7 January 1953. Lady Curzon had first heard of this from her relations in Buenos Aires. Angry and humiliated, she had written to Waugh: 'Poor Alfred does not dare call his soul his own ... [he] is very weak. Laura Hill is *determined* to get married at once. I feel if *you* would advise him to wait

25. Unpublished section of ALS to Laura Waugh, 21 December [1952]; *Letters*, p. 388.
26. Unpublished section of ALS to Laura Waugh, 26 December [1952]; *Letters*, p. 388.

until he had found a job he would listen to you.'[27] Waugh, on the contrary, advised marriage, but had smoothed over the difficulty by agreeing to be best man.

At the root of this argument lay money and, just as Waugh marshalled his Catholic troops to attack Tito, so he rallied them in support of Duggan. Hollis had already taken an interest and held out some hopes of a school-teaching post. Woodruff was alerted and unearthed an acquaintance from Gabbitas and Thring. 'There are only two things I can do,' Duggan explained to Waugh, 'milk cows and write books.'[28] But, since he now spurned the udder, had gone down without a degree and had yet to make a living wage from writing, his prospects in his fiftieth year were bleak. 'I have been practically a hermit for many years,' he explained:

> I don't know anyone else who can be trusted to behave properly in a church. If you were there, not only would you do it all in a dignified and impressive manner, but all the press photographers and columnists of London would come too, and that would be good publicity in my search for a salary.[29]

Waugh was not offended by this stark explanation. He understood the logistics of self-promotion. Alfred needed help: that was the only issue.

Waugh had offered to shorten his Goa trip so as to be back by the 7th. Duggan, refusing to allow this, had postponed the ceremony for a week. Waugh had promised to be there and someone, presumably Duggan, had leaked the news to the papers. 'Evelyn Waugh', the *Mail* reported, '. . . flies 5,000 miles from Goa . . . next week for a London wedding.'[30] Everything was set to re-launch Duggan as a 'Society' novelist. But it was not to be. Good as his word, Waugh reached Rome punctually, only to find the airport fogbound. The next morning he tried again, but there was a further twenty-four hours' delay. Sadly, he cabled that he could not get back in time. Happily, he abandoned the barbarities of air travel to complete his journey on the *Golden Arrow*.

The year 1953 began badly for Waugh and ended worse: trouble with his children, more trouble with the Inland Revenue and his agents, the next novel dragging to a dead stop, quarrels, persecution mania. Just before Waugh's departure for Goa, Peters had received a letter from Mayes's American solicitors. Mayes, having rejected 'A Pilgrim's Progress', had now rejected *Love Among the Ruins* and had exhausted his patience. He was suing through the English courts for $4,677. Peters, it seems, had held

27. Unpublished ALS, 7 December 1952, from Bodiam Manor, Robertsbridge, Sussex; BL.
28. Unpublished ALS, 7 September 1952, from Bodiam Manor etc.; BL.
29. Unpublished ALS to Evelyn Waugh, 23 October 1952, from Bodiam Manor etc.; BL.
30. *DM*, 8 January 1953, 4.

this news back so as not to spoil Waugh's holiday. But there was no escaping the spectre in January, nor the fact that the Revenue required £1,300. It was a depressing start to the year.

Waugh paid the tax but insisted that Peters fight Mayes. 'Waugh', Peters explained to Matson, 'is extremely annoyed.... The money was not an advance.... It was payment for an option.'[31] The situation was delicate. Matson had been present at Waugh's original interview with the 'good housekeeper' and Waugh thus held his American agent responsible for any confusion. For Peters, embarrassment was doubled. He wished neither to offend Matson (whose services he valued) nor Mayes, an excellent customer for other clients. 'I'll do what I can to get Mayes to call off the legal hounds,' Matson replied, 'but I'm not sanguine, not at all. A gesture, including a tangible offering could soften [him], but nothing short of that, I'm sure. He's emotional about this....'[32] So was Waugh. To him, Matson's response was disgustingly 'wet'.

On his return, Waugh had set to work dismantling engravings to illustrate *Love Among the Ruins*: 'With dazzling eyes and a magnifying glass and razor blade I attempted adaption.'[33] The task absorbed him for two months in a way that writing never could. Creating a collage from engravings of Canova's work, he reconstructed them by inking in the missing limbs and heads. Then he added the mischievous, dystopian touches: the heroine's golden beard, the signs. It was to be his last appearance as an illustrator, and a grand and witty one with those perfectly deformed neo-classical figures.[34]

He wanted to be left alone. The year's excursions were already mapped out: Easter retreat at Downside; a return trip to India, paid for, he hoped, by *Life*; a lecture tour to Buenos Aires; harvest-home holiday for Laura some time in the autumn. His literary work would consist of an essay on Goa for *Life*, odd reviews and, most important, volume two of his war saga. How differently things turned out.

Peters saw danger on the horizon: *folie de grandeur* in full sail, flying the Cross of St George. Waugh's contempt for his customers was at last seriously imperilling his livelihood. Something, at least, had to be done to placate the Americans and, when Stanley Salmen visited England, Peters saw his chance. Salmen, Managing Director of Little, Brown, had always regarded Waugh with the near-religious awe reserved for the 'real artist' who was also a best-seller. Waugh's erratic letters had flown into the Boston office, predicting disaster for his American editions. Salmen's solemn epistles had returned full of steady, schoolmasterly praise. Waugh found

31. Unpublished TccLS to Harold Matson, 20 January 1953; HRC.
32. Unpublished TccLS to A. D. Peters, 28 January 1953; HRC.
33. *Diaries*, 18 January 1953, p. 714.
34. Waugh's collages are in the Iconography Department, HRC.

him imperturbably jokeless. The idea of their spending a week-end *à deux* in the silence of Piers Court struck chill into the novelist's heart. But Salmen wanted to meet his client and Peters had suggested that this was not something to be avoided. Serious business was at stake and Waugh's financial plight left him in no position to refuse. Salmen wished to suggest something Waugh had always rejected: cheap hardback reprints of the novels. 'It seems to me', Peters remarked, 'that $13,500 free of tax is not to be sneezed at.'[35] That was just the advance. Waugh, pleading poverty ('can't entertain Americans here in winter),'[36] asked Peters to arrange a date at White's. Then, noticing to his horror that Mrs Salmen was also due, he got Peters to deposit her at the Hyde Park Hotel for Laura to entertain. The whole affair was purgatorial but he went through with it and, without argument, changed his mind about cheap editions.

Waugh's contacts with the American publishing world were now uniformly prickly. Salmen's visit coincided with the developing Mayes crisis, an ill omen for the unwary guest. 'I looked for Salmen's name among the drowned in the Irish crossing,' Waugh wrote to Peters. 'He seems to have survived so I will meet him. . . .':

> Matson's letter is sublimely smug. He seems quite unconscious of his own delinquency in the [Mayes] matter. Well, it is blackmail. We can't have an action so please make a complete settlement. . . . I wish Matson would sell 'Love Among The Ruins'. . . . I am going to propose to Salmen a book called 'A Papist Abroad' . . . Clare [Booth Luce] writes to me that Henry Luce is in a rage with me because of a conversation reported in Thomas Merton's diaries which Henry has misread so even the astute & indefatigable Matson may fail to fix a contract for India. . . .[37]

On the same day, *Life* had rejected the India idea, having earlier refused *Love Among the Ruins*. Matson explained that if Waugh wanted 'expenses' similar to those demanded for 'The American Epoch', then there was little point in proceeding: 'I know of no magazine here that will guarantee that kind of money. . . .'[38] Such deals were only available through 'personal arrangement' and Waugh, it seems, had slaughtered that golden goose. In an attempt to repair the damage with the Luces, he turned up a week later at a cocktail party given to celebrate the opening of *Life*'s London office: 'I had decided to go as a means of making friends with them. I don't think I can have achieved my object. . . . No memories of the evening.'[39]

35. Unpublished TccL, 26 January 1953; HRC.
36. Unpublished ALS to A. D. Peters, 27 January [1953], from Piers Court; *Catalogue* E783, p. 195.
37. Unpublished ALS, 2 February 1953; *Catalogue* E784, p. 195.
38. Unpublished TLS from Harold Matson to A. D. Peters, 4 February 1953; HRC.
39. *Diaries*, 13 February 1953, p. 715.

'Was our evening out hell?' he asked Diana Cooper. 'I was looking forward to it so much & what must I do but get pissed. I am so awfully sorry & ashamed.... I have a memory of ... arriving at my hotel in the middle of a Caledonian Ball with pipers in the lift & you telephoning & my thinking it was the pipers.'[40] 'Darling Bo,' she replied:

> What islands we are – never knowing what's going on in other's lands. *I* thought our dinner delightful. You were tremendously foxed at 'Time & Life', as was Ed. Stanley & others. I feared for our evening – but you were docile & deigned to be led to Wheelers. There you were sat in a corner in discreet light.... Before [the meal] I'm rather sorry to say you sobered completely.... I cried only once not from pain but emotion because you assured me so very many people dead & alive were praying for me. You suggested, without enthusiasm, following the evening up with a bottle of Pop at the Hyde Park but there is something throttling to me in its atmosphere of respectable gloom ... that I said it was better not.
>
> When I got home ... and feeling my song ½ sung I called you to give thanks, & for reminisance [*sic*], & love's sake. I got a very sharp 'These are Mr Waugh's appartments [*sic*]' & a 'hang up', a viscious [*sic*] one, because I laughed. 10 mins. later, pride successfully swallowed, I tried again, only to get 'Put me immediately onto the mannager [*sic*]' 'It's only BABY,' I whined & pleasant good nights were said....
>
> I wish you'd go to the Abbey. You say you can't bring up the pretty chickens on what you make – but £250 for 4 hours pageantry and raportage [*sic*] surely helps ... as would giving up oyster snacks at Wiltons before going to lunch or dine with friends.
>
> What of the bewitched child?[41]

For 'tremendously foxed' read 'drunk and boisterous'. 'The Luce papers are definitely unapproachable ...,' Waugh wrote to Peters, 'I made myself conspicuous at their London reception, addressing everyone as "Mrs Ambassador Luce", I am told.'[42] There was to be no lucrative contract for the lengthy article on Goa which he had rewritten on discovering the *Picture Post* one to be 'cut and garbled'.[43] Ultimately, the only paper Peters could get to publish it in England was the *Month*.[44] Waugh's journalism was

40. ALS, nd [? mid-February 1953], from Piers Court; BL; *MWMS*, p. 157.
41. ALS, 28 February [1953], from Château de St Firmin, Vineuil, Oise; BL; *MWMS*, p. 158.
42. Unpublished ALS, 22 March 1953, from Piers Court; *Catalogue* E799, p. 198. Clare Booth Luce had recently been appointed American Ambassador to Rome.
43. Unpublished APC to John Montgomery, 23 January 1953, from Piers Court; *Catalogue* E781, p. 194.
44. 'Goa: The Home of a Saint', *op. cit.*

elegantly composed but difficult to market.[45] And when offered a 'money for jam' job, he tended to refuse. The Beaverbrook press had suggested that Waugh cover the Coronation for them in June but he would not demean himself, as he told Lady Diana, by celebrating the Protestant monarchy for £250. Waugh, like Gervase Crouchback, recognized no British monarch after James II.

Lady Diana's letter offers an intriguing glimpse of his erratic personality: the benign diner-out; the savage riposte defending privacy; his taste for the hotel's 'atmosphere of respectable gloom'. Waugh's raids on London generally followed the same pattern: accumulated drunkenness over several days; collapse into maudlin loneliness; desire never to leave home again. The 'bewitched child' was Hatty, dyslexic and temporarily withdrawn from school. He loved her eccentricities and played them up to his friends, especially to Nancy, her godmother: 'Hatty has become the despair of us all.... She won't eat.... She yells. In her rare moments of self-command she is extremely droll. Do adopt her.'[46] But his favourite was, and remained, Margaret. 'My sexual passion for my ten year old daughter is obsessive,' he informed Ann Fleming. '... I can't keep my hands off her. Her school report was abusive so she is writing daily copies. At the moment she is sprawled with her nose on the paper writing: Picasso is a disgusting beast; Sartre is just an ass.'[47] This was why his daughters (and so many of his women friends) loved him. He was strict and curt, selfish about his own pleasures, but he was all the time a parodic paterfamilias, encouraging the violation of bourgeois 'correctness'. If a school were critical of his child, he would support the child – in most cases. With the boys he was more severe. Charm was the essential quality he sought and, unfortunately for Bron and, later, James, Papa could discover little of this in male adolescents.

Waugh's family at this stage was an educational disaster. Meg wrote semi-literate letters begging to be released from her convent school, and Waugh cared too much to refuse: 'I love you & will not let you be really unhappy if I can prevent it.... I really am very worried you should be unhappy, darling little girl.'[48] Meg was brought home. From June to September 1953 both younger girls were at Piers Court, sometimes taught erratically by their parents, more often left to themselves, until they went off together to St Mary's Convent at Ascot. Teresa, the eldest, was already there, unhappy (of course) and wanting to leave as soon as possible. It was

45. Cf. unpublished TLS from Gus Lobrano (of *NY*, 12 March 1953; HRC), rejecting the Goa article as 'pretty special[ized] and, aside from a few brilliant passages, not really very lively or interesting. But we'd be interested to see other travel pieces by Mr. Waugh, preferably not dealing with shrines.'
46. nd [1953]; *Letters*, p. 398.
47. 1 September [1952]; *Letters*, p. 380.
48. Whit Sunday [24 May] 1953; *Letters*, p. 402.

only with difficulty that Waugh had managed to persuade Downside to take Bron back in January, and the situation on that front soon became critical.

The divide between Waugh's public and his private world yawned ever wider. Few outsiders would have credited him with the tenderness he felt towards his family at a time when in his professional life he was becoming increasingly neurotic about money and prestige. So much depended on America. He, however, had lost all interest in the country except as a source of revenue, and America, it seems, was rapidly losing interest in him. Matson did well to get Mayes to agree that half the sum should be discounted as option money if the other half were paid immediately. Peters instructed Little, Brown to send a cheque,[49] and the matter was settled out of court. Waugh, indeed, could not have gone to law without the illegality of the station-wagon deal emerging. But it was another humiliation for which he required another scapegoat. Matson, he told Peters, was not only smug and wet, but idle and incompetent. Matson – who had set up the *Brideshead* deal and secured its author's financial future, and who had been posting clandestine shipments of cigars since 1945 – must be sacked. Waugh craved his pound of flesh. If Matson had taken any commission on the original deal with Mayes, Waugh insisted, he wanted it refunded.

Peters, dismayed and offended, refused this request,[50] but he could not dissuade Waugh from general revenge:

> While you are in New York will you please make discreet enquiries for a diligent and honest literary agent to take Matson's place. I know that my present business there is very small beer but it might grow & be worth a zealous young man's acceptance.... Laura says will you please send some tins of thin streaky high quality bacon.
>
> Since I have sweated up the anti-Tito case ad nauseam I am prepared to make money on it, if any American paper would like a diatribe.[51]

Peters replied with restrained irritation, still hoping to keep the lid on this row. Matson's behaviour had been perfectly proper and efficient. It would be extremely inconvenient to start dealing with a new American agent for a single client. Explaining the situation to Matson, he said that he had managed to persuade Waugh not to remove his custom. 'You have set me a hard task ...,' Peters wrote to Waugh, 'but I will do my best. If, in the

49. For $2,333.50, payable from the advance for the first three cheap editions.
50. Cf. unpublished TccL to Evelyn Waugh, 24 March 1953; HRC: 'I'm afraid I don't quite understand your letter. You received from Mayes the total sum of $4,677, partly in cash and partly in kind. You have refunded half, so that you retain the other half, namely $2,333.50. In my view, Matson and I are entitled to commission on this sum. We have taken commission on only $2,000, so if anybody owes anybody anything I would say that you owe us about $33!'
51. Unpublished ALS to A. D. Peters, 22 March 1953, from Piers Court; *Catalogue* E799, p. 198.

result, you find yourself no better off, you will console yourself with the conviction that you are no worse off. . . . I don't know how much of an issue Tito is in the U.S. . . .'[52] Peters knew perfectly well how little interest such an article would generate and how dangerous it might be to sales. He wanted to keep Waugh quiet for a while. Enough damage had been done in England.

The Tito tease had run on unabated for four months since that first article in the *Express*. The *New Statesman*, the *Spectator*, the *Sunday Times*, the *Sunday Express* and *The Times* had all received gruff, cocksure letters from Piers Court. Much to Waugh's delight, strong protests from the Yugoslav Embassy had arrived at the *Express* offices, accompanied by demands (ignored) that they should publish Tito's point of view. Graham Greene had pitched in on Waugh's side in the *New Statesman*, and the Catholic troops began to muster. Jim Utley of the British Legation to the Holy See wrote to assure Waugh of their appreciation. Support also came from the Church of England when Waugh found himself temporarily aligned with Dean Duncan-Jones of Chichester. Waugh was far from alone in this battle. When he travelled to Glasgow to lecture on the subject in March more than three thousand Catholics turned out.[53] By happy coincidence, the award of the James Tait Black prize to *Men At Arms* had just been announced, thus swelling Waugh's Scottish celebrity.

No one was better at whipping up a scandal. News percolated back to him that Eden was looking ill and, scenting blood, Waugh twisted the bayonet. A *Sunday Chronicle* reporter was invited to Piers Court, where he told Waugh 'that the security police are appalled at the task before them and insist on a bullet-proof car, a secret residence, a secret list of engagements'.[54] Three days later came Waugh's response:

> The possibility of a bomb being flung at Tito in London . . . is another thing that makes the invitation wildly imprudent. I am not surprised our security people are worried. . . . For if Tito were to be killed (and I have no doubt the Russians would like to arrange it) the Communists will be presented with the finest opportunity for an attack in many years. If he is not killed it is because special precautions have been taken, such precautions that his visit is quite worthless, for he won't be able to see anything at all of English life. He can't go round like the Queen of Holland and see how the ordinary people live. . . .[55]

52. Unpublished TccLS from A. D. Peters, 24 March 1953; HRC.
53. Cf. *Diaries*, 16 March 1953, p. 717. On 8 March Waugh lectured to the Catholic Truth Society in St Andrew's Hall.
54. *Ibid.*, 9 March 1953, p. 717.
55. 'It's Dangerous, Says Waugh', interview with James Dow, *Sunday Chronicle*, 15 March 1953, 1.

Any argument would do. (What did Waugh care for the 'ordinary people'?) But momentum was building and, although he was bored by the campaign, he was nevertheless enjoying a sense of national leadership. The onslaught was continued through letters to those who knew the Edens – Lady Diana, Nancy, Ann Fleming – sowing spiteful gossip. His hatred obsessed him: 'genuine public spirit', as he admitted to Nancy, 'fatally combined with the itch to have the last word.'[56] Waugh even wrote to Malcolm Muggeridge, then Editor of *Punch*, offering an article stating Tito to be a woman. Muggeridge accepted it but refused to print it until after the Marshal's departure. Waugh cancelled the piece. The whole affair was rather like that: Waugh convincing himself, as he had at school and briefly in the army, that he stood in the vanguard of a multitude of the just, applauded for his captaincy, but all the time catching hints that people did not trust his judgment.

Ultimately, he had little effect. Tito came, was met by Eden, Churchill and the Duke of Edinburgh as planned, saw and, to a large extent, conquered. There were no bombs and there was little protest. To save face, Waugh described the visit as 'an undisguised fiasco' and proclaimed himself delighted.[57] But, whatever the justice of his cause, he had ended again by appearing politically immature. Diana Cooper's response to his attempts to make bad blood was curt: 'Pipe down on Clarissa & concentrate yr. mockery on Eden. Clarissa baiting smacks to many of thwarted love.'[58] And, of course, she was right.

Peters left for America with all this buzzing in his head and small hope of finding much trade for Waugh. Matson had had enough. 'I hope you would not find it embarrassing to undertake to reconvert Evelyn Waugh to his wish for another agent . . .', he wrote. 'I don't have to tell you that there is very little for this office in the way of income.'[59] Waugh in fact owed Matson $230 and a stream of rejections had greeted *Love Among the Ruins*. It was never published as a separate volume in the States. Even so, Peters carried one piece of good news. 'If you see poor Salmen', Waugh had written, 'tell him I have begun the second volume of Magnum Opus *excellently. . . .*'[60]

56. 14 March 1953; *Letters*, p. 394.
57. ALS to Nancy Mitford, nd [March 1953], from Piers Court; *Letters*, p. 396.
58. ALS from Lady Diana Cooper, nd [March 1953], np [Château de St Firmin etc.]; BL; *MWMS*, p. 163.
59. Unpublished TLS from Harold Matson to A. D. Peters, 17 March 1953; HRC. Matson added: 'While I don't hold myself entirely blameless in the Good Housekeeping matter, neither do I find Waugh blameless and the compromise worked out should have satisfied him. As a point of interest I decline his request that I refund the commission. . . . This office charged no commission on any part of the station wagon. After having persuaded him to carry on with me, you certainly have a right to feel ungrateful; but . . . I think that . . . [this] . . . is an occasion for termination of our relationship.'
60. Unpublished ALS to A. D. Peters, 22 March 1953, *op. cit.*

Two weeks before his Glasgow lecture, Waugh had observed Lent by giving up sleeping draughts and, with a clear head, had written those brilliant opening pages designed to make Connolly (and Yorke) squirm again: 'White's in an air raid with Archie Groom [the hall porter] as hero.'[61] Concentration, however, had soon disintegrated: a month's Tito-baiting, the Downside retreat and a death in the family had forced Waugh to set his novel aside. Aunt Elsie, the last connection with Arthur Waugh's childhood home, was gone, and the Midsomer Norton house, scene of so much contentment in Evelyn's early life, was to be sold up. 'Paid a final visit to the house without emotion,' he noted. 'Collected a few objects and papers. Margaret greatly enjoyed herself among the oddments.'[62] His cold eye passed over these 'oddments', as it had over Arthur's letters in 1943, seeing them as little more than detritus. And, by an odd reflex, this inability to feel as others felt caused him pain: not envy but remorse. While he was in Goa, his mother had suffered a serious haemorrhage. She continued to live in the Hampstead flat, assisted by a resident housekeeper, Mrs Yaxley, who Waugh always referred to as her 'maid'. He occasionally visited her for an hour, only to leave ashamed of his relief to be gone. Catherine was much enfeebled, rather poor and lonely. On one occasion she wrote timorously to ask if he would buy her a pair of gloves to attend a wedding. She lived for his visits and those of the children, adoring the entire family, but rarely seeing them. She knew better, however, than to press her claims for attention. Waugh and she kept their distance as he watched her dying. For him their intimacy was irrecoverable. He was embarrassed by her 'middle-class' sentimentality.

Elsie's death caused more disruption. Alec, as head of the family, was Elsie's residuary legatee. Since he lived abroad, Evelyn had to act for him and he discovered a testamentary minefield. After Mayes and Tito, he was in no mood to brook delay from the country solicitor trying to disentangle Elsie's confused bequests. Waugh strode into the business like a colonel with a swagger stick and whacked about smartly. Those who tried to explain that matters were more complicated than he would have them, were sharply rebuked. A lengthy correspondence with his brother came close to open acrimony. As for the solicitor, Evelyn was convinced that he was not only smug and wet but idle and incompetent: another booby trying to make an ass of him – and the poor provincial whose firm had administered the sisters' legal business and their father's before them was, eventually, sacked. It was a year rich in sackings. Percy Popkin also disappeared in the purge.

61. ALS to Lady Diana Cooper, 18 March [1953], from Piers Court; BL; *MWMS*, p. 161. Waugh seems to have begun writing on 22 February 1953.
62. *Diaries*, 9 April 1953, p. 718.

Waugh wanted his (tax-free) money from the estate to set his affairs in order and suspected his Tasmanian cousin of trying to seize everything. Much more important, however, he wanted to be rid of the business, to clear his mind and return to his novel. In seven months he had completed only a few pages and wherever he looked he saw his friends industrious and successful. Nancy was deep in research for a biography of Madame de Pompadour and about to begin writing; Betjeman was secure in his role as popular poet and 'radio personality'; Greene's *The Living Room* had opened in April to excellent reviews; Powell was Literary Editor of *Punch* and was at work on *The Acceptance World*; Connolly was a senior literary critic of the Sunday press; even Duggan had a book coming out and had found employment under the magnificent title of Archivist to the *Universe*.[63] Waugh grudged none of them their triumphs. Indeed, he cheered them on and kept a benevolent eye on their progress.

He was not jealous but he was competitive, and, as we have seen, paranoid at the thought of economy. His financial position was secure so long as he could keep writing. Even at his current, extravagant rate of expenditure, he could have lived on the American money for four years without writing a word. The 'Save the Children Fund', however, had put pressure on him, for while it supplied paintings, silver and fireplaces, it could not easily supply cash. Only those books written after the Trust's execution were exempt from its conditions. He was thus looking towards his war saga to finance his old age while simultaneously sensing a steady diminution of literary power. He was also suffering the inevitable nightmare of the bully. Increasingly the world appeared to be peopled by enemies jealous of his strengths and determined upon his humiliation.

In an attempt to refresh himself for a second onslaught on *Happy Warriors* (the working title of *Officers and Gentlemen*) Waugh accepted another invitation to visit Chantilly. His children were returning for the Easter holidays and it seemed sensible to escape them for ten days. The trip, or rather the nagging memory of it, revealed the first symptoms of mental breakdown.

*

Paris was sweltering in a heat-wave, which alone was enough to put Waugh in an ill-temper. He arrived exhausted and fractious to find no dinner until midnight and Duff Cooper in combative mood. The next day, rather drunk and intolerant of Waugh's conscientious ingratitude, Cooper tore into him

63. Douglas Woodruff secured him the post. The *Universe* is a Catholic weekly and the work allowed Duggan spare time for writing.

in an 'alarming outburst of rage and hate',[64] accusing him of 'sponging'. This was bad but it was not critical. The Coopers went away for a couple of days to attend the birth of their grand-daughter, Artemis, leaving Waugh sulking, and returned to find him placable. He had visited Nancy at Versailles (where she was writing *Pompadour*) and had enjoyed himself well enough pottering round Paris. To Lady Diana's mind, the early rupture, nothing unusual with those two irascible men, was healed. Waugh was more bored than she realized ('My dreariest trip abroad since Christopher and I went to Paris together'),[65] but he was not furious.

He returned, however, irritable and unable to work in a houseful of children, to be met by a series of further frustrations. The Inland Revenue, doggedly pursuing back-taxes on the 1945 Hollywood deal, had won their case in court. In May he abandoned his proposed lecture tour of South America.[66] In June, his daughter returned for a Coronation holiday and he felt obliged to stage a mock celebration. Then Graham Greene arrived, melancholy and in need of support. Waugh had heard reports of him and Catherine renting a small house in Barbados[67] and of his telling the Italian Ambassador that he (Greene) was no longer a practising Catholic. Waugh did his best to help, saddened by this theological dilemma but also shamed by his friend's generosity: '... very sweet and modest. Always judging people by kindness.'[68] Judging people by kindness was not something which came easily to Waugh, and at this stage he found it almost impossible. Greene's visit had coincided with the publication of *Love Among the Ruins*. 'Some kind reviews ...,' Waugh noted. 'Mostly positively abusive.'[69]

This was a wild over-reaction. At the time he admitted to Greene that '*Love Among the Ruins* was a bit of nonsense begun 3 years ago & hastily

64. *Diaries*, 18 April 1953, p. 719. This was probably the occasion on which Cooper described Waugh as 'a common little man' (cf. Vol. 1, p. 475).
65. *Ibid.*, 27 April 1953, p. 720.
66. Cf. unpublished ALS to John Montgomery, nd [c. 5 May 1953], np; *Catalogue* E806, p. 199. 'The demands of Criterio [the magazine supporting the venture] have become excessive....' Jaime Portenze of *Criterio* wanted a series of different lectures. Waugh would only write one, and repeat it before different audiences. There were also problems with 'expenses'.
67. Cf. ALS from Ann Fleming, Good Friday [3 April 1953]; *LAF*, p. 126: 'The menage that interested me most however, where [*sic*] your friends Graham Greene and Mrs. Ralston [Walston] (I can never remember her name correctly). Mr. R. [W.] arrived with them but tactfully left them after a very brief stay. I immediately continued the pursuit ... their address was number one bungalow, Tower Isle Hotel. I bombard[ed] them with invitations but was unable to smoke them out, though I finally extracted an invitation to cocktails.... [The bungalow] was several unchaperoned miles from the hotel, a perfect place for lovers, two bed, two bath, one patio private beach and swimming pool. Mrs. R. was dressed as a French porter but it did little to disguise her charms. Mr. Greene was very over anxious about the making of dry martinis, and offering peanuts and quite impossible to engage in seductive conversation ... is he living in sin? is he tortured? he remained remote from all, totally polite and holding the cocktail shaker as [a] kind of defensive weapon....' Mark Amory decorously omits the sentence: 'Mr. R. ... brief stay' and alters 'their address' to 'his address'.
68. *Diaries*, 5 June 1953, p. 721. Greene arrived on the 12th.
69. *Ibid.*

finished & injudiciously published.'[70] Waugh did not 'think it quite as bad as most reviewers do',[71] but he knew it to be below par. Given that, most notices were rather good, better perhaps than he could have expected. Connolly praised the book ('Reading time: half an hour. Sensation: delight and pleasure . . .'), lamenting its slightness only courteously: 'What a waste of his time – though not of ours – this elusive pastiche of himself, this science-hater's science fiction.'[72] The *TLS* was exuberant. *The Times* liked it. The Catholic press stood by him to a man. True, *Time & Tide* found it a rather 'weary' little book[73] and there was a general feeling that the master had taken a holiday from his great work-in-progress, but then Waugh would not have disagreed with either view. The few attacks came almost entirely from a single source: the Beaverbrook group. Nancy Spain led the pack with a silly review in the *Daily Express*,[74] followed quickly by Milton Shulman in the *Sunday Express*[75] and George Malcolm Thompson in the *Evening Standard*.[76] All these, but particularly the last, offered character assassination in the place of literary criticism. It was their hostility which caused Waugh to forget the others and, quite against his normal practice, to reply.

His article, ostensibly an objective critique of the decline in standards of contemporary reviewing, reveals a man in pain. 'Reviewers', he wrote, 'can greatly encourage or cruelly wound a young writer; perhaps also a very old one, fearful of failing powers.'[77] This was the nub of the matter. At forty-nine, Waugh saw himself in the latter category. His actual age allowed him to pretend unconcern and to sidestep accusations of weakness or narcissism.[78] But the sentence is undoubtedly personal in tone. Waugh was neither weak nor vain. He was, however, vulnerable. Certain kinds of attack instantly triggered a reaction: accusations of bad faith, criticisms from friends, corrections of factual error. These he had so far been able to shrug off with an outburst of rage or a benign dismissal. He was never troubled by political guilt. But this latest assault was a long-foreseen spectre. It accused him of the worst of all horrors: becoming a bore. A change was taking place in his identity as a public figure. The licensed fool needs to

70. 5 June [1953]; *Letters*, p. 404.
71. *Ibid.*
72. *ST*, 31 May 1953, 5; *CH*, pp. 352–3.
73. 'Waugh-Weariness', *Time & Tide*, 30 May 1953, 725–6.
74. 'Nancy Spain Reads a Book in Rome, A Book that Takes Her into the Vatican: So I Yawned . . .', *DE*, 29 May 1953, 4. She reviewed three books by Catholic authors, condemning only *Love Among the Ruins* as tedious.
75. 'What a Wet Squib, Mr. Waugh!', *SE*, 31 May 1953, 8.
76. 'Why So Gloomy, Mr. Waugh?', *ES*, 3 June 1953, 10.
77. 'Mr. Waugh Replies', *Spectator*, 3 July 1953, 23–4; *EAR*, pp. 440–3.
78. *Ibid.*, p. 441: '[Reviews] do not much concern the middle-aged. For this reason I can, I hope, without rancour or egotism, examine the work of the modern reviewer in the single light of my own latest book which has been pretty generally condemned.'

be found amusing when he is trying to make people laugh. Waugh maintained his fame by virtue of his talents and, like Greene, he found himself both spiritually endangered by them and addicted to their power. During the war those glimpses of himself in mirrors had offered mildly shocking confrontations. A similar split began to reveal itself in the Beaverbrook reviews. Who did these people think they were describing? That Evelyn Waugh was utterly different from his idea of himself. His (quite legitimate) complaints are made on literary and social grounds – the 'tendency to write about the author rather than the book ... assuming a personal intimacy with him which ... they do not enjoy'[79] – but the nightmare is in plain view. 'No work done except one review,' he noted. 'Everyone eagerly on the watch for failing powers.'[80]

Waugh was convinced of a Beaverbrook conspiracy and, as Donat Gallagher, the editor of Waugh's journalism, has pointed out, we cannot be sure that this was an illusion. Shulman, apparently, 'was not aware of any directive from Lord Beaverbrook, or of any collusion among the Beaverbrook reviewers, to attack Waugh. On the other hand George Malcolm Thompson was generally believed to reflect Beaverbrook's opinions fairly accurately.'[81] It seems likely, however, that Waugh *was* at this stage deluded, vastly over-estimating the tycoon's interest in him. So far as one can tell, Beaverbrook saw the novelist as a talented pipsqueak who adopted ludicrous stances far too regularly not to expect the occasional light-hearted poke in the eye. The *Express*, having aired his early views on Tito, perhaps grew impatient with the imperious neuroticism with which Waugh had pursued his quarry elsewhere.[82] Nevertheless, the vendetta Waugh detected was probably imaginary.

With this in mind, we have a context for the next row, later in the month, with Diana Cooper. She was stunned by it. Belloc, a closer friend of hers than of Waugh's, had died in July. Waugh wrote asking if she would attend the Requiem. No, she replied, she avoided the funerals of loved-ones wherever possible: 'The idea jars upon me – exhibition of grief. The society duty side does not, in my heart, *fit*.'[83] Then, sensing that he might take offence at her evading 'society duty', she tried to explain:

79. *Ibid.*, p. 442.
80. *Diaries*, 5 June 1953, p. 722.
81. *EAR*, p. 443, n. 1.
82. Cf. 'Waugh on Tito', *DE*, 9 March 1953, 6: 'Shriller and shriller becomes the voice of Evelyn Waugh ... as Tito's visit draws closer. Yesterday in Glasgow, talking in St. Andrew's Hall, he sneered at the invitation as "one of those hit or miss after-lunch inspirations to which our Prime Minister is liable." And he confessed to his audience yesterday: "I shook hands with 'it'." A rather undergraduate remark – but still good, slashing stuff....'
83. ALS from Lady Diana Cooper, 24 July 1953, from 5 Belgrave Square, SW; BL; *MWMS*, p. 175.

> You won't see what I feel & I don't expect you to, but I do expect you to love me & my affection for you brings out the peevish. We are both spoilt babies – you are deathly proud. I'm not, but I'm vulnerable to lack of spoiling. Someone long ago said to me in Italy – 'God repudiates old women'. I don't suppose he does but most men do [,] not unnaturally.
>
> You'll see Duff at Randy's [Randolph Churchill's] on 31st. He – Randy – asked me & I would have swallowed June [his wife], line & sinker to see you – but I am taking my children to Chantilly. . . .[84]

It was a letter full of love, gossip, self-denial. She assumed their Easter skirmish to be forgotten. Waugh's reply was vicious, utterly misjudging her tone and accusing her of heresy and malice. When she responded she did so in the third person, unable even to address him by name or to sign the letter:

> Baby stupidly assumed that you would recognise Belloc's 'deathly proud' ('Godolphin Horn was nobly born') & in that light spirit the words were used. . . . She would love to think your letter . . . was not so coldly aimed to wound – arrows heavy as lead curare tipped.
>
> She can't think that she *subscribed* to the womans dictum about God & old women?[85]

She did not – as Waugh would have seen had he read carefully. His whole construction of her letter was crazy. He saw her refusal to attend the Requiem as an insult not only to Belloc but also to himself, as if his insistence on going were 'a Popish quirk'. And he went further, revising in his overheated imagination the sequence of events at Chantilly: Duff and Diana, he believed, had left the house to offend him. She was astounded. True, Waugh had offered to leave, explaining that he felt himself to be on his hosts' nerves. But she had denied this and brought him back 'to an appreciative & warm fold for a week'. Now he was telling the story in such 'a deformed way' that she could not recognize it. Duff, she admitted, had

> a well known weakness of uncontrolled rudeness – We all have grave weaknesses – Baby's is melancholia & cowardice. You have some too . . . both men in this story are exceptionally rude in cups. . . . But since recriminations are the note neither B[aby] nor D[uff] would have told all and sundry that their hosts were trying to poison them in both town and country. She will not write again – it's too painful to face the leaden answers devoid of understanding or love.[86]

84. *Ibid.*
85. ALS from Lady Diana Cooper, [29] July 1953, from 5 Belgrave Square, SW; BL; *MWMS*, p. 176.
86. *Ibid.*; mostly published in *Letters*, p. 407, n. 1.

The poisoning story, it seems, was again no joke. His Belladonna complex was emerging again.

The saga soon sailed to new heights of extravagance. Earlier in the month, Waugh had been happily contemplating a week-end at Randolph Churchill's new house. Before Lady Diana's first letter, he had written to cancel on hearing that Duff would be there. Churchill complained. Waugh explained: 'Cooper I have never tolerated except for his enchanting wife. In later years he has given up any pretence of tolerating me. My last visit to him was the occasion of his going too far.'[87]

Churchill, ever benevolent, showed this to Duff. Result: explosion, with ripples running out through the fashionable world *via* Ann Fleming's dinner table. Waugh was discomfited, furious with Churchill, and embarrassed (as Churchill had intended him to be) by the exposure of his ungentlemanly conduct, yet unable and unwilling to retract. He had been caught out in a breach of etiquette. 'I think Randolph is *too* disgusting,' Nancy wrote:

> Whatever one may think of your letter & I think you went too far really, it was quite indefensible to show it. In France that is the *one* rule, never make trouble. Nobody would ever speak to him again if he lived there. People who do that sort of thing undermine all civilized intercourse & make society impossible.... He exemplifies a sort of brutal island rudeness which is one [of] the things I have fled from.[88]

That 'brutal island rudeness' was something Waugh shared but pretended, even to himself, that he did not. He loved and hated Randolph in equal proportions.

The year had thus bled away in benign or irritable lethargy. In January he had scribbled in his diary:

> By the time I have written my letters the papers come and when I have read them it is nearly noon so I do little work before luncheon and then don't get out after luncheon and then have tired eyes by 8 o'clock and don't want to sit up reading and not sleepy so take drugs at 11. A flaw somewhere.[89]

July saw him no further on with his novel and, obsessed by his 'penury', he had begun to take desperate measures. If the glossy magazines no longer wanted his work, perhaps the BBC would? He had even volunteered to read the Goa article 'on the loudspeaker'.[90] Then Hugh Burnett had asked

87. 27 July [1953]; *Letters*, pp. 406–7.
88. Unpublished ALS from Nancy Mitford, 22 August 1953, from 10 Warwick Avenue, W2; BL. She was staying in England to attend rehearsals of her translation of *La Petite Hutte* (directed by Peter Brook), which in August 1953 was touring the provinces.
89. *Diaries*, 27 January 1953, p. 714.
90. Unpublished APCI to A. D. Peters, 8 February 1953, from Piers Court; *Catalogue* E786, p. 195.

him to contribute to the Overseas Service's 'Personal Call': 'The programme would ... be a very personal one, as though the listener were visiting you to discover the things you regard as important and necessary to you.' The series was aimed at non-British listeners in South-East Asia and intended 'to combat the many misunderstandings there about people and life in Britain today'.[91] Waugh, one might think, was a strange choice for such a task. A few months earlier he would have rejected it outright. This time he accepted and, for only fifteen guineas, conducted an interview which changed his life.

Stephen Black, the interviewer, drove down to Piers Court with a 'radio car' on 18 August, at the height of Waugh's row with the Coopers. The van was parked on the forecourt and cables run into the house. The children were at home. Intrigued by the gadgetry and somewhat in awe of Papa's celebrity, they wandered curiously round the little circus. Bron was thirteen. 'I well remember the visit ...', he wrote. 'It was the one which eventually drove my Father mad. I listened to the interview outside, standing by the recording machine in the van, where it was reproduced from within the library. My comment was that the man, later called Angel, did not seem to like my Father very much.'[92] Certainly Waugh became haunted by this experience. At the time, however, he seems merely to have been embarrassed by the invasion and by his performance. He stipulated that it should not be broadcast on any of the North American or domestic services and refused publication in the *Listener*, but no acrimonious correspondence followed.

The BBC, delighted by the recording, approached him again a fortnight later. Would he appear on *Frankly Speaking*? Black would this time be one of three interviewers: 'The usual procedure is to have a good dinner together in Broadcasting House, and then continue the conversation before a microphone in a neighbouring studio.'[93] In 1945 Waugh had ostentatiously refused to attend a similar meal before the Brains Trust. In 1953 he told Peters that, although unenthusiastic about the project, he was persuadable for a large fee, and he replied directly to the BBC asking for the date of the next broadcast so that he might judge what was required:

> I am prepared, provided the fee is adequate, to answer any ... questions on general subjects. I do not think I have the necessary talents to give the impression that I am taking part in a three-cornered intimate chat with personal friends, with the bandying about of Christian names

91. Unpublished TLS, 16 July 1953, from the BBC; BBCWAC.
92. TLS to Martin Stannard, 9 February 1989, from Combe Florey House, Combe Florey, Taunton, Somerset.
93. Unpublished TLS from J. Weltman to Evelyn Waugh, 1 September 1953; BBCWAC.

> and so forth, of the kind which deeply shocks me in some of the performances I have sometimes begun to hear.[94]

'Begun to hear' was good, but he had inserted 'do not have the necessary talents to' after having deleted 'should not find it agreeable to'. Extraordinarily, he was trying to placate 'The Broadcasting'.

Negotiations, nevertheless, came perilously close to the usual impasse. J. Weltman confirmed that there would be no 'pseudo-intimacy'.[95] Waugh replied:

> Thank you for your reassuring letter.... I am sorry to read in this morning's paper that your corporation is in financial difficulties, but I cannot accept this as a reason for the entirely inadequate sum offered for expenses.
>
> When I have paid tax & commission on the fee, I shall receive about £12.10. net. I am naturally unwilling to use this modest sum to reimburse myself for my losses in travel & accomodation [*sic*].
>
> Will you please ask Mr. Black and his companion[s] to bring their engine here, as they did before. I do not know how my cook & cellar compare with yours, but I will provide the best luncheon I can and charge you only for the ingredients.[96]

The BBC insisted on London. Waugh had been offered forty guineas, return fare and a night in town at £1. 15s. 0d. Waugh sent Peters alternative expenses totalling £8. 18s. 6d. including taxis everywhere and tips: 'If they query any item call the whole thing off. I'm not very keen on it and I won't sacrifice any comfort for their convenience.'[97] This proved unnecessary. While the BBC thought these charges 'somewhat exceptional',[98] they agreed to meet them and Waugh was committed to another inquisition, this time in Broadcasting House.

Sykes's account of all this is rather odd. He conflates the two interviews, stating that 'Frankly Speaking' was conducted at Piers Court by two interviewers, and omitting 'Personal Call' altogether. Rather than go to the script library, he invents his quotations. Ultimately, he comes down firmly on Waugh's side as the victor over fools who 'presumed that Evelyn was less intelligent than they and that this crusted conservative would be easy game....'[99] The transcript does not bear this out. Neither does the history

94. 2 September 1953; *Letters*, pp. 408–9.
95. Unpublished TLS, from J. Weltman to Evelyn Waugh, 8 September 1953; BBCWAC.
96. Unpublished ALS from Evelyn Waugh, 9 September 1953, from Piers Court; BBCWAC.
97. Unpublished APC as letter to A. D. Peters, c. 14 September 1953, from Piers Court; *Catalogue* E829, p. 202.
98. Unpublished TLS from Ronald Boswell to John Montgomery of A. D. Peters & Co., 15 September 1953; BBCWAC.
99. Sykes, p. 356.

of the recording support the notion that: 'It was like watching inexperienced toreadors taking on a bull who knew all the tricks of the ring.'[100]

Waugh went to Broadcasting House as planned on 28 September and a few days later left with Laura for her harvest-home treat – ten days of gambling in Ostend and galleries in Belgium.[101] It was a contented excursion. All the time, however, that interview kept working in his mind and, as soon as he returned, he wrote to Weltman:

> Thinking over what I said, I feel that I missed many opportunities & too often dismissed questions abruptly which should have had full answers. Is it possible to treat our performance as a rehearsal & repeat it? I should not, of course, ask for further remuneration. It is simply that I hate to leave anything shabbily done.... I would ... greatly appreciate ... the chance to do it again.[102]

This gentler Waugh was new to the BBC and pleasantly refreshing. Weltman sent a transcript and a date was fixed for a second recording (Waugh politely avoiding a second dinner):

> Need our meeting happen at night? If we meet after luncheon, I should be able to avoid the danger & expense of a night in London.... Politics & sociology are not really my subjects. I think we spent too much time on them....[103]

At the end of October, he travelled to London again. Shortly afterwards two transcripts arrived at Piers Court: one of the second attempt and one of 'our efforts to make a composite out of the two recordings. We have tried to lift one or two of the more lively exchanges from the earlier version, in order to keep the illusion of spontaneity.'[104] Weltman was uncertain whether this splicing would prove technically possible. Waugh encouraged the 'mechanics', finding the second version better than the first and the composite better than both. A couple of passages were deleted from the latter at Waugh's request and it was broadcast on 16 November.

'My broadcast was pretty dull,' he wrote to Nancy. 'They tried to make a fool of me & I don't believe they entirely succeeded.'[105] Certainly the enquiry was carefully organized to open with Waugh's attitude towards

100. *Ibid.*
101. Cf. unpublished ALS to Margaret Stephens of A. D. Peters & Co., nd [c. 21 September 1953]; *Catalogue* E831, pp. 202–3: 'I enclose my passport. I wish to visit Belgium shortly to gather material for my poems, operettas and other literary work. Will you please get your bankers to give me £100 in £5 [travellers'] cheques for this noble purpose....' The Donaldsons travelled with Waugh and Laura to Ostend and Belgium but returned early.
102. Unpublished ALS, 17 October [1953], from Piers Court; BBCWAC.
103. Unpublished ALS from Evelyn Waugh to J. Weltman, 21 October [1953], from Piers Court; BBCWAC.
104. Unpublished TLS from J. Weltman, 6 November 1953; BBCWAC.
105. 11 December [1953]; *Letters*, p. 415.

'things', questions he happily answered, and then to move gingerly on to his attitude towards people. Here one gains a distinct sense of Waugh's awkwardness. The interviewers began indirectly to press him on the contradictions between Christian ethics and conservative élitism. How did he feel about crowds? (He 'loathed crowds'.) Did he feel easy with the 'man in the street'? 'I've never met such a person.' But he surely couldn't wander round in 'a sort of Trappist condition'? He must *meet* people. No, only occasionally he would meet friends when travelling. That was delightful. Otherwise the 'prospect of just being introduced to somebody as just a person, a man, as you might say, in the street, is entirely repugnant.' Were there any sins he could excuse? 'Drunkenness.... Anger. Lust. Dishonouring their [*sic*] father and mother. Coveting their neighbour's ox, ass, wife. Killing. I think there is almost nothing I can't excuse except perhaps worshipping graven images. That seems to me idiotic.' What irritated him most? 'Bad manners, disagreeable appearance, stupidity, egoism.' And by 'disagreeable appearance' he meant ...? 'Face, hair, fingernails, teeth, clothes – everything.... I don't think one wants too much character in a woman's face....' What were the important feminine characteristics? 'Beauty, grace, humility, elegance, nice voice, a fair amount of education and intelligence. Quickness.'[106]

It is scarcely surprising that female listeners complained[107] or that Sykes complimented Waugh on beating off the Common Men.[108] Neither response, however, quite catches the tone of the exchange. For the most part, it was benevolently disposed on both sides: an amicable, if spiky, debate in which Waugh volunteered a great deal of personal information previously unknown to anyone but his family and cronies. Sykes, of course, knew nothing of the composite recording and Waugh told no one. He was, it seems, ashamed of the ease with which he had been led blundering into nonsense about 'politics and sociology'. He had had enough of vituperation and subsequent loss of friends, enough of looking foolish.

The figure described in *The Ordeal of Gilbert Pinfold* is fully formed and honestly discussed in the interview: the alienated, solitary craftsman disguised as don or colonel; the family man jovially pretending distaste for his children. Asked if he wished to convey 'novel thoughts' or a 'message', his reply was pure Pinfold: 'No, I wish to make a pleasant object. I think any work of art is something exterior to oneself, it's the making of something

106. 'Frankly Speaking', 16 November 1953; Home Service, 10.05–10.35 p.m.; BBCSL.
107. Cf. ALS from Greta Woodman, 16 November [1953]; BBCWAC: 'What a ghastly man. I bet you hated him as much as my husband and I did. I don't know how you kept your good manners, but you did.'
108. Cf. unpublished ALS from Christopher Sykes, 17 November 1953, from Silton House, Gillingham, Dorset; BL: 'Your broadcast was sublime. I thought the baiters were tossed & gored with delectable skill throughout.'

whether it's a bed-table or a book.' Asked about his children: 'Well, thank God, they don't live with me except during the holidays.' How many were there? 'It seems like hundreds, it's actually only about six. . . .' Did he play with them? 'Not when they're infantile. When they get to the age of clear speech and an appearance of reason, I associate with them – I wouldn't say I play with them. I don't bounce balls . . . or stand on my head, or carry them about on my shoulders or anything.' All this was true, but it omitted the charades and treats and teases, the funny and sympathetic letters. We should not miss the jokes at his own expense, and the pain in his admissions.

He had not, he said, succeeded in much. As a father he was distant, as a schoolboy he had been unhappy, as a soldier he had been too old to be effective; even in the hayfield with Laura he was incompetent. He liked designing gardens but everything he planted instantly died. His self-portrait has the cruel reduction of his comic fiction. It is a self-defence only in so far as he refuses to admit why anyone should love him. The man who craved love, the 'spoilt baby', was eternally at odds with the one who hated himself and hungered for contrition. The result, in public at least, was the confusing performance of one both 'deathly proud' and self-mortifyingly humble. No one could dream up an accusation he had not already levelled at himself. And the accusations, it seems, were echoing ever more resonantly in his unconscious. They were not included in the questions he was asked in these programmes. The programmes acted as a vehicle for his self-persecution.

He was, he admitted, approaching 'the dangerous age of fifty'. 'My memory is not at all hazy', he wrote to Betjeman, '– just sharp, detailed & dead wrong. This affliction leads me into countless humiliations.'[109] Waugh's deepest fear was not merely decline of mental agility but madness. Rossetti's life seemed always to have paralleled his, and Rossetti had cracked at fifty. Waugh was reading Edgar Johnson's biography of Dickens and had written to Betjeman about a possible error.[110] The poet had telegraphed confirmation. Three months later he was unable to respond so positively to a similar enquiry.

It is worth pausing over Waugh's reading of Johnson. Dickens, of course, had for thirty years been Waugh's humanist *bête noire*. He associated Boz with sentimental 'uplift', flabby writing, the mythology of progress and (possibly worst of all) the popularization of the 'traditional' British Christmas. The yo-ho-ho school of Merrie Englandism had long been an object of Waugh's contempt, and his father – an authority on Dickens –

109. 17 September 1953; *Letters*, p. 410.

110. Both Waugh's letter and Betjeman's telegram seem to have disappeared. The enquiry concerned the 'Five Sisters' window at York. Waugh remembered it as pale; Johnson described it as 'gorgeously hued'.

seemed to personify this loathsome geniality. During August, Waugh had begun an interesting correspondence with Lady Pansy Lamb, arguably his only female friend with 'intellectual' inclinations. He had written to her and Henry to celebrate their twenty-fifth wedding anniversary, after meeting them in London for the first time in years. They represented, he said, one of only four happy marriages he knew, and he enclosed a 'sentimentally moving' gift.[111] In the depths of the Cooper fiasco, Waugh was trying humbly to reclaim a lost ally – and he succeeded. Lady Pansy was touched by his loyalty.

It was all the more surprising to her, then, to find this benevolent figure opposing Dickens. Lady Pansy was a considerable expert on nineteenth-century literature and her letters to Waugh often debate the relative merits of Dickens and Ruskin. Waugh had been reading Ruskin's love-letters to Kathleen Olander, and this brief, truncated courtship between an elderly aesthete and a young girl had become an obsessive interest. Indeed, it is tempting to read his review of the book as obliquely autobiographical. When he detects, for instance, three 'quests' in Ruskin's romantic liaisons – 'Abelard in search of an Héloïse, Svengali in search of a Trilby, and the lonely little boy in search of a playmate'[112] – he calls to mind his own relationships with Teresa Jungman, Clarissa Eden and Nancy. Laura, over the years, had played all three roles. But she had offered the home and family always denied Ruskin, and this, we might think, is where the comparison collapses. Yet when Waugh says of him: 'It is not given to one man to enjoy domestic content and also the transports of aesthetic delight.... Imagine him the father of a family, and he becomes absurd', the autobiographical echoes sound again, for Waugh certainly found himself a preposterous domestic figure and increasingly the 'lonely little boy in search of a playmate'. He worshipped Ruskin and hated Dickens. Why?

Waugh had created a mythology of Victorian life centring on the 'huge euphoria of the Victorian home [which] may be attributed to the abundance of ornament.'[113] From this exuberance he saw Ruskin as excluded, a sensitive only child. Dickens, on the other hand, the supreme advocate of the tumultuous household, Waugh dismisses as a hypocrite. Reading this assault, one is struck by its resemblance to accusations Waugh had himself suffered:

111. Cf. unpublished ALS from Lady Pansy Lamb, 16 August 1953, from Whitfield, Allensmore, Herefordshire; BL. The gift was a silver coin, probably a five-shilling piece.
112. 'Ruskin and Kathleen Olander', *Spectator*, 17 July 1953, 88; review of *The Gulf of Years: Love Letters from John Ruskin to Kathleen Olander*, ed. Rayner Unwin (Allen & Unwin, 1953); *EAR*, pp. 443–4.
113. 'Those Happy Homes', 28 November 1954, 5; review of Ralph Dutton, *The Victorian Home* (Batsford, 1954); *EAR*, pp. 465–6.

> Dickens['s] . . . recreation was with a set of cronies, thinned by frequent quarrels, with whom he enjoyed boisterous games. . . . He joined the Athenaeum Club by ordinary election. . . . He appeared now and then, clothed in an unsuitable imitation of Count d'Orsay, at Lady Blessington's.[114]

The general impression is of Dickens as a vulgar 'snob', cavorting embarrassingly among the genuine 'nobs'. Dickens, he says, 'travelled a little, but always cloaked in impermeable insular smugness. He had better to have stuck to Broadstairs.'[115] The 'more we know of [him], the less we like him':

> His conduct to his wife . . . [was] deplorable. . . . He frequented the *demi-monde* with Wilkie Collins. . . . He claimed a spurious pedigree and used an illicit crest. . . . In success he was intolerably boastful, in the smallest reverse abject with self-pity. He was domineering and dishonourable in his treatment of his publishers. He was, in fact, a thumping cad.[116]

Waugh was subject to most of these accusations from outsiders who did not understand the intricate games of his relationships. (Matson, one suspects, might have added a few charges.) The review is subjective, obsessive and unfair. (Dickens, for instance, was far from 'insular', travelled widely and had a better grasp of modern foreign languages than Waugh.) Could it be that in Dickens Waugh's unconscious recognized itself: the self-made self-publicist; theatrical, lovable and with a weakness for the gentry? If this were so, it was too horrible to contemplate and his invective tries to crush the slightest association.

Waugh's reviews brought a response from Lady Pansy which perhaps disturbed him:

> You treated [Dickens] as if he were a contemporary of H. G. Wells, a worshipper of scientific Utopias, in an atheist or agnostic world, a Socialist who hypocritically made a lot of money & had a good time. Instead of which, he grew up & made his mark in an eighteenth century culture . . . where Churches were looked on as political parties, & Christianity was an affair of salvation & redemption – the Wesleyan dynamic. What separates him completely from the next generation of novelists, Meredith, Hardy, James, is his acceptance, as a matter of course, of supernatural sanctions e.g. the Last Judgement. This is the cause for the contempt that was poured on him by the intellectuals from the fifties onwards – anyone with pretensions to be[ing] a thinker

114. 'Apotheosis of an Unhappy Hypocrite', *Spectator*, 2 October 1953, 363–4; review of Edgar Johnson, *Charles Dickens* (Gollancz, 1953); *EAR*, pp. 444–7.
115. *Ibid.*, p. 445.
116. *Ibid.*, p. 446.

> was then inventing new systems & new religions. About the same time a new upper-middle class consolidated itself & began laying down the law about what gentlemen were like & what was vulgar, & how vulgar Dickens was. But it is noteworthy that the older aristocracy ... didn't find him vulgar....[117]

With few exceptions, this accurately describes Waugh's social predicament. She was effectively telling him that he had chosen for his target a man not dissimilar to himself.[118]

It was with these issues, the Cooper row and the broadcasts scratching at his ego that Waugh had climbed into his winter underclothes in late October and settled to the completion of *Happy Warriors*. The effort soon collapsed again and, after 25,000 words, stopped dead. 'I am stuck in my book from sheer boredom,' he wrote to Nancy. 'I know what to write but I just cant make the effort to write it.'[119]

Trying to cheer him up, Betjeman had offered a valuable Burges wash-hand-stand as a fiftieth birthday present. The wash-hand-stand arrived and was set splendidly against that red and gold wallpaper Betjeman had found too frightening. But there was, Waugh thought, a piece missing: '... an ornamental bronze pipe which led from the dragons mouth to the bowl below.... Did I dream this or did it exist.'[120] 'Oh no old boy,' Betjeman replied. 'There was never a pipe....'[121] It was the last day of the year; 1954 loomed ahead, promising disaster. Waugh feared he was losing his mind.

That night Duff Cooper died aboard the *Colombie*, steaming towards America, spitting blood to the incongruous accompaniment of New Year's Eve revelry next door. Lady Diana had been at his side, watching both

117. Unpublished ALS from Lady Pansy Lamb, 5 November 1953, from Coombe Bissett, Salisbury; BL.
118. Cf. also unpublished ALS from Lady Pansy Lamb, 28 November 1953, from Coombe Bissett, Salisbury; BL. Waugh had replied accusing Dickens of élitism, betrayal and parsimony. Her response might equally stand as a defence of Waugh against similar taunts: 'The [letters] to Forster, who was his literary agent, confidant & business manager, ... are almost the only egotistic ones. The amount of trouble he was prepared to take for literary protégés, or to entertain his family, or advise or help his friends, or for causes in which he was interested, was colossal. He may not have thrown money around idly but he spent himself most generously. He had an almost morbid sense of responsibility, & far from neglecting his family, worried about them too much.... It was those who didn't know him who said what an atrocious cad he was [to leave his wife].... Part of his power was due to his vitality, but it was strengthened by self-discipline. The punctuality & order he imposed on his entourage he first imposed on himself & it gave him tremendous drive, both in life & art.... [Reading] P.G. Wodehouse's Letters, I was often reminded of Dickens's advice to literary aspirants, & thought there was a good deal in common in their approach.'
119. 11 December 1953; *Letters*, p. 415.
120. ALS to [Sir] John Betjeman, 29 December [1953]; *Letters*, p. 417.
121. Unpublished ALS from [Sir] John Betjeman, 31 December 1953, from The Mead, Wantage, Berks.; BL. The wash-hand-stand was dispatched from Patrick Balfour's house in Warwick Street, London. Balfour apparently sent a piece of his ancient water closet which Betjeman confirmed 'was a ... part of the works of the wash stand' but was not the part Waugh had imagined.

their lives ebb away. The quarrel with Waugh had been resolved but, when he heard of this scene, he was ashamed. His last words to her had been critical. Resuming his diary after a six-month gap, the entries were melancholy, penitential, static: 'Clocks barely moving. Has half an hour past [*sic*]? no five minutes.'[122] 'Church again. My prayer is now only, "Here I am again. Show me what to do; help me do it."'[123] He was embroiled in another futile controversy, this time with Hugh Trevor-Roper,[124] itching for the last word. He struggled round London with the children for their Christmas treat. Then the winter closed in: 'Intense cold. Sat like a hibernating badger all day',[125] and he sank into paralysis of mind and body. Montgomery wrote enquiring about the serial possibilities of *Happy Warriors*. 'The trouble is', Waugh replied gloomily, 'that it's not finished. I promised it to C & H without fail by November 1st, then Jan. lst and it still isn't done. I feel guilty about it ... [but] I can't give an approximate date....'[126] In the meantime, to placate Salmen, he proposed the contents for an American edition of his short stories and promised an Introduction. At the end of his note he added: 'I plan shortly to go abroad to finish the second vol ... I may have recourse to you for currency.'[127]

This was news to Peters. 'If you *are* going abroad,' he replied, 'please give us as much notice as you can. It is very difficult to arrange foreign finance without warning.'[128] But Waugh could not wait. 'Oh I have been so ill ...,' he wrote to Margaret. 'First a cold & then agonising rheumatism. So I am jumping into the first ... ship ... to Ceylon. I shan't come back until I have finished my book but I hope I shall do that on the voyage.'[129]

*

The *Staffordshire* was on course from Liverpool to sail past Gibraltar to Port Said, Aden and Colombo. Four days out, Waugh wrote a disturbed and disturbing letter to Laura:

> Darling, I wish you were with me.... My rheumatism is much better – quite tolerable. It is Feb 3rd and we are not yet in the Mediterranean. My nut is clearing but feeble. It is plain that I had been accumulatively poisoning myself with chloral in the last six months.... I will come

122. *Diaries*, 2 January 1954, p. 722.
123. *Ibid.*, 3 January 1954, p. 722.
124. Cf. *Letters*, Appendix, pp. 642–7.
125. *Diaries*, 7 January 1954, p. 724.
126. Unpublished APCI, 11 January 1954, from Piers Court; *Catalogue* E845, p. 205.
127. Unpublished ANS [on TLS from Salmen dated 12 January 1954], from Piers Court; *Catalogue* E846, p. 205. *Mr. Loveday's Little Outing and Other Sad Stories* had only appeared in America in a limited edition of 700 copies during 1936.
128. Unpublished TccL, 18 January 1954; HRC.
129. nd [late January 1954]; *Letters*, p. 417.

> home and lead a luny bin life for a bit. It was at 50 that Rossettis chloral taking involved him in attempted suicide, part blindness & part paralysis. We will avoid all that. I find it hard to keep sentences connected.... It is 3 nights now since I had the last dose of sleepers.... When I wake up which I do 20 or 30 times a night I always turn to the other bed and am wretched you aren't there & puzzled that you are not – odd since we usually have different rooms.
>
> ... The chief trouble is the noise of my cabin.... To add to my balminess there are intermittent bits of 3rd Programme talks played in private cabin and two mentioned me very faintly and my p[ersecution]. m[ania]. took it for other passengers whispering about me....[130]

This was one programme he could not turn off. Those voices, so long dismissed, suppressed, invented, had returned to torment him.

The attack had begun at home. Between two sticks, he had staggered about, his joints aflame with pain, the backs of his hands blotched. During Christmas, having forced himself to a pitch of artificial gaiety, he had played charades and Up-Jenkins with his children but had caught another horrific glimpse of himself in a looking-glass, 'empurpled and wearing a paper crown'.[131] The image had frightened him, and Evelyn frightened, bemused and so thunderously depressed, had scared Laura. The doctor had been called in. Waugh failed to tell him of the fantastic concoction of sleeping draught which he took in addition to rheumatism drugs and a liberal daily intake of alcohol. It was clear to both husband and wife, however, that his reckless use of bromide and chloral was probably to blame and he promised her to ease up on it. As a result, he had taken only the dregs of his current bottle of 'sleepers' with him, determined to relinquish narcotics once aboard. He had always slept well at sea.

His last letter to his agent had begun with the old precision and had dribbled into incoherence. 'Best wishes for a happy voyage,' Peters had cabled. 'Have a thorough rest and don't worry about finishing the book until you feel disposed.'[132] A fortnight before his departure, Waugh had heard from Alec that their mother was seriously ill: breathless, legs swollen, weak heart. A day-nurse was needed in addition to Mrs Yaxley. Joan (Alec's wife) was arranging for a night-nurse. Clearly Alec was requesting assistance. Under normal circumstances. Evelyn would have rallied to the call, but his own situation was desperate. He was, it seemed, going mad while his mother was dying. An hour's visit to Highgate had satisfied protocol but, as he had hobbled out with Laura to the hired limousine,

130. 3 February 1954 [pm 9 February]; *Letters*, p. 418.
131. *The Ordeal of Gilbert Pinfold* (Chapman & Hall, 1957; reprinted Harmondsworth, Penguin Books, 1962), p. 25.
132. Unpublished cable, 29 January 1954; HRC.

both knew that he had been offensively abrupt. Laura drove with him to Euston, now earnestly trying to persuade him to postpone the trip until she could accompany him. On the platform he had dropped his sticks and tickets, mumbled and staggered. He had boarded the train scarcely conscious. A week later he abandoned the ship in Port Said – scene of that disaster during his first honeymoon when She-Evelyn had been near death – and drove to Cairo, a shaken man, having endured the most terrifying experience of his life.

The story is told in *Pinfold* and Frances Donaldson's *Portrait of a Country Neighbour*, and it is well enough known not to need repeating in detail. Briefly, Waugh suffered from traumatic aural hallucinations. He thought the telegraphist had been distributing his cables to Stephen Black and his family. According to Lady Donaldson, he thought he saw a body being transshipped on a stretcher (a memory of She-Evelyn?). He thought he overheard the torture and murder of a steward, a fearful accident which crushed a seaman, and a plot to foil the Spanish navy which was laying claim to Gibraltar. He was threatened with thrashings and sexually teased by a young woman he found attractive. And all the time there were the cacophonous accusations: he was a snob and a bully, a Fascist, a Jew, a Communist, a homosexual. He was impotent. Waugh tried to hit back. 'I used to bore the pants off . . . [the persecutors]', he later told Tom Driberg, 'by reading alternate lines of verse aloud. . . . They couldn't switch off once we were in touch.'[133] But it was no use. A fellow passenger recalled his speaking into a table lamp at mealtimes, convinced that it was a transmitter. Pinfold describes one night when, anticipating assault, he stood behind the door of his darkened cabin, alone and absurdly brave in overcoat and pyjamas, stick at the ready to repel invaders. In fact, this represented fictional compression. 'There must have been half a dozen times . . . when I rushed out with a stick, convinced that they were waiting for me – to find nobody there. I even shouted "I've got you!" Every time, by the mercy of God, there was just an empty deck . . . or I might have ended up in a strait-jacket.'[134]

Leaving the ship, he hoped to escape the voices but they followed him to his Cairo hotel. He thought himself, he wrote to Laura,

> the victim of an experiment in telepathy which made me think I really was going crazy. . . . It has made me more credulous about Tanker's box. . . . I don't know what I wrote to you on the ship or even if I wrote at all. I was semi-delirious most of the time. . . . Hand is steady today and the malevolent telepathy broken for the first time – perhaps

133. Tom Driberg, 'The Agony of Evelyn Waugh', *Sunday Dispatch*, 14 July 1957, 4.
134. *Ibid.*

> not permanently. Please don't be alarmed about the references to telepathy. I know it sounds like acute p.m. but it is real & true. A trick the existentialists invented – half mesmerism – which is most alarming when applied without warning ... to a sick man.[135]

Laura knew enough about her husband's normal 'p.m.' to realize that this was something more serious. 'Tanker' was Diana Oldridge, a neighbour who had talked of a 'black box' which could cure illness in distant animals and humans. Samples of hair or blood were inserted; the box was then supposed to emit beneficent 'life-waves'. In his right mind, Waugh had scorned the device. If he was now professing belief in its powers, it was plain to Laura that her husband *had* gone mad.

She was frightened but she did not panic. She called in Jack and Frances Donaldson, explained the matter and arranged to fly out immediately with him. In the meantime, the letters grew crazier:

> It is rather difficult to write to you because everything I say or think or read is read aloud by the group of psychologists whom I met in the ship ... the artful creatures can communicate from many hundreds of miles away. Please don't think this is balmy ... it is a fact & therefore doesn't worry me particularly.... But it is a huge relief to realize that I am merely the victim of the malice of others, not mad myself as I really feared for a few days.[136]

That came from Colombo, Ceylon, where Waugh had flown and where he had bumped into Monroe Wheeler, an amiable American art historian. They had met first at Minnie Astor's in New York. Wheeler spent some time sight-seeing with him and took him to visit George Keyt, Ceylon's most celebrated artist. Waugh arrived smartly dressed, cordial, and bearing a full whisky decanter. Keyt found him perfectly sane and was astonished to learn that he had met Waugh at the height of his terror. They discussed the development of the novel, Keyt struggling to conceal the fact that he had never read a line of Waugh's work. When Keyt '... brought in Bankim Chandra Chatterji as the innovator of the novel in India and discussed the chronicle stage of the Scott-invented novel ...', Waugh's response was abrupt – '"I don't know Indians"' – but not offensive. Indeed, he seemed 'so very normal and very nice'[137] that one is tempted to believe in temporary

135. 8 February [1954], from the Continental-Savoy Hotel, Cairo; *Letters*, pp. 418–19.
136. 12 February [1954]; from the Galle Face Hotel, Colombo; *Letters*, pp. 419–20.
137. Unpublished letters by George Keyt, quoted in memoranda to Martin Stannard, 16 February 1990 and 9 April 1990, from Mr H. A. I. Goonetileke. The latter is a close friend of Mr Keyt's and an authority on his work. Keyt was born in Kandy on 17 April 1901, of Dutch burgher parents. He developed early interests in Buddhism and was strongly influenced by the Ceylonese and Indian artistic traditions. In 1954 he lived in a house with a large studio on the outskirts of Kandy. Chatterji is a famous nineteenth-century Indian novelist.

recovery. Owing to the Queen's visit, however, most accommodation was advance-booked and Waugh soon found himself exiled to an hotel inland where the voices dogged him again.

Even in this extremity, he attempted to maintain good form, writing sympathetically to Lady Diana about her bereavement. But the voices repeated his letter word for word: 'I can't say in the presence of these eavesdroppers how much my heart and prayers are yours. They break into cackles of laughter at any expression of that kind.'[138] 'I have just got your cable urging me to return,' he wrote to Laura. 'I need no urging.... Last night I went to an Indian cinema. I saw the same film as I saw in Madura last year. Very odd as these two cinemas are the only Indian ones I have ever been to. I am still grossly afflicted....'[139] Before she could get to him, he was on the 'plane, still hallucinating.

After three days of terrifying anxiety, Laura took the train to London and arrived at the Hyde Park Hotel an hour before the car bringing Waugh from the airport. Apart from the Donaldsons, and probably her mother, she had told no one, fearful of the story reaching the press. She did not know what to expect and what she discovered was distinctly disconcerting. He was awkward with her, more than usually physically unaffectionate, explaining his condition in a strangled, high-pitched squeak. As he spoke, he insisted that everything was being repeated in his ear; Stephen Black was tormenting him.

Under instructions, Laura rang the BBC. Mr Black, she was told, was ill and in hospital. Waugh double-checked by ringing Sykes, who confirmed the story. Waugh took the news calmly and then became convinced that he was possessed by the Devil. Laura called in Fr Caraman and the three of them went to dinner. It was clearly a disturbing experience for all concerned. Waugh seemed completely deranged, even retailing uncomplimentary remarks the voices were making about Caraman. When Waugh left the table briefly, the priest asked Laura whether this behaviour were the sort of extended joke in which Waugh sometimes indulged. She paled at the suggestion. Caraman then quickly called in Dr Strauss, a Catholic psychiatrist from Bart's Hospital, who examined Waugh in the hotel. Laura and Caraman were present. Waugh responded to the questions like a child before a benevolent schoolmaster, holding nothing back, and was delighted by the diagnosis: he was not possessed but his mental equilibrium had been upset by narcotic poisoning.

Waugh left for Gloucestershire exhausted but triumphant. Laura, ever truthful, admitted to him that she had confided in the Donaldsons, but

138. ALS to Lady Diana Cooper, 18 February [1954], np [Grand Hotel, Nuwara, Eliya, Ceylon]; BL; *MWMS*, p. 188.
139. 18 February [1954], from the Grand Hotel, Nuwara, Eliya; *Letters*, p. 421.

that she had sworn them to secrecy. The matter would go no further. Far from being angry or ashamed, however, he invited them over for dinner to explain the saga as a delicious curiosity. And it did not stop there. Waugh broadcast the news among his friends. Had he been talking of someone else, he might have been accused of malicious gossip. With the voices quelled, he could stand outside himself again and unsentimentally mock the curious figure he had temporarily become. It was his way, perhaps, of burying the pain and his fears of future collapse. It was also a tactic to defuse the arguments of potential detractors in search of dirty linen. But quite apart from these motives, as a writer he was genuinely grateful for his experience: in a period of sloth and depression, he had suddenly been presented with a new subject. 'It was', Pinfold explained, 'the most exciting thing ... that ever happened to me.'[140]

Waugh's public explanation of his insanity was purely physiological and he had good medical evidence for this. In London he had a thorough check-up. His blood-test proved normal. 'In summary,' the doctor wrote, 'my conclusions about you were these':

> (1) That your recent hallucinations of hearing were due to bromide poisoning.
> (2) There is a considerable likelihood that your right antrum is infected.
> (3) and I would like to be satisfied with the integrity of your remaining teeth....
> (4) My observations on screen examination of your chest as well as the appearance of the X-rays I took, suggest very strongly that you may have ... an hiatus hernia – in plain English, that a part of your stomach slips through your diaphragm into your chest. This abnormality is often associated with lack of hydrochloric acid in the stomach, which in turn may give rise to a certain form of anaemia.
>
> ... In so far as your insomnia is concerned, my personal view is that the approach to it must be other than by narcotic drugs and I have taken up this aspect with Dr. Strauss.[141]

That was all Waugh wanted to know. He had already refused further medical investigation, much to his specialist's dismay. He wished merely to be satisfied that he was not insane. The sleeping draught was changed to paraldehyde. That, so far as he was concerned, was the end of the matter. There was to be no nonsense about psychiatric treatment.

The dust-jacket of *Pinfold* describes this extraordinary sequence of events as one in which 'the reason remains strenuously active but the information on which it acts is delusory.' One of Pinfold's tormentors distinguishes

140. *Pinfold*, *op. cit.*, p. 154.
141. Unpublished TLS from Dr Cedric Shaw, 10 March 1954, from 37 Devonshire Place, WI; BL.

between 'madness' and 'lunacy': Pinfold is already 'mad'; his torturer wishes to drive him insane. Waugh rather relished being 'mad' in the sense of 'erratic and dangerous to received opinion': this was a controlled response; he was terrified of lunacy. Beyond that point, he knew, his massive courage could not protect him. *Pinfold* is written in the form of another quest, like *Scott-King* and *Helena*, in which the hero through effort of will beats back detractors and emerges the victorious commanding officer. On numerous occasions Waugh insisted that it was an accurate account. He does, however, omit things to emphasize the completeness of this triumph. There is no mention of the psychiatrist. Returning to his unfinished novel, Pinfold puts it to one side and embarks, clear-headed, on his account of the voyage. Waugh did not, and found it difficult to reactivate *Officers and Gentlemen*. When this was published in 1955, Greene asked him why there was no indication on the wrapper that a third volume was to follow. '"I'm not sure that I'll be able to write it," he replied. "I may go off my head again, and this time permanently."'[142]

Pinfold, then, is an ingenious and deceptive autobiographical document, a further stage in the creation of a public image. Waugh had crushed the accusations back into his unconscious, pretending to his family, his public and himself that they had no relevance to his life, that they were merely the product of malice. The ship is renamed the *Caliban* and the events aboard it consigned to romance. '"What I can't understand is this,"' says Pinfold, '. . . "If I was supplying all the information to the Angels [Blacks], why did I tell them such a lot of rot? I mean to say, if I wanted to draw up an indictment of myself I could make a far blacker and more plausible case than they did."'[143] Earlier, however, Waugh allows Pinfold to give himself away more bluntly. Overhearing a conversation between two 'military gentlemen', he remarks: 'It was the sort of thing one expected to have said behind one's back – the sort of thing one said about other people.'[144] Does this not more accurately locate the style and subject matter of his voices?

Biography should not play at amateur psychoanalysis but it is impossible here to avoid some commentary on Waugh's state of mind. Any reputable psychiatrist would have told him, for instance, that he was suffering from the classic symptoms of schizophrenia. Waugh always maintained that his hallucinations stopped when he abandoned particular narcotics. But it seems more reasonable to suggest that the drugs released a barrage of self-hatred which, in his right mind, he suppressed, than that the voices were arbitrary. They were not talking 'rot'; they were abusing him as he had

142. Graham Greene, 'Both Dross and Gold', *B & B*, 22 (October 1976), 19–21; review of *Diaries*.
143. *Pinfold*, *op. cit.*, p. 155.
144. *Ibid.*, p. 57.

abused others, and they were articulating his private catalogue of self-reproach.

Read alongside the events described earlier in this chapter, *Pinfold* surely reveals itself as an intriguing glimpse of the workings of Waugh's unconscious. Ultimately it is a book about impotence: sexual and artistic impotence, impotence in the face of a host of (predominantly young) enemies determined to kick an old man when he is down. This paranoid obsession with failing powers can be seen in his dealings with Peters, Matson, the Inland Revenue and the BBC. There was no host of enemies. He either invented them or was so pertinaciously rude that he could expect no gratitude in return. As we have seen, he was by nature combative. He needed enemies. His friends had to struggle to remain on good terms as he tried, one by one, to insult them into betrayal. The novel is laced with his nightmares: exclusion from public honour;[145] guilt about his treatment of his mother, Bron and Laura; the tempting sweetness of death;[146] his sensitivity to inaccurate 'profiles' and impertinent reviews; the sexual threat of pretty young women who could so easily flatter him into romantic mood; his military incompetence; the idea that he was not trustworthy as a gentleman should be. The hallucinations, perhaps, are not so much inventions as cutting-room snippets edited out of the film of his life. Under the influence of the drug (or perhaps as a result of withdrawing from it), his unconscious flashed up scene after scene of shameful embarrassment he thought he had destroyed: the humble background; the 'cruel girls'[147] of the 1920s stabbing out their pink tongues; the attachment to Fascism; the horror of being caught out by Randolph Churchill in (and by) a betrayal of confidence.[148] Nothing comes through more strongly than 'the lonely little boy' beneath that tough cuirass of the man of the world, Hamlet in Lear's robes: 'He might be unpopular; he might be ridiculous; but he was not mad.'[149]

The point at which Waugh had stuck in his novel cannot be precisely determined, but it was certainly no more than half-way. Probably, he had faltered at the end of what became 'Book One. Happy Warriors'. This concerned the extension of Guy's Phoncy War, his entry into the Commandos and his fruitless training on the Isle of Mugg. It dealt, in short, with the period leading up to his first serious engagement with the enemy

145. Cf. the incident in which Pinfold expects to be included in the group of gentlemen selected by the captain to 'combat the Spanish navy', and is ignored (*ibid.*, pp. 82–98); also the petition attempting to exclude him from the captain's table (*ibid.*, p. 102).
146. Cf. *ibid.*, p. 102.
147. *Ibid.*, p. 105.
148. Cf. *ibid.*, pp. 82–3, where Jimmy Lance (alias John Betjeman?) and June Cumberleigh read out Pinfold's private letters.
149. *Ibid.*, p. 98.

on Crete. Is it fanciful to suggest that Waugh's imaginative saturation in his *alter ego*'s military irrelevance had contributed to the breakdown? Crouchback's quest, like Pinfold's, would lead from illusion to reality but, unlike Pinfold, neither Crouchback nor Waugh would be released from impotence. Ahead lay not action and honour but stasis and defeat. In contemplating this, was Waugh's unconscious haunted by his own wartime indignities? To write as he did from the high ground of comradeship with the professional gentlemen soldiers, he had, as it were, to divorce fiction from history and to divide his mind, obliterating the fact that these men had at best tolerated him, at worst rebuked him and refused him senior rank. '"He did pretty badly [in the army], I suppose,"' says one of Pinfold's persecutors. '"Very badly. There was a scandal in Cairo that had to be hushed up when his brigade-major shot himself."'[150] The false accusation does nothing to deflect the essence of the charge. Waugh *had* done badly. Did he dare to confront this? It seems unlikely. Instead, he tried again to suppress it and to shift the blame. But the blame would not be shifted. Unlike Ryder, and this, surely, is the crucial change in emphasis between the narrative perspective of *Brideshead* and of the war trilogy, Crouchback is complicitous in the cultural collapse of post-war Europe.

*

Waugh returned to Piers Court a thinner and a wiser man, determined never to travel alone again. Peters and McDougall spent week-ends there to judge the situation for themselves and to offer support. They left happy to see him restored but it was three months before he could report any progress with *Happy Warriors*. He lived quietly, offering public backing for Greene in his argument with the Holy Office;[151] engaging with Nancy in the 'U' and 'non "U"' debate; and helping Stopp with his book.

Waugh's chief resource and concern now was his family. Alec was in America, writing a novel at the MacDowell Colony, and at this stage, when there was a panic that Mrs Yaxley might leave to marry, Evelyn, at last, and grudgingly, offered his mother a home. Under cover of birthday greetings, he wrote to Alec confirming the offer but making it clear that:

> It would be in every way preferable for her to remain in Highgate.... The attention you give your mother must be decided by your own love & sense of duty. It is not for a younger brother to advise in this matter.... You have left your financial affairs with regard to your aunts' legacies in a most unsatisfactory state. I have engaged in much

150. *Ibid.*, pp. 103–4.
151. The Holy Office had condemned *The Power and the Glory*.

> correspondence in the matter. You should now attend to them yourself or depute a solicitor to do so.[152]

'This is a good example of my brother in a fractious mood,' Alec wrote beneath. 'He had only partially recovered from his trip to Ceylon.'

As an 'alien', Alec was allowed just ninety-three days a year in England. He had already used up twenty-eight of them. His plan was to return to France in August and to England in late October, but he was willing to disrupt this schedule. Evelyn's abrupt response had been to the enquiry: 'Is there anything that you think I can & should do about our mother?'[153] But Alec understood how to read the rebuke. The fact was that Evelyn had always believed his time to be more precious than his brother's. Such family matters had usually fallen to Alec while Evelyn had moved in a remote and grand world, or travelled, or shut himself up in the country. This time, however, Alec resisted the emotional blackmail and remained politely remote. He had a life to rebuild. At the Colony he was writing the novel which would restore his literary fortunes. He had met another writer, Virginia Sorensen, whom he hoped, eventually, to marry. Larger issues were at stake for him than for Evelyn. Big Little Brother would have to wait.

On the more immediate domestic front Waugh had other problems. Teresa turned sixteen in March and wanted to leave school. The nuns wanted her to stay on and try for Oxford. Waugh, who never disguised his amazement that anyone should think her intelligent, counselled further study, possibly to delay her return home. Throughout that summer he plodded on with the novel, finding the feminine company he craved only in Laura and Meg and odd visits from Frances Donaldson. Strauss, however, had warned Waugh that his passion for his daughter might decline as he regained his sanity – and this is precisely what happened. It was a sad loss, with nothing to fill the gap. His metropolitan friends seemed distant and, with the exception of Greene and Ann Fleming, they were cautious of him since his ordeal. Trying to console Diana Cooper, he merely wounded her further. 'I love you', she wrote, '& yet you have the power to hurt me so...':

> You have never ... known real Grief. Panic, mealancholia [*sic*], madness, night-sweats, we've all known for most of our lives, you and me particularly. I'm not sure you know human love in the way I do. You have faith & mysticism, intense inner interests – a diverting virile mind, gusto for vengence [*sic*] & destruction....
>
> What you can't imagine is a creature with a certain irredescant [*sic*]

152. Unpublished ALS, 24 June [1954], from Piers Court; *Catalogue* E1374, p. 293.
153. Unpublished ALS from Alec Waugh, 20 June 1954, np [MacDowell Colony, USA]; BL.

> aura & nothing within but a beating frightened heart built round & for Duff. I have no 'sisterhood with heavenly things' not for want of praying & trying to feel it. 'The instinct' that you call false 'to keep life as it was' is protective against madness & despair. . . .[154]

It was true: he did not know grief or that impassioned love in which the self is lost. 'O darling, O God,' he replied, 'what a shit I am! How I don't want ever to hurt you!. . . It's the fatal pen always turning kind thoughts to offence. Talking is the thing, face to your dear face.'[155] In certain areas of human experience he was, like Crouchback, sterile, impotent. No one suffered that 'false instinct' more than Waugh. The Pinfold experience, nevertheless, had changed him. Even in this stern and irritable mood, he could now turn his positive qualities to good account for his children and the Church.

*

During that summer, Laura had agreed to hold a garden fête to raise money for their local church. Waugh watched her arrangements impatiently. Finally, he stepped in and took over. The humble gathering his wife had envisaged was instantly transformed into a national event. The tincture of riotous fantasy that he brought to all his creations was infectious. It caught up the children, the press and two young American strangers.

Edward Sheehan was the impoverished foreign correspondent for a group of New England newspapers[156] and was living in a rented room in London during that humid summer. An admirer of Huxley, Greene and Waugh, Sheehan vaguely hoped to meet them. Greene and Huxley were out of the country, which left the least accessible member of the triumvirate. Sheehan scribbled a one-line postcard expecting nothing, but, like Paul Moor, was astonished by the response. Waugh enclosed an engraved invitation card and a poster. The young man was asked to display the latter in Grosvenor Square. The card read:

> Mr. & Mrs. Evelyn Waugh
>
> request the honour of your company at a Garden Fete in aid of St. Dominic's Church, to be held (weather permitting) on Saturday, August 14th, 3p.m.–7p.m. at Piers Court, Stinchcombe, Dursley.
>
> Refreshments – Children's Sports – Stalls, Etc.
>
> Admission 1/-; Children 6d.
>
> Donations gratefully accepted from those unable to be present.

154. ALS, 17 May 1954, from Château de St Firmin, Vineuil, Oise; BL; *MWMS*, p. 194.
155. ALS to Lady Diana Cooper, 22 May 1954, from Piers Court; BL; *MWMS*, p. 195.
156. Principally the *Boston Globe*.

> A small but interesting collection of Paintings, mostly Victorian narrative pictures, and of rare books, never previously exhibited, will be on view in the house 4p.m.–7p.m. (wet or fine)....[157]

'We need men of resource', Waugh wrote, 'to manage traffic, detect thieves, "bark" at sideshows, spend money, and judge children's sports. Also in the morning to help erect booths.'[158] He wanted to know if Sheehan were a conjuror, ventriloquist, contortionist or trumpet soloist. If so, these skills could be put to good use. Sheehan replied that, while possessing none of these accomplishments, he was willing to stand on his head reading selections from *Finnegans Wake*. Waugh extended the invitation to include Friday night. Clearly, he was 'more in search of a stevedore than in need of a house guest',[159] but the chance to spend an entire week-end with a literary hero was too delicious a prospect to resist.

He was not disappointed. Met at Stroud by the gardener, Sheehan was transported to the house and dumped on the doorstep. The gardener drove off. The door was locked and there was no response to the bell. Eventually Waugh opened up, solid, florid and quizzical in a red smoking-jacket, and took his American to the nightmare guest room. 'The bed was lavishly canopied, the canopy generously tasselled.... In the adjoining bathroom was a ... conventional basin with a gaping hole in it. On the basin was painted the simple inscription "Mrs Grant: *her mark*."' Then Bron, a lean, red-headed, amiable boy, knocked on the door to ask whether Sheehan wanted the housekeeper to heat water for his bath and whether he preferred his fish boiled or broiled. Downstairs again, Sheehan received the 'family treatment'. As he picked nervously at his fish, they stared at him. Waugh perched on a sofa, sipping brandy:

> The remarkable eyes came out of this far-away gaze and focussed sharply on me.
>
> 'Where are you from?' ...
>
> '... Boston.' ...
>
> 'I have been there.'
>
> 'The politics are interesting....' ...
>
> 'You like politics?' he asked, apparently intrigued.
>
> 'I love politics,' I said, plunging forward.
>
> 'I loathe politics.... Please change the subject.... You Americans.... What an extraordinary breed you are! ... While on my

157. Edward R. F. Sheehan, 'A Weekend with Waugh', *Cornhill Magazine* 171 (Summer 1960), 209–25. The poster, reproduced in *EWAHW*, p. 212, repeats this information, adding that Miss Rose Donaldson (daughter of Jack and Frances) would offer 'Personally Conducted Tours' every twenty minutes from 4.00 to 7.00 p.m.
158. *Ibid.*, 210; also *Letters*, p. 428.
159. *Ibid.*, 211.

lecture tour . . ., the enquiry most often directed at me was whether or not I slept in the nude.'[160]

The children chuckled; Laura watched the performance with 'uncritical silence'. She was, Sheehan decided, 'a woman of few words who seemed to accept those of her husband with a serenity bordering on adoration.'[161] But the American was learning the game. Already they were calling him 'Teddy' as though some extraordinary nursery toy had sprung to life in their midst. Waugh pulled down a wall-map of Piers Court's small estate, as if it might have been Blenheim Palace, and explained his tactics. '"I think we'll put Teddy in the car-park," ' he said. '"Teddy will do splendidly in the car-park. We have the special head-piece for him." '[162]

On Saturday morning the family was already at breakfast when Sheehan came down smoking a cigarette. Waugh leapt across the room in benevolent mood, snatched the offending object from his guest's lips and threw it out of a window. Afterwards Bron took him on a tour of the grounds. The front section, it seemed, was Waugh's province: the manicured lawn and the follies; the back, Laura's: hen house, pig-pens and the kitchen garden. She strode about in faded jeans organizing the domestic regime; Waugh commanded the shifting of books and furniture, the new position of each piece precisely determined as an integral part of a design. Then he took Sheehan to the toilet. While the American stood amazed at the leopard-skin throne, his host produced from a cupboard a Prussian officer's helmet surmounted by an enormous spike. This, Waugh explained, was to be worn in the car park where the guests had been promised a unicorn. Sheehan refused the honour of fabled beast. Luckily another American, Joe Crowley, turned up and was dispatched to wander dreamily on the green slope to the side of the house in horn-rimmed spectacles and spike. This left Sheehan free to observe the guests as they poured in.

Many had come from London, including William Douglas-Home for the *Sunday Express*. The Donaldsons' sixteen-year-old daughter, Rose, had been instructed by Waugh to recite a brief description of the house and its contents. The effect was that of a ventriloquist's dummy and was designed to be provocative. '"Ladies & Gentlemen, this is Sir Max Beerbohm's famous caricature of Sir Ernest Cassel. Pray notice the gross Jewish features so strongly transmitted to Lady Mountbatten". . . .'[163] In one room hung a pair of paintings by Rebecca Solomon: *The Idle Student (Reading For Pluck)* and *The Industrious Student (Reading For Honours)*. The first depicts a fashionable young man, glass in one hand, newspaper in the other, a pretty

160. *Ibid.*, 213–14.
161. *Ibid.*, 214.
162. *Ibid.*, 215.
163. ALS to Lady Diana Cooper, 29 August [1954], from Piers Court; BL; *MWMS*, p. 197.

young flower-seller looking in through an open window by his side. The second is more severe: the student, in cap and gown, is decorously paying court to a respectable young woman. '"This one is reading for honours", piped Rose, "– this one for pluck. The newspaper that can be seen ... is a kind of rag, the equivalent of, one might say, today's *Sunday Express*."'[164]

The remark did not find its way into Douglas-Home's article,[165] but he was nevertheless impressed. In the library his gaze moved respectfully round the *objets d'art*: the portrait of George III, Rossetti's *Spirit of the Rainbow*, a libellous Max Beerbohm caricature of Edward VII, a copy of Repton's *Brighton Pavilion* (the only thing guests were requested not to touch). Over the fireplace hung a panel by Martin Battersby, presented in 1953 by Chapman & Hall, which depicted in cipher Waugh's life's work.[166] The statuette of Romeo and Juliet, Miss Donaldson solemnly explained, had been inexplicably damaged by the Dominican nuns during their wartime occupation. On the stairs hung the three *Pleasures of Travel* pictures; on a landing stood the Burges wash-hand-stand, lugged there by a dutiful Sheehan. In the drawing-room was Augustus Egg's *An Afternoon on the River*, a recent purchase by the Save the Children Fund. The whole event was a huge joke to dispel the popular image of Waugh as an inaccessible ogre. Dressed that day in neat grey suit and tie, he held court, a picture of benignity, in the Greek Temple. Laura ran a roulette table with a cardboard wheel; the children took bets on a wood-louse race; for twopence one could enter a mysterious tent marked 'The Holy Friar' to discover a perforated frying pan hanging on a piece of string. The Stinchcombe Silver Band played erratically and Fr Collins had charge of a second-hand book stall where a volume on the Pope lay beside Edgar Wallace's *The India-Rubber Man*. The unicorn, under Jack Donaldson's supervision, found himself marshalling 200–300 cars. The whole atmosphere of the event was that of *Decline and Fall*. The grounds thronged with contented visitors. Waugh had paid the Poor Clares to pray for fine weather. Five minutes before opening time, the rain had stopped.

Meticulous attention to factual detail was now also a part of Waugh's regular working practice. During that summer and autumn he wrote steadily, constantly revising, and he used a research agency to check historical, meteorological and medical data. Writers and Speakers' Research[167] pro-

164. Frances Donaldson, *Portrait of a Country Neighbour* (Weidenfeld & Nicolson, 1967), p. 49. Lady Donaldson misremembers a little: the newspaper is not in the student's pocket but droops from his left hand. The paintings now hang in the University of Texas.

165. 'Waugh Locks Up His Lambs As His "Public" Tours His Treasures', *SE*, 15 August 1954, 7.

166. Waugh decided to commission Battersby after seeing similar panels in Chantilly which he had executed for Duff and Lady Diana Cooper.

167. The firm was run by the wife of the official historian of the Commandos, Joan St George Saunders, and Joan Bright Astley.

vided an excellent service with which Waugh was almost entirely satisfied. Indeed, he continued to use them until the early 1960s, when they were set to track down his genealogy for *A Little Learning*. On one occasion in 1954, however, there was a brief and revealing skirmish.

In reply to his enquiry about Crouchback's medical condition after evacuation from Crete and a week in an open boat,[168] Mrs Astley had referred Waugh to her own history of the Northumberland Hussars. This contains a description of the evacuation:

> Organization had broken down. . . . Water was the chief difficulty and they drank it from wells which they would not have looked at under normal circumstances. . . . It was the wells that were responsible for the change from decency and uniformity to an untidiness and motley. . . .
>
> On Saturday, 31st [May 1941], the . . . Hussars were told that places in a boat had been allotted for one officer and twenty men. They drew lots . . .; the boats were leaving at 3 a.m. and it was just half past two. . . . [Then] the untoward [happened]. From lower down the slope another string of men were coming in from the flank and joining in. . . . The tail of their line which moved in alongside was going faster. The two lines chased each other down the steep and narrow track to the beach. But it was too late. The last boat was pulling away and those who had got there first had taken up the space allotted.[169]

What she provided here was an alternative history to that of Waugh's fiction. The disorganization, she insisted, was not the result of cowardice but of bad drinking water and exhaustion. The collapse of discipline resulted in another regiment shoving the honourable Hussars to one side in the rush for the boats. Unknown to her, Waugh had been one of those scrambling for a place, and she embarrassed him further by emphasizing the distinction between the 'regular fighting men on Crete', debilitated by weeks of courageous rearguard action, and the 'newcomers' who had not suffered equally: '. . . if your man was an "odd man out" (i.e. a Staff Officer, a Commando, a Saboteur) then he would of course have had his wits about him and felt fairly fresh by the 31st May.' Only string-pulling, she added, by 'kindly Brigadiers watching over him in Whitehall'[170] could have secured his immediate passage home from Egypt unless he were a 'real "blighty"'.

168. Cf. *Letters*, p. 431.
169. Unpublished TLS, 26 October 1954, from Joan Bright Astley of Writers & Speakers' Research, 4 Crescent Mansions, 113 Fulham Road, SW3; BL.
170. Cf. *ibid.*: 'Only a big "string-pull" would have got him back to the U.K. . . . the majority of casualties . . . were held in hospitals in Egypt, Palestine, and then evacuated to South African Military Hospitals until the situation in England was less fraught with danger. Those fit again for active service were sent to convalescent depots and then re-drafted to units. Only the real "blighties" got home.'

Waugh was infuriated by her interference. It not only retold his account but it implicated him in dishonour, recalling the uncomfortable fact that the military in Egypt had packed him off home, unwounded, at a time when every man was needed. He did not want to know about this and rebuked the agency for meddling. In future, they sent him only the facts requested.

By 4 November he had posted the final page to the typist and was promising Chapman & Hall a 'shooting script' in a fortnight. 'It is shorter than *Men At Arms*,' he informed Peters, 'but rather better.'[171] *Happy Warriors*, he thought, would be his last novel and its completion coincided with the publication of his short stories, *Tactical Exercise*, in America. The vogue for his writing continued to wane there. Reviewers, Salmen wrote with uncharacteristic drollery, 'are unanimous in pointing out that some of the stories are good and some are bad. They are equally unanimous in disagreeing completely on which are which.'[172] Sales had only just topped 5,000 and, although this was respectable for a collection, Waugh again looked gloomily to the future. How long, he asked Peters, would the American money last exclusive of anything *Happy Warriors* might make? The answer was worrying: three years.[173] Waugh, elated to have finished the novel at all, determined to have a long rest until publication in June. But the idea soon collapsed under the cumulative weight of sorrow. On 6 December Mrs Yaxley found Catherine Waugh dead in her chair.

'My mother's death was all I could have wished for her,' he wrote to Peters. '... Alec was able to get home for the funeral....'[174] None of Waugh's children was there, nor did he make any effort to get them from school. When he and Laura had heard the news, neither rushed to London: James's first communion the following day took priority and they came up late that evening. Mrs Yaxley, it seems, was left to deal with the undertakers. Alec was left to deal with the estate. But it saddened Waugh to think that his children had never known the vivacious woman he had worshipped. 'I am afraid you will always remember her as old and feeble,' he wrote to Meg. '... She loved all you children very much. You six were her chief interest in her last years.'[175] 'Granny Waugh', as she was known in the family, had died, aged eighty-four, 'bitterly weary and irked by her depen-

171. Unpublished ALS, 4 November [1954], from Piers Court; *Catalogue* E869, p. 208.
172. Unpublished TccL from Stanley Salmen of Little, Brown, 1 November 1954; HRC.
173. Waugh's American credit stood at $47,000. American sales of *Men At Arms* (up to 5 November 1954): 19,000, earning $9,000. Sales of *Tactical Exercise* had made just $3,000. This was a far cry from the earlier success of *Brideshead* and *The Loved One*. Waugh now earned more from British than from American sales. *Men At Arms* had sold nearly 31,000 in hardback in the UK and export market. Penguin had sold 56,000.
174. Unpublished ALS, 11 December 1954; *Catalogue* E872, p. 209.
175. 11 December 1954; *Letters*, p. 434.

dent state.... So for her [death] was happy....'[176] For Waugh, however, her departure merely evoked 'regret for a lifetime of failure in affection & attention.'[177]

Christmas came and went, filling the house with children and influenza. In winter melancholy, Waugh left them for a holiday he had been planning since October: two months in Jamaica with Lord Brownlow and Ann Fleming. 'Before embarking on any ship with you', she had joked, 'I shall require a certificate guaranteeing your *mental health* and would prefer a strong male nurse to accompany us....'[178] But it was not entirely a joke for him. 'Poor Evelyn,' she wrote to her brother, 'he is deeply unhappy – bored from morning till night and has developed a personality which he hates but cannot escape from....'[179] Indeed, escape from it was now more difficult than ever. By the end of December he had decided on his next literary project and had stepped aboard a Cunarder with a quire of clean foolscap to begin *Pinfold* in the sunlight of the West Indies.

176. ALS to Nancy Mitford, 18 December 1954; *Letters*, p. 435.
177. *Ibid.*
178. *LAF*, p. 143.
179. *Ibid.*, ALS to Hugo Charteris, 14 February 1955, p. 151.

X

Papa Pug: January 1955–August 1957

Darling Laura,

. . . At present Perry and his bride[1] are alone here. Both very welcoming. . . . The house is very splendid, full of furniture and pictures & silver from Belton. The cooking awfully bad. . . . Best of all it is 600 feet up and so is cool and airy. . . . I feel full of euphoria this morning but I do not think you would be perfectly happy because we spend the evenings on the verandah and bats flies [*sic*] round us in clouds. There is to be much entertaining soon. At present all is peaceful and I intend to start writing about my lunacy soon. . . .

E.[2]

Released from the British winter, Waugh could relax for a few days in the silence of Roaring River. But this was not a mood that could long endure. As the other guests moved in, he moved out.

Ann Fleming reported Waugh's visit, saying that:

> [He] has arrived and left behaving with near-warm civility to Peter [Quennell]. . . . It was an occasion when Evelyn wished to please for he had been two weeks with the Brownlows and said it was a great intellectual strain to find words simple enough to converse with them. . . . [He] took gallantly to the underwater mask [here], but his rowing in a rubber boat over coral pinnacles became commando-courage. When his panama blew overboard, his little arms jerked up, sweeping the rocks, towards the edge of the reef and the giant breakers. I cried for mercy and said if he returned to calm water I would scramble and swim for the panama, but no sooner was swimming possible than I belly-flopped from the boat and dashed for the shore; he thought it very treacherous and was only half placated when I

1. Lord Brownlow married his second wife, an American, Dorothy Power, in 1954.
2. Unpublished ALI to Laura Waugh, 25 January 1955, from Roaring River, St Anne's Bay, Jamaica, BWI; BL.

> found him a sea-slug to squeeze – they shoot out a mile of purple ink if touched.[3]

Floating, aimless, on that dazzling sea, Waugh's thoughts were elsewhere: with his family and in his book. He found Jamaica dull. Each day, in the limpid early morning, he would write, shaping the precise self-portrait with which *Pinfold* opens. But the vagrant life no longer suited him. 'I wish your mother was here with me,' he wrote to Bron. '... I left her very cold & sad.'[4] As he relived the terrors of the previous year, a confused sense of guilt and gratitude made him eager to return. He was worried about Bron and Meg, both melancholy and subversive at school; he was also unhappy to have left before saying good-bye to them. And there was another unresolved difficulty: Nancy Spain was continuing her vendetta in the *Daily Express*.

Before his departure, Waugh had heard from Ian Gilmour[5] about this latest unwelcome publicity. 'The ... article ... was chiefly about your brother, but she made several references to you. These were not offensive but they were, I thought, pretty impertinent.'[6] Waugh did nothing about it. Three months after his return, another veiled sneer appeared in the paper, this time by Robert Pitman. Pitman, writing a 'colour piece' heralding the publication of *Officers and Gentlemen*, had thumbed through *Burke's Landed Gentry* and discovered the Waugh crest:

> ... poking from a knightly helmet stands a sheaf of corn and under it this motto: 'Industria Ditat' (Hard Work Makes You Rich).... [This] is peculiarly apt. Mr. Waugh's lineage ... is no longer than yours or mine; it brought him no riches; it certainly never landed him among the landed gentry.... [He] was reared in Golders Green. He bought Piers Court himself. He paid for his own coat of arms.... And the cash came, not from ancient fortune but from Mr. Waugh's own arduous work and from the common, book-buying millions. Mr. Waugh – the Boswell of our older aristocracy – ... is in fact something bigger, and infinitely better than the men of birth he admires. He is a self-made man.[7]

The implication seems clear: Mr Waugh should dismount from his high horse and admit to brotherhood with the 'common, book-buying millions'; Mr Waugh was a hypocrite. Pitman then drew on that bane of Waugh's

3. ALS from Ann Fleming to Hugo Charteris, 14 February 1955, from Goldeneye, Jamaica; *LAF*, pp. 150–5.
4. 22 January 1955; *Letters*, p. 438.
5. Then Editor of the *Spectator*, now Sir Ian Gilmour, a Conservative MP.
6. Unpublished ALS, 3 January 1955; BL.
7. 'Mr Waugh Makes Good', *SE*, 15 May 1955, 4.

life, the paper's press-clippings' file. The Pope anecdote[8] was trundled out like a recurring nightmare. Attention was again drawn to Waugh's divorce. The story concluded with *Men At Arms*, whose

> hero – in one critic's view – reached a degree of smug piety unrivalled outside *Tom Brown's Schooldays*.... But perhaps Mr. Waugh was pulling our legs. For his advance notice of next month's sequel to *Men At Arms* has this hint: '*Men At Arms* began with its hero inspired by illusion. *Officers and Gentlemen* ends with his deflation.'
>
> There are some who would like to apply the same process to Mr. Waugh himself – But they are wrong. For with all his faults the waspish, pompous, brilliant Mr. Waugh has become an essential mountain among our literary molehills.[9]

The ingenious final sentence kept the *Express* on the windy side of libel. There is little doubt, however, that the article was another tactical exercise in 'deflation' and Waugh, perhaps with some justification this time, detected Beaverbrook's influence.

Alec contacted his brother immediately, enclosing a letter of reply for his approval. Relations between them had been strained since their mother's death. In clearing her flat, Alec had discovered a pile of letters which opened old wounds and which he was tempted to destroy. Instead, he had set them aside for Evelyn to collect.[10] The division of portable property had also caused friction. Alec had allocated books, furniture and artefacts to various members of the family. Numerous volumes on Hampstead from their father's library had mistakenly found their way to Piers Court and Evelyn had charitably offered to burn them. Alec had stepped in to prevent sacrilege. Now, spontaneously, he was offering to close ranks against Evelyn's enemies:

> It seems to me desirable ... that the regularization of the position with the College of Heralds should be recorded as a joint operation. If you agree, I shall be delighted to send you a cheque for half the amount....
> The letter could then be phrased 'my brother and I regularized the

8. See ch. IX, p. 314 above.
9. 'Mr Waugh Makes Good', *op. cit.*
10. Cf. unpublished ALS from Alec Waugh to Evelyn Waugh, 14 December 1954, from 14A Hampstead Lane, Highgate, N6; BL: 'P.P.S.: Some of the letters in the small brown case are very personal – I nearly tore them up, as they might scratch old sores – then I thought ... suave mari magno.' Alec's Latin tag, the first words of Lucretius's *De Rerum Natura*, Bk II, is ambiguous in its application. A rough translation of the first sentence might run: 'How sweet it is when the winds stir the waters on the great sea, to gaze from the land at another's struggle, not from delight in his trouble, but because it is sweet to behold those ills from which one is free.' Alec probably chose the allusion benevolently to suggest: 'How glad I am that all those [family] troubles are behind us.'

position'. I should like anyhow to pay my share to the coat of arms.... I should have done so at the time.[11]

Evelyn was touched by this loyalty. Any rebuke, he agreed, should come from Alec rather than from himself, and Alec posted the letter. It pointed out that the arms had been regularized in 1930 and conferred on Arthur Waugh. It did not mention that, upon remarriage in 1937, Evelyn had been unduly exercised about clarifying the situation with the College. It was at this point that he had paid the money to ensure his credentials as a gentleman. Alec had been approached and asked for a half-share then, but low income and an indifference to being seen to be armigerous had allowed him to decline the offer with a clear conscience. He remained unconcerned about the crest. His financial situation, however, had suddenly improved. 'I met Peters in London,' Evelyn wrote, 'who told me the news that you have hit the jackpot with your latest novel. I am delighted & look forward eagerly to reading it.'[12] The novel, *Island in the Sun*, had appeared first in America just before *Officers and Gentlemen*.

Alec's letter had cheered Evelyn during a bad time. He had returned from Jamaica, cold and depressed, to find the precise order of his house disrupted by Highgate debris. A general election was in full swing after Churchill's resignation and Eden's succession as Prime Minister. Politics this time impinged directly upon Waugh's domestic life. Laura was absent in County Durham assisting her brother in his futile attempt to win a safe Labour seat for the Conservatives. The national result – a further swing to the right and Eden confirmed as Prime Minister – Waugh found drearily predictable and cause for further melancholy. He revised the first section of *Pinfold* and waited with some trepidation for the reception of his war novel. It was at this point, almost on the eve of publication and with the children home for the summer holidays, that persecution by the *Express* took a new turn.

Waugh's diary aptly conveys his feelings:

21 June

A telephone message at breakfast: could Miss Spain and Lord Noel-Buxton ... come to call. They were told not to.... That evening ... a hullabaloo at the front door. Miss Spain and Lord Noel-Buxton were there trying to force an entry. I sent them away and remained tremulous with rage all the evening.

11. Unpublished ALS from Alec Waugh, 16 May 1955, from Hotel King of Denmark, Holmens Kanal 15, Copenhagen, Denmark; BL.
12. Unpublished ALS to Alec Waugh, 18 May 1955, from Piers Court; BUL.

22 June
And all the next day.[13]

Laura, who had answered the telephone and passed on the message, had also opened the door. On seeing the reporters, she had sighed and leaned against the jamb. The 'hullabaloo' began with Waugh, who was heard calling from somewhere inside the house: 'Who is it? What is it?' Laura wearily recited the names. Her husband burst forth: 'Go away, go away! You read the notice, didn't you? No admittance on business!' 'I'm not on business,' Noel-Buxton replied with what he hoped was dignity. 'I'm a member of the House of Lords.' 'Go away!'[14] Waugh slammed the door. The reporters shambled back down the drive. Waugh shot out again, stumped after them and clanged the wrought-iron gates fast shut.

Two days later, in London to sign the special edition of *Officers and Gentlemen*, he was taken by Jack McDougall to his club for luncheon. There they discovered Miss Spain's version of events: two prominent columns in the *Express*. The story offered more disingenuous praise. Again file stories were constructed as shabby biography. The general tactic, as later, was to find someone sincere, gentle and with the common touch to set against Waugh the hypocrite, violent and snubbing. In this case, it was the ancient Poet Laureate, John Masefield. Spain and her Lord had first visited him and been treated royally. He liked journalists, he said, having been one himself. He had been a barman in New York before Prohibition. Miss Spain found him a 'darling man' and the three had chatted amicably over oatcakes about Roman fords, Noel-Buxton's chief interest. (During the 1950s he had several times appeared in the popular press, a damp figure wading through British rivers.)[15] Throughout the article, Noel-Buxton is presented as a farcical naïf, a character from Wodehouse. The benign eccentricities of Lord and Laureate were thus implicitly contrasted with Waugh's 'malice'. He immediately contacted Muggeridge to secure a platform for reply in *Punch*.

When the typescript arrived, Muggeridge rejected it as libellous and, on re-reading, Waugh agreed with him. Ian Gilmour's offer to publish in the *Spectator* allowed him time to stand back, cut and polish. The result was masterly, a benign and energetic dismissal, demolishing the *Express*'s main line of attack: that Waugh was indiscriminately infatuated with the aristocracy:

> The fifty or sixty thousand people in this country who alone support the Arts do not go to Lord Beaverbrook's critics for guidance. So it is that artists of all kinds form part of the battle-training of green

13. *Diaries*, p. 725.
14. Nancy Spain, 'My Pilgrimage to See Mr. Waugh', *DE*, 23 June 1955, 6.
15. Successful in fording the Humber and Severn, he had sunk in the Thames.

> reporters. 'Don't lounge about the office, lad,' the editors say, 'sit up and insult an artist.' . . . We have many sorts of lord in our country. . . . In Lord Noel-Buxton we see the lord predatory. He appears to think that his barony gives him the right to a seat at the dinner-table in any private house in the kingdom.
>
> Fear of this lord is clearly the beginning of wisdom.[16]

Waugh was delighted with this, as were his friends. Wodehouse had suffered a similar invasion:

> . . . [the reporter] prattled away all smiles and cheeriness, and sat down and wrote a stinker about me for his beastly gutter rag. . . . I was all over the bastard. . . . It just shows that the Waugh method is the only one for dealing with the *Express*. 'Ptarmigan, throw this man out and see that he lands on something sharp. . . .'[17]

It was a hot, brilliant summer. Laura was out all day in the hayfield as Waugh moved idly round the house, took long walks and anxiously watched for the post. 'I am awfully encouraged that you like *Officers & Gentlemen*,' he wrote to Bowra. 'The reviewers don't, fuck them.'[18] But so pleased was he by his triumph in the *Spectator* that even this divided reception could not spoil his mood:

> Bad reviews of *O. and G.* in England, good ones from New York. . . . Ann [Fleming] telephoned yesterday to say that Gilmour was uneasy about [Kingsley] Amis's review. . . . He need not have been. It did not disturb me at all and came unfortunately for him in the same issue as the Noel-Buxton article which shows there is life in the old dog – more than in the young. I am quite complacent about the book's quality. My only anxiety is about American sales. It would be very convenient to have another success there.[19]

For 'success' read 'blockbuster'. By normal publishing standards Waugh's novels had been continuously 'successful' and the recent publicity had boosted custom. Within a month, McDougall was reporting that sales had topped 26,000 and were cruising nicely at 800 a week. On the back of this, *Men At Arms* was moving again at 100 a week: a total of 33,000, which McDougall expected *Officers and Gentlemen* to surpass. Waugh had good reason for complacency, but he was, as usual, over-reacting to criticism.

The British reviews were by no means universally hostile. The *Manchester Guardian* had relished the novel's 'fierce gaiety' and fine writing;[20]

16. 'Awake My Soul! It Is A Lord!', *Spectator*, 8 July 1955, 36–7; *EAR*, pp. 468–70.
17. Unpublished TLS from P. G. Wodehouse, 23 July 1955, from Remsenburg, NY; BL.
18. 14 July 1955; *Letters*, p. 444.
19. *Diaries*, 11 July 1955, p. 729.
20. Norman Shrapnel, *Manchester Guardian*, 1 July 1955, 4; *CH*, pp. 365–6.

Sykes thought that this 'wild extravaganza' recalled *Black Mischief* but 'for comedy, enormity and success in ambitious effect' surpassed the earlier work.[21] Even the *TLS* considered '... the standard of Mr. Waugh's dialogue and description as high as ever ... [showing] a deeper capacity for fusing experience and entertainment.'[22] Only Amis and Connolly had expressed reservations, and both had tempered these with high praise.

Disappointed by *Men At Arms*, Connolly had looked forward 'to its successor to make amends' and discovered 'a benign lethargy which makes it slow reading'.[23] Swallowing his embarrassment, he lauded the opening scene and the last hundred pages dealing with Crete. In the intervening matter, however, he had discovered little to interest him in the relationships between the characters who seemed 'too superficial to sustain the structure'.[24] And Connolly was not alone in sensing incompleteness. Confusion arose partly from the unexpected announcement that this volume would conclude the work begun with *Men At Arms*. 'The book ends with such a tangle of loose threads', the *New York Times* remarked, 'that it is difficult to agree with Mr. Waugh that it and *Men At Arms* form a whole.'[25] Amis (who had clearly not read his dust-jacket carefully) looked only half-optimistically to 'the continuation of this saga' to pull together the 'discursive and episodic' elements of the narrative.[26]

Waugh's friends were furious with Connolly, attributing his bitchiness to the book's satire of him and to depression. (His estranged second wife had gone to live with George Weidenfeld; divorce was imminent.) Waugh could extend sympathy towards a friend in the doldrums. In Amis's piece, however, he detected a quite different note: the battle cry of a new cohort of enemies. *Lucky Jim*, published the year before and a runaway best-seller, had established Amis as a challenger to Waugh's position as the leading British humorist. The Movement was under way, with its grammar-school lads storming the portals of 'tradition'. Waugh stood fast with his stick at the ready for what he termed 'the teddy-boy school of novelist & critic'.[27] He could see nothing funny in *Lucky Jim*. Amis hoped that few would wish

21. Christopher Sykes, *Time & Tide*, 2 July 1955, 871–2; *CH*, pp. 366–9.
22. Unsigned review, *TLS*, 8 July 1955, 377.
23. *ST*, 3 July 1955, 5; *CH*, pp. 369–71.
24. *Ibid.*, p. 369.
25. Geoffrey Moore, *NYTBR*, 10 July 1955, 18; *CH*, pp. 374–6.
26. *Spectator*, 8 July 1955, 56–9; *CH*, pp. 371–4.
27. Cf. ALS to Christopher Sykes, 15 July 1955; *Letters*, p. 445: 'I have a theory about the modern Teddy-boy school of novelist & critic – Wain, Ames [*sic*] etc. It is that they all read English Literature for schools and so take against it, while good critics & writers read as a treat and a relaxation from Latin & Greek.' Five months later Waugh opened his attack on 'the new wave of philistinism', replying to Nancy Mitford's 'the English Aristocracy' in 'An Open Letter to the Honble Mrs Peter Rodd ... on a Very Serious Subject' (*Encounter*, December 1955, 11–17; revised and expanded in *Noblesse Oblige* [Hamish Hamilton, 1956], pp. 65–82): 'L'Ecole de Butler are the primal men and women of the classless society ... but of the ramifications of the social order which

to identify themselves with the neo-Jacobite, sexless Crouchback. Waugh, it seems, felt similar antipathy for Jim Dixon (who had effectively offered Hooper a voice with which to answer Ryder). Nevertheless, the essence of Amis's complaint was compliment: disappointment again at Waugh's continued suppression of 'that farcical vein which founded his reputation'.[28] In company with many others since 1945, Amis saw *A Handful of Dust* as Waugh's best and *Brideshead* as his worst book. The review was a lament for the decline of comic ferocity.

Norman Shrapnel suggested, perhaps more subtly, that 'Disorganisation is more than merely a subject for [Waugh's] fierce brand of farce; it is an expression of spiritual perversity.'[29] But it took L. P. Hartley to develop the theme:

> Your economy of means is really breath-taking.... I think it is your sincerity as an artist & a thinker that impresses me the most, for from it comes your clearness of vision & the knife-edge quality of your prose ... chaos is your subject, life without meaning – which you convey by flashes of meaning so intense that the surrounding darkness seems all the darker. And the characters, even when not meant to be sympathetic, somehow have one's sympathy – each trying in his different way to impress himself on the chaos & not quite give in to the conviction of futility – snatching humour & wit out of circumstances so supremely un-funny. There is no one who can convey as you do the desolation of the heart, deprived of everything that nourishes it.[30]

Those who saw Waugh only as a toothless lion or a lamentable lover of lords, missed this crucial point. His sense of the absurd was more strongly directed than ever upon the futility of secular experience. Supernatural reality was all, and the Nancy Spain incident marked another milestone in his cenobitic retraction. 'You may remember', he wrote to an estate agent, 'that you came here about nine years ago when I had an idea of moving to Ireland. Now I have the idea of moving anywhere. I am sick of the district.... I don't want frivolous sight-seers. Only serious lunatics....'[31] Piers Court was up for sale and Waugh was in the market for a castle with sharper palisades.

*

have obsessed some of the acutest minds of the last 150 years, they know less than of the castes of India. What can their critics hope to make of the undertones and innuendoes, the evocative reminiscent epithets of, say, Tony Powell or Leslie Hartley?' (pp. 66–7).

28. *CH*, p. 371.
29. *Ibid.*, p. 366.
30. Unpublished ALS from L. P. Hartley to Evelyn Waugh, 26 July 1955, from Avondale, Bathford, Somerset; BL. Hartley, a friend of Ann Fleming, was only a distant social acquaintance of Waugh. They admired each other's work and exchanged copies of new work after the war, but they rarely met.
31. ALS to Messrs Knight, Frank and Rutley, 4 July 1955; *Letters*, p. 443.

During that summer, Diana Cooper visited Piers Court to discover a wholly different Waugh from the man who had tormented her a year earlier: 'Thank you for my day of sweetness & light – Laura so pretty & lissom – you unpossessed & as you should always be – the dear darling Papa pug, petted ragged & loved.'[32] Waugh at home could be delightful, moving briskly about house and garden, humming hymn tunes out of key, always the master of ceremonies. Piers Court was a vital establishment. Part of his children's difficulty in dealing with school was its comparative drabness. Teresa, determined and authoritative, had settled best to formal education and became Head Girl at the Ascot convent. That summer she left to take digs in Oxford, attend a crammer's and prepare for university entrance. Meg and Hatty floundered on unhappily in her wake; Bron was enduring a difficult adolescence in his father's shadow.

From Jamaica, Waugh had written to him, offering benevolent correction of the sort Arthur Waugh had dispatched to Lancing. Arthur's prescriptions had irritated Evelyn; Evelyn's irritated Bron. 'I got the impression', Waugh wrote, 'that last term you were going a bit far in your defiance of school rules. I should hate you to be low spirited and submissive, but don't become an anarchist. Don't above all things put on side. . . . Be superior by cultivating your intellect and your taste.'[33] This was good advice perhaps, but in effect Bron was being asked not to behave as his father had done and, as schoolboys, their characters were strikingly similar.

Over the next year, relations between father and son deteriorated. Christopher Sykes's son, Mark, having been removed from Eton, was one of Bron's closer friends at Downside. The school, feeling young Waugh to be in bad company, had proposed a change of house. Evelyn had agreed without consulting Bron and the result was a sulky letter home:

> . . . Since you are obviously resolved to effect the transfer I cannot dissuade you. It is unprecedented in the history of the school to change houses outside Junior House, let alone approaching the fourth year here. You made the decision ignorant of the constitution or opinion of the school, and could not have realized how drastic such a course is . . . my circle of friends [will not] change . . ., or if it does, it will be for the worse; Carmel [?] House, under Father Aelred's ministration . . . is by far the most vicious. . . . Frankly, I would rather the ticket to Australia.[34]

32. ALS, 25 [July? 1955], from 42 Hyde Park Gate; BL; *MWMS*, p. 208.
33. 27 January 1955; *Letters*, pp. 437–8.
34. Unpublished ALS from Auberon Waugh, 21 May 1955, from Downside Numismatic Society, Stratton on the Fosse, Bath; BL.

Bron was fifteen, quick-witted, lazy, sparkish and, like his father, acutely sensitive to social distinction. The boy was already having to visit the headmaster regularly to discuss work and 'attitude', emerging from his study with the uncomfortable sensation of having been psychoanalysed. The proposed change was a further humiliation. But Papa, sternly compassionate, would not be swayed. He held Dom Aelred in the highest esteem. 'Don't write in that silly tone,' he replied:

> No one has any motive with regard to you except your own welfare. No decision is absolute yet. If you have a better suggestion ... I shall be pleased to hear it.... You have made a mess of things. At your age that is not a disaster, but you must help yourself. Your future, temporal and spiritual, is your own making. I can only provide opportunities for your achievements.[35]

It might have been Arthur writing in 1919.

Bron's spirits improved a month later with the acceptance of his first story for publication. He proposed to flood the market and make his escape as a writer. In the meantime, he accepted the transfer and continued to irritate Downside, loathing games and the Corps, joining the Empire Loyalists. Then, during the holidays, he plunged into disgrace again. Waugh was rung up by the Stroud police and informed 'that a youth had been arrested incapably drunk carrying Bron's suitcase'.[36] His parents drove over to pick him up from the cells, where they discovered him 'white and dirty and eating a bun'.[37] Waugh suspected him of stealing a bottle of gin. The Juvenile Court let him off with a ten-shilling fine, but the affair, occurring as it did at the height of the Spain–*Spectator* controversy, was embarrassing. Fortunately for Waugh, the Beaverbrook papers appear to have missed this opportunity for twisting the knife.

Try as he might, Waugh could not love his eldest son: 'In spite of my earnest prayers I was delighted to see Bron go [back to school]. The household became happy once more....'[38] The boy's letters home merely confirmed suspicion. November, apparently, brought his chief pleasure when a large portion of Downside was incinerated:

> I managed to get out of the dormitory while a riot was taking place at the other end; down in the hall I joined a group of other boys who had escaped & were busy throwing their Corps uniforms into the

35. 23 May 1955; *Letters*, p. 441.
36. *Diaries*, 25 July 1955, p. 732.
37. *Ibid.*
38. *Ibid.*, 15 August 1955, p. 737.

> blaze. I managed to grab a hose from a semi-stupefied fireman and was the first (of many) to squirt the headmaster.[39]

As flames roared fifty feet above the roof and white-hot girders smashed through the debris, Bron had never been happier.

Waugh read the letter sadly, doubtful of his son's piety and honesty: '... all stories in the papers about 40 boys being rescued by monks are quite untrue,' Bron had added. 'They were made up by myself & Mark Sykes for the reporters' benefit. I was televised ... hunting, distraught, for lost belongings. Actually we were looting the remains of the Signals room.'[40] Papa, unsmiling, wrote immediately to the school.

'I find it very hard to sum up Bron at the moment,' Dom Aelred replied:

> I don't think he is irreligious, though I don't think religion means a great deal to him ... to a boy of Bron's cast of mind religious pageantry [?] seems something bourgeois, a mere sanction imposed upon the infringement of certain ... tiresome & unexciting virtues. ... I believe we shall have just to wait and watch and pray.
>
> Lying. He has lied to me this term (to my knowledge) but when I put it to him he admitted it. I believe in his case it is fear that causes it – not fear of anything concrete but [?] just fears. He is very lacking in real confidence and so likes to appear stronger. I'll just have to work away on him. But it will have to be the work of grace – he has few natural virtues – but supernatural ones, though harder to acquire, are in the end more worthwhile.[41]

This distressing letter arrived just before Christmas and mixed awkwardly with news of Waugh's other children. Meg had won a prize in the *Observer*'s short-story competition. Teresa had won a scholarship to read history at Somerville College, Oxford.

Just before the publication of *Officers and Gentlemen* Waugh had begun his diary again. He recorded almost every day for eighteen months and the final entry, on his fifty-third birthday, reflects his eventual reconciliation with Bron. Their period of difficulty coincided with Waugh's last sustained attempt to take an interest in life beyond his gates. After 1957, the journal collapses into irregular jottings, staccato interjections, as it were, into the ceaseless drone of humbug that he heard on all sides. Dazed and baffled, he eventually turned his deaf ear to it all and tried to concentrate on his family, his work and the Church.

39. Unpublished ALS from Auberon Waugh to Evelyn Waugh, 25 November 1955, from Downside School, Stratton on the Fosse, Bath; BL.
40. *Ibid.*
41. Unpublished ALS from Dom Aelred Watkin, 22 December 1955, from Downside School etc.; BL.

In each of these areas, however, there were already difficulties. During August 1955 he had spent a week in a Folkestone hotel trying and failing to write *Pinfold*. Alone, he now merely smoked and read. Changes in the liturgy had spoilt his Easter retreat and lent weight to his fears about the erosion of Catholic solidarity. 'Every week', he noted, 'it seems I hear of a desertion. I used to see the Church as peculiar people bound by human and divine loyalties. At times it seems a nondescript crowd with comings and goings haphazard. Clarissa's apostasy was the sharpest wound of course.'[42] And, two months earlier: 'Resolved: to regard humankind with benevolence and detachment, like an elderly host whose young and indulged wife has asked a lot of people to the house whose names he does not know.'[43]

The simile was apposite. Teresa, a loyal, clever but rather haughty seventeen year old, had with her scholarship ceased to be a child. She arranged with the Stopps to visit friends of theirs in Bonn to learn German before going up in October 1956. For her trip she expected a wardrobe of new clothes and an allowance. That summer she was also due to 'come out' and to be presented at Court. A ball was required in July. At a time when Waugh's financial future looked increasingly dim, and his household was reduced to an eccentric Italian couple as gardener and cook, he found his children thrusting him towards exorbitant expense. His reward was to be introduced to the aristocratic 'pimplies' of the rock-'n'-roll generation. It seemed poor recompense but, so long as his babies stuck fast to the Faith, he could endure it all with the assistance of gin (he tried, he once joked with Diana Cooper, not to see them when he was sober). At its worst – when hideously dressed youths were invited for house-parties – he could shut himself in the library. At its best (Teresa had one friend, Alice Jolliffe, 'sweet Alice', whom he adored), he could play Basil Seal or Pinfold. But supplies of energy, sympathy and cash to gratify the young were running low. 'My children are all pretty affectionate healthy and pious', he had written to Lady Diana five years earlier, '– three of them are clever. I am glad to possess them but get little pleasure from their use – like first editions.'[44]

When Bron returned to Downside in January 1956, Waugh had already committed himself to paying £500 towards Teresa's ball. She was to share it with Susan Baring and Lady Christina McDonnell,[45] and arrangements between the three families were clearly going to consume a great part of the next six months. Waugh was not, then, in good temper when he heard of his son's latest misdemeanour. An 'obscene' letter had come to light,

42. *Diaries*, 10 January 1956, p. 751.
43. *Ibid.*, 17 November 1955, p. 747.
44. Unpublished ALS, 24 November [1950], from Piers Court; BL; *MWMS*, p. 111.
45. Daughters of, respectively, Lady Rose Baring and Lady Antrim, Christopher Sykes's sister.

written six months earlier to Bron's contemporary, Count Zamoyski's son. 'The whole tone of the letter', Dom Aelred reported, 'was that of a silly child trying to be a man of the world. Were it not so common and disgusting it would have been pathetic.'[46] Shortly afterwards Bron wrote home, asking to be removed. It was the sort of letter, Waugh admitted to himself, that he had sent to his father from Lancing and 'In the hope of understanding Bron better I read the diaries I kept at his age. I was appalled at the vulgarity and priggishness.'[47]

Bron had two A Levels and, seeing no point in acquiring two more, suggested that Papa find him a career in the hotel trade. Evelyn counselled perseverance. Bron agreed but appeared determined: '. . . the fact remains that in a class of singularly backward boys I am not among the first three. . . . You mention obeying school rules. I am convinced that school life would be insupportable without breaking them. . . .'[48] Laziness and hatred of institutional life had resulted in his low academic position. His housemaster thought him brilliant, and it came as no surprise when at this time he won the School Eloquence Prize (seconding the motion: 'Genius is akin to madness'). He was, it seems, at last beginning to listen. He found it difficult to love his father but maintained an unshakeable respect for him. Teresa's success had perhaps concentrated Bron's mind. Within a year he had himself won a scholarship. No sooner were Teresa's and Bron's educational problems resolved, however, than Meg and Harriet produced more. Poor Harriet, the nuns explained, was so enigmatic. She could understand fiction far in advance of her reading age but could neither write nor spell accurately. Could a little more encouragement be given to her?[49] And Meg, 'Darling Pig', Papa's favourite because she was so much like him – manic-depressive, utterly bored by life at thirteen years old, passionate, loyal, deeply religious – Meg was to prove the most difficult of all of his children.

Having entered manhood as Lupin-Hamlet, Waugh saw himself in his early fifties becoming Pooter-Lear. A lazy man of massive energy, his physical routine had degenerated while the high voltage of his mental life crackled on unabated. Despite the statement on the dust-jacket of *Officers and Gentlemen*, he was already planning a third volume. *Pinfold* lived with him night and day, its sentences running in his head. But he wrote very little, other than journalism and elegant prefaces. 'I don't sleep naturally,' he recorded. 'I have tried everything – exercise, cold baths, fasting, feasting, solitude, society. Always I have to take paraldehyde and sodium amytal.

46. Unpublished TLS from Dom Aelred Watkin, 21 January 1956, from Downside School etc.; BL.
47. *Diaries*, 13 February 1956, p. 754.
48. Unpublished ALS from Auberon Waugh, 19 February 1956, from Downside School etc.; BL.
49. Cf. unpublished ALS from Sister N. Mercedes, 8 January 1956, from St Mary's Convent, S. Ascot, Berks.; BL.

My life is really too empty for a diarist. The morning post, the newspaper, the crossword, gin.'[50] He looked to the new house to provide the change he needed. The increasing urbanization of Dursley, with its motor-cycles and condom factory, fuelled his longing to be gone. In search of unbreachable privacy, he expressed particular interest in establishments with private chapels. Retraction to that still centre of his faith, however, was hampered by his refusal for many months to advertise Piers Court. Serious lunatics were in short supply and negotiations and house-hunting lasted for over two years. It was with great relief during this period of limbo that he spotted two opportunities for action and revenge. John Wain and the Beaverbrook press were in the firing line.

Wain had reviewed Wodehouse's latest novel, *French Leave*, for the *Observer*, and found the book clichéd and outdated. Waugh responded with a letter to the Editor, correcting small inaccuracies. But the gist of his complaint was Wain's caddishness in daring to criticize so ancient, fecund and skilful a writer. Indirectly, this was another personal complaint. Waugh at fifty-two saw himself in much the same position as Wodehouse at seventy. Wain was of the Amis school and needed to be put in his place.

Unwilling to accept that place, the young man had replied, not unreasonably, that it was no defence of a bad book to appeal to an author's age or productivity. He made the mistake, however, of adding a light-hearted rider to the effect that this did not matter because Waugh was not a critic. Somerset Maugham, shocked by the vulgarity of novels like *Lucky Jim* and *Hurry On Down*, had recently attacked their state-educated authors (both of whom taught English in provincial universities). Waugh weighed in on Maugham's side, defending the more liberal tradition in which every gentleman used to be a 'critic'. The result, an article in the *Spectator*, was jovial and feeble, deliberately missing Wain's point, closing ranks with those writers who did not need a qualification in English Literature to know what they liked.[51] The piece has none of the scintillating acerbity of his earlier attack on Noel-Buxton or of his later one on Priestley. It turned out, however, to be of great significance because of its preamble: 'An investigation', he wrote, 'has lately been made in the book-trade to determine which literary critics have most influence on sales.... The Beaverbrook press is no longer listed as having any influence at all.'[52] Nancy Spain, who saw herself as both a good and an influential critic, was steaming with indignation.

Three weeks later she produced a riposte, 'Does a Good Word from Me

50. *Diaries*, 12 July 1955, p. 729.
51. 'Dr. Wodehouse and Mr. Wain', *Spectator*, 24 April 1956, 243–4; *EAR*, pp. 507–9.
52. *Ibid.*, p. 507.

Sell a Book?'[53] in which she picked Waugh up on his statement. *Island in the Sun* had appeared in the UK in January and had sold 60,000 copies. Its success, she said, was due largely to her favourable notice and, moreover, Alec's first-edition sales dwarfed Evelyn's. The brothers Waugh were already 'news'. Four days earlier the *Telegraph* had carried a recent photograph of them and a gossipy article about the revival of Alec's fortunes:

> Evelyn in more recent years, for reasons not purely literary, has taken the lead. Now his elder brother comes up again straight with *Island in the Sun*. That Alec, whom to read is to like and to know is to love, takes an elder-brotherly view of Evelyn, is apparent in his reference to him in this new novel.[54]

The piece characterizes Alec as charming while remaining ostentatiously silent about Evelyn.

From this point until (and beyond) his death, Waugh fell victim to similar sneers. Around this time, for instance, he had at last decided to advertise his house. 'The Waughs Move On' was the *Mail*'s headline: 'Ten-bedroom, 40-acre home is not big enough. If you have three sons and three daughters, how big a house do you need?' Attention was drawn to 'the riches – paintings, books, statues' in need of a 'new Brideshead'.[55] The yellow-press image of Waugh was green with envy and resentment. He was seen to be a fabulously wealthy, self-made hypocrite – but the backbiters had never dared say so openly. When he read Nancy Spain's piece, Waugh's eyes lit up. 'I have waited a long time to catch the *Express* in libel,' he wrote to Peters. 'I think they have done it this time.'[56]

He had to wait another year for the case to come to court. In the meantime, Teresa's social life dragged him and Laura back to Mayfair and produced gigantic bills. In March they attended a cocktail party for 250 debutantes and an equal number of young men. 'So I sat with the butler in the hall,' he wrote to Meg, 'and that is the last anyone has seen of Teresa. I suppose she was crushed to death & the corpse too flat to be recognized. About 100 dead girls were carried out & buried in a common pit. R. I. P. I shall never let you, my ewe lamb, become a debutante.'[57] He never did. He was neither able nor willing to support the full weight of upper-class expenditure for his other children.[58]

Again, Waugh's incoming correspondence for this period suggests a man

53. *DE*, 1 March 1956, 6.
54. 'One Brother and Another', *DT*, 13 March 1956. The novel speaks of Evelyn as his generation's 'mouthpiece' and 'finest flower'.
55. *DM*, 2 May 1956, 3.
56. 17 March 1956; *Letters*, p. 468.
57. 17 March 1956; *Letters*, p. 469.
58. At the time he was negotiating with Downside to take James at reduced fees as a candidate for the priesthood. In the end, he went to Stonyhurst.

far different from the pompous and greedy egotist constructed by the press. He helped pay for the education of Bridget Grant's (Laura's sister's) son. When Alec's wife, due to present Teresa at Court, had fallen ill with appendicitis the day before, Evelyn was attentive and sympathetic. Maimie Lygon, deserted by Vsevolode, neurotic and alcoholic, found in Evelyn a staunch companion to take her out to dinner and to try to fix her up with a holiday. He always stuck by Duggan. His letters to his children were compassionate and loyal; theirs to him generally addressed to 'Darling Papa'. He had arranged for Bron to enter the Blues should he choose the army as a career; he nearly ruined himself to provide for Teresa's social launch while hating every moment of it; he worshipped Meg. And all this when he had not the slightest interest in the younger generation beyond his family. 'At-a-boy', Wodehouse had replied on receiving the Wain article. 'That's the stuff to give 'em.... What a curse this new breed of Manchester Grammar School-scholarship at Oxford lads is. Kingsley Amis is another to whom we might attend some day.'[59] Much as Waugh coveted Plum's admiration, however, it was already too late for the suggested offensive. Waugh, no longer so easily irritated, wished only for complete seclusion.

Teresa's ball was the last such grand affair with which he was directly involved. Responsibilities had been divided equally: Lady Antrim to find a suitable location and decorate it; Lady Rose Baring to issue invitations; Waugh to supervise catering. In fact, most of the practical details fell to Laura, and Waugh saw his task as keeping his lackadaisical wife up to the mark. He had, he felt, enough to do with his literary work, prospective house purchasers and discussions with lawyers about the libel suit. He corresponded with Angela and 'Ran' Antrim and left Laura to deal with the 'holocaust of capons'.[60] A fortnight before the event, he sold Piers Court for £9,500 when they still had nowhere to go. 'Now', he recorded, 'as I move about the house and garden nothing irks me as it used to do. It is Mrs Gadsen's house not mine so I don't care if the stone crumbles and the tap drips and the weeds smother the beds. I am soon going. There is a meditation to be made on death on these lines.'[61] *Non enim habemus hic manentem civitatem....* Teresa's ball was to be a swan-song for those nineteen fantastical years in the old house.

Waugh prepared for 5 July by hiring the Poor Clares again: this time to pray for good weather from 7 p.m. onwards. A marquee was erected in Kensington Square and a house overlooking the gardens commandeered. Throughout the afternoon, tents, gardens and house swarmed with guests.

59. Unpublished ALS from P. G. Wodehouse, 11 March 1956, Burket Neck Lane, Remsenburg, NY; BL.
60. *Diaries*, 2 July 1956, p. 764.
61. *Ibid.*, 3 July 1956, p. 764.

Dinner was arranged in two parties, Waugh disappearing with his platoon to the Hyde Park Hotel (where non-vintage champagne was ordered for everyone but himself). At seven precisely, the weather cleared and remained fine all night – 'a remarkable performance by these excellent women',[62] he noted, and promptly sent them another £3. But cloudless skies and a fine vintage could enliven him only temporarily. Then came the dingy succession of young men who preferred dinner-jackets to tails because they wished to 'jive'. Waugh hovered paternally and in some pain on the fringes of this spectacle until 3.30 a.m., when, at last, he retired leaving the young in one another's arms. Elizabeth Pakenham, thanking him for a 'superb dance ... like an incredibly beautiful & enjoyable dream', remarked what a shame it was that 'we never actually saw *you*'.[63] Everything Waugh touched became illuminated by fantasy. But it was ultimately a dull and dutiful occasion for him, and Teresa's autocratic behaviour, particularly towards her mother, had begun to irritate him. 'Girls of 18 are always unbearable', Nancy wrote, '– Meg will be just the same. Its an unhappy time & you must try & remember that you are a Christian.... P.S. Oh is it true that at your ball a lot of *real* tarts got in through the garden & took away all the girls' partners including Leslie Hartley?'[64]

'It is not only long hair', Waugh wrote in mock despair to Penelope Betjeman, 'it is sweat and cricket shirts and woollen socks the young men have. Would I were ashes like your pa and did not see it.'[65] Meg and Harriet, shut away in Ascot and thirsting for details, were refused the tiniest encouragement towards imitation of their sister. Instead, a delicious Carrollian fantasy came from their Papa, pretending to rebuke but in fact offering a perfectly judged and tender tease.

> [It] was a great success. Teresa wore a dress of emerald green calico trimmed with zebra skin and a straw hat ... & was greatly admired.... For supper there was plenty of stout and kippers and bread & margarine and blancmange and plum jam for those who came early but it soon ran out. Your mother insisted on bringing all 14 cows.... A lot of criminals came uninvited and began robbing everyone so the police charged with truncheons and, I am sorry to say, arrested Alec Waugh and Alick Dru by mistake. They are still in prison....[66]

For Waugh, the struggle to entertain was a function of civilized discourse. As his children grew up, their steps towards the imitation of adult behaviour estranged them from him. He was happier with the lunatic logic of a

62. *Ibid.*, 5 July 1956, p. 764.
63. Unpublished ALS, 18 July 1956, from 14 Cheyne Gardens, Chelsea, SW3; BL.
64. Unpublished ALS from Nancy Mitford, 8 August 1956, from St Pierre le Château, Var; BL.
65. APCS, 3 July 1956; *Letters*, p. 473.
66. 8 July 1956; *Letters*, p. 474.

young child's imagination. His closer friends preserved that anarchic, often spiteful, humour and the love of things going wrong. Among Teresa's male contemporaries, only one engaged his attention and transported him to the world of his youth: Daphne Fielding's son, Alexander. For a moment in his company, Waugh became flirtatious, as he might have been with Richard Pares or Alastair Graham in the 1920s. After meeting the boy three days later, Waugh happily admitted that he had rather fallen in love.

*

The ball over, house-hunting began in earnest. Waugh and Laura toured the West Country with whatever children were available and settled on two leading contenders: Combe Florey House near Pixton and Bishop's Court. The first Waugh described as 'cosy, sequestered, with great possibilities',[67] but the second was grander. The children were consulted; opinions were divided. At the end of August, Laura drove to Italy with Bron and Hatty, leaving Waugh at Piers Court to polish off *Pinfold* before the move and to come to a final decision. Any disappointment Laura had felt at the uprooting of their lives had by this time been overcome and she seems to have anticipated the change with pleasure. Teresa's début had, if anything, been a greater ordeal for her mother than her father and, delighted to be released from the Mayfair circus, Laura bowled contentedly towards Portofino and wrote amusing letters home about her curious family:

> Bron was funnily boring at first through trying to be a man of the world on the subject of food & hotels & always getting it wrong. But I think he has settled down & is behaving beautifully.... Hatty ... signed her own customs form on the boat & spelt her name Harreit & couldn't understand what was wrong. She kept say[ing] 'but all the letters are there so what difference does it make'.[68]

At Piers Court Waugh settled to his novel again and tried to deal with Meg and Teresa. Teresa's main concern, it seems, was to ensure that in the new house Bron and she would have a sitting room to themselves. Meg did not know what to think. Bishop's Court had been Waugh's first choice but, unable to offer more than £11,500, he lost it and turned his attention to Combe Florey. The only member of the family seriously disappointed by this was Bron – who still lives there. Waugh bought it for £7,500 and needed the £2,000 difference.[69] The final bill for the ball came in during

67. *Diaries*, 9 July 1956, p. 765.
68. Unpublished ALS from Laura Waugh, 29 August 1956, Marche (Doubs); BL.
69. Cf. unpublished ALS to Laura Waugh, 1 September 1956, from Piers Court; BL: 'Banks [?] will buy us a house but we must pay for repairs & improvements. He says there is only £16,000 in the kitty. I thought there was twice as much.... We are going to be in rather straitened circumstances this winter unless we get damages from Nancy Spain. The film people from whom I expected

September and his share was £757 – £257 more than the original estimate and a bitter blow.

With Laura's return and the children's departure, his novel began to flow: 'I have worked hard and easily, seldom writing less than a thousand words a day. The book is too personal for me to be able to judge it.'[70] He need not have worried. 'This is terrific stuff,' McDougall wrote on receiving the first two-thirds in mid-October. 'I had not guessed Mr. Pinfold would be so accurate a portrait.'[71] The only difficulty, he pointed out, might be libel: all the figures were instantly recognizable.

*

Libel was much on Waugh's mind in October 1956. While most of his countrymen concentrated on the political crises of Suez and Hungary, Waugh's major non-literary concern was his suit against the *Express*, which he hoped would bring home a fat haunch of tax-free bacon. During the year he had already taken two 'loan' payments of £1,000 each from Peters because Combe Florey required substantial renovation and Teresa had just gone up to Oxford. At this crucial moment, the *Express* very generously libelled him again by running a story on Rebecca West's *The Meaning of Treason*. The *Express* presumably believed itself secure behind the skirts of quotation. 'Rebecca West Attacks Evelyn Waugh and Graham Greene', ran the headline and, between two rather sinister photographs of the writers, the paper repeated a damning (and much misquoted) sentence from her book: 'They have created a climate of crackbrained confusion between virtues and vices . . . a climate in which the traitor flourishes.'[72]

The Meaning of Treason had first been published in America in 1947 and in the UK in 1949. Since then, of course, much had come to light regarding espionage in the West. In 1951 Burgess and Maclean had absconded, precipitating the 'missing diplomats' scandal which had haunted the Conservative Government ever since. Eventually, in October 1955, a White Paper had been published, denying the existence of a 'Third Man', and, when bluntly asked in Parliament whether Kim Philby would be investigated, the Prime Minister had been able only to mumble a non-committal reply. It was a bad year for Eden, who was soon to resign. On 7 November, the Foreign Secretary, Harold Macmillan, had made a formal statement in the House saying, 'I have no reason to conclude that Mr Philby has at any time betrayed the interests of his country or to identify him with the

£4,000 [for *Scoop*] have not coughed up. But why should I worry you with these tedious details. I am overjoyed that you are having fun. Pray continue to do so.'

70. *Diaries*, 10 October 1956, p. 769.

71. Unpublished ALS from Jack McDougall, 17 October 1956, from Chapman & Hall, 37 Essex Street, Strand, WC2; BL.

72. *DE*, 16 October 1956, 6.

so-called "Third Man", if indeed there was one' – an amusing remark in retrospect.[73] Four months later, Burgess and Maclean had finally surfaced, brisk and healthy, at a press conference in Moscow to defend their actions. Dame Rebecca had a hot literary market, primed for the paperback reissue of her book, and she had updated it with a few revisions. Unfortunately for her, these tiny additions resulted in large subtractions.

Earlier in the year, Waugh's suspicion of a plot had grown to firm conviction after receiving a letter from Ann Fleming. A few days after the Nancy Spain article, Beaverbrook had sent Mrs Fleming a copy of *Island in the Sun*. Someone had informed him that Evelyn had been in her house at the time and that he was angered by the book's arrival. Beaverbrook rang up to check. She denied that there was any truth in the gossip. 'It's a pity [it] is not true,' he had giggled down the line, 'it's a most magnificent story . . . you know as well as I do that Alec has made more money with his books than Evelyn and Evelyn is most horribly jealous.'[74]

Evelyn had contacted Alec quickly:

> Lord Beaverbrook is a great admirer of Island in the Sun. He is obsessed by the senile aberration that you & I are inflamed my [*sic*] mutual jealously. To aggravate this imaginary condition he instructed his Miss Spain to libel me and I am suing for damages. I daresay you would prefer to keep out of it. On the other hand I suppose neither you nor your English publisher can be pleased at reading her claim that your great success is due entirely to your having given the lady a cocktail.[75]

It would indeed have been better for Alec to steer clear. The last thing he needed was to irritate the very newspapers supporting him. Cassell's would surely have advised placating Beaverbrook, and it must have depressed Alec that, even in this long-awaited triumph, his brother's shadow was again looming like Banquo's ghost. Alec knew that he had become something of a figure of fun at Piers Court. If he accepted Evelyn's oblique invitation, he would be asked to testify to his comparative failure as a writer. But he did not hesitate. On receiving the letter, he cancelled a luncheon with Nancy Spain and, again, loyally closed ranks. For his part, Evelyn defended Alec's book. Trying to curry favour, Ann Fleming had denigrated it. 'I am sorry & surprised that you can't enjoy Island in the Sun,' he replied. 'I thought it very good. My brother has lived out of England most of his life and many of his expressions are unfamiliar and

73. Philby absconded in Beirut in January 1963 while working as an *Observer* correspondent, and reappeared in Moscow in July. When asked whether Philby were the Third Man, Edward Heath, then Lord Privy Seal, replied 'Yes, sir,' in a low voice.
74. 23 March [1956]; *LAF*, p. 179.
75. Unpublished ALS to Alec Waugh, 27 March 1956, from Piers Court; private collection.

uncongenial, but the story is intricate & managed with rare competence – as well as Dr. Maugham can do. Try it again when the dexedrine is out of the system.'[76]

The article about *The Meaning of Treason* left Waugh in no doubt as to malevolent intention. This time the assassin's blade had been passed to Anthony Hern, the paper's literary editor. Beaverbrook must have been delighted by the result: not so much an article, more a way of advertising his opponent's perfidious character in Miss West's words:

> For many years ... Waugh has been implying that the worthless and dissolute are more worthy than people who are in fact worthy and who keep sober. From his works one can foretell a new hagiography in which the saints will not be depicted as giving their cloaks to poor men in the snow, but as being sadly in need of cloaks themselves, being helpless in the snow owing to alcoholic excess.[77]

Miss West lumped Waugh, Greene and Mauriac together with Gide as writers who distrusted 'sincerity':

> ... they have created an intellectual climate in which there is a crackbrained confusion between the moral and the aesthetic. ... People who practise the virtues are judged as if they had struck the sort of false attitude which betrays an incapacity for art, while the people who practise the vices are regarded as if they had shown the subtle rightness of gesture which is the sign of the born artist. ...[78]

As literary criticism there was nothing new in this. Donat O'Donnell and Kingsley Amis had made similar remarks about *Brideshead*. The context here, however, was entirely different. The suggestion was that Waugh and Greene *encouraged* treason, a view implicitly endorsed by Hern: 'That is the most devastating exposure of the essence of treachery yet made. It is devastating because it is understanding. It is understanding because Miss West speaks with the voice of humanity. ...'[79]

Waugh got his solicitors on to it immediately and, as he was packing up Piers Court at the end of October, he found himself involved in double litigation. For five weeks he had nowhere to live while builders and decorators reconstructed the library in the house where he intended to die. There, amid the workmen's continuing racket, he wrote the final chapters of *Pinfold* and waited eagerly to do battle.

The first case came to court just before Christmas: 'Waugh v. Pan Books Ltd, and Another'. Waugh's case was straightforward. He was mentioned

76. [26 March] 1956; *LAF*, pp. 180–1.
77. Quoted *DE*, 16 October 1956, 6.
78. *Ibid.*
79. *Ibid.*

for the first time in Miss West's revisions to the October 1956 edition and the passages (quoted above) were defamatory. 'In fact in only one book, *Brideshead Revisited*, . . . had the plaintiff portrayed a character who combined piety with alcoholism, and an intelligent reading of that story recorded the plaintiff's wish to show that no one, however unsuccessful by worldly standards, was outside the mercy of God.'[80] Pan Books had retreated immediately upon receiving notice of the suit, accepting that it was 'indefensible and unfair to suggest that over many years . . . Waugh had encouraged a hagiography of debauchery and . . . [had created] an intellectual climate in which traitors flourished.'[81] All unsold copies of the book were withdrawn. Waugh had no wish to persecute a fellow author and former friend. Accepting that the settlement would cause the defendants acute financial loss, he did not press for damages and settled for costs. The judge allowed the record to be withdrawn and that concluded Waugh's dealings with Miss West. The matter did not, however, rest there. If Waugh were chary of bleeding money from authors, he suffered no such scruples about press barons and a second suit was soon lodged against Beaverbrook Newspapers for printing the article. As for Dame Rebecca, she neither forgot nor forgave. When compiling the *Critical Heritage* volume on Waugh, the present author requested permission to reproduce her enthusiastic review of *Vile Bodies*.[82] At first, and for some time, she refused on the grounds that she wished in no way to be connected with such a revolting human being as Evelyn Waugh.

Waugh had left Piers Court on the last day of October for his five peripatetic weeks, beginning with visits to his 'dreadful little boy',[83] James, at Stonyhurst, and moving on to Meg and Hatty at Ascot. All three were in difficulties: James was short-sighted, dreamy and semi-literate; Hatty and Meg were proving 'a handful'[84] for the nuns. Waugh endeavoured to rally his troops but he had, after all, trained them as subversives. Shortly afterwards, in her abstracted, depressive mood, Meg succeeded in swallowing mercury by sucking it too far up a pipette. The incident inaugurated a period of crisis in her school career but, for the moment, Papa made light of her troubles. In November he went for the last time to the Easton Court Hotel with a new young friend, Paddy Leigh Fermor, to complete the rough draft of *Pinfold*. When, towards the end of the month, Waugh had

80. 'Queen's Bench Division. Mr. Evelyn Waugh's Libel Action Settled . . . Before Mr. Justice Armitage', *The Times*, 14 December 1956, 15.
81. *Ibid.*
82. See Vol. 1, pp. 195–6.
83. *Letters*, p. 478.
84. Cf. unpublished ALS from Fr Martin D'Arcy, 8 June 1957, from 114 Mount Street, London; BL: 'I gather that the nuns, though they too like her, find [Meg] a handful. I told them the best are like that.'

rejoined Laura at Pixton, he still felt that the novel required another three weeks' work.

Peaceful revision, however, was not available at this stage. He was due to move into Combe Florey House on 6 December – or, at least, to supervise the installation of the furniture – but before he could attend to this a call had come from Mells Manor. For some time, rumours of Knox's illness had been growing. Waugh went over for four days to offer support and was alarmed to discover serious deterioration in both priest and hostess. Katharine Asquith hobbled painfully on arthritic legs, selfless as ever in her devotion to Knox. He complained of indigestion, had grown crotchety and apparently careless of Katharine's suffering. Clearly he was sicker than he cared to admit. When not occupied with his translation of *The Story of a Soul*,[85] he spent his time reading, grumbling and doing *The Times* crossword. Waugh's rare visits had become increasingly important to Knox and he saw them as visits to *him* rather than to Katharine. As soon as decently possible, he would take the novelist to one side, away from women's talk, and, more often than not, insist on a shared crossword or a game of Scrabble, fiddling the scores (if Waugh is to be believed) to reduce the humiliation of defeat. A sense of defeat tortured him. His great work, the translation of the Bible, had met with a lukewarm response. His partiality for country-house life had not endeared him to his superiors and had excluded him from higher office. Waugh loved and revered 'Ronnie' but the situation was difficult and embarrassing, not least because of the cruel spectacle of this witty and brilliant man so reduced to petulance.

Waugh consoled himself by blowing the assets of the Save the Children Fund: something approaching £2,000 went on carpets, Chippendale looking-glasses and an Arthur Grimshaw painting. By February he was alarmed to learn how seriously the Little, Brown account was depleted, but he was not being entirely reckless. Three film contracts were in the offing: Rank was still pursuing *Scoop*, Sam Marx was after *A Handful of Dust* again and Luis Buñuel had promised a $10,000 advance for *The Loved One*. The first and last of these were to star Alec Guinness, who, since meeting Waugh at Edith Sitwell's reception into the Church six months earlier, had become a distant friend. Waugh admired Guinness's work and *vice versa*. This combination of talents promised a cornucopia, and Waugh's financial future

85. Cf. Evelyn Waugh, *The Life of the Right Reverend Ronald Knox* (Chapman & Hall, 1959), p. 326: '[When it was first printed in 1898, it] was believed that this was the full autobiography of St Thérèse of the Child Jesus, as she had written it and left it to her Superior. In fact, it was an abridgement and compilation from three distinct documents. Mother Agnes, the saint's sister, was their editor. She died in July 1951, and in September 1952 permission was given in Rome for the publication of the complete text.' Knox was making the English translation and, although he 'regarded it as an interruption of his major writing, ... it proved to be his last completed work.'

looked reasonably buoyant.[86] *Pinfold* was completed by the end of January and would be published and earning by July. In February the Nancy Spain libel action would come to court and Waugh believed he could not lose. Having won a Christ Church scholarship to read English Literature, Bron, a much happier young man, had left school and now lounged about the house, smoking cigars and slipping out occasionally to shoot pheasant. He was shortly to travel to Florence to stay with Harold Acton for three months, a project eagerly encouraged and illegally financed by Waugh. Apart from Knox's illness, everything was almost satisfactory, and Waugh anticipated his legal battle with relish. No Beaverbrook paper, he instructed Peters, was to be approached with the serial rights of *Pinfold*. The Grimshaw painting (a private joke?) was *Fleet Street 7 p.m.*

Sunday, 17 February 1957, found Mr and Mrs Waugh in the Hyde Park Hotel, preparing themselves with champagne. The case came up on Tuesday before Mr Justice Stable and jury. Waugh's counsel was his friend from Oxford and Nuremberg, the urbane Gerald Gardiner, QC. Beaverbrook and Spain were represented first by Sir Hartley Shawcross, QC, the Chief Prosecutor at Nuremberg, and then by Helenus Milmo, who were lodging a counter-claim against Waugh's 'Mr. Wodehouse and Dr. Wain'. Up to the last moment it appears, Beaverbrook was trying to settle out of court,[87] but, having been dragged this far, he was determined to make Waugh suffer. As Milmo remarked on the second day: 'Mr. Waugh has decided to come into this arena and since he has, we will meet him here. If he gets a bloody nose in the scrap it is his own fault.'[88] Horns were locked.

The meaning of the *Express* article, Gardiner concluded, was

> that [Waugh] was an unsuccessful and embittered writer who had made false and malicious attacks on Miss Spain in the *Spectator* by reason of personal spite against her; that he was a writer whose name carried insignificant weight with the general public, the film rights and options in whose books were not worthy of purchase, and who was not worthy of consideration for the writing of articles.[89]

This was a bit steep. The Judge was clearly beginning to despair. The first day had proceeded more along the lines of *opéra bouffe* than dignified

86. None of the film projects came to anything, but Waugh still collected considerable sums for down-payments and a 'treatment'.
87. Cf. unpublished ALS from Evelyn Waugh to A. D. Peters, 13 February 1957, from Combe Florey House, Combe Florey, Taunton, Somerset; *Catalogue* E987, p. 226; HRC.
88. 'High Court of Justice. Queen's Bench Division ... Waugh v. Beaverbrook Newspapers Ltd and Another', *The Times*, 21 February 1957, 13.
89. *Ibid.*

litigation, much to the amusement of the gallery. 'The plaintiff', Gardiner remarked,

> did not read the ... *Express*, and he had not heard of Nancy Spain, he (counsel) must confess on his behalf. Since then, counsel understood, she had taken part in panel games on television and was therefore as well known as the Prime Minister. Refusing to see an *Express* reporter was a very serious thing....[90]

The whole hilarious episode on the doorstep of Piers Court was recounted to lay the ground for more solid evidence. Miss Spain's article 'made it look as if the plaintiff's books had only sold about 40,000 copies, whereas ... his sales were about 4,280,125, of which over 2,744,000 had been published in this country and the rest in America. First edition sales amounted to 180,000.'[91]

So far so good. Then Waugh was called to the stand by Sir Hartley, and the novelist's confidence had evaporated. Shawcross had begun obliquely, by quoting reviews of Miss Spain's autobiography. Everyone seemed to think her warm-hearted, did they not? One review was by Gilbert Harding. '"Perhaps you do not approve of him?"' Waugh, flustered, did not reply. '"No, I thought you would not. (Laughter) I must not express my view of these matters. Do you think it's just possible that like so many of us you sometimes take yourself just a shade too seriously?" "No."'[92] Waugh, struggling for reticence, found himself squirming like a schoolboy.

Next came Alec and Laura. Poor Laura, dragged into the public eye again, dutifully recounted what little she knew and disappeared gratefully. But it was Alec's evidence which surely won the day. Having travelled from Tangier for the hearing, his presence was enough to undermine imputations of fraternal jealousy. And, unlike Evelyn, he conducted himself with a coolness that left no room for mockery. He had, he said, written more than forty books and had supported himself by his pen throughout his life, except when in the army. With *Island in the Sun* he had made more in a month than the total for all his other books. He had been interviewed by Miss Spain in December 1955, a month before the book's publication.

Milmo then bowled his googly. Was Mr Waugh aware that, as a gauge of literary quality, publishers would often look to first-edition sales? Alec sidestepped gracefully and cut him to the boundary. It was, he said, a misleading term. In his youth, impressions were often artificially reduced as an advertising gimmick so that a publisher could announce the seventh

90. 'Queen's Bench Division. Both of Two Writers Allege Libel by Other. Waugh v. Beaverbrook Newspapers Ltd and Another', *The Times*, 20 February 1957, 5.
91. *Ibid.*
92. 'Nancy Spain Sued for Libel by Evelyn Waugh', *DT*, 20 February 1957, 9; *CH*, pp. 513–17.

impression even before publication. This was not a direct answer and the crucial statistic – the comparative figures for the brothers' first-edition sales – was never presented by either side. It was, however, enough to close the subject. '"Mr. Waugh,"' said the Judge, warming to the Gilbert and Sullivan atmosphere, '"you must not give it all away."'[93] Cross-examined by Gardiner, Alec remarked: '"Nothing could have prevented *Island in the Sun* being an enormous success in England except a war."' '"Spelt 'W.A.R.'"' '"Yes, 'W.A.R.'"'[94] More laughter in the gallery.

'War' was the operative word in this suit. Nancy Spain had begun her article with: 'There is a war between Evelyn Waugh and me', although when she came to give evidence one might never have guessed it. She said that she thought Mr Waugh a great writer, 'simply brilliant'. What she knew of him she liked enormously. Smarting from her treatment at Piers Court? Good heavens, no: she admired him for chucking her out. True, she had written her article in response to his, but there was no question of malice. Her smiles faded a little under Gardiner's questioning.

Waugh was in an awkward position in trying to prove malice because his counsel could not decently produce Ann Fleming's letter. Gardiner, however, circumvented the problem:

> 'Have you ever discussed Mr. Evelyn Waugh with Lord Beaverbrook?'
> 'No.'
> 'Did not Lord Beaverbrook tell you that Mr. Evelyn Waugh was very jealous of his brother?'
> 'No. Certainly not.'
> 'In your book you say you love Lord Beaverbrook.'
> 'Yes.'
> 'He does not like Mr. Evelyn Waugh, does he?'
> 'I have no idea.'[95]

At least he made her lie under oath. But it was all most unsatisfactory. Having taken the precaution of promising his local priest ten per cent of any winnings, Waugh left the court feeling that supernatural aid had failed him at last. 'At the end of the first day,' he informed Nancy Mitford, 'I would have settled for a fiver.'[96]

The next day began better. Sir Hartley had to abandon the case owing to a motor-accident involving his mother-in-law. Miss Spain's counter-

93. *Op. cit.*, *The Times*, 20 February 1957, 5.
94. *Op. cit.*, *DT*, 20 February 1957, 9.
95. *Op. cit.*, *The Times*, 20 February 1957, 5.
96. [5 March] 1957; *Letters*, p. 485.

claim was heard, followed by Waugh's statement through counsel.[97] Summing up, the Judge, much to Waugh's annoyance, produced a leaden comic turn of his own. Most of the things heard during the last two days, he said, had no bearing on the case at all. The jury was not there to decide

> whether Miss Spain was ill-mannered or impudent, or whether Mr. Waugh was inhospitable or ill-tempered.... Ought any intelligent person picking up ... [her] paragraph [to] form an adverse opinion of Mr. Evelyn Waugh's books? If ... the jury ... came to that conclusion he was entitled to such compensation as they thought appropriate. It might be that the jury in this literary atmosphere might recall ... *Much Ado About Nothing*. Whether that expression applied here was exclusively a matter for them to decide.[98]

The barristers rocked with sycophantic laughter and the jury retired. For the next two hours Waugh suffered agonies of apprehension, expecting nugatory damages. On their return, they dismissed Beaverbrook's counter-claim and awarded Waugh £2,000 plus costs. Champagne flowed in White's that night but Alec was not there to share it. Having won the case for his brother, he scuttled off before a word could be exchanged.

Six weeks later the third action was settled out of court. Milmo, speaking for Beaverbrook Newspapers and Anthony Hern, accepted that the article about Rebecca West included grave libel and that it was 'particularly unfortunate' that this should have appeared while the other case was pending. The defendants agreed to publish a prominent apology in the *Express* and to pay £3,000 damages plus costs.[99] Total victory. Waugh went straight out and ordered a copy of an elaborately ugly carpet from the 1851 Great Exhibition.

*

Waugh was well pleased with his new home. Set on a wooded knoll on the edge of the hamlet of Combe Florey, it was an elegant gentleman's residence: seven principal bedrooms, four reception rooms, two bathrooms and about forty acres of land for Laura to farm. The original foundation dated from 1675, but the house had been largely rebuilt during the reign of George II. The oldest part was something of a folly: a sixteenth-century gatehouse through which visitors approached the house by a curved gravel drive. This was the nearest Waugh came to the spiked palisades. His secret hope was

97. Cf. *op. cit.*, *The Times*, 21 February 1957, 13. 'Her articles are most cleverly written and most amusing and it may well be that as a result of this case she will receive a higher post in the Beaverbrook organization. She has certainly followed in her master's footsteps.'
98. *Ibid.*
99. 'High Court of Justice, Queen's Bench Division ... Waugh v. Beaverbrook Newspapers and Another', *The Times*, 5 April 1957, 16.

to convert it into a private chapel but, when the Bishop of Clifton refused permission, he turned it over to Teresa and Bron. That eased the pressure on accommodation in the main building. Despite the newspaper accounts, Waugh had moved to a cheaper property. In typically grand style, he was trimming his sails for the rough passage into old age.

The recent publicity had made him nervous about *Pinfold.* While waiting for settlement of the third action, he had withdrawn permission for the *Spectator* to serialize the novel and requested the return of the typescript for further revisions. All earlier versions in circulation, he instructed Peters, were to be destroyed.[100] Before he had finished with it, another distress signal had come from Mells Manor. During January, Knox had gone to London for an operation to remove an obstruction in the colon and was diagnosed as suffering from malignant cancer of the liver. He was not told of this. Katharine, due to enter a nursing home herself for treatment of her arthritis, was in no condition to cope with an invalid. She had asked Waugh to take Knox somewhere to convalesce. The priest had insisted on Torquay and it was there that Waugh made his final revisions to *Pinfold* and endeavoured, to keep his dying friend amused.[101]

Laura came too for a week with 'sorrowful Ronald'.[102]

> He had lost all appetite for food, wine, tobacco; it rained almost continuously; the large, expensive hotel was uncongenial and so placed that it was impossible to walk out without encountering steps and steep hills. He drooped miserably over the table in the garish dining room, forcing himself to eat with evident revulsion.[103]

When Laura returned home, the two men went on for another equally dismal week in Sidmouth:

> Poor Ronnie cannot read for long. All he likes is to smoke a stinking pipe and to make desultory comments on the news in the paper. *The Times* crossword, done on a peculiarly laborious system, (not reading the lights for the downs ... until we have filled them in conjecturally) lasts us from nine to ten in the evening. Sometimes I walk up & down the front for half an hour.[104]

Homesick, Waugh happily abandoned this *Separate Tables* existence and took Knox back to Combe Florey for a fortnight until Katharine was ready for him. He was probably there when the news of the third libel settlement

100. Cf. unpublished APCI, 24 February 1957, from Combe Florey House; *Catalogue* E989, p. 226.
101. The novel was by this stage in galley proof, but Waugh wished to be certain that no injudicious statement prejudice his chances in the third court case. Cf. unpublished ALS to A. D. Peters, 7 March 1957, from Imperial Hotel, Torquay; *Catalogue* E992, p. 226.
102. ALS to Margaret Waugh, 10 March [1957]; *Letters*, p. 487.
103. *Ronald Knox*, *op. cit.*, p. 327.
104. ALS to Ann Fleming, 19 March [1957]; *Letters*, p. 488.

came through, a lugubrious presence blunting the edge of victory. With £5,000 tax-free booty, however, Waugh was itching for a little extravagance and on 20 May, when the motor races were safely over, he disappeared with Laura to Monte Carlo for a week.

She gambled while he strolled in the sunlit gardens. 'My idea of heaven', he wrote to Ann Fleming, 'is a Marble Hall out of season.'[105] The Hôtel du Paris was deliciously empty. Only one thing interrupted his tranquillity: Alec was in Nice with a young woman. '[She] has been a considerable concern of mine for 20 months . . .,' he wrote, trying to arrange a luncheon date, 'very argumentative but I like her – a lot. I hope this will not deter you. . . .'[106] Evelyn could hardly refuse after Alec's recent kindness but the meal, it seems, was not a success. Laura pleaded illness and stayed away. Evelyn described his brother's companion as a 'ferocious lady who is in love with C. Connolly',[107] and Alec's attempt to cement family affection failed, as indeed did his relationship with his lover. He was to wait for ever to enter his brother's confidence. On the proceeds of *Island in the Sun*, Alec set up home in Tangier, where he lived for the rest of his life, preserving his annual allowance of days in England for business and the Test cricket season. When he received his copy of *Pinfold*, he was shocked to hear of the ordeal.[108] Apparently Evelyn had said nothing of it to him.

'I'm in touch with K[atharine],' Diana Cooper had written just before the Waughs' jaunt. 'It's dreadful dreadful – I saw her twice in the nursing home and she seemed almost dead to me. Ought Ronnie to be sad to her? I think he should spare her – she broke down talking of him because she thought he was so unhappy. . . .'[109] In the meantime, Knox's physical condition had temporarily improved. The pain had subsided and he was husbanding his strength for the Romanes Lecture, which he was due to give at Oxford on 11 June. Most of it had been written during his stay at Combe Florey, a supreme effort of will, resisting lassitude and nausea. Katharine, realizing that he could collapse at any moment and trying to simulate serenity, found a loyal friend in Waugh. Before leaving for the casino, he had offered to act as literary executor,[110] thus relieving her of a huge burden. Only at the end of May, when jaundice set in, was Knox told of his condition. Like Waugh, he was sceptical of scientific opinion. Unlike him, Knox did not wish to die and insisted on a second opinion.

105. 26 May 1957; *Letters*, p. 489.
106. Unpublished ALS, [17 May 1957], from Nice RP, Alpes Maritimes; BL.
107. ALS to Ann Fleming, 26 May 1957; *Letters*, p. 489.
108. Cf. unpublished ALS from Alec Waugh to Evelyn Waugh, 20 July 1957, from Edrington etc.; BL.
109. ALS, 16 May 1957, from Château de St Firmin, Vineuil, Oise; BL; *MWMS*, p. 239.
110. Cf. unpublished ALS from Katharine Asquith, 26 May 1957, from The Manor House, Mells, Frome; BL: '. . . Ronald & I were both so touched by your suggestion. It was like you to have thought of it for both our sakes & very sweet of you. . . .'

Dom Hubert van Zeller drove him to Oxford on the 11th. He got through his lecture well: seated, a dreadful colour, but somehow picking up energy from a large and sympathetic audience, many of whom realized that they were seeing him for the last time. The next day, van Zeller accompanied him to London where Knox's old pupil, Harold Macmillan, had offered 10 Downing Street as a temporary surgery. Sir Horace Evans arrived and confirmed the earlier diagnosis. How long, Knox asked, did he have to live? Weeks or months? Sir Horace predicted the latter. Knox returned to Mells on the 13th, hoping to complete his translation of *The Imitation*, and wrote within the week to Waugh. Could he and Laura come over for a couple of nights soon? 'I am afraid your activities as my literary executor can no longer be regarded as very remote.'[111]

Unfortunately Waugh had urgent business of his own. He was completing an overdue treatment (never filmed) of *Scoop*, *Pinfold* was just a month from publication, and there were severe problems with Meg. When he did get over, ten days later, he could only spare one night to sort through the priest's literary remains. This was probably the occasion for one of Waugh's greater acts of *pietas*: his offer to write Knox's biography. Waugh had a talent for the precisely chosen gift, and no more generous an accolade could have been devised. Knox knew how difficult such a task would be for his friend and he accepted the offer without hesitation. He did not realize that this would involve Waugh's deferring the completion of his trilogy. But, then, the emaciated priest did not realize much by this stage. During July, he took to his bed. Within two months he was dead.

Altogether, despite the Beaverbrook booty, the period leading up to the publication of *Pinfold* was a melancholy one for Waugh. Meg's troubles cut him deeply, he understood her so well. Acton had written from Florence describing Bron ('he circulates on a Vespa') as 'a charming chip off the not so old block in certain ways uncannily like you.'[112] But it was in Meg that Waugh saw himself. Over the previous six months the nuns had reached successive stages of bafflement, anxiety and, finally, irritation at her behaviour. '[She] is going through a rather gloomy phase of life,' the headmistress had written after the mercury incident. 'She feels that nothing and no one, always excepting the family to whom she is devoted, is worth while.... She tells me there is [no specific reason for her misery] except for her boredom with life, unless she is at home....'[113] 'I know that Margaret finds her ideals and incentives in you ... [and she] has an astonishing clarity of outlook. She seems to have so great a grasp of the concept of infinity that

111. Unpublished ALS from Ronald Knox, 17 June [1957], from The Manor House etc.; BL.
112. Unpublished ALS, 24 March 1957, from La Pietra, Florence; BL.
113. Unpublished ALS from M. Bridget, IBVM, 20 December 1956, from St Mary's Convent, Ascot, Berks.; BL.

sometimes the very finite and humdrum doings of school life depress her excessively. . . .'[114] They had noticed this fierce family loyalty in Teresa, too, and they admired it. The pity was that it could not be extended to include the school.

By the end of May 1957, the Waughs' antipathy to education had erupted again. Meg's behaviour had deteriorated. She had broken bounds and escaped with some friends for a midnight feast on the Heath. Like Bron, she flouted the rules and expressed 'a continued and studied attitude of boredom and defiance'. 'It is so sad', the headmistress wrote, 'that she can apparently only use her strong personality in a negative and destructive way. . . .'[115] Waugh had read this in Monte Carlo, and it had rather spoiled his holiday. 'Darling Meg,' he wrote on his return:

> A sad and saddening letter from you. I am sorry you are in hot water. You do not have to tell me that you have not done anything really wicked. I know my pig. I am absolutely confident that you will never be dishonourable, impure or cruel. That is all that matters.[116]

As always in his letters to his children, Waugh struggled for the exact linguistic pitch to match the age, mood and sex of the recipient. Here he was only softly corrective. Earlier in the year, when he thought she could take it, he had teased her more sharply: 'Once upon a time there was a hideous little girl. She had flat feet, round shoulders and she bit her nails. Many observers mistook her for a pig. But her good father loved her dearly. . . .'[117] Now he recognized Meg's condition as serious 'p.m.'. She felt that everyone hated her. She wanted to leave. Waugh understood adolescent depression. He too, he told Meg, had been miserable at school; Bron had hated Downside. Both examples suggested the wisdom of patience. They could discuss her leaving during the holidays. In the meantime, he wrote to the school trying to explain his peculiar daughter.

'It is a great relief', the headmistress replied, 'to feel that you are quite aware of Margaret's state of mind and understand her so well. What you say about her self-pity and persecution mania is completely true.'[118] Meg made an effort, improved her conduct a little and soon relapsed. To encourage her, Waugh had brought her home for a week-end. But the delights of his company only intensified the misery of exile. What terrified her most was the thought of failing him. He would, she felt, be ashamed

114. Unpublished ALS from M. Bridget, IBVM, 30 December 1956, from St Mary's Convent etc.; BL.
115. Unpublished ALS from M. Bridget, IBVM, 31 May 1957, from St Mary's Convent etc.; BL.
116. 3 June [1957]; *Letters*, p. 489.
117. March 1957; *Letters*, p. 486.
118. Unpublished ALS from M. Bridget, IBVM, 9 June 1957, from St Mary's Convent etc.; BL.

of her should she prove incapable of surviving public school. 'Darling Papa,' she wrote:

> Thank you so much for last week-end – you and mummy are the kindest parents anybody could have. You are the most wonderful father. I long to leave this place because it is really the separation from you and mummy I miss more than anything. . . . Papa, please tell me truthfully soon, if you would be ashamed . . . please decide for me, I trust you, I do not trust myself.[119]

Papa decided. Unable to resist this appeal, he withdrew Meg and Harriet as from the end of the term. The headmistress seemed well satisfied. Meg, she thought, was clever; she should go to Oxford. She wished her pupil well and was glad to be rid of her. Waugh welcomed his daughters without recrimination, secretly, one suspects, rather proud of their ability to put the wind up the nuns. Meg and Hatty both had his piercing eyes and sharpness with strangers. Both, despite their school reports, were brilliant. And so it was that, as Ronnie Knox lay dying and *Pinfold* was about to astonish the literary world, the family was reunited.

*

Against his better judgement, Waugh accepted an invitation to a Foyle's Literary Luncheon on the day of publication, 19 July. It was the first and last such venture of his career. Having quarrelled with McDougall for dressing *Pinfold* so shabbily,[120] Waugh had grudgingly agreed to oil the publicity machine. In December 1956, he had marked his entry into the new house and old age by advertising in *The Times* for an ear trumpet. Offers flooded in[121] and he selected a black, Edwardian model, two feet long. It was the perfect device to signal his final separation from the world, and the Foyle's luncheon was its first outing. In future, Papa pug was to play the graceless anachronism for the unblinking eye of the press camera: dyspeptic, offensive and hugely self-important. That was just how he wanted it: *noli me tangere*.

Waugh was guest of honour. With him at the head-table sat Fr D'Arcy, Alec Guinness, Rose Macaulay, Frank Pakenham, Douglas Woodruff, Ursula Bloom, Vivien Leigh and the Duke and Duchess of Devonshire. The public paid a guinea to eat with the lions and watched bemused as a

119. Unpublished ALS, 28 June [1957], from St Mary's Convent etc.; BL.

120. Dingy brown jacket; flaccid illustration (Waugh had asked for the reproduction of a Francis Bacon painting); shoddy paper.

121. Including one from 'Debo', the Duchess of Devonshire. Angela Laycock had promised a trumpet three years earlier. When Lady Diana Cooper suggested a conventional hearing aid, he replied: 'It isn't so much the wires – it is the button in the ear that revolts me' (ALS, 23 March [1953], from Piers Court); BL; *MWMS*, p.165.

florid and elephantine Waugh, sporting red carnation and military moustache, waved his trumpet in Lady Olivier's face and she shouted responses into the bell. Then came speeches. Andrew Devonshire presided. Malcolm Muggeridge was to propose Waugh's health: a poor start. Waugh had admired Muggeridge's early writing but, meeting in Algeria during the war, they had found little to say to each other. Muggeridge's chief memory was of Waugh's gigantic shorts; Waugh's of not liking Muggeridge. Since then, the Editor of *Punch* had in Waugh's view been guilty of cowardice in the face of the enemy (Tito).

Muggeridge stood up, beaming; Waugh placed his trumpet on the table and left it there throughout the speech. Muggeridge opened by admitting that he and the principal guest were not on friendly terms and that his admiration for the novelist fell short of idolatry. There was twenty minutes of this, with Waugh glaring into space. (Asked afterwards what he thought of the toast, Waugh said that he had not heard a word of it.) When his turn came, he thanked Andrew Devonshire for taking the chair at the height of the racing season, ignored Muggeridge, and offered a startling account of the facts behind his fiction.

'Three years ago', he began, 'I had quite a new experience. I went off my head for about three weeks.'[122]

> There has been no recurrence and I went without medical treatment. . . . Many of you may be hearing voices all the time, as I did. I met various people when I was dotty and they said I looked abstracted, but they could have [had] no idea of what was going on. Look into the eyes of your neighbours – even you, ladies of the Thorpe Bay branch of the National Council of Women – and ask yourselves: 'Are you Pinfolds?'[123]

Waugh was in fine form, confusing everyone splendidly. The Thorpe Bay branch had arrived in a charabanc at the last moment, thirty-five strong. Far from being outraged, he had insisted on shaking hands with each one. Over lunch he and Lady Olivier had sung 'There's No Business Like Show Business' together. Now he was candidly admitting that *Pinfold* was autobiographical. To baffle the audience further, a consultant physician and neurologist, Sir Walter Ferguson Hannay, threw in a facetious observation: could it be that Mr Waugh was sane then and is mad now? No reply is recorded, but it was a question soon to be at the heart of a controversy with J. B. Priestley.

Waugh's admissions may have been confusing but they were not new. The dust-jacket note emphasized the author's experience of madness. As

122. 'Mr. Waugh Goes Sane', *DT*, 20 July 1957, 6. .
123. *DM*, 20 July 1957, 12.

early as April, just after the libel suits, the *Telegraph* gossip-columnist had revealed that 'After stubbornly withholding it from pilgrim journalists, ... Waugh has included in his new novel ... a curious slice of his private life.... The publishers ... hope to establish "Pinfold" as a household word meaning "half round the bend".'[124] McDougall and Waugh were quietly 'pushing' the book in an unusual fashion, perhaps hoping to forestall a bad press. The *Observer* had printed the opening section.[125] Driberg had interviewed his friend and produced a laudatory defence the previous Sunday. (Beneath a genial photograph of Waugh ran the caption '"What a horrible man," they said.')[126] But this campaign of deliberate leakage had not been entirely successful. Kenneth Allsop had scooped the reviews the day before the Foyle's gala with a large article in the *Mail.* Here the photograph glowered demoniacally above: 'Waugh, Orgies, Murder, Mutiny'. The novelist was characterized as 'a scribbling squire ... [living out his] crested, cross-patch charade, set in a draughty manor and St. James Street....'[127] Ultimately, a sympathetic review is drowned in the same sensationalist gobbledegook that had been spewed from the files for years. Little irritated Waugh more than being described as a 'squire' and no one realized better how dangerous a course he ran in giving so much of himself away in *Pinfold.*

Another ancillary difficulty had arisen through coincidence. Nine months earlier, Gabriel Fielding, the writer, had sent Waugh proofs of a first novel by a young Scottish woman.[128] Waugh had never heard of Muriel Spark, despite the fact that Greene had been quietly financing her while she recovered from a mental breakdown. *The Comforters* (1956) dealt directly with this experience: a Catholic novelist hearing voices. It would have been in Waugh's interest to do nothing to help her. Instead, he offered a glowing quotation for publicity and an equally generous review. 'It so happens', he wrote, 'that *The Comforters* came to me just as I had finished a story on a similar theme and I was struck by how much more ambitious was Miss Spark's essay and how much better she had accomplished it.'[129] Like Angus Wilson, she was astounded by his generosity. From her point of view, an established figure had singled out an unknown writer for his patronage. But it took more courage than perhaps she realized from him to say what he did. In Miss Spark he recognized a brilliant new talent. His own literary future seemed dim.

124. 'Is He Pinfold?', *DT*, 12 April 1957, 8.
125. 'Portrait of the Artist in Middle Age', *Observer*, 14 July 1957, 10.
126. 'The Agony of Evelyn Waugh', *SD*, 14 July 1957, 4.
127. 'Mr. Waugh Wields the Scalpel. This Time ... on Mr. Waugh', *DM*, 18 July 1957, 4.
128. Cf. *Letters*, p. 477.
129. 'Something Fresh', *Spectator*, 22 February 1957, 256; *EAR*, pp. 518–19.

The reviews of *Pinfold*, if anything, confirmed this foreboding. They pounced on the autobiographical element and plunged into biographical fallacy. Donat O'Donnell found the objective cruelty of Waugh's comic vision 'embarrassing' when turned to self-examination.[130] The *TLS* was quietly savage, trying to cut Waugh's talent down to size:

> It is time people stopped treating Mr. Waugh as a failed Mauriac. He is a lightweight who has suffered from being bracketed with completely different writers like ... Greene.... Like Sheridan or Fitzgerald or Max Beerbohm, [Waugh] has a freak talent and is entitled to be judged on what he writes without any attempt to relate him to trends or other writers or anything else.[131]

Waugh, it continued, had nothing to say. He was just a comic.

This notion of him as a writer of amusing squibs or romantic religious melodrama was something one might have expected from O'Donnell or Philip Toynbee. Neither had greatly admired the early work. Their dissatisfaction with *Pinfold*, however, sprang more from the fact that Waugh was still capable of shocking them. Toynbee, for example, was puzzled by Pinfold's assailants – not 'parlour pinks, pacifists, non-believers with the wrong accent or any of the other stage villains of [his] mythology' but '... upper-class thugs, anti-Semites, Fascists and bullies – just the kind of people, in fact, to whom [he] has sometimes seemed to be a little over-indulgent....'[132] Reviewers had, after Spain, to be cautious. (Driberg had insisted on Waugh's checking, and passing, his text.) But Toynbee's piece is not so much antagonistic as confused by Waugh's versatility. He had never admired Waugh's prose style but here the novelist was attempting a form of writing quite new to him and difficult to classify. Toynbee disliked what he took to be Waugh's politics, yet they apparently shared enemies. What would this extraordinary man do next?

Few, however, openly welcomed the novel and, of those who did, John Raymond of the *New Statesman* was the most generous. Raymond, who knew Nancy Mitford and had met Waugh in her company, was a recent convert. (Fr Caraman instructed him and had reported with some satisfaction the 'Catholic rot' infecting the left-wing press.)[133] The odd result for Waugh was to find *Pinfold* lauded by the *New Statesman* and (much to Ian Gilmour's embarrassment) written down by the *Spectator*. Raymond greeted Waugh's excursion into yet another literary style with delight: 'It is possible to predict a new novel by ... Greene say, a new

130. 'The Loved One', *Spectator*, 19 July 1957, 112; *CH*, pp. 380–1.
131. Unsigned review, 'Self Portrait', *TLS*, 19 July 1957, 437; *CH*, pp. 382–4.
132. 'Mr. Waugh Shifts Gears', *Observer*, 21 July 1957, 13; *CH*, pp. 386–7.
133. Cf. unpublished ALS, 9 January 1956, from 114 Mount Street, W1; B1.

Compton-Burnett, a Henry Green even, in a way that it is impossible with Waugh.'[134] Woodruff, struggling a little, found that it 'succeeds remarkably', but he remained naïvely puzzled as to why a man 'should invent unrealities about himself'.[135] *Time*, lamenting that it was not 'up to the level of the early-vintage Waugh', recommended it as 'probably the most off-beat novel of the season, and certainly Waugh's strangest.'[136] But it was a mediocre crop and the American reviews were generally unenthusiastic. With the Little, Brown money running down annually, the future again looked bleak.

It might, indeed, have looked bleaker had not Priestley injected pace into sales by writing a silly article in the *New Statesman*. An admirer of Waugh's early work, Priestley, like Amis, O'Donnell, and Toynbee, had lost faith with *Brideshead*. *Pinfold* shocked him and he decided to offer, in bluff, humanitarian fashion, a cautionary analysis, one artist to another:

> ... if Pinfold imagines his troubles are over, he is a fool. He has been warned. Because the voices talked a lot of rubbish ... he is ignoring the underlying truth ... the idea that he is not what he thinks he is.... Consciously he has rejected this idea for some time; he has drowned it in alcohol, bromide and chloral, and now it can only batter its way through to him by staging a crude drama of lunatic voices. And though they were a long way from the truth in their detailed charges, they are right, these voices, when they tell him that he is a fake.[137]

Why was he a fake? Quite simply, he was trying to combine two incompatible roles: those of artist and Catholic country gentleman. Why should he not combine these roles? Well, because they were not compatible and, moreover, this was 'really Pinfold's opinion, too'.[138] Priestley could not expect to get away with this and the response was genial, hilarious and devastating.

By way of reparation for O'Donnell's review, Gilmour was happy to offer the *Spectator* as vehicle. That was part of the joke: *not* writing for the *New Statesman*. Quickly demolishing the 'incompatible roles' argument (Priestley was himself a landed proprietor on a larger scale than Waugh), the article skips adventurously on to the sub-text of the complaint. What, he says, really 'gets Mr. Priestley's goat ... is my attempt to behave like a gentleman.'[139] In one deft move Waugh had pierced the core of the 'scribbling squire' insults and opened it to mockery:

134. 'Mr. Waugh on Deck', *NS*, 20 July 1957, 88; *CH*, pp. 384–6.
135. *Tablet*, 20 July 1957, 60.
136. 'Self-Inflicted Satire', *Time*, 12 August 1957, 92.
137. 'What Was Wrong with Pinfold', *NS*, 31 August 1957, 224; *CH*, pp. 387–92.
138. *Ibid.*, p. 389.
139. 'Anything Wrong with Priestley?', *Spectator*, 13 September 1957, 328–9; *EAR*, pp. 527–9.

> Naturally I hunger for Mr. Priestley's good opinion and would like to keep my sanity for a few more years. I am an old dog to learn new tricks but ... I should not find it beyond me to behave like a cad on occasions – there are several shining examples in the literary world. My hair grows strongly still; I could wear it long. I could hire a Teddyboy suit and lark about the dance halls with a bicycle chain. But would this satisfy Mr. Priestley? Would he not be quick to detect and denounce this new *persona*? 'There was Waugh,' he would say, 'a man of humane education and accustomed to polite society. Tried to pass as Redbrick. No wonder he's in the padded cell.'[140]

Waugh's comic genius thrived on the vulgar disruption of polite behaviour. The trick of his literary voice involved the spicing of Augustan measures with sharp doses of slang. And here he was again, the elderly literary Teddyboy, for the last time larking about the steps of the *New Statesman* with his horsewhip.

Pinfold marked another Rubicon in more ways than one. For while it was a valedictory gesture, his final black comedy, and while its pitiless self-portrait presented to many a character so dotty as to be incomprehensible, to others it opened the doors of perception – and of sympathy. If Waugh thought that he was dropping the portcullis on his life with this book, he soon learned otherwise. Several letters arrived from friends who had suffered similar torments, including Dom Aelred, Robert Henriques, Basil Bennett, Sykes, Ed Stanley and, a haunting voice from the past, John Heygate. For Lord Stanley of Alderley, *Pinfold* appeared as a corrective to White's: 'You will not accept a critical appreciation ... from one who is about to enter the same tunnel of darkness. Yours is an odd book – a curious mixture which leaves me, & my stupid friends like Randolph & Phil Dunn, un peu dans l'air ... thank you for precept & guidance.'[141] Bennett felt similarly humbled:

> I am suffering acutely at the moment & slink furtively about. I can't go into White's unless someone will come with me. I remember so many things I have done of which I am ashamed as far back as my preparatory school. I have told no one this but you.... P.S. I would like to see you soon.[142]

Pinfold released some unholy terrors. Strangers wrote, as to a Californian guru. One lady begged Waugh to tell her whether the voices were real. He replied promptly and kindly, offering comfort in her terrible isolation. Voices had prevented her sleeping for eighteen months. Another fellow-

140. *Ibid.*, p. 528.
141. Unpublished ALS, 26 July [1957], from White's; BL.
142. Unpublished ALS, 28 July [1957], from High Canfold Farm, Cranleigh, Surrey; BL.

sufferer sought succour of a different kind: Digby Goddard-Fenwick had been one of Waugh's prep-school masters at Heath Mount. He remembered Cecil Beaton as 'a very pretty, girlish youngster whose ultimate future was not difficult to forecast' and Waugh as 'a shy-sensitive freckled little fellow'. He was writing to offer sympathy. He also heard voices – and could he have £20 and a free copy? Could they meet?[143] In exorcizing his own ghosts, Waugh found himself the receiver of many more. Out of the ether they came, out of the woodwork, struggling to be heard. And this time they were not the voices of persecutors but of the persecuted, turning to him as confessor.

Waugh had never received fan-mail like this before. What had begun as a joke at his own expense, an account of an aberration brought on solely by narcotics, had described a common pattern of mental illness in others who had never touched bromide or chloral. He remained unmoved by the coincidence. There were, he thought, a thousand ways to go insane in a secular society, and the Devil stalked everywhere. 'To judge by what the papers say,' Pinfold told his wife in a cancelled conclusion, 'very nearly half the inhabitants of the kingdom are more or less barmy at one time or another.'[144] There was something satisfying to Waugh in this idea.

How accurate an account of his hallucinations is *Pinfold*? Waugh said that it represented 'almost exactly' what happened.[145] Lord Donaldson leaves us in little doubt: 'I wondered whether you cd. possibly tell the story in print as vividly as you did on your first night back, but you have succeeded wonderfully. . . . I suppose it is the only work of pure rapportage [*sic*] that you have ever written.'[146] Waugh admitted to artistic compression and we have already seen how he tinkered with revisions. Lady Donaldson herself discovered small discrepancies between her account and Pinfold's. But the Donaldsons' is powerful testimony and the result is that the book has always been read as autobiography rather than fiction. At the time, however, Greene and Powell thought it probably the best fiction Waugh had written.

There is room, surely, (not here) for a reconsideration of its fictional status. The ease with which it translated into a successful radio play testifies to the quality of its structure and dialogue.[147] Waugh's review of *The Comforters* demonstrates his fascination with Spark's self-referential tech-

143. Unpublished ALS, 24 July 1957, from 44 Dafforne Road, Tooting Bec Common, SW17; BL.
144. For a full account of the revisions see Robert Murray Davis, 'Prerogatives of the Artist: The Ordeal of Gilbert Pinfold', *Evelyn Waugh, Writer* (Pilgrim Books, 1981), p. 294.
145. 'Face to Face' interview with John Freeman, BBC TV, 26 June 1960; BBCSL.
146. Unpublished ALS, 19 July 1957, from Burden Court Farm, Tresham, Wotton-under-Edge, Glos.; BL.
147. Cf. *The Times*, 8 June 1960, 16.

nique and suggests that he was working along similar lines. The revision most assiduously tackled was that of the ending: converting it into the beginning of the book we have just read. Pinfold is thus both inside and outside his text and the tale repeats itself seamlessly. As with *Helena*, an argument can be made for *Pinfold* as a 'postmodernist' novel. B. S. Johnson and Martin Amis (both of whose writings Waugh would have loathed) later used a similar mixture of fiction and autobiography. Sir Angus Wilson has linked *Pinfold* to Kafka.[148] Much as Waugh despised 'experimental writing', his ingenuity never rested in its games with the reader. Fiction, at this stage, remained essentially a word-structure to him, good or bad according to its formal coherence. *Pinfold*, eating its tail as it does, is a brilliantly self-consuming text which eternally blurs the boundary between 'fact' and 'fiction'. However it is tackled, there will be a rich diet for future critics. The book reminded Powell of James Hogg's *Confessions of a Justified Sinner* (1894). What, for instance, are we to make of the title, echoing Meredith;[149] what of the chapter titles suggesting Joyce, Behan, Chesterton and *Punch* cartoons? As ever with Waugh's later writing, the text is pregnant with literary allusion.

Again, one person above all others was aware of these issues: Frederick Stopp. For over three years he had been tunnelling into Waugh's life and work and, at last, in the autumn of 1957, he was able to send his typescript. The conjunction of Stopp's work and the writing of *Pinfold* is interesting. Waugh was grateful in a time of siege to have so earnest and intelligent an advocate, but he wanted to make his own case first. The opening chapter of *Pinfold* is his response. Waugh's title, 'Portrait of the Artist in Middle Age', alludes directly (via Joyce) to Stopp's sub-title (*Portrait of an Artist*). It also emphasizes that the story is incomplete.

Over the years, Waugh's first biographer had moved from being 'Dr Stopp' to 'Freddie', and Waugh had been pleasantly astonished by the evidence of his allusive technique. Many references he had, of course, deliberately inserted for the 'educated reader'. Many others, however, had slipped through from the unconscious and he modestly asked Stopp not to attribute these to artistry. Overall, Waugh liked Stopp's first version and, although he thought it too long, felt churlish about suggesting cuts. McDougall suggested them for him, Stopp demolished a third of his research, and the result was a triumph. Even so, Waugh found it profoundly unsettling to be written about in this fashion. It was rather like being buried alive. The assumption behind such a book is that the subject's major work

148. Cf. Angus Wilson's review of Waugh's *Ronald Knox*, *Encounter*, January 1960, 78–80; *CH*, pp. 405–8.
149. *The Ordeal of Richard Feverel: A History of Father and Son* (1859). Gilbert Pinfold was an earlier owner of Piers Court, whose name was inscribed on one of the doors.

is complete. Waugh knew that it was not, nor was he prepared to be predictable.

In the early summer of 1957 another young American, Thomas Ryan, had written hopelessly to him begging an interview.[150] On reaching London, Ryan had fallen ill with pleurisy. Then Waugh had rung him. Was he a Catholic? Yes. Was he contagious? No. Then, Waugh said, he would just 'pop round'. Ryan staggered from his sick-bed.

It was a lively exchange. Waugh's memory clearly still played tricks, post-dating his conversion by two years. Asked whether he felt, like Graham Greene, that he was 'a writer who happens to be a Catholic' rather than a Catholic writer, he said 'No ... it would be foolish to claim I was not a Catholic writer.' Nor was he an 'intellectual'. 'That's a Marxist term that sprang up in the Middle European countries to distinguish a class, which doesn't exist here, between the worker and the bourgeoisie. I don't like the word. And certainly no one could be less an intellectual than Graham Greene.... Only mathematicians are entitled to be called intellectuals.' He preferred the term 'creative artist'. What did he think of American writers? He admired J.F. Powers's *The Presence of Grace*.[151] Hemingway was a master ('he's really at heart a Catholic author, you know'). But, no, he did not spare much time for American fiction: 'I prefer to read in my own language....' There was, he said, a fundamental difference between the two countries. The height of American culture was Boston Unitarianism; British civilization was essentially Catholic, 'part of Europe'. The English, he felt, had a 'sharper sense of reality' as a result of this. Ryan bravely confronted him with a quotation from Donat O'Donnell: 'Waugh has a private religion on which he has superimposed Catholicism, much as newly-converted pagans are said to superimpose a Christian nomenclature on their ancient cults of trees and thunder.' What did Waugh think of this? 'Nonsense.'

The interview shows Waugh comfortably settled in the eccentric logic of his private world. But perhaps his most interesting remark was thrown out towards the end: 'I have been working on a trilogy on the war but, I've put that aside ... to do a short, humorous novel [*Pinfold*]....' Did he think he would write another novel like *Brideshead*? 'Yes, I should think so. I have nothing in mind at the moment, however.'[152] No mention was made of Knox, but this was the first mention of a 'trilogy' since the publication of *Officers and Gentlemen*. As late as July 1957, Waugh had written to his

150. 'Hopelessly' because the Nancy Spain saga was also a legend in the States.

151. A book of short stories. Waugh had reviewed it favourably – 'Scenes of Clerical Life', *Commonweal*, 30 March 1956, 667–8 – but had expressed reservations about Powers's use of 'a light free, colloquial language, which is often not only unfamiliar but unintelligible.... I am sure he could write more plainly without sacrificing any of his essential artistic achievement.'

152. Thomas C. Ryan, 'A Talk with Evelyn Waugh', *The Sign*, August 1957, 41–3.

agent saying that he wanted to work on a novel (*Unconditional Surrender*) and did not wish to be disturbed.[153] All this was before his impulsive promise to write Knox's biography. The priest died on 24 August. During the same month the interview was published. But by then it was already out of date and Waugh was committed to further deferral of his *maximum opus*. Time, he felt, was running out and he wanted to concentrate all his energies upon finishing *Knox* as quickly as possible. An obsession gripped him, partly excitement, partly punctilio, partly desire to be rid of the task before his creative powers failed him. Nothing was allowed to stand in its way. That, at least, is one explanation for his extraordinary behaviour towards Bron in the following months.

153. Cf. unpublished ALS to John Montgomery of A. D. Peters & Co., 1 July 1957; *Catalogue* E1018, p. 231.

XI

Literary Garbo: September 1957–October 1961

This period began and ended with obituaries: first Knox's; finally Waugh's own with the opening pages of *A Little Learning*. Over these four years he wrote the biography, a travel book, various prefaces, articles and reviews, and his last, excellent, novel. It was a productive time. Waugh felt slothful. While many of his countrymen were celebrating a new openness and prosperity – the Wolfenden Report, Supermac and the Wind of Change, the Lady Chatterley trial, President Kennedy replacing Eisenhower, the rise of the Angry Young Men and of teenage pop-culture – Waugh saw only restriction and impoverishment. It was for him a time of death and resignation characterized by the steady collapse, like Venice sinking, of European Catholic civilization and by the dispersal of his family. Among so many skulls, the near-death of his eldest son seemed strangely insignificant.

The Priestley article was Waugh's last journalistic *jeu d'esprit*. The religious life was now his subject and obsession, his seclusion oddly projected as a cross between that of monk and vanquished celebrity. 'Oh no John no John no John no,' he had written to McDougall four months earlier, 'I won't appear on television.... [Chapman & Hall] should "plug" ... "Waugh the recluse". [Your advertising agent] must not reveal my new address. Literary Garbo.'[1] In less than three years, however, he had succumbed to this final indignity. 'Poverty', as he told John Freeman, had driven him to public exposure.

During the autumn of 1957 Waugh was a more contented man, enjoying his biographical research. When Ann Fleming visited Combe Florey she discovered a 'united clever family'.[2] Bron, like all his contemporaries, chose to complete his National Service before going up to university and had disappeared to Caterham for six months of officer-training with the Blues. Hatty and Meg were at home, attending a local day-school and receiving odd lessons from Papa. James and Septimus were still boarders, and Teresa was at Oxford. Combe Florey was a peaceful house, its tranquillity

1. [June 1957]; *Letters*, p. 492. McDougall was seeking publicity for the launch of *Pinfold*.
2. *LAF*, p. 207.

interrupted only by a small band of workmen refurbishing rooms distant from the library.

Here Waugh shuffled the conflicting images of Knox's last days. 'K[atharine Asquith]', Lady Diana Cooper had written, 'fears for his mental agony'.[3] But it was Katharine's idealized account which registered what Waugh wanted to hear:

> Towards the end every movement was an immense effort & perhaps painful.... Yet never in my presence did he utter one word of complaint. He seemed lifted out of the world. O Evelyn what is the secret! I suppose it was the climax of his long life [*sic*] surrender – to the will of God – but before he got ill he wasn't always patient like that – most of the time – but not always. I didn't realise how wonderful it was till I got ill myself.[4]

Coming from this pious, gentle woman, and probably written from her hospital bed, the letter had settled Waugh's mind about his tormented priest. The image he chose to create was that of a supremely gifted man resigned to injustice.

As with *Rossetti* and *Campion*, *Knox* reveals as much about its author as it does about its subject. Waugh constructed this life partly as castigation of his own greed for power, partly as a justification of his convert faith and aesthetic tastes. His *Sunday Times* 'Tribute' describes a man who, like Waugh, wrote in 'a language that was accurate, subtle, idiosyncratic but essentially colloquial in the idiom of his youth', a man who

> liked the classic division of mankind into the 'drastic' – the men of action and decision who know what they want and how to get it, who have little patience with the hesitation of others, who never shrink from 'making a scene' – and the 'pathetic', who take what is on the table ... who suffer neglect rather than assert their rights, who hate to inconvenience anyone.[5]

It is the philosophy of Silenus in *Decline and Fall*, separating the 'dynamic' from the 'static'. Waugh was temperamentally 'drastic' and growing ashamed of it. For years he had despised the 'pathetic' as bores. For years he had been apologizing for his aggression: 'There must be a dozen nuances I coarsely miss when I begin to offend until, splosh, I stand dashed and dazed under a Niagara of rage.'[6] But there was another aspect to this struggle for temperance. As he once wrote to Lady Diana Cooper:

3. ALS, 17 August 1957, from Rome; BL; *MWMS*, p. 244.
4. Unpublished ALS [incomplete], from Katharine Asquith, nd [late August 1957?], np [the London Hospital?]; BL.
5. 'A Tribute to Ronald Knox', *ST*, 1 September 1957, 7.
6. ALS to Lady Diana Cooper, nd [August 1953?], from Piers Court; BL; *MWMS*, p. 177.

> My chief sorrow at the moment is that, as all epigrams get attributed to Ronnie . . ., all rudeness gets attributed to me. Beasts come up to me & say: 'I heard something so amusing you said the other day' and then recount an act of hideous boorishness without the shadow of reality.[7]

Knox is pictured as a different kind of Waugh hero, 'eminently pathetic' and possessed of all the Christian virtues.

Knox, 'no obvious ascetic',[8] was a country-house priest with a keen enjoyment of upper-class society. Waugh presents him as a martyr: a rare survivor of a brilliant Oxford generation; a man who generously relinquished power in the face of neglect; a literary master who sacrificed the pleasures of pure creation for the theological tasks the Church assigned to him. The biography developed into an extension of Waugh's nostalgic mythology of an Old England which had collapsed in 1914. Knox, like Gervase Crouchback, appears as the isolated bearer of ancient values, adrift and exploited in the wasteland. With the dials of his Time Machine now set full astern, Waugh was voyaging back to 1910, to the 'exuberant intellectual and social life led in the heart of that historic, quintessential, tragic Oxford band who were soon to fall in battle; that golden roll of honour whose fame still rings clear above the whisper of envy and the thunder of subsequent national disasters.'[9]

When Knox's will was published on 4 January 1958, it was discovered that he had left Waugh all copyrights and unpublished manuscripts, but that any money received from them should go to Katharine's son, 'Trim' (the Earl of Oxford), or to his children. Waugh's later assiduous bargaining as literary executor was entirely a labour of love. The £3,000 advance was handsome but fell far short of his usual annual income. He could afford only one year to complete the work. And as this pressure mounted, so too did his emotional temperature. Throughout his correspondence about the biography, two anxieties recur: the fear of impertinent intrusion and the indignity of haste.

Waugh had five major sources: Laurence Eyres, Dom Hubert van Zeller, the Woodruffs, Lady Acton and the Prime Minister, Harold Macmillan. All offered material which required delicate handling.[10] 'I am going through the papers [Knox] left at Mells,' Waugh wrote to van Zeller in September. 'Among them are a large number of letters written to him by Daphne Acton in 1937, '38 and '39. . . . There are many references to a

7. ALS, 'Friday' [early November 1952?], from Piers Court; BL; *MWMS*, p. 150.
8. 'A Tribute to Ronald Knox', *op. cit.*, 7.
9. *Ibid.*
10. Waugh also gained useful information from Tom Driberg.

monk who, I think, must be you whose advice they sought about regulating their friendship.'[11]

Waugh found himself stumbling across potential scandal here. Daphne Strutt had married Lord Acton (whom Waugh describes as 'a light-hearted, sweet-tempered, old-fashioned, horsy young man')[12] in 1931. She was tall, sharp-witted, beautiful and came from a family of eminent scientists, fiercely opposed to Catholicism. Lord Acton was the head of the old Catholic family of Aldenham, Shropshire. One of his sisters had married Douglas Woodruff and, through him, Daphne began to take an interest in her husband's Faith. Woodruff had supplied reading lists and, in 1937, an introduction to Knox.

The attraction between 'Ronnie' and Daphne had been instantaneous. They shared an allusive wit and religious passion, and quickly found themselves devouring each other's company. Knox was forty-nine and gripped by what is now known as a 'mid-life crisis': depressed both by his lengthy tenure of Oxford's Catholic Chaplaincy and by his failure to make his mark either in the Hierarchy or in the world of letters. Lady Acton provided him with what Waugh described as a 'Second Spring'. Knox had felt alienated from young people, friendless and loveless. She recalled the gaiety and mental acuity of his generation of slaughtered friends. And for her part, she was infatuated. Married at nineteen, it seems that she had discovered little of Knox's infectious brilliance in her husband. At twenty-five, she found the priest's company irresistible. He became her instructor. On a Hellenic cruise, to the indignation of some of their fellow passengers, they spent much time alone together. On their return, she suggested that he take up residence as Chaplain to the Aldenham estate. Knox accepted. His new post, both hoped, would allow him world enough and time for Great Works. On Lady Acton's part it was a gesture of faith in his talents, unambiguously mixed with sexual attraction. The situation bristled with difficulties. But while Knox sailed through it with the innocence of a child, she became distressed. She was in love with him.

Dom Hubert was indeed the Downside monk consulted to 'regulate' this friendship. As Knox's confessor and confidant he was a crucial witness but one bound by confidentiality. He came, nevertheless, to Combe Florey for a week-end just after Christmas 1957 and provided a sheaf of notes upon which Waugh pounced eagerly. But he still needed to talk to Lady Acton, which was no easy matter. After the war the Actons had moved to Rhodesia to escape the Welfare State. Their departure had both deprived Knox of a home and concluded the 'awkwardness' with his hostess. It was at this point (1947) that Katharine Asquith had taken him in at Mells Manor and

11. 25 September 1957; *Letters*, p. 495.
12. *Ronald Knox*, *op. cit.*, p. 248.

only a few years earlier that Waugh had entered the story himself, a relative latecomer to this circle of intimates. Torn between his novelist's curiosity about the precise nature of Knox's high-voltage friendship and the horror of acting improperly, Waugh was uncertain how to proceed.

His mind was soon set at rest. During the autumn Lady Acton had begun sending him box-loads of Knox's letters. Waugh's earlier acquaintance with her had been slight, but her ebullient, open nature held nothing back, eager as she was for Waugh to immortalize her friend. In 1957 she was forty-six, settled contentedly again into her marriage with a small horde of children, and living on an estate outside Salisbury, where she helped to run a farm and mission school. What she had loved in Knox, she grew to love in Waugh, and in February 1958 he went to see her.

The fact that Waugh deigned to fly to Rhodesia and stayed for only three weeks emphasizes the exhausting haste of his project. This was no leisurely tour, taking time out at others' expense to explore the country. His 'travelling' days were over. He left in snowstorms, bearing a *pâté de foie gras* for his hostess, and returned leaving money for her to buy decent cutlery. This was a business visit, retracing Knox's footsteps of three years earlier.

Throughout, he was treated royally. Alec's son, Andrew, then ADC to the Governor-General, was on the tarmac to greet his uncle, with Daphne Acton and a box of cigars. Customs and passport control by-passed, Daphne drove Waugh forty miles in the dark to her farm: 'hideous, surrounded by the roughest rough grass.... Tin roofs, concrete walls, large bare rooms, everything painted white and awfully dirty.'[13] A rambling bungalow, it stood on a slope in a landscape of small hills. Unsupervised children, random guests and farmyard smells drifted in and out; the mission school, full of Daphne's converts, provided casual house-servants. A party-line telephone rang all day. It was a tumultuous, informal household, an outpost of the Faith which in his youth Waugh might have loved. But Rhodesia was not the exotic, transposed Barsetshire he had discovered in Kenya in 1930: 'Just as Ronnie said', he wrote to Laura, 'a wet English August, 5000 feet up.'[14]

Eager as he was to escape the plastic plates and ants in the bed, Waugh had nevertheless discovered the priceless gift of a new friendship. He described the house to Ann Fleming as 'everything that normally makes Hell' ameliorated by 'Daphne's serene sanctity radiating supernatural peace. She is the most remarkable woman I know.'[15] What delighted Waugh in one so pious was her frankness about her earlier feelings for Knox, and he returned pleasantly burdened with confidences. 'Thing is to get all facts

13. ALS to Laura Waugh, [9 February] 1958, from M'Bebi, Mazoe, S. Rhodesia; *Letters*, p. 503.
14. *Ibid.*
15. 10 March 1958; *Letters*, p. 505.

down', he informed McDougall, 'while they are in my poor nut and then spread myself being elegant.'[16] Before leaving he had written the Oxford sections. His next task was to revise them and to interview another witness.

*

Waugh wrote to 10 Downing Street and received a prompt reply:

> I am indeed glad to know that you are to write Ronnie's biography. There could be no better choice....
>
> Now as to the points you raise. First, I think the anonymity which Ronnie preserved himself in the *Spiritual Aeneid* ought to be preserved....
>
> Secondly, could you be very kind and send me the letters ... which I wrote at the time you refer to. Naturally, I can have no objection to my letters being quoted, if my name is not given. But I would just like to look at them; it is a long time ago.
>
> Thirdly, please come and see me here ... I would like to talk to you about Ronnie and tell you about Guy Lawrence....[17]

After the Tito tease, Eden baiting and twenty years' abuse of the Conservative Party, Waugh must have been pleasantly surprised by this.

In the autumn of 1910, Knox, at twenty-two, was studying for the Anglican priesthood. The Macmillans engaged him as a Classics tutor for Harold, then sixteen and preparing for an Oxford scholarship. Man and boy grew quickly to love each other. Macmillan's hero-worship was met by 'Ronnie''s delight in the company of his sharp-witted scholar. The age-gap was small. Knox was in many respects little more than a boy himself. Both were Etonians. They had much in common, not least because Macmillan's was a deeply religious nature. When their discussions strayed to Knox's High Church tastes, both found themselves inclined towards Romanism.

Macmillan's parents, fiercely Protestant and less than content with this development, perhaps entertained darker suspicions. Guy Lawrence also figured largely in Knox's emotional life. All the evidence suggests that both these friendships were affairs of the heart, intense and innocent. The Macmillans nevertheless sniffed subversion and delivered an ultimatum: Knox had either to agree to avoid religious debate or he must leave. Refusing this embargo (as they knew he must), he was dismissed and carried away a lifetime's shame at the indignity.

16. [March? 1958]; *Letters*, p. 504.
17. Unpublished TLS from Harold Macmillan, 12 March 1958, from 10 Downing Street, Whitehall; BL.

It was not long before the friendship was re-established. Knox went as chaplain to Trinity College, Oxford, in the Hilary Term of 1911 and Macmillan soon arrived as an Exhibitioner at Balliol. He attended Knox's discussion groups (principally consisting of Guy Lawrence, Edward Horner, Julian Grenfell and Charles Lister)[18] and was again infected by 'Roman fever'. Knox, of course, was then still an Anglican, but an Anglo-Catholic increasingly restive in the English Church. When his undergraduate friend tended towards 'Poping', he found himself offering tacit encouragement. Macmillan, Lawrence and Knox were all enduring similar spiritual crises simultaneously and, if anything, it seemed that Knox was the laggard in setting out for the Eternal City. Lawrence went first, in 1914, just before leaving for the trenches. Macmillan was on the brink of reception but deferred the decision until after the war. Knox thus felt under considerable pressure to maintain the courage of his convictions. It was only after three miserable years, during which he approached total loss of faith, that he finally plunged. 'It seems', Macmillan wrote at the time, '... the end of the journey has been reached – reached that is by you and Guy, while I am still ... timid, cowardly and faint.... I feel horribly now like a deserter....'[19] Lawrence was killed; Macmillan remained an Anglican.

Waugh, then, was particularly intrigued to discover the details and was pleased to be in the confidence of the Prime Minister. Like Knox, Waugh felt that 'a great part of the governing class regarded his deepest beliefs as exotic and deleterious',[20] and it was singularly gratifying to be welcomed to the heart of power by one so sympathetic. Waugh's relationship with the Churchills had been exclusively with the delinquent Randolph, and Waugh's sense of public neglect seems partly to have derived from the feeling that, like a mischievous child, he was excluded from adult counsel. At last, seeing a chance to establish his claim to national honour, he hurried to Downing Street. Macmillan was courteous, promised to dig out Knox's letters, and the novelist left anticipating elevation.

*

By early April 1958, 40,000 words were with the typist and Waugh went to Downside 'for the modern travesty of Holy Week'.[21] After another week in London, catching up on gossip through a haze of alcohol, he was back at his desk. Reports of his happiness, he informed Ann Fleming, were grossly exaggerated: 'I am a manic-depressive about money. At the moment I am depressive & think myself destitute. I find I spent over £17,000 last

18. Cf. *Ronald Knox*, pp. 60 and 125–6.
19. [September–October 1917?]; quoted *ibid*., p. 160.
20. *Ronald Knox*, p. 111.
21. Unpublished ALS to Lady Acton, 15 March 1958, from Combe Florey House; BL.

year.[22] This year I shall make 5 and pay tax on 17 – so I have reasons for depression.... Cornet Waugh is enjoying Cyprus top-hole.'[23]

Bron had just been commissioned in the Blues and posted to the latest scene of British imperial embarrassment. Like many National Servicemen, he regarded the army as less a vocation than a lark, and Papa, it seems, was not impressed by his heir's feckless exuberance. From the outset of his military career there had been ominous signs: 'I am appalled by my own incompetence.... So far 2 of us have been taken off to hospital'.[24] Six months later, touring about during leaves on his dilapidated Vespa, he seemed even less likely to make an officer. Bron was a sharp, affectionate, unathletic youth with tremendous undirected energy. He missed his 'united clever family' and he strove to be a credit to his parents. But a reckless antipathy to institutional life and an insouciant absent-mindedness were part of the boy's charm. Unluckily for Bron, he resembled the young Evelyn too closely at a time when Evelyn was developing strong similarities to his own father. Endurance tests were Bron's weakness. 'Needless to say,' he wrote, 'my resistability grading was not high.'[25]

Waugh was doubtless worried that, after the string-pulling to secure the commission, Bron would disgrace himself. Where his father was meticulous and industrious, Bron seemed inept and idle.

> The crews tinker ... with their vehicles until 12 O'clock [he wrote from Cyprus], and ... that is the end of my working day, unless we are being sent out on a patrol, road block or ambush. These occur about three times a week. We do not catch anyone. The last is the most boring as we sit all night in an olive grove from 7 p.m. to 4.30 a.m. and see no one and drink something disgusting called self-heating soup.... The day is spent sleeping, playing bridge roulette pontoon murder backgammon dumb crambo.
>
> We have to carry guns everywhere. I cannot hit a human-size target at 10 yards once in 20 shots with my absurd pistol which I am constantly in fear of losing.[26]

It might have been young Evelyn writing to his mother from Arnold House. Bombs exploded periodically, ambushes were threatened but, by and large, it was a comfortable existence. Laura was anxious; Waugh, happy for Bron to do his growing-up elsewhere, wrote the middle section of his

22. An exaggeration.
23. 21 May 1958; *Letters*, pp. 506–7.
24. ALS from Auberon Waugh, nd [September 1957?], np [Caterham?]; BL; *WTD*, p. 93.
25. ALS to Laura, Evelyn, Harriet and Margaret Waugh, 9 March 1958, from Aldershot; BL; *WTD*, p. 95.
26. ALS to Laura and Evelyn Waugh, nd [May 1958?], from Royal Horse Guards, BFPO 53 [Cyprus]; BL; *WTD*, p. 101.

book and forgot about him. A scholarship fund set up as a memorial to Knox at Trinity had received only £80 in contributions and none from the aristocracy on whom Waugh had counted so heavily. Letters to the press advertising the fund had been ignored. Waugh was irritated by the need to agitate for this cause when he wanted to concentrate on writing. Numerous embarrassing letters had to be written asking friends to cough up. And there was something else on his mind. An earlier note from Bron had ended: '... is the knighthood in the bag?'[27]

As the biography dragged on, Waugh became increasingly depressed, not only by his financial prospects but by the (in his view) irresponsible attitude of Knox's friends and relatives towards his reputation. Waugh felt unfairly burdened, just as he had when Knox was dying. And behind this complex resentment lay both his social ambition and the nightmare of time running out. He was tormented by the fear that galloping senility would claim him before national honour – and it was the latter he now craved more earnestly than riches.

> ... I decided [he wrote to McDougall] ... that I had only a year or two ahead in which I was capable of original work and I shouldn't waste that time in hack-work. Soon I shall have to jump at every chance of writing the history of insurance companies.... But ... while I have any vestige of imagination left, I must write novels.[28]

McDougall was suffering from *accidia*. So was Waugh. 'I think God sends these times', he added, 'to remind us that there is no rest except in Him. He takes away all zest in human affairs to give us the chance of seeing our immortal destiny.'[29]

Bron's zest for life thus seemed to his father both attractive and infantile, theologically immature – and so much so that he was strangely unmoved when that summer a Ministry of Defence telephone call shattered the silence of Combe Florey and he learned that Bron was confronting his immortal destiny. On 9 June he had been so seriously wounded that he was not expected to live.

Laura made immediate arrangements to fly out the next day, courtesy of the Red Cross. Waugh, more fretful than anxious, remained behind and continued writing. He disliked the back seat in any crisis, but, like Knox, could not bear the disruption of well-laid plans. Laura would have to deal with this. A certain resentment, perhaps, coloured his reaction: that his incompetent son should have chosen *this* moment; that Laura should have

27. Unpublished ALS, 27 April 1958, from Royal Horse Guards etc.; BL.
28. 18 April 1958; *Letters*, p. 507.
29. *Ibid.*, pp. 507–8. McDougall replied: 'You may be right (*you* know you are right) about my depression. But infidels can't hope for the rest you enjoy' (unpublished ALS, 22 April 1958, from Chapman & Hall; HRC).

to burden her husband with the supervision of the farm, household and children – not that he did much beyond passing on her instructions to the menials. Neither did he advertise Bron's misadventure. Friends heard about it late and, writing to offer sympathy, would receive curt notes of thanks as though they had mentioned the onset of congenital syphilis. Waugh was, it seems, not simply impatient but embarrassed.

Much to his annoyance, the newspapers discovered the story and ceaselessly publicized his address. The *Express* announced:

> Eighteen-year-old Auberon Waugh ... is dangerously ill ... following a shooting incident. He underwent an emergency operation. Red-headed Waugh ... was seriously wounded while patrolling Turkish villages. He was standing in front of a Ferret scout car when ... a Browning gun in the turret accidentally started firing. There was a stream of bullets. It is not clear whether anyone was in the turret at the time.[30]

Another report confused issues by suggesting that he had been inadvertently shot by one of his men.[31] The official press-releases offered only dignified reticence – Bron had been 'accidentally wounded' or 'struck by fire' – thus sidestepping the question of responsibility.

Laura's journey out was exhausting, but she left in the knowledge that the rest of her family were closing ranks in support. Her mother and brother (Auberon) met her at Paddington with Lieutenant Furlong who was to act as escort. After breakfast at Hendon, Furlong and Laura set off for London Airport and the VIP lounge, where she encountered and slipped past reporters, refusing an interview. Flash bulbs popped from every angle as she hurried through. Rome, Athens, Nicosia. She arrived late at Government House (where Sir Hugh and Lady Foot had offered accommodation). Finding a large dinner party in progress and no sign of her hosts, Laura drove straight to the hospital.

Bron was in an alarming condition, plugged with tubes, plastered and splinted, semi-delirious and in great pain. He was on the critical list for over a fortnight, conscious all the time and wanting to talk although breathing was agony. That first night Laura was allowed only ten minutes and returned exhausted to write home.

She was a brave, resourceful woman and, like her husband, immune to panic. A joke and a strained smile were more her style. Her letters record the precise details Waugh had trained her to include, playing up to his authority, implicitly apologetic for her absence and the additional expense. But, again, they are easy to misinterpret. These are not the writings of a

30. *DE*, 10 June 1958, 1.
31. 'Mrs Waugh Flies to Bedside of Wounded Son', *DM*, 11 June 1958, 1.

downtrodden wife but of an equal partner acutely conscious of Waugh's hair-trigger melancholia. He had been put out by his temporary eclipse as the sun around which their household revolved. She knew how to set that right: 'Please write & tell me how a lady behaves in Government House when she is exceedingly shabby & fat & has no clothes & also what sort of tips to give.'[32] Bron's accident had occurred just days before the announcement of a new Cyprus policy and a full-scale emergency was in prospect, certainly an increase in terrorist activity. Laura, not in the least frightened, seems rather to have been exhilarated by the 'flap', unable to resist a joke at Bron's expense: 'Everyone seems very jittery. The whole inner part of the town is curfewed & all cars go at 60 all the time skidding to a stop at road blockades.... There is an armoured car parked in the park of Government Ho... I will try and not stand in front of it.'[33]

Before Bron was moved to the officers' ward, Laura would wait constantly by his bed, swabbing his face, offering cold drinks and bullying the nurses; while they dressed his wounds, she would squat on the concrete outside in temperatures of over 100. Gradually, the truth about the accident emerged. At first the authorities had protected her from it. No one was to blame, they had said: it must have been the heat. Nothing like it had ever happened before. Only the last statement was true, as Bron was the first to admit: 'He says the accident was his fault & a court-martial offence if he had not been so seriously wounded.'[34] Bron, noticing something was wrong with the gun's elevation, had begun wiggling it with the barrel pointing at his chest, having absent-mindedly cocked the mechanism.

Unlike his father, Bron was always willing to see a joke at his own expense even when laughter was so painful. Throughout this ordeal his behaviour was exemplary. Laura for the first time saw her son as a pious and courageous man: 'They all praise him to the skies. When the surgeon told him they had removed his spleen ... he just said "Perhaps that will make me better tempered."'[35] The night before she wrote this he had nearly died.

At first her letters to Waugh continued in comic-apologetic vein, gossipy daily bulletins:

> They intend to remove his tubes this afternoon which they say will probably set him back a bit. Bron says I am to send an exact list of his wounds & if possible a diagram for Margaret's information as he is sure she will be keenly interested. Item 1) what has been removed 1

32. ALS from Laura Waugh, 11 June [1958], from Government House, Cyprus; BL; WTD, p. 106.
33. *Ibid.*
34. Unpublished ALS from Laura Waugh, dated 10 June but probably 12 June [1958], from Government House etc.; BL.
35. *Ibid.*

lung 1 spleen 2 ribs. Item 2) 6 bullet wounds (no bullets were removed because they all went straight through him) 4 in the chest, 1 through the shoulder & 1 through the muscular part between the thumb and 1st finger fracturing the bone leading up to the 1st finger. Here is a diagram: [rough drawing] He also had one rib that they have wired together.

He received the last sacraments before they moved him & he and the blues [*sic*] doctor recited the de Profundis as he was driven to hospital.[36]

The sub-text of this appears to have been: 'Don't be angry. Be proud.' But she soon found difficulty in containing her own irritation. She surely wanted Waugh to join her while Bron's life hung in the balance. Certainly the military authorities were at first expecting Mr Waugh rather than his wife.[37] He would not (would he?) allow his son to die on foreign soil without at least bidding him farewell? Apparently so. 'I shall go out', he told Diana Cooper, 'to travel home with Laura if he dies.'[38] Waugh made no move to fly to Cyprus during that critical fortnight and, while he wrote regularly to Laura, did not afford Bron the same privilege. Laura, as a result, became gradually emphatic as her exhaustion increased.

Bron, she explained, longed for letters. He was hot and drugged and in agony. Every other day he had to have his lung drained, 'a painful & beastly operation'.[39] All he thought about was Combe Florey and the family. Shortly before Bron was due to be removed from the danger list, abscesses began to form under the wounds in his back: 'Do please write & get other people to write it doesn't matter what . . . anything. . . . So far hes only received 2 letters 1 from you & 1 from Margaret. And as the days go by it is such a disappointment to him. . . .'[40] Waugh did as requested, asked others (Alec, Lady Acton) to pray and write, employed the Poor Clares again and corrected Laura's style. 'I am sorry you find my letters non compos,' she replied, exasperated. 'It is the great heat yesterday the temperature was 108.'[41]

At the beginning of July, Bron was posted out of danger. A week later he was flown home and hospitalized in London. Three months' painful convalescence lay ahead of him before another major operation. His father did not visit for three weeks because of a planned jaunt to Munich: a money-for-jam reading from his works, all expenses paid for him and

36. Unpublished ALS from Laura Waugh, nd [pm 15 June 1958], from Government House etc.; BL.
37. Cf. 'Evelyn Waugh May Fly to Son', *DT*, 11 June 1958, 9.
38. ALS to Lady Diana Cooper, 13 June [1958], from Combe Florey House; BL; *MWMS*, p. 255.
39. ALS from Laura Waugh, 25 June 1958, from Government House etc.; BL; *WTD*, p. 108.
40. Unpublished ALS from Laura Waugh, 21 June 1958, from Government House etc.; BL.
41. *Ibid.*

Laura, who, under the circumstances, relinquished her treat. When he wrote to welcome Bron home he explained the rota of visitors: Teresa, Laura and, finally, Papa. Sykes also looked in but it was the much-maligned Alec, and Harold Acton, who arrived regularly with presents and encouragement.

Waugh had Bron moved to Sister Agnes's Home near Broadcasting House and continued business as usual. It was a dismal period. Olivia Plunket Greene was also in terrible pain, dying heroically of breast cancer. Lady Curzon died. A few months earlier, Lord Redesdale (Nancy Mitford's father) had died. To Gwen, Alfred and Nancy, Waugh sent affectionate condolences. Where Bron was concerned, however, he was incapable of open emotion. 'The Herberts have been a great bore during Bron's lying in,' he wrote to Ann Fleming. 'Luckily they have been distracted first by Ivo de Vesci's death, then by the engagement of Anne [*sic*] Grant to an elderly penniless bachelor of good family.'[42] Waugh had bigger fish to fry and, he felt, little time to do it. *Campion*, he was enraged to discover, was to be remaindered and elaborate arrangements were made to prevent this and to produce a new edition. More important, as he told Lady Acton, 'I have come to you in the book. Now what would you like, to censure [*sic*] what I wrote or not?'[43]

She replied:

> It would be much easier for you to write this part if I were dead, wouldn't it? Let's pretend I am, but then it might work both ways and you must write charitably but firmly about my beastliness. I think the fact that Ronnie was even older when I first met him than I am now, as well as being full of grace, meant that he could behave with effortless chastity, whereas I found it more of a strain. . . .[44]

Waugh was decorous. He gave no hint of the information in this letter. Macmillan appeared disguised as 'C'. The only prospect to enliven a dull autumn was the unexpected offer by the Union Castle Line of a free cruise and £2,000 expenses in return for a travel book advertising the company. The manuscript of *Knox* was complete by December and typed by Christmas. 'Off to East Africa soon,' he wrote to Lord Kinross. 'God knows why.'[45]

*

42. 28 August 1958, from Combe Florey House; *Letters*, p. 513. Viscount de Vesci (1881–1958); Evelyn Ann Grant (d. 1984), the daughter of Bridget and niece of Laura, married [Sir] Ian Fraser who became Chairman of Rolls-Royce in 1971, and was Chairman of Lazard Brothers 1980–5.
43. 21 August 1958; *Letters*, p. 512.
44. Unpublished ALS from Lady Acton, 25 August 1958, from M'Bebi, Mazoe, S. Rhodesia; BL.
45. 31 December 1958; *Letters*, p. 516.

On 24 January, four days after resigning his commission, Bron was admitted to the Westminster Hospital for another operation and remained there for eight weeks. Waugh did not wait to follow his son's recovery. On the 28th, he entrained for Genoa, stiff of limb and in deepest winter melancholy. He had, as he wrote later, 'worked for eighteen months on the biography of a remarkable but rather low-spirited friend many years older than myself. I ... [had] read nothing and met no one except to further my work. Old letters, old dons, old clergymen ... a lowering diet when prolonged.'[46] He had no wish to add hospitals to the list. Bron would have to shift for himself.

This time Waugh set out for Rhodesia '... without preoccupations [and] with eyes reopened to the exotic.'[47] As the subsequent travelogue testifies, however, he was now just a tourist and, seeing Africa through the smoked glasses of his universal scepticism, the exotic seemed perpetually elusive. In Genoa he spent two days with Diana Cooper, who guided him to candlelit cellars and away from the marble halls in which he wished to dine. The highlight was a cemetery: the Campo Santo. It was, he proclaimed, 'a museum of mid-nineteenth century bourgeois art in the full, true sense',[48] and with death again comfortably at his elbow, he began slowly to revive.[49]

On 31 January Waugh was aboard the *Rhodesia Castle* and steaming south. The voyage replicated that of 1930–1, when, as a young and embittered man, he had travelled to Abyssinia and East Africa. He also crossed the sea-lanes of his ill-fated honeymoon cruise of 1929 and the sense of retracing steps was not lost on him. Port Said, Aden, Mombasa, Dar es Salaam, Zanzibar – at each stage the exotic flashed up before him only as memory. It was a dull, restful trip. The notes he kept for his book were later destroyed.

Appalled by his fellow travellers' 'outbreak of shorts',[50] Waugh took refuge for the best part of each day in the ship's library. There he consumed two books a day and wrote regularly to Laura. Within a week he was missing her so badly that he pleaded with her to reconsider an earlier refusal and fly out to South Africa for the return voyage. 'I hope Meg's measals [*sic*] and Bron's wounds are better,' he wrote gaily from Aden. 'I will write to them in a day or two.... Do think of the Cape Town trip.... A fortnight at sea. Sixteen days away for you.'[51] Laura, suffering from influenza, refused again. Someone had to pay the bills, tend the land and visit Bron in London.

46. *A Tourist in Africa* (Chapman & Hall, 1960), p. 13.
47. *Ibid.*
48. *Ibid.*, p. 21.
49. Cf. *ibid.*, p. 31: 'Clocks go on one hour. Sir Harold Nicolson has said that he resents this shortening of his life. I find it exhilarating; the gift of a whole precious hour totally free of delinquency and boredom. Odd that traditionally the voyage west, where days and nights get longer and longer, should symbolize the expedition to the Fortunate Isles.'
50. *Ibid.*, p. 34.
51. Unpublished ALS to Laura Waugh, 4 February [1959], from Aden; BL.

She wanted to be at home when he was discharged. The Woodruffs had been invited for Easter.

To outsiders, the cool egotism of Waugh's expenditure, when Laura had to apologize for buying a dress, often seemed outrageous. A neighbour, meeting Waugh in a first-class compartment of the London train once, had asked why Laura was not with him. 'Oh,' he replied, 'she is travelling third class.'[52] But such anecdotes, out of context, too easily miss the playfulness which coloured this marriage. (If Laura *was* travelling third class, she probably had some good reason of her own for doing so. More than likely, she was not on the train at all.) 'I am sorry you are broke,' he wrote towards the end of his African holiday. 'Peters has no money nor have I except ... expense[s] ..., so you must hang on for a week or two.'[53] Was her patience not strained to the point of indignation? Not at all. The letters he received in Africa express only misery at his absence. 'Thank you very much for your ... lovely postcard of the weeping woman ...', Margaret wrote, '– the mice soon get tired of playing and long for the cat.'[54] If Laura had much to endure from her husband, she endured it gladly. Writing to Lady Acton about Knox, Waugh once remarked: 'You gave him just the tenderness and hero-worship which he had from the 1912 undergraduates; which he needed and didn't find anywhere else.'[55] Laura offered much the same to Waugh.

As usual, Waugh's airletters acted as a composite journal and Laura was expected to file them. But he could find nothing interesting to say and, with charming insouciance, she tore off the stamps for the children, thus removing portions of text. He did not tell her that in Aden, like a latter-day Prufrock, he had searched for mermaids[56] or that he was similarly paralysed, incapable of the easy judgments of his youth, caught between the seductive authority of high culture and the exotic confusions of the bazaar.

When he came to write up his experiences, the sheer complexity of African politics defeated him. In 1931 he had offered confidently eccentric opinions on whatever crossed his path. In 1959 Africa was no longer a white

52. Interview with Hon. Mrs Gaenor Heathcoat Amory, 26 December 1976. Mrs Amory was not the neighbour.
53. Unpublished ALS, 20 March [1959], np [Bulawayo]; BL.
54. Unpublished ALS from Margaret Waugh, 19 February [1959], np [Combe Florey House]; BL.
55. 2 October [1957]; *Letters*, p. 497.
56. Two hotels he remembered had each exhibited a 'mermaid' on a previous visit. 'I had a personal interest in the mermaids, because six years ago I suffered briefly from hallucinations in the course of which I imagined myself to be in communication with a girl in Aden. She complained of having nothing to do there. I went into some detail (which I omitted from the account ... of the experience) about the rather limited diversions of the settlement. Among them I mentioned the mermaid. "It's gone, Evelyn, it's gone," she said later, in tones of reproach as though I had maliciously sought to raise false hopes of pleasure, "it isn't here any more." I was curious to discover whether in this particular as in all others my "voices" had been deceiving me. But here she spoke the plain truth' (*Tourist*, p. 37).

man's joke. Colonialism and apartheid could not be dismissed as the bugbears of lunatic liberals. He found himself in sympathy with the tribesmen and fascinated by their cults, crafts and kinships. 'The consciences of the English are unnaturally agitated by Africa,' he concluded rather hopelessly. 'The questions that greet the returned tourist are not: "Did you have a good time?" but: "What about apartheid? What about Hola? What about the imprisonment of politicians?" I can only reply: "Don't know."'[57]

He had come to loathe racism. Cecil Rhodes is seen as a pompous financier with a crazy totalitarian dream, Chief Lobengula as the victim of duplicity. 'He was personally brave, majestic, intelligent and honourable.... The white men he met were mostly scoundrels.... Contemporary accounts of Lobengula's last decade make shameful reading.'[58] Africa held up a cracked mirror to Waugh's mythology of Victorian England. The *Pax Victoriana*, he admits, was a nonsense. But he could not, had not the energy to, face these contradictions. 'Cruelty and injustice', he concluded, 'are endemic everywhere'[59] – and he left the matter there, where he always left it, with Original Sin.

He returned in early April, eager for his knighthood. Six months earlier Stopp's *Portrait* had appeared to generally appreciative reviews, consolidating Waugh's reputation. *Knox* was in the press and the Prime Minister had publicly acknowledged his support by signing a letter to *The Times* launching the Trinity scholarship.[60] Katharine Asquith thought the biography a work of genius. Waugh, at last, seemed to be in the right place at the right time, pleasing the right sort of people. He was the moving force behind Knox's 'canonization'. A week after his return, Waugh was in Oxford delivering a sonorous panegyric at the unveiling of the Arthur Pollen bust.[61]

Waugh's expectations were great. It is not difficult to imagine his anticipation when, three weeks later, just as the proofs of *Knox* were ready, a letter arrived from Downing Street:

> Sir,
>
> I am asked by the Prime Minister to inform you that he has it in mind, on the occasion of the forthcoming list of Birthday Honours,

57. *Ibid.*, pp. 164–5.
58. *Ibid.*, p. 150.
59. *Ibid.*, p. 167.
60. Cf. *Letters*, p. 509.
61. Cf. *DT*, 20 April 1959. The bust of Knox was bought from the fund, the remainder of which (£1,370) was to endow a Trinity College travel prize in biblical or classical studies. Cf. also 'In Memory of a Non-Traveller', *Observer*, 19 April 1959, 17, and 'Oxford Tribute to Mgr. Knox ...', *The Times*, 20 April 1959, 12. The text of Waugh's speech was printed as 'Ronald Knox: The Quintessence of Oxford', *Tablet*, 2 May 1959, 419.

to submit your name to the Queen with a recommendation that Her Majesty may be graciously pleased to approve that you be appointed a Commander of the Order of the British Empire. . . .'[62]

In a fury, Waugh screwed this up. Later, he flattened and filed it as testimony to another betrayal. The honour was high but, in his eyes, worthless. In writing to refuse it, he knew that he would permanently exclude himself from favour with the governing classes. It was the death blow to a lifetime's social climbing.

*

All that summer he was irritable. Tom Burns and Woodruff had given extensive help with *Knox*. Waugh picked fights with both and was an autocratic literary executor. Burns he saw as traitorous for attempting to remainder *Campion*. Woodruff, on reading *Knox* in proof, indicated errors of fact and was concerned about the acerbic attitude towards the Hierarchy. He was also worried that readers would identify 'C'. Waugh dismissed all criticism and tried to shut Burns out of the publication of Knox's sermons. In all these dealings, Fr Caraman acted as courtier, confidant and Waugh's ear to the wall of Mount Street. But even this most loyal servant had to defend Burns in this quarrel. Waugh grumbled, succumbed and, while waiting for the conclusion of a printers' strike, killed time by revising *Brideshead*.[63]

Nervous about the reception of *Knox*, angered by delays, and making lugubrious stabs at his African book, Waugh was in no mood to deal with a house full of children. Bron occupied a sofa or strolled stiffly about the grounds, impatient for Oxford where he now proposed to read PPE.[64] He planned to recuperate in Italy before going up. Teresa, about to sit her Final Schools in history, had become obsessed by Turkey[65] and by a young Rhodes Scholar. Papa approved of neither interest, and particularly the

62. Unpublished TLS from I. J. Bligh, 7 May 1959, from 10 Downing Street, Whitehall; BL.
63. McDougall had informed Waugh that *Brideshead* was out of print. A re-set edition was suggested and Waugh took the opportunity for substantial pruning. He worked quickly, splitting the spine from a hardback copy and scoring out extensive passages. Very little was added, the most significant rewriting concerning the love-making scene between Charles and Julia on the liner. Waugh's revision copy is in the HRC. For a more detailed account of the revisions see R. M. Davis, *Evelyn Waugh, Writer*, *op. cit.*, pp. 167–85. Also 'Yet Another Visit to Brideshead', *TLS*, 16 September 1960, 594, and John Coleman, *Spectator*, 29 July 1960, 187; *CH*, pp. 276–8.
64. Cf. unpublished ALS to A. L. P. Norrington, 22 April 1959, from Combe Florey House; BL.
65. Cf. *DM*, 12 February 1959, 12: 'Theresa [*sic*] Waugh, 20-year old daughter of . . . Evelyn Waugh, is "going Turkish". "It is a fascinating country. . . . When I leave Somerville College in July I'm off there to teach English. I haven't told mother yet but I don't suppose she'll mind. I'm writing. She is living in the country and father is on his way to Africa." . . . Theresa . . . is known in Oxford for her addiction to the sack dress and her interest . . . in all things Turkish. "It started last year when I went there with a party. . . . My present intention is to start work in Istanbul and work east to Persia."'

latter. After attempting to bribe her tutor with a signed copy of *Decline and Fall*, Waugh began discreet enquiries about her boyfriend.

Waugh had first encountered John D'Arms in early April, when Teresa had brought him to Combe Florey. Clearly it had not been a meeting of true minds. D'Arms was an amiable and brilliant classical scholar. He had, however, three serious defects in Waugh's eyes: he was American, Protestant and dull. The prospect of a Yank in the family appalled him. Even so, Teresa refused to be deflected and in mid-June the young man (under her instruction?) wrote an embarrassing letter to Waugh explaining that he had not seen enough of Teresa to allow the relationship to develop as he wished. Buried beneath his periphrasis was a simple and, to Waugh, simply outrageous request: D'Arms wished to take Teresa on a three-week, unchaperoned holiday to Greece.

Permission was granted (she was twenty-one) but D'Arms, he felt, would soon get his come-uppance from Teresa. Then an exuberant letter had arrived from Athens: everything between John and her was working out splendidly and, in order to see more of her, D'Arms would delay his return to America. She wanted him to spend as much of that time as possible at Combe Florey, and to invite the sort of people she wanted him to know. Could Waugh bear this?[66] An empurpled Papa lost no time in contacting Anne Fremantle and asking her to dig the dirt.[67]

Mrs Fremantle's investigations, however, only bore testimony to young John's fathomless respectability. Waugh was mildly desperate:

> I beg you not to disclose the reason for your curiosity. There is no engagement between my daughter and D'Armes [*sic*] and I hope she will lose interest in him. He is a quiet, civil, sombrely dressed young man with properly parted hair, but earnest enough to drive a daughter of mine distracted.... His father lives in Princeton & travels daily to New York. D'Armes travels third class.

'I am at work,' he concluded, 'half heartedly writing a travel book of ineffable tedium and triviality to pay for last winter abroad.'[68] The subterfuge came to nothing. Teresa, like her father, had a will of iron and that autumn she returned with D'Arms to America.

From his first meeting with this young man Waugh sensed the impending collapse of his clan. April 1959 was the last time all eight were united at Combe Florey untramelled by external loyalties. Waugh wished to preserve the moment. Shortly after D'Arms's departure, and before the calamitous Downing Street news, John Montgomery telephoned Mark Gerson to say

66. Cf. unpublished ALS from Teresa Waugh, 4 July 1959, from Hotel E E, Athens; BL.
67. Cf. 14 July 1959; *Letters*, p. 524.
68. Unpublished ALS to Anne Fremantle, 31 July 1959, from Combe Florey House; BL.

that Evelyn Waugh wished to have his household photographed. No payment was offered but, as a *quid pro quo*, Gerson could keep the copyright – a profitable deal, as it turned out. These pictures became the best-known images of the novelist and his home.

Gerson and his wife were invited for the week-end – not to stay but for two days' work – and, setting off for Somerset in their dilapidated Vauxhall Cresta, broke down on the other side of Salisbury Plain. They telephoned. The reply was cool. The family, Waugh explained, were waiting for their luncheon. An hour late, the Gersons were ushered into the dining room to be greeted by six pairs of hostile eyes. The entire brood was sitting, pointedly, at table. Waugh appeared amused to see the couple at all and embarrassed them further by insisting on pre-lunch drinks. During his sharp cross-questioning about the erratic lives of photographers, the rest of the family remained silent. Only Laura attempted to rescue her visitors with courtesy. The children took their cue from Papa. They were trained not to interrupt until he had done with his prey; their expressions were glazed, indifferent. And Gerson, eager to conclude this awful meal and begin work, soon discovered a further hiatus. After luncheon, Waugh disappeared. He remained untraceable for the rest of the day.

Laura showed her guests round the house while Gerson took interior shots: of the library, of her bedroom with its four-poster, of the Betjeman Benefaction, of a gasolier salvaged from the demolished Holborn Restaurant and re-hung over the staircase. Ironically, in his absence, Waugh was inadvertently offering Herb Mayes some late recompense. The photographs appeared over four pages in *Good Housekeeping*.[69]

Gerson had booked into the local pub and next morning was at Combe Florey early. There was still no sign of Waugh. Eventually, after luncheon, he put in an appearance, prohibiting colour film because it made him look florid. Gerson blithely loaded cameras with Ektachrome while Waugh nagged Bron to change into uniform. He soon changed back, tension sparking between father and son. But, despite these difficult circumstances, Gerson produced a brilliant series of pictures: Waugh fiercely amused in dog-tooth check; Laura grim in rough tweed; Teresa flamboyant in a print skirt; Meg self-possessed; Hatty awkward and off to one side; Bron affable, sometimes smirking; James looking pained in a rigid flannel suit; Septimus bemused. Waugh is the fulcrum of these groups, Laura their matrix. Delighted by the result, he ordered dozens of copies and was in high spirits ('The coloured transparencies please the simple peasant taste of my Italian servants')[70] – but not for long. The photographs documented the beginning of the end of his life as paterfamilias. A week later he was screwing up the

69. Also later in the *Tatler*.
70. Unpublished ALS to Mark Gerson, 29 April 1959, from Combe Florey House; private collection.

Downing Street letter. Six months hence, Teresa was in America, Meg had removed to Oxford for private coaching, Bron was up at Christ Church and Hatty had returned to Ascot. Divorced from honour, divorced from the company of his sweet Meg, with a dull book to write and money running out, Waugh's resilience began to falter. When Gerson visited him four years later he found a softer man, with a melancholic glare and a cracked smile.

Since Teresa's ball, Waugh had swayed ever closer to financial collapse and had only avoided it with the help of the Trust and his publisher's generosity. When Teresa came down from Oxford, Waugh wrote to McDougall thanking him 'for paying for her education ... her subsidy helped me keep my head above water during the last three years.'[71] In August she requested £500 to go to Boston. Waugh had educated his children to regard cost-counting as vulgar and, after his experiences with Arthur, loathed the paternal whimpering of old men down on their luck. Teresa, nevertheless, represented an exorbitant outgoing for small return. They were not close. Waugh gave her the money from the Fund and sent her to London to pick it up. Peters, he insisted, should explain the terms of the Trust clearly to her: that it was not an inheritance but money her father had earned.[72] In short, it was his money, not hers, a distinction which she apparently found difficult to comprehend. Bron, meanwhile, was relaxing in Bologna at Papa's expense and writing a novel.

> Thank you for your ... nice settlements [he wrote] ... I am very much relieved to see that I am entitled to wear a scholar's gown; it would have been very infra dig for a Waugh to have appeared as a Commoner after all this time. ... If I send an urgent telegram, could you send two five-pound notes in separate envelopes? My criminal acquaintances tell me that you should wrap the notes in carbon-paper to elude a device employed by the Excise men. ...[73]

Bron had finished half his book and was triumphantly light-hearted. Not so Papa. On the same day Peters had written: 'Yes, you have no more Little, Brown money: in fact you have [*sic*] $10,000 overdrawn.'[74] The American cash reservoir on which Waugh had depended for regular income for fourteen years was exhausted.

Waugh, less reckless than he liked to pretend, had held back Chapman & Hall's advance on *Knox* for just such an emergency. He would, he told

71. Unpublished ALS to John McDougall, 17 June 1959, from Combe Florey House; private collection. In return, it seems she was to discover new authors for Chapman & Hall, an unsuccessful enterprise.
72. Cf. unpublished APCI to A. D. Peters, 12 August 1959, from Combe Florey House; *Catalogue* E1112, p. 246.
73. ALS from Auberon Waugh, 11 August 1959, np [Bologna]; BL.; *WTD*, p. 117.
74. Unpublished ALS from A. D. Peters, 11 August 1959, from 10 Buckingham Street, Adelphi; HRC.

Peters, have to retrench, dip into the Beaverbrook damages and keep a sharp eye out for journalistic work. There was no panic but the crisis had occurred at an unfortunate moment. The final volume of the trilogy was germinating and there was another project even dearer to his heart. 'I should awfully like to write a full biography of [Holman] Hunt . . .', he told McDougall.[75] That idea was soon abandoned. Waugh accepted that, as soon as *A Tourist in Africa* was complete, he had, instead, to promise the Americans a novel.

*

By the time *Knox* appeared in early October it had already been serialized in the *Tablet* and letters were reaching Waugh suggesting further trouble. Fr Martindale, Arnold Lunn suggested, was 'outstandingly the most brilliant classical scholar of his [Oxford] generation', not Knox. Martindale had once remarked to Sir Arnold that Knox '"hates the poor. He thinks they smell". . . . I shall be amused to hear how the Hierarchy react to your very anti-mitre bias.'[76] Shortly afterwards, Mgr Barton, the senior censor, confirmed the Hierarchy's displeasure. Waugh had broken an 'unwritten law that the bishops are not criticized . . . in any public way'[77] and Barton feared that the book might be censured. As Waugh's friend, he was embarrassed by the prospect of having to perform the task himself. Waugh felt a sudden jolt of horror; not remorse for offending the mitred but rage that his exhausting campaign to establish Knox as a latter-day Newman might founder. If the Hierarchy condemned *Knox*, it would damage both its subject's memory and its author's income.

Waugh was in rebarbative mood. The book's publication had coincided with the general election and he had taken the opportunity to lampoon the Prime Minister in a contribution to the *Spectator*'s symposium of election comments. Naturally, he said, he wanted to see the Conservatives returned. He had 'bitter memories of the Attlee–Cripps regime when the kingdom seemed to be under enemy occupation.' But he had never voted and never would. Great Britain was not a democracy because 'All authority emanates from the Crown.' If he voted and the Tories won he would feel 'morally

75. *Letters*, p. 525.
76. Unpublished TLS from [Sir] Arnold Lunn, 2 September [1959], from Ski Club of Great Britain, 118 Eaton Square, SW1; BL. Sir Arnold later repeated a similar anecdote concerning Waugh: 'Once when we crossed the Atlantic together, Waugh, who was of course travelling first class, accepted an invitation to dine with me. I was travelling second class and, as he entered the dining room, he sniffed and said, "Curious how one can smell the poor." This amused me but some of those to whom I told the story were not amused. And it was that kind of person whom Waugh delighted to shock by particularly outrageous performances in his favourite comic role, the supersnob' ('Evelyn Waugh Revisited', *National Review*, 27 February 1968, 189–90).
77. Unpublished TLS, from the Right Rev. Mgr John M. T. Barton D.D., 1 October 1959, from SS Peter & Edward's Presbytery, 43 Palace Yard, Westminster, SW1; BL.

inculpated in their follies – such as their choice of Regius professors; if they failed, I should have made submission to socialist oppression by admitting the validity of popular election. I do not aspire to advise my sovereign in her choice of servants.'[78] The dig at Regius professors was effectively a subtle revenge on the man who *did* aspire to advise his sovereign and who had neglected to include Waugh among her knights. Macmillan had appointed Trevor-Roper in 1957. 'Sweet Pig,' Waugh wrote to Margaret, 'I enclose my election address. I think it is funny to hold up Trevor-Roper as Macmillan's great folly instead of Suez or Cyprus. . . .'[79]

The joke, however, soon turned sour when the enterprising Muggeridge, during a casual telephone conversation, asked Mary Herbert to confirm the identity of 'C'. Flustered, she told the truth and Muggeridge printed it in the *New Statesman*. She was mortified. Waugh was enraged. His decorous concealment suddenly appeared absurd and his own family was responsible for breaking the promised silence. Macmillan seems not to have been perturbed. By this time he had been re-elected with an increased majority and his position was unassailable. For Waugh, the incident represented further humiliation. 'I have been haunted throughout [the writing]', he had told Knox's brother, 'by the fear that older friends and, particularly, his family might think I had been impertinent.'[80] That spectre now rose again.

Waugh watched the reviews anxiously. At first they were surprisingly favourable for so overtly apologetic a work. The *TLS* regarded it as 'an extremely good biography'[81] and this was the opinion of the majority. Characteristically, Greene relished the lurid portraiture of villainy showing 'Knox meeting the meanness, jealousies and misunderstandings of the hierarchy . . . it is Mr. Waugh's great achievement that he holds the interest even of the unsympathetic.'[82] Muriel Spark, Bowra and Betjeman all applauded,[83] and when the book appeared in America in January it met with equal favour. Among the critics of the 'rationalist press' only Angus Wilson found himself unable to praise the book 'that for all its competence and high intention, seems to me dull, at times even empty.'[84] Sir Angus had waited years for a chance to record his sincere admiration of Waugh's writings and to repay the master for his muscular defence of *Hemlock and After*. Now that the chance had at last presented itself, he could regard *Knox* as little more than a dismal act of piety.

78. 'Aspirations of a Mugwump', *Spectator*, 2 October 1959, 435; *EAR*, p. 537.
79. 2 October 1959; *Letters*, p. 527.
80. Unpublished ALS to [Wilfred?] Knox, 16 May 1959, from Combe Florey House; private collection.
81. *TLS*, 9 October 1959, 569–70; *CH*, pp. 396–8.
82. *Observer*, 11 October 1959, 23; *CH*, pp. 400–1.
83. Muriel Spark, *Twentieth Century*, January 1960, 601. Maurice Bowra, *London Magazine*, December 1960, 63–5; *CH*, pp. 402–4. John Betjeman, *NY*, 23 April 1960, 174–7.
84. *Encounter*, January 1960, 78–80; *CH*, pp. 405–8.

The religious readers were more fiercely divided. 'God bless you', a priest wrote, 'and give you more tolerance and charity and take the bitterness out of your heart. . . .'[85] It was the book's thinly disguised rancour which irritated, a certain dishonesty in its tone which had even troubled the *TLS*: 'the author's slightly synthetic grumpiness [used] as evidence of his subject's views.'[86] Somehow the voices of Knox and Waugh seemed inseparable and the book advertised the priest's worldliness at the expense of his holiness. Woodruff did his best in the *Tablet*, avoiding his reservations by concentrating on style and structure.[87] Mgr Barton praised it in the *Month* suggesting quiet disagreement about the description of Cardinal Bourne.[88] Mgr Gordon Wheeler, however, corrected Waugh's interpretation of certain facts, noted his failure to examine others, and objected strongly to Bourne's having been made the villain of the piece.[89] The reception from this side of the fence was stiff and guarded, notable more for its embarrassed reticence than for the welcome Waugh had expected. It hurt him deeply.

Katharine Asquith, irritated by Woodruff's judicious coolness, sent high praise, as did Lady Peck, Alec Guinness, Sykes, Powell and Lady Acton. The fact remained, however, that the book was plagued by errors, resulting from Waugh's desire to dramatize Knox's 'tragic' exclusion from high office. Woodruff had sent him a list of corrigenda too late for inclusion in the first edition. 'Misprints and mistakes emerge daily,' Waugh wrote sadly to him. 'Two or three learned clerics read my proofs. None spotted "Hic est calix mens."'[90] He had always relied on McDougall's scholarship to preserve him from blunders. For a while he tried to bluff it out, but as the letters poured in and the list of errors mounted, he was forced to acknowledge that a revised edition was necessary. '. . . I was very glad . . . to learn that you propose making certain corrections . . .,' Archbishop Worlock wrote.

> Alas, I think that I am but one of many who feel that inaccuracies and the general tone of certain sections of your book have given its readers a wrong impression of Monsignor Knox as a priest, of his bishops and of his fellow clergy. . . . I . . . can only wish that you had felt able to accept my offer to see all these letters before the first edition was written. . . .[91]

The letters were those between Knox and Cardinal Griffin. Waugh had

85. Unpublished ALS from Fr Geoffrey Crawfurd, 17 October 1959, from Holy Family Church, 226 Trelawney Avenue, Langley, Bucks.; BL.
86. *TLS*, *op. cit.*; *CH*, p. 398.
87. *Tablet*, 10 October 1959, 857–8; *CH*, pp. 398–9.
88. *Month*, December 1959, 365–7.
89. *DR*, Winter 1959–60, 346–52.
90. Unpublished ALS to Douglas Woodruff, 12 October [1959], from Combe Florey House; private collection.
91. Unpublished TLS, 30 October 1959, from Archbishop's House, Westminster, SW1; BL.

not bothered to visit Archbishop's House to examine the file, preferring his own colourful notion of Griffin's persistent meanness towards Knox while he was translating the Bible. The relationship was characterized by Waugh as one of reciprocal animosity. Worlock's letter ran to seven typescript pages of close quotation, demonstrating that Knox and Griffin were on the friendliest of terms. Far from being cheated of his royalties, Knox had voluntarily paid them over to the Church on the grounds that he 'had developed a strong scruple against cashing in, as a private person, on the word of God.'[92] The odd result of this was that, for all Waugh's efforts to 'canonize' his subject, Knox turned out to be rather more saintly than his biographer had allowed him to be.

Waugh backed down. The second impression later that year, contained a large corrigendum slip deleting suggestions of Griffin's parsimony and ingratitude. It was another defeat. Having failed to secure social honour, Waugh had now been put firmly in his place by the governing class of his Church. And while his fortunes sank, his eldest son's rose.

*

Bron had arrived at Christ Church as *Knox* was published and rode jauntily astride his father's fame. He had returned from Italy with his novel complete. Papa, however, had got wind of its subject – in part a satire of Downside – and had issued an ultimatum: Bron was still a minor; he should not attempt publication without parental permission or the lawyers would be set on him. 'Your best course . . . will be to have it typed and send it to Peters asking him to find you a publisher without disclosing your name. It will be more gratifying to have it accepted on its own merits than on my or my brother's notoriety.'[93] The letter, it seems, was partly a joke, partly friendly advice, but also a warning to keep off the grass. The last thing Waugh wanted was his son producing a scandalous novel to cloud the anticipated glory of *Knox*. For Bron, the benefits of being 'Evelyn Waugh's son' began quickly to pall.

He put his manuscript away and settled to outdoing his father's notoriety as an undergraduate. Waugh, at least, had spent two terms with his pipe and books before discovering Harold Acton. Bron set up in elegant rooms in Meadow Building, made friends with the 'wildest richest wickedest young blood of them all',[94] Robert Corbett,[95] and from the outset regarded the university as an hotel in which he intended to be rarely sober. 'Darling Mummy and Papa' received only occasional, jubilant letters:

92. *Ibid.*, p. 4.
93. 26 August 1959; *Letters*, pp. 525–6.
94. Unpublished ALS from Auberon Waugh, 26 October 1959, np [Christ Church, Oxford]; BL.
95. Son of Lord Rowallan, Chief Scout.

> Oxford is the most tremendous fun but it cannot possibly last, and either we will all get a lot nastier or we will all be sent down very soon I fear.... Have you bottled any more sherry? If so, can I come over and pick it up? ... I would very much like to bring a few people to show off the pictures to, and Papa, and the cows, and the works. They would need no preparations, would break nothing, drop no matches. Is the thought more than you can bear? ... Poor Meg is really going through a Caterham. It is a subdued, cathartic Meg who appears from time to time.... I keep getting ludicrous messages from Pensions telling me to report unclothed to Exeter Town Hall at 8 o'clock in the morning. Must be a joke, I think.[96]

Waugh, unhappy in the role of exhibit, suffered the invasion (during which he met Mark Amory for the first time) and rather enjoyed it. Bron's pursuit of the primrose path, nevertheless, filled his father with misgiving. His heart was rather with Meg.

Clever and depressed, Meg moved uneasily on the fringes of her brother's world, awe-struck and often intimidated. Hers was a more contemplative, religious nature and her articulate shyness, a disturbing combination of modesty and wit, later caused a string of men to fall in love with her. In 1959 she was seventeen but, for several years to come, Waugh's influence was so powerful that she wanted loyally to remain Papa's little girl. It was a painful business, as both she and Bron discovered, to break free from the Combe Florey theatre and to act out of role. Nevertheless, the mental resilience developed through Waugh's playful bullying had produced a mature young woman, who, over the next two years, developed into a formidable character. 'I ... am becoming frightened of little Margaret', Ann Fleming wrote, '– what should I call her? She has tremendous poise for a British virgin.'[97] There was something of the nun about her, oddly spiced with the characteristic Waugh gaiety and charm.

> Bron is v. famous in Oxford [she wrote home] ... he is one of the bloodiest bloodies. I am learning to like music – I am sure you would if you tried – I only like violins & flutes so far but apparently I will soon love it all. Longing to see you soon, don't forget to set the prayer machinery going.[98]

The last remark referred to her impending attempt at the University entrance examinations in November. The whole family found academic

96. ALS from Auberon Waugh, nd [c. 5 November 1959], from Christ Church, Oxford; BL; partly published in *WTD*, p. 132. Mr Waugh still draws a disability pension. A 'Caterham' was an ordeal, after his experience there training with the Blues.
97. 4 February [1961]; *LAF*, p. 278.
98. November [1959], from 'Mrs Hodgson's' [25 Staverton Road, Oxford]; BL.

study irksome. Unlike Bron, however, she did not despise it and dutifully plodded. It came as no surprise when Somerville rejected her, although any disappointment she felt had long since been overshadowed by other concerns.

Three days before her first examination, Bron had been in a car with his undergraduate friends heading for a party at Viscountess Kelburn's house near Southampton. They never got there. Approaching Andover, they had collided head-on with a lorry on a perfectly straight road. The police, officially mystified by the cause of the accident, did not pursue the matter. Some important people's children were involved.[99] Both vehicles were badly damaged. Bron and the driver were trapped in the front seat and had to be released by ambulancemen. Nine days later he was still in a Winchester hospital with a fractured skull.

As Christmas approached and Waugh ground his way to the end of his African book, the news seems not to have disturbed him.[100] He feared the worst for Bron and the worst was not death but survival. Shortly after the accident Waugh promised Peters an article: 'I See Nothing But Boredom ... Everywhere'.[101] The head injury, he remarked wryly in the covering letter, had produced no noticeable alteration in Bron's behaviour.[102]

*

Waugh's article formed part of a series offering predictions for the new decade. He faced the 1960s, he said, 'with gloomy apprehensions'. It was not that he was troubled by the threat of nuclear war:

> I can see nothing objectionable in the total destruction of the earth, provided it is done ... inadvertently ... the world is going to end one day. The only certain information ... is that the catastrophe will be fiery and unexpected: the only certain instructions, that we must live each day as though it were to be our last.

No, his lament was for general impoverishment. The 'universal affluence and increased comfort'[103] of the 1950s bore no relation to Waugh's image of the contemporary world. His income, he said, was worth less than half the £3,000 a year he earned in the mid-1930s. The elaborate stratifications of the British class system, essential to the national character, were dis-

99. Simon Lennox-Boyd, son of the former Colonial Secretary; Tom Stockdale, son of the Lord Mayor of London; Toby Clarke, son of Sir Humphrey Orme Clarke; also Hercules Belleville.
100. Cf. unpublished ALS from Lady Acton to Evelyn Waugh, 27 November 1959, np [M'bebi, S. Rhodesia?]; BL: 'Bron's accident was in the *Evening Standard*. I was rather worried, but you seem to make light of it. ...'
101. *DM*, 28 December 1959, 4; *EAR*, pp. 538–40.
102. Cf. unpublished ALS to A. D. Peters, 14 December 1959, from Combe Florey House; *Catalogue* E1132, p. 249.
103. 'I See Nothing But Boredom ...', *op. cit.*, p. 538.

appearing: 'There were different vocabularies and intonations of speech; different styles of dress. Now all those things that gave salt to English life and were the raw material of the Arts are being dissolved.'[104] In the Arts, 'painting and sculpture [have] come to a dead stop all over the world'.[105] If Great Britain did produce an artist of genius he would feel alienated and either leave, or remain as an outlaw. In about ten years another world war would probably begin.

Reading this, Waugh's friends doubtless chuckled: here was Evelyn back on form: pugnacious, disingenuous. In fact, he had long-since surrendered. The article is jokeless, sincere. 'It was ten years', Waugh told Sir Arnold Lunn, 'before I could make any show of praying.'[106] But since the war, contrition had grown slowly in his heart, in direct proportion to the decline in his reverence for the British ruling class. In 1945 he had seen the aristocracy as doomed. By 1959 it no longer existed for him, and the knights and ladies had faded into the mists of his mythical Old England. Had he been invited to join them it might have been different. But he hadn't and it wasn't – and in this mood, in January 1960, he began to plan his last novel.

By the time *A Tourist in Africa* appeared in September 1960, Waugh's life had stagnated while the lives of his three elder children had changed dramatically. 'In another ten years', he told Kenneth Allsop, 'I shall be in stark penury.... Paperbacks? They bring in nothing. The royalty is 1½d. a copy, and some damn fool writes you a letter about it and you have to spend 3d. replying.'[107] The list of contemporary best-sellers provided small encouragement. The 'Braine–Wain–Amis' school, he insisted,

> have never had the faults of youth, which should be pretentiousness, affectation, over-embellishment, the use of recondite words, all being fined down by discipline and developing taste to good prose.... Nothing attracts me towards London literary life ... it is a squalid cosmopolitan city, no longer English, full of foreigners, with all the decent buildings torn down. Even the so-called Chelsea Set do not resemble the Bright Young Things of my day.... My daughter brought one of them to the house. He stole some of my books.[108]

The record was becoming wearisome. Evelyn Waugh had become that most despised opponent, the club bore.

Thirteen years later, Allsop reflected on that interview. He had arrived

104. *Ibid.*, p. 539.
105. *Ibid.*, p. 540.
106. (Sir) Arnold Lunn, 'Evelyn Waugh Revisited', *National Review*, *op. cit.*, 190.
107. Kenneth Allsop, 'The Living Arts 1960 ... Waugh Looks Forward to Poverty', *DM*, 26 April 1960, 4.
108. *Ibid.*

to discover a scuffle on the doorstep and Waugh glowering over the balustrade above his 'No Admittance on Business' plaque. '"Are you Allsop?"' he bellowed. "This uninvited person claims to be an acquaintance of yours and a photographer."'[109] As Waugh grasped the poor man's collar, the cameras round his neck danced.

Apologies were grudgingly accepted. The shaken man took his pictures and shuffled off. Waugh and Allsop settled in the library with stilton and claret. After wine and a cigar Waugh perked up and conducted his guest round the estate, discoursing amiably on his poverty. By tea-time, the journalist, well-pleased with his 'copy' but exhausted by four hours of Waugh's undivided attention, was surprised by an invitation to dinner.

He had returned at 7.30. 'The atmosphere had changed. Waugh was glum and irascible. His wife came into the sitting room. We sipped sherry. The conversation was desultory, uneasy. The dining room was cold as was the food.'[110] A young son (presumably James) joined them and, rising on a tide of alcohol, Waugh warmed to his condemnation of Braine–Wain–Amis. He recalled building the Edifice at Piers Court and advertising for skulls. The trouble was, he said, he could not get suitable ones, like that of the Editor of the *New Statesman*. Laura left the table. James had long since cleared the plates and vanished. Waugh's brief ebullience sank into tetchiness and finally slumber. Over the brandy his head had slumped on to his crumpled shirt and his guest had risen uneasily in the cold candlelight, a little squiffy and uncertain how to proceed. He 'prodded the sleeping form, now looking frail and vulnerable, but he did not stir. Feeling treacherous, I trod softly across the hall and down the steps, and drove away through the night out of that melancholy and lonely – and somewhat macabre – life on the hilltop.'[111]

*

Allsop had caught Waugh at a bad moment, at the beginning of the new tax year and just after his Downside retreat. In four months he had written nothing of his novel, having accepted another money-for-jam job, this time with the *Mail*: £2,000 for a series of four light articles, with free travel for himself and a guest. Laura and he had visited Rome, Monte Carlo and Venice. Then bad news had come from Meg, retaking her exams: 'I did them even worse than last time . . . I can't be the academic type you'll have to think of something else for me.'[112] She failed. By way of consolation,

109. 'Waugh and Peace', *ST*, 8 April 1973, 42.
110. *Ibid.*
111. *Ibid.*
112. Unpublished ALS from Margaret Waugh to Evelyn Waugh, 5 February [1960], from Nutcombe Manor, Clayhanger, Tiverton [the home of her aunt, Bridget Grant]; BL.

Papa took her on his last *Mail* jaunt to Athens and shortly afterwards explained to his agent that he wanted money badly and would accept almost any proposition. He disliked the *Mail*'s editing and titling of his pieces but needed their cash. Someone had proposed his contributing to a series which he considered 'drivel'. He accepted. He must, he explained to Peters, learn how to drivel.[113] He agreed to interviews and even went to London to record excerpts from *Vile Bodies* and *Helena*.[114] 'The choice', he explained, 'is between vanity and avarice. The avarice is not always selfish. Elderly men have many dependants. They are not to be blamed severely if they choose to sacrifice their vanity.'[115]

For Meg, he would have sacrificed anything, but as it turned out, Fr Caraman saved the day. In February he had been appointed Vice-Postulator of the Cause of the English and Welsh Martyrs. Caraman, whom Waugh once described as 'the last of the Jesuits of popular imagination',[116] was astute, 'literary' and circulated easily among the 'smart Catholic set' which Betjeman had come to despise. The young priest, always keen to be of service to the Waughs, offered Meg a job as his assistant in the Farm Street office at £10 a week. She moved to London and stayed with her cousin, Ann Fraser. Waugh thus lost Meg's company, and the relationship between priest and novelist took another step forward. 'She is a delightful girl', Waugh wrote 'but capricious & intermittently lazy. I am enormously grateful to you for finding her a task worth doing . . . and particularly one which will keep her tight bound to her Faith.'[117] Caraman found Meg equally attractive. A welcome guest at Combe Florey, he seemed almost to be assuming the position of unofficial chaplain to the family.

Around this time, early May, Waugh had begun his novel under the working title of *Sword of Honour*. The way ahead, however, was far from untroubled. James had been relegated to a dimmer set at Stonyhurst for idleness. Septimus was receiving additional tuition at All Hallows to compensate for his indolence. Teresa remained in America working for

113. Unpublished ALS to A.D. Peters, 5 April 1960, from Combe Florey House; *Catalogue* E1149, p. 252.

114. Made for Verve Records, Beverly Hills. Lawrence D. Stewart approached Waugh about this on 2 February 1960. Waugh improvised material on writing and writers to fill out the contracted time of one hour and was paid $1,000.

115. ALS to David Wright, 21 April 1960, from Combe Florey House; *Letters*, pp. 536–7. Wright, co-editor of *X*, a review of literature and the arts, had written to Waugh soliciting a contribution. Waugh refused but was so struck by the good manners of Wright's letter that he replied at length explaining why he could not afford the luxury of small-circulation publication. 'A lot is said', he wrote, 'about the "predicament" of the young writer. Perhaps you would like to hear of the "predicament" of the old . . .' (p. 536). He offered the letter, free, for publication.

116. Unpublished ALS to Fr Philip Caraman, 1 May 1959, from Combe Florey House; private collection. Waugh was congratulating him on his 'coup among the publishers' in securing a good deal on Knox's published sermons.

117. Unpublished ALS to Fr Philip Caraman, 2 May 1960, from Combe Florey House; private collection.

Little, Brown (in a job arranged by Peters) and hanging around Harvard waiting for D'Arms to complete his doctorate. (Waugh did not miss her but she showed ominous signs of hurtling towards matrimony.) Worst of all, Bron's novel had been accepted by Chapman & Hall. (Since it would now appear after his twenty-first birthday there was nothing his father could do about it.) With a £150 advance and the newspapers crooning about 'Waugh Père et Fils',[118] Bron was cock-a-hoop and intent upon launching a literary career while completing his degree. Waugh, it seems, felt threatened by this precocity at a time when his American publishers were harassing him to contract for a book a year. He could not, he explained to Peters, commit himself to such an arrangement. It would make him feel 'claustrophobic and Pinfoldian'.[119]

Waugh discovered only too many of 'the faults of youth' in Bron and found it difficult to judge *The Foxglove Saga*.[120] He thought it amusing, indeed startling for a boy of twenty, but limited. It was a reasonable first novel. There was no telling how this talent might develop. He did not wish to be uncharitable but the nightmare of Bron's overtaking him as he staggered into dotage could not easily be dispelled. His African book was small beer. It was crucial, he instructed Peters, that *Tourist* and *Foxglove* should not appear simultaneously. Comparisons would otherwise be inevitable and, on this basis, could only redound to Waugh père's discredit. He had had enough trouble recently with Alec, now a greater celebrity on the international circuit. A kindly American priest had sent Waugh an account of an interview Alec had given in Chicago. 'Mr. Waugh,' the interviewer had asked, '... whatever happened to your brother?'[121]

Bron's inconsequential epistles continued to arrive: about Candida Betjeman appearing at breakfast in evening dress and diamonds; about dances; about plans to travel to Rhodes, having no money, correcting the galley-proofs of *Foxglove*: 'I got a very brief letter from Hatty: Beast PIG Cad. HARRIET ... I have decided that when I grow up I want to be a printer....'[122] 'Dear Papa, Thank you very much for boosting *Foxglove* for the *Daily Mail*. I had a horrid little man in here from the same newspaper to whom I tried to boost it for hours, but all he was interested in was social problems....'[123] 'My examinations start tomorrow and so I am spending a

118. Cf. *DT*, 11 March 1960.
119. Unpublished ALS to A. D. Peters, c. 16 May 1960, from Combe Florey House; *Catalogue* E1151, p. 252.
120. Auberon Waugh, *The Foxglove Saga* (Chapman & Hall, 1960).
121. Unpublished TLS from Fr John Evans, 15 February 1960, from 2001 Devon Avenue, Chicago 45, Illinois; BL. Alec, alarmed by the question, replied that Evelyn had become a writer. He was then asked whether anything written by Evelyn had come up to his brother's high standard. Alec, ever loyal, replied: 'Oh yes, and far surpassed.'
122. Unpublished ALS from Auberon Waugh, nd [June 1960?], from Christ Church, Oxford; BL.
123. Unpublished ALS from Auberon Waugh, nd [June 1960?], from Christ Church etc.; BL.

quiet evening with my books. I should be disagreeably surprised if I do not distinguish myself.'[124] He was disagreeably surprised, re-sat, failed again and, refusing a third attempt, headed for London and life with the lions.[125]

Eight months earlier the BBC had approached Waugh to ask if he would appear in a 'Face to Face' interview. 'I am not keen on Mr. Burnett's television project,' he had informed Peters. '... But I may be hard up next year so don't refuse definitely.'[126] In the meantime he had reluctantly accepted £250 for Michael Bakewell's radio adaptation of *Pinfold* and instructed Peters, by way of deterrent, to demand the same fee for the interview. The BBC had called Waugh's bluff and accepted the proposition without a quibble. Waugh, rather out of countenance, had thus found himself obliged to proceed with the deal. He would meet two of them, he told Peters, in a Taunton hotel.[127] That was not satisfactory. Waugh would have to be sketched, Hugh Burnett explained, by Féliks Topolski, who was providing caption portraits for the series, and the programme must be recorded in London. Waugh had grumbled and succumbed. Very well, Burnett and Topolski could come to Combe Florey for the preliminaries.

They had arrived late to discover a disgruntled host. 'Will the studio be very hot?' he asked gravely. 'Would I need to wear my tropical clothes?' He was equally suspicious of Freeman. 'Who is this man? Will I be able to ask *him* a few questions?'[128] Shortly afterwards he wrote to Driberg: 'I have let myself in for cross-examination on Television by a man named Major Freeman who I am told was a colleague of yours in the Working Class Movement. Do you know anything damaging about him that I can introduce into our conversation if he becomes insolent?'[129] *Pinfold* had been broadcast on 7 June to enthusiastic reviews and, although Waugh refused to listen to it, the 'old BBC hands ... got a great deal of masochistic pleasure out of the opening episode ... when Pinfold is interviewed ... for a Frankly Speaking type of programme.'[130] Audience and programme-makers alike

124. ALS from Auberon Waugh to Evelyn and Laura Waugh, nd [June 1960?], from Christ Church etc.; BL; *WTD*, p. 136.
125. Cf. unpublished ALS from (Sir) Roy Harrod to Evelyn Waugh, 20 July 1960, from Bayfield Brecks, Holt, Norfolk; BL: 'I gather that Auberon did not do much work .... [He] got through his language on the first shot and got a Pass mark in logic this time (both times), failing only in poor old economics.... I am so sorry about it all.' Sir Roy, an economics don, had arranged special tuition for Bron during his last term.
126. Unpublished ALS to A. D. Peters, 14 December 1959, from Combe Florey House; *Catalogue* E1133, p. 249.
127. Cf. unpublished ALS to A. D. Peters, 28 May 1960, from Combe Florey House; *Catalogue* E1156, p. 253.
128. John Woodford, 'Mr. Waugh Succumbs', *DT*, 20 June 1960, 15.
129. 11 June 1960; *Letters*, p. 544. John Freeman was a Labour MP (1945–55), Editor of the *New Statesman* (1961–5), British Ambassador in Washington (1969–71), and Chairman and Chief Executive of London Weekend Television (1971–9).
130. 'Adapted from Waugh', *Radio Times*, 3 June 1960, 5.

now waited eagerly for the next confrontation. It was, Burnett announced, a 'major scoop'.[131]

That summer the Waughs were news. Evelyn's ordeal by television coincided with Bron's in the Examination Schools and assisted the young man's publicity-seeking. Everyone agreed that Waugh had outplayed Freeman.[132] In July the revised *Brideshead* had appeared. September saw *Tourist* on the bookstalls. Father and son, it seemed, were running neck and neck.

Tourist was Waugh's only post-war travel book and he was ashamed of it. 'I have had a travel diary published,' he wrote to Duggan, 'but I am not sending it to any of the friends I honour. It is a pot-boiler done to pay for a jaunt. . . .'[133] Reviewers were quick to note decline. The lightness of touch, the inexhaustible curiosity, the delight in the fantastic and grotesque which had sustained those works collected in *When the Going Was Good* had deserted him. 'This is Waugh . . . of the Middle-Late Mood:' wrote Basil Davidson, 'more in sorrow . . . than in wit.'[134] Connolly agreed:

> When we are young, we travel to see the world, afterwards to make sure it is still there. . . . I know the obsession by which re-visiting places where one has once felt becomes a substitute for feeling, but it does not make the best kind of travel book. In fact, *A Tourist* . . . is quite the thinnest piece of book-making which Mr. Waugh has undertaken . . . the particular pose he affects – of an elderly, infirm and irritable old buffer, quite out of touch with the times – is hardly suited to enthusiasm, a prerequisite of travel writing.[135]

It was all too true.

In a period of rather low literary achievement, however, anything from Waugh's pen merited attention. Dan Jacobson and Alan Sillitoe both dealt with the book seriously, the first seeing it as a fascinating off-shoot of the nostalgia which had coloured Waugh's fiction,[136] the second objecting to 'that curious, falsely attractive sense of tolerance of a caste-bound mind'.[137] A professor of African law found it 'well-balanced and objective',[138] while Davidson discovered numerous elementary historical blunders. Davidson

131. John Woodford, *op. cit.*, 15.
132. See Prologue, Vol. 1.
133. Unpublished ALS to Alfred Duggan, 27 September 1960, from Combe Florey House; private collection. He was writing to thank Duggan for sending his *Family Favourites*. Waugh had 'read it in proof . . . with the keenest pleasure; also with the conviction that, dealing as it does with the ever popular subject of sodomy, it is likely to be an even greater success than its predecessors.'
134. Basil Davidson, 'Mr Waugh's Africa', *NS*, 24 September 1960, 439–40; *CH*, pp. 413–14.
135. Cyril Connolly, *ST*, 25 September 1960, 27; *CH*, pp. 414–16.
136. Dan Jacobson, *Spectator*, 23 September 1960, 448; *CH*, pp. 409–11.
137. Alan Sillitoe, *Time & Tide*, 15 October 1960, 1226; *CH*, pp. 417–18.
138. Antony Allott, *Tablet*, 24 September 1960, 870; *CH*, pp. 411–12.

was closer to the mark. It was another book, like *Knox*, full of mistakes, and while *Foxglove* sold vigorously, *Tourist* foundered. After Waugh's death it was remaindered, along with *Helena*, *Love Among the Ruins*, *Pinfold* and *A Little Learning*, and gathered dust on book-dealers' shelves for a decade, waiting for the collectors.

*

Waugh blanked out the ignominy. By and large he agreed with the bad reviews. His novel was going well and he hoped to finish it by January. That would set the record straight. At the end of August he had submitted 30,000 words, under the working title of 'Conventional Weapons', taking him up to the description of Gervase Crouchback's death and Guy's spiritual enlightenment.

Reading that section alongside Waugh's letters of the period, it is difficult not to detect the author's religious struggles in his hero's:

> For many years now the direction in the *Garden of the Soul*, 'Put yourself in the presence of God', had for Guy come to mean a mere act of respect, like the signing of the Visitor's Book at an Embassy.... He reported for duty saying to God: 'I don't ask anything from you. I am here if you want me. I don't suppose I can be any use, but if there is anything I can do, let me know,' and left it at that. 'I don't ask anything from you'; that was the deadly core of his apathy.... That emptiness had been with him for years.... Enthusiasm and activity were not enough. God required more than that. He had commanded all men to ask.[139]

Waugh was writing about the supplication for Grace through humility, the courage to oppose spiritual sloth, to ask God for one's unique, and thus uniquely difficult, vocation. Waugh's profession was that of writer. It is possible that he did not now regard this as his vocation. In one sense, of course, his art fulfilled his definition of vocation as the 'small service which only he could perform, for which he had been created' and which would reveal 'his function in the divine plan'. Like Crouchback, however, he no longer expected 'a heroic destiny. Quantitative judgements did not apply.'[140] Waugh, again like his hero, seemed still to be waiting. 'All that mattered was to recognize the chance when it offered',[141] but every attempt at loyal service had been stained by his egotism. The talents which distinguished

139. *Unconditional Surrender* (Chapman & Hall, 1961; reprinted Harmondsworth, Penguin Books, 1964 and 1967), p. 66.
140. *Ibid.*
141. *Ibid.*

him corrupted his spiritual exercises. His art was a theatre of cruelty; his temperament instinctively uncharitable.

'Knox in his public utterances', Bowra had suggested in a review of Waugh's biography, 'seems sometimes to lack charity and compassion. . . .'[142] So did Waugh, but, alarmed by this construction, he had sprung to the priest's defence. 'Sanctity', he agreed, 'cannot exist without charity. That is axiomatic':

> God forbid I should start a dispute about the rights and wrongs of Franco. Of the rights and wrongs of Knox it should be remembered that undergraduate consciences were troubled in the matter, the Franco party were overwhelmingly unpopular, the French Dominicans and some men at Blackfriars were offering Catholics arguments for joining the popular side. It was Knox's duty to speak, not an officious interpolation. . . . It is true that Ronald thought it bad taste to be serious in private conversation – regrettably so I think. This would account for apparent frivolity about wars – all of which he abhorred.[143]

Waugh was effectively defending himself here. He, too, had supported Franco in the 1930s. He, too, now abhorred war while seeming to make a joke of it. Like Crouchback, his path to sanctity was obstructed by lack of charity. And while he wrestled with this, slowly becoming a more 'serious' man, his children constantly tempted him back towards irritability.

Meg alone was his consolation. 'Darling Pig', he wrote in September:

> I am glad you have lost your eyes. You are spared the sight of the cad Muggeridge.
>
> It has rained almost continuously since you left. I have made good progress with my novel but am for the moment stuck. Your sister [Hatty] and brother [James?] roll about in the kitchen & morning room, refuse all invitations to their neighbours & pretend they are not bored. . . . Bron . . . returned for a few hours yesterday & then went to London to interview possible employers. He was met with the encouraging news that *Foxglove* had found an American publisher and a good advance; also various offers from Television. So he went to his interviews weary but cheerful. . . . Septimus contracted an infection from his aunt Gabriel . . . but is now able to frequent the cinema, spreading germs. . . .[144]

142. Sir Maurice Bowra, *London Magazine*, December 1959, 63–5.
143. Unpublished ALS to Sir Maurice Bowra, 2 January 1960, from Combe Florey House; private collection.
144. Unpublished ALS to Margaret Waugh, 19 September 1960, from Combe Florey House; private collection. Margaret had left her spectacles behind; Waugh posted them on. Bron appeared on television with [Sir] John Betjeman and Lord Lloyd-George.

Family fun. Bron's name flickered through the gossip columns, a golden youth of British letters. Waugh watched it all balefully, with, perhaps, a sense of *déjà vu*. On one occasion he wrote to rebuke the *Express* for associating Bron's name with that of Prince William of Gloucester. 'I would point out', the diary editor replied, 'that the information regarding the friendship ... came among other sources from HRH Prince William and not from your son....'[145] Power, it seemed, was passing rapidly to the younger generation. 'Bron's success is most exhilarating for him,' Waugh wrote to Alec. 'I fear it may lead to disappointment later....'[146]

Meg, at nineteen, was again awkwardly on the margins of Bron's riotous life. They had always been close at home. It seemed sensible to her that they should set up house together in London. Papa strongly disapproved:

> ... First, expense. You cannot possibly hope to live on your wages in the manner you imagine. The only possible financial arrangement would be for Bron to provide what Ann Grant now provides...for £5 a week. He cannot possibly do this ... and has idiotically spent half his advances ... in buying a car....
>
> Secondly, your relationship with him. Either he treats you as he treated James when he took him to stay with a friend in Wales, or you would be a heavy burden on him. If he goes out three or four nights a week & leaves you alone you would be the first to complain of neglect. You have, so far, given no evidence of being able to keep house. Thirdly, the impermanence of Bron's plans. He may well wish to chuck his job on the Queen[147] & leave London. He is a moody, nervous boy with, so far as I have seen, no sense of responsibility. It won't, perhaps, be a bad plan for him to knock about, learn by his mistakes and acquire experience for his novels. This would not be suitable for you at your age. You still very much require a 'home atmosphere'. You are no more ready for 'independence' than the Congo.[148]

Meg capitulated. Waugh sent her £50 whenever he could to bribe her to stop smoking. But she smoked and drank and went to parties, and on one occasion in December disgraced herself in public. 'I won't scold you for being drunk,' he wrote mischievously. 'Your escapade is certain to be talked about. If you have not done so, go straight off and confess it. I hope it doesn't reach Pixton, but I fear it will.... The telephone is being moved

145. Unpublished TLS from J. D. Waddell, Diary Editor (William Hickey), 10 November 1960; from *DE*, Fleet Street, London; BL.
146. Unpublished APCI to Alec Waugh, nd [pm 25 October 1960], from Combe Florey House; private collection.
147. Auberon Waugh was working for the magazine, *Queen*.
148. Unpublished ALS to Margaret Waugh, 11 October 1960, from Combe Florey House; BL.

from the stairs to your mothers bedroom. I think the telephone-room will make a nice little bed-room for you.'[149] Waugh and Meg played elaborate charades of rewards and punishments. As a father, he was most genial when pretending to swish the rod, most awkward when Bron and Teresa refused to kiss it.

By December, Waugh's domestic irritations had rapidly mounted. That summer, Teresa had written from America informing him that she and D'Arms planned to marry at Christmas.[150] No formal permission for her hand had been sought. No mention was made of the young man's promise to receive instruction. Indeed, he now seemed uncertain whether he would. A 'mixed marriage' was entirely unacceptable to Waugh. Teresa apologized. Of course, she said, they would see to this. Then, in November, a stiff little letter had arrived from D'Arms by way of belated supplication and addressing the major causes of Waugh's displeasure: the young man planned to be received into the Roman Catholic Church at some point during the winter; Teresa had explained to him that she had no money, nor expected to receive any; there was no need to pamper a girl brought up in the rough-and-tumble of Mary Herbert's household.[151] Waugh no doubt thought the date of reception suspiciously vague and the remark about money an unconscious joke. Weddings did not come cheap. Worse still, his grandchildren would be Americans. It was a thought almost too horrible to contemplate. But there was nothing he could do about it. John and Teresa decamped to Perugia, an engaged couple, and the wedding was deferred to June.

No sooner had Waugh absorbed this shock, than another hit him. In December the *Telegraph* had employed Bron on the staff of their 'Peterborough' column. Having already written his next novel and sold the serial rights to the *Express*, he moved into an elegant apartment in Clarges Street and set up as a bachelor dandy. Some of his father's Victorian paintings decorated the walls and Bron began his own collection. As he danced his way round London, lionized at parties and pleasantly bemused by this attention, he seemed to everyone to be on course for a few reckless years. 'Bron', Waugh remarked drily in January, 'is heading for bankruptcy in fine style.'[152] Shortly afterwards, however, Waugh found himself reading an urgent message. His son wished to come down for a 'fleeting visit' to discuss something

149. Cf. unpublished ALS to Margaret Waugh, 7 December 1960, from Combe Florey House; BL.
150. Cf. unpublished ALS from Teresa Waugh, nd [July 1960?], from 73 1st Avenue, NY; BL.
151. Unpublished ALS from John D'Arms, 3 November 1960, from 159 Brattle Street, Cambridge 38, Mass.; BL.
152. Unpublished ALS to Vernon Watkinson, 26 January 1961, from Combe Florey House; private collection.

> about which I am afraid you may have misgivings, to say the least.... I propose, despite my extreme youth, my only moderately secure financial position, and my uncertain and at times *irresponsible* temperament on which it has been your painful duty from time to time to remark, to take a wife and marry her.[153]

Waugh was stunned, Bron gaily inflexible. He had met Lady Teresa Onslow, had quickly proposed and anticipated a life of industrious (but not 'grotesque') poverty. She had a private income of £600, he a salary of £1,600. The life of a wealthy bachelor, he added, is 'awfully pointless and selfish & mean.... I am extremely lucky to have such a charming and lovely girl fond of me.... My hair & teeth are falling fast.... Please take it seriously.'[154]

Waugh did. Teresa Onslow was not a Catholic. Her parents were divorced. This impetuous match must have recalled his own with She-Evelyn in 1928. Unlike Lady Burghclere, the Countess of Onslow had given her reluctant blessing, but it was a delicate situation and one which Waugh could have done without as he attempted to draw his life's work to a close. Again, however, there was nothing he could do. Lady Onslow, Bron explained, thought a July wedding would be suitable – and July it was.

When Waugh met Teresa he was pleasantly surprised: she was attractive, sharp, not only well-born but well-mannered, and she agreed to take instruction. She looked, he thought, the kind of girl who might keep his son in order. Before long, Waugh and she became rather fond of each other, a surprise, perhaps, to both since the distance between father and son increased. In November, Bron had invited his parents to an expensive twenty-first birthday party, hoping to show them off. Waugh had embarrassed and hurt him by refusing, especially as this had also kept Laura away. A horror of the press, Papa had explained, prevented his attendance. 'I am awfully sorry you can neither come ...,' Bron had replied. 'People Will Say. And lots of really quite nice people are coming. Still.' 'Nice' was his highest social accolade. He craved his father's acceptance. 'I keep buying Christmas presents for Papa,' he added, '... none for anybody else.'[155] Bron felt unfairly cast out from Combe Florey. Waugh had sold more furnishings to the Trust to raise £500 for a present but at the same time had asked Peters to put the boy in touch with an accountant. Once Bron was of age, Waugh insisted, he was on his own.[156]

153. ALS, nd [Spring 1961?], from 13 Clarges Street, Wl; BL; *WTD*, p. 151. Bron's underlining of 'irresponsible' suggests that Margaret had shown him their father's letter. See p. 434 above.
154. *Ibid.*
155. Unpublished ALS from Auberon Waugh, nd [November 1960?], [Flat 3, 26] Pont Street, [SW1]; BL.
156. Unpublished ALS, 15 November 1960, from Combe Florey House; *Catalogue* E1179, pp. 258–9.

Diffident beneath his bluster, Bron needed a 'home atmosphere' as much as Meg. Only she was welcomed back. An earlier letter from her suggests her image of Combe Florey as a paradisial retreat. 'I have heard of some good cheap houses ... and then you can come & stay for long periods spending the day in Whites & eating the delicious dinner I will cook, and Mummy can come & shop all day & we'll all go to Combe Florey for week ends.'[157] No such fairy-tale for Bron. 'I am at a loss to understand why you chose my bedroom to give to the boys,' he wrote home while pursuing Teresa, 'and you could not have chosen a room which gave more pain to at least one member of the family.... However, I must not whine on – I could not have expressed myself more strongly when the scheme was suggested ... but if it had been a scheme for keeping me out of the house it might have been successful.'[158] Papa, enraged, demanded and received an apology. 'Your brother', he wrote to Meg, 'was delirious (he says) when he wrote so impudently to your mother.'[159] Soon after this Bron had sprung the engagement and required his father to attend embarrassing interviews with Lady Onslow: 'Please make it quite plain to her that you have absolutely no capital at all....'[160] Waugh, less than comfortable explaining his poverty to the aristocracy, could not decently refuse, and so the novel increasingly fell behind schedule in this tangle of domestic arrangements. It was April before the last word was written, by which time its final title had acquired more than merely military or political significance. With that book he drew a line beneath his career as a novelist, and his detachment from the future was complete.

*

When *Unconditional Surrender* appeared in October, reviewers were uncertain what to expect. Waugh's public profile was as high and hard-etched as ever. The Freeman interview had, if anything, endeared the old dog to the great British public. In general, he appeared to be as successful, complacent and vindictively dotty as ever. He certainly appeared to be rich. His now infrequent public letters and reviews continued to whack Regius professors and Peter Quennell, and to praise the books of his titled female friends. He popped up in the newspapers as the author of light pieces on luxurious travel, at the society weddings of his children,[161] or in interviews lamenting

157. Unpublished ALS from Margaret Waugh, 13 July 1960, from The Cause of the English & Welsh Martyrs, Office of the Vice-Postulation, 31 Farm Street, W1; BL.
158. ALS from Auberon Waugh, 16 February 1961, from the *Daily Telegraph*; BL; *WTD*, p. 150.
159. Unpublished APC, nd [20 February 1961?], from Combe Florey House; private collection. Bron did not say he was delirious but in a fit of pique with the night sub-editor.
160. Unpublished ALS from Auberon Waugh, nd [February? 1961], from 13 Clarges Street, W1; BL.
161. Maria Teresa Waugh married John D'Arms on 1 June 1961; Auberon Alexander Waugh married Lady Teresa Onslow, daughter of the Earl and Countess of Onslow, at the Church of Our Lady of the Assumption, Warwick Street, a month later: 1 July 1961. The reception was at the House

his penury. During the *Lady Chatterley* trial (1960) he had been on the side of the censors. He advocated the death penalty and derided the Welfare State. A fortnight after Bron's wedding, Waugh broadcast a talk apologizing on behalf of the BBC for their unwitting complicity in Wodehouse's wartime persecution and describing him as one of the great writers of the twentieth century.[162] Many found it all a little difficult to take seriously. Evelyn Waugh seemed to his enemies a 'beat up old bastard',[163] whose prejudices had all the wit and intellectual acumen of an outmoded variety act. His last two books had been dull but he had never written a dull novel. Readers of his war saga had waited six years for its completion. Could he pull it off after so long a gap?

The answer was a resounding 'Don't know'. Distinct critical camps were again established, with the familiar arguments for and against Waugh's vision of the war and the world. Amis and Toynbee attacked him on the grounds that his literary realism was subverted by social prejudice. Crouchback's motto is, according to the first, 'It's all right when I do it';[164] according to the second, 'The man who knows a good brandy is better than the man who does not.'[165] Toynbee found the description of Gervase's funeral 'painfully gushing and ... yes, also vulgar',[166] and the whole work misanthropic. Both treated the novel as a moral statement and, apart from the technical facility of the writing, found it essentially pernicious. When the American edition appeared in 1962, Joseph Heller and Gore Vidal took a similar line although in gentler prose. Heller (whose *Catch 22* Waugh had recently refused to promote)[167] disliked Crouchback and attributed motives to him other than those acknowledged in the text; the hero is not seen as 'innocent' but by turns stupid and apathetic.[168] Vidal, who thought that the

of Lords. Lady Diana Cooper, Ann Fleming and Alec Waugh attended Teresa's wedding. Afterwards there was a ball at the Hyde Park Hotel.

162. 'An Act of Homage and Reparation to P. G. Wodehouse', BBC Home Service, 15 July 1961; reprinted *ST*, 16 July 1961; *EAR*, pp. 561–8.

163. When *Officers and Gentlemen* appeared, Waugh had written to Lady Diana Cooper: 'My unhappy novel is having the reception it deserves – large sales and sharp criticism. I am coupled always (greatly to my honour) with Hemmingway [*sic*] as a "beat up old bastard"' (ALS, 8 September [1952], from Piers Court; BL; *MWMS*, p. 143).

164. Kingsley Amis, *Spectator*, 27 October 1961, 581–2; *CH* pp. 419–24.

165. Philip Toynbee, 'Mourner for a World That Never Was', *Observer*, 29 October 1961, 21; *CH*, pp. 433–8.

166. *Ibid.* p. 437.

167. Nina Bourne of Simon & Schuster had sent this first novel to Waugh, hoping for a publicity quotation. 'I am sorry that the book fascinates you so much,' Waugh replied. '... It suffers not only from indelicacy but from prolixity. It should be cut by about a half.... You are mistaken in calling it a novel. It is a collection of sketches – often repetitious – totally without structure. Much of the dialogue is funny. You may quote me as saying: "This exposure of corruption, cowardice and incivility of American officers will outrage all friends of your country (such as myself) and greatly comfort your enemies"' (*Letters*, pp. 571–2). Miss Bourne was annoyed by Waugh's remarks and wrote to say so.

168. Joseph Heller, *Nation*, 20 January 1962, 62–3; *CH*, pp. 442–4.

trilogy had 'much to recommend it', feared that Waugh had dropped the mask of the satirist for the indulgent daydreams of the romantic, forsaking (unlike Juvenal 'his great precursor'), the 'sins of the dreadful, usable present'.[169] Two years later, the novel was still under attack. Simon Raven largely retracted his earlier favourable review on the grounds that Waugh's social commentary was simply inaccurate.[170]

There was one notable exception to this list: Cyril Connolly. He had received the book nervously on hearing that it caricatured him and *Horizon* as Everard Spruce and *Survival*. He had then approached precisely the wrong person for an opinion: Ann Fleming. Like Bowra (and Waugh), she delighted to see the faint-hearted squirm. The caricature, she replied, was most certainly based on Connolly and he slunk away, wounded. Under the circumstances, his review was astonishingly generous, especially as his editor cut fifty lines of additional praise. Connolly still had reservations about those figures whom the 'biliousness of Mr. Waugh's gaze' rendered 'dreary' (i.e. Spruce). But there was a decisive shift to the opposite camp with this piece. On re-reading all three volumes, Connolly said, 'the cumulative effect is most impressive, and it seems to me unquestionably the finest novel to have come out of the war.' He even revised his earlier complaints about *Officers and Gentlemen*, describing it as 'magnificent'.[171]

A correspondence between author and critic ensued. Waugh was furious with Mrs Fleming, conciliatory towards Connolly. 'I began to mind a little ... because Horizon had taken so much trouble with you ...,' Connolly had written before the review was published. '... I felt you did not understand how much one loved doing Horizon, that it really seemed we had a chance every month to produce something perfect ... to find out & publish what ... was good when so much else was just destruction.'[172] Thanks to Mrs Fleming's gossip-mongering, poor Connolly was constantly rung up by friends offering sympathy. But none offered more than Waugh, and their comradeship, so long in the doldrums, was re-established. Connolly was severely depressed, overwhelmed by the victory of the enemies of promise:

> I do not think posterity will ever believe in our friendship any more than someone who looked me up in the index to your biography.... I feel that doom is rushing upon us & that the west has no will to fight – surrounded by seething mobs who hate us.... It is difficult for

169. Gore Vidal, *NYTBR*, 7 January 1961, 1, 28; *CH*, pp. 438–42.
170. Simon Raven, *Spectator*, 12 June 1964, 798; *CH*, pp. 447–50.
171. Cyril Connolly, *ST*, 29 October 1961; *CH*, pp. 430–3.
172. Unpublished ALS from Cyril Connolly, 25 October [1961], from Bushey Lodge, Firle, Lewes, Sussex; BL.

> the anti-militarist son of a professional soldier to conceal his horror of khaki from his reviews![173]

Waugh perhaps sighed over the self-contradictions of the last two sentences.

Looking elsewhere among the reviews, he must also have been pleased. The Catholic intelligentsia applauded. Bernard Bergonzi thought that 'the whole work now looks a substantial achievement & one which may alter our total picture of Mr. Waugh's writings.'[174] Christopher Derrick saw the complaints about 'snobbery & romanticism' as emphasizing Waugh's own present position, 'an *avant-garde* position, a very serious and responsible one in the front rank of the contemporary movement.'[175] At last this interesting paradox was beginning to emerge. Waugh's refusal to believe in conventional heroism, Progress and rationalism allowed Derrick to label the self-proclaimed *avant-garde* as 'reactionaries'.

V. S. Pritchett's notice introduced more subtlety into this rancorous taking of sides, by suggesting that 'To object to his snobbery is as futile as objecting to cricket, for every summer the damn game comes round again whether you like it or not.' Social exclusivism, in other words, is integral to the British consciousness. It will not disappear if ignored and Waugh was entitled to write about it as an objective observer. There was no need to be affronted by this except when it became 'violent'. The point at which 'Waugh's high Romance becomes vulgar sentimentality' is when he distorts a description of snobbery to imply moral failing, even criminal tendency, in the lower classes.[176]

A discussion of Waugh's use of class distinction was often the central issue of the 'serious' notices, particularly Frank Kermode's in *Partisan Review*. Waugh had engaged in a recent dust-up with Kermode when the novelist had replied to the Professor's essay in *Encounter*, 'Mr Waugh's Cities':[177] 'Your review ... imputes to me the absurd and blasphemous opinion that divine grace is "confined" to the highest and lowest class. May I draw his attention to a book which he appears to have read with imperfect comprehension?'[178] Unabashed, Kermode continued to fight Waugh's corner. Powell, C. P. Snow, Richard Hughes and Waugh, he said later, were all writers obsessed by class, and Waugh was

> a writer of very great talent ... who has got into his books a whole self-subsistent vision. That this is to some implausible, to some repul-

173. Unpublished ALS from Cyril Connolly, nd [late October? 1961], from Bushey Lodge etc.; BL.
174. *Guardian*, 27 October 1961, 7; *CH*, pp. 423–4.
175. *Tablet*, 28 October 1961, 1024, 1026; *CH*, pp. 427–30.
176. *NS*, 27 October 1961, 603–4; *CH*, pp. 424–7.
177. *Encounter*, November 1960, 63–6, 68–70; *CH*, pp. 279–87.
178. 'Evelyn Waugh Replies', *Encounter*, December 1960, 83. Waugh quotes '"*Odi profanum volgus et arceo*" ... the See of Peter' – from *Helena*, pp. 92–3 – a passage emphasizing the interdependence of all social classes who could be 'one with the Empress Dowager in the Mystical Body'.

> sive, may matter only in the very long run; perhaps the aristocratic myth, however extreme and bizarre, ... offers possibilities of what [Henry] James called 'saturation'....[179]

The suggestion is that we should not judge according to personal, political or religious preconception but regard the value structure offered as a literary device, an extended metaphor of reality. This seems sensible. For Crouchback, the only reality is represented by the Church (parodied by the surrogate cross of the Sword of Stalingrad). To talk of the secular attitudes expressed in the novel as anything other than 'mythical' would in Waugh's own terms be a nonsense. The trilogy darkens in tone as it progresses and this development marks Guy's gradual loss of faith both in rational answers and class assumptions. Upper and lower classes are alike condemned. Only the faith survives. Ultimately, *Unconditional Surrender* is a mystical work and those who complained about the drabness of its ineffectual hero surely ignore this. The book concerns Guy's slow discovery of terrestrial impotence and spiritual vocation, his relationship to God, not man, and Kermode's notion that we should regard the hero's social attitudes as a structural myth is perhaps the most productive line of enquiry. As Bergonzi had already suggested:

> To anyone brought up as a Catholic Mr. Waugh's image of Catholicism is, to say the least, peculiar; and the same thing may well be true of his picture of the gentry. But that is beside the point; it is enough that [he] has found the myth creatively valuable.[180]

One of Waugh's greater technical achievements, however, went unnoticed. No one remembered that short story, 'Compassion', published twelve years earlier. Waugh had embarked on his complex three-decker with the idea of fleshing out Major Gordon's history. One recalls the genesis of *A Handful of Dust* in 'The Man Who Liked Dickens', and its author's desire to 'discover how the prisoner got there'.[181] The same process was repeated with *Unconditional Surrender* and 'Compassion'. Just as in 1934, the short story was spliced into the end of the novel. That earlier piece of literary dovetailing was remarkable enough but, given Waugh's skill in leading Tony Last to the point at which Henty had been lost in the jungle, the short story could be incorporated with little more than changes of name. In *Unconditional Surrender* the problems were more complex.

The conclusion, for instance, had to be held in mind over three volumes rather than one; the range of characters and historical commentary was much larger. As a result, the 'splicing' does not represent the insertion of

179. *Partisan Review*, 20 August 1962, 466–71; *CH*, pp. 445–6.
180. *Op. cit.*; *CH*, p. 423.
181. Cf. Vol. 1, pp. 379–80.

a single block but of a series of finely cut slivers of the original interspersed by new material which ties the Crouchback/Gordon experience with the Kanyis into the entire three-volume structure. It is a remarkable feat. One can dig out the original narrative, almost intact, from the fabric of the last sixty pages of 'Book Three'.[182] The tale's conclusion is rewritten to heighten tension and Crouchback's sense of helplessness; small pieces are reshaped; but the dialogue remains largely intact. There is no greater testimony to Waugh's ability to conceive and complete a structure. From the outset, it seems, and certainly from the inception of Volume Two, he knew exactly where his saga would finish, what shape his short story would give to the whole, and he would not allow 'Compassion' to be republished for precisely this reason.[183]

In its transformed state, 'Compassion' structures the coda of the trilogy. Major Gordon, like Crouchback, is not an imaginative man. Unlike him, however, Gordon has 'nothing against communists'[184] and no fixed religious belief. Crouchback wears his prejudices shyly but, almost to the end, with quiet pride. He is a traditionalist Catholic. The focus of Waugh's spiritual struggle, as we have seen, was the painful journey towards compassion and contrition. The short story ends with Gordon's sense of guilt about his political naïvety (which had allowed the Kanyis to be executed) and his turning to the padre for help. '"No suffering need ever be wasted"', says the priest. '"It is just as much a part of Charity to receive cheerfully as to give."' Gordon is jerked from his melancholy by this. '"I'd like you to tell me a bit more about that,"' he says.[185] And there the story ends. Waugh concludes with an ambiguity which relieves his hero of criminal responsibility and points him towards the Faith.

In the novel, all this is abandoned. Crouchback's (and Waugh's) spiritual crisis was more subtle. The priest's words were true but, in Crouchback's (and Waugh's) case, might be seen to counsel evasion. Without charity and compassion there could be no sanctity; the achievement of sanctity was the ultimate goal of devotion. But charity and compassion could be artfully constructed to defend failures of responsibility. Crouchback's ultimate wisdom involves his acceptance of guilt, of cowardly complicity in the face of evil, and Waugh emphasizes the point by inserting a new passage which echoes back through the novel as a *cri de coeur*. '"Is there any place that is free from evil?"' Mme Kanyi asks Crouchback:

182. Penguin edn., pp. 175–235.

183. Cf. unpublished ALS from Evelyn Waugh to A. D. Peters, nd, np, on TL from Stanley Salmen, 12 January 1954; *Catalogue* E846, p. 205. Salmen was negotiating for an American edition of Waugh's short stories. Waugh specifically excluded 'Compassion' because he thought he might use it in the concluding volume of his trilogy.

184. 'Compassion', *op. cit.*, 4.

185. *Ibid.*, 20.

'It is too simple to say that only the Nazis wanted war. These communists wanted it too. It was the only way in which they could come to power. Many of my people [the Jews] wanted it, to be revenged on the Germans, to hasten the creation of the national state. It seems to me that there was a will to war, a death wish, everywhere. Even good men thought their private honour would be satisfied by war. They could assert their manhood by killing and being killed.... Danger justified privilege. I knew Italians ... who felt this. Were there none in England?'

'God forgive me,' said Guy. 'I was one of them.'[186]

All the reviewers missed this: that the shame, the guilt at complicity and pride, the withdrawal from the struggle into the silences of religious contemplation and humdrum domesticity, all rewrite Guy's life as a history of egotism. It was the nearest Waugh came to a public apology for his own selfishness, although he felt the issue as deeply as his hero. The problem was that Crouchback was a better man than he. The last section of the novel is entitled 'The Death Wish'. To wish for death was a sin. Crouchback overcomes this despair. Waugh had yet to discover whether he could.

186. *Unconditional Surrender*, *op. cit.*, p. 232.

XII

Fin de Ligne: November 1961–April 1966

'I ... feel prostrate,' he had written a week after finishing *Unconditional Surrender*, 'as though I had walked barefoot from Aldermaston.... The last 12 months has seen a falling off of our contemporaries, ... none of them – Tony Powell, Graham Greene, John Betjeman, Nancy Mitford – at the top of their form.'[1] During 1960 Waugh had reviewed *Casanova's Chinese Restaurant*[2] and *Don't Tell Alfred*[3] with halting praise. At the end of the year Greene had sent him 'A Visit to Morin'.

'I don't take the London Magazine', he replied, 'so your Christmas story was quite new to me. It is subtle and deeply sorrowful.... I look forward to your leper novel.... I have despaired of ever arranging a meeting. I pray we run across one another soon.'[4] The tone was reserved. When the *Mail* sent the 'leper novel' (*A Burnt Out Case* [1961]), Waugh refused to review it: 'taken in conjunction with your Christmas story, this ... makes it plain that you are exasperated by the reputation which has come to you unsought as a "Catholic" writer.... I have some guilt in this matter.'[5] Waugh believed that, in promoting Greene's work during the American lecture tour, he had behaved like Rycker in the novel. Profuse apologies were offered. He prayed that 'the desperate conclusions of Morin & Querry are purely fictional.'[6] Both texts dealt with loss of faith.

The self-accusation was absurd and Greene immediately stressed this. A deeper concern, however, lay behind Waugh's letter: that Greene might be nearing apostasy. Greene replied:

> With a writer of your genius and insight I certainly would not attempt to hide behind the time old gag that an author can never be identified with his characters.... At the same time ... the parallel must not be drawn all down the line.... Fowler [in *The Quiet American* (1955)], I hope, was a more jealous man than I am, and Querry, I fear, was a

1. Unpublished ALS to Alfred Duggan, 3 April 1961, from Combe Florey House; private collection.
2. 'Marriage à la Mode – 1936', *Spectator*, 24 June 1960, 919; *EAR*, pp. 547–50.
3. *London Magazine*, December 1960, 65–8; *EAR*, pp. 553–5.
4. Unpublished ALS to Graham Greene, 11 December 1960, from Combe Florey House; private collection.
5. 3 January 1961; *Letters*, p. 557.
6. *Ibid.*

> better man than I am. I wanted to give expression to various states or moods of belief and unbelief. The doctor, whom I liked best as a realized character, represents a settled and easy atheism; the Father Superior a settled and easy belief . . .; Father Thomas an unsettled form of belief and Querry an unsettled form of disbelief. . . . Anyway . . . I do want you to believe that never for a moment have I felt other than pleasure or an interested dismay at your criticisms and never . . . anything other than affection for yourself.[7]

Waugh remained sceptical:

> I don't think you can blame people who read the book as a recantation of faith. To my mind . . . 'settled and easy atheism' is meaningless, for an atheist denies his whole purpose as a man – to love & serve God. . . . I cannot wish your book success and I will not make a sensational attack on it. . . . God forbid I should pry into the secrets of your soul. It is simply your public performance which grieves me.[8]

'This is rapidly becoming a Claudel–Gide correspondence,' Greene replied:

> I think you have carried your identification in this novel much too far. Must a Catholic be forbidden to paint the portrait of a lapsed Catholic? . . . I suggest that if you read the book again you will find in the dialogue between the doctor and Querry at the end the suggestion that Querry's lack of faith was a very superficial one – far more superficial than the doctor's atheism. If people are so impetuous as to regard this book as a recantation of faith, I cannot help it. Perhaps they will be surprised to see me at Mass.
>
> What I have disliked in some [particularly French] Catholic criticism of my work . . . is the confusion between the functions of a novelist and the functions of a moral teacher or theologian. I prefer the statement of Newman. 'I say, . . . if Literature is to be made a study of human nature, you cannot have a Christian literature. It is a contradiction in terms to attempt the sinless Literature of sinful man. You may gather together something very great and high, something higher than any Literature ever was; and when you have done so, you will find that it is not Literature at all.'
>
> I will match your quotations from Browning with Bishop Blougram:
>
> All we have gained then by our unbelief,
> Is a life of doubt diversified by faith,
> For one of faith diversified by doubt:

7. Unpublished TLS from Graham Greene, 4 January 1961, from C6 Albany, W1; BL.
8. 5 January 1961; *Letters*, pp. 559–60.

We called the chess board white, – we call it black.[9]

Waugh had effectively described Greene as a Lost Leader, after Browning's criticism of Wordsworth. 'You may well ask, what about Graham Greene's Christmas story?' he wrote to Diana Cooper.

> Is he Morin? He has now produced a novel with a precisely similar character – distinguished Papist who has lost his Faith and is disgusted with those who still look on him as a leader.... His alienist Dr Strauss kicked the bucket last week. No one to keep an eye on him now.[10]

As Waugh had faced the prospect of two of his children entering mixed marriages, this literary skirmish had wounded him and probably coloured the exegetical tone of his work in progress, 'The Death Wish'. In his early days, fighting Oldmeadow over *Black Mischief*,[11] he would have agreed with Greene and Newman. 'Literature', Waugh had stated only four months earlier, 'is simply the appropriate use of language.'[12] The Wodehouse broadcast defended his art on precisely these grounds. In his last years, however, Waugh came to believe in the need for a 'Christian Literature' and the trilogy was his contribution to it. It was no longer safe to fraternize with the rationalist enemy and bandy debating points. Waugh vigorously promoted the work of Muriel Spark and Angus Wilson. The rest he confined to the dustbin of posterity. '[Iris] Murdoch' he wrote in Driberg's copy of *Unconditional Surrender*, 'is a fraud.... [John] Mortimer must be a prize ass.'[13] But even his family dragged Waugh from his castle to the fringes of these horrors. Teresa Onslow was dubious about becoming a

9. Unpublished TLS from Graham Greene, 6 January 1961, from C6 Albany, W1; BL. Bishop Blougram is the narrator of Browning's dramatic monologue 'Bishop Blougram's Apology'.
10. 21 January 1961; *Letters*, p. 560.
11. Cf. Vol. 1, pp. 338–42.
12. ALS to Ann Fleming, 5 September 1960; *Letters*, p. 548.
13. Unpublished ALS [as dedication], nd [c. 14 October 1961], np [Combe Florey House]. Waugh had generously offered the *Spectator* a free, alternative review of Angus Wilson's *Old Men at the Zoo* (1961) (13 October 1961, 501), in response to Mortimer's review (29 September 1961, 431): '"Many writers," ... [Mortimer] says, "are not very good at anything except writing and the value of their work is often not to be judged by the quality of their thoughts." But writing is the expression of thought. There is no abstract writing. All literature implies moral standards and criticisms – the less explicit the better. Mr. Mortimer's second confusion is in his use of "symbolism". In a novel the symbols are merely the furniture of the story. They are not to be taken allegorically as in *Pilgrim's Progress*. They are not devised consciously, but arise spontaneously in the mood of composition.' Driberg had written (14 October 1961; BL) to pick Waugh up on his discussion of symbolism, citing Murdoch as a writer who alternately irritated and fascinated him by her self-conscious use of symbols. 'Symbols', Waugh replied in his dedication. 'I should have qualified my remarks by saying "good novelists". Murdoch is a fraud. E.g. her bell could not have been rung as she describes it.' Waugh was disingenuous in argument here. He had instructed Mrs Saunders to research the history of the Sword of Stalingrad before beginning *Unconditional Surrender*. Clearly this was a preconceived symbol which did not 'arise spontaneously in the mood of composition'.

Catholic; Bron's *Foxglove* had proved offensive to senior co-religionists;[14] James had drifted into an agnosticism. Only Waugh's Sweet Pig held fast to both Papa and the Faith with the uncritical fidelity he required.

By February 1961 Meg had progressed from clerical duties and relic-sorting at Farm Street to the writing of pamphlet biographies. Waugh kept a watchful eye:

> You will be welcome tomorrow. Your pamphlet [on Nicholas Owen] has the makings of good work. You must do the making. I will try to show you how. I wish to educate you, not to relieve you of labour. You are slipping in your use of pronouns & dependent clauses.[15]

Usually she could decode his affectionate refusals to express love. As the year progressed, however, she became neurotically sensitive to them. Waugh's most famous joke in this vein was to write as 'Teresa Pinfold' to Caraman, knowing that Meg would open the letter in her role as secretary and recognize the handwriting:

> Your Reverence,
> ... I have a daughter to whom I was tenderly attached and who in her youth seemed to reciprocate my affection.... She took to the use of tobacco & spirits, fell into low company and ... has repeatedly had to be rescued from debt. Her appearance is slatternly. She gave up writing to me....
> ... I ... [prayed] that I might become detached from her and indifferent to her ingratitude & lack of natural affection. This petition has been answered. I no longer have the wish to visit her....[16]

Meg did not laugh:

> Darling Papa,
> You know I love you more than anyone in the world. Please don't stop loving me. I couldn't bear it. You didn't mean that letter seriously, did you? ... it's made me dreadfully unhappy....

14. Cf. unpublished ALS from Douglas Woodruff, 13 July 1960, from 10 Evelyn Mansions, Carlisle Place, SW1; BL: '... we found the first part very entertaining but I have written to him to urge him not to publish it as it stands, but to re-write part 3. I don't suppose he will take such counsel, and if he does the burden will fall on you ... it is going to damage him to make his debut with these episodes of cold cruelty....'
15. Unpublished ALS to Margaret Waugh, nd [20 February 1961?], from Combe Florey House; private collection.
16. 5 April 1961; *Letters*, pp. 564–5. Waugh had earlier written as Teresa Pinfold defending *Foxglove* in the *Catholic Herald*. 'How nice of Miss Pinfold,' Bron responded, '– she must be an awfully good old girl – she always says such sensible things in her letters' (unpublished ALS, nd [1961?], from the *Daily Telegraph*; BL).

> Papa I'll give up living in London and come home for good if you like. I don't love any of my friends here a quarter as much as I love you. . . .[17]

Waugh grew anxious. Was the poor girl losing her sense of humour? Confidential reports ran between father and Father. Assured by Caraman that Meg's 'childish qualities' concealed 'soundness of judgement',[18] Waugh administered more slaps:

> Darling,
>
> What are you up to? Your mother got the impression ... that you intend to spend next week-end in a cottage ... unchaperoned. That won't do. I do not suspect you of fornication.... It is a matter of manners not morals. Well born, well brought up girls do not stay away with young men and well born, well brought up young men don't expect them to or respect them if they do.
>
> Your week-ends should either be spent in London resting & improving your mind at art galleries, or staying in respectable houses, or at home. . . .[19]

For a vivacious young woman in 1961, Waugh's Victorian etiquette proved stressful. Meg was caught between living as her friends did and paternal disapproval. Bron and Teresa had broken free but at a certain expense (as far as Waugh was concerned) of loyalty. Meg's fidelity to her father was absolute. The only course was a diplomatic silence about her social life, and the result was guilt.

As the correction continued, her depression increased: '. . . Please don't be cross with me because I can't bear it – life is already so bleak at the moment if you and Mummy were cross too it would be last straw for this old camel. . . .'[20] Papa wrote again to Caraman. 'Certainly', he replied, 'I have been worried about Meg's health. She is not sufficiently robust to work here ... and then go to parties four or five evenings during the week, staying up to midnight and after.'[21] Waugh proposed removing her temporarily from the relics and the flesh-pots. The *Mail* had offered a jaunt to British Guiana. If Caraman could do without her for a couple of months, Waugh intended taking her (on expenses) as his 'secretary'. Caraman approved. In the meantime, he said, he would pay her fare to Rome, where he wished her to work on the archives of the English College for her next

17. Unpublished ALS from Margaret Waugh, 6 April 1961, from 31 Farm Street, W1; BL.
18. Unpublished ALS from Fr Philip Caraman, 21 April 1961, from 31 Farm Street, W1; BL.
19. ALS to Margaret Waugh, 12 March 1961, from Combe Florey House; BL; partially reprinted Sykes, p. 454.
20. Unpublished ALS from Margaret Waugh to Evelyn Waugh, 4 September [1961], from 31 Farm Street, W1; BL.
21. Unpublished ALS from Fr Philip Caraman, 13 September 1961, from 31 Farm Street, W1; BL.

pamphlet on Ralph Sherwin. Teresa would be there. Also Caraman. Did Waugh approve? Yes, he did. Meg, perhaps, was not entirely delighted by this prospect. There was an element of her depression too deeply embarrassing to explain to either of her fathers.

*

On 26 November, Waugh and his Pig set sail for the West Indies. The ship, large and comfortable, bore the same name as that on which he and She-Evelyn had embarked for their honeymoon: the *Stella Polaris*. It was an odd and possibly unnerving coincidence since Waugh was in the process of researching his early life. As soon as the trilogy was complete, he had arranged a lucrative contract for his autobiography.[22] That, he hoped, would see him out. And as he gratefully watched the shores of England sink behind him, he prepared for another kind of honeymoon with his daughter.

Corresponding with his friends for permission to write about them, Waugh had heard more stories of decline and fall. Maimie, alcoholic, jobless, agnostic and divorced, occupied a basement flat littered with scrapbooks. Nancy's eyes were failing and she had abandoned writing fiction. Diana Cooper had returned from Paris and lived in reduced circumstances in London's Little Venice. She felt 'posthumous' and, like Connolly, was clinically depressed. Powell and Betjeman were successful but distant. Duggan, despite his friend's unstinting promotion, scarcely scraped a living from writing and Waugh had no wish to visit him. Like Meg, her father was in search of martyrs. Unlike her, he did not discover any. The 'canonization' of Knox had backfired. Even the Wodehouse affair had, to some extent, blown up in Waugh's face. The enemies he needed were no longer 'huge and hateful, all disguise cast off'. After aiming his howitzer at the *Daily Mirror*'s 'Cassandra' (William Connor) as the principal rogue in Wodehouse's defamation, Waugh must have been alarmed by a letter from his hero: 'I'm a bit concerned about this TV [radio] appearance of yours on July 15. I've just ... [heard] that you ... [are] going to make an attack on Cassandra.... And the embarrassing thing (to me) is that for several years past he and I have been great friends.'[23] Were there no good, brave causes left?

22. Cf. unpublished ALS from A. D. Peters to Evelyn Waugh, 27 April 1961; BL: 'I told ... [C. D. Hamilton, Director of *ST*] that you intended to write your autobiography in three volumes ... at two-yearly intervals. He said he was willing to buy the rights in each for five thousand pounds ... five instalments of each volume ... about twenty-five thousand words.... I am confident that we can get not less than £3,000 advance [from publishers], probably more. That would make £9,000 minimum. Little, Brown should pay $5,000 per volume, making £5,000. It is therefore safe to assume that the three volumes will bring in over £29,000 – say £5,000 a year for six years....'
23. Unpublished TLS from P. G. Wodehouse, 10 May 1961, from Remsenburg, NY; BL.

Waugh headed out into the empty ocean. The ship was half-full of elderly English and Swedes. Meg spent most of her first days aboard asleep like a cat. When she woke, she played Bingo with Papa, smoked cigars, drank schnapps and became the object of the ship's doctor's infatuation. Waugh's only discomfort was sleeplessness. On rolling seas beyond the Channel his bottle of paraldehyde had smashed. He took his pleasures sadly but he was happy enough, anxious only about one piece of unfinished business.

In September, Handasyde Buchanan, the manager of Heywood Hill's bookshop, had received Waugh's instructions to make some discreet enquiries about manuscript sales. By this stage Waugh was the legal owner of almost none of the portable property in Combe Florey. Furniture, paintings, silver – just about everything had been sold to the Trust. He had, however, one last resource. 'Look for the report in the *Times* on 13th,' he instructed Laura from mid-Atlantic, 'and telegraph if we were successful.'[24] A large, calf-bound volume had been sent to Sotheby's. As Waugh was winding up his literary estate, he began to dispose of its beginning. Collectors noted with interest that the manuscript of *Rossetti* was to be auctioned.

*

Connolly's review of *Tourist* had been uncomfortably perceptive. Waugh well knew how 'revisiting the places where one has felt becomes a substitute for feeling'. He had never travelled with Connolly's passion for landscape or women; nor did he suffer from (or suffer) Cyril's sentimental humanism. He had, nevertheless, always travelled – even in Rhodesia – to write books. Now, here he was, a plump, silver-haired paterfamilias chinking glasses with his favourite daughter over shipboard dinners and hating himself and the world for not being what they once were. Waugh had over five years of life left but less than two years of living. This was to be his last adventure.

He had prepared for it with something approaching geniality, delighted that the *Mail* should finance him so grandly. British Guiana was seeking independence. Prince Philip planned to visit the country. Waugh assumed his brief to be that of a senior commentator. Certainly his editor was deferential and other jaggers had emerged who might save him from writing the histories of insurance companies. After a lengthy pause in their friendship, Pamela Berry (Lady Hartwell) had begun to court him again with the offer of an honour he had long coveted: a place on the board of Madam Tussauds. As the wife of the Editor and Chairman of the *Daily Telegraph*, 'Pamberry' could grease the wheels of lucrative contracts. If Waugh had henceforth to earn his living as exhibit or sage, he could do

24. Unpublished ALS to Laura Waugh, 5 December 1961, on board *Stella Polaris*; BL.

worse, he thought, than to die beyond his means at the expense of national newspapers.

Shortly before leaving, he had lunched with Lady Hartwell and, among others, Stephen Spender. It was the first time they had met after more than twenty years of Waugh's literary abuse. Their hostess perhaps anticipated an amusing confrontation. But no: 'The conversation was extremely agreeable ... nothing ... acrimonious. So pleasant was it that we went on conversing till rather late.'[25] Unfortunately for the poet, this was not the end of the story.

'As I was taking my leave, E. W. suddenly remembered that he had not taken his watch to Garrards to be repaired.' There was now no time to do this before going abroad and Spender kindly offered to run the errand on his way back to the *Encounter* office. Outside, he realized how late it was.

> So I decided to take it ... the next day .... That evening my wife and I were giving a party. One of the guests, a painter, asked whether he might bring a friend.... The friend was a good-looking blond youth of somewhat suspect appearance. He helped my wife wash up the dishes, and she told me [afterwards] that he had commented on our silver [as] the 'real thing' which rather amused us. I remembered vaguely that after dinner this guest had wandered around the house. I woke at 6 a.m. and suddenly thought: 'My God! Evelyn's watch!' I ran down to my study and looked in the right-hand drawer of my desk.... The watch was gone.
>
> Later I rang my friend ... explaining what had happened. I said that if it had been my watch I would not have made a fuss, but that as it was E.W.'s we must move heaven and earth to recover it. I also rang my friend Frank Norman, ex-Borstal boy ... and a very talented writer, who was familiar with the Soho underworld and asked for his co-operation ... which, at risk to himself, he provided. Two or three days later, the front door bell ... rang, the blond young man got out of a taxi, produced the watch (which was by now sensationally broken) and said: 'Someone played a dirty trick on me the other night, slipping this into my pocket as I left your party.' Enormously relieved, I took the watch without asking any questions.[26]

Embarrassment quickly doubled. Spender instructed Garrards to post the bill to him and the watch to Waugh. They posted both to Waugh. Eventually, Spender managed to retrieve the bill and settle the matter honourably, but not before Ann Fleming had abused his confidence.

25. Unpublished TLS from Sir Stephen Spender to Martin Stannard, 3 January 1988, from 15 Loudoun Road, St John's Wood, NW8 OLS.
26. *Ibid.*

The story nicely illustrates the metropolitan malice on which Waugh had once thrived but which he was beginning to find distasteful. Any joke against the 'fuddy-duddies' – Spender, Alastair Forbes, Lucian Freud, Francis Bacon, Quennell, etc. – who dined regularly at Ann's Victoria Square house was received gratefully. Gossip spiced Waugh's solitude. But in old age he grew increasingly cautious of society's whispering gallery. In the 1960s he was a receiver rather than a transmitter. He did not snap up Mrs Fleming's bait and spread calumny about Spender. Indeed, on his return from British Guiana, he was furious to discover that a garbled version of the story had reached the papers. The tuft-hunting rivalry between the Berry and Fleming *salons* now bored him. Betrayals of confidence irritated his sense of chivalry. The gratuitous infliction of pain was no longer amusing.

Spender, 'realising that Ann ... would be greatly tickled',[27] retailed his saga as a story against himself. She immediately betrayed him by writing to Waugh:

> You refuse to meet Fuddy duddy riff raff here, but at Lady Mul-Berry's house you entrust the first fuddy duddy with an object of value. Poor Stephen has the same craven desire to please you as Connolly and Quennell ... by a miserable chance he was entertaining beatniks to dinner. Francis Bacon brought along some friend from Clapham Common ... Stephen hates unpleasantness and the poor creature was forced to [go to] Francis's studio and threaten police action if the objects were not returned.... See you in Jamaica.[28]

Waugh would have received this before departure but, much to Ann's annoyance, he did not look her up when he and Margaret were staying in Jamaica with Charles D'Costa. Ian and Ann together were strong poison, their marriage a wreck. He had a mistress on the island whom he refused not to visit. Ann's pleas for him to resist smoking, drinking and adultery were ignored. Ill, irascible and driven by the demon of the huge success of his novels, he found her demands claustrophobic. He had married her, he said, because she had 'the heart of a drum majorette'[29] but her remorseless gaiety now often fought for breath in his company. She hated Goldeneye and wanted him to sell it. He worshipped the place and would isolate himself there to hammer out what Ann termed his 'pornography'. Under these circumstances, she must have hungered for Waugh's visit. He felt happier (and Meg was safer) in more stately surroundings with Lord and Lady Hailes.

27. *Ibid.*
28. Unpublished ALS from Ann Fleming, 21 November [1961], from 16 Victoria Square, SW1; BL.
29. ALS from Ann Fleming to Clarissa Avon (Countess of Avon), 30 January [1963]; *LAF*, p. 322.

Waugh was fifty-eight, Meg nineteen. 'It is tedious for the young', he wrote six months later, 'to be constantly reminded what finer fellows their fathers were and what a much more enjoyable time we had. But there you are; we were and we did.'[30] Bron was restive under such patronage. Meg relished it. She was always attracted to older men and with Papa in sprightly mood they were like lovers. The trip was in part a performance for her benefit: an introduction to the dangerous tracks of his youth – both as a gesture of intimacy and as a demonstration that there was life in the old dog yet. None of his other children was ever invited to travel with him. He had promised luxury and hardship – 'real' travel as he had known it in 1932–3. From Georgetown he hoped to trek by mule to the interior and even did a little light training astride a barrel at Combe Florey.[31] By the time they left, however, any lingering illusions about the stimulations of rough life ahead had been dispelled.

Waugh had written to Fr Mather, then seventy-four and the oldest Jesuit in the colony. He remained the same vital, conscientious craftsman. His reply was jubilant and welcoming. It nevertheless daubed a gloomy brush across Waugh's memories. British Guiana was vastly changed. Between the Mission[32] and Boa Vista, a large industrial settlement had sprung up. Its airport and 'hotel' were only a mile distant. Everyone travelling to and from Georgetown now went by air. Barbed-wire fencing criss-crossed the savannah and, on a network of roads, Land Rovers bowled through the wasteland which in 1933 had almost cost Waugh his life. American tourists arrived with depressing frequency and bought fancy shopping bags. Politically the country was unsettled. No longer a Crown Colony, it was self-governing, and the Prime Minister, Dr Jagan, was a Marxist. His People's National Congress Party was agitating for sovereignty and black supremacy, organizing demonstrations against the Chinese immigrants and the British. Fr Mather did not like it. Neither did Waugh. There was small opportunity here for recapturing the wildness of his youth.

Although his hopes of mules and riots were disappointed, he was at least glad to be away for Christmas (Laura was giving a ball and the D'Arms family were visiting). Meg and he spent almost a fortnight with the Haileses. 'I wonder who can have told Frankie [Donaldson] that it was not nice to stay here,' he wrote home.

30. 'First Faltering Steps – 1. Drinking', in *The Compleat Imbiber -6: An Entertainment*, ed. Cyril Ray (Vista Books, 1963); *EAR*, pp. 609–11. The article was sent to Peters c. 10 July 1962; cf. *Catalogue* E1267, p. 274.

31. 'Travels with a Mule', *S. Tel.*, 26 November 1961, 28.

32. Fr Mather had returned to St Ignatius's Mission at his own request in January 1955 after a period in Georgetown.

> Only Mr. Gaikskill [*sic*], I think.... It is a lap of luxury – delicious food, flowing wine, in ones bedroom not only three sorts of bath essence but also eye lotion, Eno's fruit salt, bay rum, new toothbrushes. Huge private verandah to ones bedder. Margaret has Princess Margaret's suite and is cock-a-hoop.... Last night she was taken by the ADCs to a night club. The Haileses are not intellectual but kind & gay.[33]

And so it continued: a cossetted, VIP tour as they were passed along a chain of benevolent government officers. In British Guiana they spent ten days in Georgetown 'with Meg in indifferent health asleep most of the day. People have asked us out a lot but they are not really very interesting people.'[34] A brief visit to the north-west district of the interior was arranged with an elaborate sequence of aeroplanes, launches and jeeps. The trip was exhausting but dull. Waugh made the most of it in his *Mail* article,[35] but his letters tell the true story:

> We flit about ... and live in luxurious guest houses [he wrote to Laura], but I am awfully bored at seeing welfare activities. It is like being Princess Margaret.... We had tea with Dr Jagan & his sinister communist adviser.... I am very well. Meg is exhausted. Her chief interest is sun tan – most unbecoming of her.[36]

Apart from two attacks of nausea, only one thing had pulled him up sharply. In Georgetown he had discovered a copy of *Time* magazine with a 'silly' review of *Unconditional Surrender*[37] accompanied by 'that fatal July 1st photograph. Nothing in the tropics has been as hot as that gruesome wedding.'[38]

This now famous image haunted him for the rest of his life. On Bron's wedding day, a cameraman had caught Waugh and Laura in the street. He appeared gross and bilious in tail-coat and top hat. A pudgy left hand grasped the ear trumpet. His shoes sparkled in the sunshine. Laura, three paces behind, wore a smart spotted dress and an expression of melancholy isolation. On first seeing the picture, Waugh had been so shocked that, for some weeks, he had dieted with Lenten ferocity. He could not bear to be ugly. 'Darling Papa,' Meg had written, '... Don't be depressed about that

33. Unpublished ALS to Laura Waugh, 13 December [1961], from Governor-General's House, Trinidad; BL.
34. Unpublished ALS to Laura Waugh, 22 January [1962], from Hotel Tower, Georgetown; BL.
35. Cf. 'Here They Are, the English Lotus-Eaters ...', *DM*, 20 March 1962, 10; *EAR*, pp. 583–6.
36. 12 January [1962]; *Letters*, pp. 580–1.
37. 'A Class War', *Time*, 19 January 1962, 84. The American title of *Unconditional Surrender* was *The End of the Battle*.
38. Unpublished ALS to Laura Waugh, 22 January [1962], *op. cit.*

photograph you don't really look like that. Lord Beaverbrook distorted it on purpose.'[39]

*

In mid-February, father and daughter returned in high spirits with a consignment of baby alligators. While waiting for the *Antilles* in Trinidad, they had paid another happy visit to the Haileses, and at Combe Florey this ebullient mood continued. The *Express* reported:

> Evelyn Waugh is home from his nostalgic mule-trip to South America – terrifying his guests with a new after-dinner game . . . called 'Pencil and Paper'. Eight or ten players each write down a word, then the whole collection is handed to one competitor who has to stand up and compose a short story introducing all the words. . . . Mr. Waugh revels in the whole thing. He leaps to his feet and produces the most enthralling stories. Not all his guests share his enthusiasm.[40]

Ann Fleming soon killed this brief felicity.

She had flown home alone from Jamaica after bitter rows with Ian while, incongruously in the background, *Dr No* was being filmed. Quennell and Spender had visited Goldeneye, offering what solace they could. Inevitably, the talk had turned to Evelyn. 'Stephen . . .', she wrote, 'was told at one of the government houses where you narrowly missed each other that you had made much play with your ear trumpet and had invited Meg to tell you later of what the Governor spoke. The Governor was not hoodwinked.'[41] This apparently harmless tattle sowed a seed of self-doubt which finally broke Waugh's spirit.

In March, Lady Hartwell threw a grand London party which Waugh attended. He was having trouble with the *Mail*, who were effectively refusing to print his opinions on British Guiana, claiming that he had misunderstood his brief and commissioning instead light articles on pleasure-cruising and etiquette.[42] He saw this as a blow both to honour and

39. Unpublished ALS from Margaret Waugh, nd [July 1961], from 31 Farm Street, W1; BL.
40. 'Waugh Tests Guests', *DE*, 27 February 1962.
41. 11 March 1962; *LAF*, p. 304.
42. 'Here They Are, . . .', *op. cit.*; 'Manners and Morals', *DM*, 12 April 1962, 12; *EAR*, pp. 587–90; 'Manners and Morals – 2', *DM*, 13 April 1962, 10; *EAR*, pp. 590–2. Waugh had posted an article home 'about the places the Duke of E. will visit' (unpublished ALS to Laura Waugh, 22 January [1962], *op. cit.*). On his return he discovered that the Editor of the *Mail* had changed and that the new man (Gordon Mackenzie) appeared uncertain as to why the paper had dispatched this novelist to the tropics. On 2 March Waugh had submitted two articles: one on pleasure-cruising, the other on British Guiana. A month later, the *Mail* still seemed to be dragging its heels. They had happily printed the first piece ('Here They Are, . . .', *op. cit.*). The serious, political article, however, was savagely cut to expunge Waugh's personal reflections. He was so dismayed by the galley proof that he encouraged Peters to withdraw from the contract and place the piece elsewhere. This he did – cf. 'Return to Eldorado', *ST*, 12 August 1962, 17; *EAR*, pp. 592–6 – and also ensured that Waugh did not have to return any commission. Cf. *Letters*, pp. 583–4.

self-esteem. Doubtless he wanted to investigate alternative employment with the *Telegraph*. But there were other attractions to draw him from his lair. Nancy would be at the party; also Anthony and Violet Powell; also Ann.

He arrived drunk after six hours in White's with something already weighing heavily on his mind.

> I was sitting in the hall at 7pm [he explained afterwards to Nancy] being no trouble to anyone, when a man ... came up & said: 'Why are you alone?' 'Because no one wants to speak to me.' 'I can tell you exactly why. Because you sit there on your arse looking like a stuck pig.' That, added to a letter from Clarissa to Ann saying that the Haileses in Trinidad, whom I thought I charmed, found me a frightful bore, and Debo's idea that I am a counter-hon have worked to produce strong Pinfold feelings of persecution.[43]

This was no joke, as Nancy immediately sensed. She had thought he looked ill:

> ... what makes Ann *tell* you that some friend of an expatriate ... finds you a bore? The very last thing anyone could reproach you with.... The English must have a deep sense of insecurity to behave like this. I despise them & am far too thin-skinned to live among them.[44]

But it was no good. He would hear nothing against Ann. The truth was the truth and she appeared to be an accurate reporter. Her revelation was seen as an act of loyalty. 'I must explain about boring the Haileses', he replied, 'because it has been what young people call "traumatic"':

> ... The crucial point is that I was confident they both enjoyed my visit.... I talked loud & long & they laughed like anything. Now I find I bored them. Well of course everyone is a bore to someone. One recognizes that. But it is a ghastly thing if one loses the consciousness of being a bore. You do see it means I can never go out again.[45]

In future he preferred to dine only in intimate gatherings, preferably *à deux* with Diana Cooper and, although they rarely saw each other, it was at this point that she re-emerged as a regular confidante.

*

43. 27 March 1962; *Letters*, pp. 582–3. Mrs Fleming's letter had arrived at the height of the *Mail* crisis (cf. *Diaries*, 14 March 1962, p. 786). Waugh had recently stayed with the Duchess of Devonshire ['Debo'] at Edenson House, near Chatsworth, where the Devonshires lived from 1947 to 1959. He had been shocked by her switching on the television during dinner (cf. *Letters*, p. 585).
44. Unpublished ALS from Nancy Mitford, 29 March 1962, from 7 Rue Monsieur, Paris VII; BL.
45. ALS to Nancy Mitford, mid-April 1962; *Letters*, pp. 584–5.

As one door opened, another slammed sharply in his face. During that summer, Waugh had been negotiating for a portrait of himself and Meg, suggesting, rather to Peter Greenham's surprise, that he should paint them separately (in Somerset and London) on the same canvas. Greenham was a portraitist of royalty, currently at work on the Queen and Prince Philip. Waugh sought the best record of his love that money could buy.[46] In the face of so many betrayals, he felt closer to Meg than ever. 'Don't be a sulky bitch about your work at Farm Street,' he scolded her.

> Everyone works under criticism. It is very vulgar and unChristian to resent it. You must cure yourself of your preference for the second-rate. The first-rate are always critical and criticized. It is also very WRONG to talk of it being time you had a new job as you might say its time for a new hat. Change for the sake of change is wanton. You are fickle and capricious and feckless. But I love you.[47]

He lived for her visits amid a dismal clutter of local social engagements. She was not simply bored but irritated by the attitude of some of her colleagues. Since January, Hatty had joined the team as general dogsbody and she and Meg formed a unit. Both were disliked by some of the older members of staff. Meg also complained that she felt deserted by Bron. All the time, however, she was circling another, larger problem which she could not discuss with her father. The portrait, perhaps, was Waugh's way of jerking her from despondency. It was never painted. A fortnight later she told him her secret: she was in love and wanted to be married.

If Ann Fleming broke Waugh's spirit, Meg broke his heart. This was the end of his 'living'. 'As head of the family,' he informed Alec, 'you should know before the official announcement that . . . Margaret has contracted to marry an Irishman who hopes to be something in the city. The wedding will take place before Advent.'[48] That was all. Waugh was stunned, embittered, jealous and ashamed of these unworthy emotions. Meg had been conducting this liaison before leaving for British Guiana but had said nothing. In retrospect, the trip must have seemed less like the elaborate gift he had imagined, more like her valediction. The logistics of patronage had been reversed, as they had with the Haileses.

46. Downing College, Cambridge, had recently commissioned Greenham's famous portrait of one of Waugh's arch-enemies, F. R. Leavis for £300. Greenham met Waugh once, at the Royal Academy banquet, and was introduced to him in front of the Leavis portrait. 'What a very extraordinary picture,' Waugh remarked. Greenham was puzzled. 'What's extraordinary about it?' 'You've made him look like an intelligent man' [unpublished ALS from Peter Greenham to Martin Stannard, 18 October 1987, from the Old Dairy, Charlton-on-Otmoor, nr Oxford].
47. Unpublished ALS to Margaret Waugh, 15 July 1962, from Combe Florey House; private collection.
48. Unpublished ALS to Alec Waugh, 4 August 1962, from Combe Florey House; HRC.

In early August, Meg brought her fiancé to Combe Florey. Waugh eyed him up and produced a brave and impeccable imitation of *bonhomie*.

> I haven't really thanked you properly [she wrote on her return] for being so kind about my engagement. You are the best father anyone can ever have had in the history of the world – really no flattery or sucking up I think that. And there need be no divorce between us – I will come home just as often for week ends – Giles won't mind.[49]

'Divorce' was not too strong a word. Waugh knew that her promise was as futile as it was well-intentioned. Their intimacy was over. And when he had taken time to draw breath, he explained the situation to Diana Cooper:

> She has fallen head over heels for an Irishman, 27 years old, short, rather oriental in face, raffish, penniless, a stock-broker's clerk of ten days' experience, but a gentleman and a Catholic – name Giles FitzHerbert.[50] . . . Meg is bird-happy. . . . Let her enjoy it quick before the Light of Common Day.[51]

Shades of the prison house. Waugh's confidantes dealt delicately with the situation. 'Do I congratulate you?' Nancy asked.[52] 'My darling Bo', wrote Diana Cooper,

> – my heart shakes for you. Comes the time that I have so often dreaded for you – a time that I have known myself when one must deliver one's treasure to another with a show of generous aproval [*sic*]. . . . Age overpowers – my legs hurt wickedly. . . . I'm too ugly to strip for bathing. . . .[53]

Even Ann Fleming counterfeited sympathy: 'I condole with you on Margaret's engagement not because of her choice but because you will miss her dreadfully. . . . Did she meet him on a scoffing party? I imagine you will give her a splendid wedding, the Brompton Oratory followed by a ball at the Ritz.'[54]

To Lady Diana alone Waugh expressed his banked-up misery:

49. Unpublished ALS from Margaret Waugh, 7 August [1962], from 31 Farm Street, W1; BL.
50. Giles FitzHerbert (b. 1935) joined the Foreign Office in 1966 and is currently British Ambassador to Venezuela.
51. 16 August [1962]; *Letters*, pp. 590–1. The allusion is, of course, not so much to Wordsworth as to the second volume of Lady Diana's memoirs (1959), which concluded with the outbreak of the Second World War.
52. Unpublished ALS from Nancy Mitford, 22 August 1962, from 7 Rue Monsieur, Paris VII; BL.
53. ALS from Lady Diana Cooper, nd [25 August 1962?], from Ca' Leone Giudecca, Venice; BL; *MWMS*, p. 293.
54. 28 August [1962]; *LAF*, p. 316, 'Scoffers' in Waugh–Fleming parlance seems to have signified 'irreverent youths'.

> Your letter full of understanding. It is, to me, a bitter pill and ungilded. I would forbid the marriage if I had any other cause than jealousy & snobbery. As it is, I pretend to be complaisant. Little Meg is ripe for the kind of love I can't give her. So I am surrendering with the honours of war – without war indeed. The wedding will be at the end of October. . . . They will make all arrangements. I have given them a meagre sum of money & said spend it on trousseau or linen or festifications with bad champagne & photographers, just as you please. I will, of course, go to the church – not, I think, to any subsequent party. . . . You see I feel that with Meg I have exhausted my capacity for finding objects of love. How does one exist without them? I haven't got the Gaiety euphoria that makes old men chase tarts. My ghastly brother calls them 'pipe-lines' through which he is refuelled with youth. Not for me. . . .[55]

The 'meagre sum' was £1,000 he could ill-afford. His way of dealing with the crisis was to sublimate his feelings in his last comic fiction. 'Do you remember books I wrote about a character called "Basil Seal". . .?', he asked Lady Diana. 'I suddenly yesterday began a story about Basil Seal at 60. Jolly good so far.'[56]

When it appeared, over a year later and just before his own sixtieth birthday, his friends remarked upon certain similarities. 'I think [Basil] liked his daughter too much to want her to marry at all,' John Betjeman wrote, 'and also think that if she had to . . . marry he wanted her to marry someone rich.'[57] Nancy added:

> I don't believe young people today would care a fig [about marrying a relation] & NOR WOULD BASIL SEAL – but the trouble is Prod has turned into you & this falsifies everything. It is a great mistake . . . because never the twain could meet & its wrong to try to make them. . . . I don't believe however rich Seal was that he would have become that sort of good citizen, or broken his daughter's heart over such a silly quibble. Or was he meant to be jealous? If so we are in deep waters indeed.[58]

Waugh's reply was abrupt:

> Your odious letter was . . . [a] sharp reminder that my powers are fading and that I am a bore. All you say, I refute. . . . Old people are more interesting than young. One of the peculiar points of interest is

55. 28 August [1962]; *Letters*, p. 593.
56. *Ibid.*
57. Unpublished ALS from (Sir) John Betjeman, 23 October 1963, from Treen, Trebetherick, Wadebridge, Cornwall; BL.
58. Unpublished ALS from Nancy Mitford, 26 October 1963, from 7 Rue Monsieur, Paris VII; BL.

> to observe how after 50 they revert to the habits, mannerisms and opinions of their parents, however wild they were in youth. I see it on all sides as well as in myself.... Of course Basil was fiercely jealous.[59]

Waugh had just completed the chapter of his autobiography dealing with his father when Meg had revealed her love for FitzHerbert. Indeed, Waugh covered the expense of his gift with the fee for a rewritten version of the chapter for the *Sunday Telegraph*'s 'Father and Son' series. In that, he offered for the first time a sympathetic description of Arthur. The only sensible relationship between parent and child, Waugh suggested, was that between host and guest.[60] 'Those who most reprobate and ridicule their fathers ...', he noted in his diary, 'were not fathers themselves.'[61] McDougall referred to the short story as Waugh's 'pot of Basil', and the irony of the allusion was precise. With Meg's marriage that autumn, his literary vocation was truncated.

Ultimately, Waugh could not deny Meg his presence at the reception, which, according to Alec, was a joyous occasion.[62] But the celebrations also marked for Waugh a watershed in his relation to the Church. As his daughter set off dressed as a jockey for her honeymoon in Portofino, the Second Vatican Council was concluding three years of painful deliberation.

Waugh was not alone in feeling bereaved. Thanking Fr Caraman for his wedding address, he added:

> You have been a wonderful friend to ... [her], all the time unobtrusively standing between her and malign influences. I don't expect to be in London much this winter. If you ever feel the need of a quiet retreat from your office Laura & I would so love it if you came here.[63]

Did he sense the priest's depression? Caraman's feelings for Meg were entirely pure but nevertheless passionate. He loved her. Meg and Waugh had often joked about this 'crush'. It seemed to them deliciously innocent. Her marriage, however, had introduced a new, and awkward, factor – a husband. Between them, Waugh and Caraman had been inclined to bandy her about as a prize possession, asking each other, rather than her, whether she might do this or that. This patronage revoked, the two men shared a sense of loss which obliquely strengthened their regret over the proposed changes in the Church.

59. 29 October 1963; *Letters*, p. 614.
60. 'My Father', *S. Tel.*, 2 December 1962, 4–5.
61. *Diaries*, [October–December 1962], p. 790. Davie reads: 'ridicule their fellows'.
62. Unpublished ALS from Alec Waugh, 21 October 1962, from The Athenaeum, Pall Mall, SW1; BL.
63. Unpublished ALS to Fr Philip Caraman, 23 October 1962, from Combe Florey House; private collection.

In Caraman's case, however, there was a third, and perhaps more pressing, aspect of his discomfort, again connected with Meg. After her fortnight in Italy, she had returned, jubilant, to set up house in Westbourne Grove. Her happiness was infectious. Saturdays would often be spent with Giles, patrolling the Portobello Road in search of gruesome additions to their collection of 'stuffed scaley things': a tortoise, a crocodile, a dilapidated lizard and a rearing cobra decorated their flat.[64] During the working week, she was back with Hatty among the martyrs in Farm Street, sublimely unaware, it seems, that Caraman was approaching a nervous breakdown. In the office, resentment against the priest's favouritism had hardened into accusations of malpractice. Meg's ebullient presence and his obviously tender affection for her merely salted the wound.

Shortly after her return, Caraman took Waugh up on his offer. He needed, he said, a few days' rest. He was making disastrous mistakes at work and losing his judgment of

> persons and situations.... If nothing is said outside the house, I have no scruple in saying Mass at Combe Florey. (I could bring with me all that is needed.) Jesuits have this privilege, but the Bishops can make difficulties over it.... I have had a fascinating letter from Fr. Basset in Rome describing scenes at the Council. The accidental results of the meeting will be far greater than the intended ones....[65]

And so a pattern was established which was to prove the greatest consolation of Waugh's declining years. In Caraman he found a kindred spirit, a literary man of the Old Faith, equally comfortable with the laughter of the dinner table and the silences of monastic reflection. His suggestion suited Waugh perfectly. While Caraman was there, neither needed to leave the house. Retrenchment was complete.

*

Caraman's news about the Council was carried by Meg to Somerset[66] and probably spurred Waugh into writing his famous article, 'The Same Again, Please'.[67] If he had surrendered with the honours of war to FitzHerbert, Waugh was not prepared to do the same for the 'liturgists'. But he was in an awkward position. Since Pope John XXIII's election in 1958, Waugh had consistently advertised his support for the man. The previous incumbent, Pius XII, had held office throughout the war and governed the

64. Cf. unpublished ALS from Margaret Waugh to Evelyn Waugh, 6 November 1962, from 31 Farm Street, W1; BL.
65. Unpublished ALS from Fr Philip Caraman, 8 November 1962, from 31 Farm Street, W1; BL.
66. She went down for the week-end, 9–11 November 1962, shortly after Fr Caraman had come to dinner.
67. *Spectator*, 'The Same Again, Please', 23 November 1962, 785–8; *EAR*, pp. 602–9.

Vatican's awkward relationship with Fascism. It was to him that Waugh had reported about Croatia. Pius XII had fiercely opposed the Communist world, treating its Catholic clergy as solitary heroes of the besieged Faith. This was, of course, close to Waugh's own position at that time. He looked to Pope John, already an old man when elected, to sit tight and do nothing. Oddly, when the new Pope supported reform, Waugh's adulation was scarcely dented. Concordats with hostile governments were sought. Pope John abandoned the traditional reserve of his office and plunged happily about among his flock, visiting schools and hospitals. He was a People's Pope, a man of peasant stock whose pacific grace was an icebreaker in the frozen seas of the Cold War. In short, the moves to democratize the Church which were being discussed by the Council in 1962 had been condoned and effectively reactivated by Pope John, Waugh's 'hero'.

His article was thus quiet in tone, not least because it represented an attack on the 'Priesthood of the Laity' and is manifestly impatient with lay theologians. '. . . I know of none', he wrote, 'whose judgement I would prefer to that of the simplest parish priest.'[68] There were also the difficulties of the Pope's infallibility and the sacramental character of the Church: 'It may seem absurd to speak of "dangers" in the Council when all Catholics believe that whatever is decided in the Vatican will be the will of God.'[69] Nevertheless, dangers he saw and he was determined to speak against them.

Waugh's article casts its net far beyond the confines of strict theological debate. It represents a summation of his religious and social beliefs. The two, indeed, are indistinguishable, but not for the reasons his enemies supposed. Many of his socialist contemporaries might have said: 'You cannot be a Christian and support a hierarchical social order.' Waugh saw the case otherwise: 'A man who grudges a special and higher position to another is very far from being a Christian.'[70]

The whole discussion revolved, for him, around the concept of hierarchy. Moves were afoot to de-mystify the priest's authority, to turn him round during Mass to face his congregation, to replace Latin with vernacular languages, to encourage communal responses. Communion, it was suggested, should become a 'social meal'. And on the back of all this rode a general tendency to ecumenism. The modern scripture movement (of which Knox had been a part) had been fostered by Leo XIII and Pius XII in two encyclicals. Scholars had already scraped away the encrustations of ceremony which had grown slowly since the second century. A plainer, more 'authentic' style of worship was proposed by the liturgists, and the

68. *Ibid.*, p. 606.
69. *Ibid.*, p. 609.
70. *Ibid.*, p. 606.

services of Holy Week had been their first victim. Waugh was in the business of saving what was left.

Certain elements of his argument were predictable: Latin as a *lingua franca*, an abhorrence of any alteration to the liturgy he had always known, a hatred of 'intellectual', essentially rationalist, attacks by the laity on the mystical nature of the priest's office. But the social (and aesthetic) dimension of his argument is new, or rather clearly revealed for the first time. The impulse towards democratization and ecumenism, he implies, had been presented as a mass movement against privilege. He wonders how accurate an assessment this is. In defending hierarchy, he presents himself as 'fairly typical of English Catholics ... of that middle rank of the Church, far from her leaders, much farther from her saints; distinct, too, from the doubting, defiant, despairing souls who perform so conspicuously in contemporary fiction and drama.'[71] The latter category clearly alludes to Greene's work. Waugh was staking his claim here not only as a common man speaking to common men but as an artist addressing his public. As a writer defending Liberty, Diversity, Privacy, he had for years seen an analogy between the craftsman and the priest. And, just as he reviled the artist who attempted to dictate his audience's response, so Waugh insisted upon his right during Mass to be left alone with his God. Waugh preferred the priest's back and the obscure, time-honoured rites. He preferred also to look at the backs of other members of the congregation. The new circular Liverpool Cathedral was designed to bring the congregation, as a body, closer to the altar. Waugh felt that the sight of other faces would obstruct contemplation. His Faith and his art were essentially solitary activities. He was shy of praying aloud and found it repulsive to be dragged into communal worship.

A psychoanalyst might unearth a tangle of 'complexes' and repressions here. He might see the social climber disgusted by the taint of the 'second-rate' he had always struggled to escape; the fierce little snob counterfeiting compassion to defend his élite; the fear of crowds, perhaps agoraphobia; the buried Belladonna complex. There is no end to such speculation. But at the root of Waugh's (admittedly self-contradictory) pronouncements, surely, there is something much simpler and, at the same time, infinitely more complex: the terror of babel. One thing alone, in Waugh's view, kept men sane: the sense of unified, agreed meaning. Ultimately this 'meaning' was God. In temporal terms it was language. The post-structuralist notions of the (almost) infinite plurality of meaning would have been anathema to him. That way lay Picasso and *Finnegans Wake*. He had to see language, and the 'language' of the Church's ritual, as precise instruments. And yet (did he dare to confront this?) this position was logically absurd, and in his

71. *Ibid.*, p. 604.

art and his worship he revolted against it. In both he wished to be free to choose his own 'meanings'.

Waugh's cult of the individual, of course, and his theory of unified meaning, could marry only in a scheme which arrogated authority to selected individuals and privileged their view. This was all very well so long as he was of the elect. But his lifetime's experience had demonstrated conclusively that he was not. Beyond the literary world, few sought his counsel. Most thought him more than slightly mad and mistrusted his ability to maintain confidences. He thus found himself consistently in the schizophrenic condition of professing submission to authority while being simultaneously uncomfortable with its hierarchy. He had experienced exactly this problem with the Church, the aristocracy and the army. He craved membership of clubs, was fascinated by their etiquette and their 'language', observed them with a scrupulousness approaching lunacy, but was too intelligently disruptive (or just plain rude) not to smash up the furniture now and again.

The article, of course, presents its author not as an anarchist but as a temperate traditionalist. With an air of generous melancholy, he dares not instruct but quietly advises:

> To compare small things with great, an artist's 'inspiration' is not a process of passive acceptance of dictation. At work he makes false starts and is constrained to begin again ... so that eventually by trial and error a work of art is consummated. So with the inspired decisions of the Church. They are not revealed by a sudden clear voice from heaven. Human arguments are the means by which the truth eventually emerges. It is not really impertinent to insinuate one more human argument into the lofty deliberations.[72]

Waugh's 'human argument', however, had always been against human argument and it was the final, bitter blow that the Church should have become infected by it. Eighteen months later, after the battle was lost, he wrote in his diary:

> When I first came into the Church I was drawn, not by splendid ceremonies but by the spectacle of the priest as a craftsman. He had an important job to do which none but he was qualified for. He and his apprentice stumped up to the altar with their tools and set to work without a glance to those behind them, still less with any intention to make a personal impression on them.

72. *Ibid.*, p. 609.

> 'Participate' – the cant word – does not mean to make a row [in church] as the Germans suppose. One participates in a work of art when one studies it with reverence and understanding.[73]

The sour taste of failure was rendered all the more disgusting by the fact that, at the outset of his campaign, Waugh had again been encouraged to believe that he *was* of the elect. Advance copies of his article were sent to Rome and warmly received by Bishop Butler,[74] who circulated it in the English College. Peters had sold the piece to the *Spectator*, and Archbishop Heenan[75] wrote immediately from Rome offering his congratulations:

> There is nothing in [it] with which I don't agree. But, what a pity the voice of the laity was not heard sooner. The enthusiasts who write for the *Tablet* & *Catholic Herald* are so easily mistaken for the intelligent & alive Catholics. The real difficulty ... is that the Continentals are twisting themselves inside out to make us look as like as possible to the Protestants. How I wish we could persuade them (a large majority I fear) that to be at home with our Mass and ceremonies is far more important than being right according to the books of liturgical antiquities.[76]

Bishop Dwyer[77] and Jim Utley were equally enthusiastic. Clearly Waugh had raised the morale of the Conciliar latinists at the English College and, inspired by this, he instructed Peters to place the piece in French and German magazines regardless of fee. In America the *National Review* took it and its Editor, William F. Buckley, Jr, soon produced it as a separate pamphlet. Greene wrote offering unequivocal support. The bandwagon was rolling.

*

With something to attack, Waugh was temporarily enlivened. And there were other consolations. Ironically, at a time when he felt artistically exhausted, his stock on the literary market had never been higher. Peters could sell articles for £100 per thousand words and secured an astonishing £3,000 for the British serial rights of *Basil Seal*. Under these circumstances, Waugh felt justified in complaining about the $1,250 *Esquire* paid for the story and complacent about the £2,000 an American autobiographer

73. Easter 1964; *Diaries*, pp. 792–3.
74. The Abbot of Downside who was attending the Council.
75. Then Archbishop of Liverpool; soon after, the Cardinal Archbishop of Westminster.
76. Unpublished ALS from Archbishop Heenan, 25 November 1962, from Venerabile Collegio Inglese, Via Monserrato 45, Roma 227; BL. Heenan added: 'In my Cathedral, by the way, nobody will be looking in anyone else's face.... The High Altar is off centre & there will be no people behind it.' In its original form, Waugh's counterblast was set up in proof as two articles, but the *Spectator* reunited them for publication.
77. Bishop of Leeds.

coughed up for a short preface. Film rights were beginning to move again. Over the next year, Ivan Foxwell bought *Decline and Fall*, Sam Marx repurchased *A Handful of Dust*, and Tony Richardson took over Buñuel's contract for *The Loved One* with a cash adjustment for the author. At these prices, Waugh did not need to work hard and the months before Christmas were spent making only dilatory stabs at *A Little Learning*, obsessively trying to track down his solitary Catholic forebear, Theodosia Mahon.[78] He even entered into the spirit of Meg's menagerie, advertising on his daughter's behalf for stuffed big game, and packed Fr Caraman off to London with a monkey for the collection.

The joke, it seems, went badly wrong, although Meg enjoyed it hugely at first. Offers of beasts poured in. The press besieged her at the Farm Street office. One paper rang up to ask if they could photograph Caraman presenting her with a rhino. This was all good fun – but not to the peevish women whose impatience with the priest's 'connections' now reached new heights. A deputation registered an official complaint and the storm, at last, broke.

Just after Christmas, when Waugh was snowed up in Combe Florey, he received a letter from Meg:

> Darling Papa,
>
> Such terrible, terrible things have happened here.... What they are doing to Fr. Caraman is unbelievable – & he poor saintly darling has no resentment.
>
> He has been threatened with Osterly which is where they send disgraced priests. It all comes from **** (whom everybody hates) who has told Fr. Walsh and the Fr. Provincial
>
> a) That Fr. C. is infatuated/or makes a favourite of/with me & the staff resent it.
>
> b) That Fr. C. is hated by the staff, throws his weight around to [*sic*] much etc.
>
> The second is so ridiculously false that I could get up a petition signed by the whole staff saying we love Fr. C.... About the first – it is clearly true that I am a favourite but only **** really resents it.... And **** has been intriguing for this for months.... Hatty will be out of a job too. Apparently one of ****'s sticks was that Fr. C. employed Hatty because she was your daughter (although at the time

78. Waugh set Joan Saunders of Writer's and Speaker's Research on the trail. All he knew of Theodosia derived from his mother's memories. He had just read Cecil Woodham-Smith's *Great Hunger* and was intrigued by the account (pp. 324–5) of the murder of Major Denis Mahon of Strokestown, Co. Roscommon. Waugh believed Theodosia might be related to the murdered man, rather hoped she was, in order to add colour to his image of her as an alienated figure, clutching secretly to her crucifix. The extant correspondence with Mrs Saunders, however, records only false starts.

he knew of her lack of qualifications ...).... Fr. Caraman thinks I should stay to be sacked....[79]

Waugh received the news benevolently (Giles was in hospital and Meg under strain; she seemed to be suffering another phase of persecution mania) and Papa counselled patience:

It is not unexpected is it? We have often spoken of it in fun.... No good will be done by organizing a mutiny. I should guess that the Superiors in the Society think that too much money is being spent ... and that a much smaller staff could do all that needs doing just as efficiently. They would accordingly welcome an excuse to clear most of you girls out.

Certainly do not give notice. If you have done your work conscientiously you have nothing to reproach yourself with. If Fr. Caraman likes your company and takes you out to meals, that is his business and yours. But if you have taken advantage of his liking for you and shirked work, his distress is partly due to you and the best way you can compensate for it is to work with grim efficiency and punctuality for his successors....[80]

Meg was frenetic:

I must have explained it awfully badly – you have completely misunderstood the whole situation. There is no question of my or Hatty staying on ... they will sack us both but they would prefer us to resign – I think perhaps I ought to come to see you....[81]

By this stage, the priest, sick and desperate, had found his way to Combe Florey, and Waugh's attitude to the business had undergone violent transformation:

He has told me some of the details of his ill-treatment by his superiors. He is, as you know, accepting all with supernatural resignation in the spirit of St. Ignatius.

You, on the other hand have taken no vows of obedience and are entitled to the fair dealing you would expect in any trade. You are no longer my chattel. This is a matter for you and Giles to decide, but my advice ... is to ... get your solicitor to draw up a statement for **** to sign saying 1) that you are leaving ... for personal reasons by your own wish 2) that your work there has always been satisfactory 3) that your conduct there has shown the highest propriety 4) that

79. Unpublished ALS, 9 January 1963, from 31 Farm Street, W1; BL.
80. Unpublished ALS, 10 January [1963], from Combe Florey House; private collection.
81. Unpublished ALS, nd [c. 11 January 1963], from 31 Farm Street, W1; BL.

> ... **** believes any statements he has heard to the contrary of 3) to be false....
>
> If he signs, the paper may be of value to Fr. Caraman to submit to the General in Rome. If he refuses to sign the last two clauses, I think you might scare him by saying that his reluctance can only mean that he accuses you of improper conduct and that your husband insists on vindicating your good name publicly and that the matter will be put into the hands of your solicitor.
>
> So far as the other girls are concerned, I think you will be fully justified in fermenting mutiny.... If **** denies having trafficked in scandal, just say 'Good. I would like that in writing' and present your Magna Charter [*sic*].[82]

It was for Waugh a terrible disappointment. Throughout his Catholic life he had maintained a special admiration for the Jesuits. They represented to him an ideal hierarchy: intellectually rigorous, charitable, stoical. Now, he believed, they were abusing authority. The imputation of impropriety was absurd but none the less damaging and embarrassing for that.

The matter did not end happily. Events moved so quickly that Meg had no time to get a solicitor's draft. Her superior, she said, rang her up in great agitation, requesting an interview:

> He denied absolutely everything & more or less admitted that P.C. had been framed ... that my 'relationship' had nothing to do with it but they were using it as a means 'of getting through to him' that he must go. I said that I was not prepared to be used for getting P.C. out. He begged me not to resign – but I decided ... I must. I am afraid this has probably done Fr. C. more harm.[83]

Certainly it hardened the antagonism of his superiors. Four girls (half the staff) resigned in his support. Before a witness, Caraman was severely reprimanded by Fr Coventry for reading to Meg the section of his letter dealing with the 'relationship'. Caraman asked Waugh to approach Fr D'Arcy with a letter which could be forwarded to Rome.[84] Waugh did as requested. D'Arcy (then in America) sent a strong letter of support to the Provincial. It did not help.

82. Unpublished ALS to Margaret Waugh, 13 January [1963], from Combe Florey House; private collection.
83. Unpublished ALS from Margaret Waugh to Evelyn Waugh, 16 January [1963; misdated 16 April], from 31 Farm Street, W1; BL.
84. Cf. unpublished ALS from Fr Philip Caraman to Evelyn Waugh, 16 January 1963, from 31 Farm Street, W1; BL. The final charge read: 'The special attention you have given to Margaret Waugh has created an unhealthy atmosphere of resentment and gossip among your staff, which the more adult members are finding intolerable. I believe this to be true and not a calumny.'

At Easter he handed over the *Month* to Fr Moffat after fifteen years as Editor. In mid-April he left Farm Street for a melancholy bed-sitting room in Pimlico. Waugh wrote to Greene:

> If you are in London, be kind to Fr. Caraman. He is suffering one of those disasters which happen to Jesuits & which we outside the Society can't hope to understand. I think he is the victim of a mean little office intrigue. The result is that he is in disgrace & needs friends. I think you have rather lost sympathy with him lately, but not he with you, and it would cause great comfort if you looked him up, as though unaware of his difficulties, as a mere act of friendship.[85]

Greene promised his best efforts. But it was true, he did not share Waugh's affection for the priest, and he found it difficult to invent an excuse: '. . . I have not sought his company for so many years.'[86] In 1965, Caraman was sent to Oslo after a period of peripatetic obscurity. Waugh remained staunchly loyal, despite the deepening embarrassment of the 'relationship' in the months ahead.

*

The following nine months represented for Waugh a period of dismal recession. No sooner had Meg resigned than another family crisis blew up. Laura struggled through the snow to visit two of her husband's ancient relations, only to discover them in appalling destitution. Waugh wrote immediately to Alec: '[Uncle] George is senile, paralysed, bed-ridden & incontinent (I speak of excretions, not sexually). [Aunt] Emma is senile but still mobile. They live in the utmost squalor.'[87] The letter represented a gentle but firm demand. Waugh and Laura were shortly to holiday in Mentone, Alpes Maritimes, where he hoped to complete *A Little Learning*. He had found temporary accommodation for the decrepit couple in a nursing home to cover this period. After that, Alec was informed, he would be liable for half of any expenses.

Alec was rich again and living between America and Tangier; his estranged wife was a millionaire. He had no objection to helping. As the correspondence progressed, however, Evelyn's tone needled Alec. Evelyn had never visited George and Emma. Alec had looked in as regularly as he could, most recently only three months before, when their condition had seemed 'pathetic but not desperate'. Nevertheless, he bit his lip, paid up and tried to smooth over the awkwardness: 'Did you know that Louise

85. Unpublished APCI, nd [January 1963], from Combe Florey House; private collection.
86. Unpublished ALS from Graham Greene, 24 January 1963, from C6 Albany, W1; BL.
87. 16 January 1963; *Letters*, p. 598.

Cockburn's daughter was married to Ezra Pound's son? He runs the American school here. . . .'[88]

This was not the sort of family gossip Waugh wished to hear. The connection never found its way into his autobiography. Indeed, nothing found its way into it for a couple of months. The Mentone visit proved sterile. Nothing was written there and he returned to the twin prospect of a libel suit and Aunt Emma as a house-guest. When Uncle George died, she took up temporary residence at Combe Florey. In the meantime, the *Telegraph* had published the first instalment of *Basil Seal* and solicitors' letters had followed concerning the description of the Travellers' Club as a notorious haunt of homosexuals. The Vassall case was still news and a nervous editor had quickly altered the reference in the second part to 'Bellamy's'. (For book publication Waugh changed this again to the 'Tory Club'.)[89]

Throughout that bitter winter, Waugh became increasingly fractious. The old Pope was dying, Caraman was packing up, Alec would not do as he was told. Waugh suggested that Joan should take Aunt Emma and, when this proved impossible, he sent her back to her house, where, a year later, she set fire to the place and was asphyxiated. Even then, organizing the distribution of her property continued to irritate him until Alec explained, in an unmistakably tetchy letter, that, against their mother's wishes, he had generously disinherited himself. Evelyn was now the head of the family.[90]

From Alec's point of view, Evelyn's life appeared as glamorous and successful as ever: Easter in Rome with Diana Cooper, Florence with Harold Acton, luncheon with the Prime Minister, the award of a C.Litt. in June. Each of these, however, had disappointed Waugh. Lady Diana had been depressed; he agonized over her spiritual condition and still tried (unsuccessfully) to bully her into the Church. The recall to Admiralty House had been gratifying but Waugh had accepted the invitation as an aspect of his continuing rearguard action against the liturgists, and it was a battle that he already knew he was losing. The luncheon was in honour of the Italian Ambassador. Archbishop Heenan was there. Any chance of channelling the discussion towards Catholic issues was soon lost amid the humanist banter of Roy Thomson and Harold Nicolson. Waugh had last met Nicolson on the *Antilles*, returning from the West Indies, and had

88. Unpublished ALS from Alec Waugh, 22 January 1963, from Hotel Vélazquez Palace, Tangier, Morocco; BL.

89. William Vassall, an Admiralty clerk, had been convicted of spying for Russia on 22 October 1962. Questions were asked as to how he had become a member of the exclusive Bath Club in Brook Street, Mayfair. The secretary explained that Vassall had 'slipped in' through his membership of the Conservative Club which had merged with the Bath in 1951.

90. Cf. unpublished AL, copy of part of ALS from Alec Waugh to Evelyn Waugh, 30 March 1964, from Hotel Vélazquez Palace, Tangier, Morocco; HRC.

thought him senile. Thomson seemed brutish. Apart from the latter's 'discordant voice', Waugh found the party 'very cosy',[91] but he did not bother even to record the event in his diary.[92]

The C.Litt. was, perhaps, a rather different matter but ultimately equally bathetic. When the President of the Royal Society of Literature, R. A. Butler, wrote in March offering the Companionship, Waugh was suspicious. Here, at last, was his honour, but what was it worth? Bron acted as private detective: '... You will be easily the youngest member at 59,' he replied. '... The great objection to accepting ... is that it is ... extremely young.... The C. Litt. promises to become a minor perquisite which great men are not afraid to include among their honours....'[93] He advised his father to discover the other candidates. On learning that they included Edmund Blunden, Edith Sitwell and Aldous Huxley, Waugh hesitated, then accepted.

The 'Presentation of Scrolls' took place at the Skinners' Hall on 25 June. Butler had been called away to an urgent conference in Southern Rhodesia and Waugh's old friend the Earl of Birkenhead, Chairman of the Council, had presided.[94] It was in some respects a dismal occasion. Dame Edith was too ill to attend; Sir Osbert had suffered a 'nasty fall' and was also laid up; Huxley remained in California and was represented by Spender. Waugh had been dreading the banquet and this decimation rendered the proceedings faintly ridiculous. But Sacheverell was there for Edith, and Caraman, Laura, Meg and Ann Fleming turned up. Waugh felt among friends and appears to have been genuinely pleased with his recognition. His speech was the centrepiece of the evening. Sacheverell had ended with a joke. Edith, he said, had recently been rung up by a journalist and asked how she felt. 'How do I feel?' she said. 'I feel like an electric eel in a tank of flat fish.'[95] Applause. Waugh began: 'My Lords, Ladies and Gentlemen: I feel like a flat fish in a tank of electric eels.'[96] Laughter and applause. It was his last triumphant appearance as master of ceremonies.

Afterwards he told Sykes: 'It is a meaningless distinction without emolument, precedence or adornment, but I thought it would be stuck up to

91. *Letters*, p. 605.
92. The other guests were: John Sparrow, Lord Eccles, Aidan Crawley, Lord Drogheda, Sir Michael Adeane and Philip de Zulueta. Inviting Waugh for 22 April, de Zulueta was charmingly circumspect: 'I know that the Prime Minister would be very distressed to feel that his invitation gave you pain and would not wish you to put yourself out in order to come ...' (unpublished TLS, 3 April 1963; BL). A list of proposed guests was attached.
93. Unpublished ALS, 25 March 1963, from *Daily Telegraph*, Fleet Street, EC4; BL.
94. Waugh always attributed the offer of the honour to Birkenhead's influence.
95. *Proceedings of the Royal Society of Literature*, p. 38.
96. *Ibid.* 'The word "companionship"', he added, 'is somehow not one which one associates naturally with an author's exceptionally solitary and acrimonious trade. If we Companions had to call on one another we should have rather a long journey ... and whether we should get on awfully well when we met ... (Laughter).'

refuse.'[97] This probably understates his pleasure. A year later he was encouraging Greene to accept: 'Some years back I refused the C.B.E. from side (not good enough, I thought) and am now ashamed.'[98] But it was probably Greene's refusal which wrecked Waugh's quiet pride in his honour. Greene had been a Fellow of the Royal Society of Literature for nearly twenty years in order to contribute to its charitable funds. Fellows had not been consulted before the Companionships were inaugurated and he thought it 'pretentious nonsense' that the 'body of well-intentioned people' Waugh had cited 'should reserve [?] the right to separate ten authors from the multitude for special honour.'[99] Greene had also turned down the CBE (without shame) and admired Kipling for refusing a knighthood. It was a broadside on Waugh's hierarchical principles:

> Really you old school prefect come off it.... Many people have expressed surprise to me at your acceptance & I have defended it as an outbreak of eccentricity.... You have made yourself a little absurd by joining the octogenarians, but I love you for it.[100]

Waugh accepted the rebuke. Two years earlier he had described himself to Nancy Mitford as 'just a retired schoolmaster'[101] and, after Meg's marriage, that was precisely how he felt.

*

'... I distil a few daily drops of exquisite boredom about my early life,' he wrote to Ann Fleming in August. 'I am also writing a preface for an American edition of Galsworthy's *Man of Property*. Ever read it? Don't.'[102] As he gloomily scraped together a few hundred pounds, two more family embarrassments rose to assault his dignity. Alec wrote to say that during the next month he would be 'going through a form of legal marriage with Virginia Sorenson – an American with whom I have been co-habiting intermittently for the last nine years',[103] and Meg was enduring another crisis with Caraman.

The phrasing of Alec's letter – 'It is my hope that this covenant will not have any effect on my present way of life; I don't plan to put down roots anywhere. I am for the first time in my life doing something which I know is wrong' – was scarcely calculated to elicit Evelyn's sympathy in his current

97. Unpublished APCI to Christopher Sykes, nd [June 1963?], from Combe Florey House; private collection. Sykes had written to congratulate him.
98. 7 May 1964; *Letters*, p. 620.
99. Unpublished ALS from Graham Greene, 14 May 1964, from 130 Boulevard Malherbes, Paris 17; BL.
100. *Ibid.*
101. [Received 22 August 1962]; *Letters*, p. 591.
102. 7 August 1963; *Letters*, p. 611.
103. Unpublished ALS from Alec Waugh, 13 August 1963, from 'French Line'; BL.

ultra-montanist mood. Alec was revealing his private life to his brother for the first time for thirty years in the hope of forgiveness: 'Please say a prayer for my imperilled soul.'[104] Evelyn turned his back. From this point, and until the project was abandoned, he refused to respond, referring to Alec as 'my revolting brother'.[105]

Meg's news was still more alarming. Caraman, increasingly agitated by his uncertain future, had become a regular guest in Somerset and at Westbourne Terrace. 'My visits to Combe Florey', he wrote to Laura, 'have taken me out of myself at times when I have become afraid of doing something desperate and despairing.'[106] Waugh reciprocated the feeling, happy to have the priest pottering round the grounds pruning apple trees and 'clandestinely saying Mass in the dining room'.[107] In London, the FitzHerberts entertained him. It seemed an amicable arrangement to tide the poor man over his difficulties. Then, suddenly, the nightmarish imputations of the Farm Street *débâcle* emerged again. Meg wrote, distraught, begging Waugh's advice as to how she might keep Fr Caraman at a greater distance. She knew that his physical attentions were entirely innocent and was tortured by the idea that she might be betraying him when he needed her most, attacking his belief in his own impeccable motives. Yet it was all getting 'sloppy' and unbearable for her. Could Fr D'Arcy offer some quiet advice?[108]

Waugh could not turn his back on this. He refused, however, to suspect his friend of dubious motives. Delicate diplomacy ensued and by September the crisis was over. Meg was heavily pregnant and Caraman's demonstrations of affection abated. She wrote to thank her father for 'so much trouble' and to say that the priest 'seemed much better – I'm afraid I was rather silly – if it's only going to be an occasional outbreak I can easily bear with it. . . .'[109] But the incident had spoiled the intimacy of their triumvirate. Waugh negotiated with his local bishop for permission to build a twelve-bed vault at Combe Florey and welcomed the breath of death on his neck. 'It was fun thirty-five years ago', he noted in his diary, 'to travel far and in great discomfort to meet people whose entire conception of life and manner of expression were alien. Now one has only to leave one's gates. All fates are "worse than death".'[110]

104. *Ibid.*
105. ALS to Ann Fleming, 5 September 1963; *LAF*, p. 328. Virginia Sorenson, a Mormon, was a writer whom Alec had met at the MacDowell Colony. Although the 'form of legal marriage' was called off three months later, he married her in 1969 after Joan's death.
106. Unpublished ALS to Laura Waugh, 18 March 1963, from 31 Farm Street, W1; BL.
107. 5 December 1962; *LAF*, p. 319.
108. Unpublished ALS to Evelyn Waugh, 16 August 1963, from 15 Westbourne Terrace, W2; BL.
109. Unpublished ALS to Evelyn Waugh, 9 September 1963, from 15 Westbourne Terrace, W2; BL.
110. *Diaries*, 3 September 1963, p. 791.

The diary by this stage had faltered into random jottings. Words were failing him and, as they did, he fell increasingly into the role of 'eccentric don'. Where this was simply a matter of correcting Nancy's grammar or writing a review of a volume on Victorian book design, he could contentedly kill time. But he had set himself up as a man of classical training and something of an authority on Church history, and in both respects was soon found wanting. Usually he 'borrowed' his scholarship from friends and, so far, had carried off this act with only minor embarrassments. As the battle against the Council continued, however, he was steadily deserted by those from whom he expected support. His assumption that he represented the 'middle rank' of Catholics was attacked as plainly absurd. Worse still, the scholarly basis for his 'hierarchy' and 'babel' argument was impugned.

When, for instance, Waugh had published a letter in the *Tablet* on the Eastern Uniate Churches,[111] it had received a stiff rebuke from a scholar in Rome. The idea of the Eastern Churches as 'some sort of ancient museum piece', he said, was utterly misguided. 'The Eastern Churches have always had their Liturgy in the language of the people, fully sung and prayed by the people and Communion under both forms. They have always had concelebration by several priests. All these points seem to be exactly what the "progressives" in the Vatican Council are looking into.'[112] At the beginning of this debate, Waugh had believed himself to be in the vanguard of a popular movement supported by the Church's scholars and gentlemen. Gradually he was forced to accept that his position was thought to be eccentric.

By September 1963, he was in open disagreement with one of his former backers, the Abbot of Downside, and fiercely opposed to his apostolic and ecumenical leanings. Where Bishop Butler quoted: 'Go ye into the world and make disciples of all nations', Waugh countered with: 'Many are called but few are chosen.' He accepted that 'the truth must be accessible to all' but he believed its acceptance 'to be a matter for the individual conscience':

> The early Christians sought no accommodation with their enemies. They offered something new and quite unreconcilable with contemporary tastes and superstitions. They died to preserve their unique position in opposition to what was the spirit of their age.

111. 'The Dialogue Mass', *Tablet*, 16 March 1963, 292: 'The Eastern Uniate Churches retain ancient habits of worship which are dear to them, and liturgies which in many cases are unintelligible to the faithful. Is it not the time to seek similar privileges for Roman Catholics? Will you promote an appeal to the Holy See for the establishment of a Uniate Latin Church which shall observe all the rites as they existed in the reign of Pius IX?' Pius IX died in 1878. The (First) Vatican Council had begun its deliberations in 1869.

112. Unpublished TLS from David Kirk, 21 March 1963, from Pontificio Collegio Beda, Viale San Paolo, 18, Roma; BL.

> Instead of 'dialogue with separated brethren' why do we not revert to the old-fashioned effort to convert the Protestants, the Jews and the Heathen, to show them their errors and present disagreeable truths in full and sharp detail.
>
> I write this because ... conversions to the Church have much declined since the assembly of the Council.[113]

For many readers of the *Tablet*, this was Waugh with all disguise cast off. The humility of 'The Same Again, Please' now appeared disingenuous. The letter came dangerously close to asserting that the Church's essential attraction was its unique status separating its members from the babel of common men beyond its doors. In his article, Waugh had been forced to admit that: 'Most Christians, relying on the direct prophecies of Our Lord, expect [the reunion of Christendom] to occur in some moment of historical time.' He had, however, quickly qualified this with: 'Few believe that moment to be imminent.'[114] The truth was that he loathed the idea and was determined to obstruct ecumenism to the last breath in his body. For Waugh, the prophecy could only be fulfilled if everyone became a Roman Catholic, and, in the liberal atmosphere of the 1960s, few Church leaders were prepared to follow him down this road. Waugh's position was so awkwardly orthodox as to verge on heresy. Only one senior figure continued to offer his (confidential) support: Archbishop Heenan – and on him Waugh pinned his dying hopes for the Old Faith.

*

It was in this glum mood that Waugh read the reviews of *Basil Seal*. Book publication had been delayed to coincide with his sixtieth birthday. It was his swan-song as a writer of fiction and appeared as an expensive gift for the discriminating: a limited edition of 750 copies, numbered and signed, with a frontispiece by Kathleen Hale. In his dedication to Ann Fleming he described the story as 'a senile attempt to recapture the manner of my youth' and, as the reviews suggested, it is not much more than that: amusing, ingenious and slight.

Most notices, nevertheless, were respectful. Pritchett turned out a comic piece, pretending distress at Seal's displacement from the realm of eternal youth.[115] Jocelyn Brooke found Waugh's prose 'as impeccable as ever ... after all the Jack Murdochs and Iris Kerouacs I have been reviewing

113. 'The Council: Phase One', *Tablet*, 7 September 1963, 137. Waugh's letter was a reply to an article by the Abbot of Downside under the same title.
114. 'The Same Again, Please', *op. cit.*, p. 602.
115. *NS*, 15 November 1963, 706–7; *CH*, pp. 452–3.

lately. . . .'[116] Only the *TLS* offered harsh criticism ('a nasty little book')[117] and the general impression was of massive regard for Waugh's mastery. As pure entertainment, *Seal* came as a draught of vintage in the wastelands of experimental fiction, reassuring Waugh's public of the vitality of his wit.

It was later than they thought. By this time the rough draft of *A Little Learning* was complete and, although he toyed with the idea of adding another chapter to take the story up to 1926, he never wrote it. The autumn was spent fine-tuning what was to be his last book. To indulge John Sutro, he attended a reunion of the Oxford University Railway Club, taking Bron and Terence Greenidge along as guests, but the event proved a 'ghostly' experience and the photograph 'funny'.[118] 'We cherish our friends', he had remarked in his diary that summer, 'not for their ability to amuse us but for ours to amuse them – a diminishing number in my case.'[119]

Waugh had greeted his birthday as the death of one life and the birth of a new. Fat, lame and disgusted by his physical appearance, he had visited a health farm to shrink before taking Laura to the Flemings' new house, Sevenhampton Place, in Wiltshire. It was his last country-house excursion. Again he had found himself a flat fish in a tank of electric eels. Ian was near death, Bowra boomed, Ann was so worried that she could pay little attention to her guests. Clarissa Avon and Teresa Jungman were there. Too many of his old loves were assembled as though to bid him farewell and Waugh left them without regret, an old man again. He hated the house and had coveted only one of Ian's possessions. A few weeks later an elaborate invalid chair arrived at Combe Florey with Ian's earnest hopes that Evelyn would spend many happy years in it.

On the birth of Bron's second child in December, the *Evening Standard* dubbed Waugh a 'Literary Grandpa' and he settled uneasily into this new role, increasingly anxious about money. Whatever Peters proposed, Waugh now accepted: a book on the history of the papacy,[120] another television interview. In the West Indies, he had learned that he had indeed 'been successful' in selling the *Rossetti* manuscript. *The Times* reported that £800 had been paid by an anonymous bidder. Since the manuscript remained in Waugh's collection as the property of the Trust, the identity of this mys-

116. *Listener*, 7 November 1963, 764. Brooke, while professing neutrality about Waugh's 'romantic snobbery', clearly disliked it but was prepared to ignore the issue and concentrate on the 'dedicated artist' beneath the 'public *persona*'. Brooke had encountered Waugh's softer side. In 1961 both writers had chosen the same title, *Conventional Weapons*, for their next novel. As the senior figure, Waugh might have tried to pull rank. Instead, he generously relinquished his 'claim', saying that there was no copyright in titles and wishing Brooke the best of luck.
117. 14 November 1963, 921.
118. Unpublished ALS to Ann Fleming, 10 December 1963; private collection. The reunion, to celebrate the Club's fortieth anniversary took place on 18 November 1963.
119. *Diaries*, 10 June 1963, p. 790.
120. For Doubleday's *Mainstreams of Modern History* series.

terious purchaser seems clear. Waugh was selling it to himself, or rather to his children, tax-free. In July 1963 he had suddenly informed Peters that Laura owned the manuscript of *The Loved One* and wished to sell for £1,500. And so, he had hoped, it would continue: a steady, quiet transfer of manuscript into cash with no interference from the Inland Revenue. In September, however, Peters's accountant had insisted that these sales *were* taxable. They had stopped instantly. Much worse was to come. In February, Waugh had signed a document agreeing to Evill's replacement as co-Trustee by one R. Chantry. At the time it had seemed a mere technicality, one solicitor replacing another. Only in 1965 did it emerge as the initiation of Waugh's ultimate financial collapse.

In the meantime, he plodded on, picking up contracts wherever he could. The BBC paid £300 for his appearance on 'Monitor' and succumbed to his mischievous condition that he be interviewed either by Sykes or some pretty girl who had read all his books. That Christmas was the first Waugh had spent with his family for many years and, in early January, eager to escape, he came to London for the recording. Elizabeth Jane Howard (the future Mrs Kingsley Amis) was given the task of re-reading the novels and dealing with Waugh's 'senile vanity'. Later she complained to Ann Fleming that he had chosen all the questions, but the interview was another triumph. Here the public saw Waugh in quite another role. He was charmed. He liked nothing better than to flirt with an attractive young woman. Leering gallantly at his cool inquisitor, he inveighed against the 'gibberish' of modernism. Joyce, he said, was plainly lunatic.

Watching this, Waugh's friends must have been concerned about his health. Ann Fleming had warned him after the C.Litt. banquet that he had appeared breathless – perhaps no bad thing from her point of view since she often complained that his breath stank of paraldehyde. Here he looked decidedly infirm, an exhausted rogue jollied up by drink. Shortly afterwards, he and Laura went to Mentone again and he returned a sick man. A bed was booked in St Agnes's nursing home and Waugh only cancelled it on discovering that Randolph Churchill was an inmate. Oddly, this brought about their reconciliation after an estrangement of twelve years. Their recent correspondence had only widened the gap, Churchill requesting signed first editions to complete his collection, Waugh rebuking him for sharp practice and demanding postage and packing costs. After his recovery, on his way to spend Easter again with Diana Cooper in Rome, Waugh had been unable to resist a vicious joke at Churchill's expense. It was a 'typical triumph of modern science', he remarked to Ed Stanley, 'to find the only part of Randolph that was not malignant and remove it'.[121] Stanley repeated

121. *Diaries*, March 1964, p. 792.

the anecdote to Churchill, who had lost a lung in an operation for suspected cancer. On Waugh's return, he met him in White's, sadly enfeebled, distressed by the calumny, and Waugh's animosity had melted.

'When I saw the doctor', Waugh wrote just before his trip, 'he asked about my habits. I said "I have practically given up drinking – only about 7 bottles of wine & 3 of spirits a week." "A week? Surely you mean a month?" "No, and I smoke 30 cigars a week & take 40 grains of sodium amytal." He looked graver & graver. "Oh, yes, a bottle of paraldehyde a week." '[122] In Rome to escape 'the horrors of the English liturgy'[123] he had found Lady Diana ill and wretched. No sooner was he back than Alfred Duggan died. Waugh was learning to relish mortality and he certainly did nothing to arrest his own decline.

He wanted to die. All pleasure in his domestic life had evaporated. 'My daughter Harriet (19) is a great trial to me', he wrote to Lady Acton, '– quite pretty, very good & affectionate but stupid & dull & incompetent. My son James (17) is also a thorn. Won't go into the church or the army, smokes cigarettes & can't take his hands out of his pockets. My youngest son is a jewel but I suspect he will grow up homosexual.'[124] Poor James had written nervously to explain that he did not wish to enter Sandhurst. Waugh had screwed the letter up and, before the year was out, managed to bully the boy into uniform. Waugh's marriage, it seems, was under considerable strain during these last two years. Laura took to drinking quantities of cheap sherry and neglected the farm. 'You see that dreadful old bore,' she remarked once to Bron about his father, 'he used to be so witty and gay.'[125]

Tiny disturbances in his routine could now raise Waugh to a pitch of fury. When Aunt Emma died in May and her possessions were transferred temporarily to Combe Florey, he complained bitterly to Alec that the house had become a junk shop. Joan had done nothing, he said. Laura and Hatty had had to clean out the cottage at great personal inconvenience. He made an inventory, had the goods valued, and proposed a family auction of these largely worthless relics, the sooner the better. When Alec's children, Peter and Veronica, hurried down to stake their claim, Waugh accused them of showing 'exaggerated interest' in the property, even though his own children had already made out lists of the things they wanted. Ultimately, Waugh offered to pay three-quarters of the assessment and to take his chances at public auction. In the meantime, Alec was advised to arrive quickly in a small van.

122. ALS to Ann Fleming, 3 March 1964; *Letters*, p. 618.
123. *Ibid.*
124. 7 January 1964; *Letters*, p. 617.
125. 'The Waugh Trilogy', 'Arena', BBC TV, broadcast 18, 19, 20 April 1987.

Their letters had again reached the stage of thinly veiled acrimony. Alec must have dreaded the prospect of a final, appalling row, terminating his years of diplomacy. But Evelyn, as usual, surprised him. 'This was a very happy visit,' Alec noted. 'The last time I saw him.'[126] Three of the five instalments of *A Little Learning* had been published in the *Sunday Times* amid a tumult of publicity. Peers and politicians were holding their breath week by week. In July, Waugh had broadcast his celebration of Duggan[127] and Alec's *A Family of Islands* had appeared. There was plenty to talk about and, the centre of attraction again, Evelyn was genial. There can be little doubt, however, that the brothers remained fundamentally incompatible. *A Little Learning* was circumspect on this matter. Four years later Cyril Connolly rather cruelly recalled a joke at Alec's expense:

> I remember [Evelyn] once questioning me about Freud and asking 'What is an anal-erotic?' I explained that it was not a pejorative term and that Freud had mentioned excessive tidiness, parsimony and obstinacy as typical characteristics. Evelyn reflected. 'Then I am the brother of an anal-erotic.'[128]

With the exception of 'parsimony', the description might also have fitted Evelyn. Alec could scarcely have been described as mean but, by his brother's extravagant standards, he appeared cautious. A huge slice of Evelyn's small pleasure in life had been to astonish friends with exorbitant gifts. Now he was unable to afford them. Each time a new grandchild appeared, he sent £100 and might throw in a dinner at the Café Royal. The enormous trouble he took to assist Duggan's widow[129] testifies to an abiding generosity. But his inability to allow this free reign was a root of depression not unconnected with his terror of becoming a bore. If he could no longer give pleasure, he was as good as dead.

Shortly after Alec's departure, Waugh launched his third and final assault on the liturgists. Again Archbishop Heenan wrote in support, saying how much he regretted the influence of the 'intellectuals': 'People may call you reactionary . . . nobody can call you a fool. But do not despair. The changes are not so great as they are made to appear. . . .'[130] A correspondence ensued, Waugh hopelessly trying to encourage him to fight on. Heenan replied:

126. AN on Waugh's unpublished letter of invitation, 15 July 1964; HRC. Alec's visit was on 23 July 1964.
127. 'Alfred Duggan: An Appreciation', 2 July 1964; reprinted *Spectator*, 10 July 1964, pp. 38–9; *EAR*, pp. 625–8.
128. 'Fresh Strands on the Loom', *ST*, 22 October 1967, 155; review of *MBE*.
129. Laura Duggan was financially embarrassed after her husband's death. Waugh helped to set up a fund and wrote numerous letters to raise money for her, and for her son's education. Alfred's family, who had always disapproved of Laura, contributed nothing, another blow to Waugh's faith in the British aristocracy.
130. Unpublished ALS, 20 August 1964, from Hare Street House, Buntingford, Herts.; BL.

> Of course you are right. That is why they are playing up this People of God and Priesthood of the Laity so much. The Mass is no longer the Holy Sacrifice but the Meal at which the priest is the waiter. The bishop, I suppose, is the head waiter and the Pope the Patron.[131]

Heenan, now promoted to Cardinal Archbishop of Westminster, invited Waugh to dine in London. He went, and made his case. But it was all too late. The Archbishop's complicity seemed traitorous to Waugh and to his conservative Catholic friends. On Heenan's first letter to Waugh, Sykes later scribbled: 'He went back on all of this.'

Even before his visit, Waugh had written to D'Arcy enquiring how one might be excused from attending Mass. Since he was more than three miles from a church, he asked, did this not qualify him for a dispensation? Yes, D'Arcy replied, this was true – for those without cars. But, lest Waugh see this as a reason for selling his transport, the priest encouraged perseverance: 'I can well understand how nerve racking & almost unbearable a mass in the future in a small & modern Church might be with the priest facing the people. But I think it a terrible loss to miss the central act of our faith. . . .'[132] Waugh, of course, could say nothing of how Fr Caraman assisted him in this matter. 'Returning to London after the turmoil of Rome,' he had noted that Easter, 'I found Barchester.'[133] Neither alternative was any longer satisfactory, and with the publication of *A Little Learning* in September, his life effectively ended.

*

The book was well-received. Those holding their breath (Tom Driberg in particular) relaxed. There was always a danger of Waugh's indiscretion. Alfred Duggan's aunt had ungratefully feared this in Waugh's earlier broadcast. But they need not have worried. *A Little Learning*, although not mendacious, is decorously evasive. Waugh always requested his friends' *imprimatur*. If this were withheld, he scrapped the story. In only one respect was he indiscreet.

During 1963, the model for Captain Grimes had popped up, living in an almshouse in Winchester. Abandoning schoolmastering, W. R. B. Young had become a solicitor, this time in the legal profession. In retirement he was the same joyful paederast. Publish and be damned, he told Waugh. Then, on second thoughts, fearing the loss of his home, he had requested some reserve. The resulting anecdote nevertheless offended Katharine

131. Unpublished ALS from John Carmel [Archbishop Heenan], 28 August 1964, from Archbishop's House, Westminster, SW1; BL.
132. Unpublished ALS from Fr Martin D'Arcy, 24 August 1964, from 114 Mount Street, W1; BL.
133. *Diaries*, 1 April 1964; p. 793.

Asquith. 'Why do you put in the things that shock me?' she wrote. '... it just seems uncivilised....'[134]

The general bias of Waugh's autobiography has been described earlier.[135] The letters he received flesh this out. Alec was relieved to escape so lightly and touched by his brother's affection for Barbara Jacobs.'Reading it', he said, 'was a curious experience.... I was seeing a part of my own life from a different angle. How different our lives were! Yours ended ... where mine began – with the click of our father's latch key in the door.'[136] Powell and Greene both experienced a similar, stimulating strangeness in the description of Oxford.

> I was not [Greene wrote] suffering from any adult superiority at Oxford to explain our paths not crossing ... I belonged to a rather rigorously Balliol group of ... boisterous heterosexuals, while your path temporarily took you into the other camp. Also for a considerable period of my time ... [there] I lived in a general haze of drink. I've never drunk so much in my life since![137]

Harold Acton went into some detail about the 'other camp':

> The Oxford chapter is so vividly evocative that it left me rather sad.... Perhaps my passion for Tony [Bushell] was given undue notice in proportion to so many that were not alluded to: Cyril's for Bobby Longden, Robert [Byron]'s, Patrick [Balfour]'s, Brian [Howard]'s and Hugh [Lygon]'s promiscuities, Billy [Clonmore]'s passion for Peter Rodd (all of his acrobatic feats were inspired by love of Peter), etc. etc. Not that I care, for I am almost free of hypocrisy.[138]

Maurice Bowra was less happy (Waugh had implied that Bowra had only taken him up after he had become famous), and others also suffered.

> We were all rather wondering [Lord Clonmore wrote] what embarrassments your pen might have in store for us [concerning] ... those strange & most enjoyable & sometimes unhappy days.... Chris Hollis comes out rather hard to decipher; it is like looking at him through spectacles that don't fit one's eyes.... I wonder what he & Mrs H. think about it? ... I almost shed a tear over Crutwell [*sic*].... I can see that savage face, like some large dog on the verge of rabies....[139]

134. Unpublished ALS, 9 September 1964, from Tynts Hill, Mells, Frome, Somerset; BL.
135. Prologue, Vol. 1, pp. 4–5.
136. Unpublished ALS from Alec Waugh, 2 September 1964, from Raffles Hotel, Singapore; BL.
137. Unpublished TLS from Graham Greene, 10 September 1964, from C6 Albany, W1; BL.
138. Unpublished ALS from (Sir) Harold Acton, 25 September 1964, from La Pietra, Florence; BL.
139. Unpublished ALS, 28 September 1964, from Seagrange, Sandycove Ave E., Dun Laoghaire, Co. Dublin; BL.

The Hollises remained silent. Not so Dudley Carew: '. . . why on earth you should deliberately spit in the eye of one who has always wished you well passes my comprehension'. Waugh's Lancing acolyte was outraged by

> the contemptuous squiggle of a caricature you have drawn of our relationship, a relationship which relegates me to the position of a half-witted hanger-on you tolerantly patronized for a term or two . . . many people . . . will have little difficulty, thanks to your gratuitous clues, in identifying me with the grotesque figure of the 'boy in another house'.[140]

More than anyone, Carcw had been the guardian of Waugh's fame at Lancing. He had preserved not only Waugh's memory but also his letters, essays and stories. This collection comprises the bulk of the novelist's extant juvenilia, later sold to the University of Texas. The wound rankled but, sadly, Carew's riposte (*A Fragment of Friendship* [1974]) merely reinforced the image Waugh had created.

A Little Learning set the seal on Waugh's reputation and the general feeling was that Waugh's melancholy compassion was endearing. He was accepted as a consummate master. The predictable grumbles from Toynbee and Muggeridge were drowned in a flood of approbation. Even Pritchett and Auden forgave everything for the beauty of Waugh's prose. After Waugh had arrived at that New York party in white tie and full evening dress, Auden's only comment to Spender had been that 'he thought E. W. must be mad. Auden never complained . . . of anything that E. W. had written about him – nor did Isherwood for that matter. I think the thing is that members of my generation who were attacked by E. W., admired him immensely as a writer of genius. . . .'[141]

Many mistook Waugh's misanthropy for a pose and eagerly anticipated ripeness to come. In fact, he scarcely began his second volume.[142] There were many reasons for this: poor health, depression, pressure of other contracts. But one thing above all others, surely, baulked him. The crucial event of the next volume would inescapably have been Evelyn Gardner's desertion. That wound had never healed. Its discomfort is reflected in the novels' continuous line of faithless wives from Agatha Runcible to Virginia Troy. It is probable that, as a Catholic celebrity, he did not wish to degrade himself and his family by recalling the incident. It also seems likely that he had never dared to look its full implications in the face.

*

140. Unpublished ALS from Dudley Carew, 4 September 1964, from Goatham House, Broad Oak, Rye, Sussex; BL.
141. Unpublished TLS from Stephen Spender to Martin Stannard, 3 January 1988, *op. cit.*
142. Cf. Vol. 1 on *A Little Hope*, pp. 99–100 and 113–14.

'When you next write a book,' Ann Fleming's daughter once asked, 'couldn't you incorporate mama? She's heroine stuff – . . . gay beautiful & courageous. After all there's a touch of her in Virginia – though she's nicer. . . .'[143] More than a touch, perhaps. When she was not disseminating malice, Waugh gained a sexual thrill from her as a kind of spanking nanny. On one famous occasion at table she had banged his ear trumpet with a spoon to keep him in order. Since the death of her sister and husband, however, her courage and gaiety had sadly diminished. Only fortitude was left, enlivened by mockery, and one of her tiny, ruthless corrections proved to be the fatal pin-prick in the heart of Waugh's embattled self-esteem.

That December, he was invited as usual to Brian Franks's 'Hyde Park Vomit'. Waugh refused. 'The truth is', he wrote, 'that I am no longer sortable – deaf, toothless, without appetite, reduced to extreme exhaustion by travel. I should only be a bore and a burden.'[144] Franks encouraged him: 'That luncheon party is built around you and Bob [Laycock] . . . this premature senility (which I do not believe for a moment) is no excuse.'[145] Waugh was bribed by the offer of free accommodation. 'I accept', he replied, 'with gratitude & the repeated warning that I can only be regarded as a ghost. People get a macabre pleasure in regarding the decay of their contemporaries. That is the only pleasure I can hope to give the assembled company.'[146] When they saw him, they realized that he was telling the truth. He left the table early and retired alone to his room having eaten almost nothing.

Meeting him the night before, Diana Cooper had been equally alarmed:

> . . . I am fearful for you – having loved you for years. Lets not forget Pinfold with your laudenum [*sic*] & creme de menthe . . . till madness claimed you.
>
> You will tell me that your present symptoms are totally differant [*sic*] – but drink-drug-escape adiction [*sic*] can bring you by differant [*sic*] streams to the same Slough of Despond.[147]

He was already there. Later, with Ann Fleming, he was worse.

> You have been constantly in my prayers and thoughts [she wrote]. On leaving you in that dolorous condition, I made a further attempt to contact Laura but failed. Have you been to a dentist and a doctor?

143. Unpublished ALS from Fionn O'Neill, 20 October [1961], from 5 Eccleston Square, SW1; BL. She had just read *Unconditional Surrender*.
144. 14 November 1964; *Letters*, p. 627.
145. Unpublished ALS from Brian Franks, 17 November 1964, from 37 Duke Street, St James's, SW1; BL.
146. 20 November 1964; *Letters*, p. 627.
147. ALS from Lady Diana Cooper, nd [December? 1964], from 10 Warwick Avenue, W2; BL; *MWMS*, p. 315.

> Betjeman's teeth are as white as snow compared to yours. I did not see a toothbrush in your bedroom, do you use one?[148]

The final remarks, intended as a kindness, clearly punctured his tattered vanity. Shortly afterwards, he travelled to London again and had all his remaining teeth extracted. According to Bron, he never recovered from the operation.

Toothlessness seemed a strangely appropriate condition. A few days after the publication of *A Little Learning*, Harold Wilson had become Prime Minister and Waugh felt doomed to die, powerless, under another Socialist regime. For Waugh, it was a time of violence and betrayal, in which he had more sympathy for Profumo than for the hordes assembling for Churchill's funeral. He had seen 'satire' pass into the hands of callow youths disrespectful of tradition. His own son soon joined them on *Private Eye* and the *Daily Mirror.* A year earlier, Waugh had asked Sykes to secure Bron a job with the BBC. Entrance, Bron was informed, was now by competitive examination and, since he had already been offered employment on two national papers, he could not afford to wait. With several mouths to feed and his novels beginning to fail, he settled for a career in journalism. 'I am at a loss to understand why you should find the *Sketch* so shameful,' he had written to his father. 'It would be a worthy aim in life ... to try and bring the lower classes to their senses.'[149] Papa no longer agreed.

The last entry in the diary is for Easter 1965:

> A year in which the process of transforming the liturgy has followed a planned course. Protests avail nothing.... Pray God I will never apostatize but I can only now go to Church as an act of duty and obedience....[150]

In January he had been invited to another Foyle's luncheon, this time to launch *Objections to Roman Catholicism.* A book of essays, it contained a piece by Archbishop Thomas Roberts, S. J., which questioned the Church's authority to declare all contraception immoral. If the invitation was designed to elicit a vitriolic reaction for 'good publicity', it succeeded. 'I would gladly attend an *auto-da-fé* at which your guests were incinerated,' Waugh replied. 'But I will certainly not sit down to a social meal in their company.'[151]

'Darling Papa,' Meg had written in February, 'I was awfully upset to hear from Hatty that you weren't well & sad & depressed. Would it cheer you up if I came down ...? ... I love you so much – please don't be

148. Unpublished ALS, 8 January 1965, from Shane's Castle, Antrim, N. Ireland; BL.
149. ALS from Auberon Waugh, 29 January 1964, from 44 Chester Row, SW1; BL; *WTD*, p. 165.
150. *Diaries*, p. 793.
151. 'Book Stirs Catholics in Britain', *NYT*, 15 January 1965. The editor of the volume was Michael de la Bedoyere, formerly Editor of the *Catholic Herald*, who had supported Waugh's position on Abyssinia in the 1930s.

unhappy. Why not come & stay here & unsmother.'[152] It did no good. Signals flashed round the literary world. 'I have been ill and idle all the winter', he replied to an anxious McDougall, '– not diseased but seedy. Now I have had a lot of teeth out and new snappers substituted – very uncomfortable at present. Odd and interesting about the quotation.'[153] Waugh was trying to trace the author of the (de Musset) lyric for the title of his next volume of autobiography:

La vie est brève,
Un peu d'amour,
Un peu de rêve,
Et puis, Bonjour.

La vie est vaine,
Un peu d'espoir,
Un peu de haine,
Et puis, Bonsoir.

*

A thunderbolt had arrived from Peters in January: 'You asked me how much money there is in the Save the Children Fund. I am afraid that there will not be any money available because it now appears that Evill was mistaken in his view that ... this revenue ... was not subject to tax.'[154] Peters advised him not to draw on the fund for the foreseeable future. Enough money had been reserved to pay back-taxes for six years. This was already lost. Peters's problem was to try to persuade the inspector not to demand payment for the whole fifteen years. Waugh wrote desperately to Bron. Did he own anything that was the property of the Trust and which could be sold? Apart from one painting, he did not. 'If you are left with no furniture at all,' he replied gaily, 'we could offer you some interesting chairs from the Raban Bequest.'[155]

Peters again came to the rescue. Waugh was advised to declare the Trust rather than run the risk of being accused of concealment. There was £7,000 'in the kitty' and the six years' tax did not amount to more than £5,000. Waugh paid up and was excused the rest. But there was another day of reckoning ahead: the point at which the Trust was due to be distributed. This was when the youngest child came of age, now only six years hence. He felt desolate.

152. Unpublished ALS from Margaret Waugh, 26 February 1965, from South East House, Goffers Road, Blackheath, S3. BL.
153. Unpublished APCI to John McDougall, 10 March 1965, from Combe Florey House; private collection.
154. Unpublished TLS from A. D. Peters, 12 January 1965, from 10 Buckingham Street, WC2; BL.
155. Unpublished ALS from Auberon Waugh, 18 January 1965, from 'London 4'; BL.

> I caught a glimpse of you & Teresa on the platform at Newbury [he wrote to Bron that summer]. I was returning from a funeral – the only social function I now attend. I congratulate you on acquiring a Canaletto. . . . Some time soon either Christie or Sotheby is selling Millais's historic portrait of Ruskin. It will I fear go for much more than we can afford since the Evill debacle. . . . Your mother-in-law was making a tour of the criminal classes of Wessex & kindly included us. Neither your mama nor I have been very well lately.[156]

He watched his children sadly from a distance. He would not call out. As with Alec in the 1930s, he found himself divided from his family by tracks leading in opposite directions. In the war of patronage between father and son, Waugh could no longer pull rank, and Bron, after a lifetime's rebukes, was perhaps tempted to stand on his dignity. As the child of one aristocrat and the husband of another, was he comforted by his father's spots of commonness? There had been few enough victories for Bron in their civil war. The dust-jacket of his latest novel, *Path of Dalliance* (1964), had stated that its author 'was a born writer and writes like himself and nobody else', a vain attempt, as he admitted, to prevent critics from 'dragging in my father. Because after all it *is* so pointless to say the book isn't as good as *Brideshead Revisited*.'[157] He was irritated by the reception of his fiction. Reviewers, he thought, paid no attention to the primary function of narrative, which was to entertain. The writers he admired were Greene and Spark. As for his more celebrated contemporaries (particularly David Storey), he could not see their point. In an age of 'egalitarian' fiction, Bron's work seemed anachronistic. Yet, in trying to escape his father's shadow, he had encountered a singular problem. Waugh had moulded his son's tastes so exactly that the young man seemed to face only a ghostly future of endless imitation.

Bron did not repine. Bravado concealed a resourceful and amusing man, always pragmatic about the need to support his dependants, always industrious. He and Teresa had let their Chelsea house and rented a rectory in Chilton Foliat. Here he could escape from Fleet Street to enjoy some days each week in the country with his family. This has remained the pattern of his life. Bron was an affectionate man. He did not want to send his children away to school, having been offended by the banners hung out to celebrate his return to Downside. And, saddened to learn of his parents' illness, he offered them the dedication of *Who Are the Violets Now?* with a hint that he might make it warmer in tone. As it stood it read simply: 'For My Parents'. The hint was not taken up. 'If it fails', Bron added, 'I shall

156. Unpublished ALS to Auberon Waugh, 12 July [1965], from Combe Florey House; BL.
157. 'And Father Came Too: Auberon Waugh Interviewed by Stephanie Nettell', *Books and Bookmen*, January 1964, 9–10.

dedicate myself to some serious occupation like accountancy, or the prison service.'[158] It failed, and he dedicated himself to journalism. *Industria ditat.*

That summer Betjeman stayed at Combe Florey. Poet and novelist had not met for many years. They never met again. Waugh's days were empty save for gin and crosswords and writing the occasional letter. He rarely left the village. Betjeman was effectively separated from Penelope and involved with another woman. He was visiting the West Country to film a Unitarian chapel for the BBC, and relishing his new celebrity. It was a happy visit, and his letter to Laura offers a last glimpse of that 'delicious, remote and restful' world from which Bron now felt excluded:

> Every moment of it was an excitement for the eye, the ear & the palate. I kept thinking of Cadogan Cooper, that travel series, the drawing room carpet & the bears [?] climbing up that tile [?] in the bathroom. I love the bowered world in which you & Evelyn live there on the red sandstone ... the dark & thoughtful beauty....[159]

There is, perhaps, a suggestion of encouragement behind these compliments. Gaiety had deserted the house, and its macabre decorative jokes, never intended to be 'restful', had taken on a brooding quality. A year earlier Waugh had still been capable of fury at the persistent myth of his aping the gentry. He had even invited a reporter down to contradict it. 'This is not a country gentleman's house,' he had insisted. 'It is not full of servants. It is full of children and grandchildren.... No honest man could live in London the way I do here. I live simply. I want to save money. So that I can leave it to the Save the Children Fund.'[160] Now even that joke had soured.

During that summer, Waugh completed his last 'fictional work': the recension of his trilogy to a single volume. The work was executed quickly and brilliantly. But while his editorial skills remained as acute as ever, his imagination had died. When *Sword of Honour* appeared in September, he was reading Nigel Dennis's book on Swift and finding its subject temperamentally sympathetic. The result was his last letter to the *Tablet* attacking the liturgists: 'Some Modest Proposals From Illinois'. Waugh's élitism had recently been rebuked in *Commonweal*, the magazine he had supported in the palmier days of his enthusiasm for American Catholicism. Now he found it carrying an article by a Fr Ryan who wished to change

158. Unpublished ALS from Auberon Waugh, 13 July 1965, from The Old Rectory, Chilton Foliat, Hungerford, Berks.; BL.
159. Unpublished ALS, 17 July 1965, np [Sussex on *London Magazine* notepaper]; BL.
160. 'Words with Evelyn Waugh', *S. Tel.*, 23 August 1964, 5. The piece appeared in the 'Mandrake' column, which had the previous week carried gossip about Waugh's 'current doctrinal anti-modernismus'. A postcard had arrived in Fleet Street: '... Mandrake has written about me foolishly. I am willing to correct him....'

the catechism. 'Law, obedience, duty, and virtue' were out; 'encounter, commitment, and involvement' were in. Ryan advocated 'improvisations, impromptu additions and substitutions in the liturgy ... greater exchange among the worshippers themselves, the priest-president acting as something of a chairman and commentator.' Waugh warned his readers of 'an underground movement active almost everywhere in the Church which is far from being a bogeyman imagined by the traditionalists.'[161] The Yahoos were abroad.

Only three confidantes remained to whom he could explain his agony, Lady Acton and Penelope Betjeman having deserted his cause for the vernacular mass. 'Thc last 10 months', he told Nancy, 'have been ineffably dreary.... The buggering up of the Church is a deep sorrow to me....'[162] All three struggled to offer support. All three, however, were at best deists with a streak of agnosticism. 'I feel for you over the Church,' Nancy replied. 'Even I *mind terribly* the thought of immemorial beauty being cast away in a few months. How lucky I am to believe in God without any religious instincts or needs.'[163] There was small comfort here, or from Ann's: 'I am very sorry about the absurd democratising of your Church, it was grand and splendid and strong and now it will be weak and futile like everything else.'[164] When Diana Cooper had written requesting spiritual advice, Waugh's reply had been harsh:

> Prayer is not asking but giving. Giving your love to God asking for nothing in return.... He doesn't want sugar-babies. Have you ever experienced penitence? I doubt it. No wonder you are in the dumps. Do you believe in the Incarnation & Redemption in the full historical sense in which you believe in the Battle of el Alamein? That's important. Faith is not a mood.[165]

'O beastly Bo,' she had replied. '... That's not the way to answer those in pain.'[166] But he knew no other way, and applied the same strictures to himself when his own Faith was threatened.

161. *Tablet*, 18 September 1965, 1040. In a letter to *Commonweal* (7 January 1966, 391) Waugh defended this statement: '... the underground of which I wrote has now very much come into the open. Pope John was a conservative with little recent experience of the movements in the Church. I think he had no suspicion of the dangers of calling a general Council. I will not deny that Father John Ryan's "Post-Tribal Worship" deeply shocked me.... I cannot hope to live to see the counter-revolution. There have been many bad periods in the history of the Church. It is our misfortune to be living in one. I confess to vexation when I see it referred to as renewal.'
162. 5 September 1965; *Letters*, pp. 632–3.
163. Unpublished ALS from Nancy Mitford, 10 September 1965, from 7 Rue Monsieur, Paris VII; BL.
164. 4 October [1965]; *LAF*, p. 372.
165. 17 September 1964; *Letters*, p. 624.
166. ALS from Lady Diana Cooper, nd [c. 18 September 1964], from 10 Warwick Avenue, W2; BL; *MWMS*, p. 309. On 11 September she had written to Waugh: 'I'm a prey of neat despair.... *I could howl*. What shall I do to be saved?'

To his family, it seems, he said nothing of his fears of apostasy. He would not call out. 'I had not realised the depth of your depression . . .,' Fr D'Arcy wrote.[167] Few but Laura and Meg did, and only Meg dared to speak bluntly:

> . . . I've been thinking about you a lot – & worrying – I've never seen you so low. . . . It seemed a more abiding settled depression than ever before. Darling Papa please don't be unhappy – you may think this an impertinence but it is written in love –
>
> I think your trouble is that you don't go to the sacraments often enough. You can't expect your faith to stand these onslaughts unless you sustain it. I've been reading . . . *A Visit To Morin* & I think it's making a true point. I'm sure you'ld [*sic*] be happier if you were happier about religion. . . .[168]

Just before Christmas she wrote again:

> . . . Spending a whole day with you I suddenly realised that you were eating nothing – I knew you'd taken against food but not to that extent . . . you must literally be starving yourself to death. Please, please Papa see a doctor & a proper specialist . . . you are growing physically weaker under one's eyes. You could not begin to do another British Guiana trip today but it was only 4 years ago. And you can't really wish to kill yourself. . . .[169]

Her exhortations had little effect. Increasingly haunted by the 'Evill debacle', he accepted another two contracts, one for a work on American history, the other for Rainbird: a picture-book history of the Crusades. A friend from Rainbird, the publisher of Nancy's *The Sun King*, told her in January that Waugh's book was nearly finished. If this information came from Waugh, it was a desperate bluff. Not a word was written and in February he withdrew from the deal and had to repay the advance.

News of his ill-health again crackled through the ether. Mandrake of the *Telegraph* informed his readers that Waugh had suffered a Pinfoldian nervous collapse but was now happily working again. Alec wrote anxiously to enquire.

> As usual [his brother replied] the newspapers had got their facts wrong. It is true that all last year I was idle and low spirited but I was free from hallucinations. I had foolishly contracted to write 4 books . . . and could not face the task. Also I . . . find that the false snappers ruin my appetite for solid food. . . .[170]

167. Unpublished ALS to Evelyn Waugh, 14 September 1965, from 114 Mount Street, W1; BL.
168. Unpublished ALS from Margaret Waugh, nd [summer 1965?], from Lisbon; BL.
169. Unpublished ALS from Margaret Waugh, 19 December [1965], from South East House, Goffers Road, Blackheath, SE3; BL.
170. 6 March 1966; *Letters*, p. 637.

It was the last letter from him that Alec received.

*

That Easter, Waugh's friends were pleasantly surprised by the lighter tone of his correspondence. Meg came down to Combe Florey with Giles and their daughter, Emily, and found her father in good spirits. Hatty was also there. Fr Caraman had returned from Norway for a few days and was staying with the Herberts at Pixton. 'That Easter morning,' he wrote, 'I was driven over to Wiveliscombe [a nearby village] where E. W. attended my Mass: several others apart from those at C. Florey were also present.'[171] It was a gathering of the clan: Mary and Auberon Herbert, probably the Grants who 'wd. not have attended Mass elsewhere'.[172] The Wiveliscombe priest was Fr Formosa. Caraman said the Latin Mass in his church. It was a joyous occasion with Waugh radiating good humour.

After Mass, Caraman was driven to Combe Florey where he was to have luncheon. The meal was never served. During that morning, 10 April, Waugh pottered off somewhere, probably to the library. He was not seen alive again. When he proved difficult to trace, a search was instigated culminating at the downstairs lavatory. Inside, Laura found her husband sprawled face down. There was a gash on his forehead. It seems that he had suffered a coronary thrombosis, tried to rise and staggered forward, dashing his head against the door handle. Meg's nanny attempted the kiss of life but it was obviously too late. Caraman gave conditional absolution and the stunned family withdrew to await Fr Formosa, a doctor and an undertaker. Mrs Grant came over to pick up Caraman. 'The main anxiety after E. W.'s death', he remarks, 'was to make contact with Auberon [Waugh] lest he should first hear the news on the radio.'[173] When Bron arrived at midnight, only his brother-in-law, Giles FitzHerbert, was waiting for him. Everyone else had gone to bed, and the body had been removed.

Graham Greene heard another account and in 1983 the present author wrote to Christopher Sykes about this. 'As regards ... Waugh's last days,' he replied:

> I remember my meeting with Graham Greene who, I think, came to call on me and my late wife with his brother Hugh. You ask whether the story about Evelyn's death is true. It is.... [Fr Caraman] tried to interest me in the story ..., but I showed a marked lack of interest and ... did not listen.[174]

171. Unpublished ALS from Fr Philip Caraman, S.J., to Martin Stannard, 7 November 1989.
172. Unpublished AN from Fr Philip Caraman to Martin Stannard, nd [c. 14 November 1989].
173. Unpublished ALS, 7 November 1989, *op. cit.*
174. Unpublished TLS, 10 October 1983, from Broadwater House, 46 Broadwater Down, Tunbridge Wells, Kent.

Greene listened, and what he thought he heard was this: that Waugh had drowned in the lavatory, that there was water in his lungs and that an autopsy was necessary.

As with so many Waugh myths, this one contains only a fragment of truth. A post-mortem was necessary, but so it would have been in hundreds of similar cases where there was no witness to the death. There was no inquest. The coroner has no memory of 'suspicious circumstances' or water in the lungs. It was, perhaps, typical of Waugh (and of Greene) to continue to generate fictions. Both had, after all, spent their lives turning themselves into enigmas. And, ultimately, there remains a mystery. Greene was certain of his story. Fr Caraman denies it absolutely. The documentary evidence which might settle the matter would be in the coroner's enquiry file. Home Office circular no. 250/1967 put paid to any such easy resolution: all enquiry papers since 1875, it instructed, should be destroyed after fifteen years. The only exceptions were to be treasure-trove and cases of historical interest. Evelyn Waugh, apparently, fell into neither category. All we can say with certainty is that he died, as he had lived, alone.

Epilogue

'The Christian writer', Waugh explained in 1952, 'knows that five minutes after his death it will not matter to him in the least whether his books are a success or not. So he is naturally lazy.'[1] He was, nevertheless, jealous of his reputation and that of his friends. At the beginning of that last, blank year, Waugh had been disturbed by the obituary of Philip Dunne. On hearing that Sykes was writing to *The Times* to protest about it, Waugh abstained but added: 'I hope you will emphasize his antiquated sense of chivalry which he disguised under a pose of rascality.'[2] No such subtlety entered *The Times*'s account of Waugh's life,[3] whose celebration of one of the century's unique artists was designed more to put Waugh in his place than to place him in the hierarchy. Only Ann Fleming complained. Of the famous, Greene was alone in emphasizing that '... Waugh was the greatest novelist of my generation.'[4]

Under a blue spring sky eleven days later, the famous turned up in droves at Westminster Cathedral to hear Fr Caraman's panegyric on Waugh's loyalty. For the politicians, there was a dilemma to test their own fidelity: the date of Waugh's Requiem Mass also marked the State Opening of Parliament. Both ceremonies began at the same time: 11.30 a.m. For the writers there was, perhaps, a mischievous allusion to *Decline and Fall.* After the Last Post, the congregation lustily sang all six verses of 'O God, Our Help in Ages Past', Waugh's favourite hymn. When half-tipsy, he often used to be heard warbling it tunelessly at home.

The Cathedral authorities had granted permission, as a mark of special respect, for the Mass to be said in Latin. For John Raymond, the occasion recalled the last time he had met the novelist: in the same place after the Requiem for Knox. '[Waugh] was attired in full top-hatted mourning rig with the largest, thickest and most heavily bound dark red missal that I have ever seen.'[5] Waugh had been gratified to see the Prime Minister there. Macmillan, of course, was otherwise engaged on 21 April 1966. It was Alec who punctiliously appeared in full mourning. In addition to the family,

1. 'The Art of Literature Is Dying ...', *Catholic Herald*, 1 February 1952. Waugh was addressing the annual dinner of the Newman Society in Derby.
2. Unpublished APC to Christopher Sykes, nd [March 1965], from Combe Florey House; private collection.
3. 'Mr. Evelyn Waugh. Artist in Satiric Prose', *The Times*, 11 April 1966, 10.
4. 'Mr. Evelyn Waugh', *The Times*, 15 April 1966.
5. 'Waugh's Last Post', *NS*, 29 April 1966.

Peters, Sykes, Powell, Betjeman and Leigh Fermor turned up; also Ann Fleming and Diana Cooper. Cardinal Heenan was in the Sanctuary. Sadly, Penelope Betjeman, Nancy Mitford and Greene missed their beloved master's last farewell. The ceremony seemed to Raymond peculiarly appropriate. It was

> the feast of St. Anselm, the most intransigent of the Church's writing doctors. . . . As . . . the men in uniform bore away the coffin, one had the feeling that, whatever powers there be had arranged that Evelyn Arthur St. John Waugh should make his exit in his own characteristic manner.[6]

He was buried quietly in the West Country. His headstone reads simply: 'Evelyn Waugh. Writer'.

By July, Combe Florey was up for sale and expected to make £35,000. When Waugh's will was published that month it was discovered that he had left only £11,744 (£20,068 gross) and the *Daily Mirror* published an anonymous article entitled 'Proved again . . .: The Difficulty of Hanging On To Your Cash'. The house, it said,

> was always owned by his wife. . . . But he had set up a trust for his children composed of his collection of Victorian pictures, his silver, books and furniture. The value of the trust still has to be assessed. . . . [His] books . . . sell as well as ever, but it is unlikely their copyright will make [his widow] a rich woman. Copyrights are assessed as if they were property and are liable for death duties.[7]

Whoever distributed this information forgot to mention that nearly all of Waugh's assets were tied up in the Trust, including most of his copyrights. The £150,000 quoted as his gross earnings before tax over a lifetime's writing was a huge underestimate.

Once recovered from the initial shock, Laura was more anxious than distraught. Her faith, like Meg's, was absolute. Both wrote to friends telling them not to grieve. Waugh had wanted to die, they said, and he had died as he would have chosen: after Easter Mass with a priest in the house. They were glad it was over. But with Waugh's huge presence now absent from the house and half her family grown up and gone, Laura's introversion and innate misanthropy deepened, and for the first time in her life she grew nervous about money. 'An over-cautious lawyer', Bron remarked, 'persuaded her . . . that she was penniless. In fact she was very rich, but she took joyfully to the alternative disciplines of penury, selling most of

6. *Ibid.*
7. *Daily Mirror*, 21 July 1966, 11.

the family furniture for a song to Texas University....'[8] With the money from this sale behind her, Laura lived out her seven remaining years sadly, turning increasingly to the sherry, killing time with crosswords and jigsaws. When Combe Florey failed to reach its reserve at auction in September 1966[9] she kept the house on until Bron took it over in October 1971 and converted part of it into accommodation for her. After her death from pneumonia in June 1973, he remarked:

> ... I am not sure that her life ... was a particularly happy one. [She was] ... a more intensely private person than Evelyn Waugh – who despite all his protestations to the contrary, was in large part a public figure.... [F]or all her apparent shyness and avoidance of company, [she] was a born satirist. Behind the veil of good manners, she mocked everybody and everything.[10]

Of the children, Bron continued to cultivate notoriety as columnist and reviewer and has taken on the editorship of the *Literary Review*; Meg began a promising career as a writer with *The Man Who Was Greenmantle*,[11] but was knocked down by a car and killed in 1986; Teresa, who developed a brilliant reputation as a lawyer in America, also suffered a serious car smash; Harriet, an excellent novelist, married late; Septimus is a wood carver in the West Country; James remains (to this author at least) a mystery.

Waugh left a time-bomb in his library: the manuscript of his diary. For some months it lay there untouched. Then it went to Texas. David Astor, as Editor of the *Observer*, bought the rights from Laura shortly before her death. 'People may find it puzzling', Bron remarked, 'that the diaries were sold without any member of the family having studied them.' Each must have been constrained, he imagined, by 'a feeling of delicacy....'[12] He was not consulted over the sale, but, had he been, one suspects that he would have cut none of the references to himself. Despite his sufferings at his father's hands, Bron shared his comic relish for dirty linen, even his own, and understood, as many did not, the context in which those apparently heartless remarks should be read. 'Certainly', he wrote, 'one receives few impressions of any spontaneous gaiety or sweetness of nature, for which his friends remember him best, and which obviously made him such an agreeable companion. Similarly there have been few glimpses of the

8. Auberon Waugh, 'Laura Waugh 1916–1973', *Antigonish Review*, *op. cit.*, 27–32.
9. The house was withdrawn at £18,000. The gatehouse, which was being auctioned separately, also failed to sell and was withdrawn at £8,000.
10. Auberon Waugh, 'Laura Waugh 1916–1973', *op. cit.*
11. The biography of Aubrey Herbert, her maternal grandfather, the model for Buchan's Hannay.
12. 'My Father's Diaries', *NS*, 13 April 1973, 528–9.

kindliness, or the sudden disarming gentleness, which members of his family most particularly remember.'[13]

It is perhaps too easy to forget this. Waugh was his own worst enemy, but it was only during his last two years that he outlived his charm. The problem for the biographer is that 'disarming gentleness' is not the stuff of anecdotes. Those moments pass, if not unremarked, largely unrecorded.

Waugh's last published piece was a review of Dom Hubert van Zeller's autobiography. It is full of that hard-won compassion. Waugh clearly found the life of this artist-monk intensely sympathetic: another Merton figure but also something more. In writing of him, Waugh seems to be writing about himself and, at one point, he quotes at length as though to reinforce the point:

> 'A wish for death superseded, and in intensity vastly outmatched, the wish to grow up. The attraction has remained with me ever since. I was not unhappy. There was nothing morbid about it. There is nothing morbid now. But over the past forty-five years I do not think it has been out of my mind for as long as a single day. Earlier I had seen in growing up the means to emancipation; in 1916 I saw in death the means to a more significant emancipation. It is just that I do not much like living.'

'There will be many readers,' Waugh added, 'quite lacking in Dom Hubert's holiness, who will dimly understand and echo these words.'[14]

13. *Ibid.*, 529.
14. '*One Foot in the Cradle* by Dom Hubert van Zeller', *Downside Review*, Vol. 84, 275 (April 1966), 231–2.

Select Bibliography

[Place of publication is London unless otherwise stated.]

1. WORKS BY EVELYN WAUGH

The World to Come: A Poem in Three Cantos (privately printed, 1916).

P. R. B. An Essay on the Pre-Raphaelite Brotherhood, 1847–1854 (privately printed, Alastair Graham, 1926).

'The Balance: A Yarn of the Good Old Days of Broad Trousers and High Necked Jumpers' in *Georgian Stories 1926*, ed. Alec Waugh (Chapman & Hall, 1926).

Preface to *Thirty-Four Decorative Designs by Francis Crease* (privately printed, Oxford, A. R. Mowbray & Co.; E. W.'s preface dated August 1927).

Rossetti, His Life and Works (Duckworth, 1928; New York, Dodd, Mead & Co., 1928). Reprinted Duckworth, 1975 with an Introduction by John Bryson.

Decline and Fall, An Illustrated Novellette (Chapman & Hall, 1928; New York, Doubleday, Doran 1929; New York, Farrar & Rinehart, 1929). Revised Uniform Edition (with Preface by E. W.), Chapman & Hall, 1962. Reprinted Harmondsworth, Penguin Books, 1937.

Vile Bodies (Chapman & Hall, 1930; New York, Cape, Smith, 1930). Revised Uniform Edition (with Preface by E. W.), Chapman & Hall, 1965. Reprinted Harmondsworth, Penguin Books, 1938.

Labels, A Mediterranean Journal (Duckworth, 1930); US edition: *A Bachelor Abroad, A Mediterranean Journal* (New York, Cape, Smith, 1930). Reprinted Duckworth, 1975 with an Introduction by Kingsley Amis; reprinted Harmondsworth, Penguin Travel Library, 1985.

Remote People (Duckworth, 1931); US edition: *They Were Still Dancing* (New York, Farrar & Rinehart, 1932). Reprinted Duckworth, 1986; reprinted Harmondsworth, Penguin Travel Library, 1985.

Black Mischief (Chapman & Hall, 1932; New York, Farrar & Rinehart, 1932). Revised Uniform Edition (with Preface by E. W.), Chapman & Hall, 1962. Reprinted Harmondsworth, Penguin Books, 1938.

An Open Letter to H. E. the Cardinal Archbishop of Westminster (privately printed but not distributed. Whitefriar's Press, 1933; first published in edited version, *Letters*, 1980).

Ninety-Two Days, The Account of a Tropical Journey Through British Guiana and Part of Brazil (Duckworth, 1934; New York, Farrar & Rinehart, 1934). Reprinted Harmondsworth, Penguin Travel Library, 1986.

A Handful of Dust (Chapman & Hall, 1934; New York, Farrar & Rinehart, 1934). Revised Uniform Edition (with Preface by E. W.), Chapman & Hall, 1964. Reprinted Harmondsworth, Penguin Books, 1951.

Edmund Campion: Jesuit and Martyr (Longman, 1935; New York, Sheed & Ward, 1935). 2nd revised edition (with Preface by E. W.), Boston, Little, Brown & Co., 1946; London, Hollis & Carter, 1947. Reprinted OUP, 1980.

Mr Loveday's Little Outing and Other Sad Stories (Chapman & Hall, 1936; Boston, Little, Brown, 1936).

Waugh in Abyssinia (Longman, Green & Co., 1936; New York, Longman, Green & Co., 1936). Reprinted Methuen, 1984 and Harmondsworth, Penguin Travel Library, 1985.

Scoop: A Novel About Journalists (Chapman & Hall, 1938; Boston, Little, Brown, 1938). Revised Uniform Edition (with Preface by E. W.), Chapman & Hall, 1964. Reprinted Harmondsworth, Penguin Books, 1943.

Robbery Under Law: The Mexican Object-Lesson (Chapman & Hall, 1939); US edition: *Mexico: An Object-Lesson* (Boston, Little, Brown, 1939).

My Father's House [the first section of *Work Suspended*, later re-titled 'A Death' in the 1942 text; see below], *Horizon*, Vol. IV, No. 23 (November 1941), 329–341.

Put Out More Flags (Chapman & Hall, 1942; Boston, Little, Brown, 1942). Revised Uniform Edition (with Preface by E. W.), Chapman & Hall, 1967. Reprinted Harmondsworth, Penguin Books, 1943.

Work Suspended [limited edition of 500 copies] (Chapman & Hall, 1942; reprinted in revised version *Work Suspended and Other Stories etc.* (1949, see below) and *Tactical Exercise* (1954, see below)). Reprinted Harmondsworth, Penguin Books, 1951 (see below).

Brideshead Revisited: The Sacred and Profane Memories of Captain Charles Ryder (Chapman & Hall, 1945; Boston, Little, Brown, 1945). Revised Uniform Edition (with Preface by E. W.), Chapman & Hall, 1960. Reprinted Harmondsworth, Penguin Books, 1951; revised edition, 1962.

When the Going Was Good (Duckworth, 1946; Boston, Little, Brown, 1946). Reprinted Harmondsworth, Penguin Books, 1951.

Scott-King's Modern Europe (Chapman & Hall, 1947; Boston, Little, Brown, 1949). Reprinted in *Work Suspended and Other Stories*, Harmondsworth, Penguin Books, 1951.

Wine In Peace and War (privately printed, Saccone and Speed, Ltd, 1947).

The Loved One (Chapman & Hall, 1948; Boston, Little, Brown, 1948). Revised Uniform Edition (with Preface by E. W.), Chapman & Hall, 1965. Reprinted Harmondsworth, Penguin Books, 1951.

Work Suspended and Other Stories Written Before the Second World War (Chapman & Hall, 1949). Reprinted Harmondsworth, Penguin Books, 1951.

Helena (Chapman & Hall, 1950; Boston, Little, Brown, 1952). Reprinted Harmondsworth, Penguin Books, 1963.

Men At Arms (Chapman & Hall, 1952; Boston, Little, Brown, 1952. Reprinted Harmondsworth, Penguin Books, 1964.

The Holy Places (Queen Anne Press, 1952; New York, Queen Anne Press and British Book Center, 1953).

Love Among the Ruins: A Romance of the New Future (Chapman & Hall, 1953). Reprinted in *The Ordeal of Gilbert Pinfold*, Harmondsworth, Penguin Books, 1962.

Tactical Exercise [US edition of short stories] (Boston, Little, Brown, 1954). Eponymous story reprinted in *The Ordeal of Gilbert Pinfold*, Harmondsworth, Penguin Books, 1962.

Officers and Gentlemen (Chapman & Hall, 1955; Boston, Little, Brown, 1955). Reprinted Harmondsworth, Penguin Books, 1964.

The Ordeal of Gilbert Pinfold (Chapman & Hall, 1957; Boston, Little, Brown, 1957). Reprinted Harmondsworth, Penguin Books, 1962 with 'Tactical Exercise' and 'Love Among the Ruins'.

The Life of the Right Reverend Ronald Knox (Chapman & Hall, 1959); US edition: *Monsignor Ronald Knox* (Boston, Little, Brown, 1959).

A Tourist in Africa (Chapman & Hall, 1960; Boston, Little, Brown, 1960).

Unconditional Surrender (Chapman & Hall, 1961); US edition: *The End of the Battle* (Boston, Little, Brown, 1961). Reprinted Harmondsworth, Penguin Books, 1964.

Basil Seal Rides Again or The Rake's Regress (Chapman & Hall, 1963; Boston, Little, Brown, 1963). Reprinted in *Work Suspended and Other Stories*, Harmondsworth, Penguin Books, 1967.

A Little Learning. The First Volume of an Autobiography (Chapman & Hall, 1964; Boston, Little, Brown, 1964). Reprinted Harmondsworth, Penguin Books, 1983.

Sword of Honour. A Final Version of the Novels: Men At Arms (1952), Officers and Gentlemen (1955), and Unconditional Surrender (1961) (Chapman & Hall, 1965; Boston, Little, Brown, 1966). Reprinted Harmondsworth, Penguin Books, 1964 and 1984.

2. EVELYN WAUGH'S PRIVATE PAPERS AND JOURNALISM

Amory, Mark (ed.), *The Letters of Evelyn Waugh* (Weidenfeld and Nicolson, 1980).

Davie, Michael (ed.), *The Diaries of Evelyn Waugh* (Weidenfeld and Nicolson, 1976).

Gallagher, Donat (ed.), *The Essays, Articles and Reviews of Evelyn Waugh* (Methuen, 1983).

3. MEMOIRS, BIOGRAPHY, HISTORY

Acton, Harold, *Memoirs of an Aesthete* (Methuen, 1948).

More Memoirs of an Aesthete (Methuen, 1970).

Amory, Mark (ed.), *The Letters of Ann Fleming* (Collins, Harvill, 1985).

Beevor, Antony, *Crete. The Battle and the Resistance* (John Murray, 1991).

Bowra, C. M., *Memories* (Weidenfeld & Nicolson, 1966).

Carew, Dudley, *A Fragment of Friendship. Evelyn Waugh as a Young Man* (Everest Books, 1974).

Carpenter, Humphrey, *The Brideshead Generation* (Weidenfeld & Nicolson, 1989).

Clissold, Stephen (ed.), *Yugoslavia and The Soviet Union 1939–1973* (OUP, 1975).

Connolly, Cyril, *Previous Convictions* (New York & Evanston, Harper & Row, 1963).

Cooper, Artemis, (ed.), *Mr Wu and Mrs Stitch: The Letters of Evelyn Waugh and Diana Cooper* (Hodder & Stoughton, 1991).

Cooper, Diana, *The Light of Common Day* (Rupert Hart-Davis, 1959).

Cooper, Duff, *Old Men Forget* (Rupert Hart-Davis, 1956).

Donaldson, Frances, *Evelyn Waugh. Portrait of a Country Neighbour* (Weidenfeld & Nicolson, 1967).

Green, Henry, *Pack My Bag: A Self-Portrait* (Hogarth Press, 1940).

Greene, Graham, *Ways of Escape* (Bodley Head, 1980).

Hillier, Bevis, *Young Betjeman* (John Murray, 1988).

Hollis, Christopher, *The Seven Ages* (Heinemann, 1974).

Maclean, Fitzroy, *Eastern Approaches* (Cape 1949; reprinted Macmillan Papermac, 1982).

Mosley, Diana Mitford, *A Life of Contrasts* (Hamish Hamilton, 1977).

Loved Ones (Sidgwick & Jackson, 1985).

Nicolson, Harold, *Harold Nicolson Diaries and Letters*, ed. and condensed by Stanley Olsen (Collins, 1980).

Pakenham, Frank, *Born to Believe* (Cape, 1953).

Powell, Anthony, *To Keep the Ball Rolling. Vol. 2: Messengers of Day* (Heinemann, 1978).

Pryce-Jones, David (ed.), *Evelyn Waugh and His World* (Weidenfeld & Nicolson, 1973).

St John, John, *To The War With Waugh* (Leo Cooper, 1973).

Sherry, Norman, *The Life of Graham Greene. Vol. 1: 1904–1939* (Viking Penguin, 1989).

Sitwell, Osbert, *Laughter in the Next Room* (Macmillan, 1949).

Sykes, Christopher, *Four Studies in Loyalty* (Collins, 1946).

Evelyn Waugh: A Biography (Collins, 1975).

Waugh, Alec, *The Early Years of Alec Waugh* (Cassell, 1962).

My Brother Evelyn and Other Profiles (Cassell, 1967).

The Fatal Gift (W. H. Allen, 1973).

Waugh, Auberon, *Will This Do? The First Fifty Years of Auberon Waugh. An Autobiography* (Century, 1991).

Wilson, Edmund, *Classics and Commercials: A Literary Chronicle of the Forties* (W. H. Allen, 1951).

4. CRITICAL WORKS

Bradbury, Malcolm, *Evelyn Waugh* (Oliver & Boyd, 1964), 'Writers & Critics' series.

Carens, James F., *The Satiric Art of Evelyn Waugh* (Seattle & London, University of Washington Press, 1966).

Connolly, Cyril, *Enemies of Promise* (Routledge, 1938).

The Condemned Playground. Essays 1927–1944 (Routledge, 1945).

Cook, William J., Jr, *Masks, Modes and Morals: The Art of Evelyn Waugh* (Cranbury, N.J., Fairleigh Dickinson University Press, 1971).

Davis, Robert Murray, *Evelyn Waugh, Writer* (Oklahoma, Pilgrim Books, 1981).

De Vitis, A. A., *Roman Holiday. The Catholic Novels of Evelyn Waugh* (Vision Press, 1958).

Dyson, A. E., 'Evelyn Waugh and the Mysteriously Disappearing Hero' in *The Crazy Fabric* (Macmillan, 1965).

Eagleton, Terry, *Exiles and Emigrés* (Chatto & Windus, 1970).

Fussell, Paul, *Abroad* (OUP, 1980).

Green, Martin, *Children of the Sun. A Narrative of 'Decadence' in England After 1918* (Constable, 1977).

Greenblatt, Stephen Jay, *Three Modern Satirists: Waugh, Orwell and Huxley* (Yale University Press, 1965).

Heath, Jeffrey, *The Picturesque Prison* (Weidenfeld & Nicolson, 1982).

Hollis, Christopher, 'Evelyn Waugh' (Longman's pamphlet for British Council, 1966). 'Writers and their Work' series.

Johnstone, Richard, *The Will to Believe: Novelists of the Thirties* (OUP, 1982).

Kermode, Frank, 'Mr Waugh's Cities' in *Puzzles and Epiphanies: Essays and Reviews 1958–1961* (Routledge & Kegan Paul, 1962).

Linck, Charles E., Jr, 'The Development of Evelyn Waugh's Career: 1903–1939' (PhD thesis, University of Kansas, 1962).

Littlewood, Ian, *The Writings of Evelyn Waugh* (Oxford, Basil Blackwell, 1983).

Lodge, David, 'Evelyn Waugh' (Columbia University Press, 1971), 'Columbia Essays on Modern Writers' series.

McDonnell, Jacqueline, *Waugh on Women* (Duckworth, 1986).

McNamara, Jack Donald, 'Literary Agent A. D. Peters and Evelyn Waugh, 1928–1966: "Quantitative Judgments Don't Apply"' (PhD thesis, University of Texas at Austin, 1983).

Myers, William, 'Evelyn Waugh' in *British Writers*, Volume 7 (Scribners, 1984), pp. 289–308.

Evelyn Waugh and the Problem of Evil (Faber, 1991).

O'Donnel, Donat, *Maria Cross: Imaginative Patterns in a Group of Modern Catholic Writers* (New York, OUP, 1952).

Phillips, Gene, D., *Evelyn Waugh's Officers, Gentlemen and Rogues: The Fact Behind His Fiction* (Chicago, Nelson-Hall, 1975).

Spender, Stephen, 'The World of Evelyn Waugh' in *The Creative Element: A Study of Vision, Despair and Orthodoxy Among Some Modern Writers* (Hamish Hamilton, 1953).

Stannard, Martin (ed.), *Evelyn Waugh: The Critical Heritage* (Routledge & Kegan Paul, 1984).

Stopp, Frederick J., *Evelyn Waugh, Portrait of an Artist* (Chapman & Hall, 1958).

Tosser, Yvon, *Le Sens de l'Absurde Dans L'Oeuvre d'Evelyn Waugh* (Réproduction des Thèses, Université de Lille III, 1977).

Waley, Hubert, 'The Revival of Aesthetics' (Hogarth Press, 1926), 'Hogarth Essays' series.

5. INTERVIEWS WITH WAUGH

16 November, 1953:	Charles Wilmot, Jack Davies and Stephen Black for the 'Frankly Speaking' series, BBC Home Service; BBCSL.
26 June, 1960:	John Freeman for the 'Face to Face' series, BBC TV; BBCSL.
April 1962:	Julian Jebb for the *Paris Review*; text in *Writers At Work. The Paris Review Interviews. Third Series* (Secker & Warburg, 1968), pp. 103–114.
16 February, 1964:	Elizabeth Jane Howard for the 'Monitor' series, BBC TV.

6. CATALOGUES

Davis, Robert Murray,	*A Catalogue of the Evelyn Waugh Collection at the Humanities Research Center, The University of Texas at Austin* (New York, Whitston Publishing Co., 1981).
Davis, Robert Murray, Paul A. Doyle, Heinz Kosok, Charles E. Linck Jr,	*Evelyn Waugh: A Checklist of Primary and Secondary Material* (New York, Whitston Publishing Co., 1972).

Index

WORKS BY EVELYN WAUGH

THE FOLLOWING SECTION OF THE INDEX IS DIVIDED THUS:

1. Autobiography
2. Biography
3. Fiction
4. Short Fiction
5. Travel
6. Other Monographs
7. Non-fiction: (a) Articles; (b) Broadcasts; (c) Essays; (d) Reports; (e) Interviews; (f) Letters to newspapers and magazines; (g) Speeches; (h) Reviews; (i) Prefaces and forewords

General Index